THE LOEB CLASSICAL LIBRARY

FOUNDED BY JAMES LOEB, LL.D.

EDITED BY
G. P. GOOLD, PH.D.

ARRIAN
I

236

ARRIAN

WITH AN ENGLISH TRANSLATION

BY

P. A. BRUNT

CAMDEN PROFESSOR OF ANCIENT HISTORY
UNIVERSITY OF OXFORD

IN TWO VOLUMES

I

ANABASIS ALEXANDRI

BOOKS I–IV

CAMBRIDGE, MASSACHUSETTS
HARVARD UNIVERSITY PRESS
LONDON
WILLIAM HEINEMANN LTD
MCMLXXVI

American ISBN 0–674–99260–1
British ISBN 0 434–99236–4

Edition by E. Iliff Robson first published 1929
*Revised text and translation with new introduction,
notes and appendixes by P. A. Brunt,* 1976

Printed in Great Britain

CONTENTS

PREFACE

The Greek text is, with minor changes, that of the Teubner edition of 1967, edited by A. G. Roos and revised by G. Wirth; I am indebted to Ernst Heimeran-Verlag of Munich for permission to use it.

I must express my most grateful acknowledgments to successive editors of the Loeb Classical Library, to Professor E. H. Warmington for many improvements in the translation and to Professor G. P. Goold, and also to his wife, for care in correction of the proofs.

Brasenose College
Oxford

P. A. Brunt

INTRODUCTION

THE LIFE AND WORKS OF ARRIAN[1]

1. Lucius (or Aulus) Flavius Arrianus came, as he
told himself in his now lost Bithynian history, from
a family at Nicomedia, a Hellenized city in Bithynia,
where he was born and educated and held the priesthood of Demeter and Kore. From his name, most
fully recorded in a recently found inscription, we can
see that he was a Roman citizen; evidently his father
or grandfather had received the honour from one of
the Flavian emperors (A.D. 69–96), and he was connected with another family, the Arrii, which enjoyed
the same status. In Greek-speaking cities the
citizenship was seldom granted except to members
of the local ruling class, and Arrian's priesthood also
points to wealth and high birth. Indeed he was eli-
gible for a senatorial career at Rome itself. We
know from inscriptions and allusions in his own
works that he was governor of Cappadocia from c. A.D.
132 to 137; he had previously been consul, probably
in 129. If he reached this office at the normal age,
he would have been born not later than 89 and have
entered the senate before the death of Trajan in 117.

[1] For abbreviations and short titles see p. lxxxv. The
Teubner edition by A. G. Roos, revised by G. Wirth, Leipzig,
2 vols, 1967–8, with large bibliography, prints in vol. ii the
minor works and fragments of A. and *testimonia* to his life, on
which see esp. E. Schwartz, *RE* ii 1230 ff. = *Griechische
Geschichtsschreiber* 130 ff.; A. B. Bosworth, *CQ* 1972, 163 ff.
with two new inscriptions and further bibliography. P. A.
Stadter, *Greek Roman and Byzantine Studies* 1967, 155 ff.,
argues that Arrian was actually named Xenophon, but cf. § 6.

It has, however, recently been argued that he was admitted to the senate and rapidly promoted by Hadrian as a reward for literary productions, including the *Anabasis*.[2] Moreover, it may be that before entering the senate he had held equestrian military commissions. He could well have been somewhat older than forty in 129.

2. Before his public career began, Arrian had attended the classes of the Stoic teacher, Epictetus, at Nicopolis in Epirus, and was so impressed that probably at the end of each day he wrote down extensive notes of his master's lectures or sermons, trying to preserve what he had said word for word in the manner of Boswell. Years later, he published these *Discourses* in eight books (of which four survive), explaining in an introductory letter to Lucius Gellius that defective copies had somehow fallen into other hands; he wished that the published text should be authentic. He also wrote a Manual (*Enchiridion*) summarizing Epictetus' teaching, which is still extant. Allusions in the *Discourses* show that it was in the first decade of the second century that he sat under Epictetus. In his own age Arrian was styled a philosopher, but perhaps not only because of these writings: he also composed a little work on meteorology, which was then comprised under philosophy, and this too survives. How far he was permanently influenced by Stoicism must be doubted; I can detect no Stoic colouring in the *Anabasis*.[3]

---

[2] Trajan was very ready to promote men from the Greek world. The first view is commonly held: Bosworth advocates the second.

[3] See Oldfather's Loeb edition; F. Millar, *Journal of Roman Studies*, 1965, 141 ff. A. Bonhöffer, *Epictet und die Stoa* (1890) and *Die Ethik des Stoikers Epiktet* (1894) are fundamental on his beliefs.

3. No details are recorded of Arrian's early career in the service of Rome. The governor of Cappadocia had the task of protecting the upper Euphrates frontier with an army, including two legions, of about 20,000 men.[4] It is natural to suppose that he had obtained some military experience before he held this post, and the fact that he had himself seen the Danube and some of its tributaries (*Ind.* 4, 15) suggests service in that area, perhaps as an equestrian officer, though this inference has been challenged, and high military command was occasionally entrusted to mere civilians. Early in his tenure of the province Arrian inspected the forts on the Black Sea coast; he reported officially to Hadrian in Latin, but also presented him with a little literary work in Greek called 'The Voyage round the Black Sea' (*Periplous Euxini*), mostly culled from previous topographical writings (for he had not seen all the coasts for himself), but with some account of his own experiences and observations and special attention to works of art and antiquity that would interest the emperor. There is an old-world piety in his assertion that he will pacify a brigand tribe 'if God so wills' (11, 2, cf. *Anab.* vii 30). Later he was confronted with a serious danger of an Alan invasion, and again wrote a short description of his preparations to repel it (*Ectaxis contra Alanos*), a tract of no literary pretensions, very valuable for the evidence it provides on the Roman army in the province and on its marching and fighting practices. His fellow-countryman, Cassius Dio (*fl. c.* 200), who was to compose a biography of Arrian, now lost, says in his history that Arrian in fact deterred the Alans from attack (lxix

---

[4] See H. F. Pelham, *Essays on Roman History* 212 ff.

15, 1). He was still governor when he wrote a third treatise in 136/7 on *Tactics*; the material is mostly borrowed from earlier writers, rephrased with greater elegance, but it includes an account of contemporary methods for training cavalry.

4. There is no evidence that Arrian was employed again by Rome. He presently retired to Athens, where he was a citizen and became *archon* (chief magistrate) in 148/9. The name of Flavius Arrianus, which occurs on Athenian prytany lists, probably in 167/8 and certainly in 172/3, may be that of his son rather than his own. He is said to have lived into the reign of Marcus Aurelius (161–180), but was dead when Lucian wrote his *Alexander the False Prophet* shortly after 180. Most of his writings doubtless date from his retirement. Whether the *Anabasis* and *Indica* belong to this period will be discussed in volume II.

5. Arrian was a prolific writer, though apart from the works mentioned above and those comprised in this edition, his essay on *Hunting* (*Cynegeticus*) is the only one to survive. Mere fragments, or summaries by the ninth-century Byzantine scholar, Photius, attest his *History of Affairs after Alexander* in ten books (presumably a sequel to the *Anabasis*) which ended so abruptly in 321 B.C. that it must have been left unfinished, a *History of Parthia* in 17 books, which had reached Trajan's Parthian war in the 8th, and a *History of Bithynia* from mythical times to its annexation by Rome in 74 B.C. in eight books. His preface to this work (known from Photius) referred to lost biographies of Dion and Timoleon and implied that these lives, as well as the *Anabasis*, were exercises in historiography, preparing him for his great life-work of recording the story of his own fatherland;

this is curious, when we consider that in the *Anabasis* (i 12, cf. *preface* and vii 30) he seems to claim that that work is an inspired production, worthy of its great subject and destined to place its author among the masters of Greek literature. There was also another biography of a bandit named Tilliborus or Tillorobus of which not a word remains.

6. The connecting link between many of these varied productions may be found in Arrian's admiration for Xenophon, who also ranked both as philosopher and historian. In the *Ectaxis* he even assumes Xenophon's name (§ 10), and elsewhere he refers to him as ' the elder Xenophon ' (e.g. *Periplous* 12, 5) or ' that Xenophon ' (ib. 1, 1 etc.) or ' my namesake ' (*Cynegeticus* 22, 1). It has been inferred that he actually possessed the name from the first (it is not uncommon) or later assumed it, but this is not confirmed by any of the inscriptions in which his own name appears. Be this as it may, he claims to have ' followed the same pursuits from youth, hunting and warfare and philosophy ' (ibid. 1, 4). His work on hunting in fact recalled Xenophon's on the same subject, just as his *Discourses of Epictetus* had their counterpart in Xenophon's *Recollections of Socrates* (*Memorabilia*), while he gave to his account of Alexander the same title as Xenophon had used for his story of the Ten Thousand, to which Arrian refers in i 12, 3; ii 4, 3; 7, 8; 8, 11. In the eyes of Lucian he was a man whose whole life was concerned with culture (*paideia*) and an inscription refers to his intellectual eminence (*sophia*); he was regarded as one of the ornaments of an age to which some moderns now credit a renaissance of Greek civilization. However, his works illustrate how derivative were its ideas and literary forms; he and his con-

temporaries found their inspiration in the past. This is reflected in Arrian's style. Photius admired his clarity of diction and arrangement and held that he hit a happy mean between excessive bareness and excessive adornment,[5] but though this be granted, it is certain that except in the *Discourses* and *Manual* he adopted the style and language of the past, imitating Xenophon in particular. In the *Anabasis* he writes in the old Attic, while in the *Indica* he seeks to reproduce the Ionic of Herodotus, in each case eschewing the idioms of the living language. No doubt this was a *tour de force* and may explain his boast that he was a master of Greek speech (i 12) and his claim (vi 28, 6) that the *Indica* would be a ' Greek book ' on the theme, i.e. more literary than the memoir of Nearchus on which most of it was based.

THE TEXT OF THE *ANABASIS* AND *INDICA*

7. In the previous Loeb edition Robson followed the Didot text edited by Dübner and based on a fifteenth-century manuscript at Paris (B, called A by Dübner). However, A. G. Roos is held to have shown that this, and all other extant manuscripts, were copied from an extant codex in Vienna (A), written about A.D. 1200. In his Teubner edition (see n. 1) he, therefore, relied solely on A, where possible, except for a few passages where he considered that the true text, corrupted in A, had been preserved in ancient excerpts and quotations from Arrian. Unfortunately, A had suffered from damp, and as early as the fifteenth century the pages

[5] Teubner ed. of Arrian, vol. ii, p. LXVI f.

nearest the cover, corresponding to some two pages in this edition at the beginning of the *Anabasis* and half a page at the end of the *Indica*, were lost. Elsewhere too a later scribe (A²) wrote in, with his own hand, words which he found barely legible; where the original writing can still be made out, it proves that he was negligent and ignorant. Worse still, he tore out twenty pages, which were presumably hardest to read, and substituted his own, presumably bad, copy. The codex, thus amended or rather defaced, was transcribed in a fifteenth-century Laurentian manuscript (k), which was once regarded as primary evidence for the text. However, the remaining 36 manuscripts, of which 29 include the *Indica* as well as the *Anabasis*, were copied from A before its maltreatment, and can be used to restore A's readings, where A is lost or illegible. Roos, who divided them into two classes (the second of which was marked by certain lacunae), chose to rely mainly on B from the first class and a Laurentian manuscript (L) from the second. He had not in fact collated or even seen all these manuscripts, but further work on them is taken into account by Wirth in his revision of Roos' edition. Not being a textual critic, I have simply reprinted this revised text, with only a few changes, mostly suggested in Wirth's addenda and corrigenda (which often reveal Roos' own final judgement). The apparatus will draw attention to all these changes,[6] and occasionally to other textual points, but the student of Arrian's text must turn to the Teubner edition.

---

[6] This text differs from that of Roos in i 7, 2; 17, 2; ii 1, 4; 2,2; 23, 2; iii 6, 5 and 6; 7, 7; 11, 7 and 8; 13, 3; 20, 4; 30, 7; iv 4, 3; 5, 3; 8, 9; 12, 1; 21, 7; 23, 1; 25, 2; 28, 4 and 7; 29, 4; 30, 6. Cf. n. 99.

INTRODUCTION

THE TRANSLATION

8. Robson's translation was notoriously marred by frequent inaccuracies. None the less, I have found it a necessary economy of time to revise it rather than replace it. In trying to remove errors, I have also chosen in many places to introduce stylistic changes. Robson affected an old-world style, as indeed did Arrian. I doubt whether any translator can reproduce the kind of effect Arrian made on contemporary readers, but a systematic attempt to do this would no doubt involve him in the most careful study of (let us say) the English of Hakluyt or Clarendon, and the more successful he might be in imitation of models analogous in English to Arrian's models in Greek, the less his version would serve to make Arrian accessible to a modern English public. If we want to savour Arrian's style, we must read him in the original. But the truth is surely that he will mostly be read, alike in Greek and in translation, for what he has to tell. My object is to make that as plain as possible.

THE COMMENTARY

9. Arrian unquestionably provides us with the best evidence we have for Alexander, and a full commentary might be no less than an exhaustive, critical examination of all, or almost all, our material for Alexander's reign; this would clearly transcend any reasonable limits for a Loeb edition.[7] My purpose in the rest of this introduction and in the notes and appendixes is to explain what Arrian says, where

[7] A. B. Bosworth is preparing a full commentary.

explanation seems to be required, and to furnish some
material and guidance for an evaluation of his work.
Arrian takes for granted much that a modern reader
(and perhaps some of his own public) might not know;
in particular, he plunges into the story of Alexander's
campaigns without telling us anything about the
condition of Macedon, Greece or Persia at the time,
of the circumstances of his own accession or of the
military resources at his command. By setting the
stage in the introduction I shall incidentally explain
many allusions he makes to transactions he never
describes. To evaluate his work we have to compare it with our other accounts of Alexander. The
comparison shows clearly enough that his is the best.
Arrian himself was very conscious of this superiority
of his treatment to the histories read in his own
day, and explains it by his choice of better sources
(*preface*). It is then necessary to determine the value
of his sources, so far as possible. It will appear that
they have their defects as well as great merits, and
that the inferior accounts cannot be wholly neglected.
To facilitate detailed comparison I have given references throughout to the principal texts which the
student has to collate with Arrian's own statements,
though for brevity I have not normally noted or com-
mented on their divergences from Arrian. Crucial
questions which bear on the reliability of his sources
or on his own methods and interpretation are treated
at greater length, but from a historiographical
rather than a historical standpoint; for instance my
aim in discussing Alexander's visit to the oracle of
Ammon (Appendix V) is not to discover, if indeed it
be discoverable, what actually happened and what its
importance was for Alexander, but what the various
historians told and thought. For an assessment of

INTRODUCTION

Arrian and his main sources omissions are sometimes no less relevant than divergences from the rest of the tradition. The reader will be assisted (I hope) to form his own judgement, as he proceeds; a final statement of my own view will be deferred to the second volume, and there I shall discuss Arrian's own contribution to his theme. It will be best too to consider in that connection when he wrote the *Anabasis* and *Indica* (cf. § 1). Assuming that they are works of his full maturity, many scholars have seen them as products of a man versed in government and war. I can detect no clear evidence of this, and no grounds in the quality of Arrian's historical judgement to rule out the thesis that they were composed before he had gone far in his senatorial career.

THE SOURCES FOR THE HISTORY OF ALEXANDER

10. Archaeology, inscriptions and coins tell us little of Alexander: we have to rely mainly on literary sources, and of the many contemporary accounts of his reign, none survives; all extant narratives are rather late. (i) In the mid first century B.C. Diodorus the Sicilian composed a *Universal History* in Greek, of which book xvi deals with Philip, xvii with Alexander (there is a long lacuna, and only a table of contents shows what he recounted between winter 330/29 and summer 327), and xviii-xx with Alexander's successors. (ii) Between 29 B.C. and A.D. 226, and almost certainly in the first century A.D., Quintus Curtius Rufus wrote a Latin history of Alexander in ten books, of which the first two which went down to spring 333 are lost; there are also some later gaps. (iii) Early in the second century

A.D. Plutarch included Alexander in his *Parallel Lives*. (iv) A lost Latin Universal History written by Pompeius Trogus under Augustus was epitomized probably in the third century A.D. by Justin; his work is of small value. (v) There are of course allusions in other writers, notably the scholarly *Geography* by Strabo (*c.* A.D. 1), whose lost historical work also contained something on Alexander (ii 1, 9).[8] Naturally there must have been many other treatments of Alexander written in antiquity after Alexander's own time. We do not know which were those Arrian hoped to supersede (*pref.* 3). Even their names may not be preserved. It is significant that he himself cites the works of Aristos and Asclepiades (vii 15, 5), of which the first is almost and the second, but for his allusion, totally unknown to us. A few fragments from such shadowy or anonymous later historians still survive. Clearly the evidentiary value of all such non-contemporary historians, including Arrian himself, rests on their ability to obtain and transmit reliable contemporary information. Even if it had been the practice of classical historians to search out documentary records for the past, they could not have found much to their purpose, and at best they had to turn to contemporary narratives. Their proper course was to examine and collate such narratives, written by eye-witnesses or at least by men who had themselves been able to question eye-witnesses. (Even a companion of Alexander could not have seen and heard for himself more than a little of what occurred.) But some of them simply paraphrased,

[8] All, except Justin, in Loeb editions. On Curtius' date see D. Korzeniewski, *Die Zeit des Q. Curtius Rufus*, Köln dissertation, 1969; G. V. Sumner, *Australasian Universities Modern Language Association*, 1961; H. U. Instinsky, *Hermes* 1962. For Plutarch see J. R. Hamilton's good commentary, 1969.

summarized or expanded existing works by authors who themselves depended directly or indirectly on the primary authorities; the possibilities of error were thus multiplied at every stage, as careless or wilful omissions and additions might occur. Thus it is clear that whatever sources Curtius used he embellished what he found with all the arts of Silver Latin rhetoric, and any later writer who trusted him implicitly would be to that extent further from the truth. Still, all accounts of Alexander which are not mere fiction (see § 18) must ultimately go back to contemporary sources. Recently C. B. Welles suggested that Diodorus drew on Trogus.[9] But Trogus probably wrote after Diodorus (see Addendum, p. lxxxiv). In any case he himself must ultimately have drawn on a first-hand account, and even if Welles' theory is correct, it does nothing to discredit the orthodox hypothesis that the ultimate source of Diodorus is Clitarchus (cf., however, § 22).

11. There were many contemporary accounts of Alexander; I name only the most notable.[10] *Callisthenes* of Olynthus, Aristotle's kinsman and pupil, already an accredited historian, was taken with him by Alexander to commemorate his deeds; he perished at Alexander's hands in 327, but his narrative went down to 331 and perhaps to 329. *Anaximenes* of Lampsacus continued his history of Philip with a work on Alexander that is cited only twice. *Chares* of Mitylene, an usher in Alexander's court, is credited with at least ten books which *may* have comprised no more than a series of reminiscences and anecdotes of court life. A work by the Cynic philosopher, *Onesicritus* of Astypalaea, a pilot in

---

[9] Introd. to Loeb edition of Diodorus vol. viii.
[10] Pearson, *LH*, discusses each writer in turn.

INTRODUCTION

Alexander's Indus flotilla and in Nearchus' fleet, is cited mainly for geographical descriptions and marvels, and treated by Arrian with contempt (vi 2, 3; *Ind.* 3, 6), but it may have had a far wider scope and certainly ranged further than the memoir of his voyage by *Nearchus* himself, which was Arrian's chief source in the *Indica.*[11] *Clitarchus* of Alexandria wrote at least twelve books on Alexander; though he may not have actually served on the expedition, the suggestion that he was not a contemporary has been refuted, and he must surely have published before Ptolemy.[12] A somewhat older friend of Alexander, *Ptolemy* played a part of growing importance in the campaigns and became satrap of Egypt on Alexander's death; here he made himself an independent ruler and assumed the royal title in 304, founding a dynasty which lasted till the death of Cleopatra in 30; he more or less retired in 285, three years before his death. Since Arrian refers to him as king, it is commonly assumed that he did not write his history until after 304, and perhaps not until his years of leisure and extreme old age. These assumptions seem to me unwarranted. Naturally Arrian knew that he became king, whether or not he was so described on Arrian's copy, and Arrian's point is perhaps that the man with the qualities of a king would not tell lies; this point, if valid at all, would

[11] More on this in vol. II.
[12] Badian, *Cl. World* 1971, 37 ff., 77 ff., cf. *Proceedings of African Classical Associations*, 1965, 5 ff. (I retract the contrary view, expressed in *CQ* 1962, 141 ff., an article in which I believe I refuted the hypothesis of Tarn and others, that Diodorus and Curtius used an author who obtained valuable information from the mercenaries in Persian service; this matter will not be mentioned again.) Probably A. did not read Clitarchus, cf. vi 28, 2 n.; vii 15, 5 n.

hold good at whatever date the ' kingly man ' was
writing. Moreover, even if Arrian supposed that he
wrote when king, we do not know that the supposition
was justified by anything in Ptolemy's text. And we
have only to think of Caesar to see that the claims of
government and warfare do not exclude literary composition. Finally, *Aristobulus* too accompanied
Alexander, and was employed to repair the tomb of
Cyrus (vi 29); we do not know what professional
expertise he had, nor where he came from, but he
ultimately became a citizen of Cassandria in Macedon, founded by Antipater's son in 316; he was
writing after the battle of Ipsus in 306 (vii 18, 5, cf. 22,
5), and allegedly began only when he was eighty-
three; this, if true, tells us little, as the date of his
birth is not on record.[13]

12. The ' fragments ' of these writers are collected in
Jacoby's *Fragmente der griechischen Historiker* and have
been translated by C. A. Robinson (*The History of
Alexander the Great*, 1953). The term ' fragments '
is misleading. Very seldom do we have their actual
words as distinct from summaries or mere allusions;
thus Plutarch reports (*Alex.* 46) that Alexander was
visited by the queen of the Amazons ' as most writers
say, among whom are Clitarchus, Polyclitus, Onesicritus, Antigenes and Ister; but Aristobulus, Chares
the royal usher, Ptolemy . . . (and others) say that
this is a fiction ', and this passage is cited as a fragment of each author named. Moreover, the fragments, such as they are, may give us a very imperfect
idea of the scope and importance of their works. If
Arrian's *Anabasis* were lost, only three or four

---

[13] The best and most cautious account of all these writers
is by Pearson, *LH* (cf. E. Badian, *Studies in Greek and Roman
History* 250 ff.), though he is wrong on Clitarchus' date.

INTRODUCTION

uninformative fragments of Ptolemy would survive, and while we should know more of Aristobulus through Strabo, we might have supposed that he was primarily interested in geographical descriptions, whereas Arrian uses him for other matters as well, and in fact gives little space to geography in the *Anabasis*, as distinct from the *Indica*. Chares alone is much *quoted*, but by Athenaeus, who was interested in food, drink, luxury and the like, and excerpts passages from Chares on these topics: this may give no juster an impression of Chares' range than Strabo with his geographical theme gives of the scope of either Aristobulus or Onesicritus. Finally, the almost complete disappearance of Ptolemy's history except in the pages of Arrian must warn us not to ignore the possible importance of Anaximenes, and indeed of other writers who were with Alexander, like Polyclitus and Medeius of Larissa, who are hardly ever cited or whose sparse ' fragments ' may again be untypical.

13. Callisthenes alone is *known* to have been actually writing during the course of the campaigns.[14] By contrast Aristobulus composed his work not less than 20–30 years after the events he described, and it is generally but rashly assumed that Ptolemy too wrote after a long lapse of time. Callisthenes, it is true, need not have been the only historian actually engaged in writing in Alexander's lifetime, and others may have made contemporary notes. A historian who did neither must, when at last he came to compose, have relied on works previously published by others, on documentary evidence, on his own and others' recollections, or on all these kinds of informa-

---

[14] Cicero, *pro Archia* 24 says that Alexander had many historians with him, but this statement has perhaps no value.

tion. Now it is a marked feature of Arrian's work that he gives very detailed reports of a dry factual kind; he tells who commanded particular regiments, who were given particular provincial appointments at particular times, how many days the army took to reach a specified place or how many stades it covered. Similar information is also found in Curtius, and even in Diodorus; though the brevity of his account compels him generally to omit such data, there is enough to show that they appeared in his source.[15] All this suggests that some of the contemporary historians, including the sources of Curtius and Diodorus as well as Arrian, disposed of documentary material.

14. Both Arrian (vii 25 f.) and Plutarch (76) purport to describe Alexander's last days from 'the royal journals', to which there are a few other references elsewhere, all concerned with his spending days drinking and sleeping! We are also told that the journals were 'written up' by Eumenes, the royal secretary (who was to play a turbulent part in the struggles after Alexander's death), in collaboration with one Diodotus. It has commonly been supposed that the journals in fact recorded all important decisions made by Alexander and all notable events reported to him, as well as an account of his own actions day by day; it would seem that the Ptolemies in Egypt kept such journals, and perhaps required their officials to do so; in that case an extract preserved from such a journal of a Roman official in Egypt (Wilcken, *Chrestomathie* 41) attests a practice that conjecturally goes back to Alexander. It is further assumed that a copy of Alexander's journals came into the possession of Ptolemy, presumably in

---

[15] I shall note all such data in the commentary.

321 on the death of Perdiccas, and that he used them for his history. This hypothesis is not proved, nor probable. (*a*) The journals are cited only for Alexander's personal habits and particularly for his last days (Jacoby no. 117), not for any military or political measures; for instance Plutarch (55, 3) seeks to show the innocence of Callisthenes from a royal letter, not from the journals, and Arrian cannot resolve his doubts about Callisthenes' fate (iv 14, 3) from the journals. If Ptolemy used them here and elsewhere, he certainly never made this plain to Arrian. (*b*) It is far from clear from vii 26, 3 that even for Alexander's last days Arrian obtained his knowledge of the journals from Ptolemy (or Aristobulus) rather than directly, but it is certain that the version he knew was materially different from that known to Plutarch; neither was necessarily authentic. (*c*) If Arrian's ' documentary ' material comes from the journals through Ptolemy, we must ask how some such material also reached Diodorus and Curtius; evidently part of it was in their common source, and that source is usually taken to be Clitarchus, who must be supposed to have written before Ptolemy (cf. Curtius ix 5, 21). It seems to me clear that the so-called journals were of limited scope and circulated in different versions, which were literary compositions. Various theories have been proposed by scholars who do not accept the orthodox but (in my judgement) incorrect dogma that official journals underlie Ptolemy's history. On one view, the fact that they are not attested except for Alexander's final residence at Babylon can be readily explained: it was at Babylon that local records were kept under the old kings, as later under the Seleucids, narrating all the doings of the king; such records could have been the

basis for literary compositions. Alternatively an alleged ' record ' of Alexander's last days was circulated by Eumenes himself (or perhaps rather in his name) to show that there was no truth in the stories that Alexander had been poisoned at the instance of Antipater or others, and this ' record ' might in turn have been altered by various hands for propagandist purposes. One account of Alexander spending his time in drinking and sleeping ascribed to Eumenes (Jacoby no. 117 F. 2) might even be taken as fabrication designed to depreciate the king.[16] In any event the notion that Ptolemy's history was specially reliable because he had access, and perhaps sole access, to the king's own journals, should be given up.[17]

15. Plutarch and others often cite the letters of Alexander and other figures of his time. Some are undeniably spurious, as they contain manifest absurdities. Others make statements which are or might be true. Scholars commonly hold that each must be treated on its merits.[18] Unfortunately, we do not possess any unquestionably authentic letters, which would make stylistic tests possible. Moreover, a forger would obviously draw on histories of Alexander, and might use true information by this method. Hence we cannot properly infer that a letter must be genuine, if its statements are correct.

---

[16] A. E. Samuel, *Historia* 1965, 1 ff.; A. B. Bosworth, *CQ* 1971, 112 ff.

[17] L. Pearson, *Historia* 1955, 429 ff.; Pearson also deals with the letters and bematists' reports.

[18] This view is sometimes ascribed to J. Kaerst, *Philologus,* 1892, 602 ff. (the fundamental discussion), but this seems to me a misunderstanding of his cautiously expressed scepticism. Cf. notes on vi 1, 4; vii 12, 6 f.; the latter text does not imply that A. himself used the letters.

Now it seems that all those used by Plutarch (and others) came from one collection, and it is hard to see how genuine letters would have been mixed up with spurious letters or in what circumstances genuine private letters would have been published at all. In my judgement all should be rejected. Official letters which cities received from Alexander and inscribed (e.g. Tod 185) are another matter. So are the letters Arrian or Curtius purport to give. They also affect to record speeches and conversations in the very words of the speaker, yet it cannot be doubted that (as in other ancient histories) the words they use are their own; at most the substance may be true, or at least derived from sources they believed. This practice went back to Herodotus and Thucydides, and the latter included a letter (vii 10 ff.) which is certainly his own composition, even though it probably gives the sense of what its imputed author actually wrote. The letters Arrian puts in direct speech (ii 14; vii 23, 8) probably belong to the same genre, that is to say, like the speeches in his work, they are his own literary compositions based on the material he found in his sources; by contrast, the mere summary of a letter in ii 25 is likely to be wholly drawn from his sources. I shall discuss the speeches and letters more fully in vol. II and argue that when they are of his own composition he was apt to use material not entirely drawn from the sources he was following in the surrounding narrative.

16. One kind of documentary material does seem to have been available to the historians of Alexander, viz. the reports of ' bematists ' on marches and distances discussed in Appendix VIII.

17. From all this it follows that historians like Aristobulus who wrote some time after the events

had to rely on their own and others' recollections, on contemporary notes and on already published accounts which had come their way. Callisthenes' official record, so far as it went, must therefore have been of great value to all his successors. But we do not know that it was the only truly contemporaneous version of events. And the difficulty of understanding how minute details could be given for the period Callisthenes certainly did not cover will be mitigated by the assumption that later writers, including Clitarchus and Ptolemy, composed their stories much sooner after Alexander's death than is often assumed, or that (whenever they wrote) they could refer to their own notes made at the time.

18. Callisthenes was censured in antiquity for his rhetoric, his adulation of Alexander and (by Polybius, quite unjustly) for incompetence in military matters.[19] Clitarchus, the only other contemporary historian who is known to have been read widely for a long period, was thought to be clever but mendacious.[20] Strabo, who often cites Onesicritus, Nearchus and Aristobulus, was contemptuous of the way in which all the historians who accompanied Alexander ' toyed with facts ', glorifying Alexander, imposing fables on the credulity of their readers and contradicting each other on matters of which, as eye-witnesses, they should have been able to give true and uniform reports. He had in mind their geographical descriptions, but his criticisms have a wider relevance.[21] Onesicritus, whom he once characterizes as the arch-liar (xv 1, 28), had the audacity to tell how Alexander

---

[19] Jacoby no. 124 T. 20 f. (cf. Pearson 24); 30–32 f.; App. III.

[20] Jacoby no. 137 T. 6–9; 13.

[21] App. XII.

cohabited with the queen of the Amazons (§12); so did Clitarchus, though he (unlike Onesicritus) was perhaps not with the army at the time. Even Ptolemy and Aristobulus did not eschew the fabulous in recounting Alexander's visit to Siwah (iii 3). It is less surprising that in the end an ' Alexander-Romance ' was fashioned, perhaps by the first century B.C., which bears as little relation to the historic king as the *Chanson de Roland* to Charlemagne.[22] In his preface Arrian himself speaks with contempt of the current histories of Alexander (cf. vi 11), and with an emphasis unique in ancient historiography proclaims his reliance on the more trustworthy accounts of Ptolemy and Aristobulus.

19. I shall discuss Arrian's sources more fully in the second volume, but some preliminary observations are required here. He undertakes to record as facts what Ptolemy and Aristobulus agreed in recording and, where they differed, to select what he thinks most credible and memorable. Although he sometimes notes discrepancies between them, that is certainly not his invariable practice, nor did he promise to follow such a practice. One divergence gravely disturbed him (iv 14, 4), and it seems likely that if they had often *disagreed* he would have lost confidence in one, if not in both. I suppose, therefore, that the differences he has in mind arose mainly when one provided information that the other did not give; in such circumstances Arrian could reasonably have treated their stories as complementary. In fact neither is often cited specifically, nor when either or both are cited, is it always easy to see why; there seems to be an element of caprice. Similarly in his

[22] ed. Kroll [2], 1958; cf. R. Merkelbach, *Die Quellen des griechischen Alexanderromans*, 1954.

great book on Alexander, written for the general
reader, Wilcken gives his authority even for contro-
versial statements quite infrequently and for apparently arbitrary reasons.) However, Arrian's preface
seems to promise that all statements of fact will come
from Ptolemy or Aristobulus or both, whereas what
he derives from other sources will be given as mere
'tales' (cf. § 21). His actual practice is not quite so
simple. On the one hand, some parts of the 'factual'
narrative in books vi and vii seem to come from
Nearchus, his chief source for the *Indica*, whom he
regarded as no less reliable than Ptolemy and
Aristobulus, and with good reason; on the other
hand, there are occasions, registered in the notes,
in which 'tales' can be shown to have been told by
one or both of his main authorities.[23]

20. Most scholars assume that he normally relied
more on Ptolemy than on Aristobulus.[24] This may
be true, though it is usually taken too much for
granted. Certainly, as an old friend of Alexander
(iii 6) and a high ranking officer in his army, Ptolemy
should have been better placed to know the truth
than Aristobulus, and his military and political
experience might well have given him more insight
into matters of war and statecraft. But though
these considerations have had much weight with the
moderns, they do not seem to have occurred to
Arrian. If he shows some preference for Ptolemy

[23] ii 12, 3–5, cf. vii 14, 7 with 23, 6: i 1, 1 n. Note also that
Ptolemy or Aristobulus could record a 'tale' told at the time,
e.g. ii 3.
[24] See e.g. E. Schwartz, *RE* ii 911 ff. = *Gr. Geschichtschreiber*
119 ff. (cf. also n. 1); H. Strasburger, *Ptolemaios und Alexander*,
1934; E. Kornemann, *Die Alexandergeschichte des Königs
Ptolemaios I*, 1935 (largely refuted by Strasburger, *Gnomon*
1937, 483 ff.); G. Wirth, *RE* xxxii 2467 ff.

in the preface, it is on the ludicrous ground that as
a king he could not have lied without special dishonour.   It is also clear from comparison of Arrian's
narrative with ' fragments ' of Aristobulus preserved
elsewhere that Arrian omitted much that Aristobulus
told, particularly geographical descriptions.[25]   Unfortunately Ptolemy is so seldom cited elsewhere that
we have virtually no independent check on Arrian's
use of his work, and cannot tell how much he omitted
from it, or whether he at times silently rejected
Ptolemy in favour of Aristobulus; it would have been
perfectly in accord with his own preface if he had done
so, whenever he found Aristobulus' account more
credible or memorable.   I hope to show that Arrian
did in fact omit much ' documentary ' material; one
kind of omission is discussed in Appendix VIII (cf.
§ 56), and others will be reviewed in volume II.   On
the common view that Ptolemy was his preferred
source, these omissions may well be from Ptolemy's
history, and we certainly ought not to assume that
even if Arrian is mainly Ptolemy, Ptolemy is mostly
in Arrian.   Again, Arrian's own express avowals in
v 7, 1 and vi 2, 4 that he agrees with or follows
Ptolemy perhaps need not be given an application to
the whole history.   The importance of Aristobulus as
a source may be generally underrated; on the other
hand I have some doubt (of a subjective kind) whether
Arrian was capable of systematically collating and
dovetailing both narratives, and there are occasions
when Ptolemy is not actually cited in which he is unquestionably the authority used, at least for military

---

[25] In vii 20, 1 a ' prevalent tale ' apparently comes from
Aristobulus, and he may be the source, though unnamed, for
vi 24, 4–26, an account widely different from Ptolemy's, if that
is to be found in 23, 1–24, 1, but see discussion in vol. II.

operations in which he played a large part himself. It may then seem *probable* that Ptolemy was more extensively used than Aristobulus.

21. In his preface Arrian adds that he has also recorded, but only as tales (*legomena*), statements he found in other writers, if he thought them memorable and not entirely untrustworthy; in fact he sometimes mentions such ' tales ', only to reject them as incredible, presumably because they were so prevalent that he felt bound to notice them, or because they illustrated his contention that the usual versions of Alexander's expedition were often worthless. It is conventional to refer to the accounts of Alexander which do not depend on Ptolemy, Aristobulus or Nearchus as ' the vulgate '. This is an expression I shall use for convenience. It must not be taken to imply that the *legomena* belong to a single tradition. On the contrary, variants were numerous and outright contradictions not infrequent. It appears that though the *legomena* retailed by Arrian are sometimes found, along with many other ' tales ' that he ignored, in Diodorus, Curtius, Plutarch, Justin and elsewhere, Arrian's own versions of them are often peculiar to himself; I believe that he culled them from very late writers, those which were read in his own day, whereas our other authorities may preserve much earlier versions. This thesis again will be more fully set out in volume II, where I shall argue that Arrian never inspected any of the contemporary historians of Alexander except Ptolemy, Aristobulus and Nearchus.

22. Diodorus is generally held to have used only one source at a time, for instance in books xviii–xx the excellent contemporary historian, Hieronymus of Cardia (*c.* 360–260); evidence from these books which

bears on Alexander is of first rate value. In book xvii his one source (if this theory is correct) was also used, perhaps at second hand, by Curtius, whose account often shows striking concurrences but preserves more of the common source than Diodorus' briefer story. Curtius, it is true, must also have drawn on another tradition, perhaps Ptolemy, for he is also sometimes at variance with Diodorus. As Clitarchus is named once by Diodorus (though not in book xvii) and twice by Curtius, and as there are some (but very few) significant agreements between the fragments of his work and their accounts, he is generally identified as their common source, all the more readily as he was much read down to the first century B.C., though little respected.[26] However, since the fragments of Clitarchus are meagre, this identification adds little to the picture we can form of their common source from the works of Diodorus and Curtius alone, and it is positively harmful if it induces the error of thinking that the evidence for Alexander in antiquity came to consist only of the ' Clitarchean vulgate ' and of Arrian's chosen authorities. In fact there was a multiplicity of versions of many events, and we should not disregard any of the historians of Alexander's own time or those who may later have distorted and embellished what they read. In this edition I shall claim less knowledge of Clitarchus than most scholars profess.[27]

---

[26] Jacoby, *RE* xi 622 ff. But cf. now E. N. Borza, *Proc. of African Classical Ass.* 1968 with further bibliography.

[27] The discussion of the sources in Tarn ii 1–134 is largely discredited, see especially H. Strasburger, *Bibliotheka Orientalis* 1952, 202 ff. Even the adulation of Ptolemy (and what in Arrian is divined to be from Ptolemy), which Tarn shared with most earlier scholars, is now diminishing.

23. Arrian's account is in general at once more detailed, clear and coherent than those given by Diodorus and Curtius, and it has less of the trivial and fabulous; Ptolemy and Aristobulus were among those who denied or omitted absurd stories like that of the queen of the Amazons, such as even Onesicritus and Clitarchus, though contemporaries, retailed. So little, however, is known of their works except from Arrian that it is the qualities of his history that do most to prove their superiority as sources and confirm his judgement in relying mainly on them. However, he himself was too much of an admirer of Alexander to detect that their histories were often apologetic, especially in tendentious omissions (cf. Appendixes II, V, VI, VIII 15; XIV); nor did it occur to him that Ptolemy's version might have been affected by the feuds after Alexander's death in which he played a great part. Moreover, Arrian himself lacks some of the ' documentary ' material which other writers, notably Curtius, have preserved; it seems to me probable that he must have omitted much detail that his own main sources contained. We cannot, therefore, neglect other accounts of Alexander, even Diodorus and Curtius despite their general inferiority, and still less Plutarch and Strabo, especially when they themselves cite other contemporary authorities. Nor can it in my view be maintained that Arrian contributes much, if anything, of his own that is important to understanding Alexander. His merit was to have unearthed better accounts than were current in his day, and to have followed them without the embellishments of a Curtius, but just as his style is less brilliant than that of Curtius, so his own judgement is more naïve. He was a simple, honest soul, but no historian.

INTRODUCTION

THE MACEDONIANS[28]

24. In the time of Alexander and his father, Philip, the heart of the Macedonian kingdom with its centres at Aegae and Pella lay in the ' rich Emathian plain ' formed by the alluvial deposits of the rivers, Haliacmon, Lydias, Axius and Echedorus; it extended southwards to the vale of Tempe and eastwards to the river Strymon, with Pella as capital. It was a land rich in timber and grain, capable of supporting a fairly large population, with abundant pasturage; the military strength of the Macedonians lay above all in their cavalry. However, the mountainous cantons to the north-west, Pelagonia, Lyncestis, Orestis, Eordaea, Elimea, Tymphaea, also counted as Macedonian. These cantons in Upper Macedon had their own ' kings ' until Philip's time, who had often been able to combine a loose allegiance to their overlords at Pella with a high degree of independence. It was one of Philip's great achievements to have brought them under closer control; three of the six foot regiments Alexander took with him to Asia were recruited in Upper Macedon (D. 57, 2), and their native habitat fitted them particularly well for the mountain campaigns Alexander undertook in Iran and the Hindu Kush. The picture that Arrian (vii 9) makes Alexander draw of the primitive conditions in which the Macedonians had lived before Philip's

[28] Cf. G. T. Griffith, *GR*, 125 ff. Geography: S. Casson, *Macedonia Thrace and Illyria* 1926, chapters I–II; N. G. L. Hammond, *History of Macedonia* I, 1972, 1–213. Early history: esp. F. Geyer, *Makedonien bis zur Thronbesteigung Philipps II*, 1930. Philip: A. Momigliano, *Filippo il Macedone*, 1934; F. R. Wüst, *Philipp II von Makedonien u. Griechenland* 1938; P. Cloché, *Philippe II*, n.d.

reign (359–336), clad in skins and tending a few sheep in the mountains, can at most apply only to the people of Upper Macedon; though Philip undoubtedly encouraged urban life, and set a precedent for Alexander by founding new towns like Philippopolis that bore his name, older towns such as Pella had long existed in Lower Macedon. However, whereas Greek cities enjoyed or sought to enjoy full sovereignty, the towns in Macedon can at most have possessed local self-government as municipalities within the kingdom. A Greek would describe himself as an Athenian or a Corinthian or the like, but in Macedon a man was said to be a Macedonian, coming from such and such a town or rural canton.[29] The army was organized on a territorial basis, divided into units recruited from these urban or rural districts.[30]

25. The relics of the Macedonian language, such as the names of places and persons, both human and divine, e.g. Zeus, show that it was basically Greek with an admixture of (probably) Illyrian. However, to Greeks in the fourth century it was evidently unintelligible.[31] Macedonian institutions too, though they resembled those we find in the Homeric poems, were alien to the Greeks of Alexander's time, who were accustomed to city-states with oligarchic or democratic institutions. Hence they did not see that the Macedonians were of the same stock as themselves but at an earlier, indeed Homeric, stage of development. Demosthenes (iii 17) called Philip a barbarian, Isocrates (v 107 f.) a Greek ruling over barbarians; technically Isocrates was right, since the royal house of the Argeads, who traced their

[29] e.g. vi 28, 4; *Ind.* 18; 27, 8; Tod 164; 186.
[30] iii 16, 5, cf. i 2, 5; 12, 7; ii 9, 3; D. 57, 2.
[31] Kalléris, *Les anciens Macédoniens*, 1954.

INTRODUCTION

descent to Heracles and origin to Argos (e.g. A. ii
5, 9; iv 11, 6), had been admitted as Greeks to the
Olympic games in the fifth century.[32] In the end the
Macedonians were all to count as Greek (e.g. Polybius
ix 37), but in Alexander's time they themselves
perhaps did not wish to be so regarded, for Arrian,
following his main sources, who were Macedonian by
birth (Ptolemy) or adoption (Aristobulus and Nearchus), is normally careful to distinguish and even to
contrast Macedonians and Greeks.[33] Still the process
of Hellenization had already begun. Euripides had
produced his *Bacchae* at the Macedonian court.
Philip employed Aristotle as tutor for Alexander and,
though it is absurd to suppose that the adolescent
prince comprehended his teacher's philosophy, he was
saturated in Homer (App. IV), became a patron of
Apelles and Lysippus (i 16, 4), the best painter and
sculptor respectively of the time, and took a number
of Greek men of letters and science to Asia, notably
Callisthenes. Philip had also incorporated Greek
cities in the kingdom, and these supplied some of his
cavalry (i 2, 5; 12, 7); indeed Greeks like Nearchus
were admitted to the noble order of Companions. It
is no surprise that Ptolemy, one of the old nobility,
was himself to write a history of Alexander, obviously
inspired by Greek models. Eventually the whole
people was thoroughly Hellenized, and the Macedonian kingdoms in the near east which arose out of the
ruins of Alexander's empire were to diffuse Greek

[32] Herodotus v 20–2; viii 137–9.
[33] ii 10, 7 cf. 7, 4; iii 22, 2; iv 11, 8 (' vulgate '); v 26, 6;
27, 4 f.; 27, 8; vii 9, 4 f.; *Ind.* 18, 3 and 7 (Nearchus, cf.
18, 11). Contrast ii 14, 4: ' Macedonia and the rest of Greece ';
the words, ascribed to Al., must be A's, and reflect the later
conception.

culture among their Oriental subjects. This was how Greek became the *lingua franca* in which the Gospel could be preached centuries later, the language in which even Jews, like Paul, chose to write.

26. As we have seen, the Macedonians were governed by kings. From the earliest times they had been normally drawn from the Argead dynasty. Herodotus (viii 137–9) seems to have thought that down to his own day the crown had descended in unbroken succession from father to son. This was certainly not true in later generations. Thus Philip himself became King in preference to his elder brother's child, Amyntas, who continued to live honourably at court, till he was put out of the way after Alexander's accession (§ 46). Philip is said to have had the assent of the army, the people in arms, to his usurpation (J. vii 5, 10), and it is generally held that it was a *right* of the army to elect their kings, though only from the Argead line;[34] to my mind it is more probable that they exercised this *power*, not of right but only when the succession was disputed; that was admittedly frequent.

27. Callisthenes is reported to have said that the kings had always ruled Macedon by *nomos*, not by force (iv 11, 6). *Nomos* means both law and custom. So primitive a people as the Macedonians would not have had a code of laws: they were ruled by custom. Thus we find Alexander often performing the sacrifices that custom required.[35] Evidently the king was also the chief intermediary between his subjects and the

---

[34] So most fully F. Granier, *Die makedonische Heeresversammlung* 1931, with much evidence from the successor kingdoms which I think irrelevant to Macedon.

[35] e.g. iii 16, 9; 25, 1; 28, 4; iv 4, 1; v 3, 6; 8, 2 f.; 20, 1; 29, 2; vi 3, 1 f. (cf. *Ind.* 18, 11); vii 11, 8; 14, 1; 24, 4; 25.

gods. A few texts indicate that he was likewise the supreme judge.[36] Quintus Curtius indeed states (vi 8, 25) that it was an ancient Macedonian custom that the king could do no more than investigate capital offences and had then to bring them before the people in arms for trial. This procedure is apparently illustrated by the trials of Philotas and his supposed accomplices, and of Hermolaus and others implicated in the pages' conspiracy. But on other occasions both Alexander and later Macedonian kings executed Macedonians summarily. If the people enjoyed the customary right of which Curtius tells, it was one which the kings set at naught whenever they felt it safe.[37] Some hold that the people possessed only one other right, that of electing the kings (*supra*). More probably the kings would consult the army on any occasions when they felt themselves in need of popular consent. Otherwise they could and did act autocratically. Demosthenes says that ' Philip, a single man, decides all questions open and secret for himself; he is his own general, his own master, his own treasurer.'[38] Similarly Alexander constantly seeks the advice of a council, drawn from the nobles, but he is free to disregard it.[39]

28. In principle the king was the state. Coins

---

[36] D. xvi 93, 8; P. 43, 2; *Demetrius* 42, 4; *Moralia* 178 AF; 179 A.

[37] See iii 26 f.; iv 14, 2, but also vi 27, 4 f.; vii 8, 3. Cf. App. XI 5. Polybius v 27 is instructive. QC. vi 11, 20 and viii 6, 28 are inconsistent with viii 8, 18 and not credible as an explanation of Parmenio's killing, especially as his brother, Asander, was allowed to survive (A. iv 7, 2).

[38] i 4, cf. xviii 235.

[39] i 25, 4 f.; ii 6, 1; 16, 8 and 18, 1; 25, 2; iii 9, 3 f.; v 25–8 etc.

were issued in his name, not in that of the Macedonians.[40] Treaties were made by him and with him; it is not till the third century that we get documentary mention of the ' commonalty (*koinon*) of the Macedonians'; Arrian vii 9, 5 is anachronistic. He alone could bind his subjects by inter-state agreements. Thus the so-called League of Corinth (*infra*) could properly be described as ' Philip (or Alexander) and the Greeks'; this does not mean that the Macedonians stood outside the league: they were represented by their king.[41] However, other states would not be content with the royal oath to a treaty, if they had reason to think that he was not in full control of his people, and in the past they had sometimes extracted, or reserved the right to extract, confirmatory oaths from the king's son, or from Macedonian nobles, as well as from the king himself; even then the Macedonians as such do not appear.[42] Such arrangements were required when the king was weak, and until Philip's reign that had been common.

29. This weakness appears to have been partly due to the turbulence of the barons and disloyalty of the ' kings ' of Upper Macedon; moreover, dissidents within the realm could always look for support to the enemies who beset it on every frontier. Probably the kings had sought to counteract the disloyalty of the greater nobles by appealing to other elements in the population. This hypothesis will explain some confusing technical terms that often recur in Arrian's history.

30. There the Macedonian cavalry, thousands strong, are commonly described as ' Companions '

[40] Head, *Hist. Nummorum* 218 ff.
[41] Tod 111; 177; 183; 191, 6; cf. § 38.
[42] *SEG* x 86; Tod 129; 158.

(*hetairoi*).[43] But the same term is also used of a more limited class who attend Alexander's council, are banqueted by him or receive (in 324) Oriental brides from him; of these marriages there were only 92.[44] It seems probable that the term was first used in this narrower sense; the original 'Companions' will have been the royal *comitatus*, his entourage consisting chiefly of the principal nobles. Similarly in Homer, king Idomeneus calls himself the 'Companion' of his overlord, Agamemnon, and Patroclus and the Myrmidons are the 'Companions' of Achilles.[45] At some stage a king conferred this honorific title on all those who served him on horse, appealing to the 'knights' against the barons, but the old title continued to be used in a pregnant sense of individuals, whether or not they were actually accompanying the king, who belonged to the higher class; when Arrian says of a particular man that he was a 'Companion', he does not mean simply that he was a horseman; it is only in the plural that 'Companions' is used of the cavalry. Later on, but before Philip's reign, even the foot had been designated as 'foot-companions' (*pezetairoi*), presumably by a king who wished to broaden the basis of his power by relying

[43] Cf. i 14, 1; vii 6, 3 etc. Theopompus (Jacoby no. 115) F. 225, referring to 800 Companions in Philip's time, must have in mind an addition of so many Greeks to the cavalry force, brought about by new allotments of royal (conquered) land on condition of knight service; cf. n. 51; *SIG*³ 332. Some foreigners like Nearchus were admitted to the Companions in the narrower sense, cf. *Ind.* 17 with notes. F. Carrata-Thomes, *Il problema degli eteri nella monarchia di Alessandro Magno*, 1955, usefully assembles evidence.

[44] e.g. i 25, 4 f.; iv 8, 8; vii 4. 'Friends' is an untechnical synonym, i 25, 2 and 4.; usual in D.

[45] e.g. *Iliad* i 345; iv 266.

more on the peasants able to serve in heavy armour.[46]

31. We can actually see this process at work in 324. The grandees of the Persian court were styled ' kinsmen ' by the Persian king, and Alexander adopted this usage. But to conciliate the mutinous Macedonians at Opis, he declared that henceforth they should all be his ' kinsmen '.[47]

32. The confusion of terminology goes further.[48] At times all the squadrons of the Macedonian ' companions ' are called ' royal ', but one of them, which fought by the side of the king himself, is also called royal *par excellence* (see § 58). Again, the élite regiments of foot, the hypaspists (§ 61), can be described as ' the bodyguards ', since it was they whom the king would choose out of the foot to accompany him on some special expedition. But the same term is also applied to a group, normally restricted in number to seven (vi 28, 4), of high-ranking officers, attached to the king's person, who lose this rank, if they are given permanent posts elsewhere. Again, it is plausible to suppose that at one time they were the only ' bodyguards ' and that there was only one ' royal ' squadron. It is curious that the seven bodyguards retained their title and that the hypaspists had acquired it, though by Alexander's time neither were actually charged with the ordinary protection of the king's person, which was committed to pages (§ 34).

33. Before Philip external pressures had helped to keep Macedon and its kings weak. The country

[46] iv 23, 1, cf. Demosthenes ii 17; Anaximenes (Jacoby no. 72) F. 4. See also n. 99.

[47] vii 11, 6 cf. 11, 1; see QC. iii 3, 14 and 21.

[48] For what follows cf. Tarn ii 138–41.

was always in danger of invasions from Illyrian tribes in the north and Thracians in the east. At his accession the coast was mainly in the hands of Greek cities, some organized in the federation of the Chalcidians with a centre at Olynthus, and others under Athenian control. Macedon's neighbours freely intervened in her internal affairs. Here Philip's achievement can only be summarized. Olynthus was destroyed and all the coastal cities brought within the kingdom. The south Thracian principalities were absorbed as far as the Hellespont and Bosphorus. In the north Philip failed to establish a secure frontier, and Alexander felt it indispensable to carry the terror of his arms to the Danube before embarking for Asia; in fact his expedition served to keep the peace there throughout the rest of his reign. Some of the northern tribes had actually been reduced to vassaldom and, like the Thracians, contributed to Alexander's army. The creation of greater internal security seems to have promoted a population explosion, and the new territories incorporated in the kingdom further augmented Alexander's manpower.[49] In Mount Pangaeum Philip also discovered rich gold and silver mines which gave him abundant financial resources and provided funds for Alexander to launch his large and costly expedition.[50]

34. Early in his reign Philip had made his control of the Upper Macedonian principalities more effective. His other successes fortified his internal authority. Conquered land, for instance that of the Greek cities on the coast, became his property; by granting it in return for knight-service, he increased

---

[49] Griffith (n. 28) 129 ff.
[50] ib. 127 f.

his patronage and the strength of his cavalry.[51] Members of 'royal' lines, presumably of Upper Macedon, are said now to come from towns in the plain, Leonnatus from Pella and Perdiccas from Amphipolis;[52] presumably they had moved down to estates granted them in places where they would be more under the king's eye. Even so their fidelity might be suspect, like that of the Lyncestian princes under Alexander (§ 46). Philip also arranged that the sons of notables should be attached to his person as pages (A. iv 13, 1), and some were sent out to Alexander in Asia (D. xvii 65, 1); whether or not they came to feel affection or awe for the king, at court they were hostages for the loyalty of their fathers. In general, the conquests of both Philip and Alexander offered the nobility opportunities to gratify their taste for warfare, plunder and glory. But only a strong ruler could keep them in order. Alexander began his reign with blood and terror, his relations with many of the notables remained uneasy, and after his death when the kingship was divided between his infant son and half-wit brother, his empire was disrupted by their rivalry, in which his former officers, who appear as lay figures in the pages of Arrian, overshadowed by Alexander, displayed great talent and inordinate ambition and rancour.

35. In fact the power of the king rested essentially on his own ability and personality, especially as he lived among his companions on terms of comradeship. They shared his table and drinking bouts, and Alexander would strip to play ball-games with them (Plut. 73). Long after his time Polybius (v 27, 6)

[51] e.g. at Amphipolis, *Ind.* 18, 4 and 10; Methone, D. xvi 34; Bottiaea, *SIG*[3] 332; Griffith 134 f.; cf. n. 43.
[52] QC. x 7, 8, cf. A. vi 28, 4; *Ind.* 18, 4.

could write of the *isegoria*, the equal right to speak freely, that Macedonians had always enjoyed in addressing the king. Similarly Curtius says that though used to royal power the Macedonians ' lived in a greater shade of freedom ' than others so placed; he alleges that such freedom was reduced after the murder of Clitus, which followed a scene vividly illustrating the old practice of equality.[53] It is clear that the Companions resented the pompous trappings of Oriental monarchy which Alexander began to adopt after he could claim to have succeeded Darius as king of kings. His attempt to introduce the Persian custom of *proscynesis* (Appendix XIV) foundered on their opposition, though to the end of his reign he persisted in Orientalizing measures that were designed to win the hearts of his leading Iranian subjects. They were abandoned after his death; we can only surmise whether he would have been strong enough to surmount the resentment among Macedonians of all ranks that this policy provoked. Certainly at the Hyphasis even he had had to yield to the common objection of both officers and men to advancing further into India (v 25–9). Despite the lack of constitutional limits on his authority, enhanced as it was by his unexampled successes, Alexander discovered there that the most self-willed autocrat may at times have no choice but to defer to the strength of public opinion.

GREECE AND MACEDON[54]

36. Philip had also imposed his will on Greece. His predecessors had always had a natural desire to

[53] iv 7, 31 cf. vi 6, 2; viii 4, 30.
[54] I give no references for many statements documented in all standard works.

dominate Thessaly, immediately to the south of their kingdom. In Philip's time the Thessalians were torn by internal feuds and had lost their traditional control of the shrine of Delphi to the Phocians. By a series of interventions Philip re-established peace within the country and restored in appearance the special position of the Thessalians at the shrine. In fact he himself was now its master, all the more because he was elected *tagos* or president of the Thessalian confederation. None the less most of the Thessalians seem to have been grateful for his services. Alexander succeeded him as *tagos*, and the Thessalian cavalry, the best in Greece, who were regularly stationed on his left wing in the great battles down to 331, were one of his most valuable units. Later in his reign discontent increased in Thessaly, and the Thessalians revolted in the Lamian war which broke out in Greece just after his death, but this does not concern us here.

37. By his action against the Phocians, who were allies of Athens, and still more by seizing places on the Macedonian seaboard which Athens had held or claimed, Philip had incurred the deep hostility of the most powerful maritime city in Greece. A peace patched up in 346 was regarded by Demosthenes and his friends, who gradually came to dominate Athenian counsels, as no more than a respite during which they could prepare a war of revenge. The intrigues and coups by which Philip tried to extend his influence in Greece, perhaps to counter that of Athens, strengthened the impression that his power menaced the liberties of all Greek cities, and enabled Athens to organize a strong coalition against him.[55]

[55] Cf. Brunt, *CQ* 1969, 245 ff., also on the particularism that determined the policy of all Greek cities.

It was even joined by the Thebans, who had the best army in Greece (cf. i 9, 6); old enemies of Phocis and Athens and former allies of Philip, they had become aware that their previous dominance in central Greece had been undermined by Philip's successes. This coalition was decisively defeated at Chaeronea in 338. Under the settlement Philip imposed Athens' maritime league was dissolved, and Thebes was still more harshly treated; the Boeotian federation was freed from her control, the anti-Macedonian leaders killed or banished, and a Macedonian garrison installed in her citadel, the Cadmea (cf. i 7). Philip next settled affairs in the Peloponnese to the disadvantage of Sparta and in the interest of the cities there which were his friends, because they feared Spartan power. For the time being opposition was cowed, but Athens, Thebes and Sparta naturally resented the foreign hegemony, nor was discontent confined to them. As soon as Philip died there was a widespread movement of disaffection in Greece (§ 49); in 335 not only Athens but Elis, the Aetolians and some of the Arcadians almost came to the assistance of Thebes in her revolt (i 7, 4; 10, 1 f.), in 331 Sparta enjoyed the support of Elis and most of the Arcadians and Achaeans, while in 323 Athens was able to organize a still more formidable revolt in the Lamian war. Arrian occasionally indicates that Alexander himself was aware of such general discontent (i 7, 4; 18, 8; ii 26, 3) and of the need to terrorize the Greeks (i 29, 6), especially Athens and Sparta (ii 17). It is not disproved by flattering embassies the Greeks felt obliged to send in his honour (iii 5; vii 14; 23). Of course some Greeks were apprehensive of the ambitions of the great cities and looked for protection to Macedon (Polybius xviii 14); the bitter

feelings that Thebes had provoked by prolonged
oppression of her neighbours contributed to the
harshness of her treatment in 335 (i 8, 8; 9, 6–9), and
in 331 Antipater obtained indispensable aid against
Sparta from her old enemies in the Peloponnese,
Argos, Messene and the Arcadians who followed the
lead of Megalopolis. It was fear of Sparta that made
them loyal to Alexander (iii, 6, 3); once this had
been allayed by Sparta's crushing defeat, even Argos
and Messene were ready to rise against Macedon in
323. We may doubt if there was anywhere a
party sincerely sympathetic to Macedon, as distinct
from men who saw that the particular interests of
their own cities, or sometimes their own private
advantage, lay for the time in seeking Macedonian
support.

38. However, in 337 Philip's power enabled him to
dictate to the whole of the Greek mainland and
many of the island cities, and to organize what
moderns call the League of Corinth, since it was at
Corinth that the Greeks met by plenipotentiaries
and concluded a new ' common peace ' (cf. ii 14, 6).
This was the latest in a series of such treaties,[56] the
first of which had been imposed on the Greek world
by the combined will of the Persian king, Artaxerxes II, and Sparta in 387/6 and which was known
either as the king's peace or the peace of Antalcidas,
from the name of the Spartan diplomat concerned
(cf. ii 1, 4; 2, 2). Under that peace, as under every
' common peace ' that followed, including Philip's,
all Greek cities, great and small, were declared free
and autonomous; the fine phrase always veiled the
truth that some were in practice to be in subjection;

[56] T. T. B. Ryder, *Koine Eirene*, 1965.

in 337 Thebes was not the only city actually under the ' protection' of a Macedonian garrison. In 387/6 indeed it had been expressly provided that the Greek cities in Asia were to be excepted from the rule and subject to Persia; this was certainly not re-affirmed in 337 (§ 39). In the past there had been no machinery to enforce the preservation of peace and the principle of autonomy: now all the member states were bound to take common action for these purposes (and also to suppress internal revolutions). Such common action was to be decided by a *synedrion*, consisting of plenipotentiaries sent by the members, in conjunction with the *hegemon*, that is to say, Philip himself (and his heirs after him).[57] Thus, though the members were officially termed ' the cities that shared in the peace', in effect a league was created, and its very first act was to proclaim a common war against Persia. Hence Arrian (iii 24, 4 f.) refers to the organization as a league (*koinon*) or alliance and to the members as 'allies ' (i 9, 9; 24, 3; iii 19, 5). On Philip's death Alexander succeeded to his position as *hegemon* (§ 49, cf. ii 14, 4); though the Greeks evidently renewed their treaties with him, he already had a hereditary right to that position. All league decisions required the concurrence of the *hegemon* as well as that of a majority in the *synedrion*,[58]

[57] Cf. Tod 177 (with bibliography); the other chief texts are Ps-Demosthenes xvii (dated *c.* 330 BC), D. xvi 89, 3 (cf. xviii 56, which shows that the scheme was propounded in an edict or *diagramma* by Philip); J. ix 5; the relevance of *IG* iv[2] 1, 68 is conjectural. The articles by U. Wilcken, (1) *Sitzungsberichte München* 1917, 35 ff.; (2) *Berlin* 1922, 97 ff., (3) *ibid.* 1929, 291 ff.; 316 ff. are of fundamental importance. I pass over matters that are not directly related to understanding of Arrian. For decrees of the *synedrion* see iii 23, 8.

[58] Cf. the hegemonic position of Sparta or Athens in the

but in addition Philip seems to have been appointed
' general with full powers ', i.e. given the right to act
at his own discretion in the conduct of the war on
behalf of the league, e.g. to accept new members,
and Arrian's allusion to Alexander as ' *hegemon* with
full powers ' (vii 9, 5), incorrectly amalgamating the
two functions, suggests that he too, as we should
expect, was formally given this same role, presumably
in 336 (i 1, 2). All this explains Arrian's references
to the peace and alliance concluded by the Greeks
with the Macedonians, i.e. with their kings (iii 24, 5,
cf. § 28), and to the treaties made with him or, more
correctly, with him and the Greeks by two islands
which acceded to the league (ii 1, 4; 2, 2). The
Persian war was carried on by ' Alexander and the
Greeks except Sparta ' (i 16, 7); Sparta alone in
mainland Greece stood outside the league on the pretext given in i 1, 2, but in reality because Macedonian
power entrenched on her sovereignty and adversely
affected her interests (§ 37). Philip or Alexander
could easily have coerced her, but her manifest
hostility may have actually suited them, binding to
them other states in the Peloponnese. It can of
course be seen that the league was an instrument of
their dominance; this comes out in Arrian's statements that in 334 Alexander put Antipater in charge
of the Greeks (i 11, 3, cf. ii 2, 4; iii 16, 10; Diodorus
xviii 8, 4) and that in 324 Craterus as his successor was
' to direct the freedom (!) of the Greeks ' (vii 12, 4).
Both may have been formally designated by the

---

leagues named ' the Lacedaemonians ' (or ' Athenians ') ' and
their allies ' (see G. E. M. de Ste Croix, *Origins of the Peloponnesian War*, 1972, 303 ff., 339 f.); ' Alexander and the Greeks '
is a corresponding description. And see Tod 177, 20-2.

1

synedrion too as persons ' appointed for the common
protection ' (Ps-Demosthenes xvii 15).

39. The league had two possible pretexts for
attacking Persia. One is given only by Diodorus
(xvi 91, 2; xvii 24, 1): to free the Greeks in Asia
from Persian rule. This objective was perhaps
adopted by Alexander only after initial hesitation,
when he ordered that the cities previously subject
to Asia should be given autonomy and immunity
from tribute and that they should be governed
democratically (cf. i 18, 2). Immunity from tribute
did not mean that they were not required to make a
contribution (*syntaxis*) to war costs, which was
probably obligatory on all league cities; though
there is no testimony that the Asian cities were
admitted to the league, it is reasonable to assume
that they were. However, as Alexander came into
possession of the Persian hoards of precious metal
(App. X 3), he ceased to need Greek contributions,
and we happen to hear of his remitting that previously
demanded from Priene; in the end at least the Greek
cities gained financially from the abolition of the
tribute permanently exacted by Persia. As autonomous, the Asian cities were theoretically to be
free from interference by Alexander as king or his
satraps: in practice, they were no more exempt
from Macedonian control than those of old Greece.
Indeed, the establishment of democracies in 334
was in itself an interference in their internal affairs.
Its motive cannot have been that Alexander intrin-
sically preferred democracy (cf. v 2, 3); elsewhere
he even backed tyrants, but in Asia the oligarchs had
favoured the cause of the Persian king, who had
upheld their local authority. No doubt, however, the
overthrow of those oligarchs was of great benefit to

the Asian Greeks, and the gratitude they felt for liberation was still commemorated by cults centuries later.[59]

40. The other pretext for the league's war with Persia was retribution for the Persian invasion of Greece in 480–479.[60] Officially it was in fulfilment of this war aim that Alexander set Persepolis on fire and destroyed its temples (iii 18, 12). The war was now over for the league, and their contingents, even the valued Thessalians, were disbanded soon afterwards (iii 19, 6). Athens had suffered more than any other city from the Persian invasion (iii 18, 12), and though well aware of her hostility, Alexander sought to give colour to the Panhellenism of his enterprise by dedicating trophies at Athens after the Granicus (i 16, 7) and restoring the statues of Harmodius and Aristogiton which Xerxes had removed to Susa (iii 16, 7). He claimed to be fighting for Greece (i 29, 5) and could punish as traitors Greeks who served Darius (cf. also i 16, 6); indeed he treated any Greek cities, whether or not members of the league, which showed sympathy for Persia, as in principle liable to penalties, though he could also pardon both communities and individuals on the ground that they had acted under *force majeure*, or simply because it was in his own interest to show clemency.[61]

[59] E. Badian, *Ancient Society and Institutions, Studies presented to Victor Ehrenberg* 1966, 37 ff. cites and supersedes previous discussions. *Syntaxis*: Tod 185 (c. 332 BC), cf. A. i 26, 3 (Aspendus counted as Greek, n. 61). Cults: C. Habicht, *Gottmenschentum u. griechische Städte* 17 ff.

[60] A. ii 14; D. xvi 89; Polybius quoted in § 42.

[61] See i 16, 6 f.; 17, 2; 19, 6 (cf. 24, 4); 22, 7 and 23, 4 (Halicarnassus was Greek, *pace* Tarn ii 218, cf. Herodotus ii 178, vii 99); 26, 3 and 27, 4 on Aspendus (reputed an Argive colony, Strabo xiv 4, 2); ii 5, 5 and 8 and 12, 2 (Soli, said to have been founded by Achaeans and Rhodians, Strabo xiv

41. Isocrates had long been urging the Greeks to combine in a war of conquest against Persia, and had latterly incited Philip to lead the enterprise. But Isocrates evinced little concern for the ' enslavement ' of the Asian Greeks or desire to revenge the atrocities of the Persians in 480–479.[62]   In his conception a Panhellenic crusade would promote peace at home and provide the Greeks with new lands on which to settle their surplus population; Philip was to be content with the glory of benefiting the Greeks by victories over the barbarians.[63]   If we can believe the ' vulgate ', Callisthenes may well have shared this naïve idea, for we are told that he reminded Alexander of his original purpose, to annex ' Asia' to Greece (iv 11, 7).[64]   It is quite unlikely that either Philip or Alexander ever entertained such a purpose. They could allege Macedonian *casus belli*: in the fifth century the Persians had invaded Macedon

---

5, 8); 5, 9 (' Argive ' Mallus); 20, 3 (Cyprus); iii 24, 4 (Sinope); 23, 8 and 24, 5 (mercenaries). Note also release of Athenian captives, iii 6, 2, contrast i 29, 5 f.; he now felt conciliation of Athens to be most prudent.

[62] He alludes to these themes only in iv 155; 181; 183; 185; v 124–6 (?); xii 103; *ep.* ix 8.

[63] iv 131–3; 174; 182; 187; v (addressed to Philip) 9; 84 f.; 107 f.; 112; 120–2; 129–45.

[64] ' Asia ' means the Persian empire in Isocrates v 66; 76 and often; cf. A. ii 7, 6; 12, 5; 14, 8 f.; iii 9, 6; 18, 11; 25, 3, and presumably ii 3, 6; iv 4, 3. But in iv 15, 5 f.; v 4, 4; v 26 (three times) it includes India, cf. *Ind.* 2, 2; 3, 6, even (most clearly in v 26) beyond the utmost conceivable confines of the Persian empire; indeed the Indus was sometimes regarded as the boundary between ' India ' and that empire, cf. App. XV. Al's claim to rule all Asia thus came to be a claim to rule more than the Persian empire, though when he had failed to conquer all India (v 25 ff.), he could revert to the other sense of ' Asia ' in his boast that he had traversed all Asia and was in possession of it (Nearchus *ap. Ind.* 35, 8). Cf. n. 76.

as well as Greece, and in 340 they had helped Perinthus to repel Philip's attack; Alexander even had the impudence to add that Darius had been guilty of hostile acts against him—after Philip had already invaded Asia (ii 14, 4 f.).[65] But all these were surely pretexts. Conquest must have been the real purpose. Immediately after the Granicus Alexander began to organize provinces and collect taxes (i 17, 1–8); he continued to do so, as he advanced. In his letter to Darius he already claimed to be 'king of Asia' (ii 14, 7), and to make good this Macedonian or personal objective, he carried on the war after dismissing the league troops; indeed 'Asia' came to mean more than the Persian empire as it was in 336, or had ever been (cf. n. 64). The Greeks benefited in that his requirements for mercenaries gave many of them opportunity of employment, and that he founded cities where they were settled, but these benefits were incidental to the aggrandizement and protection of his own dominions.[66]

42. Arrian altogether fails to make Alexander's aims clear: in fact he does not discuss them. He seems to assume that the war needs no explanation. Even the *casus belli* are mentioned quite late in his narrative (ii 14), and he gives no hint that they are to be considered mere pretexts, and that some of them were simply absurd. Contrast the observation of Polybius (iii 6) that the real cause of the war lay in

---

[65] For the intervention at Perinthus perhaps authorized only by the local satrap cf. Ps-Demosthenes (Anaximenes) xi 5 f.; D. xvi 75. The date and even the historicity of the alliance between Philip and Persia it breached are disputed.

[66] Greek mercenaries proved to be unwilling settlers in Bactria and tried to make their way home in defiance of Al., cf. D. xvii 99, 5 f.; xviii 4, 8; 7, 1 ff.; QC. ix 7; to this there is a mere allusion in A. v 27, 5 (speech).

INTRODUCTION

Philip's conviction that the Persian empire was weak, that an attack on it would bring him handsome rewards and win popularity in the Greek world and that he seized on the pretext of avenging Persian ' lawlessness ' in 480.

43. Even Polybius was mistaken (like many moderns) if he thought that the war did reconcile the Greeks to Macedonian hegemony. Panhellenism derived its true force from the sense that all Greeks had certain characteristics in common which distinguished them from barbarians (Herodotus viii 144). But not the least of these characteristics was attachment to a free, independent city state. The political unity of the Greek ' nation ' would involve the sacrifice of an element essential to Greekness. This was one of the rocks on which the attempts had foundered which Greek cities, Athens and Sparta, had made to create larger political units. But the Macedonians were not even Greek: they were as barbarian in Greek eyes as the Persians. In Philip's lifetime it had still been possible to style the Persian king ' the common enemy of the Greeks ' (Demosthenes xiv 3), but such conventional language, for a century past, had not prevented Greek cities seeking aid from him, and now it was evident that the true threat to Greek liberty came from Macedon. It was in the name of liberty that Athens, Thebes and Sparta all contended with the Macedonians and they felt no shame in accepting and avowing Persian aid.[67] Arrian himself mentions the Theban appeal to ' freedom and liberty of speech, time-honoured and fine-sounding words ' (i 7, 2); there is a nuance of contempt. He does not wholly conceal the extent of

---

[67] Demosthenes x 31 ff.; D. 9, 5; 62, 1–3.

discontent in Greece, though he almost ignores the anti-Macedonian movement immediately after Philip's death (§ 49), merely alludes to Agis' revolt (Appendix VI) and has nothing on the actions of Alexander in 324 which provoked the Lamian war. But he is clearly unsympathetic to it. The ideal of the independent *polis* was remote to this Hellenized and Romanized Bithynian, and he could hardly have grasped that to contemporaries the Macedonians were not Greeks and Alexander not at all the 'national' hero that he might seem later. In the context of his general admiration for Alexander and uncritical reporting of his claim to be fighting for Greece, the reader is surely meant to feel that revolts and 'medism' were as treasonable as Alexander pretended. He cannot avoid describing the atrocious treatment of Thebes, but he conveys the impression (i 9, 6 ff.) that it was just retribution for her own misdeeds and that in any event Alexander was not primarily responsible.[68] He makes us feel that towards Athens Alexander was remarkably forbearing, failing (again like many modern scholars) to make it clear that it would have been an odd prelude to a war of retribution on Persia, if Alexander had shown severity to Persia's chief victim in 480, and, more important, that Athens was strongly fortified, that all experience before the capture of Tyre suggested that such a city could not be taken by assault, that her ships commanded the seas and could bring in supplies, and that in the event of a long siege Persian intervention east of the Aegean and further revolts in Greece were to be apprehended.[69]

[68] Contrast D. 9, 4.

[69] Cf. Polybius' mistaken view that Philip's humanity to Athens won the Athenians over (v 10). The honours paid to

44. It was not only the revolts that manifested Greek sentiments. The soldiers the league contributed to Alexander's army were neither numerous (§ 56) nor, except for the Thessalians who stood in a special relation to their *tagos* (§ 36), important. The army did indeed include a steadily growing proportion of Greek mercenaries, but they were individuals serving Alexander for pay, as their compeers served Darius.[70] On the other hand, his fleet in 334 was Greek (i 18, 4 n.), and it was inadequate: 160 ships, when Athens alone had 400 in her dockyards[71] and could have given Alexander something

Philip, and to Al. in 336 B.C. (A i. 1, 3, cf. Schaefer, *Demosthenes* iii ² 32 and 97), and to other Macedonians (Tod 180 f.), like the embassy sent in 331 (iii 6, 2), are not evidence of their true feelings. Demosthenes and his friends (i 10, 4) remained the most influential politicians at Athens, though the pro-Macedonian, Demades (i 10, 3), was useful in conducting negotiations with Macedon. The acquittal of Ctesiphon in 330 B.C. was a vindication of the past policy Demosthenes defended in his speech *On the Crown*. In 336, 335 and 331 B.C. he all but took Athens over the brink into war with Macedon; probably it was his reluctance to do so in 324 that led to his banishment at the instance of extremists. A. notes Athenian discontent in i 1, 3; 7, 4; 10, 2 ff.; 29, 5 f.; ii 17, 2; iv 10, 3 (' vulgate '), and communications with Persia in ii 15, 2; iii 24, 4 (though he ignores Demosthenes' intrigues with Persia D. 4, 7 ff.; 5, 1), and shows how Al. tried to keep Athens loyal by pressure (i 29, 5 f.) or kindness (iii 6, 12; 16, 7), cf. n. 61; in i 10, 6 he does perhaps hint at the considerations which surely determined the policy of Al. (and Philip). Cf also F. Mitchel, *Greece and Rome*, 1965, 189 ff.

[70] Numbers: § 56 f.; App. XIII; in addition on the Hydaspes Al. was joined by over 37,000 foot and 6,000 horse, D. 95, 4; QC. ix 3, 21.

[71] *IG* ii ² 1627b 266 ff.; 1628, 22 ff.; 1629 d 783 ff. She could not man and equip them all, but put 170 to sea in 322 (D. xviii 15, 8), after sustaining losses; in 323 it had been decided to equip 240 (ib. 10, 2).

approaching naval parity with the Persians. He dismissed it, keeping 20 Athenian ships, presumably as hostages. Naval inferiority distorted his strategy. For fear that the Persian navy even after Issus might stir up a great revolt in Greece and strike at his home base in Macedon, he adopted the plan of capturing the Persian naval bases and thereby bringing about the disintegration of the enemy fleet; hence, instead of pursuing Darius with his usual speed and audacity, marching at once into Mesopotamia and depriving him of the chance to mobilize new forces and fight again in conditions much less favourable to the Macedonians, he had to spend a year in the conquest of Phoenicia. Arrian explains this strategy plainly enough (ii 16, 8 n.), without drawing out its unfortunate consequences. It may be added that in 331 Alexander relied on the old Persian navy to repress his own 'allies' in Greece (iii, 6, 3), and that in 322 the Phoenicians played a decisive part in the Macedonian sea victory at Amorgos, in which the Athenian navy was finally destroyed and Salamis at last avenged.

PHILIP'S LAST YEAR AND ALEXANDER'S ACCESSION

45. By beginning his history with Alexander's accession and passing over his first actions in a few sentences (i 1, 1–3), Arrian denies his readers knowledge of events which are highly relevant to his chosen subject and to which he later makes a few, dark allusions. Having failed to show how Philip had built up the power that made Alexander's conquests possible, or to explain the genesis of the war with

Persia, he also almost conceals the initial operations of the war (Diod. xvi 91; xvii 7). In 336 Philip despatched a force of about 10,000 men (§ 56) to Asia under Parmenio and Attalus. At first they gained considerable successes; hence a party favourable to Philip gained power in his lifetime at Ephesus, only to be overmastered later by pro-Persian oligarchs (i 17, 10–12), once a Persian counter-offensive had been launched in 335 by the Greek condottiere, Memnon of Rhodes (cf. i 12, 9). But though Memnon defeated Calas, the general who had taken command of the Macedonian forces after Attalus had been murdered (§ 48) and Parmenio withdrawn, an essential bridgehead at Abydus (i 11, 6) remained in the hands of the troops Philip had sent to Asia, and they were to augment the expeditionary army which crossed there under Alexander himself in 334 (§ 56).

46. Philip had of course intended to take command himself, but delayed his own departure until after the wedding of his daughter, Cleopatra, in the late summer of 336.[72] At the wedding he was struck down by Pausanias, one of his Bodyguards (§ 32). At the instance of Antipater, one of Philip's leading advisers, his eighteen-year-old son, Alexander, was at once proclaimed king. Antipater's reward was to be left in charge of Macedon during the absences of Alexander in 335 and 334–323. Diodorus (xvi 93 f.) recounts in some detail that Pausanias acted from a

---

[72] For § 46–48 see D. xvi 91–5; xvii 2, 1; P. 9 f.; J. ix 6 f.; xi 2 and other scattered evidence, discussed by E. Badian, *Phoenix* xvii 244 ff. Cf. also J. R. Hamilton, *GR* 117 ff.; A. B. Bosworth, *CQ* 1971, 93 ff. K. Kraft, *Der ' rationale ' Alexander* 1971, ch. 1 rejects complicity of Alexander or Olympias.

personal grudge of his own, and this was the view expressed by our only contemporary source, Aristotle (*Politics* 1311 b 1), who thus gave the lie to the official version, that he was merely a tool of others. Alexander lost no time in executing as his instigators two brothers, perhaps of the old Lyncestian royal house (§ 24; 34); their guilt is assumed in i 25, where we read of the alleged treason of the third brother, Alexander, the son-in-law of Antipater, who had saved himself for the time by promptly doing homage to the new king, and had been promoted to be governor of Thrace and then to high commands in Alexander's army, only to perish later (App. XI 5). At some time before his Balkan campaign (i 5, 4 n.), Alexander also put out of the way his cousin, Amyntas who, as son of Philip's elder brother, Perdiccas II, could have been held to have the better title to the throne, and whose friend, Amyntas, son of Antiochus, fled to take service with the Persians.[73] Alexander was also to claim in 332 that the Persian king had instigated Philip's assassination; this has no credibility.

47. Aristotle was not alone in rejecting the official account. Others actually imputed guilt to Alexander himself or at least to his mother, Olympias. A motive can be assigned. Philip had had many wives or concubines besides Olympias (Athenaeus 557 b-e), but until 337 she was his queen, and Alexander the heir presumptive; indeed his only other son, Philip Arrhidaeus, who was ultimately to succeed Alexander *faute de mieux*, was a half-wit. But in that year he took a new wife, Cleopatra, called Eurydice in iii 6, 5, the niece of Attalus (§ 45); she came from the

[73] Cf. Tod 164, to be dated to 337.

Macedonian nobility, whereas Olympias was sister of Alexander, king of Epirus, and any son she might bear to Philip might have a better chance of succeeding him; since Philip was only forty-six himself, he could easily have lived long enough for such a son to reach man's estate. At the wedding banquet Attalus expressed the hope that Philip might now have a legitimate heir; Alexander resented this, and after a brawl, he and Olympias fled to Epirus (Plut. 9, 4 f.). Although he soon returned, on one view the rift had not been healed; either before or after his return his most intimate friends, including Ptolemy, were banished (iii 6, 4 f., cf. Plut. 10, 3), and his prospects of the succession may have seemed precarious. Some scholars suppose that by marrying his daughter by Olympias to her uncle, king Alexander of Epirus, Philip intended to weaken the support that her mother and brother could otherwise have expected in that quarter: this conjecture need not be correct.

48. There is no confirmation of this sinister hypothesis. It is not to be found in the fact that Alexander procured the assassination of Attalus, with the complicity of Attalus' own father-in-law, Parmenio, or that Cleopatra-Eurydice with her newborn child, perhaps a boy, Caranus, rather than a daughter (though this is not the generally accepted view), were also put out of the way. Like the removal of the Lyncestian brothers and of the prince Amyntas, these actions merely show how insecure Alexander felt, and how little scruple he had in eliminating potential rivals or enemies. The violence of Olympias is notorious. Perhaps neither would have hesitated to kill a father or husband to preserve their own position. Naturally Arrian's partial sources

would not have hinted at Alexander's guilt. It can
also be argued that it was not safe for Aristotle to
suggest their complicity. Yet he had no need to
allude to the affair at all, and his rejection of the
official version demonstrates his independence; I
doubt if he believed, or had heard, the allegations.
Moreover, it is far from clear that Philip intended
to put Alexander out of the succession on the eve of a
momentous foreign expedition, or that Alexander
would have imputed to him such a design. As the
discarded wife, Olympias had reason for vengeance,
but the stories purveyed by Justin that she avowed
her approval of Pausanias' deed are hardly credible;
that could only have cast doubt on the official account
and endangered her position and Alexander's. At
most we must pronounce the charges against both
' not proven '.

49. The past history of Macedon gave her enemies
in Greece good hope that her power would vanish with
Philip's death; anarchy might ensue, or the new
king lack ability. Alexander was young and unknown; Demosthenes spoke of him with contempt
(Aeschines iii 77; 160). News of the murder set off
an anti-Macedonian movement in Aetolia, Ambracia,
Thebes, Athens (where Demosthenes was in receipt
of Persian subsidies) and in the Peloponnese. Late
in 336 Alexander marched south and successively
obtained recognition as *hegemon* of the league in
Thessaly, in central Greece and from the *synedrion*
at Corinth.[74] In conformity with his general tendency to minimize anti-Macedonian feeling in Greece,
A. deals briefly with this expedition (i 1, 1–3), men-

---

[74] D. 3 f. (correctly analysed by Wilcken (3) in n. 57); A. i
1, 2 f. refers (by implication) to discontent only at Athens and
to Al's recognition only by the Peloponnesians.

tioning only the hostility of Sparta and Athens. The events of the next year show that in fact Alexander had not yet established his authority in Greece. For that purpose he resorted to deliberate terrorism by destroying Thebes; characteristically, A. suggests that this decision was taken by his Greek allies (i 9, 9); some of them were undoubtedly full of bitterness against Thebes, but the destruction of the city naturally required Alexander's approval. And yet opposition still continued, and broke out into the revolts led by Agis of Sparta in 331 (App. VI) and by Athens in 323, soon after Alexander's death. Until Gaugamela there appeared to be some chance of a Persian victory, and as throughout his reign Alexander was in constant danger of sudden death and had no heir, Greeks could continue to hope that, if he were removed, Macedonian dominance would be dissolved in civil wars. Such wars were in fact to tear his empire in pieces, but they began just too late to assist Athens and her friends in 323–322.

THE PERSIAN EMPIRE

50. Although Alexander was bent on conquest from the start, we have no evidence that he hoped to subdue ' Asia ' (n. 64) before the incident at Gordium (ii 3), and it was at Tyre that he first formally claimed to be ruler of all Asia (ii 14). Isocrates (v 120) had envisaged that Philip might be content with Asia Minor west of a line drawn from Sinope to Cilicia, and Parmenio is said to have advised Alexander in 332 to accept Darius' offer to cede all territory west of Euphrates (ii 25). The vast extent of the Persian empire might well have made

any more ambitious plan seem quite chimerical. Yet Cyrus, the founder of that empire, had had a power-base no greater than Alexander's, as Alexander presumably knew. The sources magnify his success, remarkable as it was on any reckoning, by inflating the numbers of the Persian armies he defeated. In reality, the Persian empire was weak when he attacked it, and its weakness was not only known in the Greek world but exaggerated, for instance by Isocrates.[75]

51. At all times it was a loosely knit structure with no ethnical, linguistic or religious ties to unite it. It was based solely on conquest, on the ' right of the stronger '. The Achaemenid kings ruled absolutely by grace of their great god, Ahura-Mazda, but they had not developed any elaborate bureaucratic or military system to support their power. Large provinces were entrusted to governors or ' satraps ', who were generally chosen from the Persian nobility, occasionally from the barons of the other Iranian peoples (Medes, Bactrians etc), and very rarely, as in Caria (cf. i 22), from local dynasts; the authority bestowed on Memnon, a Greek (i 20, 3), was exceptional. These satraps, in the fourth century at least, exercised complete military, financial and administrative control in their provinces; those on the Anatolian seaboard, of whom we know most from their relations with the Greeks, sometimes conducted a foreign policy of their own, and in conflict with each other. There was no large standing army, and military or naval forces were raised as they were required. Thus in 334 the Persian fleet, largely supplied by the cities of Phoenicia and Cyprus, was mobilized

[75] e.g. iv 135; 140-9; 182; v 95-104; xii 14.

too late to interfere with Alexander's crossing of the Hellespont, while the powerful cavalry forces of east Iran were not available to Darius before the campaign of 331 (iii 8, 2 n.). The subject peoples were obliged to contribute not only men and (where appropriate) ships for the king's service but to pay heavy tribute, a large part of which accumulated in the royal coffers to be seized by Alexander. In the west they were certainly left to manage their local affairs under a variety of institutions that the king approved. Thus the Greek cities in Asia were administered by oligarchies, the Phoenicians and Cypriotes by kings, and the Jews by a priestly hierarchy. Like the Roman emperors, the Persian kings preserved the peace, though less successfully, since revolts were frequent, but they did not, like the Romans, win the hearts of their subjects (outside Iran) by giving their leading men an increasing share in the imperial government.

52. Numerous revolts occurred in the fourth century; so far as they are known, they were of two kinds. First, satraps themselves from time to time threw off their allegiance. Second, some of the subjects sought independence. Egypt was actually free of Persian domination from 405 to 343/2, and repelled three great invasions; there was further trouble even after the reconquest, and Alexander was welcomed by the native population (iii 1, 2 n.). Even at Babylon the destruction by Xerxes of the nation's temples after a revolt in 482 had not been forgiven (iii 16, 4). In Phoenicia and Cyprus there had been formidable revolts as late as the 340s, and Sidon had been atrociously punished. Indeed it was only late in this decade that the Rhodian condottiere, Mentor, the elder brother of Darius'

general, Memnon, restored Persian authority on the west coast of Asia Minor.   Little is known of conditions further east, but before Alexander the Achaemenids had lost control of the lower Indus valley (App. XV 1).

53. Alexander could thus suppose that in the task of defeating the king's forces he would not be hampered by the hostility of the peoples whose lands he traversed but might well receive their active assistance.   In fact none of Darius' subjects actually revolted, while the satraps and Iranian nobility, who had displayed such turbulence in the recent past, remained faithful to him, until his cause was lost. Individual governors or commanders of course surrendered, as at Sardis (i 17, 3) and in Egypt (iii, 1, 2), when they had no chance of resisting, but it was only after Gaugamela that Alexander could venture on the systematic policy of employing such men in his own service; if we ignore the despatch of a satrap with an Iranian name to Cappadocia (ii 4, 2 n.), the first case is the re-appointment of Mazaeus at Babylon (iii 16, 4).   Darius, it is true, was ultimately murdered by Bessus and other Iranian nobles, but their aim was pretty clearly to continue the war under more effective leadership.   Alexander had now begun to pose as the legitimate successor of the Achaemenids [76] and to seek to win for himself the courageous and faithful service that most of the old ruling class had rendered to Darius and that he had evidently come to admire.

54. On the other hand, until 329–327 Alexander

---

[76] P. 34 says that he was formally proclaimed king of Asia (cf. n. 64) after Gaugamela.   Cf. iii 22, 4; 30, 4; iv 7, 3; vi 29, 4–30, 1; App. XIV 1 f. and 8 f.

seldom met with determined resistance from the local population; for the most part, they were evidently indifferent to a change of masters, even if they did not positively welcome it, as in Egypt. This was a factor of the utmost importance in his success. For instance, a small number of men could have held the Cilician Gates against him, and in the absence of regular Persian forces, the satrap might have employed Cilicians, if they could have been relied on. Any attempt by Persian generals to impede his advance by a ' scorched earth ' strategy was surely doomed to fail, especially in view of Alexander's strength in cavalry, unless they had had enough soldiers to carry it out without local co-operation; the peasants had no such love of Persian rule as to destroy their own food supplies.[77] For his part Alexander was bound to live off the country (we cannot imagine trains of supplies hauled hundreds of miles from Europe), and seems to have found no difficulty in obtaining what he needed. Of course it is no evidence of loyalty to Persia that some mountain peoples, who are known or can be assumed to have been recalcitrant to every imperial power, including the Persian, refused submission to him.[78] Elsewhere local resistance is very uncommon, that of Tyre and Gaza being the most remarkable, and can be explained only conjecturally, if at all. It is most surprising that there was little in Persia itself or generally in west Iran. It was not till he entered

[77] Cf. i 12, 9; iii 7, 1 n. Darius and Bessus proposed this strategy with more reason to expect success in east Iran, iii 19, 1; 28, 8.

[78] e.g. in south Anatolia, i 24 ff.; Antilebanon, ii 20, 4; Uxii, iii 17; Cossaei, vii 15. The Uxian *hillmen* had not owed allegiance to Persia, iii 17, 1; this is probably typical.

Sogdiana (Russian Turkestan) that Alexander
encountered something like national opposition and
then he had to spend two years carrying fire and
sword through the country. Obviously his advance
would have been delayed indefinitely if the other
subjects of Persia had fought as stubbornly. Even
here the resistance was probably so obdurate because
the necessary leaders were found, as they were not
in western Iran.

55. Earlier fighting between Greeks and Persians
had demonstrated that heavily armed Greek hoplites
could beat the bowmen who on horse and foot formed
the main strength of Persian armies; at any rate
this was true in narrow plains and valleys.[79] In the
fourth century the Persian kings and satraps had
themselves come to rely heavily on Greek mercenary
foot,[80] who still provided their infantry, or the best
part of it, at the Granicus and Issus. Isocrates was
doubtless not the only Greek to infer that the
Persian empire was easy prey.[81] In reality, the Greek
cities had no cavalry to equal the Persian and could
never have exploited any victories won in conditions
that favoured hoplites; to pursue the defeated enemy
and destroy his forces once for all, or to command
wide plains where they could have been encircled and
shot down, was beyond their power. Philip and
Alexander, however, had at their disposal a cavalry
force that proved superior to the Persian, and it was

[79] W. W. How, *JHS* 1923, 117 ff.

[80] H. W. Parke, *Greek Mercenary Soldiers*, 1933, chs XI and
XVI; Isocrates iv 135.

[81] See n. 75 and A. ii 7, 8 f.; in fact the Persian cavalry made
no all-out effort to destroy the Ten Thousand and were able to
prevent Agesilaus of Sparta exploiting his successes in Asia
Minor (396–395 B.C.).

this fact that made the plan of conquest feasible from the start (cf. § 64).

ALEXANDER'S ARMY[82]

56. Arrian (i 11, 3) says that Alexander marched to the Hellespont in 334 with not many more than 30,000 foot and over 5,000 horse. Contemporary historians gave the following figures,[83] rounded up or down; it is evident that Arrian adopted Ptolemy's.

	Infantry	*Cavalry*
Callisthenes	40,000	4,500
Ptolemy	30,000	5,000
Aristobulus	30,000	4,000
Anaximenes	43,000	5,500

Although Arrian frequently refers to individual units, for instance when he describes the deployment of the army in the great battles, he nowhere gives any particulars of the strength of those units, and the details that he does furnish on such occasions are in consequence almost meaningless, or would be if we lacked any information to supplement his data. It is hardly credible that his authorities, particularly Ptolemy, who were so careful to state with what units Alexander carried out this or that operation, had never given a breakdown of the army with the strength of the different units. Such a breakdown is found in summary form in Diodorus xvii 17.

---

[82] Cf. Brunt, *JHS* 1963, 27 ff. (here somewhat modified).
[83] For all these figures see Polybius xii 19, 1; Plutarch 327 D–E.

INTRODUCTION

Infantry

Macedonians	12,000
[Greek] allies	7,000
[Greek] mercenaries	5,000
Odrysians, Triballians, Illyrians [Balkan troops]	7,000
Agrianians [javelin-men] and archers	1,000
Total	32,000

Cavalry

Macedonians [i.e. Companion cavalry]	1,800
Thessalians [allies]	1,800
Other Greeks [allies]	600
Thracians, *prodromoi* and Paeonians[84]	900
Total (given by Diodorus as 4,500)	5,100

' Macedonians ' evidently refers only to the phalanx regiments, hypaspists and Companions, and not to archers (some of whom were Macedonian) nor to *prodromoi*, of whose five squadrons four were Macedonian (§ 58; 64). There is no reason to distrust the figures, especially as the totals agree with Ptolemy's. It remains, however, to account for the discrepancies in the totals given by contemporary writers. Now according to Polyaenus (v 44, 4) the advance force Philip had sent to Asia numbered 10,000, no doubt a round figure. There is no evidence or likelihood that these troops had been withdrawn: they were needed to hold the bridgehead in Asia. The advance force may well have consisted mainly of mercenaries, and in 334 Alexander demonstrably had more mercenary foot than Diodorus allows

[84] The text is corrupt; R. D. Milns' Θρᾷκες δὲ ⟨καὶ⟩ πρόδρομοι καὶ Παίονες gives the right sense (*JHS* 1966, 167 f.). The *prodromoi* are also called lancers (*sarissophoroi*), cf. i 14, 1 and 6; iii 12, 3 with QC. iv 15, 13; § 64 below.

(Arrian i 18, 1 and 5), and mercenary cavalry (i 23, 6), of whom he makes no mention. Anaximenes' total for foot, 11,000 more than that given by Diodorus and probably by Ptolemy (*ap.* i 11, 3), is plausible if the strength of this force is counted in; Callisthenes' figure is no doubt rounded down. (Both Callisthenes as reported by Polybius and Diodorus must be inaccurate in that the former purports to give the numbers before the crossing and the latter those after it.) On the other hand, Anaximenes' total for cavalry is only 400 greater than that given by Diodorus and (probably) Ptolemy, yet it seems improbable that Alexander took over no more than 400 additional horse from the advance force. As the Persians' main strength lay in cavalry, and as Philip had plenty of cavalry at his disposal, it is quite unlikely that he sent only 400 horse to Asia; 1,000 would make a better proportion. Now it may be significant that in giving his own total of the cavalry Diodorus left out 600 men, probably omitting a contingent which joined late, after a muster to which his total really relates. I conjecture that Anaximenes too made the same error, assumed that Alexander brought across only 4,500 horse, not 5,100, added 1,000 and obtained his total of 5,500, which should have been 6,100. Callisthenes and Aristobulus (the latter rounding down) likewise gave the number of those who crossed with Alexander, omitting the same contingent. It may be added that Anaximenes, when counting in the troops already in Asia before 334, probably made no allowance for losses. On this hypothesis the nominal strength of the army, once Alexander had crossed, was 43,000 foot and 6,100 horse, and its real strength somewhat less. Certainty is unattainable.

57. Before Issus Arrian records the arrival as reinforcements of only 3,000 Macedonian foot, 300 Macedonian horse and 350 Greek horse (i 29, 4). Callisthenes' total of 5,000 foot and 800 horse ' from Macedon ' (Polybius xii 19, 2) may include mercenaries, even the 300 Alexander took into his service at Miletus (i 19, 6), if he has been inaccurately reported.[85] At Gaugamela Alexander is credited with about 40,000 foot and 7,000 horse (iii 12, 5). In the interim he had been joined by 7,400 more mercenary foot (ii 20, 5; iii 5, 1; QC. iv 5, 18) and 500 Thracian horse (iii 5, 1). However, no single source records all reinforcements, and we cannot even assume that all are mentioned somewhere. Similarly our authorities minimize losses in battle and say almost nothing of losses by sickness, which modern scholars too tend to ignore, though they must have carried off far more men than fighting (cf. v 27, 5 f.); they also give only incomplete data about the size of garrisons. By the time of Gaugamela the total number of men who had ever been in the army, so far as recorded, was as follows:

Infantry: 43,000 + 12,400   55,400
Cavalry: 6,100 (5,500) + 1,300   7,400 (6,800)

It is not wholly implausible that the cavalry had suffered lower proportionate casualties than the foot, and that as they were the principal striking arm, few had been left in garrisons; only on these assumptions can we account for their reputed strength in 331. However, unrecorded reinforcements seem to me likely. For numbers after Gaugamela see Appendix XIII.

[85] R. D. Milns, *Greek Roman and Byzantine Studies* 1966, 159 ff. (against Brunt, op. cit.).

INTRODUCTION

58. At that battle the Companions formed 8 *ilai* or squadrons (iii 11, 8), of which one was the 'royal squadron', the 'King's Own Horse Guards' (iii 1, 4, etc.). Plutarch's 13 squadrons at the Granicus (16, 2) must include 5 squadrons of *prodromoi*, one Paeonian (cf. i 14, 6; iv 4, 6). Each squadron of Companions should have been on average 225 strong until the arrival of 500 more men in winter 331/0, when Alexander divided each squadron into two *lochoi* or companies (iii 6, 10; QC. v 1, 39 ff.). The whole force was under Philotas, Parmenio's son (iii 11, 8, etc.), till his execution late in 330, when Alexander divided the command between two hipparchs (commanders of cavalry), Hephaestion and 'Black' Clitus, thinking it imprudent to entrust the whole force to one man (iii 27, 4). After Clitus' murder he went further in the same direction; from late 327 we find at least 6 hipparchs, 'White' Clitus, Coenus, Craterus, Demetrius, Hephaestion and Perdiccas,[86] but in fact it seems that there were 8 hipparchies, including the *agema*, which corresponds to the old 'royal' squadron (last named as such in iii 18, 5 and anachronistically called *agema* in i 8, 3). This can be inferred from the facts that in 327 Alexander had with him half the Companions, amounting to 4 hipparchies including the *agema* (iv 22, 7; 23, 1; 24, 1), as again in 326, when his own force comprised at least 4 hipparchies (vi 16, 1 n.). The names of one hipparch and of the commander of the *agema* have not been preserved. By 324 the number had again been reduced to 4 or 5 (vii 6, 4 n.), probably as a result of losses in the Gadrosian march.

59. The squadron commanders, except for 'Black'

---

[86] iv 27, 5; v 11, 3; 12, 2; 16, 3; 21, 5; 22, 6; vi 6, 4; 8, 2.

Clitus who commanded the royal squadron, were men of little note, whereas the hipparchs after 328 were leading figures in Alexander's entourage. They bore the same grand title that had once belonged to Philotas alone. Were the old squadrons simply renamed hipparchies to correspond to the enhanced style of their commanders? They were indeed themselves divided into squadrons, as the squadrons had been divided into companies after 331/0, and Griffith contends with some force that they must have differed from the squadrons in more than name.[87] Most scholars believe that long before 324, when this is clearly attested (vii 6, 4; 8, 2 with notes), Alexander had incorporated Oriental horsemen in the hipparchies. It is indeed certain that he was using such horsemen from 330, and particularly in the Indian campaign; we hear of mounted javelin-men and mounted archers,[88] and there were no such units among his European cavalry; various troops of Scythian and east Iranian horse are also specifically named (v 11, 3). None of these units appears to belong to the hipparchies of the Companions, but Griffith remarks that we have no specific mention of any cavalry from west Iran, which had once supplied the king with crack regiments, and conjectures that *they* were incorporated in the hipparchies. Arrian refers to three hipparchies forming only part of the Companions in 329 (iii 29, 7; iv 4, 7); in the second passage we also hear of squadrons, and Griffith urges that the hipparchies are brigades divided into squadrons, some of which would be barbarian; when

[87] *JHS* 1963, 68 ff.

[88] iii 24, 1; 29, 7; iv 4, 7; 23, 1; 24, 3; 25, 6; 26, 4; 28, 8; v 11, 3; 12, 2; 16, 4; 18, 3. This explains how he had *c.* 5,000 horse at the Hydaspes, v 14, 1.

he writes (v 13, 4) of ' the *agema* of the cavalry and the best men of the remaining hipparchies ', he means the purely Macedonian squadrons by ' the best men '. By contrast, I argued that the hipparchies were still purely Macedonian but larger than the old squadrons, since Alexander had received considerable reinforcements and might have incorporated the *prodromoi*, last mentioned in 329 (iv 4, 6), in the Companions.

60. On this view the use of ' hipparchy ' in iii 29, 7; iv 4, 7 must be anachronistic, or rather (as in i 24, 3) non-technical, denoting simply a force of cavalry under one particular commander. Indeed I cannot see how the cavalry could have been organized in more than two groups technically called hipparchies, so long as there were only two hipparchs, i.e. before the death of Black Clitus in late summer 328. If Griffith is right that Orientals were already brigaded with the Companions on the Iaxartes, they must have been armed in the Macedonian fashion rather than as bowmen, since Arrian does not suggest that the hipparchies of the Companions by themselves had any answer to Scythian tactics (iv 4). Arrian's language is also gravely misleading in iv 24, 1 and vi 6, 1 and 4, unless the Orientals supposedly incorporated in the hipparchies already counted as Companions, and in that case one might have expected Macedonian opposition before the mutiny at Opis (but cf. vii 8, 2 n.). As for ' the best men ' in v 13, 4, it does not seem inconceivable that in each hipparchy the fittest and best mounted troopers had been formed into one of the squadrons, precisely in order that they might be used as Alexander did use them at the Hydaspes.[89]

---

[89] Cf. perhaps vi 21, 3, which does readily fit Griffith's view.

However, my own hypothesis is open to the objection that the Macedonian reinforcements Alexander had received by 328 were probably smaller than I had estimated, and once we allow for losses, even the incorporation of the surviving Macedonian *prodromoi*, originally perhaps 800, might not have made the hipparchies significantly stronger than the old *ilai*,[90] None the less, I still incline to the view that all references to hipparchies before Clitus' death are non-technical and that thereafter the hipparchies remained Macedonian till *c*. 324, though they were perhaps not much stronger than the *ilai*; the change of name in the units primarily reflected the change of title, and higher status, of their commanders.

61. The Macedonian foot (apart from the archers) consisted of the hypaspists (' shield-bearers ') and of the battalions (*taxeis*) of the phalanx; at Gaugamela the latter numbered 6 (iii 11, 9 f.), but at the Hydaspes 7 (v 11, 3 with 12, 1 f.); another was perhaps formed when Alexander was reinforced at Susa (iii 16, 11). Confirmation can be found. Of the 12,000 men in the phalanx of Alexander's expeditionary force (§ 56), the 6 battalions of the phalanx must account for 9,000, as the hypaspists apparently numbered 3,000. Thus each battalion was 1,500 strong. But in 330 Alexander left 6,000 of them at Ecbatana,

[90] Milns (n. 85). In particular the officers sent for reinforcements in winter 328/7 B.C. (iv 18, 3) are not known to have brought any, and they could not in any case have arrived by autumn 327 B.C., when the 8 hipparchies were in being, unless we suppose that they were already on the way from Macedon in 328 B.C. This remains *possible*, as our information on reinforcements is defective. Beloch III ² 343 conjectured that the officers concerned secured the (non-Macedonian) reinforcements which reached Alexander in India (App. XIII 8).

evidently a notional figure for 4 battalions, yet even before this force rejoined him (App. XIII 6), he had just 3 battalions under his own command (iii 23, 2; 24, 1).[91] The hypaspists were a *corps d'élite* (§ 62), sometimes called the bodyguards or royal hypaspists, or even the hypaspists of the Companions (i 14, 2); two of the three battalions were commanded by chiliarchs (iv 30, 6; v 23, 7 cf. i 22, 7), and therefore consisted of 1,000 men; the third, the *agema* or royal footguard, was presumably of the same strength, since after Alexander's time, when the whole corps was called 'Silver-shields', their number is given as 3,000. (Arrian's terminology is confusing; he can write of the *agema* and the hypaspists, meaning the other hypaspists, i 8, 3, and probably calls the *agema* alone the hypaspists.[92])

62. The Macedonian phalanx differed somewhat from the Greek. Greek hoplites, equipped with helmet, cuirass, greaves, a round shield about 3 feet across, a spear 8–9 feet long and a short sword for slashing, were usually marshalled eight deep and fought battles that were generally won 'at push of pike'. Heavily encumbered, they were not easily manoeuvrable.[93] Alexander's Greek allies, who played no important part in the war, will have been soldiers of this type. The mercenaries on both sides were probably peltasts, carrying a smaller and lighter shield (*pelta*), but a spear over 12 feet long and a sword longer than the hoplite's.[94] The Macedonian phalanx was also less heavily armoured than hoplites

[91] Milns (n. 85).

[92] Tarn ii 148 ff.

[93] A. M. Snodgrass, *Arms and Armour of the Greeks* 1967, chs III–IV, cf. How (n. 79).

[94] See Parke (n. 80) 79 f. on D. xv 44.

(cf. iii 18, 1; iv 25, 5 f.), with helmet and greaves but apparently no cuirass, and with a *pelta* about 2 feet in diameter, probably suspended from the neck, so that both arms were free to wield the formidable *sarissa*.[95] This was a lance normally 21 feet long in the second century (Polybius xviii 29), but evidently rather shorter in Alexander's time, as it was made from the hard wood of the male cornel tree, and Theophrastus, a contemporary, says that the tree had an average height of 12 cubits, the greatest length of the *sarissa* (*History of Plants* iii 12, 2). The cubit is normally equated with $1\frac{1}{2}$ feet, and Tarn's hypothesis (ii 169 f.) that the Macedonian cubit was shorter has not found favour. Hence the longest *sarissa* was 18 feet.[96] In Polybius' time the lances of the first five ranks protruded before the front line, and in Alexander's that must have been true of the first three or four. Men in the ranks behind would hold their lances upright, offering some protection against missiles. At Issus the phalanx was 8 deep, and I consider this to have been normal,[97] though it was to be deepened later. The hypaspists are often included in the phalanx (iii 11, 9; iv 28, 8; 30, 3), but that need mean only that they formed part of the infantry line. In ii 4, 3 Arrian clearly contrasts them, together with archers and javelin men, with all the other infantry as less heavily equipped, and this helps to explain why they were picked for forced marches and other special tasks; no doubt they

[95] Snodgrass 117 ff.
[96] In Alexander's time men in the front rank (cf. Asclepiodotus v) and also the *prodromoi* (§ 64) may have had shorter *sarissae*.
[97] App. III 4 (p. 461); App. IX 3. The Greek line was normally 8 deep (How cited in n. 79), though the Thebans had sometimes made it much deeper. Cf. Lane Fox 76 and 511.

were also more highly trained. Lane Fox argues from their name that they had larger and heavier shields (which might be left behind when occasion demanded) but that in compensation they did not carry the *sarissa*.[98] His account, like all others, is conjectural.[99]

63. In encounters with Greek hoplites, the phalanx had an advantage, perhaps partially offset by the heavier armour of the former, in the greater length of their lances. Persian foot, who mostly had little defensive armour and only short spears, relying chiefly on the bow, were at the mercy of either Greek or Macedonian infantry in fighting at close quarters. On the other hand, the Macedonian phalanx (like the Greek) was not easily manoeuvrable and tended to break line on rough ground.

64. In fact the decisive arm in Alexander's battles with the Persians was his cavalry.[100] It was in cav-

---

[98] Cf. J. R. Hamilton, *CQ* 1955, 218 ff.; Lane Fox 78 f. against G. T. Griffith, *Proc. of Cambridge Philol. Soc.* 1956, 3 ff.

[99] Lane Fox 512 and Bosworth, *CQ*, 1973, 245 ff., have independently urged the retention of the manuscript readings ἀσθέταιροι or ἀσθέτεροι in ii 23, 2; iv 23, 1; v 22, 6; vi 6, 1; 21, 3; vii 11, 3. Lane Fox supposes that the *asthetairoi* were less heavily armoured than the *pezetairoi* (for this there is no evidence), Bosworth, more plausibly, that they are the phalanx regiments from Upper Macedon, the *pezetairoi* those from Lower Macedon. Clearly, they would be ' Companions ' of some kind (*hetairoi*), though the force of the prefix ' ast ' is obscure. Scribes will hardly have substituted a meaningless word six times for the well-known *pezetairoi*, and I have kept the manuscript text, contrary to the practice of all modern editors in amending to πεζέταιροι.

[100] For what follows cf. J. K. Anderson, *Greek Horsemanship*, 1961, 40–78; F. E. Adcock, *The Greek and Macedonian Art of War* 1957; H. Delbrück, *Gesch. der Kriegskunst*[3] 1920, I iv and III i.

alry that the main strength of Darius' armies lay
(apart from his Greek mercenaries). Like the Persians' foot, they too relied mostly on bows and
javelins, with short spears and swords or scimitars for
hand to hand fighting.[101] In the fourth century (and
long afterwards) horses were unshod and riders had
no stirrups; and hence instead of charging like
modern cavalry with lance at rest and the full force of
man and beast behind it, they had to wield the lance
with the strength of their arms; horsemen often had
much ado to keep their seats.[102] Greek cavalry had
been used mainly for reconnaissance, for ravaging the
country or hampering similar operations by the
enemy, for pursuing a broken army or covering its
retreat, or for hurling missiles at a hoplite line;
indeed even Philip and Alexander could never
attempt a frontal cavalry assault on serried ranks of
pikes. What they did do, with success, thanks to the
high level of horsemanship their men had reached in
constant practice, was to charge the cavalry that
covered the flanks of the enemy foot, and then turn
on the foot from side or rear; finally, they completed
the destruction of the enemy by relentless pursuit.
The Macedonian Companions, and presumably the
Thessalian horse, were protected by helmet and
corselet, and armed with a lance (*dory* or *xyston*), and a
curved slashing sword (*kopis*). However, the *prodromoi* (n. 84) carried *sarissae*, presumably longer than
the lances of the rest, and requiring (like those of
the infantry) both hands to wield them; they must

---

[101] Cf. i 15, 1; so too at Issus Al. fears Persian archers
(ii 10, 3). But at Issus the Persian cavalry charged (ii 11, 2),
as also at Gaugamela (iii 13), curiously not adopting the tactics
of the Scythians (iv 4) and of Spitamenes (iv 5).

[102] Xenophon, *Anab.* ii 2, 18 f.

therefore have controlled the horses with their legs alone, which modern horsemen assure me is possible.[103] Arrian notes that at the Granicus the Persian horse were at a disadvantage, as they were less well trained, and as the Macedonians had spears of cornel wood longer than the Persian javelins (*palta*), which were doubtless designed more for throwing than for thrusting; they also carried short slashing swords (i 15, 5–8). It was not till 331 that some attempt was made to equip them with longer spears and swords and give them more defensive armour (iii 8, 2 n.).[104] Perhaps only some units were thus re-equipped; we continue to hear of Oriental light horse afterwards.[105] In that case Alexander's cavalry, though heavily outnumbered at Gaugamela (App. IX), still retained a superiority in armament as well as in training over most of their opponents; otherwise Alexander's victory must be wholly ascribed to the skill with which he deployed his forces.

65. Demosthenes had remarked that Philip's army did not consist only of a phalanx (like that of most Greek cities) but of light troops, cavalry, archers, mercenaries (i.e. peltasts), and that he was well provided with artillery (ix 49 f.; cf. A. ii 7, 8). Arrian makes Alexander refer to the value of the Balkan

[103] Cf. Lane Fox 75. See n. 96.
[104] Xenophon, *Cyropaedia* vii 1, 2 makes out that the elder Cyrus' Companions had *palta* of cornel-wood, which were used by Persian cavalry in 396 (id., *Hellenica* iii 4, 14), and bronze corselets; in 402 some of the younger Cyrus' horsemen were so protected, and their horses too were armoured (*Anab.* i 8, 6 f.). Herodotus (vii 84–6, cf. 61 ff.) tells that in 480 only some Persians and no other Oriental cavalry even had helmets; perhaps only a few Oriental horsemen, especially the nobles (cf. ix 22; A. i 15, 8), normally had much defensive armour.
[105] iv 4 f., cf. § 59.

contingents, who constituted most of the light
infantry (ii 7, 5); the Agrianian javelin-men, in particular, were a *corps d'élite*, mentioned 47 times by
Arrian (cf. iv 25, 6 n.). Alexander far excelled Philip
in the success of his siege operations, notably at
Tyre, and his ability to transport machines over
difficult mountain country is astounding.[106] But his
debt to Philip can hardly be over-estimated even in
the strictly military sphere. Philip's constant
campaigns bequeathed him a ready-made professional
army. Its discipline and manoeuvrability are seen
at the very outset of his reign (i 1, 8 f.; 6, 2 f.); his
men were already inured to long marches and to
winter operations, almost unprecedented in Greek
practice. It was in Philip's school that Alexander's
officers had been trained, many of whom were to show
remarkable ability after his own death. Speed of
movement, so striking and effective an element in
his successes, had been no less characteristic of Philip,
and the basic tactical plan of his victories over the
Persians was inherited from his father.[107] Alexander's military genius of course appeared in the way
he adapted what he had learned from Philip to the
particular conditions of his own operations.

BIBLIOGRAPHY

66. For editions of the text I refer to Roos-
Wirth's edition. The *editio princeps* was issued at
Venice in 1535 by Trincavalius; his most important

---

[106] Cf. E. W. Marsden, *Greek and Roman Artillery*, 1969,
index *s.v.* Alexander and Philip.

[107] See Demosthenes i 4; viii 11; ix 48–50; D. xvi 3; 4,
5–7; 8, 2; 84, 1 f.; 86; Polybius viii 12; Polyaenus iv 2, 10;
Frontinus, *Stratagems* iv 1, 6.

successors were Stephanus (1625), Gronovius (1704) and Krüger (1835–1851), none of whom relied on the archetypal manuscript.

67. For works on Alexander and his historians students can now turn to a full, classified bibliography by J. Seibert.[108] A survey of work since 1948 by E. Badian[109] is particularly valuable for his critical comments, but since he naturally says nothing of his own articles, I would add that no one in this period has done so much to advance our knowledge. On most subjects the basis for all new inquiries is H. Berve's collection of material about the court, army and administration and about every person who comes into the story of Alexander's reign.[110] Pearson has provided the most reliable account of the sources.[111] In the English-reading world the works of Sir William Tarn[112] have long exercised most influence, but his brilliant style, vast erudition and curious ingenuity were employed to devise an apologia for Alexander suited to modern conceptions but perhaps even more misleading than those of any ancient writer who made a hero out of the king. Safer guidance can be found in Ulrich Wilcken's introductory book;[113] though he rarely cites authorities, he not only presents a vigorous narrative but puts Alexander in the context of his age and looks forward to the

---

[108] *Alexander der Grosse (Erträge der Forschung)*, 1972

[109] *Alexander the Great 1948–1967* in *The Classical World* 1971, 37–56; 77–83.

[110] *Das Alexanderreich auf prosopographischer Grundlage*, 2 volumes, 1926. In vol. ii personages are numbered, and references to this volume are given by these numbers.

[111] *The Lost Histories of Alexander the Great*, 1960

[112] Especially *Alexander the Great*, 2 volumes, 1948.

[113] *Alexander the Great*; the English translation (1932) has been reprinted in a paperback edition.

new era which Alexander's conquests inaugurated; this is one of the great histories. For brevity I shall cite modern works rather sparingly, and generally when they give more information than I have room for, and shall normally refer only to the most important ancient evidence.

ADDENDUM (see p. xx)

Diodorus visited Egypt in 60–56 B.C.; in his history, which went down to 54 B.C., the latest event mentioned is the foundation of a Roman colony at Tauromenium, *c.* 36 B.C. (Brunt, *Italian Manpower* 597). Trogus' work, published before *c.* 2 B.C., ended in 20 B.C.; his grandfather or great-grandfather received Roman citizenship in the 70s. See *RE* V 663 (Schwartz); XXI 2300 f. (Klotz). It is at least unlikely that Diodorus did not write before Trogus.

ABBREVIATIONS AND SHORT TITLES

A. = Arrian
Al. = Alexander
Ar. = Aristobulus
D. = Diodorus

J. = Justin
P. = Plutarch, *Alexander*
Pt. = Ptolemy
QC. = Quintus Curtius

Where no other author is indicated, references in the form iii 2, 3 are to Arrian's *Anabasis*; *Ind.* refers to *Indica*.

Book numbers for all authors are in Roman numerals, and are omitted where the context shows what book is intended.

All references to D. are to book xvii, unless otherwise specified.

Beloch   K. J. Beloch, *Griechische Geschichte*[2]
Berve   H. Berve, *Das Alexanderreich* (see Introd. n. 110)
CQ   *Classical Quarterly*
Fuller   Major-General J. F. C. Fuller, *The Generalship of Alexander the Great*, 1958
GR   *Greece and Rome*, vol. XII, 2, 1965 (*Alexander the Great*)
Jacoby   F. Jacoby, *Die Fragmente der griechischen Historiker*. The historians are numbered, and I refer to them by these numbers, e.g. no. 124 (Callisthenes) T[estimonium] 1 or F[ragmentum] 1; Jacoby's numbering of volumes is confusing.
JHS   *Journal of Hellenic Studies*

ABBREVIATIONS

Lane Fox	R. Lane Fox, *Alexander the Great*, 1973
Pearson, *LH or* Pearson	L. Pearson, *The Lost Histories of Alexander the Great*, 1960
RE	Pauly-Wissowa, *Real-Encyclopädie der classischen Altertumswissenschaft*
Tarn	W. W. Tarn, *Alexander the Great* (2 vols.), 1948
Tod	M. N. Tod, *Greek Historical Inscriptions* II

ARRIAN

ANABASIS OF ALEXANDER

BOOK I

ΑΡΡΙΑΝΟΥ

ΑΛΕΞΑΝΔΡΟΥ ΑΝΑΒΑΣΕΩΣ

ΒΙΒΛΙΟΝ ΠΡΩΤΟΝ

1 Πτολεμαῖος ὁ Λάγου καὶ Ἀριστόβουλος ὁ
Ἀριστοβούλου ὅσα μὲν ταὐτὰ ἄμφω περὶ Ἀλεξάνδρου τοῦ Φιλίππου συνέγραψαν, ταῦτα ἐγὼ ὡς
πάντη ἀληθῆ ἀναγράφω, ὅσα δὲ οὐ ταὐτά, τούτων
τὰ πιστότερα ἐμοὶ φαινόμενα καὶ ἅμα ἀξι-
2 αφηγητότερα ἐπιλεξάμενος. ἄλλοι μὲν δὴ ἄλλα ὑπὲρ
Ἀλεξάνδρου ἀνέγραψαν, οὐδ᾽ ἔστιν ὑπὲρ ὅτου
πλείονες ἢ ἀξυμφωνότεροι ἐς ἀλλήλους· ἀλλ᾽ ἐμοὶ
Πτολεμαῖός τε καὶ Ἀριστόβουλος πιστότεροι
ἔδοξαν ἐς τὴν ἀφήγησιν, ὁ μὲν ὅτι συνεστράτευσε
βασιλεῖ Ἀλεξάνδρῳ, Ἀριστόβουλος, Πτολεμαῖος
δὲ πρὸς τῷ ξυστρατεῦσαι ὅτι καὶ αὐτῷ βασιλεῖ
ὄντι αἰσχρότερον ἤ τῳ ἄλλῳ ψεύσασθαι ἦν· ἄμφω
δέ, ὅτι τετελευτηκότος ἤδη Ἀλεξάνδρου ξυγγρά-
φουσιν [ὅτε] αὐτοῖς ἥ τε ἀνάγκη καὶ ὁ μισθὸς τοῦ
3 ἄλλως τι ἢ ὡς συνηνέχθη ξυγγράψαι ἀπῆν. ἔστι δὲ
ἃ καὶ πρὸς ἄλλων ξυγγεγραμμένα, ὅτι καὶ αὐτὰ
ἀξιαφήγητά τέ μοι ἔδοξε καὶ οὐ πάντη ἄπιστα, ὡς
λεγόμενα μόνον ὑπὲρ Ἀλεξάνδρου ἀνέγραψα.
ὅστις δὲ θαυμάσεται ἀνθ᾽ ὅτου ἐπὶ τοσοῖσδε
συγγραφεῦσι καὶ ἐμοὶ ἐπὶ νοῦν ἦλθεν ἥδε ἡ συγ-

---

* See p. lxxxv for abbreviations and short titles, Introd.
30–2; 58–62 for technical Macedonian terms, App. VIII 1 for
the meaning of ' stade ' (normally ·185 km.).

ARRIAN

ANABASIS OF ALEXANDER*

BOOK I

PREFACE

Wherever Ptolemy son of Lagus and Aristobulus son of Aristobulus have both given the same accounts of Alexander son of Philip, it is my practice to record what they say as completely true, but where they differ, to select the version I regard as more trustworthy and also better worth telling. In fact other 2 writers have given a variety of accounts of Alexander, nor is there any other figure of whom there are more historians who are more contradictory of each other, but in my view Ptolemy and Aristobulus are more trustworthy in their narrative, since Aristobulus took part in king Alexander's expedition, and Ptolemy not only did the same, but as he himself was a king, mendacity would have been more dishonourable for him than for anyone else; again, both wrote when Alexander was dead and neither was under any constraint or hope of gain to make him set down anything but what actually happened. However, I have also 3 recorded some statements made in other accounts of others, when I thought them worth mention and not entirely untrustworthy, but only as tales told of Alexander. Anyone who is surprised that with so many historians already in the field it should have

3

γραφή, τά τε ἐκείνων πάντα τις ἀναλεξάμενος καὶ
τοῖσδε τοῖς ἡμετέροις ἐντυχὼν οὕτω θαυμαζέτω.

1. Λέγεται δὴ Φίλιππος μὲν τελευτῆσαι ἐπὶ
ἄρχοντος Πυθοδήλου Ἀθήνησι· παραλαβόντα δὲ
τὴν βασιλείαν Ἀλέξανδρον, παῖδα ὄντα Φιλίππου,
ἐς Πελοπόννησον παρελθεῖν· εἶναι δὲ τότε ἀμφὶ τὰ
2 εἴκοσιν ἔτη Ἀλέξανδρον. ἐνταῦθα ξυναγαγόντα
τοὺς Ἕλληνας, ὅσοι ἐντὸς Πελοποννήσου ἦσαν,
αἰτεῖν παρ' αὐτῶν τὴν ἡγεμονίαν τῆς ἐπὶ τοὺς
Πέρσας στρατιᾶς, ἥντινα Φιλίππῳ ἤδη ἔδοσαν· καὶ
αἰτήσαντα λαβεῖν παρ' ἑκάστων πλὴν Λακεδαιμο-
νίων· Λακεδαιμονίους δὲ ἀποκρίνασθαι μὴ εἶναί
σφισι πάτριον ἀκολουθεῖν ἄλλοις, ἀλλ' αὐτοὺς
3 ἄλλων ἐξηγεῖσθαι. νεωτερίσαι δὲ ἄττα καὶ τῶν
Ἀθηναίων τὴν πόλιν. ἀλλὰ Ἀθηναίους γε τῇ
πρώτῃ ἐφόδῳ Ἀλεξάνδρου ἐκπλαγέντας καὶ πλείονα
ἔτι τῶν Φιλίππῳ δοθέντων Ἀλεξάνδρῳ εἰς τιμὴν
συγχωρῆσαι. ἐπανελθόντα δὲ ἐς Μακεδονίαν ἐν
παρασκευῇ εἶναι τοῦ ἐς τὴν Ἀσίαν στόλου.

4 Ἅμα δὲ τῷ ἦρι ἐλαύνειν ἐπὶ Θρᾴκης, ἐς Τριβαλλοὺς καὶ Ἰλλυριούς, ὅτι τε νεωτερίζειν ἐπύθετο
Ἰλλυριούς τε καὶ Τριβαλλούς, καὶ ἅμα ὁμόρους
ὄντας οὐκ ἐδόκει ὑπολείπεσθαι ὅτι μὴ πάντῃ
ταπεινωθέντας οὕτω μακρὰν ἀπὸ τῆς οἰκείας στελ-
5 λόμενον. ὁρμηθέντα δὴ ἐξ Ἀμφιπόλεως ἐμβαλεῖν
εἰς Θρᾴκην τὴν τῶν αὐτονόμων καλουμένων

---

[1] For A's sources Introd. 10–23; a fuller discussion will
appear in vol. II.
[2] The 'tale' is apparently not from the 'vulgate', but
rather what all tell; §1–3 summarize well-known facts

occurred to me too to compose this history should express his surprise only after perusing all their works and then reading mine.[1]

1. Now we are told[2] that the death of Philip occurred in the archonship of Pythodelus at Athens; then about twenty, Alexander succeeded, as Philip's son, and arrived in the Peloponnesus. There he assembled the Peloponnesian Greeks and requested from them the leadership of the Persian expedition, which they had already granted to Philip. Each people agreed except the Lacedaemonians, who replied that their country's tradition did not permit them to follow others; it was theirs to take the lead. At Athens too there was a revolutionary movement, but the Athenians collapsed at Alexander's first approach and conceded to him honours still greater than had been given to Philip. Alexander returned to Macedonia and began to get ready for the Asian expedition. At the advent of spring[3] he marched towards Thrace against the Triballi and Illyrians, since he learned that they were restless; moreover, as they marched with his borders, he did not think it well to leave them behind him, when going on an expedition so far from home, unless they had been thoroughly humbled. Starting from Amphipolis, he invaded the part of Thrace that belongs to the independent

336 B.C.

2

3

4 335 B.C.

5

(Introd. 38, 49); § 4-ch. 6 at end give a seamless narrative in which direct speech replaces indirect at the end of 1,5, presumably from Pt./Ar.; Pt. is actually cited in 2, 7 and followed in 4, 6-8.

[3] Perhaps this suggests too early a date; 4, 1 may indicate that it was early June when Al. was on the Danube; 5, 9 that the harvest was already in near Pellium; Thebes did not fall till October (10, 2 n.).

Θρακῶν, Φιλίππους πόλιν ἐν ἀριστερᾷ ἔχοντα καὶ τὸν Ὄρβηλον τὸ ὄρος. διαβὰς δὲ τὸν Νέστον ποταμὸν λέγουσιν, ὅτι δεκαταῖος ἀφίκετο ἐπὶ τὸ
6 ὄρος τὸν Αἶμον. καὶ ἐνταῦθα ἀπήντων αὐτῷ κατὰ τὰ στενὰ τῆς ἀνόδου τῆς ἐπὶ τὸ ὄρος τῶν τε †ἐμπόρων¹ πολλοὶ ὡπλισμένοι καὶ οἱ Φρᾶκες οἱ αὐτόνομοι, παρεσκευασμένοι εἴργειν τοῦ πρόσω κατειληφότες τὴν ἄκραν τοῦ Αἴμου τὸν στόλον,
7 παρ' ἣν ἦν τῷ στρατεύματι ἡ πάροδος. ξυναγαγόντες δὲ ἁμάξας καὶ προβαλόμενοι πρὸ σφῶν ἅμα μὲν χάρακι ἐχρῶντο ταῖς ἁμάξαις ἐς τὸ ἀπομάχεσθαι ἀπ' αὐτῶν, εἰ βιάζοιντο, ἅμα δὲ ἐν νῷ εἶχον ἐπαφιέναι ἀνιοῦσιν ᾗ ἀποτομώτατον τοῦ ὄρους ἐπὶ τὴν φάλαγγα τῶν Μακεδόνων τὰς ἁμάξας. γνώμην δὲ πεποίηντο ὅτι ὅσῳ πυκνοτέρᾳ τῇ φάλαγγι καταφερόμεναι συμμίξουσιν αἱ ἅμαξαι, τοσῷδε μᾶλλόν τι διασκεδάσουσιν αὐτὴν βίᾳ ἐμπεσοῦσαι.
8 Ἀλεξάνδρῳ δὲ βουλὴ γίγνεται ὅπως ἀσφαλέστατα ὑπερβαλεῖ τὸ ὄρος· καὶ ἐπειδὴ ἐδόκει διακινδυνευτέα, οὐ γὰρ εἶναι ἄλλῃ τὴν πάροδον, παραγγέλλει τοῖς ὁπλίταις, ὁπότε καταφέροιντο κατὰ τοῦ ὀρθίου αἱ ἅμαξαι, ὅσοις μὲν ὁδὸς πλατεῖα οὖσα παρέχοι λῦσαι τὴν τάξιν, τούτους δὲ διαχω-
9 ρῆσαι, ὡς δι' αὐτῶν ἐκπεσεῖν τὰς ἁμάξας· ὅσοι δὲ περικαταλαμβάνοιντο, ξυννεύσαντας, τοὺς δὲ καὶ πεσόντας ἐς γῆν, συγκλεῖσαι ἐς ἀκριβὲς τὰς ἀσπίδας, τοῦ κατ' αὐτῶν φερομένας τὰς ἁμάξας καὶ τῇ ῥύμῃ κατὰ τὸ εἰκὸς ὑπερπηδώσας ἀβλαβῶς ἐπελ-

---

¹ corrupt. Editors have proposed βαρβάρων, ἐγχωρίων, ἐμπείρων, ἐκ τῶν ὀρῶν, ὁμόρων, ὀρείων, ἐκεῖ ἐμπόρων.

Thracians,[4] with Philippi and Mount Orbelus on his
left. Then he crossed the river Nestus and is said
in ten days to have reached Mount Haemus
[Great Balkan mountain], where he was met in the 6
defile of the approach to the mountains by many of
the . . . [5] in arms and by the independent Thracians;
prepared to bar his advance, they had occupied the
height of Haemus on the line of the army's march.
They collected carts and set them up in their front as 7
a stockade from which to put up a defence, if they
were pressed; but it was also in their mind to launch
the carts at the Macedonian phalanx as the troops
mounted the slope just where the mountain was most
precipitous. Their idea was that the closer packed
the phalanx when the descending carts charged it,
the more their violent descent would scatter it.

Alexander consulted how he could most safely 8
cross the ridge; and since he saw that the risk must
be run, for there was no way round, he sent orders
to his hoplites that whenever the carts tumbled down
the slope, those who were on level ground and could
break formation were to part to right and left,
leaving an avenue for the carts; those caught in the 9
narrows were to crouch close together; and some
were actually to fall to the ground and link their
shields closely together so that when the carts came
at them they were likely to bound over them by their

---

[4] As distinguished from the Thracian principalities near the
coast which Philip had annexed. For this campaign, cf.
Introd. 33; D. 8, 1; P. 11; Strabo vii 3, 8. Al.'s route from
Amphipolis is unclear, see Seibert (Introd. n. 108) 78; the
Lyginus (2, 1) and Peuce are not certainly identified. At this
time the Triballi extended from round Sofia to the Danube,
perhaps as far as Silistria (RE VI A 2392 ff.).

[5] See textual note; the MS reading ' merchants ' is sense-
ess; editors propose ' local barbarians ' or the like.

θεῖν. καὶ οὕτω ξυνέβη ὅπως παρήνεσέ τε ᾿Αλέ-
10 ξανδρος καὶ εἴκασεν. οἱ μὲν γὰρ διέσχον τὴν
φάλαγγα, αἱ δ᾿ ὑπὲρ τῶν ἀσπίδων ἐπικυλισθεῖσαι
ὀλίγα ἔβλαψαν· ἀπέθανε δὲ οὐδεὶς ὑπὸ ταῖς
ἁμάξαις. ἔνθα δὴ οἱ Μακεδόνες θαρσήσαντες, ὅτι
ἀβλαβεῖς αὐτοῖς, ἃς μάλιστα ἐδεδίεσαν, αἱ ἅμαξαι
ἐγένοντο, σὺν βοῇ ἐς τοὺς Θρᾷκας ἐνέβαλον.
11 ᾿Αλέξανδρος δὲ τοὺς τοξότας μὲν ἀπὸ τοῦ δεξιοῦ
κέρως πρὸ τῆς ἄλλης φάλαγγος, ὅτι ταύτῃ εὐπορώτερα ἦν, ἐλθεῖν ἐκέλευσε καὶ ἐκτοξεύειν ἐς τοὺς
Θρᾷκας ὅπῃ προσφέροιντο· αὐτὸς δὲ ἀναλαβὼν τὸ
ἄγημα καὶ τοὺς ὑπασπιστὰς καὶ τοὺς ᾿Αγριᾶνας
12 κατὰ τὸ εὐώνυμον ἦγεν. ἔνθα δὴ οἱ τοξόται βάλ-
λοντες τοὺς προεκθέοντας τῶν Θρᾳκῶν ἀνέστελλον·
καὶ ἡ φάλαγξ προσμίξασα οὐ χαλεπῶς ἐξέωσεν ἐκ
τῆς χώρας ἀνθρώπους ψιλοὺς καὶ κακῶς ὡπλισμένους βαρβάρους, ὥστε ᾿Αλέξανδρον ἀπὸ τοῦ
εὐωνύμου ἐπάγοντα οὐκέτι ἐδέξαντο, ἀλλὰ ῥίψαντες
ὡς ἑκάστοις προὐχώρει τὰ ὅπλα κατὰ τοῦ ὄρους
13 ἔφυγον. καὶ ἀπέθανον μὲν αὐτῶν ἐς χιλίους καὶ
πεντακοσίους, ζῶντες δὲ ἄνδρες μὲν ὀλίγοι ἐλήφθησαν δι᾿ ὠκύτητα καὶ τῆς χώρας ἐμπειρίαν,
γυναῖκες δὲ ὅσαι ξυνείποντο αὐτοῖς ἑάλωσαν πᾶσαι,
καὶ τὰ παιδάρια καὶ ἡ λεία πᾶσα ἑάλω.

2. ᾿Αλέξανδρος δὲ τὴν μὲν λείαν ὀπίσω ἀπέπεμψεν ἐς τὰς πόλεις τὰς ἐπὶ θαλάσσῃ, Λυσανίᾳ καὶ
Φιλώτᾳ παραδοὺς διατίθεσθαι· αὐτὸς δὲ τὸ ἄκρον
ὑπερβαλὼν προῄει διὰ τοῦ Αἵμου ἐς Τριβαλλούς,
καὶ ἀφικνεῖται ἐπὶ τὸν Λύγινον ποταμόν· ἀπέχει δὲ
οὗτος ἀπὸ τοῦ ῎Ιστρου ὡς ἐπὶ τὸν Αἷμον ἰόντι
2 σταθμοὺς τρεῖς. Σύρμος δὲ ὁ τῶν Τριβαλλῶν
βασιλεύς, ἐκ πολλοῦ πυνθανόμενος τοῦ ᾿Αλεξάνδρου

gathered impetus and pass without doing harm. The   335
event corresponded to Alexander's advice and   B.C.
conjecture. Part of the phalanx divided, while the 10
carts sliding over the shields of the others did little
harm; not one man perished beneath them. The
Macedonians now took heart, finding that the carts
they had most dreaded proved harmless, and they
charged the Thracians, shouting as they did so.
Alexander ordered the archers from the right wing 11
to the front of the phalanx as on that side it was
easier to shoot at the Thracians wherever they
attacked. He himself took the *agema*, the hypaspists
and the Agrianians and led them on the left. Then 12
by their volleys the archers held back those Thracians
who were rushing forward and the phalanx, coming
to close quarters, easily drove from their position men
who were lightly clad and ill-armed barbarians; so
they did not await the charge of Alexander on the left,
but casting away their arms as best they could fled
down the mountain-side. Some fifteen hundred 13
perished; few were captured alive, by reason of their
speed and their knowledge of the country; the
women, however, who followed them were all taken,
with the children and all their impedimenta.

2. Alexander sent the booty back to the cities on the
coast, appointing Lysanias and Philotas [1] to deal
with it; he himself crossed the ridge, marched over
Haemus against the Triballians, and arrived at the
river Lyginus; as you approach the Haemus, it is
three days' march from the Ister (Danube). Syrmus, 2
King of the Triballians, learning some time before

---

[1] Berve no. 805; Parmenio's son (ib. no. 802) is probably
meant in § 5.

τὸν στόλον, γυναῖκας μὲν καὶ παῖδας τῶν Τριβαλλῶν προὔπεμψεν ἐπὶ τὸν Ἴστρον διαβαίνειν κελεύσας τὸν ποταμὸν ἐς νῆσόν τινα τῶν ἐν τῷ
3 Ἴστρῳ· Πεύκη ὄνομα τῇ νήσῳ ἐστίν. ἐς ταύτην
δὲ τὴν νῆσον καὶ οἱ Θρᾷκες οἱ πρόσχωροι τοῖς
Τριβαλλοῖς προσάγοντος Ἀλεξάνδρου ἐκ πολλοῦ
συμπεφευγότες ἦσαν καὶ αὐτὸς ὁ Σύρμος ἐς ταύτην
ξυμπεφεύγει ξὺν τοῖς ἀμφ' αὐτόν· τὸ δὲ πολὺ
πλῆθος τῶν Τριβαλλῶν ἔφυγεν ὀπίσω ἐπὶ τὸν
ποταμόν, ἔνθενπερ τῇ προτεραίᾳ ὡρμήθη Ἀλέξανδρος.

4 Ὡς δὲ ἔμαθεν αὐτῶν τὴν ὁρμήν, καὶ αὐτὸς ὑπο-
στρέψας τὸ ἔμπαλιν ἐπὶ τοὺς Τριβαλλοὺς ἦγεν, καὶ
καταλαμβάνει καταστρατοπεδεύοντας ἤδη. καὶ οἱ
μὲν καταληφθέντες πρὸς τῷ νάπει τῷ παρὰ τὸν
ποταμὸν παρετάσσοντο· Ἀλέξανδρος δὲ καὶ αὐτὸς
τὴν μὲν φάλαγγα ἐς βάθος ἐκτάξας ἐπῆγε, τοὺς
τοξότας δὲ καὶ τοὺς σφενδονήτας προεκθέοντας
ἐκέλευσεν ἐκτοξεύειν τε καὶ σφενδονᾶν ἐς τοὺς
βαρβάρους, εἴ πως προκαλέσαιτο αὐτοὺς ἐς τὰ ψιλὰ
5 ἐκ τοῦ νάπους. οἱ δὲ ὡς ἐντὸς βέλους ἐγένοντο,
παιόμενοι ἐξέθεον ἐπὶ τοὺς τοξότας, ὅπως ἐς
χεῖρας ξυμμίξειαν γυμνοῖς οὖσι τοῖς τοξόταις.
Ἀλέξανδρος δὲ ὡς προήγαγεν αὐτοὺς ἐκ τῆς νάπης
ἔξω, Φιλώταν μὲν ἀναλαβόντα τοὺς ἐκ τῆς ἄνωθεν
Μακεδονίας ἱππέας προσέταξεν ἐμβάλλειν κατὰ τὸ
κέρας τὸ δεξιόν, ᾗπερ μάλιστα προυκεχωρήκεσαν
ἐν τῇ ἐκδρομῇ. Ἡρακλείδην δὲ καὶ Σώπολιν τοὺς
ἐκ Βοττιαίας τε καὶ Ἀμφιπόλεως ἱππέας κατὰ τὸ
6 εὐώνυμον κέρας ἐπάγειν ἔταξε. τὴν δὲ φάλαγγα
τῶν πεζῶν καὶ τὴν ἄλλην ἵππον πρὸ τῆς φάλαγγος
παρατείνας κατὰ μέσους ἐπῆγε. καὶ ἔστε μὲν

of Alexander's march, sent on the women and 335 B.C. children to the Ister, ordering them to cross to an island in the river called Peuce.   To this island the 3 Thracians who are neighbours to the Triballians had also fled some time before on Alexander's approach, and Syrmus and his men now joined them there; but the mass of the Triballians fled back to the river from which Alexander had started out the day before.

Hearing of their move, Alexander turned back in 4 person to attack the Triballians, and found them already encamping.   Caught as they were, they formed line near the glen by the river; but Alexander threw his phalanx into deep formation and led it against them in person, ordering the bowmen and slingers to run out ahead and discharge their arrows and stones on the barbarians, to see if he could provoke them into the open out of the glen.   When 5 they were in range and came under fire, they ran out against the bowmen to come to grips with them, unarmed as bowmen are.   But having drawn them out of the glen, Alexander ordered Philotas to take the cavalry of upper Macedonia and charge their right wing, where they had advanced farthest in their outward rush.   Heracleides and Sopolis were ordered to lead the cavalry from Bottiaea and Amphipolis against the left wing.   The infantry phalanx and 6 the remaining cavalry, which he deployed in advance of the phalanx, he led against the centre.   While the

ἀκροβολισμὸς παρ᾽ ἑκατέρων ἦν, οἱ Τριβαλλοὶ οὐ
μεῖον εἶχον· ὡς δὲ ἥ τε φάλαγξ πυκνὴ ἐνέβαλλεν ἐς
αὐτοὺς ἐρρωμένως καὶ οἱ ἱππεῖς οὐκ ἀκοντισμῷ
ἔτι, ἀλλ᾽ αὐτοῖς τοῖς ἵπποις ὠθοῦντες ἄλλῃ καὶ
ἄλλῃ προσέπιπτον, τότε δὴ ἐτράπησαν διὰ τοῦ
7 νάπους εἰς τὸν ποταμόν. καὶ ἀποθνήσκουσι μὲν
τρισχίλιοι ἐν τῇ φυγῇ, ζῶντες δὲ ὀλίγοι καὶ τούτων
ἐλήφθησαν, ὅτι ὕλη τε δασεῖα πρὸ τοῦ ποταμοῦ ἦν
καὶ νὺξ ἐπιγενομένη τὴν ἀκρίβειαν τῆς διώξεως
ἀφείλετο τοὺς Μακεδόνας. αὐτῶν δὲ Μακεδόνων
τελευτῆσαι λέγει Πτολεμαῖος ἱππέας μὲν ἔνδεκα,
πεζοὺς δὲ ἀμφὶ τοὺς τεσσαράκοντα.

3. Ἀπὸ δὲ τῆς μάχης τριταῖος ἀφικνεῖται Ἀλέξανδρος ἐπὶ τὸν ποταμὸν τὸν Ἴστρον, ποταμῶν
τῶν κατὰ τὴν Εὐρώπην μέγιστον ὄντα καὶ πλείστην
γῆν ἐπερχόμενον καὶ ἔθνη μαχιμώτατα ἀπεί-
ργοντα, τὰ μὲν πολλὰ Κελτικά, ὅθεν γε καὶ αἱ
πηγαὶ αὐτῷ ἀνίσχουσιν, ὧν τελευταίους Κουάδους
2 καὶ Μαρκομάνους· ἐπὶ δὲ Σαυρομάτων μοῖραν,
Ἰάζυγας· ἐπὶ δὲ Γέτας τοὺς ἀπαθανατίζοντας·
ἐπὶ δὲ Σαυρομάτας τοὺς πολλούς· ἐπὶ δὲ Σκύθας
ἔστε ἐπὶ τὰς ἐκβολάς, ἵνα ἐκδιδοῖ κατὰ πέντε
3 στόματα ἐς τὸν Εὔξεινον πόντον. ἐνταῦθα καταλαμβάνει αὐτῷ ἡκούσας ναῦς μακρὰς ἐκ Βυζαντίου
διὰ τοῦ πόντου τοῦ Εὐξείνου κατὰ τὸν ποταμόν.
ταύτας ἐμπλήσας τοξοτῶν τε καὶ ὁπλιτῶν τῇ νήσῳ
ἐπέπλει, ἵνα οἱ Τριβαλλοί τε καὶ οἱ Θρᾷκες
ξυμπεφευγότες ἦσαν, καὶ ἐπειρᾶτο βιάζεσθαι τὴν

---

[2] Pt. is perhaps cited because A. felt that such precise figures
needed justification.

[1] An explanatory note by A. The Quadi and Marcomanni

battle was still at long range, the Triballians did not have the worst of it, but when the phalanx in close formation charged them in full force and the cavalry, no longer shooting, but actually thrusting them with their horses, fell on them here, there and everywhere, they turned in flight through the glen to the river. Three thousand perished in the flight, but 7 only a few were captured alive, as the wood in front of the river was dense, and as nightfall prevented the Macedonians from any thorough pursuit. Of the Macedonians, according to Ptolemy, eleven cavalrymen and about forty foot-soldiers were killed.[2]

3. On the third day after the battle Alexander reached the Ister, the greatest river of Europe, traversing the greatest tract of country and acting as a barrier to the most warlike tribes, Celts for the most part [1]—its springs rising in Celtic territory; the farthest of these peoples are the Quadi and Marcomanni; then it passes the Iazyges, a branch of 2 the Sauromatae, the Getae who call themselves immortals,[2] most of the Sauromatae, and the Scythians down to the outlets, where it runs through five mouths into the Black Sea. There Alexander 3 found at the mouth of the river warships come to join him from Byzantium through the Black Sea. He manned them with archers and hoplites and sailed against the island where the Triballians and Thracians had taken refuge, and attempted to force

were important in his time, not Al's. They were German, the Getae Thracian; ' Celts ' often has no precise ethnic or linguistic significance for Greeks, but denotes northern barbarians, sometimes Germans, though Ephorus (Jacoby no. 70 F. 30) in the fourth century put Celts in the western extremity of the world, Scythians in the north; the last term is used indifferently of all nomads.

[2] Belief in immortality: Herodotus iv 93 f.

4 ἀπόβασιν. οἱ δὲ βάρβαροι ἀπήντων ἐπὶ τὸν
ποταμόν, ὅπῃ αἱ νῆες προσπίπτοιεν· αἱ δὲ ὀλίγαι τε
ἦσαν καὶ ἡ στρατιὰ οὐ πολλὴ ⟨ἡ⟩ ἐπ' αὐτῶν, καὶ
τῆς νήσου τὰ πολλὰ ἀπότομα ἐς προσβολήν, καὶ τὸ
ῥεῦμα τοῦ ποταμοῦ τὸ παρ' αὐτήν, οἷα δὴ ἐς στενὸν
συγκεκλεισμένον, ὀξὺ καὶ ἄπορον προσφέρεσθαι.

5 Ἔνθα δὴ Ἀλέξανδρος ἀπαγαγὼν τὰς ναῦς ἔγνω
διαβαίνειν τὸν Ἴστρον ἐπὶ τοὺς Γέτας τοὺς πέραν
τοῦ Ἴστρου ᾠκισμένους, ὅτι τε συνειλεγμένους
ἑώρα πολλοὺς ἐπὶ τῇ ὄχθῃ τοῦ Ἴστρου, ὡς
εἴρξοντας, εἰ διαβαίνοι, — ἦσαν γὰρ ἱππεῖς μὲν ἐς
τετρακισχιλίους, πεζοὶ δὲ πλείους τῶν μυρίων —
καὶ ἅμα πόθος ἔλαβεν αὐτὸν ἐπέκεινα τοῦ Ἴστρου
6 ἐλθεῖν. τῶν μὲν δὴ νεῶν ἐπέβη αὐτός· τὰς δὲ
διφθέρας, ὑφ' αἷς ἐσκήνουν, τῆς κάρφης πληρώσας
καὶ ὅσα μονόξυλα πλοῖα ἐκ τῆς χώρας ξυναγαγών
— ἦν δὲ καὶ τούτων εὐπορία πολλή, ὅτι τούτοις
χρῶνται οἱ πρόσοικοι τῷ Ἴστρῳ ἐφ' ἁλιείᾳ τε τῇ
ἐκ τοῦ Ἴστρου καὶ εἴποτε παρ' ἀλλήλους ἀνὰ τὸν
ποταμὸν στέλλοιντο καὶ λῃστεύοντες ἀπ' αὐτῶν οἱ
πολλοί — ταῦτα ὡς πλεῖστα ξυναγαγὼν διεβίβαζεν
ἐπ' αὐτῶν τῆς στρατιᾶς ὅσους δυνατὸν ἦν ἐν τῷ
τοιῷδε τρόπῳ. καὶ γίγνονται οἱ διαβάντες ἅμα
Ἀλεξάνδρῳ ἱππεῖς μὲν ἐς χιλίους καὶ πεντακοσίους,
πεζοὶ δὲ ἐς τετρακισχιλίους.

4. Διέβαλον δὲ τῆς νυκτὸς ᾗ λήιον ἦν σίτου
βαθύ· καὶ ταύτῃ μᾶλλόν τι ἔλαθον προσχόντες τῇ
ὄχθῃ. ὑπὸ δὲ τὴν ἕω Ἀλέξανδρος διὰ τοῦ ληίου
ἦγε, παραγγείλας τοῖς πεζοῖς πλαγίαις ταῖς σαρίσσαις ἐπικλίνοντας τὸν σῖτον οὕτω προάγειν ἐς τὰ
οὐκ ἐργάσιμα. οἱ δὲ ἱππεῖς ἔστε μὲν διὰ τοῦ ληίου
2 προῄει ἡ φάλαγξ ἐφείποντο· ὡς δὲ ἐκ τῶν

a landing. The barbarians, however, came down to 4 335
the river-side wherever the ships touched land; B.C.
these were few in number, and carried only a small
force; the island was for the most part steep for
landing; and the current past the island, as was
natural in a narrow strait, was swift and difficult
to contend with.

Thereupon Alexander withdrew his ships and de- 5
cided to cross the Ister to attack the Getae settled on
the farther side, both because he saw a large force of
them gathered on the bank, to repel him, should he
cross—there were about four thousand mounted men,
and more than ten thousand on foot—and also because he had been seized with a longing [3] to go
beyond the river. He himself embarked in the fleet; 6
he filled the leather tent covers with hay, collected
as many as possible of the boats from the countryside made from single tree trunks (they were plenti-
ful, for the river-side dwellers use them for fishing, at
times for river expeditions among themselves, and
even more for thieving), and ferried across as much of
his force as he could in this way. About fifteen
hundred cavalry and four thousand foot-soldiers
crossed with him.

4. The crossing was made at night where there
was a deep cornfield, and this concealed them more,
as they reached the bank. About dawn, Alexander
led the troops through the field, ordering the infantry to smooth down the corn with their spears,
held obliquely, and so advance to untilled ground.
As long as the phalanx was marching through the
corn the cavalry followed; but when they emerged 2

[3] Appendix V 3.

ἐργασίμων ἐξήλασαν, τὴν μὲν ἵππον ἐπὶ τὸ δεξιὸν
κέρας αὐτὸς Ἀλέξανδρος παρήγαγεν, τὴν φάλαγγα
3 δὲ ἐν πλαισίῳ Νικάνορα ἄγειν ἐκέλευσε. καὶ οἱ
Γέται οὐδὲ τὴν πρώτην ἐμβολὴν τῶν ἱππέων
ἐδέξαντο· παράδοξος μὲν γὰρ αὐτοῖς ἡ τόλμα
ἐφάνη τοῦ Ἀλεξάνδρου, ὅτι εὐμαρῶς οὕτως τὸν
μέγιστον τῶν ποταμῶν διεβεβήκει ἐν μιᾷ νυκτὶ τὸν
Ἴστρον οὐ γεφυρώσας τὸν πόρον, φοβερὰ δὲ καὶ
τῆς φάλαγγος ἡ ξύγκλεισις, βιαία δὲ ἡ τῶν ἱππέων
4 ἐμβολή. καὶ τὰ μὲν πρῶτα ἐς τὴν πόλιν καταφεύγουσιν, ᾗ δὴ ἀπεῖχεν αὐτοῖς ὅσον παρασάγγην
τοῦ Ἴστρου· ὡς δὲ ἐπάγοντα εἶδον σπουδῇ
Ἀλέξανδρον τὴν μὲν φάλαγγα παρὰ τὸν ποταμόν,
ὡς μὴ κυκλωθεῖέν πῃ οἱ πεζοὶ ἐνεδρευσάντων τῶν
Γετῶν, τοὺς ἱππέας δὲ κατὰ μέτωπον, λείπουσιν αὖ
καὶ τὴν πόλιν οἱ Γέται κακῶς τετειχισμένην, ἀνα-
λαβόντες τῶν παιδαρίων καὶ τῶν γυναικῶν ἐπὶ τοὺς
5 ἵππους ὅσα φέρειν οἱ ἵπποι ἠδύναντο· ἦν δὲ αὐτοῖς
ἡ ὁρμὴ ὡς πορρωτάτω ἀπὸ τοῦ ποταμοῦ ἐς τὰ
ἔρημα. Ἀλέξανδρος δὲ τήν τε πόλιν λαμβάνει καὶ
τὴν λείαν πᾶσαν ὅσην οἱ Γέται ὑπελίποντο. καὶ
τὴν μὲν λείαν Μελεάγρῳ καὶ Φιλίππῳ ἐπαναγαγεῖν
δίδωσιν, αὐτὸς δὲ κατασκάψας τὴν πόλιν θύει τε
ἐπὶ τῇ ὄχθῃ τοῦ Ἴστρου Διὶ Σωτῆρι καὶ Ἡρακλεῖ
καὶ αὐτῷ τῷ Ἴστρῳ, ὅτι οὐκ ἄπορος αὐτῷ ἐγένετο,
καὶ ἐπανάγει αὐτῆς ἡμέρας σώους σύμπαντας ἐπὶ
τὸ στρατόπεδον.

6   Ἐνταῦθα ἀφίκοντο πρέσβεις ὡς Ἀλέξανδρον
παρά τε τῶν ἄλλων ὅσα αὐτόνομα ἔθνη προσοικεῖ
τῷ Ἴστρῳ καὶ παρὰ Σύρμου τοῦ Τριβαλλῶν
βασιλέως· καὶ παρὰ Κελτῶν δὲ τῶν ἐπὶ τῷ Ἰονίῳ
κόλπῳ ᾠκισμένων ἧκον· μεγάλοι οἱ Κελτοὶ τὰ

from the tilled land, Alexander in person took off the
the cavalry to the right wing, ordering Nicanor
to lead the phalanx in rectangular formation. The 3
Getae did not even withstand the first charge of the
cavalry; for Alexander's bold stroke came as a
great shock to them, in crossing the Ister, the
greatest of rivers, so easily in one night without
bridging the stream; the solidity of the phalanx was
terrifying, and the onslaught of the cavalry violent.
They first took refuge in the city, about a parasang [1] 4
away from the Ister; then, seeing that Alexander
was rapidly bringing up his phalanx along the river,
so that the infantry might not be encircled by an
ambush of the Getae, with the cavalry on the front,
the Getae in their turn deserted their city, which
was feebly fortified, taking up on horseback as many
of the women and children as the horses could carry;
and then marched as far as possible away from the 5
river towards the desert. Alexander captured the
city and all the plunder the Getae left behind.
This plunder he ordered Meleager and Philip to take
to the base; he himself razed the city and sacrificed
on the bank of the Ister to Zeus the Preserver and
Heracles and Ister himself, for permitting the
passage. Then the same day he took all his force
safe and sound back to the camp.

At this juncture ambassadors came to Alexander 6
from Syrmus, King of the Triballi and from the other
self-governing tribes near the Ister; others from
the Celts settled on the Ionian gulf [Adriatic].

[1] The use of this Persian term (part of a day's march, c.
5-6 km) is strange.

σώματα καὶ μέγα ἐπὶ σφίσι φρονοῦντες· πάντες δὲ
φιλίας τῆς Ἀλεξάνδρου ἐφιέμενοι ἥκειν ἔφασαν.
7 καὶ πᾶσιν ἔδωκε πίστεις Ἀλέξανδρος καὶ ἔλαβε·
τοὺς Κελτοὺς δὲ καὶ ἤρετο, ὅ τι μάλιστα δεδίττεται
αὐτοὺς τῶν ἀνθρωπίνων, ἐλπίσας ὅτι μέγα ὄνομα τὸ
αὐτοῦ καὶ ἐς Κελτοὺς καὶ ἔτι προσωτέρω ἥκει καὶ
8 ὅτι αὐτὸν μάλιστα πάντων δεδιέναι φήσουσι. τῷ
δὲ παρ' ἐλπίδα ξυνέβη τῶν Κελτῶν ἡ ἀπόκρισις.
οἷα γὰρ πόρρω τε ᾠκισμένοι Ἀλεξάνδρου καὶ
χωρία δύσπορα οἰκοῦντες καὶ Ἀλεξάνδρου ἐς ἄλλα
τὴν ὁρμὴν ὁρῶντες ἔφασαν δεδιέναι μήποτε ὁ
οὐρανὸς αὐτοῖς ἐμπέσοι, Ἀλέξανδρόν τε ἀγασθέντες
οὔτε δέει οὔτε κατ' ὠφέλειαν πρεσβεῦσαι παρ'
αὐτόν. καὶ τούτους φίλους τε ὀνομάσας καὶ
ξυμμάχους ποιησάμενος ὀπίσω ἀπέπεμψε, το-
σοῦτον ὑπειπὼν ὅτι ἀλαζόνες Κελτοί εἰσιν.

5. Αὐτὸς δὲ ἐπ' Ἀγριάνων καὶ Παιόνων προὔ-
χώρει. ἔνθα δὴ ἄγγελοι ἀφίκοντο αὐτῷ Κλεῖτόν τε
τὸν Βαρδύλεω ἀφεστάναι ἀγγέλλοντες καὶ Γλαυκίαν προσκεχωρηκέναι αὐτῷ τὸν Ταυλαντίων
βασιλέα· οἱ δὲ καὶ τοὺς Αὐταριάτας ἐπιθήσεσθαι
αὐτῷ κατὰ τὴν πορείαν ἐξήγγελλον· ὧν δὴ ἕνεκα
2 κατὰ σπουδὴν ἐδόκει ἀναζευγνύναι. Λάγγαρος δὲ
ὁ τῶν Ἀγριάνων βασιλεὺς ἤδη μὲν καὶ Φιλίππου
ζῶντος ἀσπαζόμενος Ἀλέξανδρον δῆλος ἦν καὶ
ἰδίᾳ ἐπρέσβευσε παρ' αὐτόν, τότε δὲ παρῆν αὐτῷ
μετὰ τῶν ὑπασπιστῶν, ὅσους τε καλλίστους καὶ

---

² §6–8 from Pt. (Strabo vii 3, 8).
¹ Striking SW for the upper Strymon (Struma) and Axius
(Vardar) valleys. For chapters 5 and 6 in general see N. G.
L. Hammond, *JHS* 1974, with full topographic discussion,

335
B.C.

The Celts were of great height and had a high conceit of themselves; but all professed to have come in desire for Alexander's friendship, and with all he 7 exchanged pledges. Of the Celts he enquired what mortal thing they most dreaded, hoping that his own great name had reached the Celts and gone still farther, and that they would say that they dreaded him more than anything else. Their 8 answer, however, was not what he expected, for, living in difficult country far from Alexander, and seeing that his aim lay elsewhere, they said that their greatest dread was that the sky would fall upon them, and that, while they admired Alexander, neither fear nor interest had prompted their embassy.[2] He declared them his friends, made them his allies and sent them home, only remarking, ' What braggarts Celts are! '

5. He then advanced towards the Agrianians and Paeonians.[1] There messengers reached him with the news that Clitus, son of Bardylis, was in revolt, and that Glaucias, king of the Taulantians, had joined him.[2] They also told him that the Autariates were going to attack him on his march. For these reasons he decided to move rapidly. Langarus, 2 king of the Agrianians, had shown his regard for Alexander even in Philip's lifetime, had been on an embassy to him personally, and was now in attendance on him with the finest and best-armed hypas-

which I was able to see in typescript, but which is too complex to summarize here.

[2] Bardylis is presumably ' the Illyrian king ' decisively beaten by Philip in 358 (D. xvi 4); Hammond argues that he and Clitus were kings of the Dardanians on the upper Vardar and White Drin, and that the Taulantii dwelt round Tiranë in Albania (*Annual of British School at Athens* 1966, 243 ff.). The Autariatae are placed on the upper Neretsa (Naron).

3 εὐοπλοτάτους ἀμφ' αὐτὸν εἶχε· καὶ ἐπειδὴ ἔμαθεν
ὑπὲρ τῶν Αὐταριατῶν πυνθανόμενον Ἀλέξανδρον,
οἵτινές τε καὶ ὁπόσοι εἶεν, οὐκ ἔφη χρῆναι ἐν λόγῳ
τίθεσθαι Αὐταριάτας· εἶναι γὰρ ἀπολεμωτάτους
τῶν ταύτῃ· καὶ αὐτὸς ἐμβαλεῖν ἐς τὴν χώραν
αὐτῶν, ὡς ἀμφὶ τὰ σφέτερα μᾶλλόν τι ἔχοιεν. καὶ
κελεύσαντος Ἀλεξάνδρου ἐσβάλλει ἐς αὐτοὺς καὶ
ἐμβαλὼν ἦγε καὶ ἔφερε τὴν χώραν αὐτῶν.

4 Αὐταριᾶται μὲν δὴ ἀμφὶ τὰ αὑτῶν εἶχον· Λάγγαρος δὲ τά τε ἄλλα ἐτιμήθη μεγάλως πρὸς
Ἀλεξάνδρου καὶ δῶρα ἔλαβεν, ὅσα μέγιστα παρὰ
βασιλεῖ τῷ Μακεδόνων νομίζεται· καὶ τὴν ἀδελφὴν
τὴν Ἀλεξάνδρου Κύναν καὶ ταύτην ὡμολόγησε
δώσειν αὐτῷ ἐς Πέλλαν ἀφικομένῳ Ἀλέξανδρος.

5 Ἀλλὰ Λάγγαρος μὲν ἐπανελθὼν οἴκαδε νόσῳ
ἐτελεύτησεν. Ἀλέξανδρος δὲ παρὰ τὸν Ἐριγόνα
ποταμὸν πορευόμενος ἐς Πέλλιον πόλιν ἐστέλλετο.
ταύτην γὰρ κατειλήφει ὁ Κλεῖτος ὡς ὀχυρωτάτην
τῆς χώρας· καὶ πρὸς ταύτην ὡς ἧκεν Ἀλέξανδρος,
καταστρατοπεδεύσας πρὸς τῷ Ἐορδαϊκῷ ποταμῷ

6 τῇ ὑστεραίᾳ ἐγνώκει προσβάλλειν τῷ τείχει. οἱ δὲ
ἀμφὶ τὸν Κλεῖτον τὰ κύκλῳ τῆς πόλεως ὄρη
ὑπερδέξιά τε ὄντα καὶ δασέα κατεῖχον, ὡς πάντοθεν
ἐπιτίθεσθαι τοῖς Μακεδόσιν, εἰ τῇ πόλει προσβάλ-
λοιεν· Γλαυκίας δὲ αὐτῷ ὁ τῶν Ταυλαντίων

7 βασιλεὺς οὔπω παρῆν. Ἀλέξανδρος μὲν δὴ τῇ
πόλει προσῆγεν· οἱ δὲ πολέμιοι σφαγιασάμενοι
παῖδας τρεῖς καὶ κόρας ἴσας τὸν ἀριθμὸν καὶ κριοὺς
μέλανας τρεῖς, ὥρμηντο μὲν ὡς δεξόμενοι ἐς χεῖρας
τοὺς Μακεδόνας· ὁμοῦ δὲ γενομένων ἐξέλιπον
καίτοι καρτερὰ ὄντα τὰ κατειλημμένα πρὸς σφῶν

pists he had; and when he learnt that Alexander was 3
enquiring who the Autariates were and how numerous, he told him not to trouble about them, as they
were the least warlike of the tribesmen in those
parts; he would himself invade their country, so that
they might be preoccupied with their own affairs.
On Alexander's instructions he invaded and devas-
tated their country. Thus the Autariates were kept 4
busy at home. Langarus received great honours
from Alexander and what were considered at the
court of Macedon the greatest gifts. Alexander
actually promised to wed his sister Cyna [3] to him,
when he came to Pella. However, after reaching 5
home, Langarus sickened and died.

Alexander, marching along the river Erigon
[Cerna Reka], made for Pellium, a city Clitus had
occupied, as the strongest in the country. When
he reached it, he camped by the river Eordaicus
[Devoll] and decided to assault the wall next day.[4]
Clitus' forces held the heights surrounding the city, 6
which were commanding and thickly wooded, so as to
attack the Macedonians from all sides, if they made
the assault on the city, but Glaucias, king of the
Taulantians, was not yet present. Alexander 7
proceeded against this city, on which the enemy
sacrificed three boys and three girls and three black
rams, and advanced to close combat with the Macedonians; but once engaged, they deserted the

335
B.C.

[3] Or Cynnana, previously married to Al's cousin, Amyntas
(Introd. 46). The Agrianians, a Paeonian branch of the
Thracians on the upper Strymon, provided a valuable con-
tingent for the Asian expedition.

[4] Hammond (§1 n.) places Pellium by the modern Goricë
about 25 km S.E. of Lake Ochrid in the fertile plain of Poloskë
watered by the river Devoll (Eordaicus); the operations can
only be followed with maps as detailed as he supplies.

χωρία, ὥστε καὶ τὰ σφάγια αὐτῶν κατελήφθη ἔτι κείμενα.

8 Ταύτῃ μὲν δὴ τῇ ἡμέρᾳ κατακλείσας αὐτοὺς ἐς τὴν πόλιν καὶ στρατοπεδευσάμενος πρὸς τῷ τείχει ἐγνώκει περιτειχισμῷ ἀποκλεῖσαι αὐτούς· τῇ δὲ ὑστεραίᾳ παρῆν μετὰ πολλῆς δυνάμεως Γλαυκίας ὁ τῶν Ταυλαντίων βασιλεύς. ἔνθα δὴ Ἀλέξανδρος τὴν μὲν πόλιν ἀπέγνω ἑλεῖν ἂν ξὺν τῇ παρούσῃ δυνάμει, πολλῶν μὲν ἐς αὐτὴν καὶ μαχίμων ξυμπεφευγότων, πολλῶν δὲ ἅμα τῷ Γλαυκίᾳ προσκεισομένων, εἰ αὐτὸς τῷ τείχει προσμάχοιτο.

9 Φιλώταν δὲ ἀναλαβόντα τῶν ἱππέων ὅσους ἐς προφυλακὴν καὶ τὰ ὑποζύγια τὰ ἐκ τοῦ στρατοπέδου ἐς ἐπισιτισμὸν ἔπεμπε. καὶ ὁ Γλαυκίας μαθὼν τὴν ὁρμὴν τῶν ἀμφὶ Φιλώταν ἐξελαύνει ἐπ' αὐτούς, καὶ καταλαμβάνει τὰ κύκλῳ ὄρη τοῦ πεδίου, ὅθεν οἱ ξὺν Φιλώτᾳ ἐπισιτιεῖσθαι ἔμελλον.

10 Ἀλέξανδρος δέ, ἐπειδὴ ἀπηγγέλθη αὐτῷ, ὅτι κινδυνεύουσιν οἵ τε ἱππεῖς καὶ τὰ ὑποζύγια, εἰ νὺξ αὐτοὺς καταλήψεται, αὐτὸς μὲν ἀναλαβὼν τούς τε ὑπασπιστὰς καὶ τοὺς τοξότας καὶ τοὺς Ἀγριᾶνας καὶ ἱππέας ἐς τετρακοσίους ἐβοήθει σπουδῇ· τὸ δὲ ἄλλο στράτευμα πρὸς τῇ πόλει ἀπέλιπεν, ὡς μὴ ἀποχωρήσαντος παντὸς τοῦ στρατοῦ καὶ οἱ ἐκ τῆς πόλεως ἐπιδραμόντες τοῖς ἀμφὶ Γλαυκίαν συμ-

11 μίξειαν. ἔνθα δὴ Γλαυκίας προσάγοντα Ἀλέξανδρον αἰσθόμενος ἐκλείπει τὰ ὄρη· οἱ δὲ ξὺν Φιλώτᾳ ἀσφαλῶς ἐπὶ τὸ στρατόπεδον διεσώθησαν. ἐδόκουν δ' ἔτι τὸν Ἀλέξανδρον ἐν δυσχωρίᾳ

12 ἀπειληφέναι οἱ ἀμφὶ τὸν Κλεῖτον καὶ Γλαυκίαν· τά τε γὰρ ὄρη τὰ ὑπερδέξια κατεῖχον πολλοῖς μὲν ἱππεῦσι, πολλοῖς δὲ ἀκοντισταῖς καὶ σφενδονήταις

positions they had occupied, strong as they were, so that their victims were found still lying there.

On this day then Alexander shut them up in their 8 city and camped by the wall, intending to cut them off by a circumvallation, but next day Glaucias, king of the Taulantians, appeared with a large force. Thereupon Alexander gave up the idea of taking the city with the forces at his disposal, as many fighting men had taken refuge inside, and Glaucias' strong force would fall upon him, should he assault the wall. He sent Philotas to obtain food with as many horse- 9 men as he needed for a screen, and all the baggage animals from the camp. Glaucias, on learning of this move of Philotas, set off to attack his troops, and occupied the heights encircling the plain where Philotas' troops were to obtain food. When it was 10 reported to Alexander that the cavalry and baggage animals would be in danger, if night overtook them, he himself went with the hypaspists, archers and Agrianians and some four hundred horsemen at full speed to their aid, leaving the rest of the army near the city, as there was a risk that, if the whole force had withdrawn, the enemy in the city might have sallied out and joined with Glaucias' forces. As 11 a result, on seeing Alexander's approach, Glaucias abandoned the heights, and Philotas and his party got safe back to the camp. Clitus and Glaucias with their troops still appeared to have caught Alexander in a disadvantageous position; they held 12 the commanding heights with many horsemen, javelin-men, and slingers, as well as a large number

καὶ ὁπλίταις δὲ οὐκ ὀλίγοις, καὶ οἱ ἐν τῇ πόλει
κατειλημμένοι προσκείσεσθαι ἀπαλλαττομένοις
ἤμελλον· τά τε χωρία δι' ὧν ἡ πάροδος ἦν τῷ
Ἀλεξάνδρῳ στενὰ καὶ ὑλώδη ἐφαίνετο, τῇ μὲν πρὸς
τοῦ ποταμοῦ ἀπειργόμενα, τῇ δὲ ὄρος ὑπερύψηλον
ἦν καὶ κρημνοὶ πρὸς τοῦ ὄρους, ὥστε οὐδὲ ἐπὶ
τεσσάρων ἀσπίδων ἂν τῷ στρατεύματι ἡ πάροδος
ἐγένετο.

6. Ἔνθα δὴ ἐκτάσσει τὸν στρατὸν Ἀλέξανδρος
ἕως ἑκατὸν καὶ εἴκοσι τὸ βάθος τῆς φάλαγγος.
ἐπὶ τὸ κέρας δὲ ἑκατέρωθεν διακοσίους ἱππέας
ἐπιτάξας παρήγγελλε σιγῇ ἔχειν τὸ παραγγελ-
2 λόμενον ὀξέως δεχομένους. καὶ τὰ μὲν πρῶτα
ἐσήμηνεν ὀρθὰ ἀνατεῖναι τὰ δόρατα τοὺς ὁπλίτας,
ἔπειτα ἀπὸ ξυνθήματος ἀποτεῖναι ἐς προβολήν, καὶ
νῦν μὲν ἐς τὸ δεξιὸν ἐγκλῖναι τῶν δοράτων τὴν
σύγκλεισιν, αὖθις δὲ ἐπὶ τὰ ἀριστερά. καὶ αὐτὴν
δὲ τὴν φάλαγγα ἔς τε τὸ πρόσω ὀξέως ἐκίνησε καὶ
3 ἐπὶ τὰ κέρατα ἄλλοτε ἄλλη παρήγαγε. καὶ οὕτω
πολλὰς τάξεις τάξας τε καὶ μετακοσμήσας ἐν
ὀλίγῳ χρόνῳ, κατὰ τὸ εὐώνυμον οἷον ἔμβολον
ποιήσας τῆς φάλαγγος ἐπῆγεν ἐπὶ τοὺς πολεμίους.
οἱ δὲ πάλαι μὲν ἐθαύμαζον τήν τε ὀξύτητα ὁρῶντες
καὶ τὸν κόσμον τῶν δρωμένων· τότε δὲ προσάγοντας ἤδη τοὺς ἀμφὶ Ἀλέξανδρον οὐκ ἐδέξαντο,
4 ἀλλὰ λείπουσι τοὺς πρώτους λόφους. ὁ δὲ καὶ
ἐπαλαλάξαι ἐκέλευσε τοὺς Μακεδόνας καὶ τοῖς δό-
ρασι δουπῆσαι πρὸς τὰς ἀσπίδας· οἱ δὲ Ταυλάντιοι
ἔτι μᾶλλον ἐκπλαγέντες πρὸς τῆς βοῆς ὡς πρὸς τὴν
πόλιν ἐπανήγαγον σπουδῇ τὸν στρατόν.

5 Ἀλέξανδρος δὲ λόφον τινὰς κατέχοντας ἰδὼν οὐ
πολλοὺς τῶν πολεμίων, παρ' ὃν αὐτῷ ἡ πάροδος

335
B.C.

of hoplites, and the forces enclosed in the city were
likely to attack as Alexander's men drew off, while the
ground through which Alexander must pass seemed
narrow and forested, bounded on the one side by the
river, and on the other by a lofty mountain and cliffs
on the side of the mountain, so that the army could
not have passed through even four abreast.

6. In the circumstances Alexander drew up his
phalanx with a depth of 120 files. On either wing
he posted 200 horsemen, bidding them keep silent
and smartly obey the word of command; the hoplites 2
were ordered first to raise their spears upright, and
then, on the word, to lower them for a charge,
swinging their serried points first to the right, then
to the left; he moved the phalanx itself smartly
forward, and then wheeled it alternately to right and
left. Thus he deployed and manoeuvred it in many 3
difficult formations in a brief time, and then making
a kind of wedge from his phalanx on the left, he led
it to the attack. The enemy, long bewildered both
at the smartness and the discipline of the drill, did
not await the approach of Alexander's troops, but
abandoned the first hills. Alexander ordered the 4
Macedonians to raise their battle-cry and clang their
spears upon their shields, and the Taulantians, even
more terrified at the noise, hastily withdrew back to
the city.

Alexander saw that a few of the enemy were hold- 5
ing a hill on his line of march, and ordered his

ARRIAN

ἐγίγνετο, παρήγγειλε τοῖς σωματοφύλαξι καὶ τοῖς
ἀμφ' αὑτὸν ἑταίροις, ἀναλαβόντας τὰς ἀσπίδας
ἀναβαίνειν ἐπὶ τοὺς ἵππους καὶ ἐλαύνειν ἐπὶ τὸν
γήλοφον· ἐκεῖσε δὲ ἐλθόντας, εἰ ὑπομένοιεν οἱ
κατειληφότες τὸ χωρίον, τοὺς ἡμίσεας καταπηδῆσαι
ἀπὸ τῶν ἵππων καὶ ἀναμιχθέντας τοῖς ἱππεῦσι
6 πεζοὺς μάχεσθαι. οἱ δὲ πολέμιοι τὴν ὁρμὴν τὴν
Ἀλεξάνδρου ἰδόντες λείπουσι τὸν γήλοφον καὶ
παρεκκλίνουσιν ἐφ' ἑκάτερα τῶν ὀρῶν. ἔνθα δὴ
καταλαβὼν Ἀλέξανδρος τὸν γήλοφον σὺν τοῖς
ἑταίροις τούς τε Ἀγριᾶνας μεταπέμπεται καὶ τοὺς
τοξότας, ὄντας ἐς δισχιλίους· τοὺς δὲ ὑπασπιστὰς
διαβαίνειν τὸν ποταμὸν ἐκέλευσε καὶ ἐπὶ τούτοις
τὰς τάξεις τῶν Μακεδόνων· ὁπότε δὲ διαβάντες
τύχοιεν, ἐπ' ἀσπίδα ἐκτάσσεσθαι, ὡς πυκνὴν εὐθὺς
διαβάντων φαίνεσθαι τὴν φάλαγγα· αὐτὸς δὲ ἐν
προφυλακῇ ὢν ἀπὸ τοῦ λόφου ἀφεώρα τῶν
7 πολεμίων τὴν ὁρμήν. οἱ δέ, ὁρῶντες διαβαίνουσαν
τὴν δύναμιν, κατὰ τὰ ὄρη ἀντεπῇσαν, ὡς τοῖς μετὰ
Ἀλεξάνδρου ἐπιθησόμενοι τελευταίοις ἀποχω-
ροῦσιν. ὁ δὲ πελαζόντων ἤδη αὐτὸς ἐκθεῖ σὺν τοῖς
ἀμφ' αὑτόν, καὶ ἡ φάλαγξ, ὡς διὰ τοῦ ποταμοῦ ἐπι-
ιοῦσα, ἐπηλάλαξεν· οἱ δὲ πολέμιοι πάντων ἐπὶ
σφᾶς ἐλαυνόντων ἐγκλίναντες ἔφευγον· καὶ ἐν
τούτῳ ἐπῆγεν Ἀλέξανδρος τούς τε Ἀγριᾶνας καὶ
τοὺς τοξότας δρόμῳ ὡς ἐπὶ τὸν ποταμόν. καὶ
8 πρῶτος μὲν αὐτὸς φθάσας διαβαίνει· τοῖς τελευταίοις δὲ ὡς εἶδεν ἐπικειμένους τοὺς πολεμίους
ἐπιστήσας ἐπὶ τῇ ὄχθῃ τὰς μηχανὰς ἐξακοντίζειν
ὡς πορρωτάτω ἀπ' αὐτῶν ἐκέλευσεν ὅσα ἀπὸ
μηχανῶν βέλη ἐξακοντίζεται, καὶ τοὺς τοξότας δὲ
ἐκ μέσου τοῦ ποταμοῦ ἐκτοξεύειν, ἐπεσβάντας καὶ

335
B.C.

bodyguards [1] and the Companions with him to take their shields, mount and charge the hill; on reaching it, supposing those who held it should stand their ground, half were to dismount and, mingling with the cavalry, fight on foot. But the enemy, observing 6 Alexander's onset, abandoned the hill and withdrew to the mountains on either side. So after occupying the hill with his Companions, Alexander sent for the Agrianians and the archers, up to the number of two thousand; the hypaspists were ordered to cross the river, and the battalions of the Macedonian phalanx to follow them. Once across, they were to extend to the left, so that the phalanx might appear solid the moment they had crossed. He himself was in an advanced covering position, watching the enemy's movement from the hill. On seeing the force 7 crossing, the enemy charged down the mountain with the idea of attacking the last of Alexander's troops to withdraw. When they were already close, he himself with the troops he had with him ran out, and the phalanx coming to the attack through the river raised its battle-cry; under this combined onslaught the enemy broke and fled, whereupon Alexander brought up the Agrianians and the archers at the double in the direction of the river. He himself got over first, but seeing the enemy 8 pressing on the hindmost, he set up his engines on the bank and ordered every kind of missile to be discharged from them at furthest range, and the archers to shoot from mid-river, as they too had

---

[1] i.e. the hypaspists.

τούτους. καὶ οἱ μὲν ἀμφὶ τὸν Γλαυκίαν εἴσω
βέλους παρελθεῖν οὐκ ἐτόλμων, οἱ Μακεδόνες δὲ ἐν
τούτῳ ἀσφαλῶς ἐπέρασαν τὸν ποταμόν, ὥστε
οὐδεὶς ἀπέθανεν ἐν τῇ ἀποχωρήσει αὐτῶν.

9 Τρίτῃ δὲ ἀπ' ἐκείνης ἡμέρᾳ καταμαθὼν Ἀλέξανδρος κακῶς αὐλιζομένους τοὺς ἀμφὶ Κλεῖτον καὶ
Γλαυκίαν, καὶ οὔτε φυλακὰς ἐν τῇ τάξει αὐτοῖς
φυλαττομένας οὔτε χάρακα ἢ τάφρον προβε-
βλημένους, οἷα δὴ ξὺν φόβῳ ἀπηλλάχθαι οἰομένων
Ἀλέξανδρον, ἐς μῆκός τε οὐκ ὠφέλιμον ἀποτετα-
[γ]μένην αὐτοῖς τὴν τάξιν, ὑπὸ νύκτα ἔτι λαθὼν
διαβαίνει τὸν ποταμόν, τούς τε ὑπασπιστὰς ἅμα οἷ
ἄγων καὶ τοὺς Ἀγριᾶνας καὶ τοὺς τοξότας καὶ τὴν
10 Περδίκκου καὶ Κοίνου τάξιν. καὶ προσετέτακτο
μὲν ἀκολουθεῖν τὴν ἄλλην στρατιάν· ὡς δὲ καιρὸν
εἶδεν εἰς ἐπίθεσιν, οὐ προσμείνας ὁμοῦ γενέσθαι
πάντας ἐφῆκε τοὺς τοξότας καὶ τοὺς Ἀγριᾶνας· οἱ
δὲ ἀπροσδόκητοί τε ἐπιπεσόντες καὶ φάλαγγι κατὰ
κέρας, ᾗπερ ἀσθενεστάτοις αὐτοῖς καρτερωτάτῃ τῇ
ἐμβολῇ προσμίξειν ἔμελλον, τοὺς μὲν ἔτι ἐν ταῖς
εὐναῖς κατέκτεινον, τοὺς δὲ φεύγοντας εὐμαρῶς
αἱροῦντες, ὥστε πολλοὶ μὲν αὐτοῦ ἐγκατελήφθησαν
καὶ ἀπέθανον, πολλοὶ δὲ ἐν τῇ ἀποχωρήσει ἀτάκτῳ
καὶ φοβερᾷ γενομένῃ· οὐκ ὀλίγοι δὲ καὶ ζῶντες
11 ἐλήφθησαν. ἐγένετο δὲ ἡ δίωξις τοῖς ἀμφὶ
Ἀλέξανδρον μέχρι πρὸς τὰ ὄρη τῶν Ταυλαντίων·
ὅσοι δὲ καὶ ἀπέφυγον αὐτῶν, γυμνοὶ τῶν ὅπλων
διεσώθησαν. Κλεῖτος δὲ ἐς τὴν πόλιν τὸ πρῶτον
καταφυγὼν ἐμπρήσας τὴν πόλιν ἀπηλλάγη παρὰ
Γλαυκίαν ἐς Ταυλαντίους.

7. Ἐν τούτῳ δὲ τῶν φυγάδων τινὲς τῶν ἐκ
Θηβῶν φευγόντων παρελθόντες νύκτωρ ἐς τὰς

breasted the stream. Glaucias' troops did not
venture within range; the Macedonians meanwhile
crossed the river safely and lost not a man in the
withdrawal.

On the third day after this Alexander learned 9
that Clitus' and Glaucias' troops were carelessly
bivouacked, no sentry posts in due order, no palisade,
no trench in front of them—for they thought that
Alexander had retreated in panic—and their line
unduly elongated; he crossed the river unobserved
under cover of night with the hypaspists, Agrianians,
archers and the battalion of Perdiccas and Coenus.[2]
He had left orders for the rest of the army to follow, 10
but seeing an opportunity for attack, he did not
wait for all to join him, but sent on all the archers
and Agrianians: his forces attacked when not expected and in deep formation on the flank of the
line, where they were likely to make the strongest
onslaught on the enemy at his weakest point;
they killed several in their beds and easily seized the
fugitives, so that many were caught and killed
there and then, and many others in panic-stricken
and headlong flight; a good number too were taken
alive. Alexander's men carried on the pursuit of 11
the Taulantians as far as the mountains; those
who did escape survived with the loss of their arms.
Clitus, who had originally taken refuge in the city,
set fire to it and fled to Glaucias among the Taulantians.

7. Meanwhile some of the exiles from Thebes
slipped into Thebes by night on the invitation of

---

[2] Later they each command a battalion. A. is doubtless
careless and should have written ' battalions '.

Φήβας, ἐπαγ⟨αγ⟩ομένων τινῶν αὐτοὺς ἐπὶ νεωτε-
ρισμῷ ἐκ τῆς πόλεως, Ἀμύνταν μὲν καὶ Τιμόλαον
τῶν τὴν Καδμείαν ἐχόντων οὐδὲν ὑποτοπήσαντας
πολέμιον ἔξω τῆς Καδμείας ἀπέκτειναν ξυλ-
2 λαβόντες· ἐς δὲ τὴν ἐκκλησίαν παρελθόντες ἐπῆραν
τοὺς Θηβαίους ἀποστῆναι ἀπὸ Ἀλεξάνδρου, ἐλευ-
θερίαν τε⟨καὶ παρρησίαν [1]⟩ προϊσχόμενοι, παλαιὰ
καὶ καλὰ ὀνόματα, καὶ τῆς βαρύτητος τῶν Μακεδόνων ἤδη ποτὲ ἀπαλλαγῆναι. πιθανώτεροι δὲ ἐς
τὸ πλῆθος ἐφαίνοντο τεθνηκέναι Ἀλέξανδρον
3 ἰσχυριζόμενοι ἐν Ἰλλυριοῖς· καὶ γὰρ καὶ πολὺς ὁ
λόγος οὗτος καὶ παρὰ πολλῶν ἐφοίτα, ὅτι τε
χρόνον ἀπῆν οὐκ ὀλίγον καὶ ὅτι οὐδεμία ἀγγελία
παρ' αὐτοῦ ἀφῖκτο, ὥστε, ὅπερ φιλεῖ ἐν τοῖς
τοιοῖσδε, οὐ γιγνώσκοντες τὰ ὄντα τὰ μάλιστα καθ'
ἡδονήν σφισιν εἴκαζον.

4 Πυθομένῳ δὲ Ἀλεξάνδρῳ τὰ τῶν Θηβαίων
οὐδαμῶς ἐδόκει ἀμελητέα εἶναι, τήν τε τῶν
Ἀθηναίων πόλιν δι' ὑποψίας ἐκ πολλοῦ ἔχοντι καὶ
τῶν Θηβαίων τὸ τόλμημα οὐ φαῦλον ποιουμένῳ, εἰ
Λακεδαιμόνιοί τε πάλαι ἤδη ταῖς γνώμαις ἀφεστηκότες καί τινες καὶ ἄλλοι τῶν ἐν Πελοποννήσῳ
καὶ Αἰτωλοὶ οὐ βέβαιοι ὄντες συνεπιλήψονται τοῦ
5 νεωτερισμοῦ τοῖς Θηβαίοις. ἄγων δὴ παρὰ τὴν
Ἐορδαίαν τε καὶ τὴν Ἐλιμιῶτιν καὶ παρὰ τὰ τῆς
Στυμφαίας καὶ Παρ⟨α⟩υαίας ἄκρα ἑβδομαῖος
ἀφικνεῖται ἐς Πέλινναν τῆς Θετταλίας. ἔνθεν δὲ
ὁρμηθεὶς ἕκτῃ ἡμέρᾳ ἐσβάλλει ἐς τὴν Βοιωτίαν,
ὥστε οὐ πρόσθεν οἱ Θηβαῖοι ἔμαθον εἴσω Πυλῶν
παρεληλυθότα αὐτὸν πρὶν ἐν Ὀγχηστῷ γενέσθαι

[1] So Krüger.

persons in the city with revolutionary designs, and
seized and killed Amyntas and Timolaus, members
of the force occupying the Cadmea, who had no
suspicion of hostile movement outside.[1] Then 2
appearing in the assembly they incited the Thebans
to rebel against Alexander, on the pretence of
freedom and of liberty of speech—time-honoured
and fine sounding words: now at last had come the
time to shake off Macedon's heavy yoke. They
won readier trust from the populace by affirming that
Alexander had died in Illyria: in fact this was com- 3
mon talk, and many put it about; he had been long
away and no word had come from him, so that, in
ignorance of the facts, they conjectured (as often
happens in such cases) what they most desired.[2]

Alexander hearing of what occurred at Thebes was 4
fully convinced that it had to be taken seriously; for
he had long had suspicions of Athens, and was much
concerned about the Theban coup, in case the
Lacedaemonians (long ago rebels at heart) as well as
some other Peloponnesians and the Aetolians, who
were unreliable, should join in the revolutionary
movement of the Thebans.[3] He marched, therefore, 5
past Eordaea and Elimiotis, and the heights of
Stymphaea and Paravaea, and on the seventh day
reached Pelinna in Thessaly. Thence in five days he
entered Boeotia, so that the Thebans did not learn
that he was within the Gates until he arrived, with

335
B.C.

---

[1] For other accounts of and allusions to the revolt of Thebes
see Aeschines iii 239 f.; Dinarchus, *contra Demosthenem* 10; 18;
D. 8–14; P. 11–13 (and his life of Demosthenes 23); J xi 3 f.
Cf. Introd. 37 f.; 43; 49. A. omits the story of Timoclea from
Ar. (F. 2), though it illustrates Al's magnanimity.

[2] Cf. Thuc. iv 108, 4.

[3] Introd. 37; 49.

6 ξὺν τῇ στρατιᾷ πάσῃ. καὶ τότε δὲ οἱ πράξαντες
τὴν ἀπόστασιν στράτευμα ἐκ Μακεδονίας Ἀντιπάτρου ἀφῖχθαι ἔφασκον, αὐτὸν δὲ Ἀλέξανδρον
τεθνάναι ἰσχυρίζοντο, καὶ τοῖς ἀπαγγέλλουσιν ὅτι
οὗτος αὐτὸς προσάγει Ἀλέξανδρος χαλεπῶς εἶχον·
ἄλλον γάρ τινα ἥκειν Ἀλέξανδρον τὸν Ἀερόπου.

7 Ὁ δὲ Ἀλέξανδρος ἐξ Ὀγχηστοῦ ἄρας τῇ
ὑστεραίᾳ προσῆγε πρὸς τὴν πόλιν τῶν Θηβαίων
κατὰ τὸ τοῦ Ἰολάου τέμενος· οὗ δὴ καὶ ἐστρατοπέδευσεν, ἐνδιδοὺς ἔτι τοῖς Θηβαίοις τριβήν, εἰ
μεταγνόντες ἐπὶ τοῖς κακῶς ἐγνωσμένοις πρεσβεύ-
8 σαιντο παρ' αὐτόν. οἱ δὲ τοσούτου ἐδέησαν
ἐνδόσιμόν τι παρασχεῖν ἐς ξύμβασιν, ὥστε ἐκθέοντες ἐκ τῆς πόλεως οἵ τε ἱππεῖς καὶ τῶν ψιλῶν οὐκ
ὀλίγοι ἔστε ἐπὶ τὸ στρατόπεδον ἠκροβολίζοντο ἐς
τὰς προφυλακάς, καί τινας καὶ ἀπέκτειναν οὐ πολ-
9 λοὺς τῶν Μακεδόνων. καὶ Ἀλέξανδρος ἐκπέμπει
τῶν ψιλῶν καὶ τοξοτῶν, ὥστε αὐτῶν ἀναστεῖλαι
τὴν ἐκδρομήν· καὶ οὗτοι οὐ χαλεπῶς ἀνέστειλαν
ἤδη τῷ στρατοπέδῳ αὐτῷ προσφερομένους. τῇ δὲ
ὑστεραίᾳ ἀναλαβὼν τὴν στρατιὰν πᾶσαν καὶ
περιελθὼν κατὰ τὰς πύλας τὰς φερούσας ἐπ'
Ἐλευθεράς τε καὶ τὴν Ἀττικήν, οὐδὲ τότε
προσέμιξε τοῖς τείχεσιν αὐτοῖς, ἀλλ' ἐστρατοπέδευσεν οὐ πολὺ ἀπέχων τῆς Καδμείας, ὥστε ἐγγὺς
εἶναι ὠφέλειαν τῶν Μακεδόνων τοῖς τὴν Καδμείαν
10 ἔχουσιν. οἱ γὰρ Θηβαῖοι τὴν Καδμείαν διπλῷ
χάρακι ἐφρούρουν ἀποτειχίσαντες, ὡς μήτε ἔξωθέν
τινα τοῖς ἐγκατειλημμένοις δύνασθαι ἐπωφελεῖν,
μήτε αὐτοὺς ἐκθέοντας βλάπτειν τι σφᾶς, ὁπότε

---

[4] In 339 with Thermopylae held by Thebes Philip had come

all his force, at Onchestus.[4]   At that time the authors   6   335
of the revolt were saying that a force of Antipater   B.C.
had come from Macedon, but confidently affirmed
that Alexander himself was dead, getting annoyed
at anyone who reported Alexander's own proximity
at the head of his men: it was, said they, a different
Alexander, the son of Aeropus.[5]

Alexander left Onchestus and next day reached   7
Thebes, near the enclosure of Iolaus, where he
encamped, giving the Thebans a period of grace, in
case they should repent of their bad decisions and
send an embassy to him.   They were so far from   8
making any concession that might lead to an agreement that their cavalry and many of their light
troops sallied out against the camp, discharged
volleys at the outposts, and actually killed a few
Macedonians.   Alexander sent out some of his   9
light troops and archers to hold up their sally; they
easily checked the Thebans, who by now were
approaching the camp.   Next day Alexander moved
his whole force and came round to the gates leading
to Eleutherae and Attica, yet even then he did
not actually assault the walls, but pitched camp
not far from the Cadmea, so that support would be
close at hand for its Macedonian garrison.   The   10
Thebans were investing the Cadmea with a double
stockade, so that no one from without could help
those shut up inside, nor could they sally out and

---

south through Heraclea, the Asopus pass and Cytinium
(Beloch iii 563).   Crossing Thessaly by an unusual easterly
route, Al. may well have done the same for the purpose of a
surprise; in that case the ' Gates ' do not refer to Thermopylae
but to the pass south of Heraclea.

[5] As in 334-323 B.C., Antipater had evidently been left in
charge of Macedon.   Alexander the Lyncestian: Introd. 46.

τοῖς ἔξω πολεμίοις προσφέροιντο. Ἀλέξανδρος δέ
—ἔτι γὰρ τοῖς Θηβαίοις διὰ φιλίας ἐλθεῖν μᾶλλόν τι
ἢ διὰ κινδύνου ἤθελε—διέτριβε πρὸς τῇ Καδμείᾳ
11 κατεστρατοπεδευκώς. ἔνθα δὴ τῶν Θηβαίων οἱ
μὲν τὰ βέλτιστα ἐς τὸ κοινὸν γιγνώσκοντες ἐξελθεῖν
ὥρμηντο παρ' Ἀλέξανδρον καὶ εὑρέσθαι συγ-
γνώμην τῷ πλήθει τῶν Θηβαίων τῆς ἀποστάσεως·
οἱ φυγάδες δὲ καὶ ὅσοι τοὺς φυγάδας ἐπικεκλημένοι
ἦσαν, οὐδενὸς φιλανθρώπου τυχεῖν ἂν παρ' Ἀλεξάνδρου ἀξιοῦντες, ἄλλως τε καὶ βοιωταρχοῦντες
ἔστιν οἳ αὐτῶν, παντάπασιν ἐνῆγον τὸ πλῆθος ἐς
τὸν πόλεμον. Ἀλέξανδρος δὲ οὐδ' ὣς τῇ πόλει
προσέβαλλεν.

8. Ἀλλὰ λέγει Πτολεμαῖος ὁ Λάγου, ὅτι
Περδίκκας, προτεταγμένος τῆς φυλακῆς τοῦ
στρατοπέδου σὺν τῇ αὑτοῦ τάξει καὶ τοῦ χάρακος
τῶν πολεμίων οὐ πολὺ ἀφεστηκώς, οὐ προσμείνας
παρ' Ἀλεξάνδρου τὸ ἐς τὴν μάχην ξύνθημα αὐτὸς
πρῶτος προσέμιξε τῷ χάρακι καὶ διασπάσας αὐτὸν
2 ἐνέβαλεν ἐς τῶν Θηβαίων τὴν προφυλακήν. τούτῳ
δὲ ἑπόμενος Ἀμύντας ὁ Ἀνδρομένους, ὅτι καὶ
ξυντεταγμένος τῷ Περδίκκᾳ ἦν, ἐπήγαγε καὶ αὐτὸς
τὴν αὑτοῦ τάξιν, ὡς εἶδε τὸν Περδίκκαν προ-
εληλυθότα εἴσω τοῦ χάρακος. ταῦτα δὲ ἰδὼν
Ἀλέξανδρος, ὡς μὴ μόνοι ἀποληφθέντες πρὸς τῶν
Θηβαίων κινδυνεύσειαν, ἐπῆγε τὴν ἄλλην στρατιάν.
3 καὶ τοὺς μὲν τοξότας καὶ τοὺς Ἀγριᾶνας ἐκδραμεῖν
ἐσήμηνεν εἴσω τοῦ χάρακος, τὸ δὲ ἄγημά τε καὶ
τοὺς ὑπασπιστὰς ἔτι ἔξω κατεῖχεν. ἔνθα δὴ

335
B.C.

harm the Thebans when engaged with their enemies without. But Alexander still hoped to win Theban friendship rather than to incur any danger and waited, encamped near the citadel. At this point 11 those Thebans who best saw the city's advantage were anxious to go out to Alexander and obtain pardon for the Theban people for their revolt; but the exiles and those who had called them in, not expecting to receive kind treatment from Alexander, especially some of them who were Boeotarchs, used every method of urging their countrymen to war. Yet even so Alexander did not attack.[6]

8. Ptolemy son of Lagus, however, says that Perdiccas, who was officer in charge of the camp guard with his own battalion and lay not far from the enemy palisade, did not await Alexander's signal for battle, but himself first attacked the palisade and tearing it apart broke in upon the Theban advance guard.[1] Amyntas son of Andromenes followed, as he was 2 brigaded with Perdiccas, and led on his own battalion when he saw Perdiccas had advanced within the palisade. Seeing this, Alexander brought up the rest of the army, so that they might not be stranded and at the mercy of the Thebans. He ordered 3 the archers and Agrianians to run out in advance

---

[6] Contrast D. 9, 6. Boeotarchs were magistrates of the federation of Boeotian cities, long dominated by Thebes. Some hold that Philip in 338 dissolved this federation, in which case Thebes on her revolt had sought to revive it.

[1] Perdiccas (Berve no. 627 cf. Introd. 34), a figure of growing importance under Al., became virtual ruler of the empire outside Greece and Macedon, on his death. Pt., who played a large part in encompassing his ruin in 321, may have sought to shift any blame for the sack of Thebes from Al. (cf. 7, 7–11), on to his enemy's unauthorized impetuosity; D. 12, 3 says that P. acted under orders. Cf 21, 1 f. for more indiscipline in his regiment.

ARRIAN

Περδίκκας [μὲν] τοῦ δευτέρου χάρακος εἴσω
παρελθεῖν βιαζόμενος αὐτὸς μὲν βληθεὶς πίπτει
αὐτοῦ καὶ ἀποκομίζεται κακῶς ἔχων ἐπὶ τὸ
στρατόπεδον, καὶ χαλεπῶς διεσώθη ἀπὸ τοῦ
τραύματος· τοὺς μέντοι Θηβαίους ἐς τὴν κοίλην
ὁδὸν τὴν κατὰ τὸ Ἡράκλειον φέρουσαν οἱ ἅμα
αὐτῷ εἰσπεσόντες ὁμοῦ τοῖς παρ' Ἀλεξάνδρου
4 τοξόταις συνέκλεισαν. καὶ ἔστε μὲν πρὸς τὸ
Ἡράκλειον ἀναχωροῦσιν εἵποντο τοῖς Θηβαίοις,
ἐντεῦθεν δὲ ἐπιστρεψάντων αὖθις σὺν βοῇ τῶν
Θηβαίων φυγὴ τῶν Μακεδόνων γίγνεται· καὶ
Εὐρυβώτας τε ὁ Κρὴς πίπτει ὁ τοξάρχης καὶ αὐτῶν
τῶν τοξοτῶν ἐς ἑβδομήκοντα· οἱ δὲ λοιποὶ
κατέφυγον πρὸς τὸ ἄγημα τὸ τῶν Μακεδόνων καὶ
5 τοὺς ὑπασπιστὰς τοὺς βασιλικούς. κἂν τούτῳ
Ἀλέξανδρος τοὺς μὲν αὐτοῦ φεύγοντας κατιδών,
τοὺς Θηβαίους δὲ λελυκότας ἐν τῇ διώξει τὴν
τάξιν, ἐμβάλλει ἐς αὐτοὺς συντεταγμένῃ τῇ
φάλαγγι· οἱ δὲ ὠθοῦσι τοὺς Θηβαίους εἴσω τῶν
πυλῶν· καὶ τοῖς Θηβαίοις ἐς τοσόνδε ἡ φυγὴ
φοβερὰ ἐγίγνετο, ὥστε διὰ τῶν πυλῶν ὠθούμενοι
ἐς τὴν πόλιν οὐκ ἔφθησαν συγκλεῖσαι τὰς πύλας.
ἀλλὰ συνεσπίπτουσι γὰρ αὐτοῖς εἴσω τοῦ τείχους
ὅσοι τῶν Μακεδόνων ἐγγὺς φευγόντων εἴχοντο, ἅτε
καὶ τῶν τειχῶν διὰ τὰς προφυλακὰς τὰς πολλὰς
6 ἐρήμων ὄντων. καὶ παρελθόντες ἐς τὴν Καδμείαν
οἱ μὲν ἐκεῖθεν κατὰ τὸ Ἀμφεῖον σὺν τοῖς κατέχουσι
τὴν Καδμείαν ἐξέβαινον ἐς τὴν ἄλλην πόλιν, οἱ δὲ
κατὰ τὰ τείχη, ἐχόμενα ἤδη πρὸς τῶν συνεισπε-
σόντων τοῖς φεύγουσιν, ὑπερβάντες ἐς τὴν ἀγορὰν
7 δρόμῳ ἐφέροντο. καὶ ὀλίγον μέν τινα χρόνον
ἔμειναν οἱ τεταγμένοι τῶν Θηβαίων κατὰ τὸ

335
B.C.

behind the palisade; but he still retained the *agema* and hypaspists outside. Then Perdiccas, trying to force his way into the second palisade, was wounded and fell on the spot; he was borne off to the camp in a serious condition; only with difficulty was he healed of his wound. The troops who had broken in with him along with Alexander's archers hemmed the Thebans into the sunken road leading down by the Heracleum; so long as the Thebans were in re- 4 treat towards the Heracleum, the Macedonians followed; but then the Thebans turned at bay with shouting, and the Macedonians took flight. Eurybotas the Cretan, commander of the archers, fell with about seventy of his men; the rest took refuge with the Macedonian *agema*, and the royal hypaspists. At 5 this point Alexander, seeing that his own men were in flight and that the Thebans had broken formation in the pursuit, charged them with phalanx in battle order. The Thebans were pushed inside the gates; their flight became a panic, so that while being thrust through the gates into the city they could not shut them in time. The Macedonians who were pressing on the fugitives passed with them inside the wall; the walls were undefended on account of the large number of advanced posts. Some Macedonians reached the Cadmea and thence 6 went along the Ampheum,[2] joined by the garrison of the Cadmea, and entered the rest of the city; those on the walls, already held by the troops that had poured in together with the fugitives, crossed over and rushed to the market-place. For a short while 7 the Theban armed forces stood their ground by the

---

[2] A hill continuing the Cadmea northwards.

Ἀμφεῖον· ὡς δὲ πανταχόθεν αὐτοῖς οἱ Μακεδόνες καὶ Ἀλέξανδρος ἄλλοτε ἄλλῃ ἐπιφαινόμενος προσέκειντο, οἱ μὲν ἱππεῖς τῶν Θηβαίων διεκπεσόντες διὰ τῆς πόλεως ἐς τὸ πεδίον ἐξέπιπτον, οἱ δὲ πεζοὶ

8 ὡς ἑκάστοις προὐχώρει ἐσῴζοντο. ἔνθα δὴ ὀργῇ οὐχ οὕτως τι οἱ Μακεδόνες, ἀλλὰ Φωκεῖς τε καὶ Πλαταιεῖς καὶ οἱ ἄλλοι δὲ Βοιωτοὶ οὐδὲ ἀμυνομένους τοὺς Θηβαίους ἔτι οὐδενὶ κόσμῳ ἔκτεινον, τοὺς μὲν ἐν ταῖς οἰκίαις ἐπεισπίπτοντες, οὓς δὲ ἐς ἀλκὴν τετραμμένους, τοὺς δὲ καὶ πρὸς ἱεροῖς ἱκετεύοντας, οὔτε γυναικῶν οὔτε παίδων φειδόμενοι.

9. Καὶ πάθος τοῦτο Ἑλληνικὸν μεγέθει τε τῆς ἁλούσης πόλεως καὶ ὀξύτητι τοῦ ἔργου, οὐχ ἥκιστα δὲ τῷ παραλόγῳ ἔς τε τοὺς παθόντας καὶ τοὺς δράσαντας, οὐ μεῖόν τι τοὺς ἄλλους Ἕλληνας ἢ καὶ

2 αὐτοὺς τοὺς μετασχόντας τοῦ ἔργου ἐξέπληξε. τὰ μὲν γὰρ περὶ Σικελίαν Ἀθηναίοις ξυνενεχθέντα, εἰ καὶ πλήθει τῶν ἀπολομένων οὐ μείονα τὴν ξυμφορὰν τῇ πόλει ἤνεγκεν, ἀλλὰ τῷ τε πόρρω ἀπὸ τῆς οἰκείας διαφθαρῆναι αὐτοῖς τὸν στρατόν, καὶ τὸν πολὺν ξυμμαχικὸν μᾶλλον ἢ οἰκεῖον ὄντα, καὶ τῷ τὴν πόλιν αὐτοῖς περιλειφθῆναι, ὡς καὶ ἐς ὕστερον ἐπὶ πολὺ τῷ πολέμῳ ἀντισχεῖν Λακεδαιμονίοις τε καὶ τοῖς ξυμμάχοις καὶ μεγάλῳ βασιλεῖ πολεμοῦντας, οὔτε αὐτοῖς τοῖς παθοῦσιν ἴσην τὴν αἴσθησιν τῆς ξυμφορᾶς προσέθηκεν, οὔτε τοῖς ἄλλοις Ἕλλησιν τὴν ἐπὶ τῷ πάθει ἔκπληξιν ὁμοίαν

3 παρέσχε. καὶ τὸ ἐν Αἰγὸς ποταμοῖς αὖθις Ἀθηναίων πταῖσμα ναυτικόν τε ἦν καὶ ἡ πόλις οὐδὲν ἄλλο ὅτι μὴ τῶν μακρῶν τειχῶν καθαιρέσει

Ampheum, but as the Macedonians pressed on them
from all sides, and Alexander appeared, now here,
now there, the Theban cavalry, pushing their way
through the city, streamed out upon the plain;
with the infantry it was *sauve qui peut*. And then,
in hot blood, it was not so much the Macedonians as
Phocians and Plataeans and the other Boeotians [3]
who slaughtered the Thebans without restraint,
even when they no longer offered resistance, some
in their houses, which they broke into, some showing
fight; others actually suppliant at the shrines;—they
spared neither woman nor child.

9. This Greek disaster, because of the size of the
captured city, the sharpness of the action, and not
least the general unexpectedness of the event, both
to victors and victims, horrified the other Greeks as
much as those who had a hand in it.[1] The misfortunes
of the Athenians in Sicily brought no less a disaster
upon their city measured by the number of the dead,
yet their army was destroyed far from home; it was
mainly composed of allies rather than of citizens,
and their city was left them, so that they held out
long afterwards in the war against Sparta, her
allies, and Persia; even this disaster did not make
the victims themselves equally conscious of misfortune, and did not strike the other Greeks with
like horror at the catastrophe. Again, the Athenian
defeat at Aegospotami was at sea, and though the
city was humbled, yet it only suffered from the

335
B.C.

8

2 [413
B.C.]

3 [405
B.C.]

---

[3] Exonerating the Macedonians, cf. 9, 6, *contra* D. 13, 1,
though D. too admits (13, 5 f.) that the Thespians, Plataeans
and Orchomenians worked off old grudges on the Thebans.
Note also ii 15, 3 f.
[1] §1–5 seem to give A's own reflections, 6–8 recite the
charges apparently made against Thebes by Al's Greek allies,
cf. D. 14, 1–4.

ARRIAN

καὶ νεῶν τῶν πολλῶν παραδόσει καὶ στερήσει τῆς
ἀρχῆς ἐς ταπεινότητα ἀφικομένη τό τε σχῆμα τὸ
πάτριον ὅμως ἐφύλαξε καὶ τὴν δύναμιν οὐ διὰ
μακροῦ τὴν πάλαι ἀνέλαβεν, ὡς τά τε μακρὰ τείχη
ἐκτειχίσαι καὶ τῆς θαλάσσης αὖθις ἐπικρατῆσαι καὶ
τοὺς τότε φοβερούς σφισι Λακεδαιμονίους καὶ παρ'
ὀλίγον ἐλθόντας ἀφανίσαι τὴν πόλιν αὐτοὺς ἐν τῷ
μέρει ἐκ τῶν ἐσχάτων κινδύνων διασώσασθαι.

4 Λακεδαιμονίων τε αὖ τὸ κατὰ Λεῦκτρα καὶ
Μαντίνειαν πταῖσμα τῷ παραλόγῳ μᾶλλόν τι τῆς
ξυμφορᾶς ἢ τῷ πλήθει τῶν [τε] ἀπολομένων τοὺς
Λακεδαιμονίους ἐξέπληξεν· ἥ τε ξὺν Ἐπαμεινώνδᾳ
Βοιωτῶν καὶ Ἀρκάδων γενομένη προσβολὴ πρὸς
τὴν Σπάρτην καὶ αὐτὴ τῷ ἀήθει τῆς ὄψεως μᾶλλον
ἢ τῇ ἀκριβείᾳ τοῦ κινδύνου αὐτούς τε τοὺς Λακεδαιμονίους καὶ τοὺς ξυμμετασχόντας αὐτοῖς τῶν τότε
5 πραγμάτων ἐφόβησεν. ἡ δὲ δὴ Πλαταιῶν ἅλωσις
τῆς πόλεως τῇ σμικρότητι . . . τῶν ἐγκατα-
ληφθέντων, ὅτι οἱ πολλοὶ αὐτῶν διαπεφεύγεσαν
πάλαι ἐς τὰς Ἀθήνας, οὐ μέγα πάθημα ἐγένετο.
καὶ ἡ Μήλου καὶ Σκιώνης ἅλωσις, νησιωτικά τε
πολίσματα ἦν καὶ τοῖς δράσασιν αἰσχύνην μᾶλλόν
τι προσέβαλεν ἢ ἐς τὸ ξύμπαν Ἑλληνικὸν μέγαν
τὸν παράλογον παρέσχε.

6 Θηβαίοις δὲ τὰ τῆς ἀποστάσεως ὀξέα καὶ ξὺν
οὐδενὶ λογισμῷ γενόμενα, καὶ ἡ ἅλωσις δι' ὀλίγου
τε καὶ οὐ ξὺν πόνῳ τῶν ἑλόντων ξυνενεχθεῖσα, καὶ
ὁ φόνος ⟨ὁ⟩ πολύς, οἷα δὴ ἐξ ὁμοφύλων τε καὶ
παλαιὰς ἀπεχθείας ἐπεξιόντων, καὶ ὁ τῆς πόλεως
παντελὴς ἀνδραποδισμός, δυνάμει τε καὶ δόξῃ ἐς
τὰ πολέμια τῶν τότε προεχούσης ἐν τοῖς Ἕλλησιν,
οὐκ ἔξω τοῦ εἰκότος ἐς μῆνιν τὴν ἀπὸ τοῦ θείου

destruction of its long walls, the surrender of most of
its ships, and the loss of its empire, it retained its
ancestral form, and soon recovered its old strength;
the Athenians rebuilt their long walls, recovered
dominion on the sea, and themselves in turn saved
from the most extreme danger the Lacedaemonians,
who had inspired such terror and had come so near
to annihilating Athens. The defeat of the Lace- 4
daemonians themselves at Leuctra and Mantinea
came as a great shock to them rather by the unexpectedness of the disaster than by the number
of the dead, while the onslaught of Epaminondas with
his Boeotians and Arcadians on Sparta scared the
Spartans and their then allies rather by the strange-
ness of such a sight than by the measure of the
danger. The capture, again, of Plataea was no 5
great tragedy because of the smallness of the city
and . . . [2] of those captured in the city—the greater
number having fled long before to Athens. Finally,
the capture of Melos and Scione, which were little
island towns, brought more shame to the perpetrators
than any great shock to the whole Greek world.

With Thebes, on the other hand, the hastiness 6
and lack of consideration in the revolt, her sudden
capture, with so little trouble to the victors, the great
massacre, a natural act to kindred people working
off old feuds, the complete enslavement of the city,
then foremost in Greece for power and military
prestige, were quite naturally set down to divine
wrath: Thebes, men said, had thus paid the price,

335
B.C.

[393
B.C.]

[371,
362 B.C.]

[370-
369 B.C.]

5 [427
B.C.]

[416, 421
B.C.]

[2] The lacuna presumably mentioned the small number of
prisoners.

7 ἀνηνέχθη, ὡς τῆς τε ἐν τῷ Μηδικῷ πολέμῳ
προδοσίας τῶν Ἑλλήνων διὰ μακροῦ ταύτην δίκην
ἐκτίσαντας Θηβαίους, καὶ τῆς Πλαταιῶν ἔν τε ταῖς
σπονδαῖς καταλήψεως καὶ τοῦ παντελοῦς ἀνδραποδισμοῦ τῆς πόλεως, καὶ τῆς τῶν παραδόντων
σφᾶς Λακεδαιμονίοις οὐχ Ἑλληνικῆς γενομένης διὰ
Θηβαίους σφαγῆς, καὶ τοῦ χωρίου τῆς ἐρημώσεως,
ἐν ὅτῳ οἱ Ἕλληνες παραταξάμενοι Μήδοις
ἀπώσαντο τῆς Ἑλλάδος τὸν κίνδυνον, καὶ ὅτι
Ἀθηναίους αὐτοὶ τῇ ψήφῳ ἀπώλλυον, ὅτε ὑπὲρ
ἀνδραποδισμοῦ τῆς πόλεως γνώμη προὐτέθη ἐν
8 τοῖς Λακεδαιμονίων ξυμμάχοις. ἐπεὶ καὶ πρὸ τῆς
ξυμφορᾶς πολλὰ ἀπὸ τοῦ θείου ἐπισημῆναι ἐλέγετο,
ἃ δὴ ἐν μὲν τῷ παραυτίκα ἠμελήθη, ὕστερον δὲ ἡ
μνήμη αὐτὰ ἐς λογισμὸν τοῦ ἐκ πάλαι ἐπὶ τοῖς
ξυνενεχθεῖσιν προσημανθῆναι ἀνήνεγκεν.

9 Τοῖς δὲ μετασχοῦσι τοῦ ἔργου ξυμμάχοις, οἷς δὴ
καὶ ἐπέτρεψεν Ἀλέξανδρος τὰ κατὰ τὰς Θήβας
διαθεῖναι, τὴν μὲν Καδμείαν φρουρᾷ κατέχειν
ἔδοξε, τὴν πόλιν δὲ κατασκάψαι ἐς ἔδαφος καὶ τὴν
χώραν κατανεῖμαι τοῖς ξυμμάχοις, ὅση μὴ ἱερὰ
αὐτῆς· παῖδας δὲ καὶ γυναῖκας καὶ ὅσοι ὑπελείποντο Θηβαίων, πλὴν τῶν ἱερέων τε καὶ ἱερειῶν καὶ
ὅσοι ξένοι Φιλίππου ἢ Ἀλεξάνδρου ἢ ὅσοι πρόξενοι
10 Μακεδόνων ἐγένοντο, ἀνδραποδίσαι. καὶ τὴν Πινδάρου δὲ τοῦ ποιητοῦ οἰκίαν καὶ τοὺς ἀπογόνους
τοῦ Πινδάρου λέγουσιν ὅτι διεφύλαξεν Ἀλέξανδρος
αἰδοῖ τῇ Πινδάρου. ἐπὶ τούτοις Ὀρχόμενόν τε καὶ
Πλαταιὰς ἀναστῆσαί τε καὶ τειχίσαι οἱ ξύμμαχοι
ἔγνωσαν.

10. Ἐς δὲ τοὺς ἄλλους Ἕλληνας ὡς ἐξηγγέλθη

at length, for betraying the Greek cause in the Persian wars, for seizing Plataea in time of truce, for completely enslaving the Plataeans, for her responsibility for the un-Greek massacre of men who had surrendered to Sparta, and for the desolation of the Plataean countryside, on which the Greeks, ranged shoulder to shoulder against Persia, had repelled the common danger of Greece, and last, for voting for the destruction of Athens when a motion was put before the allies of Sparta that the Athenians should be sold into slavery. People said that the coming disaster cast its shadow before, in many divine warnings neglected then, but the memory of them later made people realize that there had long been prognostications, now confirmed by the event.

The allies who took part in the action, to whom Alexander actually entrusted the settlement of Thebes,[3] decided to garrison the Cadmea, but to raze the city to the ground, and to apportion its land among the allies, in so far as it had not been consecrated, and to enslave the women and children and any Theban survivors, save for priests and priestesses, and any guest-friends of Philip or Alexander, or *proxenoi*[4] of Macedonians. They say[5] that Alexander saved the poet Pindar's house and any of his descendants out of reverence for Pindar. Besides this, the allies determined to rebuild and fortify Orchomenus and Plataea.[6]

10. When the fate of Thebes was notified to the

---

[3] D. 14, 4 makes this a formal decree of the *synedrion* (Introd. 38), but still ascribes the real decision to Al., who wished to terrorize the Greeks, cf. P. 11, 5.

[4] Citizens who performed consular functions for members of particular foreign communities.

[5] Cf. P. 11, 6; ' vulgate ', unless ' they ' are Pt. and Ar.

[6] Previously destroyed by Thebes.

τῶν Θηβαίων τὸ πάθος, Ἀρκάδες μὲν, ὅσοι
βοηθήσοντες Θηβαίοις ἀπὸ τῆς οἰκείας ὡρμήθησαν,
θάνατον κατεψηφίσαντο τῶν ἐπαράντων σφᾶς ἐς
τὴν βοήθειαν· Ἠλεῖοι δὲ τοὺς φυγάδας σφῶν
κατεδέξαντο, ὅτι ἐπιτήδειοι Ἀλεξάνδρῳ ἦσαν·

2 Αἰτωλοὶ δὲ πρεσβείας σφῶν κατὰ ἔθνη πέμψαντες
ξυγγνώμης τυχεῖν ἐδέοντο, ὅτι καὶ αὐτοί τι πρὸς τὰ
παρὰ τῶν Θηβαίων ἀπαγγελθέντα ἐνεωτέρισαν·
Ἀθηναῖοι δέ, μυστηρίων τῶν μεγάλων ἀγομένων
ὡς ἧκόν τινες τῶν Θηβαίων ἐξ αὐτοῦ τοῦ ἔργου, τὰ
μὲν μυστήρια ἐκπλαγέντες ἐξέλιπον, ἐκ δὲ τῶν

3 ἀγρῶν ἐσκευαγώγουν ἐς τὴν πόλιν. ὁ δῆμος δὲ ἐς
ἐκκλησίαν συνελθὼν Δημάδου γράψαντος δέκα
πρέσβεις ἐκ πάντων Ἀθηναίων ἐπιλεξάμενος
πέμπει παρὰ Ἀλέξανδρον, οὕστινας ἐπιτηδειοτά-
τους Ἀλεξάνδρῳ ἐγίγνωσκον, ὅτι τε σῶος ἐξ
Ἰλλυριῶν καὶ Τριβαλλῶν ἐπανῆλθε χαίρειν τὸν
δῆμον τῶν Ἀθηναίων οὐκ ἐν καιρῷ ἀπαγγελοῦν-
τας καὶ ὅτι Θηβαίους τοῦ νεωτερισμοῦ ἐτιμω-

4 ρήσατο. ὁ δὲ τὰ μὲν ἄλλα φιλανθρώπως πρὸς τὴν
πρεσβείαν ἀπεκρίνατο, ἐπιστολὴν δὲ γράψας πρὸς
τὸν δῆμον ἐξῄτει τοὺς ἀμφὶ Δημοσθένην καὶ
Λυκοῦργον· καὶ Ὑπερείδην δὲ ἐξῄτει καὶ Πο-
λύευκτον καὶ Χάρητα καὶ Χαρίδημον καὶ Ἐφιάλτην

5 καὶ Διότιμον καὶ Μοιροκλέα· τούτους γὰρ
αἰτίους εἶναι τῆς τε ἐν Χαιρωνείᾳ ξυμφορᾶς τῇ
πόλει γενομένης καὶ τῶν ὕστερον ἐπὶ τῇ Φιλίππου

---

[1] Introd. 37.
[2] Early Oct. 335.
[3] Plut. *Dem.* 23 says that Idomeneus and Duris (third-
century writers) gave 10 names (cf. D. 15, 1, perhaps those in

other Greeks, the Arcadians who had left home to help Thebes condemned to death those who had persuaded them to take this step, while the Eleans restored their own exiles, as they were persons ready to serve Alexander.[1] The Aetolians sent embassies, tribe by tribe, and begged forgiveness for revolting on the news brought from Thebes. The Athenians, who were celebrating their great mysteries[2] when some of the Thebans arrived hot foot from the action, abandoned the mysteries in consternation and began to get in their belongings from the country into the city. The people met in an assembly, and on the motion of Demades chose ten ambassadors from the whole body of citizens, men known to be most acceptable to Alexander, and sent them to him bearing the city's rather belated congratulations on his safe return from the Illyrians and Triballians and on his punishment of the Theban revolt. Alexander replied in a friendly way to the embassy, except that he wrote a letter to the city demanding the surrender of Demosthenes and Lycurgus, as well as Hyperides, Polyceutas, Chares, Charidemus, Ephialtes, Diotimus and Moerocles,[3] whom he held responsible for the city's disaster at Chaeronea and for the wrongs later committed,

335
B.C.

2

3

4

5

[338
B.C.]

Suidas *s.v.* Antipatros), but that the majority and best of the sources gave eight, which he lists; he then reports a *mot* of Demosthenes from Ar. (F. 3). If P. had read Ar., it follows that Ar. either gave no names, or the eight P. lists, which exclude Hyperides, Chares, Diotimus and Moerocles and include two not listed by A. In that case, as A. does not cite the ' vulgate ', he must be following Pt., without mentioning the discrepancy with Ar. A's list agrees with that in Suidas, if Thrasybulus has dropped out of A's manuscripts and if we amend Patrocles to Moerocles in Suidas. See also Introd. n. 69.

45

τελευτῇ πλημμεληθέντων ἔς τε αὐτὸν καὶ ἐς
Φίλιππον· καὶ Θηβαίοις δὲ τῆς [τε] ἀποστάσεως
ἀπέφαινεν αἰτίους οὐ μεῖον ἢ τοὺς αὐτῶν Θηβαίων
6 νεωτερίσαντας. Ἀθηναῖοι δὲ τοὺς μὲν ἄνδρας οὐκ
ἐξέδοσαν, πρεσβεύονται δὲ αὖθις παρὰ Ἀλέξανδρον, ἀφεῖναι δεόμενοι τὴν ὀργὴν τοῖς ἐξαι-
τηθεῖσι· καὶ Ἀλέξανδρος ἀφῆκε, τυχὸν μὲν αἰδοῖ
τῆς πόλεως, τυχὸν δὲ σπουδῇ τοῦ ἐς τὴν Ἀσίαν
στόλου, οὐκ ἐθέλων οὐδὲν ὕποπτον ἐν τοῖς Ἕλλησιν ὑπολείπεσθαι. Χαρίδημον μέντοι μόνον τῶν
ἐξαιτηθέντων τε καὶ οὐ δοθέντων φεύγειν ἐκέλευσε·
καὶ φεύγει Χαρίδημος ἐς τὴν Ἀσίαν παρὰ βασιλέα
Δαρεῖον.

11. Ταῦτα δὲ διαπραξάμενος ἐπανῆλθεν εἰς
Μακεδονίαν· καὶ τῷ τε Διὶ τῷ Ὀλυμπίῳ τὴν
θυσίαν τὴν ἀπ' Ἀρχελάου ἔτι καθεστῶσαν ἔθυσε
καὶ τὸν ἀγῶνα ἐν Αἰγαῖς διέθηκε τὰ Ὀλύμπια· οἱ
δὲ καὶ ταῖς Μούσαις λέγουσιν ὅτι ἀγῶνα ἐποίησε.
2 καὶ ἐν τούτῳ ἀγγέλλεται τὸ Ὀρφέως τοῦ Οἰάγρου
τοῦ Θρᾳκὸς ἄγαλμα τὸ ἐν Πιερίδι ἱδρῶσαι
ξυνεχῶς· καὶ ἄλλοι ἄλλα ἐπεθείαζον τῶν μάντεων,
Ἀρίστανδρος δέ, ἀνὴρ Τελμισσεύς, μάντις, θαρρεῖν
ἐκέλευσεν Ἀλέξανδρον· δηλοῦσθαι γάρ, ὅτι ποι-
ηταῖς ἐπῶν τε καὶ μελῶν καὶ ὅσοι ἀμφὶ ᾠδὴν
ἔχουσι πολὺς πόνος ἔσται ποιεῖν τε καὶ ᾄδειν
Ἀλέξανδρον καὶ τὰ Ἀλεξάνδρου ἔργα.
3 Ἅμα δὲ τῷ ἦρι ἀρχομένῳ ἐξελαύνει ἐφ' Ἑλλησπόντου, τὰ μὲν κατὰ Μακεδονίαν τε καὶ τοὺς
Ἕλληνας Ἀντιπάτρῳ ἐπιτρέψας, αὐτὸς δὲ ἄγων
πεζοὺς μὲν σὺν ψιλοῖς τε καὶ τοξόταις οὐ πολλῷ

---

[4] Cf P. 13, 1 f. Only a hint of the difficulty of reducing
Athens, Introd. 43.

at Philip's death, against himself and Philip. He 335
also showed that they were just as guilty of the B.C.
Theban rebellion as the Theban revolutionaries
themselves. The Athenians did not give up the 6
men, but sent a second embassy to Alexander, begging him to relent to those whose surrender he had
demanded. Alexander did so, whether from reverence for Athens, or because he was anxious to hurry
on his Asian expedition and did not wish to leave
any ill-feeling behind in Greece.[4] Charidemus
alone, however, of those men whose surrender he had
demanded but not obtained, he ordered to be exiled;
and he took refuge in Asia with King Darius.[5]

11. After completing these operations Alexander
returned to Macedonia, where he offered the traditional sacrifice (established by Archelaus) to
Olympian Zeus and celebrated the Olympian games
at Aegae: others add[1] that he held games in honour
of the Muses. Meanwhile, it was reported that 2
the statue of Orpheus, son of Oeagrus the Thracian,
in Pieria, had sweated continuously; the seers
interpreted this variously, but Aristander of Telmissus
encouraged Alexander by saying that it meant that
makers of epics and choric songs and writers of
odes would be hard at work on poetry and hymns
honouring Alexander and his exploits.

In early spring he marched to the Hellespont, 3 334
leaving Macedonian and Greek affairs in charge B.C.
of Antipater. His infantry including light troops
and archers numbered not much above thirty thou-

---

[5] This well-known general was allegedly first honoured,
then executed by Darius, D. 30; QC. iii 2, 10 ff. (with variants).
[1] 'Vulgate', cf. D. 16, 3 f. A. omits D's story (16, 1 f.)
that Al. rejected the advice of Parmenio and Antipater to
defer the expedition till he had married and had a son.

πλείους τῶν τρισμυρίων, ἱππέας δὲ ὑπὲρ τοὺς
πεντακισχιλίους. ἦν δὲ αὐτῷ ὁ στόλος παρὰ τὴν
λίμνην τὴν Κερκινῖτιν ὡς ἐπ᾽ Ἀμφίπολιν καὶ τοῦ
4 Στρυμόνος ποταμοῦ τὰς ἐκβολάς. διαβὰς δὲ τὸν
Στρυμόνα παρήμειβε τὸ Πάγγαιον ὄρος τὴν ὡς ἐπ᾽
Ἄβδηρα καὶ Μαρώνειαν, πόλεις Ἑλληνίδας ἐπὶ
θαλάσσῃ ᾠκισμένας. ἔνθεν δὲ ἐπὶ τὸν Ἕβρον
ποταμὸν ἀφικόμενος διαβαίνει καὶ τὸν Ἕβρον
5 εὐπετῶς. ἐκεῖθεν δὲ διὰ τῆς Παιτικῆς ἐπὶ τὸν
Μέλανα ποταμὸν ἔρχεται. διαβὰς δὲ καὶ τὸν
Μέλανα ἐς Σηστὸν ἀφικνεῖται ἐν εἴκοσι ταῖς
πάσαις ἡμέραις ἀπὸ τῆς οἴκοθεν ἐξορμήσεως.
ἐλθὼν δὲ ἐς Ἐλαιοῦντα θύει Πρωτεσιλάῳ ἐπὶ τῷ
τάφῳ τοῦ Πρωτεσιλάου, ὅτι καὶ Πρωτεσίλαος
πρῶτος ἐδόκει ἐκβῆναι ἐς τὴν Ἀσίαν τῶν Ἑλλήνων
τῶν ἅμα Ἀγαμέμνονι ἐς Ἴλιον στρατευσάντων.
καὶ ὁ νοῦς τῆς θυσίας ἦν ἐπιτυχεστέραν οἷ γενέσθαι
ἢ Πρωτεσιλάῳ τὴν ἀπόβασιν.

6 Παρμενίων μὲν δὴ τῶν τε πεζῶν τοὺς πολλοὺς
καὶ τὴν ἵππον διαβιβάσαι ἐτάχθη ἐκ Σηστοῦ ἐς
Ἄβυδον· καὶ διέβησαν τριήρεσι μὲν ἑκατὸν καὶ
ἑξήκοντα πλοίοις δὲ ἄλλοις πολλοῖς στρογγύλοις.
Ἀλέξανδρον δὲ ἐξ Ἐλαιοῦντος ἐς τὸν Ἀχαιῶν
λιμένα κατᾶραι ὁ πλείων λόγος κατέχει, καὶ αὐτόν
τε κυβερνῶντα τὴν στρατηγίδα ναῦν διαβάλλειν
καί, ἐπειδὴ κατὰ μέσον τὸν πόρον τοῦ Ἑλλησπόντου ἐγένετο, σφάξαντα ταῦρον τῷ Ποσειδῶνι
καὶ Νηρηῖσι σπένδειν ἐκ χρυσῆς φιάλης ἐς τὸν
7 πόντον. λέγουσι δὲ καὶ πρῶτον ἐκ τῆς νεὼς σὺν
τοῖς ὅπλοις ἐκβῆναι αὐτὸν ἐς τὴν γῆν τὴν Ἀσίαν

---

2 Numbers: Introd. 56. **Pt.** and Ar. agreed as to the foot;

sand, his cavalry over five thousand.[2] His route was
past Lake Cercinitis in the direction of Amphipolis
and the delta of the river Strymon [Struma]. He
crossed the Strymon and passed Mount Pangaeum,
on the way to Abdera and Maronea, Greek cities
settled by the sea. Thence he reached the Hebrus
[Maritza] and crossed it with ease; from there he
went through Paetice to the Black River, crossed it,
and reached Sestus twenty days in all after starting
from home.[3] Arriving at Elaeus, he sacrificed to
Protesilaus at his tomb, since he was thought to be
the first to disembark on Asian soil of the Greeks who
fought with Agamemnon against Troy. The intention of the sacrifice was that his own landing on Asian
soil might be luckier than that of Protesilaus.

Parmenio was appointed to see to the ferrying
over from Sestus to Abydos of the cavalry and most
of the infantry; they crossed in a hundred and sixty
triremes [4] and in a good number of cargo boats.
According to the prevalent story[5] Alexander made
from Elaeus for the Achaean harbour, and steered
the admiral's ship himself when he crossed, sacrificing
a bull to Posidon and the Nereids in the midst of the
Hellespont strait, and pouring into the sea a drink
offering from a golden bowl. They also say that he
was the first to disembark on Asian soil armed *cap-*

4

5

6

7

A. ignores Ar's variant (4,000) for horse, and his statement that
he had only 70 Talents (*contra* vii 9, 6; for other variants,
P. 15), though this deserved full treatment; initial costs
were inevitably heavy; hence in 334 shortage of cash, cf. i 20;
vii 9. 6; App. II 1.

[3] Landing in Asia, D. 17–18, 1; P. 15. For § 5–8 see App.
IV 1 f.

[4] App. II 1.

[5] ' Vulgate ' to end of ch.

49

καὶ βωμοὺς ἱδρύσασθαι ὅθεν τε ἐστάλη ἐκ τῆς
Εὐρώπης καὶ ὅπου ἐξέβη τῆς Ἀσίας Διὸς ἀπο-
βατηρίου καὶ Ἀθηνᾶς καὶ Ἡρακλέους. ἀνελθόντα
δὲ ἐς Ἴλιον τῇ τε Ἀθηνᾷ θῦσαι τῇ Ἰλιάδι, καὶ τὴν
πανοπλίαν τὴν αὑτοῦ ἀναθεῖναι ἐς τὸν νεών, καὶ
καθελεῖν ἀντὶ ταύτης τῶν ἱερῶν τινα ὅπλων ἔτι ἐκ
8 τοῦ Τρωικοῦ ἔργου σωζόμενα. καὶ ταῦτα λέγουσιν
ὅτι οἱ ὑπασπισταὶ ἔφερον πρὸ αὐτοῦ ἐς τὰς μάχας.
θῦσαι δὲ αὐτὸν καὶ Πριάμῳ ἐπὶ τοῦ βωμοῦ τοῦ
Διὸς τοῦ Ἑρκείου λόγος κατέχει, μῆνιν Πριάμου
παραιτούμενον τῷ Νεοπτολέμου γένει, ὃ δὴ ἐς
αὐτὸν καθῆκεν.

12. Ἀνιόντα δ' αὐτὸν ἐς Ἴλιον Μενοίτιός τε ὁ
κυβερνήτης χρυσῷ στεφάνῳ ἐστεφάνωσε καὶ ἐπὶ
τούτῳ Χάρης ὁ Ἀθηναῖος ἐκ Σιγείου ἐλθὼν καί
τινες καὶ ἄλλοι, οἱ μὲν Ἕλληνες, οἱ δὲ ἐπιχώριοι·
. . . οἱ δέ, ὅτι καὶ τὸν Ἀχιλλέως ἄρα τάφον
ἐστεφάνωσεν· Ἡφαιστίωνα δὲ λέγουσιν ὅτι τοῦ
Πατρόκλου τὸν τάφον ἐστεφάνωσε· καὶ εὐδαι-
μόνισεν ἄρα, ὡς λόγος, Ἀλέξανδρος Ἀχιλλέα, ὅτι
2 Ὁμήρου κήρυκος ἐς τὴν ἔπειτα μνήμην ἔτυχε. καὶ
μέντοι καὶ ἦν Ἀλεξάνδρῳ οὐχ ἥκιστα τούτου
ἕνεκα εὐδαιμονιστέος Ἀχιλλεύς, ὅτι αὐτῷ γε
Ἀλεξάνδρῳ, οὐ κατὰ τὴν ἄλλην ἐπιτυχίαν, τὸ
χωρίον τοῦτο ἐκλιπὲς ξυνέβη οὐδὲ ἐξηνέχθη ἐς
ἀνθρώπους τὰ Ἀλεξάνδρου ἔργα ἐπαξίως, οὔτ' οὖν
καταλογάδην, οὔτε τις ἐν μέτρῳ ἐποίησεν· ἀλλ'
οὐδὲ ἐν μέλει ᾔσθη Ἀλέξανδρος, ἐν ὅτῳ Ἱέρων τε
καὶ Γέλων καὶ Θήρων καὶ πολλοὶ ἄλλοι οὐδέν τι
Ἀλεξάνδρῳ ἐπεοικότες, ὥστε πολὺ μεῖον γιγνώ-
σκεται τὰ Ἀλεξάνδρου ἢ τὰ φαυλότατα τῶν πάλαι
3 ἔργων· ὁπότε καὶ ἡ τῶν μυρίων ξὺν Κύρῳ ἄνοδος

à-pie, that he set up altars both where he started from Europe and where he landed in Asia to Zeus of Safe Landings, Athena, and Heracles, and that he then went up to Troy, and sacrificed to the Trojan Athena, dedicated his full armour in the temple, and took down in its place some of the dedicated arms yet remaining from the Trojan war, which, it is said, the hypaspists henceforth used to carry before him into battle. Then he sacrificed also to Priam at the altar of Zeus of Enclosures (so runs the story), praying Priam not to vent his anger on the race of Neoptolemus, of which he himself was a scion. 8

12. When Alexander reached Troy Menoetius the pilot crowned him with a golden wreath and then Chares the Athenian[1] arrived from Sigeum with others, Greeks or natives of the place . . .[2] Some say that Alexander crowned the tomb of Achilles, while Hephaestion, others say, placed a wreath on Patroclus' tomb; and Alexander, so the story goes, blessed Achilles for having Homer to proclaim his fame to posterity.[3] Alexander might well have counted Achilles happy on this score, since, fortunate as Alexander was in other ways, there was a great gap left here, and Alexander's exploits were never celebrated as they deserved, either in prose or verse; there were not even choral lyrics for Alexander as for Hiero, Gelo, Thero and many others not to be compared with him, so that Alexander's exploits are far less known than very minor deeds of old times. Why, 3

---

[1] The Athenian general, earlier (10, 4) and later (iii 2, 6) hostile.

[2] The text has a lacuna.

[3] ' Vulgate ', as often with variant versions; A's own reflections follow. (Hephaestion was Al's most intimate friend.)

ἐπὶ βασιλέα Ἀρτοξέρξην καὶ τὰ Κλεάρχου τε καὶ
τῶν ἅμα αὐτῷ ἁλόντων παθήματα καὶ ἡ κατάβασις
αὐτῶν ἐκείνων, ἣν Ξενοφῶν αὐτοὺς κατήγαγε, πολύ
τι ἐπιφανέστερα ἐς ἀνθρώπους Ξενοφῶντος ἕνεκά
ἐστιν ἢ Ἀλέξανδρός τε καὶ τὰ Ἀλεξάνδρου
4 ἔργα. καίτοι Ἀλέξανδρος οὔτε ξὺν ἄλλῳ ἐστρά-
τευσεν, οὔτε φεύγων μέγαν βασιλέα τοὺς τῇ
καθόδῳ τῇ ἐπὶ θάλασσαν ἐμποδὼν γιγνομένους
ἐκράτησεν· ἀλλ' οὐκ ἔστιν ὅστις ἄλλος εἷς ἀνὴρ
τοσαῦτα ἢ τηλικαῦτα ἔργα κατὰ πλῆθος ἢ μέγεθος
ἐν Ἕλλησιν ἢ βαρβάροις ἀπεδείξατο. ἔνθεν καὶ
αὐτὸς ὁρμηθῆναί φημι ἐς τήνδε τὴν ξυγγραφήν, οὐκ
ἀπαξιώσας ἐμαυτὸν φανερὰ καταστήσειν ἐς ἀνθρώ-
5 πους τὰ Ἀλεξάνδρου ἔργα. ὅστις δὲ ὢν ταῦτα
ὑπὲρ ἐμαυτοῦ γιγνώσκω, τὸ μὲν ὄνομα οὐδὲ
δέομαι ἀναγράψαι, οὐδὲ γὰρ οὐδὲ ἄγνωστον ἐς
ἀνθρώπους ἐστίν, οὐδὲ πατρίδα ἥτις μοί ἐστιν οὐδὲ
γένος τὸ ἐμόν, οὐδὲ εἰ δή τινα ἀρχὴν ἐν τῇ ἐμαυτοῦ
ἦρξα· ἀλλ' ἐκεῖνο ἀναγράφω, ὅτι ἐμοὶ πατρίς τε
καὶ γένος καὶ ἀρχαὶ οἵδε οἱ λόγοι εἰσί τε καὶ ἀπὸ
νέου ἔτι ἐγένοντο. καὶ ἐπὶ τῷδε οὐκ ἀπαξιῶ
ἐμαυτὸν τῶν πρώτων ἐν τῇ φωνῇ τῇ Ἑλλάδι, εἴπερ
οὖν καὶ Ἀλέξανδρον τῶν ἐν τοῖς ὅπλοις.
6 Ἐξ Ἰλίου δὲ ἐς Ἀρίσβην ἧκεν, οὗ πᾶσα ἡ
δύναμις αὐτῷ διαβεβηκυῖα τὸν Ἑλλήσποντον
ἐστρατοπεδεύκει, καὶ τῇ ὑστεραίᾳ ἐς Περκώτην·
τῇ δὲ ἄλλῃ Λάμψακον παραμείψας πρὸς τῷ
Πρακτίῳ [1] ποταμῷ ἐστρατοπέδευσεν, ὃς ῥέων ἐκ
τῶν ὀρῶν τῶν Ἰδαίων ἐκδιδοῖ ἐς θάλασσαν τὴν
μεταξὺ τοῦ Ἑλλησπόντου τε καὶ τοῦ Εὐξείνου
πόντου. ἔνθεν δὲ ἐς Ἕρμωτον ἀφίκετο, Κολωνὰς

---

[1] Freinsheim; προσακτίῳ A: παρ' ἀκτήν Lane Fox 515.

334
B.C.

[401
B.C.]

the march up into Asia of the Ten Thousand with
Cyrus against King Artaxerxes, the sufferings of
Clearchus and those captured with him, and the
descent to the sea of those Ten Thousand under
the leadership of Xenophon, are, thanks to Xenophon,
far better known to the world than Alexander and
Alexander's exploits. Yet Alexander did not take 4
the field in another's army; he did not flee from the
Great King, defeating only those who tried to stop
the march down to the sea; no other single man
performed such remarkable deeds, whether in
number or magnitude, among either Greeks or
barbarians. That, I declare, is why I myself have
embarked on this history, not judging myself unworthy to make Alexander's deeds known to men.
Whoever I may be, this I know in my favour; I need 5
not write my name, for it is not at all unknown
among men, nor my country nor my family nor any
office I may have held in my own land; this I do set
on paper, that country, family, and offices I find and
have found from my youth in these tales. That is
why I think myself not unworthy of the masters of
Greek speech, since my subject Alexander was
among the masters of warfare.[4]

From Ilium Alexander came to Arisbe, where his 6
whole force had encamped after crossing the Hellespont; next day to Percote, the next he passed
Lampsacus and camped by the river Practius, which
flows from Mount Ida and runs into the sea that
lies between the Hellespont and the Black Sea.
Then he reached Hermotus, passing by Colonae.

---

[4] I shall discuss this in an Appendix on A's career in vol. II.
For the striking and strange language (derived from *Iliad*
vi 429 f.) cf. Aelius Aristides xxxiii 20; I owe these references
to E. Bowie.

7 πόλιν παραμείψας. σκοποὶ δὲ αὐτῷ ἐπέμποντο
πρὸ τοῦ στρατεύματος· καὶ τούτων ἡγεμὼν ἦν
᾿Αμύντας ὁ ᾿Αρραβαίου, ἔχων τῶν τε ἑταίρων τὴν
ἴλην τὴν ἐξ ᾿Απολλωνίας, ἧς ἰλάρχης ἦν Σωκράτης
ὁ Σάθωνος, καὶ τῶν προδρόμων καλουμένων ἴλας
τέσσαρας. κατὰ δὲ τὴν πάροδον Πρίαπον πόλιν
ἐνδοθεῖσαν πρὸς τῶν ἐνοικούντων τοὺς παραληψο-
μένους ἀπέστειλε σὺν Πανηγόρῳ τῷ Λυκαγόρου,
ἑνὶ τῶν ἑταίρων.

8 Περσῶν δὲ στρατηγοὶ ἦσαν ᾿Αρσάμης καὶ
῾Ρεομίθρης καὶ Πετήνης καὶ Νιφάτης καὶ ξὺν
τούτοις Σπιθριδάτης ὁ Λυδίας καὶ ᾿Ιωνίας σατράπης
καὶ ᾿Αρσίτης ὁ τῆς πρὸς ῾Ελλησπόντῳ Φρυγίας
ὕπαρχος. οὗτοι δὲ πρὸς Ζελείᾳ πόλει κατεστρατο-
πεδευκότες ἦσαν ξὺν τῇ ἵππῳ τε τῇ βαρβαρικῇ καὶ
9 τοῖς ῞Ελλησι τοῖς μισθοφόροις. βουλευομένοις δὲ
αὐτοῖς ὑπὲρ τῶν παρόντων, ἐπειδὴ ᾿Αλέξανδρος
διαβεβηκὼς ἠγγέλλετο, Μέμνων ὁ ῾Ρόδιος παρῄνει
μὴ διὰ κινδύνου ἰέναι πρὸς τοὺς Μακεδόνας, τῷ τε
πεζῷ πολὺ περιόντας σφῶν καὶ αὐτοῦ ᾿Αλεξάνδρου
παρόντος, αὐτοῖς δὲ ἀπόντος Δαρείου· προϊόντας
δὲ τόν τε χιλὸν ἀφανίζειν καταπατοῦντας τῇ ἵππῳ
καὶ τὸν ἐν τῇ γῇ καρπὸν ἐμπιπράναι, μηδὲ τῶν
πόλεων αὐτῶν φειδομένους. οὐ γὰρ μενεῖν ἐν
τῇ χώρᾳ ᾿Αλέξανδρον ἀπορίᾳ τῶν ἐπιτηδείων.
10 ᾿Αρσίτην δὲ λέγεται εἰπεῖν ἐν τῷ συλλόγῳ τῶν
Περσῶν, ὅτι οὐκ ἂν περιίδοι μίαν οἰκίαν ἐμπρησθεῖ-
σαν τῶν ὑπὸ οἷ τεταγμένων ἀνθρώπων· καὶ τοὺς
Πέρσας ᾿Αρσίτῃ προσθέσθαι, ὅτι καὶ ὕποπτόν τι
αὐτοῖς ἦν ἐς τὸν Μέμνονα τριβὰς ἐμποιεῖν ἑκόντα
τῷ πολέμῳ τῆς ἐκ βασιλέως τιμῆς οὕνεκα.

7   334 B.C.

He sent scouts ahead of the army; Amyntas, son of Arrabaeus, led them with the squadron of Companions from Apollonia, whose squadron leader was Socrates, son of Sathon, with four squadrons of the so-called *prodromoi*. On his march the city of Priapus was surrendered to him by the citizens, and he sent a party to take it over under Panegorus son of Lycagorus, one of the Companions.

The Persian commanders were Arsames, Rheomithres, Petenes, Niphates, and with them Spithridates the satrap of Lydia and Ionia and Arsites the hyparch [5] of Hellespontine Phrygia. They had already encamped by the city of Zeleia with the barbarian cavalry and the mercenary Greeks. They held a council of war when Alexander's crossing was reported and Memnon of Rhodes advised them to run no risk against the Macedonians, as the latter were far superior in infantry, while Alexander was present and Darius absent on their own side; they had far best march on, destroying the fodder by trampling it with their cavalry, and burning the growing crops, not even sparing the very cities; then Alexander would not stay in the country for want of provisions. However, it is said that Arsites stated in the Persian council that he would not suffer one house to be burned belonging to his subjects, and that the Persians supported Arsites, suspecting Memnon of deliberately holding up warlike operations for the sake of the honour he held from the king.[6]

---

[5] Properly an official subordinate to a satrap, but here, as in iv 18, **3** (cf. iii 16, 4), meaning a satrap.

[6] On Memnon (brother-in-law of Artabazus, iii 21, 4 n.) and his strategy cf. Introd. §45; 54.

13. Ἐν τούτῳ δὲ Ἀλέξανδρος προὐχώρει ἐπὶ τὸν Γράνικον ποταμὸν συντεταγμένῳ τῷ στρατῷ, διπλῆν μὲν τὴν φάλαγγα τῶν ὁπλιτῶν τάξας, τοὺς δὲ ἱππέας κατὰ τὰ κέρατα ἄγων, τὰ σκευοφόρα δὲ κατόπιν ἐπιτάξας ἕπεσθαι· τοὺς δὲ προκατασκεφομένους τὰ τῶν πολεμίων ἦγεν αὐτῷ Ἡγέλοχος, ἱππέας μὲν ἔχων τοὺς σαρισσοφόρους, τῶν 2 δὲ ψιλῶν ἐς πεντακοσίους. καὶ Ἀλέξανδρός τε οὐ πολὺ ἀπεῖχε τοῦ ποταμοῦ τοῦ Γρανίκου καὶ οἱ ἀπὸ τῶν σκοπῶν σπουδῇ ἐλαύνοντες ἀπήγγελλον ἐπὶ τῷ Γρανίκῳ πέραν τοὺς Πέρσας ἐφεστάναι τεταγμένους ὡς ἐς μάχην. ἔνθα δὴ Ἀλέξανδρος μὲν τὴν στρατιὰν πᾶσαν συνέταττεν ὡς μαχουμένους· Παρμενίων δὲ προσελθὼν λέγει Ἀλεξάνδρῳ τάδε.

3 " 'Ἐμοὶ δοκεῖ, βασιλεῦ, ἀγαθὸν εἶναι ἐν τῷ παρόντι καταστρατοπεδεῦσαι ἐπὶ τοῦ ποταμοῦ τῇ ὄχθῃ ὡς ἔχομεν. τοὺς γὰρ πολεμίους οὐ δοκῶ τολμήσειν πολὺ τῷ πεζῷ λειπομένους πλησίον ἡμῶν αὐλισθῆναι, καὶ ταύτῃ παρέξειν ἕωθεν εὐπετῶς τῷ στρατῷ διαβαλεῖν τὸν πόρον· ὑποφθάσομεν γὰρ αὐτοὶ περάσαντες πρὶν ἐκείνους ἐς 4 τάξιν καθίστασθαι. νῦν δὲ οὐκ ἀκινδύνως μοι δοκοῦμεν ἐπιχειρήσειν τῷ ἔργῳ, ὅτι οὐχ οἷόν τε ἐν μετώπῳ διὰ τοῦ ποταμοῦ ἄγειν τὸν στρατόν. πολλὰ μὲν γὰρ αὐτοῦ ὁρᾶται βαθέα, αἱ δὲ ὄχθαι αὗται ὁρᾷς ὅτι ὑπερύψηλοι καὶ κρημνώδεις εἰσὶν αἱ 5 αὐτῶν· ἀτάκτως τε οὖν καὶ κατὰ κέρας, ᾗπερ ἀσθενέστατον, ἐκβαίνουσιν ἐπικείσονται ἐς φάλαγγα ξυντεταγμένοι τῶν πολεμίων οἱ ἱππεῖς· καὶ τὸ πρῶτον σφάλμα ἔς τε τὰ παρόντα χαλεπὸν καὶ ἐς τὴν ὑπὲρ παντὸς τοῦ πολέμου κρίσιν σφαλερόν.' "

6 Ἀλέξανδρος δέ, "ταῦτα μέν", ἔφη, "ὦ Παρμε-

13. Meanwhile, Alexander was advancing to the river Granicus [1] with his force all ready for battle, after drawing up his hoplites in two lines, with the cavalry on the wings, and ordering the baggage train to follow behind. The reconnoitring force was under the command of Hegelochus, with the lancers as cavalry, and five hundred light troops. Alexander was not far from the river Granicus, when some of the scouts, riding in at full speed, reported that the Persians were drawn up for battle on the farther bank of the Granicus. Alexander then formed the whole army for battle; but Parmenio came forward and said:

'My view, sir, is that we should encamp at once on the river bank, as we are; the enemy outnumbered in infantry will, I believe, not dare to bivouac near us; and this will make it easy for the army to cross at dawn; we shall be across ourselves before they get into order. As things are, I feel that we should run great risk in taking action, since we cannot take the army across the river on a wide front, for one can see that many parts of it are deep; its banks, as you see, are very high, sometimes like cliffs. As we emerge in disorder and in column, the weakest of formations, the enemy cavalry in good solid order will charge: the initial disaster would be damaging at present, and most harmful for the general result of the war.'

Alexander, however, replied: 'All this I know,

---

[1] For chs 13-16 see App. I. The battle was fought in May-June. The Granicus descends from Mt. Ida to the Propontis.

νίων, γιγνώσκω· αἰσχύνομαι δέ, εἰ τὸν μὲν
Ἑλλήσποντον διέβην εὐπετῶς, τοῦτο δέ, σμικρὸν
ῥεῦμα,—οὕτω τῷ ὀνόματι τὸν Γράνικον ἐκφαυ-
λίσας,—εἴρξει ἡμᾶς τὸ μὴ οὐ διαβῆναι ὡς ἔχομεν.
7 καὶ τοῦτο οὔτε πρὸς Μακεδόνων τῆς δόξης οὔτε
πρὸς τῆς ἐμῆς ἐς τοὺς κινδύνους ὀξύτητος ποιοῦμαι·
ἀναθαρρήσειν τε δοκῶ τοὺς Πέρσας ⟨ὡς⟩ ἀξιομά-
χους Μακεδόσιν ὄντας, ὅτι οὐδὲν ἄξιον τοῦ σφῶν
δέους ἐν τῷ παραυτίκα ἔπαθον."

14. Ταῦτα εἰπὼν Παρμενίωνα μὲν ἐπὶ τὸ
εὐώνυμον κέρας πέμπει ἡγησόμενον, αὐτὸς δὲ ἐπὶ
τὸ δεξιὸν παρῆγε. προετάχθησαν δὲ αὐτῷ
τοῦ μὲν δεξιοῦ Φιλώτας ὁ Παρμενίωνος, ἔχων
τοὺς ἑταίρους τοὺς ἱππέας καὶ τοὺς τοξότας καὶ
τοὺς Ἀγριᾶνας τοὺς ἀκοντιστάς· Ἀμύντας δὲ ὁ
Ἀρραβαίου τούς τε σαρισσοφόρους ἱππέας ἔχων
Φιλώτᾳ ἐπετάχθη καὶ τοὺς Παίονας καὶ τὴν ἴλην
2 τὴν Σωκράτους. ἐχόμενοι δὲ τούτων ἐτάχθησαν οἱ
ὑπασπισταὶ τῶν ἑταίρων, ὧν ἡγεῖτο Νικάνωρ ὁ
Παρμενίωνος· ἐπὶ δὲ τούτοις ἡ Περδίκκου τοῦ
Ὀρόντου φάλαγξ· ἐπὶ δὲ ἡ Κοίνου τοῦ Πολε-
μοκράτους· [ἐπὶ δὲ ἡ Κρατεροῦ τοῦ Ἀλεξάνδρου·]
ἐπὶ δὲ ἡ Ἀμύντου τοῦ Ἀνδρομένους· ἐπὶ δὲ ὧν
3 Φίλιππος ὁ Ἀμύντου ἦρχε. τοῦ δὲ εὐωνύμου
πρῶτοι μὲν οἱ Θετταλοὶ ἱππεῖς ἐτάχθησαν, ὧν
ἡγεῖτο Κάλας ὁ Ἁρπάλου· ἐπὶ δὲ τούτοις οἱ
ξύμμαχοι ἱππεῖς, ὧν ἦρχε Φίλιππος ὁ Μενελάου·
ἐπὶ δὲ τούτοις οἱ Θρᾷκες, ὧν ἦρχεν Ἀγάθων·
ἐχόμενοι δὲ τούτων πεζοὶ ἥ τε Κρατεροῦ φάλαγξ
καὶ ἡ Μελεάγρου καὶ ἡ Φιλίππου ἔστε ἐπὶ τὸ μέσον
τῆς ξυμπάσης τάξεως.

Parmenio, but I should feel ashamed if after crossing the Hellespont easily, this petty stream (by this epithet did he belittle the Granicus) hinders us from crossing, just as we are. I consider this unworthy 7 either of the prestige of the Macedonians or of my own celerity in dealing with dangers; I believe it would encourage the Persians to think themselves equal to fighting the Macedonians, since they have not experienced any immediate disaster to justify their alarm.'

14. After saying this, he sent off Parmenio to lead the left wing; he himself passed along to the right. In front of his right he had already posted Philotas son of Parmenio, with the Companion cavalry, the archers, and the Agrianian javelin-men. Next to Philotas Amyntas son of Arrabaeus was posted, with the lancers,[1] the Paeonians and Socrates' squadron. Next to them were marshalled the hypaspists of the 2 Companions, led by Nicanor son of Parmenio; beside these was the phalanx [2] of Perdiccas son of Orontes, then that of Coenus son of Polemocrates, [then that of Craterus son of Alexander,] [3] then that of Amyntas son of Andromenes, then the troops under Philip son of Amyntas. On the left wing the 3 Thessalian cavalry came first, commanded by Calas son of Harpalus, next, the allied cavalry under Philip son of Menelaus, then the Thracians under Agatho; on their right were the infantry, the phalanx regiments of Craterus, of Meleager and of Philip,[4] up to the centre of the whole line.

[1] Amyntas: App. XI 5. 'Lancers': Introd. § 58; 64.

[2] i.e. a battalion of the Foot-Companions, Introd. § 61.

[3] Craterus was on the left (§ 3), as in other battles, ii 8, 4; iii 11, 10. Hence, these words are interpolated.

[4] A. mentions Philip's battalion twice, counting first from the right, then from the left.

4   Περσῶν δὲ ἱππεῖς μὲν ἦσαν ἐς δισμυρίους, ξένοι
δὲ πεζοὶ μισθοφόροι ὀλίγον ἀποδέοντες δισμυρίων·
ἐτάχθησαν δὲ τὴν μὲν ἵππον παρατείναντες τῷ
ποταμῷ κατὰ τὴν ὄχθην ἐπὶ φάλαγγα μακράν, τοὺς
δὲ πεζοὺς κατόπιν τῶν ἱππέων· καὶ γὰρ ὑπερδέξια
ἦν τὰ ὑπὲρ τὴν ὄχθην χωρία. ᾗ δὲ Ἀλέξανδρον
αὐτὸν καθεώρων—δῆλος γὰρ ἦν τῶν τε ὅπλων τῇ
λαμπρότητι καὶ τῶν ἀμφ᾽ αὐτὸν τῇ σὺν ἐκπλήξει
θεραπείᾳ—κατὰ τὸ εὐώνυμον [μὲν] σφῶν ἐπέχοντα,
ταύτῃ πυκνὰς ἐπέταξαν τῇ ὄχθῃ τὰς ἴλας τῶν
ἱππέων.

5   Χρόνον μὲν δὴ ἀμφότερα τὰ στρατεύματα ἐπ᾽
ἄκρου τοῦ ποταμοῦ ἐφεστῶτες ὑπὸ τοῦ τὸ μέλλον
ὀκνεῖν ἡσυχίαν ἦγον καὶ σιγὴ ἦν πολλὴ ἀφ᾽
ἑκατέρων. οἱ γὰρ Πέρσαι προσέμενον τοὺς Μακεδόνας, ὁπότε ἐσβήσονται ἐς τὸν πόρον, ὡς ἐπικει-
6   σόμενοι ἐκβαίνουσιν· Ἀλέξανδρος δὲ ἀναπηδήσας
ἐπὶ τὸν ἵππον καὶ τοῖς ἀμφ᾽ αὐτὸν ἐγκελευσάμενος
ἕπεσθαί τε καὶ ἄνδρας ἀγαθοὺς γίγνεσθαι, τοὺς μὲν
προδρόμους ἱππέας καὶ μὴν καὶ τοὺς Παίονας
προεμβαλεῖν ἐς τὸν ποταμὸν ἔχοντα Ἀμύνταν τὸν
Ἀρραβαίου ⟨ἔταξε⟩ καὶ τῶν πεζῶν μίαν τάξιν, καὶ
πρὸ τούτων τὴν Σωκράτους ἴλην Πτολεμαῖον τὸν
Φιλίππου ἄγοντα, ἣ δὴ καὶ ἐτύγχανε τὴν ἡγεμονίαν
τοῦ ἱππικοῦ παντὸς ἔχουσα[ν] ἐκείνῃ τῇ ἡμέρᾳ·
7   αὐτὸς δὲ ἄγων τὸ δεξιὸν κέρας ὑπὸ σαλπίγγων τε
καὶ τῷ Ἐνυαλίῳ ἀλαλάζοντας ἐμβαίνει ἐς τὸν
πόρον, λοξὴν ἀεὶ παρατείνων τὴν τάξιν, ᾗ παρεῖλκε
τὸ ῥεῦμα, ἵνα δὴ μὴ ἐκβαίνοντι αὐτῷ οἱ Πέρσαι
κατὰ κέρας προσπίπτοιεν, ἀλλὰ καὶ αὐτὸς ὡς
ἀνυστὸν τῇ φάλαγγι προσμίξῃ αὐτοῖς.

15. Οἱ δὲ Πέρσαι, ᾗ πρῶτοι οἱ ἀμφὶ Ἀμύνταν

The Persians had about 20,000 cavalry, and little 4 334
short of the same number of foreign mercenary   B.C.
infantry. They were drawn up with the cavalry
in an extended phalanx, on the bank parallel to the
river, the infantry behind them; the land above
the bank was high and commanding. Where they
observed Alexander himself—he was unmistakable,
from the splendour of his equipment and the en-
thusiasm of the men in attendance round him—
aiming at their left, they massed their cavalry squadrons on the bank there.

For some time the two forces on the river's brink, 5
dreading to precipitate the event, remained still
and in deep silence on either side. For the Persians
were waiting for the Macedonians, so as to fall on
them emerging from the river, whenever they attempted the crossing; but Alexander leapt on his 6
horse, and calling on his suite to follow and show
themselves brave men and true, ordered the *prodromoi*
and the Paeonians to plunge first into the stream,
under command of Amyntas son of Arrabaeus, with
one battalion of the infantry and in advance Socrates' squadron under Ptolemy son of Philip (this
was on the list as leading the whole cavalry on that
day); then he himself, leading the right wing, with 7
bugles sounding, and the battle cry going up to the
God of Battles, went into the stream, continually
extending his troops obliquely in the direction in
which the current was pulling them, so that the
Persians should not fall on him in column as he
emerged, but that he himself might attack them, as
far as might be, in deep formation.

15. At the point where the vanguard under Amyntas

καὶ Σωκράτην προσέσχον τῇ ὄχθῃ, ταύτῃ καὶ αὐτοὶ
ἄνωθεν ἔβαλλον, οἱ μὲν αὐτῶν ἀπὸ τῆς ὄχθης ἐξ
ὑπερδεξίου ἐς τὸν ποταμὸν ἐσακοντίζοντες, οἱ δὲ
κατὰ τὰ χθαμαλώτερα αὐτῆς ἔστε ἐπὶ τὸ ὕδωρ
2 καταβαίνοντες. καὶ ἦν τῶν τε ἱππέων ὠθισμός,
τῶν μὲν ἐκβαίνειν ἐκ τοῦ ποταμοῦ, τῶν δ' εἴργειν
τὴν ἔκβασιν, καὶ παλτῶν ἀπὸ μὲν τῶν Περσῶν
πολλὴ ἄφεσις, οἱ Μακεδόνες δὲ ξὺν τοῖς δόρασιν
ἐμάχοντο. ἀλλὰ τῷ τε πλήθει πολὺ ἐλαττούμενοι
⟨οἱ⟩ Μακεδόνες ἐκακοπάθουν ἐν τῇ πρώτῃ προσβολῇ, καὶ αὐτοὶ ἐξ οὐ βεβαίου τε καὶ ἅμα κάτωθεν
ἐκ τοῦ ποταμοῦ ἀμυνόμενοι, οἱ δὲ Πέρσαι ἐξ
ὑπερδεξίου τῆς ὄχθης· ἄλλως τε καὶ τὸ κράτιστον
τῆς Περσικῆς ἵππου ταύτῃ ἐπετέτακτο, οἵ τε
Μέμνονος παῖδες καὶ αὐτὸς Μέμνων μετὰ τούτων
3 ἐκινδύνευε. καὶ οἱ μὲν πρῶτοι τῶν Μακεδόνων
ξυμμίξαντες τοῖς Πέρσαις κατεκόπησαν πρὸς
αὐτῶν, ἄνδρες ἀγαθοὶ γενόμενοι, ὅσοι γε μὴ πρὸς
Ἀλέξανδρον πελάζοντα ἀπέκλιναν αὐτῶν. Ἀλέξανδρος γὰρ ἤδη πλησίον ἦν, ἅμα οἷ ἄγων τὸ κέρας
τὸ δεξιόν, καὶ ἐμβάλλει ἐς τοὺς Πέρσας πρῶτος,
ἵνα τὸ πᾶν στῖφος τῆς ἵππου καὶ αὐτοὶ οἱ ἡγεμόνες
τῶν Περσῶν τεταγμένοι ἦσαν· καὶ περὶ αὐτὸν
4 ξυνειστήκει μάχη καρτερά· καὶ ἐν τούτῳ ἄλλαι ἐπ'
ἄλλαις τῶν τάξεων τοῖς Μακεδόσι διέβαινον οὐ
χαλεπῶς ἤδη. καὶ ἦν μὲν ἀπὸ τῶν ἵππων ἡ μάχη,
πεζομαχίᾳ δὲ μᾶλλόν τι ἐῴκει. ξυνεχόμενοι γὰρ
ἵπποι τε ἵπποις καὶ ἄνδρες ἀνδράσιν ἠγωνίζοντο, οἱ
μέν ἐξῶσαι εἰς ἅπαν ἀπὸ τῆς ὄχθης καὶ ἐς τὸ
πεδίον βιάσασθαι τοὺς Πέρσας, οἱ Μακεδόνες, οἱ δὲ
εἶρξαί τε αὐτῶν τὴν ἔκβασιν, οἱ Πέρσαι, καὶ ἐς τὸν
5 ποταμὸν αὖθις ἀπώσασθαι. καὶ ἐκ τούτου ἐπλεο-

and Socrates touched the bank, the Persians shot volleys on them from above, some hurling their javelins
into the river from their commanding position on
the bank, others going down to the stream on the
more level ground. There was a great shoving by 2
the cavalry, as some were trying to get out of the
river, others to stop them, great showers of Persian
javelins, much thrusting of Macedonian spears. But
the Macedonians, much outnumbered, came off badly
in the first onslaught; they were defending themselves from the river on ground that was not firm and
was beneath the enemy's while the Persians had the
advantage of the bank; in particular, the flower of
the Persian cavalry was posted here, and Memnon's
sons and Memnon himself ventured their lives with
them. The first Macedonians who came to grips
with the Persians were cut down, despite their valour, 3
save those of them who fell back on Alexander as he
approached. For he was already near, with the right
wing which he was leading, and he charged the Persians at the head of his men just where cavalry were
massed and the Persian commanders were posted.
A fierce fight raged round him; and meanwhile the 4
Macedonians, battalion after battalion, kept crossing, a task now not so difficult. Though the fighting
was on horseback, it was more like an infantry battle,
horse entangled with horse, man with man in the
struggle, the Macedonians trying to push the Persians once and for all from the bank and force them on
to the level ground, the Persians trying to bar their
landing and thrust them back again into the river.

νέκτουν ἤδη οἱ σὺν Ἀλεξάνδρῳ τῇ τε ἄλλῃ ῥώμῃ καὶ ἐμπειρίᾳ καὶ ὅτι ξυστοῖς κρανεΐνοις πρὸς παλτὰ ἐμάχοντο.

6 Ἔνθα δὴ καὶ Ἀλεξάνδρῳ ξυντρίβεται τὸ δόρυ ἐν τῇ μάχῃ· ὁ δὲ Ἀρέτην ᾔτει δόρυ ἕτερον, ἀναβολέα τῶν βασιλικῶν· τῷ δὲ καὶ αὐτῷ πονουμένῳ συντετριμμένον τὸ δόρυ ἦν, ὁ δὲ τῷ ἡμίσει κεκλασμένου τοῦ δόρατος οὐκ ἀφανῶς ἐμάχετο, καὶ τοῦτο δείξας Ἀλεξάνδρῳ ἄλλον αἰτεῖν ἐκέλευεν· Δημάρατος δέ, ἀνὴρ Κορίνθιος, τῶν ἀμφ' αὐτὸν ἑταίρων,

7 δίδωσιν αὐτῷ τὸ αὑτοῦ δόρυ. καὶ ὃς ἀναλαβὼν καὶ ἰδὼν Μιθριδάτην τὸν Δαρείου γαμβρὸν πολὺ πρὸ τῶν ἄλλων προϊππεύοντα καὶ ἐπάγοντα ἅμα οἷ ὥσπερ ἔμβολον τῶν ἱππέων ἐξελαύνει καὶ αὐτὸς πρὸ τῶν ἄλλων, καὶ παίσας ἐς τὸ πρόσωπον τῷ δόρατι καταβάλλει τὸν Μιθριδάτην. ἐν δὲ τούτῳ Ῥοισάκης μὲν ἐπελαύνει τῷ Ἀλεξάνδρῳ καὶ παίει

8 Ἀλεξάνδρου τὴν κεφαλὴν τῇ κοπίδι· καὶ τοῦ μὲν κράνους τι ἀπέθραυσε, τὴν πληγὴν δὲ ἔσχε τὸ κράνος. καὶ καταβάλλει καὶ τοῦτον Ἀλέξανδρος παίσας τῷ ξυστῷ διὰ τοῦ θώρακος ἐς τὸ στέρνον. Σπιθριδάτης δὲ ἀνετέτατο μὲν ἤδη ἐπ' Ἀλέξανδρον ὄπισθεν τὴν κοπίδα, ὑποφθάσας δὲ αὐτὸν Κλεῖτος ὁ Δρωπίδου παίει κατὰ τοῦ ὤμου καὶ ἀποκόπτει τὸν ὦμον τοῦ Σπιθριδάτου ξὺν τῇ κοπίδι· καὶ ἐν τούτῳ ἐπεκβαίνοντες ἀεὶ τῶν ἱππέων ὅσοις προυχώρει κατὰ τὸν ποταμὸν προσεγίγνοντο τοῖς ἀμφ' Ἀλέξανδρον.

16. Καὶ οἱ Πέρσαι παιόμενοί τε πανταχόθεν ἤδη ἐς τὰ πρόσωπα αὐτοί τε καὶ ἵπποι τοῖς ξυστοῖς καὶ πρὸς τῶν ἱππέων ἐξωθούμενοι, πολλὰ δὲ καὶ πρὸς τῶν ψιλῶν ἀναμεμιγμένων τοῖς ἱππεῦσι βλαπτό-

Already, however, Alexander's men were getting the 5 334
best of it, not only through their strength and experi-   B.C.
ence but because they were fighting with cornel-
wood lances against short javelins.

At this point in the *mêlée* Alexander's lance was 6
broken in the battle; he called on Aretas, a groom
of the royal suite, for another, but Aretas had also
snapped his lance, and was hard pressed, though
putting up a brave fight with the half of his broken
weapon. Showing this to Alexander, he told him to
call on someone else. Demaratus of Corinth, one of
his Companions, gave him his own lance. Alexander 7
grasped it and seeing Mithridates, son-in-law of
Dareius, riding far ahead of the line and leading
on a wedge shaped body of horse, charged out alone
in advance of his own men, thrust his lance into
Mithridates' face and hurled him to the ground.
Then Rhoesaces rode at Alexander, and struck him
on the head with his scimitar; though he sheared 8
off part of the helmet, still the helmet parried the
blow. Alexander hurled him too to the ground,
piercing with his lance through the cuirass into his
chest. Spithridates had already raised his scimitar
against Alexander from behind when Clitus son of
Dropides, slipping in first, struck Spithridates' shoulder with his scimitar and cut it off. Meanwhile
cavalry who made good their way down stream kept
coming up and joining the band round Alexander.[1]

16. The Persians were now being roughly handled
from all quarters; they and their horses were struck
in the face with lances, they were being pushed
back by the cavalry, and were suffering heavily from

---

[1] D's parallel account (ch. 20) has some differences in
names and other details. On weapons used see Introd. 63f.

μένοι ἐγκλίνουσι ταύτῃ πρῶτον, ᾗ Ἀλέξανδρος
προεκινδύνευεν. ὡς δὲ τὸ μέσον ἐνεδεδώκει αὐτοῖς,
παρερρήγνυτο δὴ καὶ τὰ ἐφ᾽ ἑκάτερα τῆς ἵππου,
2 καὶ ἦν δὴ φυγὴ καρτερά. τῶν μὲν δὴ ἱππέων τῶν
Περσῶν ἀπέθανον εἰς χιλίους. οὐ γὰρ πολλὴ ἡ
δίωξις ἐγένετο, ὅτι ἐξετράπη Ἀλέξανδρος ἐπὶ τοὺς
ξένους τοὺς μισθοφόρους· ὧν τὸ στῖφος, ᾗ τὸ
πρῶτον ἐτάχθη, ἐκπλήξει μᾶλλόν τι τοῦ παραλόγου
ἢ λογισμῷ βεβαίῳ ἔμενεν· καὶ τούτοις τήν τε
φάλαγγα ἐπαγαγὼν καὶ τοὺς ἱππέας πάντῃ προσπεσεῖν κελεύσας ἐν μέσῳ δι᾽ ὀλίγου κατακόπτει
αὐτούς, ὥστε διέφυγε μὲν οὐδείς, ὅτι μὴ διέλαθέ
τις ἐν τοῖς νεκροῖς, ἐζωγρήθησαν δὲ ἀμφὶ τοὺς
3 δισχιλίους. ἔπεσον δὲ καὶ ἡγεμόνες τῶν Περσῶν
Νιφάτης τε καὶ Πετήνης καὶ Σπιθριδάτης ὁ
Λυδίας σατράπης καὶ ὁ τῶν Καππαδοκῶν ὕπαρχος
Μιθροβουζάνης καὶ Μιθριδάτης ὁ Δαρείου γαμβρὸς
καὶ Ἀρβουπάλης ὁ Δαρείου τοῦ Ἀρτοξέρξου
παῖς καὶ Φαρνάκης, ἀδελφὸς οὗτος τῆς Δαρείου
γυναικός, καὶ ὁ τῶν ξένων ἡγεμὼν Ὠμάρης.
Ἀρσίτης δὲ ἐκ μὲν τῆς μάχης φεύγει ἐς Φρυγίαν,
ἐκεῖ δὲ ἀποθνήσκει αὐτὸς πρὸς αὑτοῦ, ὡς λόγος,
ὅτι αἴτιος ἐδόκει Πέρσαις γενέσθαι τοῦ ἐν τῷ τότε
πταίσματος.
4   Μακεδόνων δὲ τῶν μὲν ἑταίρων ἀμφὶ τοὺς εἴκοσι
καὶ πέντε ἐν τῇ πρώτῃ προσβολῇ ἀπέθανον· καὶ
τούτων χαλκαῖ εἰκόνες ἐν Δίῳ ἑστᾶσιν, Ἀλεξάνδρου κελεύσαντος Λύσιππον ποιῆσαι, ὅσπερ καὶ
Ἀλέξανδρον μόνος προκριθεὶς ἐποίει· τῶν δὲ
ἄλλων ἱππέων ὑπὲρ τοὺς ἑξήκοντα, πεζοὶ δὲ ἐς τοὺς

the light troops, who had intermingled with the
cavalry, and so they began to give way, first at the
point where Alexander was in the front of the line.
But when their centre had given way, then the
cavalry wings also were broken, and they really
turned to flight in earnest. About a thousand 2
Persian horsemen perished; there was not a long
pursuit, since Alexander turned against the foreign
mercenary troops. Their serried ranks stood where
they had been first drawn up, not so much from
steadiness based on calculation as because they were
stunned by the unexpectedness of the situation.
Bringing his phalanx to bear on them and bidding
the cavalry fall on them from all quarters, he hemmed
them in and soon massacred them; not one got away
except by escaping notice among the dead, and some
two thousand were taken prisoners. Of Persian 3
commanders there fell Niphates, Petenes, Spithridates, satrap of Lydia, Mithrobuzanes the Cappadocian hyparch, Mithridates, son-in-law of Darius,
Arbupales son of Darius who was son of Artaxerxes,[1]
Pharnaces, brother of Darius' wife, and Omares,
commander of the mercenaries. Arsites fled from
the battle into Phrygia, but there died by his own
hand, it is said because the blame of the present
blunder seemed to the Persians to lie at his door.

On the Macedonian side about twenty-five of the 4
Companions fell in the first shock. There are brazen
statues of them set up at Dium; Alexander gave the
order to Lysippus,[2] the only sculptor he would select
to portray himself. Of the rest of the cavalry more

---

[1] i.e. king Artaxerxes II (404–358 B.C.).
[2] Lysippus was the greatest sculptor of the day. A. is
unaware that the statues had been removed to Rome in
146 B.C., cf. A. B. Bosworth, *CQ* 1972, 173 (giving 148 B.C.).

5 τριάκοντα. καὶ τούτους τῇ ὑστεραίᾳ ἔθαψεν
Ἀλέξανδρος ξὺν τοῖς ὅπλοις τε καὶ ἄλλῳ κόσμῳ·
γονεῦσι δὲ αὐτῶν καὶ παισὶ τῶν τε κατὰ τὴν χώραν
ἀτέλειαν ἔδωκε καὶ ὅσαι ἄλλαι ἢ τῷ σώματι
λειτουργίαι ἢ κατὰ τὰς κτήσεις ἑκάστων εἰσφοραί.
καὶ τῶν τετρωμένων δὲ πολλὴν πρόνοιαν ἔσχεν,
ἐπελθών τε αὐτὸς ἑκάστους καὶ τὰ τραύματα ἰδὼν
καὶ ὅπως τις ἐτρώθη ἐρόμενος καὶ ὅ τι πράττων
6 εἰπεῖν τε καὶ ἀλαζονεύσασθαί οἱ παρασχών. ὁ δὲ
καὶ τῶν Περσῶν τοὺς ἡγεμόνας ἔθαψεν· ἔθαψε δὲ
καὶ τοὺς μισθοφόρους Ἕλληνας, οἳ ξὺν τοῖς πολεμίοις στρατεύοντες ἀπέθανον· ὅσους δὲ αὐτῶν
αἰχμαλώτους ἔλαβε, τούτους δὲ δήσας ἐν πέδαις
εἰς Μακεδονίαν ἀπέπεμψεν ἐργάζεσθαι, ὅτι παρὰ
τὰ κοινῇ δόξαντα τοῖς Ἕλλησιν Ἕλληνες ὄντες
ἐναντία τῇ Ἑλλάδι ὑπὲρ τῶν βαρβάρων ἐμάχοντο.
7 ἀποπέμπει δὲ καὶ εἰς Ἀθήνας τριακοσίας πανο-
πλίας Περσικὰς ἀνάθημα εἶναι τῇ Ἀθηνᾷ ἐν πόλει·
καὶ ἐπίγραμμα ἐπιγραφῆναι ἐκέλευσε τόδε· Ἀλέξανδρος Φιλίππου καὶ οἱ Ἕλληνες πλὴν Λακεδαιμονίων ἀπὸ τῶν βαρβάρων τῶν τὴν Ἀσίαν
κατοικούντων.

17. Καταστήσας δὲ Κάλαν σατραπεύειν ἧς
Ἀρσίτης ἦρχε καὶ τοὺς φόρους τοὺς αὐτοὺς ἀποφέρειν τάξας, οὕσπερ Δαρείῳ ἔφερον, ὅσοι μὲν τῶν
βαρβάρων κατιόντες, ἐκ τῶν ὀρῶν ἐνεχείριζον
σφᾶς, τούτους μὲν ἀπαλλάττεσθαι ἐπὶ τὰ αὑτῶν
2 ἑκάστους ἐκέλευεν, Ζελείτας δὲ ἀφῆκε τῆς αἰτίας,
ὅτι πρὸς βίαν ἔγνω συστρατεῦσαι τοῖς βαρβάροις·
Δασκύλιον δὲ παραληψόμενον Παρμενίωνα ἐκπέμ-

---

[3] Ar. ap. P. 16, 7 said that Al. lost only 25 of his cavalry and
9 footmen.   Probably he did not include any non-Macedonians,

than sixty perished, and about thirty infantry.[3] 334
Alexander buried them next day with their arms 5 B.C.
and other accoutrements; to their parents and
children he gave remission of land taxes and of all
other personal services and property taxes. He
took great care of the wounded, visiting each man
himself, examining their wounds, asking how they
were received, and allowing them to recount and
boast of their exploits. He also buried the Persian 6
commanders and the mercenary Greeks who fell in
the enemy ranks; the prisoners were sent in chains
to Macedonia to hard labour, because though
Greeks they had violated the common resolutions
of the Greeks by fighting with barbarians against
Greece. He sent to Athens three hundred Persian 7
panoplies to be set up to Athena in the acropolis;
he ordered this inscription to be attached: ' Alexander son of Philip and the Greeks, except the
Lacedaemonians, set up these spoils from the barbarians dwelling in Asia'.[4]

17. Alexander then made Calas satrap of the
territory Arsites ruled, ordering the inhabitants to
pay the same taxes as they used to pay to Darius;[1]
natives who came down from the hills and gave themselves up were told to return home. He exempted 2
the city of Zeleia[2] from blame, because he recognized that it had been impressed to fight on the
barbarian side. He also sent Parmenio to take over

---

for the first figure coincides with A's 25 Companions. It looks
as if A's data come from Pt. as his other main source.
    [4] P. 16, 8 has the same formula (from Ar.?). Cf. Introd.
§ 28; 38. For Athenian prisoners see i 29, 5; Introd n. 69.
    [1] See Introd. § 41; Badian, *GR* 166 ff.
    [2] By implication, not otherwise confirmed, Zeleia ranked as
Greek.

πει· καὶ παραλαμβάνει [1] Δασκύλιον Παρμενίων
ἐκλιπόντων τῶν φρουρῶν.

3   Αὐτὸς δὲ ἐπὶ Σάρδεων προὐχώρει· καὶ ἀπέχοντος
αὐτοῦ ὅσον ἑβδομήκοντα σταδίους Σάρδεων ἧκον
παρ' αὐτὸν Μιθρήνης τε ὁ φρούραρχος τῆς ἀκρο-
πόλεως τῆς ἐν Σάρδεσι καὶ Σαρδιανῶν οἱ δυνατώ-
τατοι, ἐνδιδόντες οἱ μὲν τὴν πόλιν, ὁ δὲ Μιθρήνης
4 τὴν ἄκραν καὶ τὰ χρήματα. Ἀλέξανδρος δὲ αὐτὸς
μὲν κατεστρατοπέδευσεν ἐπὶ τῷ Ἕρμῳ ποταμῷ·
ἀπέχει δὲ ὁ Ἕρμος ἀπὸ Σάρδεων σταδίους ὅσον
εἴκοσιν· Ἀμύνταν δὲ τὸν Ἀνδρομένους τὴν ἄκραν
παραληψόμενον ἐκπέμπει ἐς Σάρδεις· καὶ Μιθρήνην
μὲν ἐν τιμῇ ἅμα οἷ ἦγεν, Σαρδιανοὺς δὲ καὶ τοὺς
ἄλλους Λυδοὺς τοῖς νόμοις τε τοῖς πάλαι Λυδῶν
χρῆσθαι ἔδωκεν καὶ ἐλευθέρους εἶναι ἀφῆκεν.
5 ἀνῆλθε δὲ καὶ αὐτὸς εἰς τὴν ἄκραν, ἵνα τὸ φρούριον
ἦν τῶν Περσῶν· καὶ ἔδοξεν αὐτῷ ὀχυρὸν τὸ
χωρίον· ὑπερύψηλόν τε γὰρ ἦν καὶ ἀπότομον πάντῃ
καὶ τριπλᾷ τείχει πεφραγμένον· αὐτὸς δὲ ἐπὶ τῇ
ἄκρᾳ ναόν τε οἰκοδομῆσαι Διὸς Ὀλυμπίου ἐπενόει
6 καὶ βωμὸν ἱδρύσασθαι. σκοποῦντι δὲ αὐτῷ τῆς
ἄκρας ὅπερ ἐπιτηδειότατον χωρίον ὥρᾳ ἔτους
ἐξαίφνης χειμὼν ἐπιγίνεται καὶ βρονταὶ σκληραὶ
καὶ ὕδωρ ἐξ οὐρανοῦ πίπτει, οὗ τὰ τῶν Λυδῶν
βασίλεια· Ἀλεξάνδρῳ δὲ ἔδοξεν ἐκ θεοῦ σημαν-
θῆναι, ἵνα χρὴ οἰκοδομεῖσθαι τῷ Διὶ τὸν νεών, καὶ
7 οὕτως ἐκέλευσε. κατέλιπε δὲ τῆς μὲν ἄκρας τῆς
Σάρδεων ἐπιμελητὴν Παυσανίαν τῶν ἑταίρων, τῶν
δὲ φόρων τῆς συντάξεώς τε καὶ ἀποφορᾶς Νικίαν,
Ἄσανδρον δὲ τὸν Φιλώτα Λυδίας καὶ τῆς ἄλλης τῆς

---

[1] παραλαμβάνει. Roos prints παραληψόμενον, which seems
to be meaningless dittography.

Dascylion, and this he duly did, the guards having evacuated the place.

He himself marched towards Sardis; and when 3 he was still about seventy stades away he was met by Mithrenes, commander of the citadel garrison, and the chief citizens of Sardis; they gave up the city, and Mithrenes the citadel and treasury.[3] Alexander 4 himself camped on the Hermus river, which runs about twenty stades from Sardis, but sent Amyntas, son of Andromenes, to Sardis to take over the citadel; Mithrenes remained with him, with the honours of his rank, while the Sardians and the other Lydians were granted the use of the old Lydian customs, and allowed to be free.[4] Alexander himself ascended to 5 the citadel, where the Persian garrison was stationed. He noted the strength of the position, which was very high, sheer on every side, and fortified all round with a triple wall. He was thinking of building a temple on the citadel to Olympian Zeus, and of setting up an altar near it, but as he was surveying the citadel 6 for the best place, suddenly (it was summer-time) a storm broke with heavy crashes of thunder and violent rain, just where the palace of the Lydian kings was; Alexander supposed that here was a divine intimation where he must build the temple of Zeus, and gave orders accordingly. He left as 7 commandant of the citadel Pausanias, one of the Companions, put Nicias in charge of the assessment and receipt of tribute, and appointed Asander, son

[3] D. 21, 7; P. 17, 1.
[4] i.e. allowed local self-government; the Persians are unlikely to have denied such rights.

Σπιθριδάτου ἀρχῆς, δοὺς αὐτῷ ἱππέας τε καὶ
ψιλοὺς ὅσοι ἱκανοὶ πρὸς τὰ παρόντα ἐδόκουν.

8 Κάλαν δὲ καὶ Ἀλέξανδρον τὸν Ἀερόπου ἐπὶ τὴν
χώραν τὴν Μέμνονος ἐκπέμπει, ἄγοντας τούς τε
Πελοποννησίους καὶ τῶν ἄλλων ξυμμάχων τοὺς
πολλοὺς πλὴν Ἀργείων· οὗτοι δὲ ἐν Σάρδεσι
κατελείφθησαν τὴν ἄκραν φυλάττειν.

9 Ἐν τούτῳ δέ, ὡς τὰ ὑπὲρ τῆς ἱππομαχίας
ἐξηγγέλθη, οἵ τε τὴν Ἔφεσον φρουροῦντες μισθοφόροι ᾤχοντο φεύγοντες, δύο τριήρεις τῶν
Ἐφεσίων λαβόντες, καὶ ξὺν αὐτοῖς Ἀμύντας ὁ
Ἀντιόχου, ὃς ἔφυγεν ἐκ Μακεδονίας Ἀλέξανδρον,
παθὼν μὲν οὐδὲν πρὸς᾽ Ἀλεξάνδρου, δυσνοίᾳ δὲ τῇ
πρὸς Ἀλέξανδρον καὶ αὐτὸς ἀπαξιώσας τι παθεῖν
πρὸς αὐτοῦ ἄχαρι.

10 Τετάρτῃ δὲ ἡμέρᾳ ἐς Ἔφεσον ἀφικόμενος τούς τε
φυγάδας, ὅσοι δι᾽ αὐτὸν ἐξέπεσον τῆς πόλεως,
κατήγαγε καὶ τὴν ὀλιγαρχίαν καταλύσας δημοκρα-
τίαν κατέστησε· τοὺς δὲ φόρους, ὅσους τοῖς
βαρβάροις ἀπέφερον, τῇ Ἀρτέμιδι ξυντελεῖν ἐκέ-
11 λευσεν. ὁ δὲ δῆμος ὁ τῶν Ἐφεσίων, ὡς ἀφῃρέθη
αὐτοῖς ὁ ἀπὸ τῶν ὀλίγων φόβος, τούς τε Μέμνονα
ἐπαγομένους καὶ τοὺς τὸ ἱερὸν συλήσαντας τῆς
Ἀρτέμιδος καὶ τοὺς τὴν εἰκόνα τὴν Φιλίππου τὴν
ἐν τῷ ἱερῷ καταβαλόντας καὶ τὸν τάφον ἐκ τῆς
ἀγορᾶς ἀνορύξαντας τὸν Ἡροπύθου τοῦ ἐλευ-
12 θερώσαντος τὴν πόλιν ὥρμησαν ἀποκτεῖναι. καὶ
Σύρφακα μὲν καὶ τὸν παῖδα αὐτοῦ Πελάγοντα καὶ
τοὺς τῶν ἀδελφῶν τοῦ Σύρφακος παῖδας ἐκ τοῦ
ἱεροῦ ἐξαγαγόντες κατέλευσαν· τοὺς δὲ ἄλλους
διεκώλυσεν Ἀλέξανδρος προσωτέρω ἐπιζητεῖν καὶ
τιμωρεῖσθαι, γνοὺς ὅτι ὁμοῦ τοῖς αἰτίοις καὶ οὐ

of Philotas, governor of Lydia and the rest of   334
Spithridates' district with cavalry and light troops   B.C.
that seemed sufficient for present needs. Calas   8
and Alexander son of Acropus were sent to Memnon's country,[5] with the Peloponnesians and the
greater part of the allies except the Argives who were
left in Sardis to garrison the citadel.

Meanwhile, when the news of the cavalry engage-   9
ment came through, the mercenary troops garrisoning
Ephesus made off, taking two Ephesian triremes;
along with them went Amyntas son of Antiochus [6]
who had fled from Macedon to avoid Alexander;
he had not actually suffered at Alexander's hands,
but he was disaffected and did not think he deserved
to suffer harm at his hands. Alexander reached 10
Ephesus on the fourth day, restored the exiles who
had been turned out of the city on his account, destroyed the oligarchy, and established a democracy;
he also ordered them to contribute to Artemis the
taxes they had been paying to the barbarians. The 11
Ephesian populace, relieved from fear of the oligarchs,
rushed to kill those who had been for calling in
Memnon, those who had plundered the temple of
Artemis, and those who threw down the statue
of Philip in the temple and dug up the tomb of
Heropythes, the liberator of the city, in the market-
place. Syrphax, his son Pelagon, and the sons of 12
the brothers of Syrphax were pulled from the temple
and stoned: but Alexander prevented further in-
quiry or punishment, knowing that once permission
was given the people would put to death innocent

[5] Apparently in the Troad, Polyaenus iv 3, 15; Strabo xiii
1, 11.
[6] Introd. 46.

ξὺν δίκῃ τινάς, τοὺς μὲν κατ' ἔχθραν, τοὺς δὲ κατὰ ἁρπαγὴν χρημάτων ἀποκτενεῖ, ξυγχωρηθὲν αὐτῷ, ὁ δῆμος. καὶ εἰ δή τῳ ἄλλῳ, καὶ τοῖς ἐν Ἐφέσῳ πραχθεῖσιν Ἀλέξανδρος ἐν τῷ τότε εὐδοκίμει.

18. Ἐν τούτῳ δὲ ἐκ Μαγνησίας τε καὶ Τράλλεων παρ' αὐτὸν ἦκον ἐνδιδόντες τὰς πόλεις· καὶ ὃς πέμπει Παρμενίωνα, δοὺς αὐτῷ δισχιλίους καὶ πεντακοσίους πεζοὺς τῶν ξένων καὶ Μακεδόνας παραπλησίους, ἱππέας δὲ τῶν ἑταίρων ἐς διακοσίους. Ἀλκίμαχον δὲ τὸν Ἀγαθοκλέους ἐπὶ τὰς Αἰολίδας τε πόλεις ξὺν δυνάμει οὐκ ἐλάττονι ἐξέπεμψε καὶ ὅσαι Ἰωνικαὶ ὑπὸ τοῖς βαρβάροις ἔτι
2 ἦσαν. καὶ τὰς μὲν ὀλιγαρχίας πανταχοῦ καταλύειν ἐκέλευσεν, δημοκρατίας δὲ [τε] ἐγκαθιστάναι καὶ τοὺς νόμους τοὺς σφῶν ἑκάστοις ἀποδοῦναι, καὶ τοὺς φόρους ἀνεῖναι, ὅσους τοῖς βαρβάροις ἀπέφερον. αὐτὸς δὲ ὑπομείνας ἐν Ἐφέσῳ θυσίαν τε ἔθυσε τῇ Ἀρτέμιδι καὶ πομπὴν ἔπεμψε ξὺν τῇ στρατιᾷ πάσῃ ὡπλισμένῃ τε καὶ ὡς ἐς μάχην ξυντεταγμένῃ.
3 Τῇ δὲ ὑστεραίᾳ ἀναλαβὼν τῶν τε πεζῶν τοὺς λοιποὺς καὶ τοὺς τοξότας καὶ τοὺς Ἀγριᾶνας καὶ τοὺς Θρᾷκας ἱππέας καὶ τῶν ἑταίρων τήν τε βασιλικὴν ἴλην καὶ πρὸς ταύτῃ τρεῖς ἄλλας ἐπὶ Μιλήτου ἐστέλλετο· καὶ τὴν μὲν ἔξω[δον] καλουμένην πόλιν ἐξ ἐφόδου ἔλαβεν ἐκλιπούσης τῆς φυλακῆς· ἐνταῦθα δὲ καταστρατοπεδεύσας ἔγνω ἀποτειχίζειν
4 τὴν εἴσω πόλιν. Ἡγησίστρατος γάρ, ὅτῳ ἡ φρουρὰ ἡ Μιλησίων ἐκ βασιλέως ἐπετέτραπτο, πρόσθεν γράμματα παρ' Ἀλέξανδρον ἔπεμπεν ἐνδιδοὺς τὴν Μίλητον· τότε δὲ ἀναθαρρήσας ἐπὶ τῷ Περσῶν στρατῷ οὐ μακρὰν ὄντι διασώζειν τοῖς

men along with the guilty, from private hatred or in order to seize their property. Seldom did Alexander win a higher reputation than he did on that occasion by his treatment of Ephesus.[7]

18. About this time representatives of Magnesia and Tralles came to Alexander to hand over their cities; so he sent Parmenio with 2,500 mercenary infantry and as many Macedonians, and 200 of the Companion horse. He sent also Alcimachus son of Agathocles, with at least an equal force, to the Aeolian cities and to any Ionian towns still subject to the barbarians. He ordered the oligarchies 2 everywhere to be overthrown and democracies to be established; he restored its own laws to each city and remitted the tribute they used to pay to the barbarians.[1] He himself remained in Ephesus and sacrificed to Artemis and held a great procession with his troops armed *cap-à-pie* in full battle order.

Next day he took the remainder of the infantry, 3 the archers, the Agrianians, the Thracian horse, the royal squadron of the Companions and three others in addition, and marched against Miletus.[2] He captured in his stride what they called the outer city, which the garrison had abandoned, and camping there, decided to invest the inner city. For Hegesi- 4 stratus, to whom Darius had entrusted command of the Milesian garrison, had previously sent a letter to Alexander surrendering the city, but he had taken heart again, because the Persian force was no distance

---

[7] Al. and Ephesus: E. Badian, cited in Introd. n. 59.
[1] Introd. 39 and last note.
[2] D. 22 thinks Memnon was in command at Miletus. A. omits some description of Miletus in Ar. F. 6.

Πέρσαις ἐπενόει τὴν πόλιν. Νικάνωρ δὲ τὸ
Ἑλληνικὸν ναυτικὸν ἄγων ὑποφθάνει τοὺς Πέρσας
τρισὶν ἡμέραις πρότερος καταπλεύσας ἢ τοὺς
Πέρσας Μιλήτῳ προσχεῖν, καὶ ὁρμίζεται ναυσὶν
ἑξήκοντα καὶ ἑκατὸν ἐν τῇ νήσῳ τῇ Λάδῃ· κεῖται
5 δὲ αὕτη ἐπὶ τῇ Μιλήτῳ. αἱ δὲ τῶν Περσῶν νῆες
ὑστερήσασαι, ἐπειδὴ ἔμαθον οἱ ναύαρχοι τῶν ἀμφὶ
Νικάνορα τὴν ἐν τῇ Λάδῃ προκαταγωγήν, πρὸς τῇ
Μυκάλῃ τῷ ὄρει ὡρμίσθησαν. τὴν γὰρ Λάδην τὴν
νῆσον προκατειλήφει Ἀλέξανδρος, οὐ τῶν νεῶν
μόνον τῇ ἐγκαθορμίσει, ἀλλὰ καὶ τοὺς Θρᾷκας καὶ
τῶν ἄλλων ξένων ἐς τετρακισχιλίους διαβιβάσας ἐς
αὐτήν. ἦσαν δὲ τῶν βαρβάρων αἱ νῆες ἀμφὶ τὰς
τετρακοσίας.

6 Παρμενίων μὲν δὴ καὶ ὡς παρῄνει Ἀλεξάνδρῳ
ναυμαχεῖν, τά τε ἄλλα κρατήσειν τῷ ναυτικῷ τοὺς
Ἕλληνας ἐπελπίζων καί τι καὶ θεῖον ἀνέπειθεν
αὐτόν, ὅτι ἀετὸς ὤφθη καθήμενος ἐπὶ τοῦ αἰγιαλοῦ
κατὰ πρύμναν τῶν Ἀλεξάνδρου νεῶν. καὶ γὰρ δὴ
νικήσαντας μὲν μεγάλα ὠφεληθήσεσθαι ἐς τὰ ὅλα,
νικηθεῖσι δὲ οὐ παρὰ μέγα ἔσεσθαι τὸ πταῖσμα·
καὶ ὡς γὰρ θαλασσοκρατεῖν τοὺς Πέρσας. καὶ
αὐτὸς δὲ ἔφη ἐπιβῆναι ἐθέλειν τῶν νεῶν καὶ τοῦ
7 κινδύνου μετέχειν. Ἀλέξανδρος δὲ τῇ τε γνώμῃ
ἁμαρτάνειν ἔφη Παρμενίωνα καὶ τοῦ σημείου τῇ οὐ
κατὰ τὸ εἰκὸς ξυμβλήσει· ὀλίγαις τε γὰρ ναυσὶ
πρὸς πολλῷ πλείους ξὺν οὐδενὶ λογισμῷ ναυμα-
χήσειν καὶ οὐ μεμελετηκότι τῷ σφῶν ναυτικῷ
⟨πρὸς⟩ προησκημένον τὸ τῶν Κυπρίων τε καὶ
8 Φοινίκων· τήν τε ἐμπειρίαν τῶν Μακεδόνων καὶ
τὴν τόλμαν ἐν ἀβεβαίῳ χωρίῳ οὐκ ἐθέλειν παραδοῦναι τοῖς βαρβάροις· καὶ ἡττηθεῖσι τῇ ναυμαχίᾳ οὐ

away; his intention was now to save the city for Persia.
Nicanor, however, brought up the Greek fleet,[3]
reached Miletus by sea three days before the
Persians put in, and anchored with 160 ships at the
island of Lade off Miletus. The Persian fleet were too 5
late, and when their commanders learnt that Nicanor
had already put in at Lade, they anchored under
Mount Mycale. For by seizing Lade Alexander
had forestalled them, not only anchoring his fleet
there, but also transporting the Thracians and about
4000 of the other mercenaries to the island. The
barbarians had about 400 ships.

Parmenio, notwithstanding, urged Alexander to 6
fight by sea; he expected the Greeks to win with
their fleet for various reasons, and in particular he used
an omen to persuade him: an eagle had been seen
perching on the shore astern of Alexander's ships.
If they won, he argued, it would be of great advantage to the expedition generally, whereas a defeat
would not be very serious; for even as things were
the Persians held supremacy at sea. He said that
he was willing even to embark himself and share the
peril. Alexander, however, said that Parmenio's 7
judgment was at fault, and his interpretation of the
omen improbable; it would be wholly irrational to
fight a much greater fleet with an inferior one, and
face the trained Cyprian and Phoenician fleet with
his own, which was unpractised. He would not risk 8
sacrificing the experience and daring of the Macedonians to the barbarians on so uncertain an element;

[3] Cf. §6; 19, 7. Evidently the fleet was mainly provided by
the Greek allies (cf. QC. iii 1, 20), since A. is careful to distinguish Greeks from Macedonians (Introd. n. 33), though
Macedonians would presumably serve as marines in a battle
(§8). Numbers of Greek and Persian ships: App. II 1. Cf.
Introd. 44.

μικρὰν τὴν βλάβην ἔσεσθαι ἐς τοῦ πολέμου τὴν
πρώτην δόξαν, τά τε ἄλλα καὶ τοὺς Ἕλληνας
νεωτεριεῖν πρὸς τοῦ ναυτικοῦ πταίσματος τὴν
9 ἐξαγγελίαν ἐπαρθέντας. ταῦτα μὲν τῷ λογισμῷ
ξυντιθεὶς οὐκ ἐν καιρῷ ἀπέφαινε ναυμαχεῖν· τὸ
θεῖον δὲ αὐτὸς ἄλλῃ ἐξηγεῖσθαι· εἶναι μὲν γὰρ πρὸς
αὐτοῦ τὸν ἀετόν, ἀλλ' ὅτι ἐπὶ γῇ καθήμενος
ἐφαίνετο, δοκεῖν οἱ μᾶλλόν τι σημαίνειν, ὅτι ἐκ γῆς
κρατήσει τοῦ Περσῶν ναυτικοῦ.

19. Καὶ ἐν τούτῳ Γλαύκιππος, ἀνὴρ τῶν δοκί-
μων ἐν Μιλήτῳ, ἐκπεμφθεὶς παρὰ Ἀλέξανδρον
παρὰ τοῦ δήμου τε καὶ τῶν ξένων τῶν μισθοφόρων,
οἷς μᾶλλόν τι ἐπετέτραπτο ἡ πόλις, τά τε τείχη
ἔφη ἐθέλειν τοὺς Μιλησίους καὶ τοὺς λιμένας
παρέχειν κοινοὺς Ἀλεξάνδρῳ καὶ Πέρσαις καὶ τὴν
2 πολιορκίαν ἐπὶ τούτοις λύειν ἠξίου. Ἀλέξανδρος
δὲ Γλαυκίππῳ μὲν προστάσσει ἀπαλλάττεσθαι κατὰ
τάχος ἐς τὴν πόλιν καὶ Μιλησίοις ἀπαγγέλλειν
παρασκευάζεσθαι ὡς μαχουμένους ἕωθεν. αὐτὸς δ'
ἐπιστήσας τῷ τείχει μηχανάς, καὶ τὰ μὲν καταβα-
λὼν δι' ὀλίγου τῶν τειχῶν, τὰ δὲ κατασείσας ἐπὶ
πολὺ προσῆγε τὴν στρατιὰν ὡς ἐπιβησομένους ᾗ
κατερήριπτο ἢ ἐσεσάλευτο τὸ τεῖχος, ἐφομαρτού-
ντων καὶ μόνον οὐ θεωμένων τῶν Περσῶν ἀπὸ τῆς
Μυκάλης πολιορκουμένους τοὺς φίλους σφῶν καὶ
ξυμμάχους.

3 Ἐν τούτῳ δὲ καὶ οἱ ἀμφὶ Νικάνορα ἀπὸ τῆς
Λάδης τὴν ὁρμὴν τῶν ξὺν Ἀλεξάνδρῳ κατιδόντες
ἐς τὸν λιμένα ἐπέπλεον τῶν Μιλησίων παρὰ γῆν τὴν
εἰρεσίαν ποιούμενοι, καὶ κατὰ τὸ στόμα τοῦ
λιμένος, ᾗπερ τὸ στενότατον ἦν, ἀντιπρώρους βύζην
τὰς τριήρεις ὁρμίσαντες ἀποκεκλείκεσαν τῷ μὲν

if they lost the engagement, it would be a serious 334 B.C. blow to their initial prestige in the war, especially with the Greeks also ready to blaze into revolt at the news of a naval defeat. Adducing these rational 9 arguments, he showed that it was no time to fight by sea, and that he interpreted the omen differently: the eagle was indeed on his side but, since it was seen sitting on the land, it rather meant (he thought) that he would beat the Persian fleet from the land.[4]

19. Meanwhile, Glaucippus, one of the notables of Miletus, was sent to Alexander by the people and the foreign mercenaries to whose care the city had been chiefly entrusted, and declared that the citizens were prepared to open their walls and harbours to Alexander and the Persians in common; he demanded that on these terms he should raise the siege. Alexander, however, ordered Glaucippus to leave 2 without delay for the city and tell the Milesians to be ready to fight at dawn. He personally saw to engines being set against the wall and, after knocking down part of the walling for a little way, and shattering it over a great distance, he brought up his force to be ready to go over where the wall had been demolished or shaken, though the Persians from Mycale were close by and all but witnesses of the siege of their friends and allies.

At this point Nicanor's fleet from Lade, which 3 had sighted Alexander's attack and sailed into the harbour of Miletus, rowing along the coast, jammed their triremes, with prows facing an enemy attack, at the narrowest part of the entrance, and so barred

[4] Cf. 20, 1.

Περσικῷ ναυτικῷ τὸν λιμένα, τοῖς Μιλησίοις δὲ
4 τὴν ἐκ τῶν Περσῶν ὠφέλειαν. ἔνθα οἱ Μιλήσιοί τε
καὶ οἱ μισθοφόροι πανταχόθεν ἤδη προσκειμένων
σφίσι τῶν Μακεδόνων οἱ μὲν αὐτῶν ῥιπτοῦντες
σφᾶς ἐν τῇ θαλάσσῃ ἐπὶ τῶν ἀσπίδων ὑπτίων ἐς
νησῖδά τινα ἀνώνυμον τῇ πόλει ἐπικειμένην διε-
νήχοντο, οἱ δὲ ἐς κελήτια ἐμβαίνοντες καὶ ἐπειγόμενοι ὑποφθάσαι τὰς τριήρεις τῶν Μακεδόνων
ἐγκατελήφθησαν ἐν τῷ στόματι τοῦ λιμένος πρὸς
τῶν τριήρων· οἱ δὲ πολλοὶ ἐν αὐτῇ τῇ πόλει
ἀπώλοντο.

5 Ἀλέξανδρος δὲ ἐχομένης ἤδη τῆς πόλεως ἐπὶ
τοὺς ἐς τὴν νῆσον καταπεφευγότας ἐπέπλει αὐτός,
κλίμακας φέρειν ἐπὶ τὰς πρῴρας τῶν τριήρων
κελεύσας, ὡς κατὰ τὰ ἀπότομα τῆς νήσου, καθάπερ
πρὸς τεῖχος, ἐκ τῶν νεῶν τὴν ἀπόβασιν ποιησόμε-
6 νος. ὡς δὲ διακινδυνεύειν ἐθέλοντας τοὺς ἐν τῇ
νήσῳ ἑώρα, οἶκτος λαμβάνει αὐτὸν τῶν ἀνδρῶν, ὅτι
γενναῖοί τε καὶ πιστοὶ αὐτῷ ἐφαίνοντο, καὶ
σπένδεται πρὸς αὐτοὺς ἐπὶ τῷδε ὡς αὑτῷ ξυστρα-
τεύειν· ἦσαν δὲ οὗτοι μισθοφόροι Ἕλληνες ἐς
τριακοσίους. αὐτοὺς δὲ Μιλησίους, ὅσοι μὴ ἐν τῇ
καταλήψει τῆς πόλεως ἔπεσον, ἀφῆκεν καὶ ἐλευθέρους εἶναι ἔδωκεν.

7 Οἱ δὲ βάρβαροι ἀπὸ τῆς Μυκάλης ὁρμώμενοι τὰς
μὲν ἡμέρας ἐπέπλεον τῷ Ἑλληνικῷ ναυτικῷ,
προκαλέσεσθαι ἐς ναυμαχίαν ἐλπίζοντες· τὰς δὲ
νύκτας πρὸς τῇ Μυκάλῃ οὐκ ἐν καλῷ ὡρμίζοντο,
ὅτι ὑδρεύεσθαι ἀπὸ τοῦ Μαιάνδρου ποταμοῦ τῶν
8 ἐκβολῶν διὰ μακροῦ ἠναγκάζοντο. Ἀλέξανδρος δὲ
ταῖς μὲν ναυσὶ τὸν λιμένα ἐφύλαττε τῶν Μιλησίων,
ὡς μὴ βιάσαιντο οἱ βάρβαροι τὸν ἔσπλουν, ἐκπέμ-

the harbour against the Persian fleet, and cut off Persian help for Miletus. Then, as the Milesians 4 and mercenaries were hard pressed on all sides by the Macedonians, some threw themselves into the sea and inverting their shields paddled over to a little nameless island off the city, while others got into small boats and hurried to get in front of the Macedonian triremes, but were caught by them at the harbour entrance; the greatest number perished in the city itself.

With the city now under control, Alexander sailed 5 in person against those who had fled to the islet, ordering ladders to be brought to the bows of the triremes, so as to disembark from the ships on the cliffs of the island as if on a city wall. But when he 6 saw that the men on the island were going to fight to the death, he was seized with pity for them, as fine, loyal soldiers, and made terms with them on which they should join his forces; there were about 300 of these Greek mercenaries. The Milesians themselves who had not fallen at the city's capture were released and granted their freedom.

The Persians with Mycale as a base by day-time 7 used to sail towards the Greek navy,[1] hoping to provoke an engagement; but at night they could not ride in comfort at Mycale, because they were obliged to get water from the mouths of the Maeander, some way off. While guarding the harbour of 8 Miletus with his fleet, so that the Persians might not force the entrance, Alexander sent Philotas to

---

[1] Cf. 18, 4 n.

πει δ' ἐς τὴν Μυκάλην Φιλώταν, ἄγοντα τούς τε
ἱππέας καὶ τῶν πεζῶν τάξεις τρεῖς, παραγγείλας
εἴργειν τῆς ἀποβάσεως τοὺς ἀπὸ τῶν νεῶν. οἱ δέ,
ὕδατός τε σπάνει καὶ τῶν ἄλλων ἐπιτηδείων οὐδὲν
ἄλλο ὅτι μὴ πολιορκούμενοι ἐν ταῖς ναυσίν, ἐς
Σάμον ἀπέπλευσαν. ἐκεῖθεν δὲ ἐπισιτισάμενοι
9 αὖθις ἐπέπλεον τῇ Μιλήτῳ· καὶ τὰς μὲν πολλὰς
τῶν νεῶν πρὸ τοῦ λιμένος ἐν μετεώρῳ παρέταξαν,
εἴ πῃ ἐκκαλέσαιντο ἐς τὸ πέλαγος τοὺς Μακεδόνας,
πέντε δὲ αὐτῶν εἰσέπλευσαν ἐς τὸν μεταξὺ τῆς τε
Λάδης νήσου καὶ τοῦ στρατοπέδου λιμένα, ἐλπί-
σαντες κενὰς καταλήψεσθαι τὰς Ἀλεξάνδρου ναῦς,
ὅτι τοὺς ναύτας ἀποσκεδάννυσθαι τὸ πολὺ ἀπὸ τῶν
νεῶν τοὺς μὲν ἐπὶ φρυγανισμῷ, τοὺς δὲ ἐπὶ
ξυγκομιδῇ τῶν ἐπιτηδείων, τοὺς δὲ καὶ ἐς προνο-
10 μὰς ταττομένους, πεπυσμένοι ἦσαν. ἀλλὰ μέρος
μέν τι ἀπῆν τῶν ναυτῶν, ἐκ δὲ τῶν παρόντων
ξυμπληρώσας Ἀλέξανδρος δέκα ναῦς, ὡς προσ-
πλεούσας τὰς πέντε τῶν Περσῶν κατεῖδε, πέμπει
ἐπ' αὐτὰς κατὰ σπουδήν, ἐμβάλλειν ἀντιπρώρους
κελεύσας. οἱ δὲ ἐν ταῖς πέντε ναυσὶ τῶν Περσῶν,
ὡς παρ' ἐλπίδα ἀναγομένους τοὺς Μακεδόνας ἐπὶ
σφᾶς εἶδον, ὑποστρέψαντες ἐκ πολλοῦ ἔφευγον πρὸς
11 τὸ ἄλλο ναυτικόν. καὶ ἡ μὲν Ἰασσέων ναῦς
ἁλίσκεται αὐτοῖς ἀνδράσιν ἐν τῇ φυγῇ, οὐ ταχυναυ-
τοῦσα· αἱ δὲ τέσσαρες ἔφθασαν καταφυγεῖν ἐς τὰς
οἰκείας τριήρεις. οὕτω μὲν δὴ ἀπέπλευσαν ἄπρακτοι ἐκ Μιλήτου οἱ Πέρσαι.

20. Ἀλέξανδρος δὲ καταλῦσαι ἔγνω τὸ ναυτικὸν
χρημάτων τε ἐν τῷ τότε ἀπορίᾳ καὶ ἅμα οὐκ
ἀξιόμαχον ὁρῶν τὸ αὑτοῦ ναυτικὸν τῷ Περσικῷ,
οὔκουν ἐθέλων οὐδὲ μέρει τινὶ τῆς στρατιᾶς κινδυ-

Mycale with the cavalry and three battalions of
infantry, instructing him to hinder the Persians
from disembarking. So, from want of water and
other necessities, they were as good as besieged in
their ships, and sailed off to Samos; after provisioning there, they made for Miletus again. They 9
drew up most of their ships in line out at sea opposite
the harbour, hoping to provoke the Macedonians to
action in the open water; but five ships slipped into
the harbour between Lade and the camp, hoping to
capture Alexander's ships unmanned, as they had
learned that most of the crews had scattered, away
from the ships, under instructions to get firewood
or collect provisions or fodder. But though a certain 10
number of sailors were absent, Alexander had manned
ten ships with the available hands, which he sent,
when he sighted the five Persian ships bearing down,
to meet them at full speed with orders to ram, head
on. The crews of the five Persian ships, seeing the
Macedonians making for them (the last thing they
expected), doubled back, while still far off, and
joined the main fleet. One ship (manned by 11
Iassians) was captured with its crew in the retreat,
as it was a slow sailer; the other four got safe to their
own triremes. Hence the Persians sailed away
from Miletus without success.[2]

20. Alexander now decided to disband his navy, as
he was then short of money and also perceived that
his fleet could not face an action with the Persian
navy; he was unwilling to risk disaster with even part
of his forces. Further, he reflected that as he now

[2] D. 22 is vague on operations at Miletus.

νεύειν. ἄλλως τε ἐπενόει, κατέχων ἤδη τῷ πεζῷ
τὴν 'Ασίαν, ὅτι οὔτε ναυτικοῦ ἔτι δέοιτο, τάς τε
παραλίους πόλεις λαβὼν καταλύσει τὸ Περσῶν
ναυτικόν, οὔτε ὁπόθεν τὰς ὑπηρεσίας συμπληρώ-
σουσιν οὔτε ὅποι τῆς 'Ασίας προσέξουσιν ἔχοντας.
καὶ τὸν ἀετὸν ταύτῃ συνέβαλλεν, ὅτι ἐσήμηνεν
αὐτῷ ἐκ τῆς γῆς κρατήσειν τῶν νεῶν.

2   Ταῦτα δὲ διαπραξάμενος ἐπὶ Καρίας ἐστέλλετο,
ὅτι ἐν 'Αλικαρνασσῷ συνεστηκέναι οὐ φαύλην
δύναμιν τῶν τε βαρβάρων καὶ ξένων ἐξηγγέλλετο.
ὅσαι δὲ ἐν μέσῳ πόλεις Μιλήτου τε καὶ 'Αλικαρνασ-
σοῦ, ταύτας ἐξ ἐφόδου λαβὼν καταστρατοπεδεύει
πρὸς 'Αλικαρνασσῷ, ἀπέχων τῆς πόλεως ἐς πέντε
3   μάλιστα σταδίους, ὡς ἐπὶ χρονίῳ πολιορκίᾳ. ἥ τε
γὰρ φύσις τοῦ χωρίου ὀχυρὸν ἐποίει αὐτὸ καὶ ὅπῃ
τι ἐνδεῖν ὡς πρὸς ἀσφάλειαν ἐφαίνετο, ξύμπαντα
ταῦτα Μέμνων τε αὐτὸς παρών, ἤδη ἀποδεδειγ-
μένος πρὸς Δαρείου τῆς τε κάτω 'Ασίας καὶ τοῦ
ναυτικοῦ παντὸς ἡγεμών, ἐκ πολλοῦ παρεσκευάκει,
καὶ στρατιῶται πολλοὶ μὲν ξένοι μισθοφόροι ἐν
τῇ πόλει ἐγκατελείφθησαν, πολλοὶ δὲ καὶ Περσῶν
αὐτῶν, αἵ τε τριήρεις ἐφώρμουν τῷ λιμένι, ὡς καὶ
ἀπὸ τῶν ναυτῶν πολλὴν ὠφέλειαν γίγνεσθαι ἐς τὰ
ἔργα.

4   Τῇ μὲν δὴ πρώτῃ ἡμέρᾳ προσάγοντος 'Αλεξάνδρου τῷ τείχει κατὰ τὰς ἐπὶ Μύλασα φερούσας
πύλας ἐκδρομή τε γίγνεται τῶν ἐκ τῆς πόλεως καὶ
ἀκροβολισμός· καὶ τούτους οὐ χαλεπῶς ἀνέστειλάν
τε οἱ παρ' 'Αλεξάνδρου ἀντεκδραμόντες καὶ ἐς τὴν
πόλιν κατέκλεισαν.

5   Οὐ πολλαῖς δὲ ὕστερον ἡμέραις 'Αλέξανδρος
ἀναλαβὼν τούς τε ὑπασπιστὰς καὶ τὴν τῶν ἑταίρων

controlled Asia with his land troops, he no longer needed a navy, and that by capturing the cities on the coast he would break up the Persian fleet, since they would have nowhere to make up their crews from, and no place in Asia where they could put in. This was what he took the eagle to mean; he was to overcome the ships from dry land.[1]

When he had carried out this decision, he marched 2 towards Caria, on reports that a considerable force of barbarians and mercenaries had mustered at Halicarnassus.[2] He captured on the march the cities between Miletus and Halicarnassus, and encamped against Halicarnassus, at about five stades distance, settling down for a long siege. For the nature of the 3 site made it strong, and where any defect in its security was apparent, Memnon, who was present in person and had now been appointed by Darius to the command of lower Asia and the whole fleet,[3] had made all the necessary preparations long ago; a large force of foreign mercenaries had been left in the city, with many of the Persians themselves; the triremes were guarding the harbour, so that the sailors too lent much assistance to the operations.

On the first day, as Alexander was approaching the 4 wall near the gate leading to Mylasa, there was a sally from the men in the city and volleying at safe distance; Alexander's troops had no difficulty in driving back the assailants by a counter charge, and shut them up in the city.

A few days later Alexander took the hypaspists, the 5 Companion cavalry and the infantry battalions of

[1] At present Al. was probably thinking only of the coast of Asia Minor; after Issus he continued the same strategy (ii 17). Cf. D. 22, 5-23, 3; P. 17, 2; Introd. 44; App. II.

[2] For operations in Caria cf. D. 23, 4-27, 6.

[3] D. 23, 5 f.

ἵππον καὶ τὴν Ἀμύντου τε καὶ Περδίκκου καὶ
Μελάγρου τάξιν τὴν πεζικὴν καὶ πρὸς τούτοις τοὺς
τοξότας καὶ τοὺς Ἀγριᾶνας περιῆλθε τῆς πόλεως
ἐς τὸ πρὸς Μύνδον μέρος, τό τε τεῖχος κατοψό-
μενος, εἰ ταύτῃ ἐπιμαχώτερον τυγχάνει ὂν ἐς τὴν
προσβολήν, καὶ ἅμα εἰ τὴν Μύνδον ἐξ ἐπιδρομῆς
δύναιτο λαθὼν κατασχεῖν· ἔσεσθαι γὰρ οὐ σμικρὰν
τὴν ὠφέλειαν ἐς τὴν τῆς Ἁλικαρνασσοῦ πολιορκίαν τὴν Μύνδον οἰκείαν γενομένην· καί τι ⟨καὶ⟩
ἐνεδίδοτο αὐτῷ ἐκ τῶν Μυνδίων, εἰ λάθοι νυκτὸς
6 προσελθών. αὐτὸς μὲν δὴ κατὰ τὰ ξυγκείμενα
ἀμφὶ μέσας νύκτας προσῆλθε τῷ τείχει· ὡς δὲ
οὐδὲν ἐνεδίδοτο ἀπὸ τῶν ἔνδον, αἵ τε μηχαναὶ καὶ αἱ
κλίμακες αὐτῷ οὐ παρῆσαν, οἷα δὴ οὐκ ἐπὶ πολιορκίαν σταλέντι, ἀλλ’ ὡς ἐπὶ προδοσίᾳ ἐνδιδομένης
τῆς πόλεως, προσήγαγε καὶ ὡς τῶν Μακεδόνων
τὴν φάλαγγα, ὑπορύττειν κελεύσας τὸ τεῖχος. καὶ
ἕνα γε πύργον κατέβαλον οἱ Μακεδόνες, οὐ μέντοι
7 ἐγύμνωσέ γε τὸ τεῖχος πεσών· καὶ οἱ ἐκ τῆς
πόλεως ἅμα εὐρώστως ἀμυνόμενοι καὶ ἐκ τῆς
Ἁλικαρνασσοῦ κατὰ θάλασσαν πολλοὶ ἤδη παρα-
βεβοηθηκότες ἄπορον ἐποίησαν τῷ Ἀλεξάνδρῳ τὴν
αὐτοσχέδιόν τε καὶ ἐξ ἐπιδρομῆς κατάληψιν τῆς
Μύνδου. οὕτω μὲν δὴ ἐπανέρχεται Ἀλέξανδρος
οὐδὲν πράξας, ὧν ἕνεκα ὡρμήθη, καὶ τῇ πολιορκίᾳ
τῆς Ἁλικαρνασσοῦ αὖθις προσεῖχε.
8 Καὶ πρῶτα μὲν τὴν τάφρον, ἣ πρὸ τῆς πόλεως
ὀρώρυκτο αὐτοῖς, πλάτος μὲν τριάκοντα μάλιστα
πηχῶν, τὸ δὲ βάθος ἐς πεντεκαίδεκα, ἐχώννυε, τοῦ
ῥᾳδίαν εἶναι τὴν προσαγωγὴν τῶν τε πύργων, ἀφ’
ὧν ἔμελλε τοὺς ἀκροβολισμοὺς ἐς τοὺς προμαχομένους τοῦ τείχους ποιεῖσθαι, καὶ τῶν ἄλλων

Amyntas, Perdiccas, and Meleager, with the archers
also and the Agrianes, and went round the city to
the side that lay towards Myndus,[4] to reconnoitre the
wall in case it should prove more open to an assault
there, and also to see if perhaps he could capture
Myndus by a sudden raid. The possession of
Myndus, he thought, would be a great help to the
siege of Halicarnassus. A proposal of surrender
had been received from the Myndians, provided
he could approach secretly by night. He there- 6
fore in person approached the wall about midnight,
as agreed; but there was no sign of surrender from
the people inside; his engines and ladders had been
left behind, naturally enough, since he had not come
for a siege, but to receive a treacherous surrender
of the city. None the less he brought up the Macedonian phalanx with orders to sap the wall. They did
bring down one tower, but its fall did not strip the
wall; the citizens resisted stubbornly, and by this 7
time numerous troops had sailed up from Halicarnassus and deprived Alexander of the means of
rushing the capture of Myndus without preparation. So Alexander retreated without effecting his
purpose, and concentrated once more on the siege
of Halicarnassus.

First he began to fill up the moat they had dug 8
before the city, about 30 cubits broad and 15 deep, so
as to facilitate the approach of the siege-towers,
from which he intended to shower missiles on the
defenders of the wall, and of the other engines with

A Carian town.

9 μηχανῶν, αἷς κατασείειν ἐπενόει τὸ τεῖχος. καὶ ἥ
τε τάφρος αὐτῷ ἐχώσθη οὐ χαλεπῶς καὶ οἱ πύργοι
προσήγοντο ἤδη. οἱ δὲ ἐκ τῆς Ἁλικαρνασσοῦ
νυκτὸς ἐκδραμόντες, ὡς ἐμπρῆσαι τούς τε πύργους
καὶ ὅσαι ἄλλαι μηχαναὶ προσηγμέναι ἢ οὐ πόρρω
τοῦ προ⟨σ⟩άγεσθαι ἦσαν, ὑπὸ τῶν φυλακῶν τε
τῶν Μακεδόνων καὶ ὅσοι ἐν αὐτῷ τῷ ἔργῳ
ἐξεγερθέντες παρεβοήθησαν οὐ χαλεπῶς κατεκλεί-
10 σθησαν ἐς τὰ τείχη αὖθις. καὶ ἀπέθανον αὐτῶν
ἄλλοι τε ἐς ἑβδομήκοντα καὶ ἑκατὸν καὶ Νεοπτόλεμος ὁ Ἀρραβαίου, τοῦ Ἀμύντου ἀδελφός, τῶν
παρὰ Δαρεῖον αὐτομολησάντων· τῶν δὲ Ἀλεξάνδρου στρατιωτῶν ἀπέθανον μὲν ἐς ἑκκαίδεκα,
τραυματίαι δὲ ἐγένοντο ἐς τριακοσίους, ὅτι ἐν νυκτὶ
γενομένης τῆς ἐκδρομῆς ἀφυλακτότεροι ἐς τὸ
τιτρώσκεσθαι ἦσαν.

21. Οὐ πολλαῖς δὲ ἡμέραις ὕστερον δύο τῶν
Μακεδόνων ὁπλῖται ἐκ τῆς [ὕστερον] Περδίκκου
τάξεως ξυσκηνοῦντές τε καὶ ἅμα ξυμπίνοντες
αὐτόν τε καὶ τὰ αὐτοῦ ἑκάτερος ἐπὶ μέγα τῷ λόγῳ
ἦγεν. ἔνθα δὴ φιλοτιμία τε ἐσπίπτει αὐτοῖς, καί τι
καὶ ὁ οἶνος ὑπεθέρμαινεν, ὥστε ὁπλισάμενοι αὐτοὶ
ἐπὶ σφῶν προσβάλλουσι τῷ τείχει κατὰ τὴν ἄκραν
τὴν πρὸς Μύλασα μάλιστα τετραμμένην, ὡς
ἐπίδειξιν τῆς σφῶν ῥώμης μᾶλλόν τι ἢ πρὸς
πολεμίους μετὰ κινδύνου τὸν ἀγῶνα ποιησόμενοι.
2 καὶ τούτους κατιδόντες τινὲς τῶν ἐκ τῆς πόλεως
δύο τε ὄντας καὶ οὐ ξὺν λογισμῷ προσφερομένους
τῷ τείχει ἐπεκθέουσιν. οἱ δὲ τοὺς μὲν ἐγγὺς πελάσαντας ἀπέκτειναν, πρὸς δὲ τοὺς ἀφεστηκότας

---

[5] See E. W. Marsden, *Greek and Roman Artillery*, esp. ch. II
and p. 101. For plan see Fuller 201.

which he designed to batter down the wall.[5] The 9   334
ditch was filled up by him without difficulty and he   B.C.
began at once to bring up the towers. The garrison
of Halicarnassus, however, made a night sally, to
burn the towers and the other engines which had
been brought up, or were nearly in position. But
they were easily enclosed again in their city walls
by the Macedonian guards and others who were
aroused in the course of the action itself and rushed
to their help. They lost up to 170 men, including 10
Neoptolemus son of Arrabaeus, brother of Amyntas,
one of those who had deserted to Darius: up to
sixteen of Alexander's troops fell, but three hundred
were wounded, since the sally was at night and they
were less protected against wounds.[6]

21. Not many days after, two Macedonian men-
at-arms of Perdiccas' battalion, who were bivouacked
and drinking together, were each boasting of his
own prowess and actions: rivalry arose, assisted by
the heating fumes of wine; so they armed themselves and attacked the wall by the height which
looks chiefly towards Mylasa, their idea being to
exhibit their strength rather than to force a perilous
encounter with the enemy.[1] Some of those in the 2
city sighted them, only two men rashly approaching
the wall, and made a dash out at them. But they
killed those who came up close and discharged

---

[6] D. 24, 4–25, 5 supplements § 7–10, but makes Neoptolemus
fall on the Macedonian side, rightly according to Welles *ad loc.*
since Amyntas remained in Al's favour; but he is last mentioned in 28, 4, and Alexander the Lyncestian was still employed after his brothers had been executed for treason (25);
an error in A's Macedonian sources is less likely than a careless
assumption by D. that a Macedonian notable *must* have fought
for Alexander.

[1] D. 25, 5 f.

ἠκροβολίζοντο, πλεονεκτούμενοι τῷ τε πλήθει καὶ
τοῦ χωρίου τῇ χαλεπότητι, ὅτι ἐξ ὑπερδεξίου τοῖς
πολεμίοις ἡ ἐπιδρομή τε καὶ ὁ ἀκροβολισμὸς

3 ἐγίνετο. καὶ ἐν τούτῳ ἀντεκθέουσί τινες καὶ ἄλλοι
τῶν τοῦ Περδίκκου στρατιωτῶν, καὶ ἀπὸ τῆς
Ἁλικαρνασσοῦ ἄλλοι καὶ ξυμπίπτει μάχη καρτερὰ
πρὸς τῷ τείχει· καὶ κατακλείονται αὖθις πρὸς τῶν
Μακεδόνων εἴσω τῶν πυλῶν οἱ ἐπεκδραμόντες.

4 παρ' ὀλίγον δὲ ἦλθε καὶ ἁλῶναι ἡ πόλις. τά τε
γὰρ τείχη ἐν τῷ τότε οὐκ ἐν ἀκριβεῖ φυλακῇ ἦν καὶ
δύο πύργοι καὶ μεσοπύργιον ἐς ἔδαφος καταπεπτω-
κότα οὐ χαλεπὴν ἂν τῷ στρατεύματι, εἰ ἅπαν προσήψατο τοῦ ἔργου, τὴν ἐς τὸ τεῖχος πάροδον παρέσχε, καὶ ὁ τρίτος πύργος κατασεσεισμένος οὐδὲ οὗτος
χαλεπῶς ἂν ἠρίφθη ὑπορυσσόμενος· ἀλλὰ ἔφθησαν
γὰρ ἀντὶ τοῦ πεπτωκότος τείχους ἔσωθεν πλίνθινον
μηνοειδὲς ἀντοικοδομησάμενοι οὐ χαλεπῶς ὑπὸ
πολυχειρίας.

5 Καὶ τούτῳ ἐπῆγε τῇ ὑστεραίᾳ τὰς μηχανὰς
Ἀλέξανδρος· καὶ ἐκδρομὴ αὖθις γίγνεται τῶν ἐκ
τῆς πόλεως ἐπὶ τῷ ἐμπρῆσαι τὰς μηχανάς. καὶ
μέρος μέν τι τῶν πλησίον τοῦ τείχους γέρρων καὶ
ἑνὸς τῶν πύργων τῶν ξυλίνων κατεκαύθη, τὰ δὲ
ἄλλα διεφύλαξαν οἱ περὶ Φιλώταν τε καὶ Ἑλλά-
νικον, οἷς ἡ φυλακὴ αὐτῶν ἐπετέτραπτο· ὡς δὲ καὶ
Ἀλέξανδρος ἐπεφάνη ἐν τῇ ἐκδρομῇ, τάς τε δᾷδας,
ὅσας ἔχοντες ἐκβεβοηθήκεσαν, ἀφέντες καὶ τὰ ὅπλα
οἱ πολλοὶ αὐτῶν ῥίψαντες εἴσω τοῦ τείχους

6 ἔφευγον. καίτοι τά γε πρῶτα τῇ φύσει τε τοῦ
χωρίου, ὑπερδεξίου ὄντος, ἐπεκράτουν καὶ οὐ κατὰ
μέτωπον μόνον ἠκροβολίζοντο ἐς τοὺς προμαχομένους τῶν μηχανῶν, ἀλλὰ καὶ ἐκ τῶν πύργων, οἳ

missiles at the more distant enemies, though they 334
were at a disadvantage in numbers and in the diffi- B.C.
culty of the ground; the enemy could charge or volley
on them from above. At this point more of Perdiccas' 3
men hurried up, and others from the city too, and a
stiff fight was joined near the wall. Once more the
Macedonians drove the sallying force back inside the
gates, and indeed the city was not far from being
captured. For at the time the walls were not care- 4
fully guarded, and as two towers and one intervening curtain [2] had fallen to their foundations,
the approach to the wall would have been easy for
the army, if all had applied themselves to the business. The third tower, moreover, had been badly
shaken, and if undermined would itself easily have
been brought down, but the besieged anticipated
this by building on the inner side, in place of the
wall where it had collapsed, a crescent-shaped brick
structure; [3] as they had many hands, this was easy
work.

Next day Alexander brought up his engines against 5
this wall; again a sally was made by those in the city
to burn them. Part of the fence of mantlets near the
walls and part of one of the wooden towers were
burnt down; the rest was saved by Philotas and
Hellanicus and their men, who had been entrusted
with their protection. But when Alexander also
appeared in the sally, they dropped the torches
with which they had rushed out to attack, and most
cast away their arms and escaped within the wall. [4]
Yet at first, from the nature of their commanding 6
position, the besieged had the best of it, and they used
to fire at the force protecting the engines not
only from in front but also from the towers which

[2] D. 25, 5.   [3] D. 26, 6.   [4] Not in D.

δὴ ἑκατέρωθεν τοῦ ἐρηριμμένου τείχους αὐτοὶ
ὑπολελειμμένοι ἐκ πλαγίου τε καὶ μόνον οὐ κατὰ
νώτου παρεῖχον ἀκροβολίζεσθαι ἐς τοὺς τῷ
ἀντῳκοδομημένῳ τείχει προσάγοντας.

22. Οὐ πολλαῖς δὲ ὕστερον ἡμέραις ἐπάγοντος
αὖθις Ἀλεξάνδρου τὰς μηχανὰς τῷ πλινθίνῳ τῷ
ἐντὸς τείχει καὶ αὐτοῦ ἐφεστηκότος τῷ ἔργῳ,
ἐκδρομὴ γίνεται πανδημεὶ ἐκ τῆς πόλεως, τῶν μὲν
κατὰ τὸ ἐρηριμμένον τεῖχος, ᾗ αὐτὸς Ἀλέξανδρος
ἐπετέτακτο, τῶν δὲ κατὰ τὸ Τρίπυλον, ᾗ οὐδὲ πάνυ
2   τι προσδεχομένοις τοῖς Μακεδόσιν ἦν. καὶ οἱ μὲν
δᾷδάς τε ταῖς μηχαναῖς ἐνέβαλλον καὶ ὅσα ἄλλα ἐς
τὸ ἐξάψαι τε φλόγα καὶ ἐπὶ μέγα προκαλέσασθαι,
τῶν δὲ ἀμφ᾽ Ἀλέξανδρον αὐτῶν τε ἐμβαλλόντων ἐς
αὐτοὺς ἐρρωμένως καὶ ταῖς μηχαναῖς ἀπὸ τῶν
πύργων λίθων τε μεγάλων ἀφιεμένων καὶ βελῶν
ἐξακοντιζομένων οὐ χαλεπῶς ἀπεστράφησάν τε καὶ
3   ἔφυγον ἐς τὴν πόλιν. καὶ φόνος ταύτῃ οὐκ ὀλίγος
ἐγένετο, ὅσῳ πλείονές τε καὶ ξὺν μείζονι τῇ τόλμῃ
ἐξέδραμον. οἱ μὲν γὰρ εἰς χεῖρας ἐλθόντες τοῖς
Μακεδόσιν ἀπέθανον, οἱ δὲ ἀμφὶ τῷ τείχει τῷ
καταπεπτωκότι, στενωτέρας τε ἢ κατὰ τὸ πλῆθος
αὐτῶν τῆς παρόδου οὔσης καὶ τῶν κατερηριμμένων
τοῦ τείχους χαλεπὴν τὴν ὑπέρβασιν αὐτοῖς παρε-
χόντων.

4   Τοῖς δὲ κατὰ τὸ Τρίπυλον ἐκδραμοῦσιν ἀπήντα
Πτολεμαῖος ὁ σωματοφύλαξ ὁ βασιλικός, τήν τε
Ἀδαίου καὶ Τιμάνδρου ἅμα οἱ τάξιν ἄγων καὶ
ἔστιν οὓς τῶν ψιλῶν· καὶ οὗτοι οὐδὲ αὐτοὶ χαλεπῶς
5   ἐτρέψαντο τοὺς ἐκ τῆς πόλεως. ξυνέβη δὲ καὶ
τούτοις ἐν τῇ ἀποχωρήσει κατὰ στενὴν γέφυραν τὴν
ἐπὶ τῆς τάφρου πεποιημένην φεύγουσι τήν τε

had been left standing on either side of the breach
and which made it possible to fire from the flanks
and almost at the back of those assailing the replace-
ment wall.

22. A few days afterwards Alexander again brought
up his engines to the inner brick wall, taking charge
of operations himself, and there was a sally from the
city in full force; [1] some of the enemy attacked near
the breach, where Alexander had himself taken up
position, others at the triple gate, the last place the
Macedonians looked for a sally. Some flung torches 2
on the siege engines, and anything else which might
light a flame and make a great blaze; but Alexander's immediate supports counter-attacked vigorously; large stones were hurled by the engines from
the towers, missiles were showered in volleys, and the
besieged were easily repulsed and fled into the city.
Here there was great carnage, proportionate to their 3
number and the greater boldness of their sally. Some
fell in hand-to-hand fight with the Macedonians,
others round the fallen wall, where the passage was
too narrow to admit such a number and the fallen
parts of the wall made it difficult to pass over them.

As for those who sallied by the triple gate, Ptole- 4
maeus, the royal bodyguard, met them, bringing up
the battalions of Adaeus and Timander and some
of the light troops; they too had no difficulty in
driving back the sallying party, who in fact also 5
suffered in the retreat over a narrow bridge thrown
across the moat, which gave way under their numbers;

---

[1] D. 26 with variant details; he makes the Athenian
Ephialtes (A. i 10, 4) the leader.

γέφυραν αὐτὴν ὑπὸ πλήθους ξυντρῖψαι καὶ πολλοὺς
αὐτῶν ἐς τὴν τάφρον ἐμπεσόντας τοὺς μὲν ὑπὸ
σφῶν καταπατηθέντας διαφθαρῆναι, τοὺς δὲ καὶ
6 ἄνωθεν ὑπὸ τῶν Μακεδόνων βαλλομένους. ὁ
πλεῖστος δὲ φόνος περὶ ταῖς πύλαις αὐταῖς ξυνέβη,
ὅτι ἡ ξύγκλεισις τῶν πυλῶν φοβερά τε καὶ πρὸ τοῦ
καιροῦ γενομένη, δεισάντων μὴ συνεισπέσοιεν τοῖς
φεύγουσιν ἐχόμενοι αὐτῶν οἱ Μακεδόνες, πολλοὺς
καὶ τῶν φιλίων τῆς εἰσόδου ἀπέκλεισεν, οὓς πρὸς
7 αὐτοῖς τοῖς τείχεσιν οἱ Μακεδόνες διέφθειραν. καὶ
παρ᾽ ὀλίγον ἧκεν ἁλῶναι ἡ πόλις, εἰ μὴ ᾽Αλέξανδρος
ἀνεκαλέσατο τὸ στράτευμα, ἔτι διασῶσαι ἐθέλων
τὴν ᾽Αλικαρνασσόν, εἴ τι φίλιον ἐνδοθείη ἐκ τῶν
᾽Αλικαρνασσέων. ἀπέθανον δὲ τῶν μὲν ἐκ τῆς
πόλεως ἐς χιλίους, τῶν δὲ ξὺν ᾽Αλεξάνδρῳ ἀμφὶ
τοὺς τεσσαράκοντα, καὶ ἐν τούτοις Πτολεμαῖός τε
ὁ σωματοφύλαξ καὶ Κλέαρχος ὁ τοξάρχης καὶ
᾽Αδαῖος ⟨ὁ⟩ χιλιάρχης, οὗτοι καὶ ἄλλοι τῶν οὐκ
ἠμελημένων Μακεδόνων.

23. Ἔνθα δὴ ξυνελθόντες οἱ ἡγεμόνες τῶν
Περσῶν, ᾽Οροντοβάτης τε καὶ Μέμνων, καὶ ἐκ τῶν
παρόντων γνόντες σφᾶς τε οὐ δυναμένους ἐπὶ πολὺ
ἀντέχειν τῇ πολιορκίᾳ καὶ τοῦ τείχους τὸ μέν τι
καταπεπτωκὸς ἤδη ὁρῶντες, τὸ δὲ καὶ κατασεσει-
σμένον, πολλοὺς δὲ τῶν στρατιωτῶν ἐν ταῖς
ἐκδρομαῖς τοὺς μὲν διεφθαρμένους, τοὺς δὲ καὶ ὑπὸ
2 τοῦ τετρῶσθαι ἀπομάχους ὄντας, ταῦτα ἐν νῷ
λαβόντες ἀμφὶ δευτέραν φυλακὴν τῆς νυκτὸς τόν τε
ξύλινον πύργον, ὃν αὐτοὶ ἀντῳκοδόμησαν ταῖς
μηχαναῖς τῶν πολεμίων, ἐμπιπρᾶσι καὶ τὰς στοάς,
ἐν αἷς τὰ βέλη αὐτοῖς ἀπέκειτο. ἐνέβαλον δὲ καὶ
3 ταῖς οἰκίαις πῦρ ταῖς πλησίον τοῦ τείχους· τῶν δὲ

334
B.C.

many fell into the moat and some of them were
trampled to death by their comrades, and others shot
down by the Macedonians from above. The greatest 6
slaughter was round about the gates themselves; for
they were shut prematurely in panic, as the defenders feared that the Macedonians also might
enter, pressing hard upon the fugitives; thus many
friends were shut out, to be destroyed by their foes
close to the walls themselves. The city indeed 7
came near to capture, had not Alexander sounded
the retreat, in a desire even now to save Halicarnassus
if the citizens would surrender amicably. About a
thousand of the garrison perished and about forty
of Alexander's forces, including Ptolemaeus the
bodyguard, Clearchus, the commander of the
archers, Addaeus, a chiliarch, and other Macedonians of repute.

23. The leaders of the Persians, Orontobates
and Memnon, now met and decided that as things
were they could not long hold out against the siege,
with part of the wall gone, as they saw, and part
badly shaken, many soldiers lost in the sallies, many
disabled by wounds. With all this in mind, about 2
the second watch of the night they burned the
wooden tower they themselves had built to oppose
the enemy engines and the sheds in which their
missiles were stored. They also fired all houses
near the walls, while others caught alight from 3

καὶ προσήψατο ἡ φλὸξ ἀπό τε τῶν στοῶν καὶ τοῦ
πύργου πολλὴ ἀπενεχθεῖσα καί τι καὶ τοῦ ἀνέμου
ταύτῃ ἐπιφέροντος· αὐτῶν δὲ οἱ μὲν ἐς τὴν ἄκραν
τὴν ἐν τῇ νήσῳ ἀπεχώρησαν, οἱ δὲ ἐς τὴν Σαλμα-
4 κίδα, ἄκραν οὕτω καλουμένην. Ἀλεξάνδρῳ δὲ ὡς
ἐξηγγέλθη ταῦτα πρός τινων αὐτομολησάντων ἐκ
τοῦ ἔργου καὶ τὸ πῦρ πολὺ καθεώρα αὐτός, καίτοι
ἀμφὶ μέσας που νύκτας ἦν τὸ γιγνόμενον, ὁ δὲ καὶ
ὣς ἐξαγαγὼν τοὺς Μακεδόνας τοὺς μὲν ἔτι
ἐμπιπράντας τὴν πόλιν ἔκτεινεν, ὅσοι δὲ ἐν ταῖς
οἰκίαις καταλαμβάνοιντο τῶν Ἁλικαρνασσέων,
τούτους δὲ σώζειν παρήγγειλεν.
5   Ἤδη τε ἠὼς ὑπέφαινε καὶ κατιδὼν τὰς ἄκρας, ἃς
οἵ τε Πέρσαι καὶ οἱ μισθοφόροι κατειλήφεσαν,
ταύτας μὲν ἀπέγνω πολιορκεῖν, τριβήν τε ἐπινοῶν
οὐκ ὀλίγην ἔσεσθαί οἱ ἀμφ' αὐτὰς τῇ φύσει τῶν
χωρίων καὶ οὐ παρὰ μέγα εἶναι ἐξελόντι οἱ τὴν
6 πόλιν ἤδη πᾶσαν. θάψας δὲ τοὺς ἀποθανόντας ἐν
τῇ νυκτὶ τὰς μὲν μηχανὰς ἐς Τράλλεις ἀπαγαγεῖν
ἐκέλευσε τοὺς ἐπ' αὐταῖς τεταγμένους, αὐτὸς δὲ τὴν
πόλιν ἐς ἔδαφος κατασκάψας αὐτῆς τε ταύτης καὶ
τῆς ἄλλης Καρίας φυλακὴν ἐγκαταλιπὼν ξένους
μὲν πεζοὺς τρισχιλίους, ἱππέας δὲ ἐς διακοσίους
καὶ Πτολεμαῖον ἡγεμόνα αὐτῶν ἐπὶ Φρυγίας
7 ἐστέλλετο. τῆς δὲ Καρίας ξυμπάσης σατραπεύειν
ἔταξεν Ἄδαν, θυγατέρα μὲν Ἑκατόμνω, γυναῖκα
δὲ Ἰδριέως, ὃς καὶ ἀδελφὸς αὐτῇ ὢν κατὰ νόμον
τῶν Καρῶν ξυνῴκει. καὶ ὁ μὲν Ἰδριεὺς τελευτῶν
ταύτῃ ἐπέτρεψε τὰ πράγματα, νενομισμένον ἐν

---

[1] D. 27, 5 (most of the forces allegedly evacuated to Cos).
[2] Cf. ii 5, 7: Ptolemaeus (Berve no. 674, not the historian)

the sheds and the tower, where the blaze was
furious and wafted by the wind in this direction.
They themselves retreated, some to the citadel on
the island and others to the height called Salmacis.[1]
When this news was reported to Alexander by men   4
who deserted in this action, and when he himself saw
the fire spreading, though all this took place about
midnight, none the less he brought out his Macedonians and put to the sword those who were still
setting fire to the city; he gave orders that Hali-
carnassians found in their houses should be spared.

Dawn was breaking; and observing the heights   5
which the Persians and the mercenaries had seized,
he decided not to besiege them, considering that it
would mean much delay for him round about the
heights, owing to the nature of the ground, and no
great advantage now he had captured the whole city.
He buried those who had fallen during the night,   6
ordered the troops placed in charge of the siege
engines to remove them to Tralles, himself razed the
city to the ground and, to guard it and the rest of
Caria, left three thousand mercenary foot and two
hundred horse under Ptolemaeus, while he set out for
Phrygia.[2]   As satrap of all Caria he appointed Ada,   7
daughter of Hecatomnos, wife of Hidrieus;[3] though
her brother, he had lived with her in accordance with
Carian custom.   On his death Hidrieus had handed
over affairs to her; from Semiramis[4] down, it had

was made general in Caria, as Ada (§8), like other ' native '
satraps Al. appointed, would only have had civil power.   Al.
proceeded towards Phrygia only by a very devious route.

[3] D. 24, 2 f. puts this before the fall of Halicarnassus.   The
Carians, and their local dynasty, were partly Hellenized, cf.
Tod 138, 155.

[4] A legendary figure probably based on Sammuramat, queen
regent of Assyria, 810-805 B.C.

τῇ Ἀσίᾳ ἔτι ἀπὸ Σεμιράμεως καὶ γυναῖκας ἄρχειν
ἀνδρῶν. Πιξώδαρος δὲ τὴν μὲν ἐκβάλλει τῆς
8 ἀρχῆς, αὐτὸς δὲ κατεῖχε τὰ πράγματα. τελευτήσαντος δὲ Πιξωδάρου Ὀροντοβάτης τὴν Καρῶν
ἀρχὴν ἐκ βασιλέως πεμφθεὶς εἶχε, γαμβρὸς ὢν
Πιξωδάρου. Ἄδα δὲ Ἄλινδα μόνον κατεῖχε,
χωρίον τῆς Καρίας ἐν τοῖς ὀχυρώτατον, καὶ
ἐσβαλόντι Ἀλεξάνδρῳ ἐς Καρίαν ἀπήντα, τά τε
Ἄλινδα ἐνδιδοῦσα καὶ παῖδά οἱ τιθεμένη Ἀλέξανδρον. καὶ Ἀλέξανδρος τά τε Ἄλινδα αὐτῇ
ἐπέτρεψε καὶ τὸ ὄνομα τοῦ παιδὸς οὐκ ἀπηξίωσε,
καί ἐπειδὴ Ἁλικαρνασσόν τε ἐξεῖλε καὶ τῆς ἄλλης
Καρίας ἐπεκράτησεν, αὐτῇ ἄρχειν ἁπάσης ἔδωκε.
24. Τῶν Μακεδόνων δὲ ἔστιν οἳ συνεστρατευ-
μένοι Ἀλεξάνδρῳ ἦσαν νεωστὶ πρὸ τῆς στρατιᾶς
γεγαμηκότες· καὶ τούτων ἔγνω οὐκ ἀμελητέα
εἶναί οἱ Ἀλέξανδρος, ἀλλ᾽ ἐκπέμπει γὰρ αὐτοὺς ἐκ
Καρίας διαχειμάσοντας ἐν Μακεδονίᾳ ἅμα ταῖς
γυναιξίν, ἐπιτάξας αὐτοῖς Πτολεμαῖόν τε τὸν
Σελεύκου, ἕνα τῶν σωματοφυλάκων τῶν βασιλικῶν, καὶ τῶν στρατηγῶν Κοῖνόν τε τὸν Πολεμοκράτους καὶ Μελέαγρον τὸν Νεοπτολέμου, ὅτι καὶ
2 αὐτοὶ τῶν νεογάμων ἦσαν, προστάξας, ἐπειδὰν
αὐτοί τε ἐπανίωσι καὶ τοὺς μετὰ σφῶν ἐκπεμφθέν-
τας ἐπαναγάγωσι, καταλέξαι ἱππέας τε καὶ πεζοὺς
ἐκ τῆς χώρας ὅσους πλείστους. καὶ τῷ ἔργῳ
τῷδε, εἴπερ τινὶ ἄλλῳ, εὐδοκίμησε παρὰ Μακεδόσιν
Ἀλέξανδρος. ἔπεμψε δὲ καὶ Κλέανδρον τὸν
Πολεμοκράτους ἐπὶ ξυλλογῇ στρατιωτῶν εἰς
Πελοπόννησον.
3 Παρμενίωνα δὲ πέμπει ἐπὶ Σάρδεων, δοὺς αὐτῷ
τῶν τε ἑταίρων ἱππαρχίαν καὶ τοὺς Θετταλοὺς

334
B.C.

been accepted in Asia that women should actually rule men. Pixodarus, however, turned her out of the government and held power himself. On his death Orontobates, his brother-in-law, was sent down by the king and assumed the government. Ada meanwhile held only Alinda, the strongest fortress in Caria; and when Alexander entered Caria she went to meet him, surrendering Alinda and adopting Alexander as her son. Alexander gave Alinda to her charge, and did not reject the title of son, and when he had taken Halicarnassus and become master of the rest of Caria, made her ruler of the whole country.

24. Some of the Macedonians serving under Alexander had recently married before taking the field; Alexander thought he ought to consider these men, and sent them off from Caria to spend the winter with their wives in Macedonia, putting them under Ptolemaeus son of Seleucus, one of the royal Bodyguards, and attaching to him two of his generals, Coenus son of Polemocrates and Meleager son of Neoptolemus, as they themselves were among the newly wed. He directed them, when they returned and brought back their party, to enrol as many horse and foot from the country as they could. Alexander gained as much popularity by this act among the Macedonians as by any other. He also sent Cleander son of Polemocrates to the Peloponnese to collect troops.[1]

Parmenio was sent to Sardis, with a hipparchy of the Companions, the Thessalian cavalry, the other

---

[1] QC. iii 1, 1 (not in D.).

ἱππέας καὶ τοὺς ἄλλους ξυμμάχους καὶ τὰς
ἁμάξας ἄγειν· καὶ κελεύει προϊέναι ἀπὸ Σάρδεων
ἐπὶ Φρυγίαν. αὐτὸς δὲ ἐπὶ Λυκίας τε καὶ Παμφυ-
λίας ᾔει, ὡς τῆς παραλίου κρατήσας ἀχρεῖον
4 καταστῆσαι τοῖς πολεμίοις τὸ ναυτικόν. καὶ
πρῶτον μὲν ἐν παρόδῳ Ὕπαρνα, χωρίον ὀχυρόν,
φυλακὴν ἔχον ξένους μισθοφόρους, ἐξ ἐφόδου
ἔλαβεν· οἱ δ' ἐκ τῆς ἄκρας ξένοι ὑπόσπονδοι
ἐξῆλθον. ἔπειτα εἰσβαλὼν εἰς Λυκίαν Τελμισσέας μὲν ὁμολογίᾳ προσηγάγετο, περάσας δὲ τὸν
Ξάνθον ποταμὸν Πίναρα καὶ Ξάνθον τὴν πόλιν καὶ
Πάταρα ἐνδοθέντα ἔλαβε καὶ ἄλλα ἐλάττω πολίσματα ἐς τριάκοντα.

5   Ταῦτα καταπράξας ἐν ἀκμῇ ἤδη τοῦ χειμῶνος ἐς
τὴν Μιλυάδα καλουμένην χώραν ἐσβάλλει, ἥ ἐστι
μὲν τῆς μεγάλης Φρυγίας, ξυνετέλει δὲ ἐς τὴν
Λυκίαν τότε, οὕτως ἐκ βασιλέως μεγάλου τεταγ-
μένον. καὶ ἐνταῦθα Φασηλιτῶν πρέσβεις ἧκον
περὶ φιλίας τε καὶ χρυσῷ στεφάνῳ στεφανῶσαι
Ἀλέξανδρον· καὶ ὑπὲρ τῶν αὐτῶν ἐπικηρυκευό-
μενοι ἐπρέσβευον Λυκίων τῶν κάτω οἱ πολλοί.
6 Ἀλέξανδρος δὲ Φασηλίτας τε καὶ Λυκίους παραδοῦναι τὰς πόλεις τοῖς ἐπὶ τοῦτο στελλομένοις
ἐκέλευσε· καὶ παρεδόθησαν ξύμπασαι. αὐτὸς δὲ
ὀλίγον ὕστερον ἐς τὴν Φασηλίδα παραγενόμενος
συνεξαιρεῖ αὐτοῖς φρούριον ὀχυρόν, ἐπιτετειχι-
σμένον τῇ χώρᾳ πρὸς Πισιδῶν, ὅθεν ὁρμώμενοι οἱ

----

[2] D. 27, 6 (vague). Hipparchy: Introd. 60.

[3] D. 27. 7, cf. 31. 3 ff., takes Al. along the coast to Cilicia
in 334! 28 has the story of a Lycian hill-town not in A.,
whose account in 24, 4–29, 6 is virtually all that we know of

allies and the waggons, and given orders to proceed   334
from Sardis to Phrygia. ² He himself went towards   B.C.
Lycia and Pamphylia, so as to gain control of the
coast and render the enemy's navy useless.³ On   4
his route he first took in his stride Hyparna, a strong   334-3
place with a mercenary garrison; the mercenaries   B.C.
received terms and marched out of the citadel.
Then on entering Lycia he took over the Telmis-
seans by surrender, and after crossing the Xanthus
he received Pinara and the city of Xanthus and Patara
in submission with about thirty smaller little towns.

By the time he had completed all this it was the   5
depth of winter, but he attacked the Milyan territory,
as it is called; it belongs to Greater Phrygia, but
was then reckoned part of Lycia by the Persian
king's orders. There envoys from Phaselis came to
offer friendly relations and to crown Alexander with
a gold crown; most of the Lower Lycians also
sent envoys with overtures on the same matters.
Alexander ordered Phaselis and the Lycians to hand   6
over their cities to those appointed for the purpose;
and all were handed over. He came soon after to
Phaselis, and, along with these places, took a strong
outpost, fortified to threaten this district by Pisidians,

the operations described, from autumn 334 (24, 1) to spring
333, cf. also P. 17, 2–18, 1. The routes taken are often unclear
(cf. Freya Stark, *JHS* 1958, 102 ff.), and Al's aims have never
been explained; most of his marching was in the interior, and
the coastal cities were not important as naval bases or suppliers
of ships to Persia; it may be relevant that Phaselis (a Greek
city) lay on the sea-route between Athens and Egypt, a potential supplier of Athens' essential grain imports. Al.
evidently planned to unite with Parmenio and the newly
married in Phrygia (i 29, 4 f.). A. neglects to record the
appointment of Nearchus as satrap of Lycia (iii 6, 6).

ARRIAN

βάρβαροι πολλὰ ἔβλαπτον τῶν Φασηλιτῶν τοὺς τὴν
γῆν ἐργαζομένους.

25. Ἔτι δὲ αὐτῷ περὶ τὴν Φασηλίδα ὄντι
ἐξαγγέλλεται Ἀλέξανδρον τὸν Ἀερόπου ἐπιβουλεύ-
ειν, τά τε ἄλλα τῶν ἑταίρων ὄντα καὶ ἐν τῷ τότε
Θεσσαλῶν τῆς ἵππου ἄρχοντα. ἦν μὲν δὴ ὁ
Ἀλέξανδρος οὗτος ἀδελφὸς Ἡρομένους τε καὶ
Ἀρραβαίου τῶν ξυνεπιλαβόντων τῆς σφαγῆς τῆς
2 Φιλίππου· καὶ τότε αἰτίαν σχόντα αὐτὸν Ἀλέξανδρος ἀφῆκεν, ὅτι ἐν πρώτοις τε ἀφίκετο τῶν
φίλων παρ’ αὐτόν, ἐπειδὴ Φίλιππος ἐτελεύτησε, καὶ
τὸν θώρακα συνενδὺς συνηκολούθησεν αὐτῷ εἰς τὰ
βασίλεια· ὕστερον δὲ καὶ ἐν τιμῇ ἀμφ’ αὐτὸν εἶχε,
στρατηγόν τε ἐπὶ Θρᾴκης στείλας καὶ ἐπειδὴ
Κάλας ὁ τῶν Θετταλῶν ἵππαρχος ἐπὶ σατραπείᾳ
ἐξεπέμφθη, αὐτὸν ἀπέδειξεν ἄρχειν τῆς Θεσσαλικῆς
ἵππου. τὰ δὲ τῆς ἐπιβουλῆς ἐξηγγέλθη ὧδε.

3 Δαρεῖος, ἐπειδὴ Ἀμύντας αὐτομολήσας παρ’
αὐτὸν λόγους τέ τινας καὶ γράμματα παρὰ τοῦ
Ἀλεξάνδρου τούτου ἐκόμισε, καταπέμπει ἐπὶ
θάλασσαν Σισίνην, ἄνδρα Πέρσην τῶν ἀμφ’ αὐτὸν
πιστῶν, πρόφασιν μὲν παρὰ Ἀτιζύην τὸν Φρυγίας
σατράπην, τῇ δὲ ἀληθείᾳ τῷ Ἀλεξάνδρῳ τούτῳ
συνεσόμενον καὶ πίστεις δώσοντα, εἰ ἀποκτείνει⟨ε⟩
βασιλέα Ἀλέξανδρον, αὐτὸν βασιλέα καταστήσειν
Μακεδονίας καὶ χρυσίου τάλαντα πρὸς τῇ βασιλείᾳ
4 ἐπιδώσειν χίλια. ὁ δὲ Σισίνης ἁλοὺς πρὸς Παρμενίωνος λέγει πρὸς Παρμενίωνα ὧν ἕνεκα ἀπεστάλη·
καὶ τοῦτον ἐν φυλακῇ πέμπει Παρμενίων παρ’
Ἀλέξανδρον, καὶ πυνθάνεται ταὐτὰ παρ’ αὐτοῦ
Ἀλέξανδρος. ξυναγαγὼν δὲ τοὺς φίλους βουλὴν
προὐτίθει, ὅ τι χρὴ ὑπὲρ Ἀλεξάνδρου γνῶναι.

a base from which the barbarians did much injury to the people of Phaselis tilling the soil.

334–3 B.C.

25. While Alexander was still operating round Phaselis it was reported to him that his namesake, son of Aeropus, was conspiring; he was one of the Companions, and at the time commander of the Thessalian cavalry. This Alexander was brother to Heromenes and Arrabaeus, who had a part in the murder of Philip. Though he was implicated at the time, Alexander let him off, since he had been among the first of his friends to rally to him on Philip's death, and had put on his cuirass and accompanied Alexander into the palace; later Alexander had even held him in honour near his person, had sent him to command in Thrace, and when Calas, commander of the Thessalian cavalry, had been transferred to a satrapy,[1] appointed him commander of the Thessalian horse. The story of the plot was reported as follows.

Darius, when Amyntas deserted to him bringing overtures and a letter from this Alexander, sent Sisines, a trusty Persian from his suite, to the sea. The pretext was that he was to visit Atizyes, satrap of Phrygia, but in fact he was to meet this Alexander and give him assurances that if he assassinated Alexander the king, the Persian king would make him king of Macedonia and give him a thousand gold Talents as well. Sisines fell into Parmenio's hands and revealed to him the object of his mission; and Parmenio sent him under escort to Alexander, who heard the same story from him. So he called together his friends, to consider what should be de-

_____
[1] 17, 1.

5 καὶ ἐδόκει τοῖς ἑταίροις μήτε πάλαι εὖ βεβουλεῦ-
σθαι τὸ κράτιστον τοῦ ἱππικοῦ ἀνδρὶ οὐ πιστῷ
ἐπιτρέψας, νῦν τε χρῆναι αὐτὸν κατὰ τάχος ἐκπο-
δὼν ποιεῖσθαι, πρὶν καὶ ἐπιτηδειότερον γενόμενον
6 τοῖς Θετταλοῖς ξὺν αὐτοῖς τι νεωτερίσαι. καί τι
καὶ θεῖον ἐφόβει αὐτούς. ἔτι γὰρ πολιορκοῦντος
αὐτοῦ Ἀλεξάνδρου Ἁλικαρνασσὸν ἀναπαύεσθαι
μὲν ἐν μεσημβρίᾳ, χελιδόνα δὲ περιπέτεσθαι ὑπὲρ
τῆς κεφαλῆς τρύζουσαν μεγάλα καὶ τῆς εὐνῆς ἄλλῃ
καὶ ἄλλῃ ἐπικαθίζειν, θορυβωδέστερον ἢ κατὰ τὸ
7 εἰωθὸς ᾄδουσαν· τὸν δὲ ὑπὸ καμάτου ἐγερθῆναι
μὲν ἀδυνάτως ἔχειν ἐκ τοῦ ὕπνου, ἐνοχλούμενον δὲ
πρὸς τῆς φωνῆς τῇ χειρὶ οὐ βαρέως ἀποσοβῆσαι
τὴν χελιδόνα· τὴν δὲ τοσούτου ἄρα δεῆσαι
ἀποφυγεῖν πληγεῖσαν, ὥστε ἐπὶ τῆς κεφαλῆς αὐτῆς
τοῦ Ἀλεξάνδρου καθημένην μὴ πρόσθεν ἀνεῖναι
8 πρὶν παντελῶς ἐξεγερθῆναι Ἀλέξανδρον. καὶ
Ἀλέξανδρος οὐ φαῦλον ποιησάμενος τὸ τῆς
χελιδόνος ἀνεκοίνωσεν Ἀριστάνδρῳ τῷ Τελμισσεῖ,
μάντει· Ἀρίστανδρον δὲ ἐπιβουλὴν μὲν ἔκ του τῶν
φίλων σημαίνεσθαι αὐτῷ εἰπεῖν, σημαίνεσθαι δὲ
καί, ὅτι καταφανὴς ἔσται. τὴν γὰρ χελιδόνα
σύντροφόν τε εἶναι ὄρνιθα καὶ εὔνουν ἀνθρώποις καὶ
λάλον μᾶλλον ἢ ἄλλην ὄρνιθα.
9 Ταῦτά τε οὖν καὶ τὰ ἀπὸ τοῦ Πέρσου ξυνθεὶς
πέμπει ὡς Παρμενίωνα Ἀμφοτερὸν τὸν Ἀλεξάνδρου μὲν παῖδα, ἀδελφὸν δὲ Κρατεροῦ. καὶ
ξυμπέμπει αὐτῷ τῶν Περγαίων τινὰς τὴν ὁδὸν
ἡγησομένους. καὶ ὁ Ἀμφοτερὸς στολὴν ἐνδὺς
ἐπιχώριον, [καὶ] ὡς μὴ γνώριμος εἶναι κατὰ τὴν
10 ὁδόν, λανθάνει ἀφικόμενος παρὰ Παρμενίωνα· καὶ
γράμματα μὲν οὐ κομίζει παρὰ Ἀλεξάνδρου· οὐ

5 334-3
B.C.

cided about Alexander. The Companions held
that he had originally acted unwisely in committing
the best of the cavalry to an untrustworthy officer,
and that he should now get rid of him as soon as
possible, before he became more popular with the
Thessalians and secured their help for a revolution.
They were also troubled by an omen: while Alex- 6
ander was still besieging Halicarnassus and was
taking his midday rest, a swallow circled over his
head chattering loudly, and perched here and there
on his bed; its song was noisier than the usual
swallow's twittering. Alexander was too weary to 7
awaken, but troubled by the sound, he gently brushed
the swallow away; but the bird would not fly off when
hit; rather it perched on Alexander's very head
and kept on till Alexander was fully awake. Alex- 8
ander took the incident seriously and informed
Aristander of Telmissus, a seer; he replied that it
meant a plot on the part of one of his friends but
also that the plot would come to light. For the
swallow is a domestic bird, friendly to man, and
more talkative than any other bird.

Putting this together with the Persian's story, he 9
sent Amphoterus son of Alexander, brother of
Craterus, to Parmenio with some Pergaeans as guides.
Amphoterus wore a native dress, so as not to be
recognized on the journey, and so reached Parmenio
safely. He brought no letter from King Alexander; 10
it was thought unwise to write plainly in a matter

ARRIAN

γὰρ ἔδοξε γράφειν ὑπὲρ οὐδενὸς τοιούτου ἐς τὸ
ἐμφανές· τὰ δὲ ἀπὸ γλώσσης οἱ ἐντεταλμένα
ἐξήγγειλεν, καὶ οὕτω ξυλλαμβάνεται ὁ Ἀλέξανδρος οὗτος καὶ ἐν φυλακῇ ἦν.

26. Ἀλέξανδρος δὲ ἄρας ἐκ Φασηλίδος μέρος
μέν τι τῆς στρατιᾶς διὰ τῶν ὀρῶν πέμπει ἐπὶ
Πέργης, ᾗ ὡδοπεποιήκεσαν αὐτῷ οἱ Θρᾷκες χαλεπὴν
ἄλλως καὶ μακρὰν οὖσαν τὴν πάροδον· αὐτὸς δὲ
παρὰ τὴν θάλασσαν διὰ τοῦ αἰγιαλοῦ ἦγε τοὺς
ἀμφ' αὐτόν. ἔστι δὲ ταύτῃ ἡ ὁδὸς οὐκ ἄλλως ὅτι
μὴ τῶν ἀπ' ἄρκτου ἀνέμων πνεόντων· εἰ δὲ νότοι
κατέχοιεν, ἀπόρως ἔχει διὰ τοῦ αἰγιαλοῦ ὁδοιπο-
2 ρεῖν. τῷ δὲ ἐκ νότων σκληροὶ βορραῖ ἐπιπνεύ-
σαντες, οὐκ ἄνευ τοῦ θείου, ὡς αὐτός τε καὶ οἱ
ἀμφ' αὐτὸν ἐξηγοῦντο, εὐμαρῆ καὶ ταχεῖαν τὴν
πάροδον παρέσχον. ἐκ Πέργης δὲ ὡς προῄει,
ἐντυγχάνουσιν αὐτῷ κατὰ τὴν ὁδὸν πρέσβεις
Ἀσπενδίων αὐτοκράτορες, τὴν μὲν πόλιν ἐνδιδό-
3 ντες, φρουρὰν δὲ μὴ εἰσάγειν δεόμενοι. καὶ περὶ
μὲν τῆς φρουρᾶς πράξαντες ἀπῆλθον, ὅσα ἠξίουν·
πεντήκοντα δὲ τάλαντα κελεύει τῇ στρατιᾷ δοῦναι
αὐτοῖς ἐς μισθὸν καὶ τοὺς ἵππους, οὓς δασμὸν
βασιλεῖ ἔτρεφον. οἱ δὲ ὑπέρ τε τοῦ ἀργυρίου καὶ
τοὺς ἵππους παραδώσειν ξυνθέμενοι ἀπῆλθον.

4 Ἀλέξανδρος δὲ ἐπὶ Σίδης ᾔει. εἰσὶ δὲ οἱ
Σιδῆται Κυμαῖοι ἐκ Κύμης τῆς Αἰολίδος· καὶ
οὗτοι λέγουσιν ὑπὲρ σφῶν τόνδε τὸν λόγον, ὅτι, ὡς
κατῆράν τε ἐς τὴν γῆν ἐκείνην οἱ πρῶτοι ἐκ Κύμης

---

[2] For this Alexander and Amyntas see Introd. 46 and
Appendix XI 5.
[1] This ' miracle ', when the sea did ' obeisance ' to Al.
(Callisthenes F. 31, *not* a quotation of his words), is said to

of this sort; but he gave a verbal message as
directed. As a result the other Alexander was
arrested and kept under guard.[2]

26. Leaving Phaselis, Alexander sent part of
his force through the mountain passes towards
Perge, where the Thracians had made him a road,
the approach being otherwise difficult and long. He
himself led his men by the sea along the shore, a
route practicable only with north winds blowing;
south winds make the passage along the shore impossible. There had been southerlies but a north
wind had set in, not without divine interposition, as
Alexander and his followers interpreted it, and made
the passage easy and swift.[1] As he went on from
Perge, plenipotentiaries from Aspendus met him
on the way surrendering their city, but begging it
might not be garrisoned. This point about the
garrison they won; but Alexander ordered them to
provide fifty Talents for the army as pay, with the
horses they bred as tribute to the King of Persia.[2]
They agreed on the money and to hand over horses,
and left.

Alexander now went towards Side,[3] whose inhabitants are Cymaeans from Aeolian Cyme; according to their own account of themselves, when
the first emigrants from Cyme put into land and

have appeared in all the histories of Al. (Josephus, *Bell. Jud.*
ii 348) and was ridiculed by Menander (died *c.* 290 B.C.), fr. 924
Koch; but cf. P. 17 (no mention in a supposed letter of Al.);
Strabo xiv, 3, 9.

[2] Introd. 39.

[3] Al. seems to have by-passed Aspendus as well as Syllium,
keeping closer to the coast, on his march further east to Side,
whence he returned towards Syllium and Perge (27, 5), again
by-passing Aspendus, until he marched back against that city
on news of its disloyalty.

σταλέντες καὶ ἐπὶ οἰκισμῷ ἐξέβησαν, αὐτίκα τὴν
μὲν Ἑλλάδα γλῶσσαν ἐξελάθοντο, εὐθὺς δὲ
βάρβαρον φωνὴν ἵεσαν, οὐδὲ τῶν προσχώρων
βαρβάρων, ἀλλὰ ἰδίαν σφῶν οὔπω πρόσθεν οὖσαν
τὴν φωνήν· καὶ ἔκτοτε οὐ κατὰ τοὺς ἄλλους
5 προσχώρους Σιδῆται ἐβαρβάριζον. καταλιπὼν δὲ
φρουρὰν ἐν Σίδῃ προῆει ἐπὶ Σύλλιον, χωρίον
ὀχυρὸν καὶ φρουρὰν ἔχον ξένων μισθοφόρων καὶ
αὐτῶν τῶν ἐπιχωρίων βαρβάρων. ἀλλ' οὔτε τὸ
Σύλλιον ἐξ ἐφόδου αὐτοσχεδίου ἠδυνήθη λαβεῖν,
ἐπεί τ' ἠγγέλθη αὐτῷ κατὰ τὴν ὁδὸν τοὺς Ἀσπεν-
δίους ὅτι οὐδὲν τῶν ξυγκειμένων πρᾶξαι ἐθέλοιεν,
οὔτε τοὺς ἵππους παραδοῦναι τοῖς πεμφθεῖσιν οὔτε
ἀπαριθμῆσαι τὰ χρήματα, καὶ τὰ ἐκ τῆς χώρας ὅτι
ἀνασκευασάμενοι ἐς τὴν πόλιν τάς τε πύλας ἀποκε-
κλείκασι τοῖς παρὰ Ἀλεξάνδρου καὶ τὰ τείχη, ὅπῃ
πεπονηκότα ἦν, ἐπισκευάζουσι, ταῦτα πυθόμενος
ἐπὶ Ἀσπένδου ἀνεζεύγνυεν.

27. Ὤικισται δὲ τῆς Ἀσπένδου τὰ μὲν πολλὰ
ἐπὶ ἄκρᾳ ὀχυρᾷ καὶ ἀποτόμῳ καὶ παρ' αὐτὴν τὴν
ἄκραν ὁ Εὐρυμέδων ποταμὸς ῥεῖ· ἦσαν δὲ αὐτοῖς
καὶ περὶ τῇ ἄκρᾳ ἐν τῷ χθαμαλῷ οὐκ ὀλίγαι
οἰκήσεις καὶ τεῖχος περιεβέβλητο αὐταῖς οὐ μέγα.
2 τὸ μὲν δὴ τεῖχος εὐθύς, ὡς προσάγοντα Ἀλέξανδρον ἔγνωσαν, ἐκλείπουσιν ὅσοι ἐπῴκουν καὶ
τὰς οἰκίας, ὅσας ἐν τῷ χθαμαλῷ ᾠκισμένας οὐκ
ἐδόκουν διαφυλάξαι ἂν δύνασθαι· αὐτοὶ δὲ ἐς τὴν
ἄκραν ξυμφεύγουσιν. Ἀλέξανδρος δὲ ὡς ἀφίκετο
ξὺν τῇ δυνάμει, εἴσω τοῦ ἐρήμου τείχους παρελθὼν
κατεστρατοπέδευσεν ἐν ταῖς οἰκίαις ταῖς καταλε-
3 λειμμέναις πρὸς τῶν Ἀσπενδίων. οἱ δὲ Ἀσπένδιοι
ὡς εἶδον αὐτόν τε Ἀλέξανδρον παρ' ἐλπίδα

334–3
B.C.

disembarked to found a colony, they at once forgot
their native tongue and talked a foreign language
straight away, and not that of the neighbouring
barbarians, but their own idiom, in fact a new dialect;
and from that time the people of Side spoke like
barbarians but not like the other peoples of the
neighbourhood. Alexander left a guard at Side and 5
went on to Syllium, a strong place with a garrison
of foreign mercenaries and of barbarians too from
those parts. But he could not take Syllium at the
first assault without preparation, and, when it was
reported to him on his march that the Aspendians
were unwilling to carry out any of the terms of the
pact, would not hand over the horses to the party
sent to fetch them, nor pay the money, and had
packed up and brought their belongings in to the
city from the countryside, had shut their gates
upon Alexander's envoys, and were repairing dilapi-
dations in their walls, the news made him march
towards Aspendus.

27. Aspendus is built, for the most part, on a strong
hill-top, sheer, with the river Eurymedon flowing
right past the height. Round this hill-top on the
flat, they had a number of dwellings surrounded
by a low wall. As soon as they were aware of 2
Alexander's approach, the inhabitants deserted this
wall, as well as the houses built on the level which
they thought it impossible to defend; they all took
refuge on the hill-top. On arriving with his force,
Alexander penetrated within the deserted wall and
camped in the houses abandoned by the Aspendians. When the citizens saw with surprise Alexan- 3
der present in person and his army all round them,

ARRIAN

ἥκοντα καὶ τὸ στρατόπεδον ἐν κύκλῳ σφῶν πάντῃ,
πέμψαντες πρέσβεις ἐδέοντο ἐφ' οἷσπερ τὸ πρότερον
ξυμβῆναι. καὶ Ἀλέξανδρος τό τε χωρίον ἰσχυρὸν
ἰδὼν καὶ αὐτὸς ὡς οὐκ ἐπὶ χρόνιον πολιορκίαν
παρεσκευασμένος ἐπὶ τοῖς αὐτοῖς μὲν οὐδὲ ὡς
4 ξυνέβη πρὸς αὐτούς· ὁμήρους δὲ δοῦναι σφῶν τοὺς
δυνατωτάτους ἐκέλευσεν καὶ τοὺς ἵππους, οὓς
πρόσθεν ὡμολόγησαν, καὶ ἑκατὸν τάλαντα ἀντὶ
τῶν πεντήκοντα, καὶ πείθεσθαι τῷ σατράπῃ τῷ
⟨ὑπ'⟩ Ἀλεξάνδρου ταχθέντι καὶ φόρους ἀποφέρειν
ὅσα ἔτη Μακεδόσι, καὶ ὑπὲρ τῆς χώρας διακρι-
θῆναι, ἣν τῶν προσχώρων οὖσαν βίᾳ κατέχειν ἐν
αἰτίᾳ ἦσαν.

5 Ὡς δὲ πάντα οἱ ἐπεχώρησαν, ἀνέζευξεν ἐς
Πέργην, κἀκεῖθεν ἐς Φρυγίαν ὥρμητο· ἦν δὲ αὐτῷ
ἡ πορεία παρὰ Τελμισσὸν πόλιν. οἱ δὲ ἄνθρωποι
οὗτοι τὸ μὲν γένος Πισίδαι εἰσὶ βάρβαροι, χωρίον
δὲ οἰκοῦσιν ὑπερύψηλον καὶ πάντῃ ἀπότομον, καὶ ἡ
6 ὁδὸς παρὰ τὴν πόλιν χαλεπή. καθήκει γὰρ ἐκ τῆς
πόλεως ὄρος ἔστε ἐπὶ τὴν ὁδόν, καὶ τοῦτο μὲν
αὐτοῦ ἐν τῇ ὁδῷ ἀποπαύεται, ἀντίπορον δὲ αὐτῷ
ἄλλο ὄρος ἐστὶν οὐ μεῖον ἀπότομον. καὶ ταῦτα τὰ
ὄρη ὥσπερ πύλας ποιεῖ ἐπὶ τῇ ὁδῷ, καὶ ἔστιν
ὀλίγη φυλακῇ κατέχοντας τὰ ὄρη ταῦτα ἄπορον
ποιεῖν τὴν πάροδον. καὶ τότε οἱ Τελμισσεῖς
πανδημεὶ ἐκβεβοηθηκότες ἀμφότερα τὰ ὄρη κατεῖ-
7 χον. ταῦτα δὴ ἰδὼν Ἀλέξανδρος στρατοπεδεύ-
εσθαι αὐτοῦ, ὅπως εἶχον, ἐκέλευε τοὺς Μακεδόνας,
γνούς, ὅτι οὐ μενοῦσι πανδημεὶ οἱ Τελμισσεῖς
αὐλιζομένους σφᾶς ἰδόντες, ἀλλ' ἀποχωρήσουσιν ἐς
τὴν πόλιν πλησίον οὖσαν οἱ πολλοὶ αὐτῶν, ὅσον
φυλακὴν καταλιπόντες ἐπὶ τοῖς ὄρεσι. καὶ ξυνέβη

they sent envoys to beg for an agreement on their old terms. Alexander saw that the position was strong, and that he was not prepared for a long siege, yet even so he refused a pact with them on the same conditions. He demanded their most influ- 4 ential men as hostages, the horses they had previously promised and a hundred Talents in place of fifty; they were to be subject to the satrap appointed by him, and pay yearly tribute to Macedon and an adjudication was to be held about the territory they were accused of having annexed by violence from their neighbours.

When all this had been conceded, he moved to 5 Perge and thence began his march to Phrygia, which led past the city of Telmissus.[1] The Telmissians are Pisidian barbarians in origin, and inhabit a very high position, precipitous all round; the road past the city is difficult. A mountain stretches down 6 from the city to the road, and there ends; but opposite is another, equally abrupt. These mountains virtually make gates on the road, and a small guard can prevent all approach by holding them. On this occasion the Telmissians came out in full force and occupied both mountains. Seeing this, 7 Alexander ordered the Macedonians to camp where they were, knowing that the Telmissians, on seeing them in bivouacks, would not wait there in full force, but would for the most part drift away to the city close by, leaving only a guard on the mountains.

---

[1] Properly Termessus (coins and inscriptions).

ὅπως εἴκαζεν· οἱ μὲν γὰρ πολλοὶ αὐτῶν ἀπῆλθον,
8 αἱ φυλακαὶ δὲ ἐγκατέμειναν. καὶ ἐπὶ τούτους
εὐθὺς ἀναλαβὼν τούς τε τοξότας καὶ τὰς τῶν
ἀκοντιστῶν τάξεις καὶ τῶν ὁπλιτῶν ὅσοι κουφό-
τεροι ἐπήγαγεν. οἱ δὲ οὐκ ἔμειναν βαλλόμενοι,
ἀλλὰ ἔλιπον τὸ χωρίον· καὶ Ἀλέξανδρος ὑπερβαλὼν τὰ στενὰ πρὸς τῇ πόλει κατεστρατοπέδευσε.
28. Καὶ ἐνταῦθα ἀφικνοῦνται παρ' αὐτὸν Σελ-
γέων πρέσβεις. οἱ δέ εἰσι καὶ αὐτοὶ Πισίδαι
βάρβαροι καὶ πόλιν μεγάλην οἰκοῦσιν καὶ αὐτοὶ
μάχιμοί εἰσιν· ὅτι δὲ πολέμιοι τοῖς Τελμισσεῦσιν
ἐκ παλαιοῦ ἐτύγχανον, ὑπὲρ φιλίας πρὸς Ἀλέξανδρον πεπρεσβευμένοι ἦσαν. καὶ πρὸς τούτους
σπένδεται Ἀλέξανδρος, καὶ ἐκ τούτου πιστοῖς ἐς
2 ἄπαντα ἐχρήσατο. τὴν Τελμισσὸν δὲ ἀπέγνω
ἑλεῖν ἂν ἐν ὀλίγῳ χρόνῳ, ἀλλ' ἐπὶ Σαγαλασσοῦ
ἐστέλλετο. ἦν δὲ καὶ αὕτη οὐ μικρὰ πόλις·
Πισίδαι καὶ ταύτην ᾤκουν, καὶ ἐδόκουν πάντων
Πισιδῶν μαχίμων ὄντων αὐτοὶ εἶναι [οἱ] μαχιμώ-
τατοι· καὶ τότε τὸν λόφον τὸν πρὸ τῆς πόλεως, ὅτι
καὶ οὗτος οὐ μεῖον τοῦ τείχους ὀχυρὸς ἐς τὸ
3 ἀπομάχεσθαι ἦν, κατειληφότες προσέμενον. Ἀλέξανδρος δὲ τὴν μὲν φάλαγγα τῶν Μακεδόνων
τάττει ὧδε· ἐπὶ μὲν τοῦ δεξιοῦ κέρως, ἵνα καὶ
αὐτὸς ἐπετέτακτο, τοὺς ὑπασπιστὰς εἶχεν, ἐχομένους δὲ τούτων τοὺς πεζεταίρους ἔστε ἐπὶ τὸ
εὐώνυμον παρατείνας, ὡς ἑκάστοις τῶν στρατηγῶν
4 ἡ ἡγεμονία τῆς τάξεως ἐν τῇ τότε ἡμέρᾳ ἦν. ἐπὶ
δὲ τῷ εὐωνύμῳ ἐπέταξεν ἡγεμόνα Ἀμύνταν τὸν
Ἀρραβαίου. προετάχθησαν δὲ αὐτῷ τοῦ μὲν
δεξιοῦ κέρως οἵ τε τοξόται καὶ οἱ Ἀγριᾶνες, τοῦ δὲ
εὐωνύμου οἱ ἀκοντισταὶ οἱ Θρᾷκες, ὧν ἡγεῖτο

His guess proved right; most of them left, the
guards remained. At once he took the archers, the 8
javelin battalions, and the lighter armed hoplites
and led them against the guards, who did not stand
firm at the volleys but left their position. Alexander
passed the narrows and encamped near the city.

28. At this point arrived envoys from the Selgians,
who are also barbarian Pisidians with a large city, a
warlike people; they were old enemies of the Telmissians and that is why they had sent an embassy to
Alexander to ask for his friendship. Alexander made
a treaty with them, and thereafter found them
wholly trustworthy allies. He concluded that the 2
capture of Telmissus would be a long business, and
moved on to Sagalassus, also a large city, inhabited
by Pisidians who were thought to be the most
warlike of this warlike people; on this occasion they
had occupied the hill in front of the city which was
as strong for defensive operations as the wall itself,
and held their ground. Alexander deployed the 3
Macedonian phalanx as follows: on the right wing,
where he had stationed himself, he had the hypaspists,
and next to them the foot-companions, extended to
the left wing, each battalion under the commanders
in the order of precedence for the day. On the left 4
he placed Amyntas son of Arrabaeus in command.
In front of the right wing were posted the archers
and the Agrianians, of the left the Thracian javelin-

Σιτάλκης· οἱ γὰρ ἱππεῖς αὐτῷ οὐκ ὠφέλιμοι ἐν τῇ
δυσχωρίᾳ ἦσαν. τοῖς Πισίδαις δὲ καὶ Τελμισσεῖς
προσβεβοηθηκότες ξυνετάξαντο.

5 Ἤδη τε οἱ ἀμφ' Ἀλέξανδρον προσβεβληκότες
τῷ ὄρει, ὅπερ κατεῖχον οἱ Πισίδαι, κατ' αὐτὸ τὸ
ἀποτομώτατον τῆς ἀνόδου ἦσαν, καὶ ἐν τούτῳ
ἐπιτίθενται αὐτοῖς οἱ βάρβαροι λόχοις κατὰ κέρας
ἑκάτερον, ᾗ σφίσι μὲν εὐπροσοδώτατον ἦν, τοῖς
πολεμίοις δὲ χαλεπωτάτη ἡ πρόσβασις. καὶ τοὺς
μὲν τοξότας, οἷα δὴ οὔτε ἀκριβῶς ὡπλισμένους καὶ
πρώτους πελάσαντας, ἐτρέψαντο, οἱ δὲ Ἀγριᾶνες
6 ἔμειναν. ἐγγὺς γὰρ ἤδη καὶ ἡ φάλαγξ τῶν
Μακεδόνων προσῆγε καὶ πρὸ αὐτῆς Ἀλέξανδρος
ἐφαίνετο. ὡς δὲ ἐν χερσὶν ἡ μάχη ἐγένετο, γυμνοί
τε οἱ βάρβαροι ὄντες ὁπλίταις προσεφέροντο καὶ
πάντῃ κατατιτρωσκόμενοι ἔπιπτον [δὲ], ἐνταῦθα
7 δὴ ἐγκλίνουσιν· καὶ ἀπέθανον μὲν αὐτῶν ἐς πεντακοσίους, . . . κοῦφοι γὰρ ὄντες καὶ ἔμπειροι τῶν
χωρίων οὐ χαλεπῶς ἀπεχώρουν· καὶ οἱ Μακεδόνες
διὰ βαρύτητα τῶν ὅπλων καὶ ἀπειρίαν τῶν ὁδῶν οὐ
8 θαρραλέοι ἐς τὸ διώκειν ἦσαν. Ἀλέξανδρος δὲ
ἐχόμενος τῶν φευγόντων τὴν πόλιν αὐτῶν αἱρεῖ
κατὰ κράτος. τῶν δὲ ξὺν αὐτῷ Κλέανδρός τε ὁ
στρατηγὸς τῶν τοξοτῶν ἀποθνήσκει καὶ τῶν ἄλλων
ἀμφὶ τοὺς εἴκοσιν. Ἀλέξανδρος δὲ ἐπὶ τοὺς
ἄλλους Πισίδας ἦγε· καὶ τὰ μέν τινα τῶν φρου-
ρίων βίᾳ ἐξεῖλε, τὰ δὲ ὁμολογίᾳ προσηγάγετο.

29. Ἐντεῦθεν δὲ ᾔει ἐπὶ Φρυγίας παρὰ τὴν
λίμνην, ᾗ ὄνομα Ἀσκανία, ἐν ᾗ ἅλες πήγνυνται
αὐτόματοι, καὶ τούτοις χρῶνται οἱ ἐπιχώριοι οὐδὲ
θαλάσσης τι ἐπὶ τούτῳ δέονται· καὶ ἀφικνεῖται ἐς
Κελαινὰς πεμπταῖος. ἐν δὲ ταῖς Κελαιναῖς ἄκρα ἦν

men under Sitalces. The cavalry were of no use to
him in this rough country. The Pisidians' line
included Telmissians who had come to their help.

In their assault on the height held by the Pisidians,
Alexander's troops had already reached the steepest
part of the ascent when barbarians in bands attacked
them on either wing, where they could best approach
and the Macedonians found the means to advance
hardest. They drove back the archers, as they were
lightly armed and first to make contact; but the
Agrianians held firm. For the Macedonian phalanx
was already coming up, and Alexander himself was
visible at its head. Once hand-to-hand fighting
had begun, the barbarians who had no protective
armour and were engaged with hoplites were wounded
and fell on all sides and at length gave way. Some
five hundred perished.[1] . . . Unencumbered and
knowing the country, they got away easily; from
weight of armour and ignorance of the paths the
Macedonians had little heart for the pursuit. Alexander, however, kept on the heels of the fugitives
and stormed the city, losing Cleander, the commander of the archers, and some twenty more of his
followers. Then he attacked the remaining Pisidians,
captured some of their forts and received the surrender of others.

29. Thence he passed into Phrygia by Lake Ascania,
where salt crystallizes naturally, and is used by the
inhabitants, who thus need no sea salt; in four days
he reached Celaenae, where a citadel sheer on every
side was held under orders from the satrap of Phrygia

[1] The number of prisoners was given in the lacuna.

πάντη ἀπότομος, καὶ ταύτην φυλακὴ κατεῖχεν ἐκ
τοῦ σατράπου τῆς Φρυγίας Κᾶρες μὲν χίλιοι,
2 Ἕλληνες δὲ μισθοφόροι ἑκατόν. καὶ οὗτοι πρεσβεύονται παρ᾽ Ἀλέξανδρον, ἐπαγγελλόμενοι, εἰ
μὴ ἀφίκοιτό σφισι βοήθεια ἐν ἡμέρᾳ ᾗ ξυνέκειτο,
φράσαντες τὴν ἡμέραν, ὅτι παραδώσουσι τὸ
χωρίον. καὶ ἔδοξε ταῦτα Ἀλεξάνδρῳ ὠφελι-
μώτερα ἢ πολιορκεῖν ἄπορον πάντη προσφέρεσθαι
3 τὴν ἄκραν. πρὸς μὲν δὴ ταῖς Κελαιναῖς φυλακὴν
καταλείπει στρατιώτας ἐς χιλίους καὶ πεντακοσίους.
μείνας δὲ αὐτοῦ ἡμέρας δέκα καὶ σατράπην ἀπο-
δείξας Φρυγίας Ἀντίγονον τὸν Φιλίππου, ἐπὶ δὲ
τοὺς συμμάχους ἀντ᾽ ἐκείνου στρατηγὸν Βάλακρον
τὸν Ἀμύντου ἐπιτάξας, αὐτὸς ἐπὶ Γορδίου ἐστέλλετο. καὶ Παρμενίωνι ἐπέστειλεν, ἄγοντα ἅμα οἱ
τὴν δύναμιν ἐκεῖσε ἀπαντᾶν· καὶ ἀπήντα ξὺν τῇ
4 δυνάμει Παρμενίων. καὶ οἱ νεόγαμοι δὲ οἱ ἐπὶ
Μακεδονίας σταλέντες εἰς Γόρδιον ἧκον καὶ ξὺν
αὐτοῖς ἄλλη στρατιὰ καταλεχθεῖσα, ἣν ἦγε Πτολεμαῖός τε ὁ Σελεύκου καὶ Κοῖνος ὁ Πολεμοκράτους καὶ Μελέαγρος ὁ Νεοπτολέμου, πεζοὶ μὲν
Μακεδόνες τρισχίλιοι, ἱππεῖς δὲ ἐς τριακοσίους καὶ
Θεσσαλῶν ἱππεῖς διακόσιοι, Ἠλείων δὲ ἑκατὸν καὶ
πεντήκοντα, ὧν ἡγεῖτο Ἀλκίας Ἠλεῖος.

Τὸ δὲ Γόρδιον ἔστι μὲν τῆς Φρυγίας τῆς ἐφ᾽
Ἑλλησπόντου, κεῖται δὲ ἐπὶ τοῦ Σαγγαρίου
ποταμοῦ· τοῦ δὲ Σαγγαρίου αἱ μὲν πηγαὶ ἐκ
Φρυγίας εἰσίν, αὐτὸς δὲ διὰ τῆς Θρᾳκῶν τῶν

---

[1] QC. iii 1, 1–8 (Celaenae surrendered after expiry of time
limit of 60 days); iv 1, 35 says that Antigonus later sent on to
Alexander most of the troops left to him.

[2] Wrongly styled satrap of Lydia by QC. iv 1, 34 f. (cf. ii

by a garrison of a thousand Carians and a hundred
Greek mercenaries. They sent envoys to Alexander, 2
offering, in case help did not come to them on a day
previously appointed (the date was specified), to
surrender the position. Alexander thought this
more advantageous than a siege of a height in-
accessible on every side. So he left 1,500 troops 3
as a guard over Celaenae.[1] After waiting there
ten days and appointing Antigonus son of Philip
satrap of Phrygia,[2] and replacing him as commander
of the allies by Balacrus son of Amyntas, he in person
set out for Gordium, ordering Parmenio to meet
him there bringing his force with him, as he did.
The recently married Macedonians who had gone to 4
Macedonia also came to Gordium,[3] and with them a
freshly levied army, led by Ptolemaeus son of
Seleucus, Coenus son of Polemocrates and Meleager
son of Neoptolemus; there were 3,000 Macedonian
foot, 300 horse, 200 Thessalian horse, 150 Eleians
under Alcias of Elis.[4]

Gordium is in Hellespontine Phrygia on the river 5
Sangarius, the springs of which are in Phrygia; it

4, 2 n.), he was prominent after Al's death, almost reunited the
empire under his rule and was the ancestor of the kings of
Macedon, 284-168 B.C.

[3] As Gordium is 500 miles from Pella, they could not have
arrived before May 333 B.C. On Al's arrival, he presumably
lost little time before 'loosing' the Gordian knot (ii 3, 1)
and then set out 'next day' (ii 4, 1); he too then did not reach
Gordium before May. K. Kraft, Der ' rationale' Alexander
86 ff., reasonably suggests that Gordium was made the rendez-
vous (cf. 24, 3 n.), as a place on the main road from Syria to
the Hellespont, where Al. could withstand any Persian
counter-offensive, and that his unwillingness to tarry in
besieging Telmissus and Celaenae was due to his need to meet
the rest of his forces there at the appointed time.

[4] See Introd. 57.

Βιθυνῶν χώρας ἐξίησιν ἐς τὸν Εὔξεινον πόντον. ἐνταῦθα καὶ Ἀθηναίων πρεσβεία παρ' Ἀλέξανδρον ἀφίκετο, δεόμενοι Ἀλεξάνδρου ἀφεῖναί σφισι τοὺς αἰχμαλώτους, οἳ ἐπὶ Γρανίκῳ ποταμῷ ἐλήφθησαν Ἀθηναίων ξυστρατευόμενοι τοῖς Πέρσαις καὶ τότε ἐν Μακεδονίᾳ ξὺν τοῖς δισχιλίοις δεδεμένοι ἦσαν·

6 καὶ ὑπὲρ αὐτῶν ἄπρακτοι ἐν τῷ τότε ἀπῆλθον. οὐ γὰρ ἐδόκει ἀσφαλὲς εἶναι Ἀλεξάνδρῳ ἔτι ξυνεστῶτος τοῦ πρὸς τὸν Πέρσην πολέμου ἀνεῖναί τι τοῦ φόβου τοῖς Ἕλλησιν, ὅσοι ἐναντία τῇ Ἑλλάδι στρατεύεσθαι ὑπὲρ τῶν βαρβάρων οὐκ ἀπηξίωσαν· ἀλλ' ἀποκρίνεται, ἐπειδὰν τὰ παρόντα καλῶς γένηται, τότε ἥκειν ὑπὲρ τῶν αὐτῶν πρεσβευομένους.

runs through Bithynian Thrace into the Black Sea. An embassy also arrived there from Athens, begging Alexander to let them have the Athenian prisoners captured at the Granicus fighting on the Persian side and now under chains in Macedonia with the 2,000 captives. Their request on the prisoners' 6 behalf was not granted for the time being, and they departed.[5] Alexander did not think it safe, with the Persian war still in progress, to relax intimidation of the Greeks who did not scruple to fight for the barbarians against Greece; but he answered that when circumstances were favourable they were to approach him again on the same subject.

[5] Cf. iii 6, 2, Introd. n. 69. QC. iii 1, 9 says he now (apparently before arrival at Gordium) promised to restore all Greeks to their homes at the end of the war.

BOOK II

ΒΙΒΛΙΟΝ ΔΕΥΤΕΡΟΝ

1. Ἐκ δὲ τούτου Μέμνων τοῦ τε ναυτικοῦ παντὸς ἡγεμὼν ἐκ βασιλέως Δαρείου καθεστηκὼς καὶ τῆς παραλίου ξυμπάσης, ὡς ἐς Μακεδονίαν τε καὶ τὴν Ἑλλάδα ἀποστρέψων τὸν πόλεμον, Χίον μὲν λαμβάνει προδοσίᾳ ἐνδοθεῖσαν, ἔνθεν δὲ ἐπὶ Λέσβου πλεύσας, ὡς οὐ προσεῖχον αὐτῷ οἱ Μιτυληναῖοι, τὰς ἄλλας πόλεις τῆς Λέσβου προσ-
2 ηγάγετο. ταύτας δὲ παραστησάμενος καὶ προσχὼν τῇ Μιτυλήνῃ τὴν μὲν πόλιν χάρακι διπλῷ ἐκ θαλάσσης ἐς θάλασσαν ἀπετείχισε, στρατόπεδα δὲ πέντε ἐποικοδομησάμενος τῆς γῆς ἐκράτει οὐ χαλεπῶς. καὶ μέρος μέν τι τῶν νεῶν τὸν λιμένα αὐτῶν ἐφύλασσε, τὰς δὲ ἐπὶ τὴν ἄκραν τῆς Λέσβου τὸ Σίγριον, ἵνα ἡ προσβολὴ μάλιστά ἐστι ταῖς ἀπό τε Χίου καὶ ἀπὸ Γεραιστοῦ καὶ Μαλέας ὁλκάσιν, ἀποστείλας τὸν παράπλουν ἐν φυλακῇ εἶχεν, ὡς μή τινα ὠφέλειαν κατὰ θάλασσαν γίγνεσθαι τοῖς
3 Μιτυληναίοις. καὶ ἐν τούτῳ αὐτὸς μὲν νόσῳ τελευτᾷ, καὶ εἴπερ τι ἄλλο καὶ τοῦτο ἐν τῷ τότε ἔβλαψε τὰ βασιλέως πράγματα. Αὐτοφραδάτης δὲ καὶ Φαρνάβαζος ὁ Ἀρταβάζου, ὅτῳ καὶ ἐπέτρεψε τελευτῶν ὁ Μέμνων τὴν αὑτοῦ ἀρχὴν ἔστε Δαρεῖόν τι ὑπὲρ αὐτῆς γνῶναι, ἀδελφιδῷ αὑτοῦ ὄντι, οὗτοι
4 τῇ πολιορκίᾳ οὐκ ἀρρώστως προσέκειντο. καὶ οἱ Μιτυληναῖοι τῆς τε γῆς εἰργόμενοι καὶ ἀπὸ θαλάσσης πολλαῖς ναυσὶν ἐφορμούσαις φρουρούμενοι πέμψαντες παρὰ τὸν Φαρνάβαζον ὁμολογίας ἐποιήσαντο, τοὺς μὲν ξένους τοὺς παρ' Ἀλεξάνδρου

BOOK II

1. Subsequently Memnon, who had been appointed 333 B.C. by Darius commander-in-chief of the whole navy and all the coast, sought to divert the war into Macedonia and Greece,[1] and captured Chios, delivered over by treachery; thence he sailed to Lesbos, and though Mitylene did not adhere to him, he won over the remaining cities of Lesbos. After securing 2 their support, he put in at Mitylene, fenced off the city by a double stockade from sea to sea, built up five camps and had no trouble in mastering its territory. While part of his fleet guarded the Mitylenean harbour, other ships were despatched to Sigrium, the promontory of Lesbos, where cargo vessels from Chios and Geraistus and Malea usually approach, and so guarded the sea-route, to prevent help coming to Mitylene by sea. While thus engaged, Memnon 3 fell ill and died, the severest blow during this period to the Persian cause. But the blockade was vigorously carried on by Autophradates and Pharnabazus son of Artabazus, to whom, as his nephew, Memnon handed over his command at death, pending Darius' decision on the matter. As the people of 4 Mitylene were kept out of their land and guarded on the seaward side by many ships anchored offshore, they sent to Pharnabazus, and made an agreement to send away the mercenaries whom Alexander had

---

[1] For chs. 1 and 2 see generally Appendix II.

σφίσι κατὰ συμμαχίαν ἥκοντας ἀπελθεῖν, Μιτυληναίους δὲ καθελεῖν μὲν τὰς πρὸς ᾿Αλέξανδρόν
σφισι γενομένας στήλας, ξυμμάχους δὲ εἶναι
Δαρείου κατὰ τὴν εἰρήνην τὴν ἐπ᾿ ᾿Ανταλκίδου
γενομένην πρὸς βασιλέα [Δαρεῖον], [1] τοὺς φυγάδας
δὲ αὐτῶν κατιέναι ἐπὶ τοῖς ἡμίσεσι τῶν τότε
5 ὄντων, ὅτε ἔφευγον. ἐπὶ τούτοις μὲν δὴ ἡ ξύμ-
βασις τοῖς Μιτυληναίοις πρὸς τοὺς Πέρσας ξυνέβη.
Φαρνάβαζος δὲ καὶ Αὐτοφραδάτης, ὡς παρῆλθον
ἅπαξ εἴσω τῆς πόλεως, φρουράν τε ἐς αὐτὴν
εἰσήγαγον καὶ φρούραρχον ἐπ᾿ αὐτῇ Λυκομήδην
῾Ρόδιον, καὶ τύραννον ἐγκατέστησαν τῇ πόλει
Διογένην, ἕνα τῶν φυγάδων, χρήματά τε εἰσέπραξαν
τοὺς Μιτυληναίους τὰ μὲν βίᾳ ἀφελόμενοι τοὺς
ἔχοντας, τὰ δὲ ἐς τὸ κοινὸν ἐπιβαλόντες.

2. Ταῦτα δὲ διαπραξάμενοι Φαρνάβαζος μὲν
ἔπλει ἐπὶ Λυκίας ἄγων τοὺς ξένους τοὺς μισθοφόρους, Αὐτοφραδάτης δὲ ἐπὶ τὰς ἄλλας νήσους.
καὶ ἐν τούτῳ καταπέμπει Δαρεῖος Θυμώνδαν τὸν
Μέντορος, αὐτὸν μὲν τοὺς ξένους παρὰ Φαρναβάζου
παραληψόμενον καὶ ἀνάξοντα παρὰ βασιλέα, Φαρ-
ναβάζῳ ⟨δὲ⟩ ἐροῦντα ἄρχειν ὅσων Μέμνων
2 ἦρχεν· καὶ παραδοὺς τούτῳ τοὺς ξένους Φαρνάβαζος ἔπλει παρ᾿ Αὐτοφραδάτην ἐπὶ τὰς ναῦς.
ὡς δὲ ὁμοῦ ἐγένοντο, δέκα μὲν ναῦς στέλλουσιν ἐπὶ
τὰς Κυκλάδας νήσους Δατάμην ἄνδρα Πέρσην
ἄγοντα, αὐτοὶ δὲ ναυσὶν ἑκατὸν ἐπὶ Τενέδου

---

[1] Δαρεῖον, a gloss, unless an error by Arrian (cf. also ch.
2, 2); the king concerned was Artaxerxes.

---

[2] See Introd. 38.   A. should have written ' agreement with
Alexander and the Greeks ', cf. 2, 2.   Here as in 2. 2, Darius is
an error (perhaps a scribal gloss) for Artaxerxes II, the king

despatched to fight for them under their alliance, destroy the pillars on which their agreement with Alexander was inscribed, and become allies of Darius on the basis of the peace of Antalcidas with (the Persian) king [Darius];[2] the exiles were to return with possession of half the property they had held at the time of their exile. Though these were the terms of the Mitylenean agreement with the Persians, Pharnabazus and Autophradates, once within the city, put in a garrison under the command of Lycomedes of Rhodes, and made Diogenes, one of the exiles, tyrant over the city: they also exacted money from Mitylene, taking part from the rich citizens by force and the rest by imposing a levy on the community.[3]

2. After this success Pharnabazus sailed for Lycia with the foreign mercenaries, Autophradates to the other islands. At this juncture Darius sent Thymondas son of Mentor[1] to take over himself the mercenaries from Pharnabazus and lead them up-country to Darius, and to instruct Pharnabazus to take over Memnon's command.[2] Pharnabazus handed over the mercenaries, and sailed to join Autophradates and the fleet. Once together, they sent ten ships to the Cyclades under Datames, a Persian, while they themselves proceeded with a

reigning in 387 B.C. In fact, the Peace of Antalcidas left island cities, like Mitylene and Tenedos, free of Persian control; no doubt the Persian commanders deliberately misconstrued its terms.

[3] Cf. iii 2, 6; for other Lesbian cities iii 2, 4; QC. iv 5, 19 ff.; Tod 191.

[1] Memnon's deceased brother.

[2] Cf. QC. iii 3, 1. D. 30–31, 1 and QC. iii 2 report with variants Darius' mobilization and decision to fight Al. in person.

ἔπλευσαν· κατακομισθέντες δὲ τῆς Τενέδου εἰς τὸν
Βόρειον καλούμενον λιμένα πέμπουσι παρὰ τοὺς
Τενεδίους καὶ κελεύουσι τὰς στήλας τὰς πρὸς
᾽Αλέξανδρον καὶ τοὺς Ἕλληνας γενομένας σφίσι,
ταύτας μὲν καθελεῖν, πρὸς Δαρεῖον δὲ ἄγειν τὴν
εἰρήνην, ἣν ἐπὶ ᾽Ανταλκίδου [Δαρείῳ] [1] συνέθεντο.

3 Τενεδίοις δὲ τὰ μὲν τῆς εὐνοίας ἐς ᾽Αλέξανδρόν τε
καὶ τοὺς Ἕλληνας ἐποίει μᾶλλον, ἐν δὲ τῷ παρόντι
ἄπορον ἄλλως ἐδόκει ὅτι μὴ προσχωρήσαντας τοῖς
Πέρσαις σώζεσθαι· ἐπεὶ οὐδὲ Ἡγελόχῳ, ὅτῳ
προσετέτακτο ⟨ὑπ'⟩ ᾽Αλεξάνδρου αὖθις ξυναγαγεῖν
δύναμιν ναυτικήν, τοσαύτη ξυνηγμένη ἦν ὡς δι'
ὀλίγου προσδοκᾶν ἔσεσθαι ἄν σφισι παρ' αὐτοῦ
τινα ὠφέλειαν. οὕτω μὲν δὴ οἱ ἀμφὶ Φαρνάβαζον
τοὺς Τενεδίους φόβῳ μᾶλλον ἢ ἐθέλοντας παρε-
στήσαντο.

4 ᾽Εν δὲ τούτῳ Πρωτέας ὁ ᾽Ανδρονίκου ἐτύγχανε
μέν ξυναγαγὼν ἐξ Εὐβοίας τε καὶ Πελοποννήσου
ναῦς μακρὰς ὑπὸ ᾽Αντιπάτρου τεταγμένος, ὡς
εἶναί τινα ταῖς τε νήσοις φυλακὴν καὶ αὐτῇ τῇ
Ἑλλάδι, εἰ, καθάπερ ἐξηγγέλλετο, ἐπιπλέοιεν οἱ
βάρβαροι· πυθόμενος δὲ Δατάμην περὶ Σίφνον
ὁρμεῖν δέκα ναυσίν, αὐτὸς ἔχων πεντεκαίδεκα
νυκτὸς ἀνάγεται ἀπὸ Χαλκίδος τῆς ἐπὶ τῷ
5 Εὐρίπῳ· καὶ προσχὼν ἔωθεν Κύθνῳ τῇ νήσῳ τὴν
μὲν ἡμέραν αὐτοῦ αὐλίζεται, ὡς σαφέστερόν τε
διαπυθέσθαι τὰ περὶ τῶν δέκα νεῶν καὶ ἅμα ἐν
νυκτὶ φοβερώτερον προσπεσεῖν τοῖς Φοίνιξιν· ὡς
δὲ ἔμαθε σαφῶς τὸν Δατάμην ξὺν ταῖς ναυσὶν ἐν
Σίφνῳ ὁρμοῦντα, ἐπιπλεύσας ἔτι νυκτὸς ὑπ' αὐτὴν
τὴν ἔω καὶ ἀπροσδοκήτοις ἐπιπεσὼν ὀκτὼ μὲν ναῦς

[1] Δαρείῳ, see on ch. 1, 4.

333
B.C.

hundred sail to Tenedos. They came to port in the
'north harbour' of Tenedos and ordered the city
to destroy the inscribed pillars of the agreement
concluded by Tenedos with Alexander and the
Greeks, and to observe the peace of Antalcidas
[made with Darius].[3] The inclination of Tenedos 3
was rather towards Alexander and the Greeks;
but at the moment there seemed no hope of safety
but in joining the Persians, since Hegelochus, who
had received orders from Alexander to re-assemble
a fleet, had not raised a force sufficient to make
them expect any speedy help from him. It was in
this way, rather by terrorism than by their consent,
that Pharnabazus brought Tenedos over.

Meanwhile Proteas son of Andronicus had col- 4
lected certain ships of the line from Euboea and the
Peloponnese under a commission from Antipater,
in order to protect the islands and mainland of
Greece, in case, as reports suggested, the Persians
descended there. On learning that Datames was
anchored near Siphnos with ten ships, he weighed
anchor with fifteen sail by night from Chalcis on the
Euripus. At dawn he put in at the island of Cythnus, 5
and encamped there during the day-time, to get
clearer intelligence about the ten ships, and also to
attack the Phoenicians, and by night, to create
greater alarm. When he found for certain that
Datames was anchored with the ships at Siphnos, he
sailed there, while it was still night, attacked just at
dawn when the enemy were expecting nothing, and

---

[3] Cf. ch. 1, 4 n.

αὐτοῖς ἀνδράσιν ἔλαβε, Δατάμης δὲ μετὰ δυοῖν τριήροιν ἐν τῇ πρώτῃ προσμίξει τῶν ἅμα Πρωτέᾳ νεῶν ὑπεκφυγὼν ἀπεσώθη πρὸς τὸ ἄλλο ναυτικόν.

3. Ἀλέξανδρος δὲ ὡς ἐς Γόρδιον παρῆλθε, πόθος λαμβάνει αὐτὸν ἀνελθόντα ἐς τὴν ἄκραν, ἵνα καὶ τὰ βασίλεια ἦν τὰ Γορδίου καὶ τοῦ παιδὸς αὐτοῦ Μίδου, τὴν ἅμαξαν ἰδεῖν τὴν Γορδίου καὶ τοῦ ζυγοῦ

2 τῆς ἁμάξης τὸν δεσμόν. λόγος δὲ περὶ τῆς ἁμάξης ἐκείνης παρὰ τοῖς προσχώροις πολὺς κατεῖχε, Γόρδιον εἶναι τῶν πάλαι Φρυγῶν ἄνδρα πένητα καὶ ὀλίγην εἶναι αὐτῷ γῆν ἐργάζεσθαι καὶ ζεύγη βοῶν δύο· καὶ τῷ μὲν ἀροτριᾶν, τῷ δὲ ἁμαξεύειν τὸν

3 Γόρδιον. καί ποτε ἀροῦντος αὐτοῦ ἐπιστῆναι ἐπὶ τὸν ζυγὸν ἀετὸν καὶ ἐπιμεῖναι ἔστε ἐπὶ βουλυτὸν καθήμενον· τὸν δὲ ἐκπλαγέντα τῇ ὄψει ἰέναι κοινώσοντα ὑπὲρ τοῦ θείου παρὰ τοὺς Τελμισσέας τοὺς μάντεις· εἶναι γὰρ τοὺς Τελμισσέας σοφοὺς τὰ θεῖα ἐξηγεῖσθαι καί σφισιν ἀπὸ γένους δεδόσθαι αὐτοῖς καὶ γυναιξὶν καὶ παισὶ τὴν μαντείαν.

4 προσάγοντα δὲ κώμῃ τινὶ τῶν Τελμισσέων ἐντυχεῖν παρθένῳ ὑδρευομένῃ καὶ πρὸς ταύτην εἰπεῖν ὅπως οἱ τὸ τοῦ ἀετοῦ ἔσχε· τὴν δέ, εἶναι γὰρ καὶ αὐτὴν τοῦ μαντικοῦ γένους, θύειν κελεῦσαι τῷ Διὶ τῷ βασιλεῖ, ἐπανελθόντα ἐς τὸν τόπον αὐτόν. καί, δεηθῆναι γὰρ αὐτῆς Γόρδιον τὴν θυσίαν ξυνεπισπομένην οἱ αὐτὴν ἐξηγήσασθαι, θῦσαί τε ὅπως ἐκείνη ὑπετίθετο τὸν Γόρδιον καὶ ξυγγενέσθαι ἐπὶ γάμῳ τῇ παιδὶ καὶ γενέσθαι αὐτοῖν παῖδα Μίδαν ὄνομα.

5 ἤδη τε ἄνδρα εἶναι τὸν Μίδαν καλὸν καὶ γενναῖον καὶ ἐν τούτῳ στάσει πιέζεσθαι ἐν σφίσι τοὺς Φρύγας, καὶ γενέσθαι αὐτοῖς χρησμόν, ὅτι ἅμαξα ἄξει αὐτοῖς βασιλέα καὶ ὅτι οὗτος αὐτοῖς καταπαύ-

captured eight ships with their crews; Datames with
two triremes escaped in the first encounter with
Proteas' ships and safely joined the rest of the fleet.

3. When Alexander reached Gordium, he was seized
with a longing [1] to ascend to the acropolis, where
the palace of Gordius and his son Midas was situated,
and to see Gordius' waggon and the knot of the
waggon's yoke. There was a widespread local 2
tradition [2] about that waggon; Gordius, they said,
was a poor man among the old Phrygians, who tilled
a small amount of land with two yoke of oxen, one
for the plough and one to drive his waggon. Once, 3
as he was ploughing, an eagle settled on the yoke
and stayed sitting there, till it was time to loose the
oxen; Gordius was astonished at the sight, and went
off to consult the Telmissian prophets about the
prodigy; for they were skilled in the interpretation
of prodigies, inheriting, women and children too, the
prophetic gift. Approaching a Telmissian village, 4
he met a girl drawing water and told her his story of
the eagle; she too was of the prophetic line, and told
him to return to the exact spot and sacrifice to Zeus
the King. So then Gordius begged her to come
along with him and prescribe the sacrifice; he
sacrificed as she directed, and married the girl; they
had a son called Midas. Midas was already a grown 5
man, handsome and noble, when the Phrygians were
in trouble among themselves with civil strife; they
received an oracle that a waggon would bring them a

---

[1] Appendix V 3.
[2] This tale is not from the ' Vulgate ', but was recounted by
at least one of A's main sources.

σει τὴν στάσιν. ἔτι δὲ περὶ αὐτῶν τούτων βουλευομένοις ἐλθεῖν τὸν Μίδαν ὁμοῦ τῷ πατρὶ καὶ τῇ
μητρὶ καὶ ἐπιστῆναι τῇ ἐκκλησίᾳ αὐτῇ ἁμάξῃ.

6 τοὺς δὲ ξυμβαλόντας τὸ μαντεῖον τοῦτον ἐκεῖνον
γνῶναι ὄντα, ὅντινα ὁ θεὸς αὐτοῖς ἔφραζεν,
ὅτι ἄξει ἡ ἅμαξα· καὶ καταστῆσαι μὲν αὐτοὺς
βασιλέα τὸν Μίδαν, Μίδαν δὲ αὐτοῖς τὴν στάσιν
καταπαῦσαι, καὶ τὴν ἅμαξαν τοῦ πατρὸς ἐν τῇ ἄκρᾳ
ἀναθεῖναι χαριστήρια τῷ Διὶ τῷ βασιλεῖ ἐπὶ τοῦ
ἀετοῦ τῇ πομπῇ. πρὸς δὲ δὴ τούτοις καὶ τόδε περὶ
τῆς ἁμάξης ἐμυθεύετο, ὅστις λύσειε τοῦ ζυγοῦ τῆς
ἁμάξης τὸν δεσμόν, τοῦτον χρῆναι ἄρξαι τῆς

7 Ἀσίας. ἦν δὲ ὁ δεσμὸς ἐκ φλοιοῦ κρανίας καὶ
τούτου οὔτε τέλος οὔτε ἀρχὴ ἐφαίνετο. Ἀλέξανδρος δὲ ὡς ἀπόρως μὲν εἶχεν ἐξευρεῖν λύσιν τοῦ
δεσμοῦ, ἄλυτον δὲ περιιδεῖν οὐκ ἤθελε, μή τινα καὶ
τοῦτο ἐς τοὺς πολλοὺς κίνησιν ἐργάσηται, οἱ μὲν
λέγουσιν, ὅτι παίσας τῷ ξίφει διέκοψε τὸν δεσμὸν
καὶ λελύσθαι ἔφη· Ἀριστόβουλος δὲ λέγει ἐξελό-
ντα τὸν ἕστορα τοῦ ῥυμοῦ, ὃς ἦν τύλος διαβε-
βλημένος διὰ τοῦ ῥυμοῦ διαμπάξ, ξυνέχων τὸν
δεσμόν, ἐξελκύσαι ἔξω τοῦ ῥυμοῦ τὸ⟨ν⟩ ζυγόν.

8 ὅπως μὲν δὴ ἐπράχθη τὰ ἀμφὶ τῷ δεσμῷ τούτῳ
Ἀλεξάνδρῳ οὐκ ἔχω ἰσχυρίσασθαι. ἀπηλλάγη δ᾽
οὖν ἀπὸ τῆς ἁμάξης αὐτός τε καὶ οἱ ἀμφ᾽ αὐτὸν ὡς
τοῦ λογίου τοῦ ἐπὶ τῇ λύσει τοῦ δεσμοῦ ξυμβεβη-
κότος. καὶ γὰρ καὶ τῆς νυκτὸς ἐκείνης βρονταί τε
καὶ σέλας ἐξ οὐρανοῦ ἐπεσήμηναν· καὶ ἐπὶ τούτοις
ἔθυε τῇ ὑστεραίᾳ Ἀλέξανδρος τοῖς φήνασι θεοῖς τά
τε σημεῖα καὶ τοῦ δεσμοῦ τὴν λύσιν.

---

[3] P. 18 also cites Ar. against the general view that Al. cut
the knot (QC. iii 1. 14–19; J. xi 7). Pt. evidently did not

king and he would put an end to the strife. While
they were still discussing this, Midas arrived with
his parents and stopped, waggon and all, for the
assembly to see. The Phrygians, interpreting this 6
oracle, decided that he was the man who the gods had
told them would come in a waggon, and made him
king, and he put an end to the civil strife. He set up
his father's waggon in the acropolis as a thank-offering
to Zeus the King for sending the eagle. Over and
above this there was a legend about the waggon,
that anyone who untied the knot of the yoke would
rule Asia. The knot was of cornel bark, and you 7
could not see where it began or ended. Alexander
was unable to find how to untie the knot but unwilling to leave it tied, in case this caused a dis-
turbance among the masses; some say that he struck
it with his sword, cut the knot, and said it was now
untied—but Aristobulus says that he took out the
pole-pin, a bolt driven right through the pole, holding
the knot together, and so removed the yoke from the
pole. I cannot say with confidence what Alexander 8
actually did about this knot, but he and his suite
certainly left the waggon with the impression that
the oracle about the undoing of the knot had been
fulfilled, and in fact that night there was thunder and
lightning, a further sign from heaven; so Alexander
in thanksgiving offered sacrifice next day to whatever
gods had shown the signs and the way to undo the knot.[3]

confirm Ar., hence A's hesitation. Yet A. is confident about
the impression made on Al. and his suite, and about the
subsequent omen and sacrifice; on these matters Pt. must have
agreed with Ar., and he cannot then have ignored the incident,
but just failed to say *how* Al. loosed the knot; for a curious
parallel, v 7, 1. Al's success doubtless encouraged his claim
after Issus to be lord of 'Asia' (14, 7 f., apparently from Pt.
and/or Ar. cf. QC, P. and J.; iii 15, 5 n.). See Introd. n. 64.

4. Αὐτὸς δὲ τῇ ὑστεραίᾳ ἐπ' Ἀγκύρας τῆς Γαλατικῆς ἐστέλλετο· κἀκεῖ αὐτῷ πρεσβεία ἀφικνεῖται Παφλαγόνων, τό τε ἔθνος ἐνδιδόντων καὶ ἐς ὁμολογίαν ξυμβαινόντων· ἐς δὲ τὴν χώραν 2 ξὺν τῇ δυνάμει μὴ ἐσβαλεῖν ἐδέοντο. τούτοις μὲν δὴ προστάσσει Ἀλέξανδρος ὑπακούειν Κάλᾳ τῷ σατράπῃ τῷ Φρυγίας. αὐτὸς δὲ ἐπὶ Καππαδοκίας ἐλάσας ξύμπασαν τὴν ἐντὸς Ἅλυος ποταμοῦ προσηγάγετο καὶ ἔτι ὑπὲρ τὸν Ἅλυν πολλήν· καταστήσας δὲ Καππαδοκῶν Σαβίκταν σατράπην 3 αὐτὸς προῆγεν ἐπὶ τὰς πύλας τὰς Κιλικίας. καὶ ἀφικόμενος ἐπὶ τὸ Κύρου τοῦ ξὺν Ξενοφῶντι στρατόπεδον, ὡς κατεχομένας τὰς πύλας φυλακαῖς ἰσχυραῖς εἶδε, Παρμενίωνα μὲν αὐτοῦ καταλείπει σὺν ταῖς τάξεσι τῶν πεζῶν, ὅσοι βαρύτερον ὡπλισμένοι ἦσαν. αὐτὸς δὲ ἀμφὶ πρώτην φυλακὴν ἀναλαβὼν τούς τε ὑπασπιστὰς καὶ τοὺς τοξότας καὶ τοὺς Ἀγριᾶνας προῆγε τῆς νυκτὸς ἐπὶ τὰς πύλας, 4 ὡς οὐ προσδεχομένοις τοῖς φύλαξιν ἐπιπεσεῖν. καὶ προσάγων μὲν οὐκ ἔλαθεν, ἐς ἴσον δὲ αὐτῷ κατέστη ἡ τόλμα. οἱ γὰρ φύλακες αἰσθόμενοι Ἀλέξανδρον αὐτὸν προσάγοντα λιπόντες τὴν φυλακὴν ᾤχοντο φεύγοντες. τῇ δὲ ὑστεραίᾳ ἅμα τῇ ἕῳ ξὺν τῇ δυνάμει πάσῃ ὑπερβαλὼν τὰς πύλας κατέβαινεν ἐς 5 τὴν Κιλικίαν. καὶ ἐνταῦθα ἀγγέλλεται αὐτῷ Ἀρσάμης ὅτι πρόσθεν μὲν ἐπενόει διασώζειν Πέρσαις τὴν Ταρσόν, ὡς δὲ ὑπερβεβληκότα ἤδη τὰς πύλας ἐπύθετο Ἀλέξανδρον ἐκλιπεῖν ἐν νῷ ἔχειν τὴν πόλιν· δεδιέναι οὖν τοὺς Ταρσέας μὴ ἐφ' ἁρπαγὴν τραπεὶς οὕτω τὴν ἀπόλειψιν τῆς Ταρσοῦ ποιήσηται. 6 ταῦτα ἀκούσας δρόμῳ ἦγεν ἐπὶ τὴν Ταρσὸν τούς τε

4. Next day Alexander set out for Ancyra in Galatia; there a Paphlagonian embassy met him who offered their people's submission and agreed to terms; they begged him not to enter their country in force. Alexander instructed them to take orders 2 from Calas, satrap of Phrygia. He himself marched to Cappadocia, won over all the country this side of the river Halys and much beyond it. He made Sabictas satrap of Cappadocia and pushed on himself to the Cilician Gates.[1] When he reached the camp 3 of Cyrus, who had been with Xenophon, and saw that the Gates were strongly held, he left Parmenio there with the heavier-armed foot-battalions, while he himself, about the first watch, took the hypaspists, archers and Agrianians, and marched by night to the Gates, meaning to take the guards unawares. His march was detected, but his daring counted just 4 as much in his favour; the guards, observing that he was leading in person, left their posts in flight. Next day at dawn he passed the Gates with his full force and descended into Cilicia. There it was 5 reported to him that Arsames, who had previously planned to save Tarsus for the Persians, after learning that Alexander had already passed the Gates, was intending to abandon the city, and that the Tarsians were therefore afraid Arsames would resort to plunder before deserting it. Hearing this, Alexander led on 6

---

[1] QC. iii 1, 22–4; 4, 1 (with 'Abistamenes' for 'Sabictas'); P. 18, 3; Introd. 53. Al. never entered Paphlagonia and would have traversed only a small part of Cappadocia on the direct route from Ancyra to the Cilician Gates; the Cappadocians had to be defeated by Antigonus in Phrygia after Issus (QC. iv 1, 34, cf. A. R. Burn, *JHS* 1952, 81 ff., an important event doubtless ignored in A's main sources, because it was not part of Al's own story), fought for Darius at Gaugamela (A. iii 11, 7), and were subdued only after Al's death (D. xviii 3, 1; 16).

ἱππέας καὶ τῶν ψιλῶν ὅσοι κουφότατοι, ὥστε ὁ
Ἀρσάμης μαθὼν αὐτοῦ τὴν ὁρμὴν σπουδῇ φεύγει
ἐκ τῆς Ταρσοῦ παρὰ βασιλέα Δαρεῖον οὐδὲν
βλάψας τὴν πόλιν.

7   Ἀλέξανδρος δέ, ὡς μὲν Ἀριστοβούλῳ λέλεκται,
ὑπὸ καμάτου ἐνόσησεν, οἱ δὲ ἐς τὸν Κύδνον [τὸν]
ποταμὸν λέγουσι ῥίψαντα νήξασθαι, ἐπιθυμήσαντα
τοῦ ὕδατος, ἱδρῶντα καὶ καύματι ἐχόμενον. ὁ δὲ
Κύδνος ῥέει διὰ μέσης τῆς πόλεως· οἷα δὲ ἐκ τοῦ
Ταύρου ὄρους τῶν πηγῶν οἱ ἀνισχουσῶν καὶ διὰ
χώρου καθαροῦ ῥέων, ψυχρός τέ ἐστι καὶ τὸ ὕδωρ
8   καθαρός· σπασμῷ τε οὖν ἔχεσθαι Ἀλέξανδρον καὶ
θέρμαις ἰσχυραῖς καὶ ἀγρυπνίᾳ ξυνεχεῖ· καὶ τοὺς
μὲν ἄλλους ἰατροὺς οὐκ οἴεσθαι εἶναι βιώσιμον,
Φίλιππον δὲ Ἀκαρνᾶνα, ἰατρόν, ξυνόντα Ἀλεξάνδρῳ καὶ τά τε ἀμφὶ ἰατρικὴν ἐς τὰ μάλιστα
πιστευόμενον καὶ τὰ ἄλλα οὐκ ἀδόκιμον ἐν τῷ
στρατῷ ὄντα, καθῆραι ἐθέλειν Ἀλέξανδρον φαρ-
9   μάκῳ· καὶ τὸν κελεύειν καθῆραι. τὸν μὲν δὴ
παρασκευάζειν τὴν κύλικα, ἐν τούτῳ δὲ Ἀλεξάνδρῳ δοθῆναι ἐπιστολὴν παρὰ Παρμενίωνος φυλά-
ξασθαι Φίλιππον· ἀκούειν γὰρ διεφθάρθαι ὑπὸ
Δαρείου χρήμασιν ὥστε φαρμάκῳ ἀποκτεῖναι
Ἀλέξανδρον. τὸν δὲ ἀναγνόντα τὴν ἐπιστολὴν καὶ
ἔτι μετὰ χεῖρας ἔχοντα αὐτὸν μὲν λαβεῖν τὴν
κύλικα ἐν ᾗ ἦν τὸ φάρμακον, τὴν ἐπιστολὴν δὲ τῷ
10   Φιλίππῳ δοῦναι ἀναγνῶναι. καὶ ὁμοῦ τόν τε
Ἀλέξανδρον πίνειν καὶ τὸν Φίλιππον ἀναγινώσκειν
τὰ παρὰ τοῦ Παρμενίωνος. Φίλιππον δὲ εὐθὺς
ἔνδηλον γενέσθαι, ὅτι καλῶς οἱ ἔχει τὰ τοῦ φαρμά-
κου· οὐ γὰρ ἐκπλαγῆναι πρὸς τὴν ἐπιστολήν, ἀλλὰ
τοσόνδε μόνον παρακαλέσαι Ἀλέξανδρον, καὶ ἐς τὰ

the cavalry and the most mobile of the light troops
at full speed to Tarsus, so that Arsames learning of
his onrush fled to King Darius without harming
the city.[2]

Here Alexander fell ill, from fatigue according to
Aristobulus, but others tell the following story.[3]
Alexander dived into the river Cydnus and had a
swim; he wanted the bathe as he was in a sweat and
overcome by heat. The Cydnus runs right through
the city, and as its springs are in Mount Taurus and
it runs through open country, it is cold and its water
is clear. Alexander therefore caught a cramp, and
suffered from violent fever and continuous sleepless-
ness. All his physicians gave him up except Philip,
an Acarnanian doctor in his suite who was very much
trusted in medical matters, and in general enjoyed
honour in the army; he proposed a strong purge, and
Alexander told him to administer it. He was
making up the draught when a note was given
Alexander from Parmenio, ' Beware of Philip! I
hear that Darius has bribed him to poison you.'
Alexander read the letter, and still holding it, took
the cup with the draught and gave the note to Philip
to read; at one and the same moment Alexander
drank the dose and Philip read Parmenio's note.
Philip at once made it clear that all was well with the
dose; he was not panic-struck at the letter, but
simply re-assured Alexander and told him to follow

7

8

9

10

---

[2] QC. iii 4, 2–15; J. xi 8, 1 f.; cf. Xenophon, *Anabasis*
i 2, 21 on the Cilician Gates.
[3] ' Vulgate ' (§7–11); D. 31, 4–6, QC. iii 5 f.; J. xi 8, 3 ff.
differ in detail; P. 19 gives Ar's account without naming him.

ἄλλα οἱ πείθεσθαι ὅσα ἐπαγγέλλοιτο· σωθήσεσθαι
11 γὰρ πειθόμενον. καὶ τὸν μὲν καθαρθῆναί τε καὶ
ῥαΐσαι αὐτῷ τὸ νόσημα, Φιλίππῳ δὲ ἐπιδεῖξαι, ὅτι
πιστός ἐστιν αὐτῷ φίλος, καὶ τοῖς ἄλλοις δὲ τοῖς
ἀμφ' αὐτόν, ὅτι αὐτοῖς τε τοῖς φίλοις βέβαιος εἰς τὸ
ἀνύποπτον τυγχάνει ὢν καὶ πρὸς τὸ ἀποθανεῖν
ἐρρωμένος.

5. Ἐκ δὲ τούτου Παρμενίωνα μὲν πέμπει ἐπὶ
τὰς ἄλλας πύλας, αἳ δὴ ὁρίζουσι τὴν Κιλίκων τε
καὶ Ἀσσυρίων χώραν, προκαταλαβεῖν καὶ φυλάσσειν τὴν πάροδον, δοὺς αὐτῷ τῶν τε ξυμμάχων
τοὺς πεζοὺς καὶ τοὺς Ἕλληνας τοὺς μισθοφόρους
καὶ τοὺς Θρᾷκας, ὧν Σιτάλκης ἡγεῖτο, καὶ τοὺς
2 ἱππέας δὲ τοὺς Θεσσαλούς. αὐτὸς δὲ ὕστερος ἄρας
ἐκ Ταρσοῦ τῇ μὲν πρώτῃ ἐς Ἀγχίαλον πόλιν
ἀφικνεῖται. ταύτην δὲ Σαρδανάπαλον κτίσαι τὸν
Ἀσσύριον λόγος· καὶ τῷ περιβόλῳ δὲ καὶ τοῖς
θεμελίοις τῶν τειχῶν δήλη ἐστὶ μεγάλη τε πόλις
3 κτισθεῖσα καὶ ἐπὶ μέγα ἐλθοῦσα δυνάμεως. καὶ τὸ
μνῆμα τοῦ Σαρδαναπάλου ἐγγὺς ἦν τῶν τειχῶν τῆς
Ἀγχιάλου· καὶ αὐτὸς ἐφειστήκει ἐπ' αὐτῷ Σαρδανάπαλος συμβεβληκὼς τὰς χεῖρας ἀλλήλαις ὡς
μάλιστα ἐς κρότον συμβάλλονται, καὶ ἐπίγραμμα
4 ἐπεγέγραπτο αὐτῷ Ἀσσύρια γράμματα· οἱ μὲν
Ἀσσύριοι καὶ μέτρον ἔφασκον ἐπεῖναι τῷ ἐπιγράμ-
ματι, ὁ δὲ νοῦς ἦν αὐτῷ ὃν ἔφραζε τὰ ἔπη, ὅτι
Σαρδανάπαλος ὁ Ἀνακυνδαράξου παῖς Ἀγχίαλον
καὶ Ταρσὸν ἐν ἡμέρᾳ μιᾷ ἐδείματο. σὺ δέ, ὦ ξένε,
ἔσθιε καὶ πῖνε καὶ παῖζε, ὡς τἆλλα τὰ ἀνθρώπινα
οὐκ ὄντα τούτου ἄξια· τὸν ψόφον αἰνισσόμενος,
ὅνπερ αἱ χεῖρες ἐπὶ τῷ κρότῳ ποιοῦσι· καὶ τὸ

any further instructions from him; if he did so, he would recover. The purge worked and eased the illness; and Alexander showed Philip that as his friend he trusted him, and his suite in general that he was resolute in refusing to suspect his friends and steadfast in the face of death.

5. Next he sent Parmenio to the other Gates which divide the Cilician and Assyrian lands, to seize the passage before the enemy and guard it, giving him the allied infantry, the Greek mercenaries, the Thracians under Sitalces and the Thessalian horse.[1] Later on he left Tarsus and on the first day reached Anchialus, founded, as legend says, by Sardanapalus the Assyrian. The circumference and the foundations of the walls show that the city was large when founded, and grew to great power. Sardanapalus' monument was near the walls of Anchialus; over it stood Sardanapalus himself, his hands joined just as if to clap, and an epitaph was inscribed in the Assyrian script; the Assyrians said that it was in verse. In any case its meaning according to the words was: ' Sardanapalus son of Anakyndaraxes built Anchialus and Tarsus in one day; you, stranger, eat, drink and be merry, since other human things are not worth *this* '—the riddle referring to the noise of a

11

2

3

4

---

[1] For Issus campaign see App. III and VIII 3. Nothing of value in J. xi 9, little in P. 20. I shall note parallels to A. in D. and QC. (book iii throughout) without pointing out all divergencies. Parmenio's mission: QC. 7, 6 (put too late in D. 32, 2).

παῖζε ῥᾳδιουργότερον ἐγγεγράφθαι ἔφασαν τῷ
Ἀσσυρίῳ ὀνόματι.

5 Ἐκ δὲ τῆς Ἀγχιάλου ἐς Σόλους ἀφίκετο· καὶ
φρουρὰν ἐσήγαγεν ἐς Σόλους καὶ ἐπέβαλεν αὐτοῖς
τάλαντα διακόσια ἀργυρίου ζημίαν, ὅτι πρὸς τοὺς
6 Πέρσας μᾶλλόν τι τὸν νοῦν εἶχον. ἔνθεν δὲ
ἀναλαβὼν τῶν μὲν πεζῶν τῶν Μακεδόνων τρεῖς
τάξεις, τοὺς τοξότας δὲ πάντας καὶ τοὺς Ἀγριᾶνας
ἐξελαύνει ἐπὶ τοὺς τὰ ὄρη κατέχοντας Κίλικας.
καὶ ἐν ἑπτὰ ταῖς πάσαις ἡμέραις τοὺς μὲν βίᾳ
ἐξελών, τοὺς δὲ ὁμολογίᾳ παραστησάμενος ἐπαν-
7 ῆκεν ἐς τοὺς Σόλους. καὶ ἐνταῦθα μανθάνει
Πτολεμαῖον καὶ Ἄσανδρον ὅτι ἐκράτησαν Ὀροντο-
βάτου τοῦ Πέρσου, ὃς τήν τε ἄκραν τῆς Ἁλικαρνασσοῦ ἐφύλασσε καὶ Μύνδον καὶ Καῦνον καὶ
Θήραν καὶ Καλλίπολιν κατεῖχε· προσῆκτο δὲ καὶ
Κῶ καὶ Τριόπιον. τοῦτον ἡττῆσθαι ἔγραφον μάχῃ
μεγάλῃ· καὶ ἀποθανεῖν μὲν τῶν ἀμφ᾽ αὐτὸν
πεζοὺς ἐς ἑπτακοσίους καὶ ἱππέας ἐς πεντήκοντα,
8 ἁλῶναι δὲ οὐκ ἐλάττους τῶν χιλίων. Ἀλέξανδρος δὲ
ἐν Σόλοις θύσας τε τῷ Ἀσκληπιῷ καὶ πομπεύσας
αὐτός τε καὶ ἡ στρατιὰ πᾶσα καὶ λαμπάδα ἐπιτε-
λέσας καὶ ἀγῶνα διαθεὶς γυμνικὸν καὶ μουσικὸν
Σολεῦσι μὲν δημοκρατεῖσθαι ἔδωκεν· αὐτὸς δὲ
ἀναζεύξας ἐς Ταρσὸν τοὺς μὲν ἱππέας ἀπέστειλεν
Φιλώτᾳ δοὺς ἄγειν διὰ τοῦ Ἀλη[ν]ίου πεδίου ἐπὶ
9 τὸν ποταμὸν τὸν Πύραμον, αὐτὸς δὲ σὺν τοῖς
πεζοῖς καὶ τῇ ἴλῃ τῇ βασιλικῇ ἐς Μάγαρσον ἧκεν
καὶ τῇ Ἀθηνᾷ τῇ Μαγαρσίδι ἔθυσεν. ἔνθεν δὲ ἐς
Μαλλὸν ἀφίκετο καὶ Ἀμφιλόχῳ ὅσα ἥρωι ἐνήγισε·
καὶ στασιάζοντας καταλαβὼν τὴν στάσιν αὐτοῖς

hand-clap. (It was said that the words 'be merry'
had a less delicate original in the Assyrian.)[2]

From Anchialus he reached Soli; he put a garrison
in the place, and fined them two hundred silver
Talents, because they were inclined to favour Persia.[3]
From there he took three battalions of the Macedonian infantry, all the archers, and the Agrianians,
and marched against the Cilicians holding the heights.
In no more than seven days he drove some of them out,
induced others to enter into agreements, and
returned to Soli.[4] There he learnt that Ptolemaeus
and Asander had conquered Orontobates the Persian,
who had been defending the citadel of Halicarnassus,
was in control of Myndus, Caunus, Thera and Calli-
polis, and had won over Cos and Triopium. The
letter stated that they had beaten him in a great
battle with a loss of about 700 foot and 50 cavalry,
and taken at least 1,000 prisoners.[5] At Soli Alexander sacrificed to Asclepius and held a procession
of his whole army, with a torch relay race and
athletic and musical competitions.[6] He granted a
democracy to Soli. He then proceeded to Tarsus
and sent off the cavalry, commissioning Philotas to
conduct them to the river Pyramus through the
Aleian plain, while he himself went with the infantry
and the royal squadron to Magarsus and sacrificed to
Athena of Magarsus. He next arrived at Mallus and
made offerings for the dead to Amphilochus as a hero;
he found the Mallians torn by factions and put a stop

5

6

7

8

9

---

[2] Ar. F. 9 (Strabo xiv 5, 9; Athenaeus 530 A–B; A. is fullest),
derived probably from Callisthenes (F. 34).
[3] QC. 7, 2. Soli is treated as Greek, cf. 12, 2; Introd. n.
61.
[4] Not in QC.
[5] QC. 7, 4. Cf. App. II 2.
[6] QC. 7, 3 and 5 takes Al. straight to Mallus.

κατέπαυσε· καὶ τοὺς φόρους, οὓς βασιλεῖ Δαρείῳ
ἀπέφερον, ἀνῆκεν, ὅτι ᾿Αργείων μὲν Μαλλωταὶ
ἄποικοι ἦσαν, αὐτὸς δὲ ἀπ᾽ ῎Αργους τῶν ῾Ηρα-
κλειδῶν εἶναι ἠξίου.

6. ῎Ετι δὲ ἐν Μαλλῷ ὄντι αὐτῷ ἀγγέλλεται
Δαρεῖον ἐν Σώχοις ξὺν τῇ πάσῃ δυνάμει στρατοπεδεύειν. ὁ δὲ χῶρος οὗτός ἐστι μὲν τῆς ᾿Ασ-
συρίας γῆς, ἀπέχει δὲ τῶν πυλῶν τῶν ᾿Ασσυρίων
ἐς δύο μάλιστα σταθμούς. ἔνθα δὴ ξυναγαγὼν
τοὺς ἑταίρους φράζει αὐτοῖς τὰ ἐξηγγελμένα ὑπὲρ
Δαρείου τε καὶ τῆς στρατιᾶς τῆς Δαρείου. οἱ δὲ
2 αὐτόθεν ὡς εἶχεν ἄγειν ἐκέλευον. ὁ δὲ τότε μὲν
ἐπαινέσας αὐτοὺς διέλυσε τὸν ξύλλογον, τῇ δὲ
ὑστεραίᾳ προ[σ]ῆγεν ὡς ἐπὶ Δαρεῖόν τε καὶ τοὺς
Πέρσας. δευτεραῖος δὲ ὑπερβαλὼν τὰς πύλας
ἐστρατοπέδευσε πρὸς Μυριάνδρῳ πόλει· καὶ τῆς
νυκτὸς χειμὼν ἐπιγίγνεται σκληρὸς καὶ ὕδωρ τε ἐξ
οὐρανοῦ καὶ πνεῦμα βίαιον· τοῦτο κατέσχεν ἐν τῷ
στρατοπέδῳ ᾿Αλέξανδρον.

3 Δαρεῖος δὲ τέως μὲν ξὺν τῇ στρατιᾷ διέτριβεν,
ἐπιλεξάμενος τῆς ᾿Ασσυρίας γῆς πεδίον πάντῃ
ἀναπεπταμένον καὶ τῷ τε πλήθει τῆς στρατιᾶς
ἐπιτήδειον καὶ ἐνιππάσασθαι τῇ ἵππῳ ξύμφορον.
καὶ τοῦτο τὸ χωρίον ξυνεβούλευσεν αὐτῷ μὴ ἀπολείπειν ᾿Αμύντας ὁ ᾿Αντιόχου, ὁ παρὰ ᾿Αλεξάνδρου
αὐτόμολος· εἶναι γὰρ τὴν εὐρυχωρίαν πρὸς τοῦ
πλήθους τε καὶ τῆς σκευῆς τῶν Περσῶν. καὶ
4 ἔμενε Δαρεῖος. ὡς δὲ ᾿Αλεξάνδρῳ πολλὴ μὲν [ἡ]
ἐν Ταρσῷ τριβὴ ἐπὶ τῇ νόσῳ ἐγίνετο, οὐκ ὀλίγη δὲ
ἐν Σόλοις, ἵνα ἔθυέ τε καὶ ἐπόμπευε, καὶ ἐπὶ τοὺς
ὀρεινοὺς Κίλικας διέτριψεν ἐξελάσας, τοῦτο ἔσφη-
λεν Δαρεῖον τῆς γνώμης· καὶ αὐτός τε, ὅ τι περ

to them; he remitted the tribute paid to Darius, 333
since Mallus was a colony of Argos, and he himself B.C.
claimed descent from the Argive Heraclidae.[7]

6. Alexander was still at Mallus when a report
came that Darius with his full force was encamped
at Sochi, a place in Assyrian territory, about two
marching days from the Assyrian Gates. Alexander therefore assembled the Companions and told
them the news of Darius and his army, on which they
urged him to advance without more ado. He then 2
thanked them and dismissed the council and marched
next day to attack Darius and the Persians. On the
second day he passed the Gates and camped near a
city called Myriandrus, and in the night a severe
storm came on with rain, and a violent gale, which
kept Alexander in his camp.[1]

Darius meanwhile was marking time with his army. 3
He had selected a plain in the Assyrian land open all
round, convenient for the great number of his army
and suitable for the manoeuvres of his cavalry.
Amyntas son of Antiochus, the deserter from Alexander, advised him not to leave this place; there
was, he said, elbow-room favourable for the numbers
and equipment of the Persians.[2] So Darius stayed
where he was. But as Alexander spent a long time 4
in Tarsus on account of his illness, and a good deal at
Soli, where he sacrificed and held the parade, and was
delayed by his raid on the Cilician hillmen,[3] all this
made Darius waver in his decision. He himself was

[7] Al. treats Mallus as Greek, like its 'founder', Amphilochus.
[1] D. 32, 2; QC. 7, 6–10; App. III 3.
[2] P. 20, 1; QC. 8, 1–11 is very different.
[3] See Appendix VIII 3. For Darius' mobilization, D. 30 f.;
QC. iii 2 f.

ἥδιστον ἦν δοξασθέν, ἐς τοῦτο οὐκ ἀκουσίως
ὑπήχθη καὶ ὑπὸ τῶν καθ' ἡδονὴν ξυνόντων τε καὶ
ξυνεσομένων ἐπὶ κακῷ τοῖς ἀεὶ βασιλεύουσιν
ἐπαιρόμενος ἔγνω μηκέτι Ἀλέξανδρον ἐθέλειν
5 προϊέναι τοῦ πρόσω, ἀλλ' ὀκνεῖν γὰρ πυνθανόμενον
ὅτι αὐτὸς προσάγοι· καταπατήσειν τε τῇ ἵππῳ
τῶν Μακεδόνων τὴν στρατιὰν ἄλλος ἄλλοθεν αὐτῷ
6 ἐπαίροντες ἔλεγον· καίτοι γε Ἀμύντας ἥξειν τε
Ἀλέξανδρον ἰσχυρίζετο, ὅπου ἂν πύθηται Δαρεῖον
ὄντα, καὶ αὐτοῦ προσμένειν ἐκέλευεν. ἀλλὰ τὰ
χείρω μᾶλλον, ὅτι καὶ ἐν τῷ παραυτίκα ἡδίω
ἀκοῦσαι ἦν, ἔπειθε· καί τι καὶ δαιμόνιον τυχὸν
ἦγεν αὐτὸν εἰς ἐκεῖνον τὸν χῶρον, οὗ μήτε ἐκ τῆς
ἵππου πολλὴ ὠφέλεια αὐτῷ ἐγένετο, μήτε ἐκ τοῦ
πλήθους αὐτοῦ τῶν τε ἀνθρώπων καὶ τῶν ἀκοντίων
τε καὶ τοξευμάτων, μηδὲ τὴν λαμπρότητα αὐτὴν
τῆς στρατιᾶς ἐπιδεῖξαι ἠδυνήθη, ἀλλὰ Ἀλεξάνδρῳ
τε καὶ τοῖς ἀμφ' αὐτὸν εὐμαρῶς τὴν νίκην παρέ-
7 δωκεν. ἐχρῆν γὰρ ἤδη καὶ Πέρσας πρὸς Μακεδόνων ἀφαιρεθῆναι τῆς Ἀσίας τὴν ἀρχήν, καθάπερ
οὖν Μῆδοι μὲν πρὸς Περσῶν ἀφῃρέθησαν, πρὸς
Μήδων δὲ ἔτι ἔμπροσθεν Ἀσσύριοι.

7. Ὑπερβαλὼν δὴ τὸ ὄρος Δαρεῖος τὸ κατὰ τὰς
πύλας τὰς Ἀμανικὰς καλουμένας ὡς ἐπὶ Ἰσσὸν
προῆγε· καὶ ἐγένετο κατόπιν Ἀλεξάνδρου λαθών.
τὴν δὲ Ἰσσὸν κατασχών, ὅσους διὰ νόσον ὑπολε-
λειμμένους αὐτοῦ τῶν Μακεδόνων κατέλαβε,
τούτους χαλεπῶς αἰκισάμενος ἀπέκτεινεν· ἐς δὲ
τὴν ὑστεραίαν προὐχώρει ἐπὶ τὸν ποταμὸν τὸν
2 Πίναρον. καὶ Ἀλέξανδρος ὡς ἤκουσεν ἐν τῷ
ὄπισθεν αὐτοῦ ὄντα Δαρεῖον, ἐπεὶ οὐ πιστὸς αὐτῷ
ὁ λόγος ἐφαίνετο, ἀναβιβάσας εἰς τριακόντορον τῶν

readily induced to adopt any opinion it was most
agreeable to hold; and ingratiating courtiers, such
as do and will haunt each successive king to his
detriment,[4] encouraged him to conclude that Alexander was no longer willing to advance further, but 5
was hesitating on hearing of Darius' own approach.
On all sides they egged him on, telling him that he
would trample the Macedonian force underfoot with
his cavalry.[5] Amyntas, however, persisted that 6
Alexander would come wherever he found Darius to
be, and urged him to remain where he was. But the
worse counsels prevailed, as they were more agreeable to hear at the time; moreover, some divine
power led Darius into the very position where his
cavalry did not much help him, nor the number of
his men and javelins and arrows, where he could
make no display even of the splendour of his army,
but delivered the victory easily to Alexander and
his force. In fact it was destined that the Persians 7
should forfeit the sovereignty of Asia to Macedonians,
just as Medes had lost it to Persians, and Assyrians
even earlier to Medes.[6]

7. Darius then crossed the mountains by the so-
called Amanian Gates, advanced towards Issus and
slipped in behind Alexander. On seizing Issus, he
savagely tortured and killed all the invalid Macedonians left behind there whom he captured. Next
day he advanced to the river Pinarus.[1] Alexander 2
heard that Darius was in his rear but did not credit
the report; he embarked some of the Companions

---

[4] A's own comment, cf. iv 8, 3.
[5] So at this time Demosthene was predicting, Aeschines,
iii 164.
[6] More of A's own comment.
[1] QC. 8, 13–15.

ἑταίρων τινὰς ἀποπέμπει ὀπίσω ἐπὶ Ἰσσόν, κατα-
σκεψομένους εἰ τὰ ὄντα ἐξαγγέλλεται. οἱ δὲ
ἀναπλεύσαντες τῇ τριακοντόρῳ, ὅτι κολπώδης ἦν ἡ
ταύτῃ θάλασσα, μᾶλλόν τι εὐπετῶς κατέμαθον
αὐτοῦ στρατοπεδεύοντας τοὺς Πέρσας· καὶ ἀπαγγέλλουσιν Ἀλεξάνδρῳ ἐν χερσὶν εἶναι Δαρεῖον.

3 Ὁ δὲ συγκαλέσας στρατηγούς τε καὶ ἰλάρχας καὶ
τῶν ξυμμάχων τοὺς ἡγεμόνας παρεκάλει θαρρεῖν
μὲν ἐκ τῶν ἤδη σφίσι καλῶς κεκινδυνευμένων καὶ
ὅτι πρὸς νενικημένους ὁ ἀγὼν νενικηκόσιν αὐτοῖς
ἔσται καὶ ὅτι ὁ θεὸς ὑπὲρ σφῶν στρατηγεῖ ἄμεινον,
ἐπὶ νοῦν Δαρείῳ ἀγαγὼν καθεῖρξαι τὴν δύναμιν ἐκ
τῆς εὐρυχωρίας ἐς τὰ στενόπορα, ἵνα σφίσι μὲν
ξύμμετρον τὸ χωρίον ἀναπτύξαι τὴν φάλαγγα, τοῖς
δὲ ἀχρεῖον τὸ πλῆθος [ὅτι] ἔσται τῇ μάχῃ, οὔτε τὰ
4 σώματα οὔτε τὰς γνώμας παραπλησίοις. Μακεδόνας τε γὰρ Πέρσαις καὶ Μήδοις, ἐκ πάνυ πολλοῦ
τρυφῶσιν, αὐτοὺς ἐν τοῖς πόνοις τοῖς πολεμικοῖς
πάλαι ἤδη μετὰ κινδύνων ἀσκουμένους, ἄλλως τε
καὶ δούλοις ἀνθρώποις ἐλευθέρους, ἐς χεῖρας ἥξειν·
ὅσοι τε Ἕλληνες Ἕλλησιν, οὐχ ὑπὲρ τῶν αὐτῶν
μαχεῖσθαι, ἀλλὰ τοὺς μὲν ξὺν Δαρείῳ ἐπὶ μισθῷ
καὶ οὐδὲ τούτῳ πολλῷ κινδυνεύοντας, τοὺς δὲ ξὺν
σφίσιν ὑπὲρ τῆς Ἑλλάδος ἑκόντας ἀμυνομένους·
5 βαρβάρων τε αὖ Θρᾷκας καὶ Παίονας καὶ Ἰλ-
λυριοὺς καὶ Ἀγριᾶνας τοὺς εὐρωστοτάτους τε τῶν
κατὰ τὴν Εὐρώπην καὶ μαχιμωτάτους πρὸς τὰ

---

[2] Ib. 16–19.

[3] Sections 3–7 are naturally taken as derived from a speech
in Pt. or Ar., contrast 8 f. The speech (3) takes their view of
the tactical situation (6, 3 but the ' favour of God ' is also in

in a thirty-oared ship and sent them back to Issus, **333** to see if it was true. They discovered the more **B.C.** easily that the Persians were camped there, since the sea takes the form of a bay there, and reported to Alexander that Darius was at hand.[2]

Alexander summoned the generals, squadron **3** leaders and officers of the allies [3] and urged them to be confident in view of the dangers they had successfully surmounted in the past; already conquerors they were to fight men they had conquered, and God was a better strategist on their own side, putting it into Darius' mind to bring his force out of the open country and hem it into the narrow pass, an area just the size for the deployment of their phalanx; in the battle the Persians would have no benefit from their numbers, while their physique and morale were no match for their own. 'We Macedonians,' he continued, 'are to fight **4** Medes and Persians, nations long steeped in luxury, while we have now long been inured to danger by the exertions of campaigning. Above all it will be a fight of free men against slaves. And so far as Greek will meet Greek, they will not be fighting for like causes; those with Darius will be risking their lives for pay, and poor pay too; the Greeks on our side will fight as volunteers in the cause of Greece. As for our bar- **5** barian troops, Thracians, Paeonians, Illyrians, Agrianians, the most robust and warlike races of Europe,

D. 33, 1), makes their kind of distinction between Greeks and Macedonians (4 cf. 10, 7, but note iv 11, 8 from 'vulgate'), stresses the value of the Balkan troops which they would have appreciated more than a later writer (5), and has their figure for mercenaries at the Granicus (6, cf. App. I 1). The suggestion in 7 that Issus would decide the war proved false, but could easily have been voiced at the time. QC. viii 20 f. alleges that Al. lost confidence at this juncture. Cf. 10, 2 n.

ARRIAN

ἀπονώτατά τε καὶ μαλακώτατα τῆς Ἀσίας γένη
ἀντιτάξεσθαι· ἐπὶ δὲ Ἀλέξανδρον ἀντιστρατηγεῖν
6 Δαρείῳ. ταῦτα μὲν οὖν ἐς πλεονεξίαν τοῦ ἀγῶνος
ἐπεξῄει. τὰ δὲ ἆθλα ὅτι μεγάλα ἔσται σφίσι τοῦ
κινδύνου ἐπεδείκνυεν. οὐ γὰρ τοὺς σατράπας τοὺς
Δαρείου ἐν τῷ τότε κρατήσειν, οὐδὲ τὴν ἵππον τὴν
ἐπὶ Γρανίκῳ ταχθεῖσαν, οὐδὲ τοὺς δισμυρίους
ξένους τοὺς μισθοφόρους, ἀλλὰ Περσῶν τε ὅ τι περ
ὄφελος καὶ Μήδων καὶ ὅσα ἄλλα ἔθνη Πέρσαις καὶ
Μήδοις ὑπήκοα ἐποικεῖ τὴν Ἀσίαν καὶ αὐτὸν μέγαν
βασιλέα παρόντα, καὶ ὡς οὐδὲν ὑπολειφθήσεταί
σφισιν ἐπὶ τῷδε τῷ ἀγῶνι ὅτι μὴ κρατεῖν τῆς
Ἀσίας ξυμπάσης καὶ πέρας τοῖς πολλοῖς πόνοις
7 ἐπιθεῖναι. ἐπὶ τούτοις δὲ τῶν τε ἐς τὸ κοινὸν ξὺν
λαμπρότητι ἤδη πεπραγμένων ὑπεμίμνησκεν καὶ εἰ
δή τῳ ἰδίᾳ τι διαπρεπὲς ἐς κάλλος τετολμημένον,
ὀνομαστὶ ἕκαστον ἐπὶ τῷ ἔργῳ ἀνακαλῶν. καὶ τὸ
αὑτοῦ οὐκ ἀκίνδυνον ἐν ταῖς μάχαις ὡς ἀνεπαχθέ-
8 στατα ἐπεξῄει. λέγεται δὲ καὶ Ξενοφῶντος καὶ
τῶν ἅμα Ξενοφῶντι μυρίων ἐς μνήμην ἐλθεῖν, ὡς
οὐδέν τι οὔτε κατὰ πλῆθος οὔτε κατὰ τὴν ἄλλην
ἀξίωσιν σφίσιν ἐπεοικότες, οὐδὲ ἱππέων αὐτοῖς
παρόντων Θεσσαλῶν, οὐδὲ Βοιωτῶν ἢ Πελοποννησίων, οὐδὲ Μακεδόνων ἢ Θρᾳκῶν, οὐδὲ ὅση ἄλλη
σφίσιν ἵππος ξυντέτακται, οὐδὲ τοξοτῶν ἢ σφενδο-
νητῶν, ὅτι μὴ Κρητῶν ἢ Ῥοδίων ὀλίγων, καὶ
τούτων ἐν τῷ κινδύνῳ ὑπὸ Ξενοφῶντος αὐτοσχε-
9 διασθέντων, οἱ δὲ βασιλέα τε ξὺν πάσῃ τῇ δυνάμει
πρὸς Βαβυλῶνι αὐτῇ ἐτρέψαντο καὶ ἔθνη ὅσα
κατιόντων ἐς τὸν Εὔξεινον πόντον καθ᾽ ὁδὸν σφίσιν
ἐπεγένετο νικῶντες ἐπῆλθον· ὅσα τε ἄλλα ἐν τῷ
τοιῷδε πρὸ τῶν κινδύνων ἐς παράκλησιν ἀνδράσιν

will be ranged against the most indolent and softest
tribes of Asia. In addition you have Alexander
commanding against Darius.' Besides rehearsing 6
these advantages they had in the contest, he pointed
out the greatness of the rewards for which they
were incurring danger. It was not Darius' satraps
whom they were now to overcome, nor the cavalry
that lined the Granicus, nor the twenty thousand
foreign mercenaries, but the flower of Medes and
Persians and all their subject nations living in Asia;
the Great King was there himself; nothing remained after this final struggle but to rule the whole
of Asia and set an end to their long exertions. In 7
addition, he reminded them of all they had already
achieved with brilliant success for the common
cause, and cited any noble act of personal daring,
naming both the deed and the man; with the utmost
delicacy he mentioned the dangers he himself had
faced in battles. He is also said to have recalled [4] 8
that Xenophon and his Ten Thousand, though
they were not to be compared to themselves in number and other qualities, with no cavalry, Thessalian,
Boeotian, Peloponnesian, Macedonian or Thracian,
nor such other horse as they now had in their own
ranks, no archers or slingers, save a few Cretans
and Rhodians, and those hastily scraped together
by Xenophon in the crisis. Yet the Ten Thousand 9
routed the Great King with his whole power near
Babylon itself, and victoriously attacked the various
other tribes which barred their way as they descended
to the Black Sea. He also told them of anything else
which at such a time, before dangers, a brave general

---

[4] ' Vulgate '. Not necessarily false; Al. is likely to have
read Xenophon. A's source here in sections 8 f., as in 3–7,
is apparently not that followed by QC., cf. 10, 2 n.

ἀγαθοῖς ἐξ ἀγαθοῦ ἡγεμόνος παραινεῖσθαι εἰκός. οἱ δὲ ἄλλος ἄλλοθεν δεξιούμενοί τε τὸν βασιλέα καὶ τῷ λόγῳ ἐπαίροντες ἄγειν ἤδη ἐκέλευον.

8. Ὁ δὲ τότε μὲν δειπνοποιεῖσθαι παραγγέλλει, προπέμπει δὲ ὡς ἐπὶ τὰς πύλας τῶν τε ἱππέων ὀλίγους καὶ τῶν τοξοτῶν προκατασκεψομένους τὴν ὁδὸν τὴν ὀπίσω [ὡς ἐπὶ τὰς πύλας]· καὶ αὐτὸς τῆς νυκτὸς ἀναλαβὼν τὴν στρατιὰν πᾶσαν ᾔει, ὡς 2 κατασχεῖν αὖθις τὰς πύλας. ὡς δὲ ἀμφὶ μέσας νύκτας ἐκράτησεν αὖθις τῶν παρόδων, ἀνέπαυε τὴν στρατιὰν τὸ λοιπὸν τῆς νυκτὸς αὐτοῦ ἐπὶ τῶν πετρῶν, προφυλακὰς ἀκριβεῖς καταστησάμενος. ὑπὸ δὲ τὴν ἕω κατῄει ἀπὸ τῶν πυλῶν κατὰ τὴν ὁδόν· καὶ ἕως μὲν πάντῃ στενόπορα ἦν τὰ χωρία, ἐπὶ κέρως ἦγεν, ὡς δὲ διεχώρει ἐς πλάτος, ἀνέπτυσσεν ἀεὶ τὸ κέρας ἐς φάλαγγα, ἄλλην καὶ ἄλλην τῶν ὁπλιτῶν τάξιν παράγων, τῇ μὲν ὡς ἐπὶ τὸ ὄρος, ἐν 3 ἀριστερᾷ δὲ ὡς ἐπὶ τὴν θάλασσαν. οἱ δὲ ἱππεῖς αὐτῷ τέως μὲν κατόπιν τῶν πεζῶν τεταγμένοι ἦσαν, ὡς δὲ ἐς τὴν εὐρυχωρίαν προῄεσαν, συνέτασσεν ἤδη τὴν στρατιὰν ὡς ἐς μάχην, πρώτους μὲν ἐπὶ τοῦ δεξιοῦ κέρως πρὸς τῷ ὄρει τῶν πεζῶν τό τε ἄγημα καὶ τοὺς ὑπασπιστάς, ὧν ἡγεῖτο Νικάνωρ ὁ Παρμενίωνος, ἐχομένην δὲ τούτων τὴν Κοίνου τάξιν, ἐπὶ δὲ τούτοις τὴν Περδίκκου. οὗτοι μὲν ἔστε ἐπὶ τὸ μέσον τῶν ὁπλιτῶν ἀπὸ τοῦ δεξιοῦ 4 ἀρξαμένῳ τεταγμένοι ἦσαν. ἐπὶ δὲ τοῦ εὐωνύμου πρώτη μὲν ἡ Ἀμύντου τάξις ἦν, ἐπὶ δὲ ἡ Πτολεμαίου, ἐχομένη δὲ ταύτης ἡ Μελεάγρου. τοῦ δὲ εὐωνύμου τοῖς πεζοῖς μὲν Κρατερὸς ἐπετέτακτο

---

[1] Contrast QC. 8, 22–3.

would naturally tell brave men by way of encouragement. They crowded round and clasped their king's
hand, and with cries of encouragement urged him
to lead them on at once.

8. For the moment, however, Alexander told his
troops to take their meal, but he sent a few horsemen
and archers on [towards the Gates] to reconnoitre the
road that lay behind them; then at nightfall he himself marched with his whole force to seize the Gates
again. When about midnight he was in possession of 2
the passes once more, he rested his army for the
remainder of the night there on the crags, after
carefully setting outposts.[1] Just upon dawn he
descended from the Gates along the road; as long as
the defile enclosed on every side remained narrow,
he led the army in column, but when it grew broader,
he deployed his column continuously into a phalanx,
bringing up battalion after battalion of hoplites, on
the right up to the ridge, and on the left up to the
sea. His cavalry so far had been ranged behind the 3
infantry, but when they moved forward into open
ground, he at once drew up his army in battle order;[2]
on the right wing towards the mountain ridge he
placed first of the infantry the *agema* and hypaspists
under Nicanor son of Parmenio, next to them Coenus'
battalion, and then that of Perdiccas. From right to
left these regiments stretched to the centre of the
hoplites. On the left, Amyntas' battalion came first, 4
then Ptolemaeus', and next Meleager's. Craterus[3]
had been put in command of the infantry on the left

[2] QC. 8, 24; 9, 12 (muddled). D. 33, 1 puts the horse in
front.

[3] A. obscures the fact that Craterus also had a battalion
(i 14, 3; iii 11, 10). Battle order: QC. 9, 7–9.

ἄρχειν, τοῦ δὲ ξύμπαντος εὐωνύμου Παρμενίων
ἡγεῖτο· καὶ παρήγγελτο αὐτῷ μὴ ἀπολείπειν τὴν
θάλασσαν, ὡς μὴ κυκλωθεῖεν ἐκ τῶν βαρβάρων,
ὅτι πάντῃ ὑπερφαλαγγήσειν αὐτῶν διὰ πλῆθος
ἤμελλον.

5 Δαρεῖος δέ, ἐπειδὴ ἐξηγγέλθη αὐτῷ προσάγων
ἤδη Ἀλέξανδρος ὡς ἐς μάχην, τῶν μὲν ἱππέων
διαβιβάζει πέραν τοῦ ποταμοῦ τοῦ Πινάρου ἐς
τρισμυρίους μάλιστα τὸν ἀριθμὸν καὶ μετὰ τούτων
τῶν ψιλῶν ἐς δισμυρίους, ὅπως τὴν λοιπὴν δύναμιν
6 καθ᾽ ἡσυχίαν συντάξειε. καὶ πρώτους μὲν τοῦ
ὁπλιτικοῦ τοὺς Ἕλληνας τοὺς μισθοφόρους ἔταξεν
ἐς τρισμυρίους κατὰ τὴν φάλαγγα τῶν Μακεδόνων·
ἐπὶ δὲ τούτοις τῶν Καρδάκ[κ]ων καλουμένων
ἔνθεν καὶ ἔνθεν ἐς ἑξακισμυρίους· ὁπλῖται δὲ ἦσαν
καὶ οὗτοι. τοσούτους γὰρ ἐπὶ φάλαγγος ἁπλῆς
7 ἐδέχετο τὸ χωρίον, ἵνα ἐτάσσοντο. ἐπέταξε δὲ καὶ
τῷ ὄρει τῷ ἐν ἀριστερᾷ σφῶν κατὰ τὸ Ἀλεξάνδρου
δεξιὸν ἐς δισμυρίους· καὶ τούτων ἔστιν οἳ κατὰ
νώτου ἐγένοντο τῆς Ἀλεξάνδρου στρατιᾶς. τὸ γὰρ
ὄρος ἵνα ἐπετάχθησαν πῇ μὲν διεχώρει ἐς βάθος καὶ
κολπῶδές τι αὐτοῦ ὥσπερ ἐν θαλάσσῃ ἐγίγνετο,
ἔπειτα ἐς ἐπικαμπὴν προϊὸν τοὺς ἐπὶ ταῖς ὑπωρείαις τεταγμένους κατόπιν τοῦ δεξιοῦ κέρως τοῦ
8 Ἀλεξάνδρου ἐποίει. τὸ δὲ ἄλλο πλῆθος αὐτοῦ
ψιλῶν τε καὶ ὁπλιτῶν, κατὰ ἔθνη συντεταγμένον ἐς
βάθος οὐκ ὠφέλιμον, ὄπισθεν ἦν τῶν Ἑλλήνων τῶν
μισθοφόρων καὶ τοῦ ἐπὶ φάλαγγος τεταγμένου
βαρβαρικοῦ. ἐλέγετο γὰρ ἡ πᾶσα ξὺν Δαρείῳ
στρατιὰ μάλιστα ἐς ἑξήκοντα μυριάδας μαχίμους
εἶναι.

9 Ἀλέξανδρος δέ, ὡς αὐτῷ πρόσω ἰόντι τὸ

and Parmenio of the entire left wing, with orders 333
not to edge away from the sea, for fear the bar- B.C.
barians should surround them, since with their great
numbers they were likely to overlap them on all sides.

When the approach of Alexander in battle order 5
was reported to Darius, he sent about 30,000 of his
cavalry across the river Pinarus with 20,000 light
infantry, so that he might deploy the rest at his
leisure. He placed the Greek mercenaries, about 6
30,000, foremost of his hoplites facing the Macedonian
phalanx; next, on either side, 60,000 of the so-called
Cardaces, who were also hoplites; this was the
number which the ground where they stood allowed
to be posted in one line. He also stationed about 7
20,000 men on the ridge on his left over against
Alexander's right; some of these actually got to the
rear of Alexander's force, since the mountain ridge
where they were posted was deeply indented in one
part and formed something like a bay as in the sea;
then bending outwards again it brought those posted
on the foothills to the rear of Alexander's right wing.
The general mass of his light and heavy troops, ar- 8
ranged by their nations in such depth that they were
useless, was behind the Greek mercenaries and the
barbarian [4] force drawn up in phalanx formation.
Darius' whole force was said to amount to some
600,000 fighting men.[5]

Alexander, however, finding the ground opening 9

[4] Darius' dispositions: QC. 8, 24–9, 6 (cf. 2 *passim*). On
numbers cf. App. III 5. The mercenaries are unlikely to have
numbered 30,000, cf. H. W. Parke, *Greek Mercenary Soldiers*
183 f.

[5] Not ' Vulgate ' but a report in A's main source(s).

χωρίον διέσχεν ὀλίγον ἐς πλάτος, παρήγαγε τοὺς
ἱππέας, τούς τε ἑταίρους καλουμένους καὶ τοὺς
Θεσσαλοὺς καὶ τοὺς Μακεδόνας.[1] καὶ τούτους μὲν
ἐπὶ τῷ δεξιῷ κέρᾳ ἅμα οἱ ἔταξε, τοὺς δὲ ἐκ
Πελοποννήσου καὶ τὸ ἄλλο τὸ συμμαχικὸν ἐπὶ τὸ
εὐώνυμον πέμπει ὡς Παρμενίωνα.

10 Δαρεῖος δέ, ὡς συντεταγμένη ἤδη ἦν αὐτῷ ἡ
φάλαγξ, τοὺς ἱππέας, οὕστινας πρὸ τοῦ ποταμοῦ
ἐπὶ τῷδε προτετάχει ὅπως ἀσφαλῶς αὐτῷ ἡ
ἔκταξις τῆς στρατιᾶς γένοιτο, ἀνεκάλεσεν ἀπὸ
ξυνθήματος. καὶ τούτων τοὺς μὲν πολλοὺς ἐπὶ τῷ
δεξιῷ κέρατι πρὸς τῇ θαλάσσῃ κατὰ Παρμενίωνα
ἔταξεν, ὅτι ταύτῃ μᾶλλόν τι ἱππάσιμα ἦν, μέρος δέ
τι αὐτῶν καὶ ἐπὶ τὸ εὐώνυμον πρὸς τὰ ὄρη παρ-
11 ήγαγεν. ὡς δὲ ἀχρεῖοι ἐνταῦθα διὰ στενότητα
τῶν χωρίων ἐφαίνοντο, καὶ τούτων τοὺς πολλοὺς
παριππεῦσαι ἐπὶ τὸ δεξιὸν κέρας σφῶν ἐκέλευσεν.
αὐτὸς δὲ Δαρεῖος τὸ μέσον τῆς πάσης τάξεως
ἐπεῖχεν, καθάπερ νόμος τοῖς Περσῶν βασιλεῦσι
τετάχθαι· καὶ τὸν νοῦν τῆς τάξεως ταύτης
Ξενοφῶν ὁ τοῦ Γρύλλου ἀναγέγραφεν.

9. Ἐν τούτῳ δὲ Ἀλέξανδρος κατιδὼν ὀλίγου
πᾶσαν τὴν τῶν Περσῶν ἵππον μετακεχωρηκυῖαν
ἐπὶ τὸ εὐώνυμον τὸ ἑαυτοῦ ὡς πρὸς τὴν θάλασσαν,
αὐτῷ δὲ τοὺς Πελοποννησίους μόνους καὶ τοὺς
ἄλλους τῶν ξυμμάχων ἱππέας ταύτῃ τεταγμένους,
πέμπει κατὰ τάχος τοὺς Θεσσαλοὺς ἱππέας ἐπὶ τὸ
εὐώνυμον, κελεύσας μὴ πρὸ τοῦ μετώπου τῆς
πάσης τάξεως παριππεῦσαι, τοῦ μὴ καταφανεῖς
τοῖς πολεμίοις γενέσθαι μεταχωροῦντας, ἀλλὰ

[1] See historical note.

outwards a little as he went forward, brought into
line his cavalry, the so-called Companions, the
Thessalians and the . . . whom he posted with himself on the right wing while the Peloponnesians and
other allies were sent to Parmenio on the left.[6]

His phalanx once in due order, Darius recalled by 10
signal the cavalry he had placed in front of the river [7]
to cover the deployment of the army and posted
most of them opposite Parmenio on the right wing by
the sea, because it was rather better ground for
cavalry, though some were sent to the left wing near
the hills. But as they appeared useless there for want 11
of space, he ordered most of them too to ride round
to their right wing. Darius himself held the centre
of his whole host, the customary position for Persian
kings; Xenophon son of Gryllus has recorded the
purpose of the arrangement.[8]

9. At this Alexander, observing that nearly all
the Persian cavalry had been transferred to his left,
resting on the sea, while he had only the Peloponnesians and the other allied horse on this side, despatched the Thessalian cavalry at full speed to the
left, with orders not to ride in front of the line, so
that their change of position might not be sighted by
the enemy, but to pass unobserved behind the

---

[6] QC. 9, 8. I have marked a lacuna where the MSS read
'Macedonians'; some other cavalry units must be meant,
perhaps *prodromoi* (9, 2).
[7] QC. 8, 27 f. confuses this force with the outflanking force
on the Persian left.
[8] Xen., *Anab.* i 8, 21 f. Contrast QC. 9, 4.

2 κατόπιν τῆς φάλαγγος ἀφανῶς διελθεῖν. προέταξε
δὲ τῶν μὲν ἱππέων κατὰ τὸ δεξιὸν τοὺς προδρόμους, ὧν ἡγεῖτο Πρωτόμαχος, καὶ τοὺς
Παίονας, ὧν ἡγεῖτο Ἀρίστων, τῶν δὲ πεζῶν τοὺς
τοξότας, ὧν ἦρχεν Ἀντίοχος· τοὺς δὲ Ἀγριᾶνας,
ὧν ἦρχεν Ἄτταλος, καὶ τῶν ἱππέων τινὰς καὶ τῶν
τοξοτῶν ἐς ἐπικαμπὴν πρὸς τὸ ὄρος τὸ κατὰ νώτου
ἔταξεν, ὥστε κατὰ τὸ δεξιὸν αὐτῷ τὴν φάλαγγα ἐς
δύο κέρατα διέχουσαν τετάχθαι, τὸ μὲν ὡς πρὸς
Δαρεῖόν τε καὶ τοὺς πέραν τοῦ ποταμοῦ τοὺς
πάντας Πέρσας, τὸ δὲ ὡς πρὸς τοὺς ἐπὶ τῷ ὄρει
3 κατὰ νώτου σφῶν τεταγμένους. τοῦ δὲ εὐωνύμου
προετάχθησαν τῶν μὲν πεζῶν οἵ τε Κρῆτες
τοξόται καὶ οἱ Θρᾷκες, ὧν ἡγεῖτο Σιτάλκης, πρὸ
τούτων δὲ ἡ ἵππος ἡ κατὰ τὸ εὐώνυμον. οἱ δὲ
μισθοφόροι ξένοι πᾶσιν ἐπετάχθησαν. ἐπεὶ δὲ οὔτε
πυκνὴ αὐτῷ ἡ φάλαγξ κατὰ τὸ δεξιὸν τὸ ἑαυτοῦ
ἐφαίνετο, πολύ τε ταύτῃ ὑπερφαλαγγήσειν οἱ
Πέρσαι ἐδόκουν, ἐκ τοῦ μέσου ἐκέλευσε δύο ἴλας
τῶν ἑταίρων, τήν τε Ἀνθεμουσίαν, ἧς ἰλάρχης ἦν
Περοίδας ὁ Μενεσθέως, καὶ τὴν Λευγαίαν καλουμένην, ἧς ἡγεῖτο Παντόρδανος ὁ Κλεάνδρου, ἐπὶ τὸ
4 δεξιὸν ἀφανῶς παρελθεῖν. καὶ τοὺς τοξότας δὲ καὶ
μέρος τῶν Ἀγριάνων καὶ τῶν Ἑλλήνων μισθοφόρων ἔστιν οὓς κατὰ τὸ δεξιὸν τὸ αὐτοῦ ἐπὶ
μετώπου παραγαγὼν ἐξέτεινεν ὑπὲρ τὸ τῶν
Περσῶν κέρας τὴν φάλαγγα. ἐπεὶ γὰρ οἱ ὑπὲρ τοῦ
ὄρους τεταγμένοι οὔτε κατῄεσαν, ἐκδρομῆς τε ἐπ᾽
αὐτοὺς τῶν Ἀγριάνων καὶ τῶν τοξοτῶν ὀλίγων
κατὰ πρόσταξιν Ἀλεξάνδρου γενομένης ῥᾳδίως

---

[1] QC. 11, 3, though in 11, 13 f. he unintelligibly separates

phalanx.[1] He posted the *prodromoi* under Proto-   2 333
machus' command in front of the cavalry on the right,   B.C.
with the Paeonians led by Ariston, and in front of his
foot the archers commanded by Antiochus. The
Agrianians under Attalus, with some of the cavalry
and archers, he threw back at an angle with the
heights in his rear, so that on his right wing his
line forked into two parts, one facing Darius and
the main body of Persians across the river, the other
towards the force posted in the Macedonian rear in
the heights. On the left wing of the infantry the   3
Cretan archers and the Thracians under Sitalces had
been posted in front, with the cavalry of the left wing
further in advance. The foreign mercenaries were
drawn up in support of the whole line. But as his
phalanx did not seem very solid on his right, and
the Persians seemed likely to overlap them con-
siderably there, he ordered two squadrons of the
Companions from the centre, that from Anthemus,
commanded by Peroedes son of Menestheus, and
that called the Leugaean, under Pantordanus son of
Cleander, to transfer unobserved to the right wing.[2]
He brought over the archers and some of the Agrian-   4
ians and Greek mercenaries to the front of his
right and so extended his phalanx to out-flank the
Persian wing. For since the troops posted on the
heights had not descended, but on a sally made by
the Agrianians and a few archers at Alexander's
order, had been easily dislodged from the foothills

Parmenio from the Thessalians. D. 37, 2 also puts them on
the left. QC. 9, 9 f. has some of the following details, not
making it clear that they represent last minute changes.
   [2] This move was no doubt consequential on taking the
Thessalians out of the line on the right.

ἀπὸ τῆς ὑπωρ⟨ε⟩ίας ἀνασταλέντες ἐς τὸ ἄκρον
ἀνέφυγον, ἔγνω καὶ τοῖς κατ᾽ αὐτοὺς τεταγμένοις
δυνατὸς ὢν χρήσασθαι ἐς ἀναπλήρωσιν τῆς φάλαγ-
γος· ἐκείνοις δὲ ἱππέας τρικοσίους ἐπιτάξαι
ἐξήρκεσεν.

10. Οὕτω δὴ τεταγμένους χρόνον μέν τινα
προῆγεν ἀναπαύων, ὥστε καὶ πάνυ ἔδοξε σχολαία
γενέσθαι αὐτῷ ἡ πρόσοδος· τοὺς γὰρ βαρβάρους,
ὅπως τὰ πρῶτα ἐτάχθησαν, οὐκέτι ἀντεπῆγε
Δαρεῖος, ἀλλ᾽ ἐπὶ τοῦ ποταμοῦ ταῖς ὄχθαις, πολλαχῇ μὲν ἀποκρήμνοις οὔσαις, ἔστι δὲ ὅπου καὶ
χάρακα παρατείνας αὐταῖς ἵνα εὐεφοδώτερα ἐφαίνετο, οὕτως ἔμενεν· καὶ ταύτῃ εὐθὺς δῆλος ἐγένετο
τοῖς ἀμφ᾽ Ἀλέξανδρον τῇ γνώμῃ δεδουλωμένος.
2 ὡς δὲ ὁμοῦ ἤδη ἦν τὰ στρατόπεδα, ἐνταῦθα παριπ-
πεύων πάντῃ Ἀλέξανδρος παρεκάλει ἄνδρας ἀγαθοὺς γίγνεσθαι, οὐ τῶν ἡγεμόνων μόνον τὰ ὀνόματα
ξὺν τῷ πρέποντι κόσμῳ ἀνακαλῶν, ἀλλὰ καὶ
ἰλάρχας μὲν καὶ λοχαγοὺς ὀνομαστὶ καὶ τῶν ξένων τῶν
μισθοφόρων, ὅσοι κατ᾽ ἀξίωσιν ἤ τινα ἀρετὴν
γνωριμώτεροι ἦσαν· καὶ αὐτῷ πανταχόθεν βοὴ
ἐγίνετο μὴ διατρίβειν, ἀλλὰ ἐσβάλλειν ἐς τοὺς
3 πολεμίους. ὁ δὲ ἦγεν ἐν τάξει ἔτι, τὰ μὲν πρῶτα,
καίπερ ἐν ἀπόπτῳ ἤδη ἔχων τὴν Δαρείου δύναμιν,
βάδην, τοῦ μὴ διασπασθῆναί τι ἐν τῇ ξυντονωτέρᾳ
πορείᾳ κυμῆναν τῆς φάλαγγος· ὡς δὲ ἐντὸς
βέλους ἐγίγνοντο, πρῶτοι δὴ οἱ κατὰ Ἀλέξανδρον
καὶ αὐτὸς Ἀλέξανδρος ἐπὶ τοῦ δεξιοῦ τεταγμένος

---

³ QC. 9, 11 (put too early).
¹ Not ' many ', but some banks are 3–4 metres high, too
steep for the phalanx to have descended from them; they had
to go round; hence breaks in the line (§ 5).

and had fled to the summit,[3] Alexander decided that
he could use those who had been posted to hold
them in check to fill up his phalanx. To watch the
hill-troops he reckoned it enough to tell off three
hundred horsemen.

10. His forces thus marshalled, Alexander led them
on for some time with halts, so that their advance
seemed quite a leisurely affair. Once the barbarians had taken up their first positions, Darius made
no further advance; he remained on the river bank,
which was in many [1] places precipitous, in some parts
building up a stockade, where it appeared more
accessible. This made it plain to Alexander and his
staff that Darius was in spirit a beaten man. When 2
the two armies were close, Alexander rode all along
his front and bade them be good men and true,
calling aloud with all proper distinctions the names
not only of generals but even of commanders of
squadrons and companies, as well as any of the
mercenaries who were conspicuous for rank or for
any brave action.[2] An answering cry went up
from all sides to delay no longer, but to charge the
enemy.[3] He continued to lead on in line, at marching 3
pace at first, though he now had Darius' force in view,
to avoid any part of the phalanx fluctuating in a more
rapid advance and so breaking apart. Once within
missile range, Alexander himself and his entourage
were the first, stationed on the right, to charge in the

[2] QC. 10, 3–10 here interpolates a speech by Al., which
seems to derive from a source common to J. xi 9, 3 ff., not
followed in A. 6, 3 ff.

[3] From this point the narrative in QC. 11 resembles that in
D. 33 f. (cf. also 10, 1 f. with D. 33, 4) and departs widely
from A., giving no clear picture. To allow time for Al's march,
the battle must have begun at or after 1 p.m.

δρόμῳ ἐς τὸν ποταμὸν ἐνέβαλον, ὡς τῇ τε ὀξύτητι
τῆς ἐφόδου ἐκπλῆξαι τοὺς Πέρσας καὶ τοῦ θᾶσσον
ἐς χεῖρας ἐλθόντας ὀλίγα πρὸς τῶν τοξοτῶν
βλάπτεσθαι. καὶ ξυνέβη ὅπως εἴκασεν Ἀλέξαν-
4 δρος. εὐθὺς γὰρ ὡς ἐν χερσὶν ἡ μάχη ἐγένετο,
τρέπονται τοῦ Περσικοῦ στρατεύματος οἱ τῷ
ἀριστερῷ κέρᾳ ἐπιτεταγμένοι· καὶ ταύτῃ μὲν
λαμπρῶς ἐνίκα Ἀλέξανδρός τε καὶ οἱ ἀμφ' αὐτόν.
οἱ δὲ Ἕλληνες οἱ μισθοφόροι οἱ ξὺν Δαρείῳ, ᾗ
διέσχε τῶν Μακεδόνων ἡ φάλαγξ ὡς ἐπὶ τὸ δεξιὸν
5 κέρας παρραγεῖσα, ὅτι Ἀλέξανδρος μὲν σπουδῇ
ἐς τὸν ποταμὸν ἐμβαλὼν καὶ ἐν χερσὶ τὴν μάχην
ποιήσας ἐξώθει ἤδη τοὺς ταύτῃ τεταγμένους τῶν
Περσῶν, οἱ δὲ κατὰ μέσον τῶν Μακεδόνων οὔτε
τῇ ἴσῃ σπουδῇ ἥψαντο τοῦ ἔργου καὶ πολλαχῇ
χρημνώδεσι ταῖς ὄχθαις ἐντυγχάνοντες τὸ μέτωπον
τῆς φάλαγγος οὐ δυνατοὶ ἐγένοντο ἐν τῇ αὐτῇ
τάξει διασώσασθαι, — ταύτῃ ἐμβάλλουσιν οἱ Ἕλληνες τοῖς Μακεδόσιν ᾗ μάλιστα διεσπασμένην
6 αὐτοῖς τὴν φάλαγγα κατεῖδον. καὶ τὸ ἔργον
ἐνταῦθα καρτερὸν ἦν, τῶν μὲν ἐς τὸν ποταμὸν
ἀπώσασθαι τοὺς Μακεδόνας καὶ τὴν νίκην τοῖς ἤδη
φεύγουσι σφῶν ἀνασώσασθαι, τῶν Μακεδόνων δὲ
τῆς τε Ἀλεξάνδρου ἤδη φαινομένης εὐπραγίας μὴ
λειφθῆναι καὶ τὴν δόξαν τῆς φάλαγγος, ὡς ἀμάχου
7 δὴ ἐς τὸ τότε διαβεβοημένης, μὴ ἀφανίσαι. καί τι
καὶ τοῖς γένεσι τῷ τε Ἑλληνικῷ καὶ τῷ Μακε-
δονικῷ φιλοτιμίας ἐνέπεσεν ἐς ἀλλήλους. καὶ
ἐνταῦθα πίπτει Πτολεμαῖός τε ὁ Σελεύκου, ἀνὴρ
ἀγαθὸς γενόμενος, καὶ ἄλλοι ἐς εἴκοσι μάλιστα καὶ
ἑκατὸν τῶν οὐκ ἠμελημένων Μακεδόνων.

11. Ἐν τούτῳ δὲ αἱ ἀπὸ τοῦ δεξιοῦ κέρως

river, in order to strike panic into the Persians by the rapidity of the attack, and by coming more quickly to close quarters to reduce losses from the Persian archers. Everything happened as Alexander guessed. The moment the battle was joined 4 hand-to-hand, the Persian left gave way; and here Alexander and his followers won a brilliant success. But Darius' Greek mercenaries attacked the Macedonian phalanx, where a gap appeared as it broke formation on the right; while Alexander plunged 5 impetuously into the river, came to close quarters with the Persians posted here, and was pushing them back, the Macedonian centre did not set to with equal impetus, and finding the river banks precipitous in many places, were unable to maintain their front in unbroken line; and the Greeks attacked where they saw that the phalanx had been particularly torn apart. There the action was severe, the Greeks 6 tried to push off the Macedonians into the river and to restore victory to their own side who were already in flight, while the Macedonians sought to rival the success of Alexander, which was already apparent, and to preserve the reputation of the phalanx, whose sheer invincibility had hitherto been on everyone's lips. There was also some emulation 7 between antagonists of the Greek and Macedonian races.[4] Here it was that Ptolemaeus son of Seleucus fell, after showing himself a brave man, and about a hundred and twenty Macedonians of note.

11. At this point the battalions on the right wing,

---

[4] Cf. Introd. n. 33.

τάξεις, τετραμμένους ἤδη τοὺς κατὰ σφᾶς τῶν
Περσῶν ὁρῶντες, ἐπὶ τοὺς ξένους τε τοὺς μισθοφόρους τοὺς Δαρείου καὶ τὸ πονούμενον σφῶν
ἐπικάμψαντες ἀπό τε τοῦ ποταμοῦ ἀπώσαντο
αὐτούς, καὶ κατὰ τὸ παρερρωγὸς τοῦ Περσικοῦ
στρατεύματος ὑπερφαλαγγήσαντες ἐς τὰ πλάγια
2 ἐμβεβληκότες ἤδη ἔκοπτον τοὺς ξένους· καὶ οἱ
ἱππεῖς δὲ οἱ τῶν Περσῶν κατὰ τοὺς Θεσσαλοὺς
τεταγμένοι οὐκ ἔμειναν ἐντὸς τοῦ ποταμοῦ ἐν αὐτῷ
τῷ ἔργῳ, ἀλλ᾽ ἐπιδιαβάντες εὐρώστως ἐνέβαλον ἐς
τὰς ἴλας τῶν Θετταλῶν. καὶ ταύτῃ ξυνέστη
ἱππομαχία καρτερά, οὐδὲ πρόσθεν ἐνέκλιναν οἱ
Πέρσαι πρὶν Δαρεῖόν τε πεφευγότα ᾔσθοντο καὶ
πρὶν ἀπορραγῆναι σφῶν τοὺς μισθοφόρους συγκο-
3 πέντας ὑπὸ τῆς φάλαγγος. τότε δὲ ἤδη λαμπρά τε
καὶ ἐκ πάντων ἡ φυγὴ ἐγίγνετο· καὶ οἵ τε τῶν
Περσῶν ἵπποι ἐν τῇ ἀναχωρήσει ἐκακοπάθουν
βαρέως ὡπλισμένους τοὺς ἀμβάτας σφῶν φέροντες,
καὶ αὐτοὶ οἱ ἱππεῖς κατὰ στενὰς ὁδοὺς πλήθει τε
πολλοὶ καὶ πεφοβημένως ξὺν ἀταξίᾳ ἀποχωροῦντες
οὐ μεῖον ἀπ᾽ ἀλλήλων καταπατούμενοι ἢ πρὸς τῶν
διωκόντων πολεμίων ἐβλάπτοντο. καὶ οἱ Θεσσαλοὶ
εὐρώστως αὐτοῖς ἐπέκειντο, ὥστε οὐ μείων ἢ
τῶν πεζῶν φόνος ἐν τῇ φυγῇ τῶν ἱππέων ἐγίγνετο.
4 Δαρεῖος δέ, ὡς αὐτῷ τὸ πρῶτον ὑπ᾽ Ἀλεξάνδρου ἐφοβήθη τὸ κέρας τὸ εὐώνυμον καὶ ταύτῃ
ἀπορρηγνύμενον κατεῖδε τοῦ ἄλλου στρατοπέδου,
εὐθὺς ὡς εἶχεν ἐπὶ τοῦ ἅρματος ξὺν τοῖς πρώτοις
5 ἔφευγε. καὶ ἔστε μὲν ὁμαλοῖς χωρίοις ἐν τῇ φυγῇ

---

[1] Cf. D. 33, 2; QC. 11, 14 f.; P. 24, 1.
[2] QC. 11, 18 says that they got away in good order; for
survivors App. VI 2.

seeing that the Persians opposed to them were already routed, bent round towards Darius' foreign mercenaries, where their own centre was hard pressed, drove them from the river, and then over-lapping the now broken part of the Persian army, attacked in the flank and in a trice were cutting down the mercenaries. The Persian cavalry posted opposite to the Thessalians did not keep their ground behind the river, once the engagement had actually begun, but crossed manfully and charged the Thessalian squadrons, and here there was a desperate cavalry fight;[1] the Persians did not give way till they realized that Darius had fled and till their mercenaries were cut off, mowed down by the phalanx.[2] But then the rout was patent and universal. The Persian horses suffered much in the retreat, with their riders heavily armoured, while the riders too, hurrying by narrow paths in a crowded horde in terror and disorder, suffered as heavy losses from being ridden over by one another as from the pursuit of their enemies. The Thessalians fell on them with vigour, and there was as much slaughter in the cavalry-flight as in the infantry.

As for Darius, the moment his left wing was panic-stricken by Alexander and he saw it thus cut off from the rest of his army, he fled just as he was in his chariot, in the van of the fugitives.[3] So long as he

---

[3] A's sources make Darius a poltroon; in the 'Vulgate' (D. and QC.) he fights bravely; the contemporary, Chares (P. 20, 4), made him give Al. the wound he received in the battle (A. 12, 1); this must be false, though not refuted by a so-called letter of Al. (P. 20, 5, cf. Introd. 15); but it tended to Al's greater glory, if Darius was a Hector to his Achilles, and Al. himself treated Darius with posthumous respect (iii 22, 1; 23, 7; 25, 8; 30, 4), thus perhaps stimulating Chares' invention. Cf. App. IX 4.

ἐπετύγχανεν, ἐπὶ τοῦ ἅρματος διεσώζετο, ὡς δὲ
φάραγξί τε καὶ ἄλλαις δυσχωρίαις ἐνέκυρσε, τὸ μὲν
ἅρμα ἀπολείπει αὐτοῦ καὶ τὴν ἀσπίδα καὶ τὸν
κάνδυν ἐκδύς· ὁ δὲ καὶ τὸ τόξον ἀπολείπει ἐπὶ τοῦ
ἅρματος· αὐτὸς δὲ ἵππου ἐπιβὰς ἔφευγε· καὶ ἡ
νὺξ οὐ διὰ μακροῦ ἐπιγενομένη ἀφείλετο αὐτὸν τὸ
6 πρὸς Ἀλεξάνδρου ἁλῶναι. Ἀλέξανδρος γὰρ ἔστε
μὲν φάος ἦν ἀνὰ κράτος ἐδίωκεν, ὡς δὲ συνεσκό-
ταζέ τε ἤδη καὶ τὰ πρὸ ποδῶν ἀφανῆ ἦν, εἰς τὸ
ἔμπαλιν ἀπετρέπετο ὡς ἐπὶ τὸ στρατόπεδον· τὸ
μέντοι ἅρμα τοῦ Δαρείου ἔλαβε καὶ τὴν ἀσπίδα ἐπ’
7 αὐτῷ καὶ τὸν κάνδυν καὶ τὸ τόξον. καὶ γὰρ καὶ ἡ
δίωξις βραδυτέρα αὐτῷ ἐγεγόνει, ὅτι ἐν τῇ πρώτῃ
παραρρήξει τῆς φάλαγγος ἐπιστρέψας καὶ αὐτὸς οὐ
πρόσθεν ἐς τὸ διώκειν ἐτράπετο πρὶν τούς τε
μισθοφόρους τοὺς ξένους καὶ τὸ τῶν Περσῶν
ἱππικὸν ἀπὸ τοῦ ποταμοῦ ἀπωσθέντας κατεῖδε.
8 Τῶν δὲ Περσῶν ἀπέθανον Ἀρσάμης μὲν καὶ
Ῥεομίθρης καὶ Ἀτιζύης τῶν ἐπὶ Γρανίκῳ ἡγησαμένων τοῦ ἱππικοῦ· ἀποθνῄσκει δὲ καὶ Σαυάκης ὁ
Αἰγύπτου σατράπης καὶ Βουβάκης τῶν ἐντίμων
Περσῶν· τὸ δὲ ἄλλο πλῆθος εἰς δέκα μάλιστα
μυριάδας καὶ ἐν τούτοις ἱππεῖς ὑπὲρ τοὺς μυρίους,
ὥστε λέγει Πτολεμαῖος ὁ Λάγου ξυνεπισπόμενος
τότε Ἀλεξάνδρῳ τοὺς μετὰ σφῶν διώκοντας
Δαρεῖον, ὡς ἐπὶ φάραγγί τινι ἐν τῇ διώξει ἐγέ-
9 νοντο, ἐπὶ τῶν νεκρῶν διαβῆναι τὴν φάραγγα. τό
τε στρατόπεδον τὸ Δαρείου εὐθὺς ἐξ ἐφόδου ἑάλω

---

⁴ *Contra* D. 37, 2, but cf. 35, 1, QC. 12, 1. With nightfall about 6 p.m., the battle and pursuit might have lasted
4–5 hours. Most of the fugitives, all on the left and centre,

found level ground in his flight, he was safe in his
chariot; but when he came to gullies and other
difficult patches, he left his chariot there, threw away
his shield and mantle, left even his bow in the chariot,
and fled on horseback; only night, speedily falling,
saved him from becoming Alexander's captive, since 6
Alexander pursued with all his might as long as daylight held, but when it was growing dark and he could
not see his way, turned back towards the camp,[4]
though he took Darius' chariot, and with it his shield,
mantle and bow. The fact is that his pursuit had 7
become slower because he had wheeled back when
the phalanx first broke formation and had not himself
turned to pursue till he had seen the mercenaries and
the Persian cavalry driven back from the river.[5]

The Persians killed included Arsames, Rheomithres 8
and Atizyes who had been among the cavalry commanders on the Granicus, and also Savaces the satrap
of Egypt and Bubaces among the Persian nobles;
as for the rank and file, some 100,000 fell, including
over 10,000 cavalry, so that Ptolemy son of Lagos,
who was then with Alexander, says that the pur-
suers of Darius meeting a deep gully in the pursuit
crossed it over bodies of the dead.[6] Darius' camp 9
was stormed at once, and captured with his mother,

---

must have fled towards the Toprak Kalessi Pass, about 200
stades from the battle (App. III 3).

[5] So QC. 11, 16.

[6] Different names in D. 34,5; QC. 11, 10; same Persian totals
in D. 36, 6; QC. 11, 27; P. 20, 5; J. XI 9, 10 (except that he
includes 40,000 prisoners)—all incredible; on unreliability of
casualty figures see my *Italian Manpower*, App. 28. Macedonian losses: about 450 killed or missing in D. and QC., 280
in J., 1,000 foot and 200 horse in the fragment of an unknown
historian (Jacoby no. 148, 44); A. 10, 7 does not purport to
give the total.

καὶ ἡ μήτηρ καὶ ἡ γυνή, αὐτὴ δὲ καὶ ἀδελφὴ
Δαρείου, καὶ υἱὸς Δαρείου νήπιος· καὶ θυγατέρες
δύο ἑάλωσαν καὶ ἄλλαι ἀμφ' αὐτὰς Περσῶν τῶν
ὁμοτίμων γυναῖκες οὐ πολλαί. οἱ γὰρ ἄλλοι
Πέρσαι τὰς γυναῖκας σφῶν ξὺν τῇ ἄλλῃ κατασκευῇ
10 ἐς Δαμασκὸν ἔτυχον ἐσταλκότες· ἐπεὶ καὶ Δαρεῖος
τῶν τε χρημάτων τὰ πολλὰ καὶ ὅσα ἄλλα μεγάλῳ
βασιλεῖ ἐς πολυτελῆ δίαιταν καὶ στρατευομένῳ
ὅμως συνέπεται πεπόμφει ἐς Δαμασκόν, ὥστε ἐν
τῷ στρατεύματι οὐ πλείονα ἢ τρισχίλια τάλαντα
ἑάλω. ἀλλὰ καὶ τὰ ἐν Δαμασκῷ χρήματα ὀλίγον
ὕστερον ἑάλω ὑπὸ Παρμενίωνος ἐπ' αὐτὸ τοῦτο
σταλέντος. τοῦτο τὸ τέλος τῇ μάχῃ ἐκείνῃ ἐγένετο
ἐπὶ ἄρχοντος Ἀθηναίοις Νικοκράτους μηνὸς Μαι-
μακτηριῶνος.

12. Τῇ δὲ ὑστεραίᾳ, καίπερ τετρωμένος τὸν
μηρὸν ξίφει Ἀλέξανδρος, ὁ δὲ τοὺς τραυματίας
ἐπῆλθε, καὶ τοὺς νεκροὺς ξυναγαγὼν ἔθαψε
μεγαλοπρεπῶς ξὺν τῇ δυνάμει πάσῃ ἐκτεταγμένῃ
ὡς λαμπρότατα ἐς πόλεμον· καὶ λόγῳ τε ἐπεκόσ-
μησεν ὅσοις τι διαπρεπὲς ἔργον ἐν τῇ μάχῃ ἢ
αὐτὸς ξυνέγνω εἰργασμένον ἢ ἀκοῇ συμφωνού-
μενον ἔμαθεν, καὶ χρημάτων ἐπιδόσει ὡς ἑκάστους
2 ξὺν τῇ ἀξίᾳ ἐτίμησεν. καὶ Κιλικίας μὲν ἀπο-
δεικνύει σατράπην Βάλακρον τὸν Νικάνορος, ἕνα
τῶν σωματοφυλάκων τῶν βασιλικῶν, ἀντὶ δὲ
τούτου ἐς τοὺς σωματοφύλακας κατέλεξε Μένητα
τὸν Διονυσίου· ἀντὶ δὲ Πτολεμαίου τοῦ Σελεύκου

---

[7] D. 35 f.; QC. 11, 20 ff.; P. 20, 6–21 with elaborations.

[8] A. characteristically mentions this only when it becomes
relevant to Al's doings, cf. P. 20, 6; contrast D. 32, 3; QC.
8, 12.

wife, who was also his sister, and his infant son; two
daughters were taken too, with a few noble Persian
ladies in their suite.[7]   The other Persians had in fact
despatched their women-folk and baggage to
Damascus; Darius too had sent there the greater 10
part of his money and everything else a great king
takes with him even on campaign for his extravagant
way of living; so [8] they found no more than three
thousand Talents in the camp.   However, the money
at Damascus too was captured soon after by Parmenio,
who was specially detailed for the purpose.[9]   So
ended this battle, fought in the archonship at Athens
of Nicocrates and in the month Maimacterion.[10]

12. Next day, despite a sword wound in his thigh,
Alexander went round to see the wounded; he
gathered together the dead and gave them a splendid
military funeral, the whole army marshalled in their
finest battle array.   His speech contained citations
of all whom he knew, from his own eyes or from the
agreed report of others, to have distinguished themselves in the battle; he honoured each of them by
a donation suitable to their worth.   He appointed 2
as satrap of Cilicia Balacrus son of Nicanor,[1] one of
the royal bodyguards; and selected Menes son of
Dionysius to take his place among the bodyguards;
and in place of Ptolemaeus son of Seleucus, who had

---

[9] QC. 13, with much detail, giving 2600 Talents in coins and
500 lbs of silver. Parmenio was sent over 200 miles ahead of
the main army.

[10] The Attic month corresponding to Nov./Dec. 333 B.C.,
but Beloch, III 2, 304 ff. gives reasons for thinking that A.
has sometimes falsely converted Macedonian months in his
sources into Attic, and that Issus was fought in October;
the Persian fleet was still at sea (13, 5) a little later. QC.
8, 8 makes winter imminent.

[1] D. xviii 22, 1.

τοῦ ἀποθανόντος ἐν τῇ μάχῃ Πολυπέρχοντα τὸν
Σιμμίου ἄρχειν ἀπέδειξε τῆς ἐκείνου τάξεως. καὶ
Σολεῦσι τά τε πεντήκοντα τάλαντα, ἃ ἔτι ἐνδεᾶ
ἦν ἐκ τῶν ἐπιβληθέντων σφίσι χρημάτων, ἀνῆκεν
καὶ τοὺς ὁμήρους ἀπέδωκεν.

3 Ὁ δὲ οὐδὲ τῆς μητρὸς τῆς Δαρείου οὐδὲ τῆς
γυναικὸς ἢ τῶν παίδων ἠμέλησεν. ἀλλὰ λέγουσί
τινες τῶν τὰ Ἀλεξάνδρου γραψάντων τῆς νυκτὸς
αὐτῆς, ᾗ ἀπὸ τῆς διώξεως τῆς Δαρείου ἐπανῆκεν,
ἐς τὴν σκηνὴν παρελθόντα αὐτὸν τὴν Δαρείου, ἥτις
αὐτῷ ἐξῃρημένη ἦν, ἀκοῦσαι γυναικῶν οἰμωγὴν
καὶ ἄλλον τοιοῦτον θόρυβον οὐ πόρρω τῆς σκηνῆς·
4 πυθέσθαι οὖν αἵτινες γυναῖκες καὶ ἀνθ' ὅτου οὕτως
ἐγγὺς παρασκηνοῦσι· καί τινα ἐξαγγεῖλαι, ὅτι· ὦ
βασιλεῦ, ἡ μήτηρ τε καὶ ἡ γυνὴ Δαρείου καὶ οἱ
παῖδες, ὡς ἐξηγγέλθη αὐταῖς ὅτι τὸ τόξον τε τοῦ
Δαρείου ἔχεις καὶ τὸν κάνδυν τὸν βασιλικὸν καὶ ἡ
ἀσπὶς ὅτι κεκόμισται ὀπίσω ἡ Δαρείου, ὡς ἐπὶ
5 τεθνεῶτι Δαρείῳ ἀνοιμώζουσιν. ταῦτα ἀκούσαντα
Ἀλέξανδρον πέμψαι πρὸς αὐτὰς Λεοννάτον, ἕνα
τῶν ἑταίρων, ἐντειλάμενον φράσαι ὅτι ζῇ Δαρεῖος,
τὰ δὲ ὅπλα καὶ τὸν κάνδυν ὅτι φεύγων ἀπέλιπεν ἐπὶ
τῷ ἅρματι καὶ ταῦτα ὅτι μόνα ἔχει Ἀλέξανδρος.
καὶ Λεοννάτον παρελθόντα ἐς τὴν σκηνὴν τά τε
περὶ Δαρείου εἰπεῖν καὶ ὅτι τὴν θεραπείαν αὐταῖς
ξυγχωρεῖ Ἀλέξανδρος τὴν βασιλικὴν καὶ τὸν ἄλλον
κόσμον καὶ καλεῖσθαι βασιλίσσας, ἐπεὶ οὐδὲ κατὰ
ἔχθραν οἱ γενέσθαι τὸν πόλεμον πρὸς Δαρεῖον,
ἀλλ' ὑπὲρ τῆς ἀρχῆς τῆς Ἀσίας διαπεπολεμῆσθαι
6 ἐννόμως. ταῦτα μὲν Πτολεμαῖος καὶ Ἀριστόβουλος λέγουσι· λόγος δὲ ἔχει καὶ αὐτὸν Ἀλέξανδρον τῇ ὑστεραίᾳ ἐλθεῖν εἴσω ξὺν Ἡφαιστίωνι

fallen in the battle, he appointed Polyperchon son of 333
Simmias commander of his battalion.   To the citizens   B.C.
of Soli he remitted the fifty Talents still due from the
fine he had imposed on them, and restored their
hostages.

Nor did he neglect Darius' mother, wife, or 3
children.   Now, some of the accounts of Alexander
relate that the very night after his return from the
pursuit of Darius he entered Darius' tent, which
had been put aside for his own use, and heard a
lament and other confused sounds of women's voices
near the tent; he enquired what women they were 4
and why they were accommodated so near him; and
was told, 'Sire, it is Darius' mother, wife and children;
as they have heard that you are in possession of his
bow and royal mantle and that his shield has been
brought back, they are mourning his death.'   On 5
hearing this, Alexander sent Leonnatus, one of the
Companions, to them with instructions to tell them
that Darius was alive and had left his arms and
mantle in the chariot while escaping, and that
these were all Alexander had.   Leonnatus entered
the tent and gave Alexander's message about Darius,
adding that Alexander granted them the right of
royal state and all other marks of royalty, with the
title of queens, since he had not made war with
Darius from personal enmity but had fought for
the sovereignty of Asia lawfully.   This is the 6
account of Ptolemaeus and Aristobulus;   there is,
however, a story[2] that next day Alexander himself

[2] 'Vulgate'. Cf. D. 37, 3–38, 3; QC. 11, 24–6; 12, 1–26;
P. 21.

μόνῳ τῶν ἑταίρων· καὶ τὴν μητέρα τὴν Δαρείου
ἀμφιγνοήσασαν ὅστις ὁ βασιλεὺς εἴη αὐτοῖν,
ἐστάλθαι γὰρ ἄμφω τῷ αὐτῷ κόσμῳ, τὴν δὲ
Ἡφαιστίωνι προσελθεῖν καὶ προσκυνῆσαι, ὅτι
7 μείζων ἐφάνη ἐκεῖνος. ὡς δὲ ὁ Ἡφαιστίων τε
ὀπίσω ὑπεχώρησε καί τις τῶν ἀμφ' αὐτήν, τὸν
Ἀλέξανδρον δείξας, ἐκεῖνον ἔφη εἶναι Ἀλέξανδρον,
τὴν μὲν καταιδεσθεῖσαν τῇ διαμαρτίᾳ ὑποχωρεῖν,
Ἀλέξανδρον δὲ οὐ φάναι αὐτὴν ἁμαρτεῖν· καὶ γὰρ
8 ἐκεῖνον εἶναι Ἀλέξανδρον. καὶ ταῦτα ἐγὼ οὔθ' ὡς
ἀληθῆ οὔτε ὡς πάντῃ ἄπιστα ἀνέγραψα. ἀλλ' εἴτε
οὕτως ἐπράχθη, ἐπαινῶ Ἀλέξανδρον τῆς τε ἐς τὰς
γυναῖκας κατοικτίσεως καὶ τῆς ἐς τὸν ἑταῖρον
πίστεως καὶ τιμῆς· εἴτε πιθανὸς δοκεῖ τοῖς συγ-
γράψασιν Ἀλέξανδρος ὡς καὶ ταῦτα ἂν πράξας καὶ
εἰπών, καὶ ἐπὶ τῷδε ἐπαινῶ Ἀλέξανδρον.

13. Δαρεῖος δὲ τὴν μὲν νύκτα ξὺν ὀλίγοις τοῖς
ἀμφ' αὐτὸν ἔφυγε, τῇ δὲ ἡμέρᾳ ἀναλαμβάνων ἀεὶ
τῶν τε Περσῶν τοὺς διασωθέντας ἐκ τῆς μάχης καὶ
τῶν ξένων τῶν μισθοφόρων, ἐς τετρακισχιλίους
ἔχων τοὺς πάντας, ὡς ἐπὶ Θάψακόν τε πόλιν καὶ
τὸν Εὐφράτην ποταμὸν σπουδῇ ἤλαυνεν, ὡς
τάχιστα μέσον αὐτοῦ τε καὶ Ἀλεξάνδρου τὸν
2 Εὐφράτην ποιῆσαι. Ἀμύντας δὲ ὁ Ἀντιόχου καὶ
Θυμώνδας ὁ Μέντορος καὶ Ἀριστομήδης ὁ Φεραῖος
καὶ Βιάνωρ ὁ Ἀκαρνάν, ξυμπάντες οὗτοι αὐτόμο-
λοι, μετὰ τῶν ἀμφ' αὐτοὺς στρατιωτῶν ὡς
ὀκτακισχιλίων εὐθὺς ὡς τεταγμένοι ἦσαν κατὰ τὰ
ὄρη φεύγοντες ἀφίκοντο ἐς Τρίπολιν τῆς Φοινίκης·

---

³ A's reflections may be compared with those of D., QC. and
P. (cited above); P. praises him for not enjoying any of the

visited the tent with Hephaestion and no other
Companion; and Darius' mother, not knowing which
of the two was the king, as both were dressed alike,
approached Hephaestion and did him obeisance,
since he appeared the taller. Hephaestion drew 7
back, and one of her attendants pointed to Alexander
and said he was the king; she drew back in confusion
at her mistake, but Alexander remarked that she
had made no mistake, for Hephaestion was also an
Alexander. I have written this down without as- 8
serting its truth or total incredibility. If it really
happened, I approve of Alexander's compassion for
the women and of the trust and honour bestowed
on his companion. If the historians of Alexander
think it plausible that he would have acted and
spoken in this way, I approve of Alexander on that
ground too.[3]

13. Darius fled through the night with a handful
of his suite, but in the daylight he kept picking up
Persians who had got off safe from the battle and also
some of the foreign mercenaries; and with a body of
about 4,000 in all he rode at full speed for the city of
Thapsacus and the river Euphrates, meaning to put
the river between Alexander and himself as soon
as possible.[1] Amyntas son of Antiochus, Thymondas 2
son of Mentor, Aristomedes of Pherae and Bianor the
Acarnanian, all deserters to Darius, with their troops
to the number of 8,000, fled straight to the hills at
once in the order in which they had been drawn

women, except Barsine, daughter of Artabazus (iii 21, 4 n.).:
Ar. attested Al's liaison with her, and a son, Heracles, claimed
the Macedonian throne in 309; Tarn ii 330 ff. rejects the story,
but see my article in *Rivista di filologia classica* 1975, 22 ff.
Cf. also iv 19, 6–20, 3.
[1] QC. iv 1, 1–3 (4,000 ' Greeks ', i.e. mercenaries).

3 καὶ ἐνταῦθα καταλαβόντες τὰς ναῦς νενεωλκημένας
ἐφ᾽ ὧν πρόσθεν ἐκ Λέσβου διακεκομισμένοι ἦσαν,
τούτων ὅσαι μὲν ἱκαναί σφισιν ἐς τὴν κομιδὴν
ἐδόκουν, ταύτας καθελκύσαντες, τὰς δὲ ἄλλας
αὐτοῦ ἐν τοῖς νεωρίοις κατακαύσαντες, ὡς μὴ
παρασχεῖν ταχεῖαν σφῶν τὴν δίωξιν, ἐπὶ Κύπρου
ἔφευγον καὶ ἐκεῖθεν εἰς Αἴγυπτον, ἵναπερ ὀλίγον
ὕστερον πολυπραγμονῶν τι Ἀμύντας ἀποθνήσκει
ὑπὸ τῶν ἐγχωρίων.

4 Φαρνάβαζος δὲ καὶ Αὐτοφραδάτης τέως μὲν περὶ
τὴν Χίον διέτριβον· καταστήσαντες δὲ φρουρὰν τῆς
Χίου τὰς μέν τινας τῶν νεῶν ἐς Κῶν καὶ Ἁλικαρνασσὸν ἔστειλαν, αὐτοὶ δὲ ἑκατὸν ναυσὶ ταῖς
ἄριστα πλεούσαις ἀναγ⟨αγ⟩όμενοι ἐς Σίφνον
κατέσχον. καὶ παρ᾽ αὐτοὺς ἀφικνεῖται Ἆγις ὁ
Λακεδαιμονίων βασιλεὺς ἐπὶ μιᾶς τριήρους, χρήματά τε αἰτήσων ἐς τὸν πόλεμον καὶ δύναμιν
ναυτικήν τε καὶ πεζικὴν ὅσην πλείστην ἀξιώσων
5 συμπέμψαι οἱ ἐς τὴν Πελοπόννησον. καὶ ἐν τούτῳ
ἀγγελία αὐτοῖς ἔρχεται τῆς μάχης τῆς πρὸς Ἰσσῷ
γενομένης. ἐκπλαγέντες δὲ πρὸς τὰ ἐξαγγελθέντα
Φαρνάβαζος μὲν σὺν δώδεκα τριήρεσι καὶ τῶν
μισθοφόρων ξένων ξὺν χιλίοις καὶ πεντακοσίοις ἐπὶ Χίου ἐστάλη, δείσας μή τι πρὸς τὴν
6 ἀγγελίαν τῆς ἥττης οἱ Χῖοι νεωτερίσωσιν. Ἆγις
δὲ παρ᾽ Αὐτοφραδάτου τάλαντα ἀργυρίου λαβὼν
τριάκοντα καὶ τριήρεις δέκα, ταύτας μὲν Ἱππίαν
ἄξοντα ἀποστέλλει παρὰ τὸν ἀδελφὸν τὸν αὐτοῦ
Ἀγησίλαον ἐπὶ Ταίναρον· καὶ παραγγέλλειν
ἐκέλευσεν Ἀγησιλάῳ, διδόντα τοῖς ναύταις ἐντελῆ
τὸν μισθὸν πλεῖν τὴν ταχίστην ἐπὶ Κρήτης, ὡς τὰ
ἐκεῖ καταστησόμενον. αὐτὸς δὲ τότε μὲν αὐτοῦ ἐν

up, and reached Tripolis in Phoenicia. There they 3 333
seized the ships that had been hauled ashore and had B.C.
previously brought them from Lesbos, launched as
many of them as they thought enough for their transport, burnt the rest there in the dockyards, to prevent
speedy pursuit of them, and fled to Cyprus and
thence to Egypt, where a little later Amyntas, stirring
up some trouble or other, was killed by the natives.[2]

Meanwhile Pharnabazus and Autophradates had 4
been waiting at Chios; after installing a garrison at
Chios, they sent part of their fleet to Cos and Halicarnassus, while they themselves put to sea with
the hundred best-sailing ships and arrived at Siphnus.
They were met by Agis king of Sparta with a single 5
trireme; he came to ask them to give him funds for
the war and to send as many ships and men as possible
to him in the Peloponnese. Just at this moment came
the news of the battle of Issus. Utterly dumb-
founded at the news, Pharnabazus with twelve
triremes and fifteen hundred of the foreign mercenaries made for Chios, fearing that the Chians would
rebel on the news of the defeat. Agis got thirty 6
silver Talents from Autophradates and ten triremes
and despatched Hippias to take them to his brother
Agesilaus at Taenarum. He ordered him to tell
Agesilaus to pay the crews in full and sail as quickly
as possible to Crete, to settle things there. He
himself remained for the present there at Siphnos

[2] D. 48, 1–3; QC. iv 1, 27–33; App. VI 2.

ταῖς νήσοις ὑπέμενεν, ὕστερον δὲ εἰς Ἁλικαρνασσὸν
παρ' Αὐτοφραδάτην ἀφίκετο.

7   Ἀλέξανδρος δὲ σατράπην μὲν Συρίᾳ τῇ κοίλῃ
Μένωνα τὸν Κερδίμμα ἐπέταξε δοὺς αὐτῷ εἰς
φυλακὴν τῆς χώρας τοὺς τῶν ξυμμάχων ἱππέας,
αὐτὸς δὲ ἐπὶ Φοινίκης ἤει. καὶ ἀπαντᾷ αὐτῷ κατὰ
τὴν ὁδὸν Στράτων ὁ Γηροστράτου παῖς τοῦ
Ἀραδίων τε καὶ τῶν Ἀράδῳ προσοίκων βασιλέως·
ὁ δὲ Γηρόστρατος αὐτὸς μετ' Αὐτοφραδάτου ἔπλει
ἐπὶ τῶν νεῶν, καὶ οἱ ἄλλοι οἵ τε τῶν Φοινίκων καὶ
οἱ τῶν Κυπρίων βασιλεῖς καὶ αὐτοὶ Αὐτοφραδάτῃ
8   ξυνέπλεον. Στράτων δὲ Ἀλεξάνδρῳ ἐντυχὼν στε-
φανοῖ χρυσῷ στεφάνῳ αὐτὸν καὶ τήν τε Ἄραδον
αὐτῷ τὴν νῆσον καὶ τὴν Μάραθον τὴν καταντικρὺ
τῆς Ἀράδου ἐν τῇ ἠπείρῳ ᾠκισμένην, πόλιν
μεγάλην καὶ εὐδαίμονα, καὶ Σιγῶνα καὶ Μαριάμ-
μην πόλιν καὶ τἆλλα ὅσα τῆς σφῶν ἐπικρατείας
ἐνδίδωσιν.

14. Ἔτι δὲ ἐν Μαράθῳ Ἀλεξάνδρου ὄντος
ἀφίκοντο παρὰ Δαρείου πρέσβεις, ἐπιστολήν τε
κομίζοντες Δαρείου καὶ αὐτοὶ ἀπὸ γλώσσης
δεησόμενοι ἀφεῖναι Δαρείῳ τὴν μητέρα καὶ τὴν
2   γυναῖκα καὶ τοὺς παῖδας. ἐδήλου δὲ ἡ ἐπιστολή,
ὅτι Φιλίππῳ τε πρὸς Ἀρτοξέρξην φιλία καὶ
ξυμμαχία ἐγένετο καὶ, ἐπειδὴ Ἀρσῆς ὁ υἱὸς
Ἀρτοξέρξου ἐβασίλευσεν, ὅτι Φίλιππος ἀδικίας
πρῶτος ἐς βασιλέα Ἀρσῆν ἦρξεν οὐδὲν ἄχαρι ἐκ
Περσῶν παθών. ἐξ οὗ δὲ αὐτὸς βασιλεύει Περσῶν,

---

[3] App. II and VI.

[4] A. presumably so describes north Syria, as distinct from
the Phoenician coast and Palestine, which were parts of
'Syria', cf. A. B. Bosworth, *CQ* 1975 and iii 6, 8 n.

among the islands, but later joined Autophradates at Halicarnassus.[3]

Alexander appointed Menon son of Cerdimmas as satrap of 'hollow' Syria,[4] giving him the allied cavalry to protect the country, while he himself proceeded towards Phoenicia. On his way he was met by Straton son of Gerostratus, king of the Aradians and people near Aradus; Gerostratus himself was sailing with Autophradates, like the rest of the Phoenician and Cypriot kings. On meeting Alexander, Straton crowned him with a golden crown and surrendered to him the island of Aradus and Marathus which lay opposite it on the mainland, a large and prosperous city, with Sigon and the city of Mariamme and all the other places under his control.

8

14. While Alexander was still at Marathus, envoys reached him from Darius, bringing a letter from him;[1] they were themselves to plead by word of mouth for the release to Darius of his mother, wife and children. The letter argued as follows: Philip had been in peace and alliance with Artaxerxes,[2] and when Arses son of Artaxerxes became king,[3] Philip first did wrong to King Arses, although he had sustained no injury from the Persians. From the

2

---

[1] Significant variants in D. 39; QC. iv 1, 7 ff.; J. xi 12. D. makes Al. substitute a fictitious letter from Darius and reply to it. G. T. Griffith, *Proceedings of Cambridge Philological Society* 1968, 33 ff. conjectures that A. used the fictitious letter. A. appears to be following his main sources, though the summary of Darius' letter and the 'text' of Al's will be in his own words (Introd. 15). Al's letter contains several allusions to 'facts' otherwise unattested; if they are really fictitious, they may be Al's own propaganda.

[2] Introd. n. 65.

[3] 338–336 B.C. Philip's invasion of Asia preceded Darius' accession, D. 5; Beloch, III [2] 2, 310.

οὔτε πέμψαι τινὰ Ἀλέξανδρον παρ' αὐτὸν ἐς
βεβαίωσιν τῆς πάλαι οὔσης φιλίας τε καὶ ξυμμαχίας, διαβῆναί τε ξὺν στρατιᾷ ἐς τὴν Ἀσίαν καὶ
3 πολλὰ κακὰ ἐργάσασθαι Πέρσας. τούτου ἕνεκα
καταβῆναι αὐτὸς τῇ χώρᾳ ἀμυνῶν καὶ τὴν ἀρχὴν
τὴν πατρῴαν ἀνασώσων. τὴν μὲν δὴ μάχην ὡς
θεῶν τῳ ἔδοξεν οὕτω κριθῆναι, αὐτὸς δὲ βασιλεὺς
παρὰ βασιλέως γυναῖκά τε τὴν αὑτοῦ αἰτεῖν καὶ
μητέρα καὶ παῖδας τοὺς ἁλόντας, καὶ φιλίαν
ἐθέλειν ποιήσασθαι πρὸς Ἀλέξανδρον καὶ ξύμ-
μαχος εἶναι Ἀλεξάνδρῳ· καὶ ὑπὲρ τούτων πέμπειν
ἠξίου Ἀλέξανδρον παρ' αὐτὸν ξὺν Μενίσκῳ τε καὶ
Ἀρσίμᾳ τοῖς ἀγγέλοις τοῖς ἐκ Περσῶν ἥκουσι τοὺς
τὰ πιστὰ ληψομένους τε καὶ ὑπὲρ Ἀλεξάνδρου
δώσοντας.
4 Πρὸς ταῦτα ἀντιγράφει Ἀλέξανδρος καὶ ξυμπέμπει τοῖς παρὰ Δαρείου ἐλθοῦσι Θέρσιππον, παραγγείλας τὴν ἐπιστολὴν δοῦναι Δαρείῳ, αὐτὸν δὲ μὴ
διαλέγεσθαι ὑπὲρ μηδενός. ἡ δὲ ἐπιστολὴ ἡ
Ἀλεξάνδρου ἔχει ὧδε· Οἱ ὑμέτεροι πρόγονοι
ἐλθόντες εἰς Μακεδονίαν καὶ εἰς τὴν ἄλλην Ἑλλάδα
κακῶς ἐποίησαν ἡμᾶς οὐδὲν προηδικημένοι· ἐγὼ
δὲ τῶν Ἑλλήνων ἡγεμὼν κατασταθεὶς καὶ τιμω-
ρήσασθαι βουλόμενος Πέρσας διέβην ἐς τὴν
5 Ἀσίαν, ὑπαρξάντων ὑμῶν. καὶ γὰρ Περινθίοις
ἐβοηθήσατε, οἳ τὸν ἐμὸν πατέρα ἠδίκουν, καὶ εἰς
Θράκην, ἧς ἡμεῖς ἤρχομεν, δύναμιν ἔπεμψεν
Ὦχος. τοῦ δὲ πατρὸς ἀποθανόντος ὑπὸ τῶν
ἐπιβουλευσάντων, οὓς ὑμεῖς συνετάξατε, ὡς αὐτοὶ
ἐν ταῖς ἐπιστολαῖς πρὸς ἅπαντας ἐκομπάσατε, καὶ
Ἀρσὴν ἀποκτείναντός σου μετὰ Βαγώου, καὶ τὴν
ἀρχὴν κατασχόντος οὐ δικαίως οὐδὲ κατὰ τὸν

time Darius had been King of Persia, Alexander had
sent no envoy to him to confirm the ancient friendship
and alliance, but had crossed with an army into Asia
and had done great harm to the Persians. That was
why Darius had come down to defend his country
and to rescue his ancestral dominion. The battle
had been decided as some god had willed; but as a
king he begged a king to restore his captive mother,
wife and children; and he was ready to make friendship and an alliance with Alexander, and for these
arrangements he thought it fitting that Alexander
should send to him along with Meniscus and Arsimes
(the envoys who had come from Persia) persons
appointed to exchange pledges.

Alexander wrote a reply and sent Thersippus along
with Darius' envoys with instructions to deliver the
letter, but not to discuss anything with Darius.
This is how Alexander's letter runs: ' Your ancestors invaded Macedonia and the rest of Greece
and did us great harm, though we had done them no
prior injury; I have been appointed *hegemon* of the
Greeks, and invaded Asia in the desire to take vengeance on Persia for *your* aggressions. For you
assisted Perinthus, which wronged my father, and
Ochus sent a force into Thrace, which was under our
rule.[4] My father was murdered by conspirators,
whom you Persians organized, as you yourselves
boasted in your letters to all the world;[5] you
assassinated Arses with the help of Bagoas, and
seized the throne unjustly and in actual contra-

332
B.C.

[480–
479 B.C.]

---

[4] Introd. n. 65.   Nothing is known of an invasion of Thrace.
[5] Introd. 46.

Περσῶν νόμον, ἀλλὰ ἀδικοῦντος Πέρσας, καὶ ὑπὲρ
ἐμοῦ πρὸς τοὺς Ἕλληνας γράμματα οὐκ ἐπιτήδεια
6 διαπέμποντος, ὅπως πρός με πολεμῶσι, καὶ
χρήματα ἀποστέλλοντος πρὸς Λακεδαιμονίους καὶ
ἄλλους τινὰς τῶν Ἑλλήνων, καὶ τῶν μὲν ἄλλων
πόλεων οὐδεμιᾶς δεχομένης, Λακεδαιμονίων δὲ
λαβόντων, καὶ τῶν παρὰ σοῦ πεμφθέντων τοὺς
ἐμοὺς φίλους διαφθειράντων καὶ τὴν εἰρήνην, ἣν
τοῖς Ἕλλησι κατεσκεύασα, διαλύειν ἐπιχειρούντων,
ἐστράτευσα ἐπὶ σὲ ὑπάρξαντος σοῦ τῆς ἔχθρας.
7 ἐπεὶ δὲ μάχῃ νενίκηκα πρότερον μὲν τοὺς σοὺς
στρατηγοὺς καὶ σατράπας, νῦν δὲ σὲ καὶ τὴν μετὰ
σοῦ δύναμιν, καὶ τὴν χώραν ἔχω τῶν θεῶν μοι
δόντων, ὅσοι τῶν μετὰ σοῦ παραταξαμένων μὴ ἐν
τῇ μάχῃ ἀπέθανον, ἀλλὰ παρ' ἐμὲ κατέφυγον,
τούτων ἐπιμέλομαι καὶ οὐκ ἄκοντες παρ' ἐμοί
εἰσιν, ἀλλὰ αὐτοὶ ἑκόντες ξυστρατεύονται μετ'
8 ἐμοῦ. ὡς οὖν ἐμοῦ τῆς Ἀσίας ἁπάσης κυρίου
ὄντος ἧκε πρὸς ἐμέ. εἰ δὲ φοβῇ μὴ ἐλθὼν πάθῃς
τι ἐξ ἐμοῦ ἄχαρι, πέμπε τινὰς τῶν φίλων τὰ πιστὰ
ληψομένους. ἐλθὼν δὲ πρός με τὴν μητέρα καὶ τὴν
γυναῖκα καὶ τοὺς παῖδας καὶ εἰ ἄλλο τι θέλεις αἴτει
καὶ λάμβανε. ὅ τι γὰρ ἂν πείθῃς ἐμὲ ἔσται σοι.
9 καὶ τοῦ λοιποῦ ὅταν πέμπῃς παρ' ἐμέ, ὡς πρὸς
βασιλέα τῆς Ἀσίας πέμπε, μηδὲ [ἃ] ἐξ ἴσου
ἐπίστελλε, ἀλλ' ὡς κυρίῳ ὄντι πάντων τῶν σῶν
φράζε εἴ του δέῃ· εἰ δὲ μή, ἐγὼ βουλεύσομαι περὶ
σοῦ ὡς ἀδικοῦντος. εἰ δ' ἀντιλέγεις περὶ τῆς
βασιλείας, ὑπομείνας ἔτι ἀγώνισαι περὶ αὐτῆς καὶ
μὴ φεῦγε, ὡς ἐγὼ ἐπὶ σὲ πορεύομαι οὗ ἂν ᾖς.

15. Πρὸς μὲν Δαρεῖον ταῦτ' ἐπέστειλεν. ἐπεὶ δ'
ἔμαθεν τά τε χρήματα ὅσα σὺν Κωφῆνι τῷ

332
B.C.

vention of Persian law, doing wrong to Persians;
you sent unfriendly letters to the Greeks about me, 6
urging them to make war on me. You despatched
sums of money to the Lacedaemonians and certain
other Greeks, which no other city accepted but the
Lacedaemonians. Your envoys destroyed my friends
and sought to destroy the peace I had established
in Greece.[6] Although I marched against you, it was
you that started the quarrel. As I have conquered 7
in battle first your generals and satraps, and now
yourself and your own force, and am in possession
of the country by the gift of heaven, I hold myself
responsible for all of your troops who did not die
in the field but took refuge with me; they are
with me of their own free will, and voluntarily
serve in my army. You must then regard me as 8
Lord of all Asia and come to me. If you fear that
by coming you may receive some harm at my hands,
send some of your friends to receive pledges. Ask
for your mother, wife and children and what you
will, when you have come, and you will receive them.
You shall have whatever you persuade me to give.
And in future when you send to me, make your 9
addresses to the king of Asia,[7] and do not correspond
as an equal, but tell me, as lord of all your possessions,
what you need; otherwise I shall make plans to deal
with you as a wrongdoer. But if you claim the kingship, stand your ground and fight for it and do not
flee, as I shall pursue you wherever you are.'

15. This was Alexander's letter to Darius.[1] When
he learned that the moneys Darius had sent with

---

[6] Persian attempts to foster Greek resistance to Macedon
all seem to be later than Philip's invasion!

[7] QC. iv 1, 7 and 13 f. with different details.

[1] All this is apparently from A's main source.

Ἀρταβάζου ἀποπεπόμφει εἰς Δαμασκὸν Δαρεῖος
ὅτι ἑάλωκε, καὶ ὅσοι Περσῶν ἀμφ' αὐτὰ ἐγκατελείφθησαν ξὺν τῇ ἄλλῃ βασιλικῇ κατασκευῇ ὅτι καὶ
οὗτοι ἑάλωσαν, ταῦτα μὲν ὀπίσω κομίσαντα ἐς
2 Δαμασκὸν Παρμενίωνα φυλάσσειν ἐκέλευε. τοὺς
δὲ πρέσβεις τῶν Ἑλλήνων οἳ πρὸς Δαρεῖον πρὸ τῆς
μάχης ἀφιγμένοι ἦσαν, ἐπεὶ καὶ τούτους ἑαλωκέναι
ἔμαθεν, παρ' αὐτὸν πέμπειν ἐκέλευεν. ἦσαν δὲ
Εὐθυκλῆς μὲν Σπαρτιάτης, Θεσσαλίσκος δὲ Ἰσμη-
νίου καὶ Διονυσόδωρος Ὀλυμπιονίκης Θηβαῖοι,
Ἰφικράτης δὲ ὁ Ἰφικράτους τοῦ στρατηγοῦ
3 Ἀθηναῖος. καὶ οὗτοι ὡς ἧκον παρὰ Ἀλέξανδρον,
Θεσσαλίσκον μὲν καὶ Διονυσόδωρον καίπερ Θηβαίους ὄντας εὐθὺς ἀφῆκεν, τὸ μέν τι κατοικτίσει
τῶν Θηβῶν, τὸ δὲ ὅτι συγγνωστὰ δεδρακέναι
ἐφαίνοντο, ἠνδραποδισμένης ὑπὸ Μακεδόνων τῆς
πατρίδος σφίσιν τε ἥντινα ἠδύναντο ὠφέλειαν
εὑρισκόμενοι καὶ εἰ δή τινα καὶ τῇ πατρίδι ἐκ
4 Περσῶν καὶ Δαρείου· ταῦτα μὲν ὑπὲρ ἀμφοῖν
ἐπιεικῆ ἐνθυμηθείς, ἰδίᾳ δὲ Θεσσαλίσκου μὲν αἰδοῖ
τοῦ γένους ἀφιέναι εἶπεν, ὅτι τῶν ἐπιφανῶν
Θηβαίων ἦν, Διονυσόδωρον δὲ ἐπὶ τῇ νίκῃ τῶν
Ὀλυμπίων. Ἰφικράτην δὲ φιλίᾳ τε τῆς Ἀθηναίων
πόλεως καὶ μνήμῃ τῆς δόξης τοῦ πατρὸς ζῶντά τε
ἀμφ' αὐτὸν ἔχων ἐς τὰ μάλιστα ἐτίμησε καὶ νόσῳ
τελευτήσαντος τὰ ὀστᾶ ἐς τὰς Ἀθήνας τοῖς πρὸς
5 γένους ἀπέπεμψεν. Εὐθυκλέα δὲ Λακεδαιμόνιόν τε
ὄντα, πόλεως περιφανῶς ἐχθρᾶς ἐν τῷ τότε, καὶ
αὐτὸν οὐδὲν ἰδίᾳ εὑρισκόμενον ἐς ξυγγνώμην ὅ τι
καὶ λόγου ἄξιον, τὰ μὲν πρῶτα ἐν φυλακῇ ἀδέσμῳ
εἶχεν, ὕστερον δέ, ὡς ἐπὶ μέγα εὐτύχει, καὶ τοῦτον
ἀφῆκεν.

Cophen son of Artabazus to Damascus had been seized, and that all the Persians left to guard them had also been seized with the rest of the royal equipage, he ordered Parmenio to take the spoils back to Damascus and guard them there. As for the Greek envoys who had reached Darius before the battle, when he learned that they too had been captured, he ordered them to be sent to him. They were Euthycles the Spartiate, Thessaliscus son of Ismenias and Dionysodorus, an Olympian victor, from Thebes, and Iphicrates son of Iphicrates the general from Athens.[2] When they reached Alexander, he at once dismissed Thessaliscus and Dionysodorus, Thebans as they were, partly from compassion for Thebes and partly because he thought that they had acted pardonably, since their country had been enslaved by Macedonians and they were looking for any conceivable help they could get for themselves and for their country too from Darius and Persia; he took a kindly view of the doings of both, but privately he said that he was releasing Thessaliscus from regard for his family, since he was one of the Theban nobles, and Dionysodorus because of his victory at Olympia. From friendship for Athens and remembrance of his father's fame, he kept Iphicrates in attendance and paid him special honour; when he died, he sent back his bones to his relatives at Athens. Euthycles, however, as a Lacedaemonian, from a city conspicuously hostile to him at the moment, and as a person unable to produce any reasonable claim to individual pardon, was at first kept under guard, though not in bonds; but later, when successes crowded in on Alexander, he too was released.

332
B.C.

2

3

4

5

[2] Apart from Iphicrates, QC. iii **13**, **15** gives different names.

6 Ἐκ Μαράθου δὲ ὁρμηθεὶς Βύβλον τε λαμβάνει
ὁμολογίᾳ ἐνδοθεῖσαν καὶ Σιδῶνα αὐτῶν Σιδωνίων
ἐπικαλεσαμένων κατὰ ἔχθος τὸ Περσῶν καὶ
Δαρείου. ἐντεῦθεν δὲ προὐχώρει ὡς ἐπὶ Τύρον·
καὶ ἐντυγχάνουσιν αὐτῷ κατὰ τὴν ὁδὸν πρέσβεις
Τυρίων ἀπὸ τοῦ κοινοῦ ἐσταλμένοι ὡς ἐγνωκότων
Τυρίων πράσσειν ὅ τι ἂν ἐπαγγέλλῃ Ἀλέξανδρος.
7 ὁ δὲ τήν τε πόλιν ἐπαινέσας καὶ τοὺς πρέσβεις (καὶ
γὰρ ἦσαν τῶν ἐπιφανῶν ἐν Τύρῳ οἵ τε ἄλλοι καὶ ὁ
τοῦ βασιλέως τῶν Τυρίων παῖς. αὐτὸς δὲ ὁ
βασιλεὺς Ἀζέμιλκος μετ' Αὐτοφραδάτου ἔπλει)
ἐκέλευσεν ἐπανελθόντας φράσαι Τυρίοις, ὅτι ἐθέλοι
παρελθὼν ἐς τὴν πόλιν θῦσαι τῷ Ἡρακλεῖ.

16. Ἔστι γὰρ ἐν Τύρῳ ἱερὸν Ἡρακλέους παλαιό-
τατον ὧν μνήμη ἀνθρωπίνη διασώζεται, οὐ τοῦ
Ἀργείου Ἡρακλέους τοῦ Ἀλκμήνης· πολλαῖς γὰρ
γενεαῖς πρότερον τιμᾶται ἐν Τύρῳ Ἡρακλῆς ἢ
Κάδμον ἐκ Φοινίκης ὁρμηθέντα Θήβας κατασχεῖν
καὶ τὴν παῖδα Κάδμῳ τὴν Σεμέλην γενέσθαι, ἐξ ἧς
2 καὶ ὁ τοῦ Διὸς Διόνυσος γίγνεται. Διόνυσος μὲν
δὴ τρίτος ἂν ἀπὸ Κάδμου εἴη, κατὰ Λάβδακον τὸν
Πολυδώρου τοῦ Κάδμου παῖδα, Ἡρακλῆς δὲ ὁ
Ἀργεῖος κατ' Οἰδίποδα μάλιστα τὸν Λαΐου.
σέβουσι δὲ καὶ Αἰγύπτιοι ἄλλον Ἡρακλέα, οὐχ
3 ὅνπερ Τύριοι ἢ Ἕλληνες, ἀλλὰ λέγει Ἡρόδοτος,
ὅτι τῶν δώδεκα θεῶν Ἡρακλέα ἄγουσιν Αἰγύπτιοι,
καθάπερ καὶ Ἀθηναῖοι Διόνυσον τὸν Διὸς καὶ
Κόρης σέβουσιν, ἄλλον τοῦτον Διόνυσον· καὶ ὁ
Ἴακχος ὁ μυστικὸς τούτῳ τῷ Διονύσῳ, οὐχὶ τῷ
4 Θηβαίῳ, ἐπᾴδεται. ὡς τόν γε ἐν Ταρτησσῷ πρὸς

Alexander marched from Marathus and received   6   332
the surrender of Byblus and Sidon; the Sidonians   B.C.
who loathed Persia and Darius called him in themselves.[3] Thence he proceeded towards Tyre, and on
the way Tyrian envoys met him, sent by the community to say that Tyre had decided to accept
Alexander's orders.   He commended both the city   7
and its envoys—for they were Tyrian nobles and
included the son of their king, Azemilcus, who was
himself at sea with Autophradates' fleet—and told
them to return and inform the Tyrians that he proposed to visit Tyre and sacrifice to Heracles.[4]

16. At Tyre there is the most ancient temple of
Heracles of which there is any human recollection,
not the Argive Heracles, son of Alcmene, for a
Heracles was honoured at Tyre many generations
before Cadmus sailed from Phoenicia, occupied
Thebes, and had a daughter Semele, mother of Diony-
sus son of Zeus.   For Dionysus would appear to be in   2
the third generation from Cadmus, along with Lab-
dacus son of Polydorus, son of Cadmus; while the
Argive Heracles was probably a contemporary of
Oedipus son of Laius.   The Egyptians too worship
another Heracles, different from the Heracles of
Tyre and the Heracles of Greece; Herodotus [1] says   3
that the Egyptians reckon him one of the Twelve
Deities, just as the Athenians worship a different
Dionysus, son of Zeus and Kore.   It is to him, not the
Theban Dionysus, that the mystic chant ' Iacchus '
is sung.[2]   I think that the Heracles honoured by the   4

---

[3] QC. iv 1, 15.   Sidon had suffered much in 344/3 B.C. for
revolting from Persia.   Cf. 24, 5 n.

[4] D. 40, 2; QC. iv 2, 1–5, also for ch. 16, 7 ff.

[1] ii 43, § 1–6 are clearly A's own digression, cf. App. IV, 4.

[2] *Oxf. Class. Dict.* s.v. Iacchus.

Ἰβήρων τιμώμενον Ἡρακλέα, ἵνα καὶ στῆλαί τινες
Ἡρακλέους ὠνομασμέναι εἰσί, δοκῶ ἐγὼ τὸν
Τύριον εἶναι Ἡρακλέα, ὅτι Φοινίκων κτίσμα ἡ
Ταρτησσὸς καὶ τῷ Φοινίκων νόμῳ ὅ τε νεὼς
πεποίηται τῷ Ἡρακλεῖ τῷ ἐκεῖ καὶ αἱ θυσίαι
5 θύονται. Γηρυόνην δέ, ἐφ᾿ ὅντινα ὁ Ἀργεῖος
Ἡρακλῆς ἐστάλη πρὸς Εὐρυσθέως τὰς βοῦς
ἀπελάσαι τὰς Γηρυόνου καὶ ἀγαγεῖν ἐς Μυκήνας,
οὐδέν τι προσήκειν τῇ γῇ τῇ Ἰβήρων Ἑκαταῖος ὁ
λογοποιὸς λέγει, οὐδὲ ἐπὶ νῆσόν τινα Ἐρύθειαν
⟨τῆς⟩ ἔξω τῆς μεγάλης θαλάσσης σταλῆναι
Ἡρακλέα, ἀλλὰ τῆς ἠπείρου τῆς περὶ Ἀμπρακίαν
τε καὶ Ἀμφιλόχους βασιλέα γενέσθαι Γηρυόνην
καὶ ἐκ τῆς ἠπείρου ταύτης ἀπελάσαι Ἡρακλέα τὰς
6 βοῦς, οὐδὲ τοῦτον φαῦλον ἆθλον τιθέμενον. οἶδα
δὲ ἐγὼ καὶ εἰς τοῦτο ἔτι εὔβοτον τὴν ἤπειρον
ταύτην καὶ βοῦς τρέφουσαν καλλίστας· καὶ ἐς
Εὐρυσθέα τῶν μὲν ἐξ Ἠπείρου βοῶν κλέος
ἀφῖχθαι καὶ τοῦ βασιλέως τῆς Ἠπείρου τὸ ὄνομα
τὸν Γηρυόνην οὐκ ἔξω τοῦ εἰκότος τίθεμαι· τῶν δὲ
ἐσχάτων τῆς Εὐρώπης Ἰβήρων οὔτ᾿ ἂν τοῦ βασιλέως τὸ ὄνομα γιγνώσκειν Εὐρυσθέα, οὔτε εἰ βοῦς
καλαὶ ἐν τῇ χώρᾳ ταύτῃ νέμονται, εἰ μή τις τὴν
Ἥραν τούτοις ἐπάγων, ὡς αὐτὴν ταῦτα Ἡρακλεῖ
δι᾿ Εὐρυσθέως ἐπαγγέλλουσαν, τὸ οὐ πιστὸν τοῦ
λόγου ἀποκρύπτειν ἐθέλοι τῷ μύθῳ.
7 Τούτῳ τῷ Ἡρακλεῖ τῷ Τυρίῳ ἔφη ἐθέλειν
θῦσαι Ἀλέξανδρος. ὡς δὲ ἀπηγγέλθη ταῦτα πρὸς
τῶν πρέσβεων εἰς τὴν Τύρον, τὰ μὲν ἄλλα ἔδοξέ
σφισι ποιεῖν ὅ τι περ ἐπαγγέλλοι Ἀλέξανδρος, ἐς

---

³ This Iberian kingdom in south Spain was often confused

Iberians at Tartessus, where certain Pillars have also been named after him, is the Tyrian Heracles, since Tartessus is a Phoenician foundation [3] and it is in the Phoenician style that the temple of Heracles there has been built and that the sacrifices are offered. Moreover, Geryones against whom the Argive Heracles was sent by Eurystheus, to drive off his oxen and bring them to Mycenae, has no connection with Iberia according to Hecataeus the historian [4]; nor in his view was Heracles sent to an island, Erytheia, beyond the Great Sea, but Geryones was king of the mainland in the region of Ambracia and the Amphilochi, and it was from this mainland here that Heracles drove off the oxen; and that was in itself no mean prize-task that he set himself either. What I do know [5] is that this part of the mainland is capital pasture to this very day and rears excellent oxen; and I reckon it quite likely that the fame of these mainland oxen reached Eurystheus together with the name of the king of the mainland, Geryones; but I feel sure that Eurystheus would not have known the name of the king of the Iberians, right at the ends of Europe, nor whether there were fine cattle in those parts, unless anyone cares to bring in Hera and suppose that she passed on the news of them to Heracles through Eurystheus, and so to veil the unlikeliness of the tale with legend. [6]

It was to this Tyrian Heracles that Alexander said he wished to sacrifice. When this was announced at Tyre by the envoys, the Tyrians decided to obey

in Roman times with the Phoenician colony of Gades (e.g. Sallust, *Histories* ii 5; Cicero, *de senectute* 69), which had a famous temple of Heracles (Melkarth).

[4] Jacoby no. 1, F. 26. H. flourished c. 500 B.C.

[5] Presumably from autopsy.

[6] A. does not question but rationalizes the old legends.

δὲ τὴν πόλιν μήτε τινὰ Περσῶν μήτε Μακεδόνων δέχεσθαι, ὡς τοῦτο ἔς τε τὰ παρόντα τῷ λόγῳ εὐπρεπέστατον καὶ ἐς τοῦ πολέμου τὴν κρίσιν, ἄδηλον ἔτι οὖσαν, ἀσφαλέστατόν σφισι γνωσόμενοι.

8 ὡς δὲ ἐξηγγέλθη Ἀλεξάνδρῳ τὰ ἐκ τῆς Τύρου, τοὺς μὲν πρέσβεις πρὸς ὀργὴν ὀπίσω ἀπέπεμψεν, αὐτὸς δὲ συναγαγὼν τούς τε ἑταίρους καὶ τοὺς ἡγεμόνας τῆς στρατιᾶς καὶ ταξιάρχας καὶ ἰλάρχας ἔλεξεν ὧδε.

17. "Ανδρες φίλοι καὶ ξύμμαχοι, ἡμῖν οὔτε τὴν ἐπ' Αἰγύπτου πορείαν ἀσφαλῆ ὁρῶ θαλασσοκρατούντων Περσῶν, Δαρεῖόν τε διώκειν ὑπολειπομένους αὐτήν τε ὀπίσω τὴν τῶν Τυρίων πόλιν ἀμφίβολον καὶ Αἴγυπτον καὶ Κύπρον ἐχομένας πρὸς Περσῶν, οὐδὲ τοῦτο ἀσφαλὲς ἔς τε τὰ ἄλλα

2 καὶ μάλιστα δὴ ἐς τὰ Ἑλληνικὰ πράγματα, μή ποτε ἄρα ἐπικρατήσαντες αὖθις τῶν ἐπὶ θαλάσσῃ χωρίων οἱ Πέρσαι, προχωρησάντων ἡμῶν ξὺν τῇ δυνάμει ὡς ἐπὶ Βαβυλῶνά τε καὶ Δαρεῖον, αὐτοὶ ξὺν πλείονι στόλῳ μετ[αγ]άγοιεν τὸν πόλεμον ἐς τὴν Ἑλλάδα, Λακεδαιμονίων μὲν ἐκ τοῦ εὐθέος ἡμῖν πολεμούντων, τῆς δὲ Ἀθηναίων πόλεως φόβῳ μᾶλλόν τι ἢ εὐνοίᾳ τῇ πρὸς ἡμᾶς πρὸς τὸ παρὸν

3 κατεχομένης. ἐξαιρεθείσης δὲ Τύρου ἥ τε Φοινίκη ἔχοιτο ἂν πᾶσα καὶ τὸ ναυτικὸν ὅπερ πλεῖστόν τε καὶ κράτιστον τοῦ Περσικοῦ, τὸ Φοινίκων, παρ' ἡμᾶς μεταχωρήσειν εἰκός· οὐ γὰρ ἀνέξονται οὔτε οἱ ἐρέται οὔθ' οἱ ἐπιβάται Φοίνικες ἐχομένων σφίσι τῶν πόλεων αὐτοὶ ὑπὲρ ἄλλων πλέοντες κινδυνεύειν· Κύπρος δὲ ἐπὶ τῷδε ἢ οὐ χαλεπῶς ἡμῖν προσχωρήσει ἢ ἐξ ἐπίπλου εὐμαρῶς ληφθήσεται.

4 καὶ ταῖς τε ἐκ Μακεδονίας ναυσὶ καὶ ταῖς Φοινίσ-

all Alexander's other commands, but not to admit
any Persians or Macedonians within their city, as this
decision would be the easiest to excuse in the existing
circumstances, and safest for the future and for the
issue of the war, which was still obscure. When
Alexander received this answer, he angrily sent back
the envoys, and assembling the Companions and
the generals of the army, with the battalion and
squadron commanders, made the following speech.[7]

17. ' My friends and allies, so long as Persia is supreme at sea I am aware that we cannot march in safety
to Egypt. Nor, again, is it safe to pursue Darius,
leaving in our rear the city of Tyre itself with its
allegiance doubtful and Egypt and Cyprus still in
Persia's hands, especially in view of the state of
Greek affairs; the Persians might again secure control
of the coastal places, when we have advanced in full
force against Babylon and Darius, and with a larger
expedition transfer the war into Greece, where the
Lacedaemonians are openly at war with us, while
Athens is kept in control for the present by fear
rather than goodwill towards us. But with Tyre
once destroyed, Phoenicia would all be in our hands,
and the best and strongest part of the Persian navy,
the Phoenician, would probably come over to us.
For if their cities are in our hands neither rowers
nor marines from Phoenicia will tolerate dangers at
sea for the sake of others. After this Cyprus will
either readily come over to our side or be captured
easily by naval attack. Then if we keep the sea with

---

[7] The speech is apparently based on A's main source(s);
no mention of Heracles but an explanation of Al's strategy
(cf. i 18, 9; 20, 1; 24, 3; Introd. 44).

σαις πλεόντων ἡμῶν τὴν θάλασσαν καὶ Κύπρου ἅμα
προσγενομένης θαλασσοκρατοῖμέν τε ἂν βεβαίως
καὶ ὁ ἐς Αἴγυπτον στόλος εὐμαρῶς ἡμῖν ἐν ταὐτῷ
γίγνεται. Αἴγυπτον δὲ παραστησαμένοις ὑπέρ τε
τῆς Ἑλλάδος καὶ τῆς οἰκείας οὐδὲν ἔτι ὕποπτον
ὑπολείπεται, τόν τε ἐπὶ Βαβυλῶνος στόλον μετὰ
τοῦ ἐς τὰ οἴκοι ἀσφαλοῦς καὶ ξὺν μείζονι ἅμα
ἀξιώσει ποιησόμεθα ἀποτετμημένοι τήν τε θάλασσαν Περσῶν ξύμπασαν καὶ τὴν ἐπὶ τάδε τοῦ
Εὐφράτου γῆν.

18. Ταῦτα λέγων οὐ χαλεπῶς ἔπειθεν ἐπιχειρεῖν
τῇ Τύρῳ· καί τι καὶ θεῖον ἀνέπειθεν αὐτόν, ὅτι
ἐνύπνιον αὐτῆς ἐκείνης τῆς νυκτὸς ἐδόκει αὐτὸς μὲν
τῷ τείχει προσάγειν τῶν Τυρίων, τὸν δὲ Ἡρακλέα
δεξιοῦσθαί τε αὐτὸν καὶ ἀνάγειν ἐς τὴν πόλιν. καὶ
τοῦτο ἐξηγεῖτο Ἀρίστανδρος ὡς ξὺν πόνῳ ἁλωσο-
μένην τὴν Τύρον, ὅτι καὶ τὰ τοῦ Ἡρακλέους ἔργα
ξὺν πόνῳ ἐγένετο. καὶ γὰρ καὶ μέγα ἔργον τῆς
2 Τύρου ἡ πολιορκία ἐφαίνετο. νῆσός τε γὰρ αὐτοῖς
ἡ πόλις ἦν καὶ τείχεσιν ὑψηλοῖς πάντη ὠχύρωτο·
καὶ τὰ ἀπὸ θαλάσσης πρὸς τῶν Τυρίων μᾶλλόν τι
ἐν τῷ τότε ἐφαίνετο, τῶν τε Περσῶν ἔτι θαλασσοκρατούντων καὶ αὐτοῖς τοῖς Τυρίοις νεῶν ἔτι
πολλῶν περιουσῶν.

3 Ὡς δὲ ταῦτα ὅμως ἐκράτησε, χῶμα ἔγνω
χωννύναι ἐκ τῆς ἠπείρου ὡς ἐπὶ τὴν πόλιν. ἔστι
δὲ πορθμὸς τεναγώδης τὸ χωρίον καὶ τὰ μὲν πρὸς
τῇ ἠπείρῳ τῆς θαλάσσης βραχέα καὶ πηλώδη
αὐτοῦ, τὰ δὲ πρὸς αὐτῇ τῇ πόλει, ἵνα τὸ βαθύτατον

---

[1] QC. iv 2, 17: P. 24, 3 put this later in the siege.
[2] It lasted 6 or 7 months, D. 46, 5; QC. iv 4, 9; P. 24, 3,

332
B.C.

our Macedonian ships, and the Phoenician, and with
Cyprus ours as well, we should hold the sea-power
securely, and our expedition to Egypt would be easy
on the very same account. But once we have
brought Egypt over, we shall have no cause of uneasiness for Greece and our own home, and we shall
make the expedition to Babylon, with safety at home
as well as enhanced prestige, with the whole sea and
all the country this side of Euphrates cut off from
Persia.'

18. With these words Alexander easily won over
his staff to the attack on Tyre. In some degree an
omen influenced him, for in a dream that very night
he found himself approaching the wall of Tyre,
and there was Heracles, stretching out his right hand,
and conducting him into the city. Aristander
interpreted this dream to mean that Tyre would
be taken, but with an effort, for Heracles' achievements involved effort.[1] The fact is that the siege of
Tyre was manifestly a large task.[2] The city was an 2
island, and had been fortified all round with high
walls; and at that time the advantage by sea apparently lay with Tyre, as the Persians were still
supreme at sea and the Tyrians also still had many
ships available.

But as Alexander's arguments, none the less, won 3
the day, he decided to build a mole from the mainland
to the city.[3] The place is one where people cross
over shoal-water; it has shallows and patches of mud
towards the mainland; next to the city itself where

c. Feb.–Aug. 332 B.C., cf. 24, 6 n. For its course cf. D. 40–46;
QC. iv 2–4; P. 24 f. Al's artillery: Marsden (cf. i 20, 8 n.),
esp. 61 f. 102 f. Plan: Fuller 209.
[3] Four stades, D. 40, 4; QC 2, 6.

τοῦ διάπλου, τριῶν μάλιστα ὀργυιῶν τὸ βάθος.
ἀλλὰ λίθων τε πολλῶν ἀφθονία ἦν καὶ ὕλης, ἥντινα
τοῖς λίθοις ἄνωθεν ἐπεφόρουν, χάρακές τε οὐ
χαλεπῶς κατεπήγνυντο ἐν τῷ πηλῷ καὶ αὐτὸς ὁ
πηλὸς ξύνδεσμος τοῖς λίθοις ἐς τὸ ἐπιμένειν
4 ἐγίγνετο. καὶ προθυμία τῶν τε Μακεδόνων ἐς τὸ
ἔργον καὶ Ἀλεξάνδρου πολλὴ ἦν παρόντος τε καὶ
αὐτοῦ ἕκαστα ἐξηγουμένου καὶ τὰ μὲν λόγῳ
ἐπαίροντος, τὰ δὲ καὶ χρήμασι τούς τι ἐκπρεπέ-
στερον κατ' ἀρετὴν πονουμένους ἐπικουφίζοντος.
ἀλλ' ἔστε μὲν τὸ πρὸς τῇ ἠπείρῳ ἐχώννυτο, οὐ
χαλεπῶς προὐχώρει τὸ ἔργον, ἐπὶ βάθος τε ὀλίγον
5 χωννύμενον καὶ οὐδενὸς ἐξείργοντος. ὡς δὲ τῷ τε
βαθυτέρῳ ἤδη ἐπέλαζον καὶ ἅμα τῇ πόλει αὐτῇ
ἐγγὺς ἐγίγνοντο, ἀπό τε τῶν τειχῶν ὑψηλῶν ὄντων
βαλλόμενοι ἐκακοπάθουν, ἅτε καὶ ἐπ' ἐργασίᾳ
μᾶλλόν τι ἢ ὡς ἐς μάχην ἀκριβῶς ἐσταλμένοι, καὶ
ταῖς τριήρεσιν ἄλλη καὶ ἄλλη τοῦ χώματος
ἐπιπλέοντες οἱ Τύριοι, ἅτε δὴ θαλασσοκρατοῦντες
ἔτι, ἄπορον πολλαχῇ τὴν πρόσχωσιν τοῖς Μακε-
6 δόσιν ἐποίουν. καὶ οἱ Μακεδόνες πύργους ἐπ'
ἄκρου τοῦ χώματος, ὅ τι περ προκεχωρήκει αὐτοῖς
ἐπὶ πολὺ τῆς θαλάσσης, ἐπέστησαν δύο καὶ μηχανὰς
ἐπὶ τοῖς πύργοις. προκαλύμματα δὲ δέρρεις καὶ
διφθέραι αὐτοῖς ἦσαν, ὡς μήτε πυρφόροις βέλεσιν
ἀπὸ τοῦ τείχους βάλλεσθαι, τοῖς τε ἐργαζομένοις
προβολὴν ἐν τῷ αὐτῷ εἶναι πρὸς τὰ τοξεύματα·
ἅμα τε ὅσοι προσπλέοντες τῶν Τυρίων ἔβλαπτον
τοὺς χωννύντας, ἀπὸ τῶν πύργων βαλλόμενοι οὐ
χαλεπῶς ἀνασταλήσεσθαι ἔμελλον.

19. Οἱ δὲ Τύριοι πρὸς ταῦτα ἀντιμηχανῶνται
τοιόνδε. ναῦν ἱππαγωγὸν κλημάτων τε ξηρῶν καὶ

the crossing is deepest, the water is about three
fathoms deep. But there was plenty of stones and
wood, which they heaped on to the stones; then it
was easy to fix stakes in the mud, and the mud
itself made a stable binding for the stones. The 4
Macedonians were very eager for the work, like
Alexander; he was present directing each step himself, inspired the men with his words and encouraged
their exertions by gifts to those who did work of
exceptional merit. As long as the building of the
mole was near the mainland, the operation went
forward without difficulty; for the depth of the pile
was not great, and no resistance was offered. But 5
once they got into deeper water and also nearer the
city, they were greatly distressed by volleys from
the high walls, especially as they were properly clad
for labouring rather than for fighting; and the Tyrians
sailed up in their triremes here and there by the
mole, being still masters of the sea, and in many
places made it impossible for the Macedonians to
build up the mole. The Macedonians set two towers 6
on the mole, which had now run far out into the sea,
with engines on the towers, and covered them with
hides and skins, to prevent their being pelted with
fire-darts from the wall, and to screen the workers
also against arrows; besides, any Tyrians who
rowed up and tried to injure the men building the
mole would receive volleys from the towers and
would probably be easily repulsed.[4]

19. The Tyrians, however, took a counter step;[1]
they filled a cavalry transport-ship with dry boughs

[4] D. 40, 4–41; QC 2, 8–24 supply other details.
[1] QC. 3, 1 ff. (in Al's absence, 20, 4 below); ignored by D.
QC. 3, 9 f. tells of other Tyrian devices.

ARRIAN

ἄλλης ὕλης εὐφλέκτου ἐμπλήσαντες δύο ἱστοὺς ἐπὶ
τῇ πρώρᾳ καταπηγνύουσι καὶ ἐν κύκλῳ περιφράσ-
σουσιν ἐς ὅσον μακρότατον, ὡς φορυτόν τε ταύτῃ
καὶ δᾷδας ὅσας πλείστας δέξασθαι· πρὸς δὲ πίσσαν
τε καὶ θεῖον καὶ ὅσα ἄλλα ἐς τὸ παρακαλέσαι
2 μεγάλην φλόγα ἐπὶ ταύτῃ ἐπεφόρησαν. παρέτειναν
δὲ καὶ κεραίαν διπλῆν ἐπὶ τοῖς ἱστοῖς ἀμφοτέροις,
καὶ ἀπὸ ταύτης ἐξήρτησαν ἐν λέβησιν ὅσα ἐπιχυ-
θέντα ἢ ἐπιβληθέντα ἐπὶ μέγα τὴν φλόγα ἐξάψειν
ἔμελλεν, ἕρματά τε ἐς τὴν πρύμναν ἐνέθεσαν, τοῦ
ἐξᾶραι ἐς ὕψος τὴν πρώραν πιεζομένης κατὰ
3 πρύμναν τῆς νεώς. ἔπειτα ἄνεμον τηρήσαντες ὡς
ἐπὶ τὸ χῶμα ἐπιφέροντα ἐξάψαντες τριήρεσι τὴν
ναῦν κατ' οὐρὰν εἷλκον. ὡς δὲ ἐπέλαζον ἤδη τῷ τε
χώματι καὶ τοῖς πύργοις, πῦρ ἐμβαλόντες ἐς τὴν
ὕλην καὶ ὡς βιαιότατα ἅμα ταῖς τριήρεσιν ἐπανελ-
κύσαντες τὴν ναῦν ἐνσείουσιν ἄκρῳ τῷ χώματι·
αὐτοὶ δὲ οἱ ἐν τῇ νηὶ καιομένῃ ἤδη ἐξενήξαντο οὐ
4 χαλεπῶς. καὶ ἐν τούτῳ ἥ τε φλὸξ πολλὴ ἐνέπιπτε
τοῖς πύργοις καὶ αἱ κεραῖαι περικλασθεῖσαι ἐξέχεαν
ἐς τὸ πῦρ ὅσα ἐς ἔξαψιν τῆς φλογὸς παρεσκευασ-
μένα ἦν. οἱ δ' ἀπὸ τῶν τριήρων πλησίον τοῦ
χώματος ἀνακωχεύοντες ἐτόξευον ἐς τοὺς πύργους,
ὡς μὴ ἀσφαλὲς εἶναι πελάσαι ὅσοι σβεστήριόν τι τῇ
5 φλογὶ ἐπέφερον. καὶ ἐν τούτῳ κατεχομένων ἤδη
ἐκ τοῦ πυρὸς τῶν πύργων ἐκδραμόντες ἐκ τῆς
πόλεως πολλοὶ καὶ ἐς κέλητια ἐμβάντες ἄλλῃ καὶ
ἄλλῃ ἐποκείλαντες τοῦ χώματος τόν τε χάρακα οὐ
χαλεπῶς διέσπασαν τὸν πρὸ αὐτοῦ προβεβλημένον
καὶ τὰς μηχανὰς ξυμπάσας κατέφλεξαν, ὅσας μὴ
6 ἀπὸ τῆς νεὼς πῦρ ἐπέσχεν. Ἀλέξανδρος δὲ τό τε
χῶμα ἀπὸ τῆς ἠπείρου ἀρξαμένους πλατύτερον

190

and other combustible wood, fixed two masts in the
bows, and built bulwarks round, extended as far
as possible, so that it would contain the greatest
amount of chips and shavings and torches; to say
nothing of pitch, sulphur, and anything else to stir a
great blaze, which they added liberally. They 2
lashed a double yardarm to each mast, and hung
from it in cauldrons anything which could be poured
or thrown on to increase the flame, and they bal-
lasted the stern to lift the bows as high as possible by
the weight aft. Then they waited for a wind blowing 3
towards the mole and, making fast hawsers, towed
the transport astern with triremes. When they
got near the mole and the towers, they lit the
material, hauled with the triremes as violently as
possible and dashed the ship on to the edge of the
mole. The crew of the ship, already ablaze, swam
off without difficulty. At this point a great flame was 4
falling on the towers, and as the yards broke, they
poured on to the fire the material that had been made
ready to feed the flame. The men in the triremes
lay to near the mole, and shot at the towers, so that
it was not safe for anyone to get near with materials
to quench the fire. At this stage, the towers being 5
well alight, the citizens sallied out in large numbers,
jumping into small boats, and put in at different parts
of the mole, where they easily tore down the palisade
set up to protect it and burned all the engines which
had not been caught by fire from the ship. Alex- 6
ander, however, ordered his men to make the mole

χωννύναι, ὡς πλείονας δέξασθαι πύργους, καὶ τοὺς μηχανοποιοὺς μηχανὰς ἄλλας κατασκευάζειν ἐκέλευσεν. ὡς δὲ ταῦτα παρεσκευάζετο, αὐτὸς τούς τε ὑπασπιστὰς ἀναλαβὼν καὶ τοὺς Ἀγριᾶνας ἐπὶ Σιδῶνος ἐστάλη, ὡς ἀθροίσων ἐκεῖ ὅσαι ἤδη ἦσαν αὐτῷ τριήρεις, ὅτι ἀπορώτερα τὰ τῆς πολιορκίας ἐφαίνετο θαλασσοκρατούντων τῶν Τυρίων.

20. Ἐν τούτῳ δὲ Γηρόστρατός τε ὁ Ἀράδου βασιλεὺς καὶ Ἔννυλος ὁ Βύβλου ὡς ἔμαθον τὰς πόλεις σφῶν ὑπ' Ἀλεξάνδρου ἐχομένας, ἀπολιπόντες Αὐτοφραδάτην τε καὶ τὰς ξὺν αὐτῷ νέας παρ' Ἀλέξανδρον ξὺν τῷ ναυτικῷ τῷ σφετέρῳ ἀφίκοντο καὶ αἱ τῶν Σιδωνίων τριήρεις σὺν αὐτοῖς, ὥστε Φοινίκων μὲν νῆες ὀγδοήκοντα μάλιστα αὐτῷ 2 παρεγένοντο. ἧκον δὲ ἐν ταῖς αὐταῖς ἡμέραις καὶ ἐκ Ῥόδου τριήρεις ἥ τε περίπολος καλουμένη καὶ ξὺν ταύτῃ ἄλλαι ἐννέα, καὶ ἐκ Σόλων καὶ Μαλλοῦ τρεῖς καὶ Λύκιαι δέκα, ἐκ Μακεδονίας δὲ πεντηκόντορος, ἐφ' ἧς Πρωτέας ὁ Ἀνδρονίκου ἐπέπλει. 3 οὐ πολλῷ δὲ ὕστερον καὶ οἱ τῆς Κύπρου βασιλεῖς ἐς τὴν Σιδῶνα κατέσχον ναυσὶν ἑκατὸν μάλιστα καὶ εἴκοσιν, ἐπειδὴ τήν τε ἧσσαν τὴν κατ' Ἰσσὸν Δαρείου ἐπύθοντο καὶ ἡ Φοινίκη πᾶσα ἐχομένη ἤδη ὑπὸ Ἀλεξάνδρου ἐφόβει αὐτούς. καὶ τούτοις πᾶσιν ἔδωκεν Ἀλέξανδρος ἄδειαν τῶν πρόσθεν, ὅτι ὑπ' ἀνάγκης μᾶλλόν τι ἢ κατὰ γνώμην τὴν σφῶν ἐδόκουν ξυνταχθῆναι τοῖς Πέρσαις ἐς τὸ ναυτικόν.

4 Ἐν ᾧ δὲ αἵ τε μηχαναὶ αὐτῷ ξυνεπήγνυντο καὶ αἱ νῆες ὡς εἰς ἐπίπλουν τε καὶ ναυμαχίας ἀπόπειραν ἐξηρτύοντο, ἐν τούτῳ δὲ ἀναλαβὼν τῶν τε ἱππέων ἴλας ἔστιν ἃς καὶ τοὺς ὑπασπιστὰς καὶ τοὺς

broader starting from the mainland, so as to hold
more towers, and the engineers to construct new
engines.[2] While these were being got ready, he
made for Sidon with the hypaspists and the Agrianians, to collect all the triremes he already had there,
since the siege seemed unlikely to succeed as long as
the Tyrians were masters of the sea.[3]

20. At this time Gerostratus king of Aradus and
Enylus of Byblus, on learning that Alexander held
their cities, left Autophradates and his ships and
joined Alexander with their own fleet, along with the
Sidonian triremes; thus some eighty Phoenician
sail came over to him. In the same days nine 2
triremes came from Rhodes, in addition to their
state guardship, three from Soli and Mallus and ten
from Lycia, and a fifty-oar ship from Macedon, its
captain being Proteus son of Andronicus. Soon 3
afterwards the kings of Cyprus put in at Sidon with
about 120 sail; they had learnt of Darius' defeat at
Issus, and were alarmed at the whole of Phoenicia
being already in Alexander's power.[1] To all of them
Alexander let bygones be bygones, supposing that it
was rather from necessity than their own choice that
they had contributed to the Persian fleet.

While his engines were being fitted together, and 4
his ships were being equipped for attack and for
trying the issue of a naval battle, Alexander marched
with some of the cavalry squadrons, the hypaspists,

---

[2] QC. 3, 8 ff.
[3] Omitted in other accounts.
[1] QC. 3, 11 notes only the arrival of 120 ships from Cyprus;
D. 42, 3 presupposes, without explaining, Al's later command
of the sea.

Ἀγριᾶνάς τε καὶ τοὺς τοξότας ἐπ' Ἀραβίας στέλ-
λεται εἰς τὸν Ἀντιλίβανον καλούμενον τὸ ὄρος·
5 καὶ τὰ μὲν βίᾳ, τῶν ταύτῃ ἐξελών, τὰ δὲ ὁμολογίᾳ
παραστησάμενος ἐν δέκα ἡμέραις ἐπανῆγεν ἐς τὴν
Σιδῶνα, καὶ καταλαμβάνει Κλέανδρον τὸν Πολεμοκράτους ἐκ Πελοποννήσου ἥκοντα καὶ ξὺν αὐτῷ
μισθοφόρους Ἕλληνας ἐς τετρακισχιλίους.

6 Ὡς δὲ συνετέτακτο αὐτῷ τὸ ναυτικόν, ἐπιβιβάσας τοῖς καταστρώμασι τῶν ὑπασπιστῶν ὅσοι
ἱκανοὶ ἐδόκουν ἐς τὸ ἔργον, εἰ μὴ διέκπλοις
μᾶλλόν τι ἢ ἐν χερσὶν ἡ ναυμαχία γίγνοιτο, ἄρας ἐκ
τῆς Σιδῶνος ἐπέπλει τῇ Τύρῳ ξυντεταγμέναις ταῖς
ναυσίν, αὐτὸς μὲν κατὰ τὸ δεξιὸν κέρας, ὃ δὴ ἐς τὸ
πέλαγος αὐτῷ ἀνεῖχε, καὶ ξὺν αὐτῷ οἵ τε Κυπρίων
βασιλεῖς καὶ ὅσοι Φοινίκων, πλὴν Πνυταγόρου.
οὗτος δὲ καὶ Κρατερὸς τὸ εὐώνυμον κέρας εἶχον
7 τῆς πάσης τάξεως. τοῖς δὲ Τυρίοις πρότερον μὲν
ναυμαχεῖν ἐγνωσμένον ἦν, εἰ κατὰ θάλασσαν ἐπι-
πλέοι σφίσιν Ἀλέξανδρος, τότε δὲ πλῆθος νεῶν
πολὺ ἀπροσδοκήτως κατιδόντες (οὐ γάρ πω
πεπυσμένοι ἦσαν τάς τε Κυπρίων ναῦς καὶ τὰς
8 Φοινίκων ξυμπάσας Ἀλέξανδρον ἔχοντα) καὶ ἅμα
ξυντεταγμένως τοῦ ἐπίπλου γιγνομένου (ὀλίγον γὰρ
πρὶν προσχεῖν τῇ πόλει ἀνεκώχευσαν ἔτι πελάγιαι
αἱ ξὺν Ἀλεξάνδρῳ νῆες, εἴ πως ἄρα ἐς ναυμαχίαν
τοὺς Τυρίους προκαλέσαιντο, ἔπειτα οὕτως ξυνταξάμενοι, ὡς οὐκ ἀντανήγοντο, πολλῷ τῷ ῥοθίῳ
ἐπέπλεον)—ταῦτα ὁρῶντες οἱ Τύριοι ναυμαχεῖν μὲν
ἀπέγνωσαν, τριήρεσι δὲ ὅσας τῶν λιμένων τὰ
στόματα ἐδέχοντο βύζην τὸν ἔσπλουν φραξάμενοι

---

² Cf. 19, 1 n, and P. 24, 6 (anecdotes from Chares); QC. 2, 24

the Agrianians and the archers in the direction of
Arabia to the mountain called Antilebanon.[2] Here
he stormed and destroyed some places and brought
others to terms; in ten days he was back at Sidon,
and found that Cleander son of Polemocrates had
arrived from the Peloponnese with four thousand
Greek mercenaries.[3]

When his fleet was organized, he put on deck as
many of the hypaspists as he thought sufficient for
the action (in case the engagement were not rather a
matter of breaking the line of ships than of hand-
to-hand fighting), and weighing anchor sailed from
Sidon to Tyre with his ships in formation; himself
on the right wing, that is, seaward, with the Cyprian
kings and all the Phoenicians, except Pnytagoras
who with Craterus commanded the left wing of the
whole line. The Tyrians had previously decided
to give battle by sea, if Alexander attacked them
there. But when they sighted an armada far beyond
their estimate—for they had not been apprized earlier
that the Cyprian and the Phoenician ships were all
with Alexander—and observed the sea-attack coming
in regular order—just before closing on the city
Alexander's ships, while still in the open sea, had lain
to, hoping to draw out the Tyrians to an engagement,
and then, as they did not put out in their original
order, came on with a loud din of oars and waves—
the Tyrians, observing all this, refused a sea-battle,
but used as many of the triremes as the mouths of
their harbours would hold to block the entrances

6

7

8

and 3, 1, explaining that the natives were interfering with the
dispatch of timber from Lebanon (cf. 2, 18), not Antilebanon,
and stating that Perdiccas and Craterus were left in command.
 [3] QC. 3, 11 makes them arrive with the ships from Cyprus.

ἐφύλασσον, ὡς μὴ ἐς τῶν λιμένων τινὰ ἐγκαθορμισθῆναι τῶν πολεμίων τὸν στόλον.

9 Ἀλέξανδρος δέ, ὡς οὐκ ἀντανήγοντο οἱ Τύριοι, ἐπέπλει τῇ πόλει· καὶ ἐς μὲν τὸν λιμένα τὸν πρὸς Σιδῶνος βιάζεσθαι ἀπέγνω διὰ στενότητα τοῦ στόματος καὶ ἅμα ἀντιπρώροις τριήρεσι πολλαῖς ὁρῶν πεφραγμένον τὸν ἔσπλουν, τρεῖς δὲ τὰς ἐξωτάτω ἐφορμούσας τῷ στόματι τριήρεις προσπεσόντες οἱ Φοίνικες καὶ ἀντίπρωροι ἐμβαλόντες καταδύουσιν· οἱ δὲ ἐν ταῖς ναυσὶν οὐ χαλεπῶς 10 ἀπενήξαντο ἐς τὴν γῆν φιλίαν οὖσαν. τότε μὲν δὴ οὐ πόρρω τοῦ ποιητοῦ χώματος κατὰ τὸν αἰγιαλόν, ἵνα σκέπη τῶν ἀνέμων ἐφαίνετο, οἱ σὺν Ἀλεξάνδρῳ ὡρμίσαντο· τῇ δὲ ὑστεραίᾳ τοὺς μὲν Κυπρίους ξὺν ταῖς σφετέραις ναυσὶ καὶ Ἀνδρομάχῳ τῷ ναυάρχῳ κατὰ τὸν λιμένα τὸν ἐκ Σιδῶνος φέροντα ἐκέλευσεν ἐφορμεῖν τῇ πόλει, τοὺς δὲ Φοίνικας κατὰ τὸν ἐπέκεινα τοῦ χώματος τὸν πρὸς Αἴγυπτον ἀνέχοντα, ἵνα καὶ αὐτῷ ἡ σκηνὴ ἦν.

21. Ἤδη δὲ καὶ μηχανοποιῶν αὐτῷ πολλῶν ἔκ τε Κύπρου καὶ Φοινίκης ἁπάσης συλλελεγμένων μηχαναὶ πολλαὶ συμπεπηγμέναι ἦσαν, αἱ μὲν ἐπὶ τοῦ χώματος, αἱ δὲ ἐπὶ τῶν ἱππαγωγῶν νεῶν, ἃς ἐκ Σιδῶνος ἅμα οἷ ἐκόμισεν, αἱ δὲ ἐπὶ τῶν τριήρων 2 ὅσαι αὐτῶν οὐ ταχυναυτοῦσαι ἦσαν. ὡς δὲ παρεσκεύαστο ἤδη ξύμπαντα, προσῆγον τὰς μηχανὰς κατά τε τὸ ποιητὸν χῶμα καὶ ἀπὸ τῶν νεῶν ἄλλη καὶ ἄλλη τοῦ τείχους προσορμιζομένων τε καὶ ἀποπειρωμένων τοῦ τείχους.

3 Οἱ δὲ Τύριοι ἐπί τε τῶν ἐπάλξεων τῶν κατὰ τὸ

---

[4] With §6–9 cf. D. 42, 3; QC. 3, 11 f. D. 42, 3 puts the incident in 9 rather later.

closely, and kept guard to prevent the enemy fleet
from anchoring in any of the harbours.[4]

When the Tyrians refused battle, Alexander sailed 9
against the city; he decided not to force an entry
into the harbour facing Sidon because of the narrowness of its mouth, and also because entry was blocked
with numerous triremes, bows on, though the
Phoenicians did charge, bow to bow, the three triremes
moored farthest out and sank them; their crews
swam away comfortably to the friendly shore. For 10
the time being Alexander's fleet came to anchor
near the new-made mole along the shore, where there
seemed to be protection from the winds. Next day
Alexander ordered the Cyprians, with their contingent of ships and with Andromachus the admiral,
to blockade the city at the harbour that faced Sidon,
and the Phoenicians to do the same at the harbour
on the other side of the mole, facing Egypt, where
his own tent was.

21. By this time many engineers had been collected from Cyprus and the whole of Phoenicia,[1]
and many engines had been fitted together on the
mole or on the horse-transports Alexander had
brought with him from Sidon or on the slower
triremes. When everything was now ready, they 2
brought forward the engines down the new-made
mole and from the ships which were anchored alongside the wall at various points and were testing it
out.[2]

The Tyrians set wooden towers on the battlements 3

---

[1] D. 41, 3, 43, 1 and 44, 7 stresses the importance to the
defence of the number of engineers at Tyre.
[2] QC. 3, 13 makes the battering begin the day after the ships
arrived; but 3, 13–4, 4, like D. 42, 5–45, 7 (divergent in details),
ignore the operations A. describes (§ 3–7) and describe others.

ARRIAN

χῶμα πύργους ξυλίνους ἐπέστησαν, ὡς ἀπομάχεσθαι ἀπ᾽ αὐτῶν, καὶ εἴ πῃ ἄλλῃ αἱ μηχαναὶ
προσήγοντο, βέλεσί τε ἠμύνοντο καὶ πυρφόροις
οἰστοῖς ἔβαλλον αὐτὰς τὰς ναῦς, ὥστε φόβον
4 παρέχειν τοῖς Μακεδόσι πελάζειν τῷ τείχει. ἦν δὲ
αὐτοῖς καὶ τὰ τείχη τὰ κατὰ τὸ χῶμα τό τε ὕψος
εἰς πεντήκοντα καὶ ἑκατὸν μάλιστα πόδας καὶ ἐς
πλάτος ξύμμετρον λίθοις μεγάλοις ἐν γύψῳ κειμέ-
νοις ξυμπεπηγότα. ταῖς δὲ ἱππαγωγοῖς τε καὶ ταῖς
τριήρεσι τῶν Μακεδόνων, ὅσαι τὰς μηχανὰς προσῆγον τῷ τείχει, καὶ ταύτῃ οὐκ εὔπορον ἐγίγνετο
πελάζειν τῇ πόλει, ὅτι λίθοι πολλοὶ ἐς τὸ πέλαγος
προβεβλημένοι ἐξεῖργον αὐτῶν τὴν ἐγγὺς προσβο-
5 λήν. καὶ τούτους Ἀλέξανδρος ἔγνω ἐξελκύσαι ἐκ
τῆς θαλάσσης· ἠνύετο δὲ χαλεπῶς τοῦτο τὸ ἔργον,
οἷα δὴ ἀπὸ νεῶν καὶ οὐκ ἀπὸ γῆς βεβαίου γιγνό-
μενον· ἄλλως τε καὶ οἱ Τύριοι ναῦς καταφράξαντες
παρὰ τὰς ἀγκύρας ἐπῆγον τῶν τριήρων καὶ
ὑποτέμνοντες τὰς σχοίνους τῶν ἀγκυρῶν ἄπορον
τὴν προσόρμισιν ταῖς πολεμίαις ναυσὶν ἐποίουν.
6 Ἀλέξανδρος δὲ τριακοντόρους πολλὰς ἐς τὸν αὐτὸν
τρόπον φράξας ἐπέστησεν ἐγκαρσίας πρὸ τῶν
ἀγκυρῶν, ὡς ἀπ᾽ αὐτῶν ἀναστέλλεσθαι τὸν
ἐπίπλουν τῶν νεῶν. ἀλλὰ καὶ ὡς ὕφαλοι κολυμ-
βηταὶ τὰς σχοίνους αὐτοῖς ὑπέτεμνον. οἱ δὲ
ἁλύσεσιν ἀντὶ σχοίνων εἰς τὰς ἀγκύρας χρώμενοι,
οἱ Μακεδόνες, καθίεσαν, ὥστε μηδὲν ἔτι πλέον τοῖς
7 κολυμβηταῖς γίγνεσθαι. ἐξάπτοντες οὖν βρόχους
τῶν λίθων ἀπὸ τοῦ χώματος ἀνέσπων αὐτοὺς ἔξω
τῆς θαλάσσης, ἔπειτα μηχαναῖς μετεωρίσαντες κατὰ
βάθους ἀφίεσαν, ἵνα οὐκέτι προβεβλημένοι βλάψειν
ἔμελλον. ὅπου δὲ καθαρὸν πεποίητο τῶν προβόλων

facing the mole, from which to fight; and wherever
else the engines were brought up, they defended
themselves with missiles and shot fiery arrows at the
ships themselves, so as to deter the Macedonians
from an approach to the wall. The walls facing the 4
mole were about 150 feet high and of corresponding
breadth, constructed of big blocks of stone fitted
in mortar. The Macedonian horse-transports and
triremes, which were bringing up engines against
the wall, found it hard to approach the city at this
point, since heaps of stones cast into the sea in front
of it prevented a close attack. Alexander deter- 5
mined to drag these stones out of the sea, but this
work made slow progress as it was carried on from
ships and not from firm land, especially as the
Tyrians had protected some of their ships with armour and bore down on the anchors of the triremes
and cut the cables, thus making it impossible for the
enemy ships to lie near by. Alexander protected 6
several thirty-oar boats in the same way, and laid
them athwart in front of the anchors to repel the
attack of the Tyrian ships. Even so, divers would
swim under the surface and cut the ropes. The
Macedonians then substituted chains for ropes in
anchoring, and lowered them, so that the divers had
no further success. From the mole then they cast 7
nooses round the stones, drew them out of the sea,
and then lifting them on high with engines let them
drop into deep water, where they were not likely to
be in the way and do any more harm. Where they

τὸ τεῖχος, οὐ χαλεπῶς ἤδη ταύτῃ αἱ νῆες προσεῖχον.

8 Οἱ δὲ Τύριοι πάντῃ ἄποροι γιγνόμενοι ἔγνωσαν
ἐπίπλουν ποιήσασθαι ταῖς Κυπρίαις ναυσίν, αἳ κατὰ
τὸν λιμένα ἐφώρμουν τὸν ἐς Σιδῶνα τετραμμένον·
ἐκ πολλοῦ δὴ καταπετάσαντες τὸ στόμα τοῦ
λιμένος ἱστίοις, τοῦ μὴ καταφανῆ γενέσθαι τῶν
τριήρων τὴν πλήρωσιν, ἀμφὶ μέσον ἡμέρας, ὁπότε
οἵ τε ναῦται ἐπὶ τὰ ἀναγκαῖα ἐσκεδασμένοι ἦσαν
καὶ Ἀλέξανδρος ἐν τούτῳ μάλιστα ἀπὸ τοῦ ἐπὶ
θάτερα τῆς πόλεως ναυτικοῦ ἐπὶ τὴν σκηνὴν
9 ἀπεχώρει, πληρώσαντες πεντήρεις μὲν τρεῖς καὶ
τετρήρεις ἴσας, τριήρεις δὲ ἑπτὰ ὡς ἀκριβεστάτοις
τε τοῖς πληρώμασι καὶ τοῖς ἀπὸ τῶν καταστρωμάτων μάχεσθαι μέλλουσιν εὐοπλοτάτοις καὶ ἅμα
εὐθαρσεστάτοις ἐς τοὺς ναυτικοὺς ἀγῶνας, τὰ μὲν
πρῶτα ἀτρέμα τῇ εἰρεσίᾳ ἐπὶ μιᾶς νεὼς ἐξέπλεον
ἄνευ κελευστῶν τὰς κώπας παραφέροντες· ὡς δὲ
ἐπέστρεφον ἤδη ἐπὶ τοὺς Κυπρίους καὶ ἐγγὺς τοῦ
καθορᾶσθαι ἦσαν, τότε δὴ ξὺν βοῇ τε πολλῇ καὶ
ἐγκελευσμῷ ἐς ἀλλήλους καὶ ἅμα τῇ εἰρεσίᾳ
ξυντόνῳ ἐπεφέροντο.

22. Ξυνέβη δὲ ἐκείνῃ τῇ ἡμέρᾳ Ἀλέξανδρον
ἀποχωρῆσαι μὲν ἐπὶ τὴν σκηνήν, οὐ διατρίψαντα δὲ
κατὰ τὸ εἰωθὸς δι' ὀλίγου ἐπὶ τὰς ναῦς ἐπανελθεῖν.
2 οἱ δὲ Τύριοι προσπεσόντες ἀπροσδοκήτως ταῖς
ναυσὶν ὁρμούσαις καὶ ταῖς μὲν πάντῃ κεναῖς
ἐπιτυχόντες, τῶν δ' ὑπ' αὐτὴν τὴν βοὴν καὶ τὸν
ἐπίπλουν χαλεπῶς ἐκ τῶν παρόντων πληρουμένων,
τήν τε Πνυταγόρου τοῦ βασιλέως πεντήρη εὐθὺς
ὑπὸ τῇ πρώτῃ ἐμβολῇ κατέδυσαν καὶ τὴν Ἀνδρο-
κλέους τοῦ Ἀμαθουσίου καὶ τὴν Πασικράτους τοῦ

332
B.C.

had cleared the approach to the wall of obstructions, the ships at last lay alongside quite easily.

The Tyrians, now becoming hard pressed in every way, determined to attack the Cyprian vessels blockading the harbour facing Sidon.[3] For a long time they kept sails stretched in front of the harbour mouth, so that the manning of the triremes should not be seen, and about midday, when the sailors had scattered on necessary business and Alexander had just left the fleet on the other side of the city for his tent, they manned three quinqueremes, as many quadriremes and seven triremes, with their smartest crews and the best-armed marines to fight from the decks, men who were also boldest in sea-fights, and at first quietly paddled[4] out in line ahead, without anyone to call the stroke; but once they began to turn towards the Cyprian ships and were nearly in view, they came on with much shouting and calling of the time among themselves, rowing with unified stroke.

22. It so happened that on that day Alexander, after retiring to his tent, did not rest there as usual, but returned to the ships quite soon. The Tyrian attack on the anchored ships was unexpected; they found some quite empty, others were being manned with difficulty in the middle of the noise and attack by any who chanced to be there, and at the first charge the quinqueremes of King Pnytagoras, Androcles of Amathus and Pasicrates of Curium

---

[3] QC. 4, 5–9 (different account of sortie); nothing in D.

[4] Professor Warmington suggests that the Greek means that they were not even rowing gently but holding their oars motionless, propelled by wind or current, or at most making occasional strokes for momentum. I feel no certainty on the exact sense.

Κουριέως, τὰς δὲ ἄλλας ἐς τὸν αἰγιαλὸν ἐξωθοῦντες ἔκοπτον.

3 Ἀλέξανδρος δὲ ὡς ἤσθετο τὸν ἔκπλουν τῶν Τυρίων τριήρων, τὰς μὲν πολλὰς τῶν ξὺν αὐτῷ νεῶν, ὅπως ἑκάστη πληρωθείη, ἐπὶ τῷ στόματι τοῦ λιμένος ἀνακωχεύειν ἔταξεν, ὡς μὴ καὶ ἄλλαι ἐκπλεύσειαν τῶν Τυρίων νῆες· αὐτὸς δὲ πεντήρεις τε τὰς ξὺν αὐτῷ ἀναλαβὼν καὶ τῶν τριήρων ἐς πέντε μάλιστα, ὅσαι ἔφθασαν αὐτῷ κατὰ τάχος πληρωθῆναι, περιέπλει τὴν πόλιν ὡς ἐπὶ τοὺς
4 ἐκπεπλευκότας τῶν Τυρίων. οἱ δὲ ἀπὸ τοῦ τείχους, τόν τε ἐπίπλουν τῶν πολεμίων κατιδόντες καὶ Ἀλέξανδρον αὐτὸν ἐπὶ τῶν νεῶν, βοῇ τε ἐπανάγειν ἐνεκελεύοντο τοῖς ἐκ τῶν σφετέρων νεῶν καὶ ὡς οὐκ ἐξακουστὸν ἦν ὑπὸ θορύβου ξυνεχομένων ἐν τῷ ἔργῳ, σημείοις ἄλλοις καὶ ἄλλοις ἐπεκάλουν ἐς τὴν ἀναχώρησιν. οἱ δὲ ὀψέ ποτε αἰσθόμενοι τὸν ἐπίπλουν τῶν ἀμφ᾽ Ἀλέξανδρον ὑποστρέψαντες ἐς τὸν
5 λιμένα ἔφευγον. καὶ ὀλίγαι μὲν τῶν νεῶν φθάνουσιν ὑπεκφυγοῦσαι, ταῖς δὲ πλείοσιν ἐμβαλοῦσαι αἱ ξὺν Ἀλεξάνδρῳ τὰς μὲν αὐτῶν ἄπλους ἐποίησαν, πεντήρης δέ τις καὶ τετρήρης αὐτῶν ἐπ᾽ αὐτῷ τῷ στόματι τοῦ λιμένος ἐλήφθησαν. φόνος δὲ τῶν ἐπιβατῶν οὐ πολὺς ἐγένετο. ὡς γὰρ ᾔσθοντο ἐχομένας τὰς ναῦς ἀπενήξαντο οὐ χαλεπῶς ἐς τὸν λιμένα.

6 Ὡς δὲ οὐδεμία ἔτι τοῖς Τυρίοις ἐκ τῶν νεῶν ὠφέλεια ἦν, ἐπῆγον ἤδη οἱ Μακεδόνες τὰς μηχανὰς τῷ τείχει αὐτῶν. κατὰ μὲν δὴ τὸ χῶμα προσαγόμεναι διὰ ἰσχὺν τοῦ τείχους οὐδὲν ἤνυον ὅ τι καὶ λόγου ἄξιον, οἱ δὲ κατὰ τὸ πρὸς Σιδῶνα τετραμμένον τῆς πόλεως τῶν νεῶν τινας τῶν μηχανοφό-

were sunk and the rest driven ashore and broken up.

But when Alexander observed the sally of the 3 Tyrian triremes, while directing most of the ships with him to lie to at the harbour mouth as soon as each was manned, to prevent any other Tyrian ships sailing out, he took what quinqueremes he had and some five triremes, which had got their crews on board in all haste, and sailed round the city against the Tyrians who had sailed out. The Tyrians on the 4 wall, seeing the enemy attack and Alexander himself aboard, shouted orders to the men on their own ships to put about, and as this did not reach the hearing, in the confusion, of men pre-occupied in the action, they used various signals to recall them, but it was too late when they noticed the attack of Alexander's ships; they went about and made for refuge in the harbour; few of the ships managed to get to safety 5 in time, most were rammed by Alexander's ships, some put out of action, and a quinquereme and quadrireme captured at the very entrance of the harbour. There was no great slaughter of the crews; as soon as they saw that their ships were caught, they swam off without much difficulty into the harbour.

Now that the Tyrians could look for no help from 6 their ships, the Macedonians began to bring up their engines against the wall.[1] When moved up along the mole, they had no success worth mention, owing to the strength of the wall, while on the side of the city looking towards Sidon, where they brought up some

[1] Nothing in D. or QC. corresponds to § 6 f.

7 ρων προσῆγον. ὡς δὲ οὐδὲ ταύτῃ ἤνυεν, ἐς τὸ
πρὸς νότον αὖ ἄνεμον καὶ πρὸς Αἴγυπτον ἀνέχον
τεῖχος μετῄει πάντῃ ἀποπειρώμενος τοῦ ἔργου.
καὶ ἐνταῦθα πρῶτον κατεσείσθη τε τὸ τεῖχος ἐπὶ
μέγα καί τι καὶ κατηρίφθη αὐτοῦ παρραγέν.
τότε μὲν δὴ ὅσον ἐπιβαλὼν γεφύρας ᾗ ἐρήριπτο τοῦ
τείχους ἀπεπειράθη ἐς ὀλίγον τῆς προσβολῆς· καὶ
οἱ Τύριοι οὐ χαλεπῶς ἀπεκρούσαντο τοὺς Μακεδόνας.

23. Τρίτῃ δὲ ἀπὸ ταύτης ἡμέρᾳ νηνεμίαν τε
φυλάξας καὶ παρακαλέσας τοὺς ἡγεμόνας τῶν
τάξεων ἐς τὸ ἔργον ἐπῆγε τῇ πόλει ἐπὶ τῶν νεῶν
τὰς μηχανάς. καὶ πρῶτα μὲν κατέσεισε τοῦ
τείχους ἐπὶ μέγα, ὡς δὲ ἀποχρῶν εἰς πλάτος ἐφάνη
τὸ παρερρηγμένον, τὰς μὲν μηχανοφόρους ναῦς
2 ἐπανάγειν ἐκέλευσεν· ὁ δὲ δύο ἄλλας ἐπῆγεν, αἳ
τὰς γεφύρας αὐτῷ ἔφερον, ἃς δὴ ἐπιβάλλειν ἐπενόει
τῷ κατερρηγμένῳ τοῦ τείχους. καὶ τὴν μὲν μίαν
τῶν νεῶν οἱ ὑπασπισταὶ ἔλαβον, ᾗ ἐπετέτακτο
Ἄδμητος, τὴν ἑτέραν δὲ ἡ Κοίνου τάξις οἱ ἀσθέτεροι[1] καλούμενοι, καὶ αὐτὸς ξὺν τοῖς ὑπασπισταῖς
3 ἐπιβήσεσθαι τοῦ τείχους ᾗ παρείκοι ἔμελλεν. τὰς
τριήρεις δὲ τὰς μὲν ἐπιπλεῖν κατὰ τοὺς λιμένας
ἀμφοτέρους ἐκέλευσεν, εἴ πως πρὸς σφᾶς τετραμμένων τῶν Τυρίων βιάσαιντο τὸν ἔσπλουν· ὅσαι δὲ
αὐτῶν βέλη ἀπὸ μηχανῶν βαλλόμενα εἶχον ἢ ὅσαι
τοξόται ἐπὶ τῶν καταστρωμάτων ἔφερον, ταύτας
δὲ ἐκέλευσεν ἐν κύκλῳ περιπλεούσας τὸ τεῖχος
ἐποκέλλειν τε ὅπῃ παρείκοι καὶ ἀνακωχεύειν ἐντὸς
βέλους, ἔστε τὸ ἐποκεῖλαι ἄπορον γίγνοιτο, ὡς

---

[1] Editors generally amend to πεζέταιροι, but cf. Introd. n. 99.

of their ships carrying engines, they again did not
succeed, so Alexander turned to the south and the
wall facing Egypt, and tested the work at every
point. It was here that the wall was first badly
shaken and in part broken down by a rent. At that
time Alexander made a slight and tentative attack,
going so far as to throw gangways over the broken
part of the wall: the Tyrians, however, easily repulsed the Macedonians.

23. Two days afterwards,[1] having waited till he got
a calm, and urged his battalion commanders to
action, Alexander brought up the engines on board
the ships against the city. First he battered
down the wall for a good space. But when the
breach seemed wide enough, he ordered the engine-
carrying ships to back water; and sent in two
others, carrying his gangways, which he intended
to let fall where the wall was breached. The
hypaspists took over one of the ships, Admetus being
its captain; the other was manned by Coenus' battalion of the so-called *astheteroi*.[2] Alexander himself
intended to mount on the wall with his hypaspists
where practicable. Some of his triremes were
ordered to sail round about each harbour, in case they
might force an entrance by sea while the Tyrians
were occupied with his own party. Other triremes,
which had missiles to fire from engines on board or
which carried archers on the decks, were ordered to
circle about the wall, run ashore wherever possible, or
lie to within range, so long as it was impracticable to
run ashore. In this way the Tyrians would be under

---

[1] Vague accounts of final assault, diverging from A., in D.
46; QC. 4, 10 ff. (two days after naval sortie). J. xi 10, 14
makes Tyre fall by treachery.

[2] See Introd. n. 99.

πανταχόθεν βαλλομένους τοὺς Τυρίους ἐν τῷ δεινῷ
ἀμφιβόλους γίγνεσθαι.

4 Ὡς δὲ αἵ τε νῆες αἱ σὺν Ἀλεξάνδρῳ προσέσχον
τῇ πόλει καὶ αἱ γέφυραι ἐπεβλήθησαν τῷ τείχει
ἀπ' αὐτῶν, ἐνταῦθα οἱ ὑπασπισταὶ εὐρώστως κατὰ
ταύτας ἀνέβαινον ἐπὶ τὸ τεῖχος. ὅ τε γὰρ Ἄδμητος
ἀνὴρ ἀγαθὸς ἐν τῷ τότε ἐγένετο καὶ ἅμα Ἀλέξανδρος εἵπετο αὐτοῖς, τοῦ τε ἔργου αὐτοῦ καρτερῶς
ἁπτόμενος καὶ θεατὴς τῶν ἄλλων ὅτῳ τι λαμπρὸν
5 κατ' ἀρετὴν ἐν τῷ κινδύνῳ ἐτολμᾶτο. καὶ ταύτῃ
πρῶτον ᾗ ἐπετέτακτο Ἀλέξανδρος ἐλήφθη τὸ
τεῖχος, οὐ χαλεπῶς ἀποκρουσθέντων ἀπ' αὐτοῦ
τῶν Τυρίων, ἐπειδὴ πρῶτον βεβαίῳ τε καὶ ἅμα οὐ
πάντῃ ἀποτόμῳ τῇ προσβάσει ἐχρήσαντο οἱ Μακεδόνες. καὶ Ἄδμητος μὲν πρῶτος ἐπιβὰς τοῦ
τείχους καὶ τοῖς ἀμφ' αὐτὸν ἐγκελευόμενος ἐπιβαί-
6 νειν βληθεὶς λόγχῃ ἀποθνήσκει αὐτοῦ· ἐπὶ δὲ αὐτῷ
Ἀλέξανδρος ἔσχε τὸ τεῖχος ξὺν τοῖς ἑταίροις. ὡς
δὲ εἴχοντο αὐτῷ πύργοι τε ἔστιν οἳ καὶ μεταπύργια,
αὐτὸς μὲν παρῄει διὰ τῶν ἐπάλξεων ὡς ἐπὶ τὰ
βασίλεια, ὅτι ταύτῃ εὐπορωτέρα ἐφαίνετο ἐς τὴν
πόλιν ἡ κάθοδος.

24. Οἱ δὲ ἐπὶ τῶν νεῶν, οἵ τε Φοίνικες κατὰ τὸν
λιμένα τὸν πρὸς Αἰγύπτου, καθ' ὅνπερ καὶ ἐφορ-
μοῦντες ἐτύγχανον, βιασάμενοι καὶ τὰ κλεῖθρα
διασπάσαντες ἔκοπτον τὰς ναῦς ἐν τῷ λιμένι, ταῖς
μὲν μετεώροις ἐμβάλλοντες, τὰς δὲ ἐς τὴν γῆν
ἐξωθοῦντες, καὶ οἱ Κύπριοι κατὰ τὸν ἄλλον λιμένα
τὸν ἐκ Σιδῶνος φέροντα οὐδὲ κλεῖθρον τοῦτόν γε
ἔχοντα εἰσπλεύσαντες εἷλον εὐθὺς ταύτῃ τὴν πόλιν.

2 τὸ δὲ πλῆθος τῶν Τυρίων τὸ μὲν τεῖχος, ὡς
ἐχόμενον εἶδον, ἐκλείπουσιν, ἀθροισθέντες δὲ κατὰ

fire from all sides and not know where to turn in the 332
crisis.   B.C.

As soon as Alexander's ships closed upon the city 4
and the gangways were let down on the wall from
them, the hypaspists went down them gallantly on
to the wall; Admetus then showed his courage and
Alexander too was there with them, taking a stren-
uous part in the action itself and keeping his eyes
open for any conspicuous display of courage, and
daring by others in the danger. The part of the 5
wall captured first was, in fact, that where Alexander
had posted himself; the Tyrians were easily pushed
off it, since for the first time the Macedonians had
access that was secure and not absolutely sheer.
Admetus, first on the wall, was wounded by a spear
while calling on his men to mount, and died there;[3]
Alexander followed him and seized the wall with 6
the Companions. When some of the towers and the
curtains between them were in his possession, he
passed on through the battlements towards the royal
quarters; this way it appeared that descent into the
city was easier.

24. To turn to the ships and their crews, the
Phoenicians who were moored near the harbour
facing Egypt, forcing their way and tearing asunder
the booms, battered the ships in the harbour, ram-
ming some afloat, and driving others ashore; the
Cyprians by the other harbour in the direction of
Sidon, which did not even have a boom, sailed in and
at once captured the city on this side. The main 2
body of the Tyrians deserted the wall when they saw

[3] D. 45, 6 kills off Admetus earlier in the siege.

τὸ ᾿Αγηνόριον καλούμενον ἐπέστρεψαν ταύτῃ ἐπὶ
τοὺς Μακεδόνας. καὶ ᾿Αλέξανδρος ξὺν τοῖς ὑπασπισταῖς ἐπὶ τούτους χωρήσας τοὺς μὲν αὐτοῦ
μαχομένους διέφθειρεν αὐτῶν, τοῖς δὲ φεύγουσιν
3 ἐφείπετο. καὶ φόνος ἦν πολύς, τῶν τε ἀπὸ τοῦ
λιμένος ἐχόντων ἤδη τὴν πόλιν καὶ τῆς Κοίνου
τάξεως παρεληλυθυίας ἐς αὐτήν. ὀργῇ γὰρ ἐχώρουν
ἐπὶ πᾶν οἱ Μακεδόνες, τῆς τε πολιορκίας τῇ τριβῇ
ἀχθόμενοι καὶ ὅτι λαβόντες τινὰς αὐτῶν οἱ Τύριοι
πλέοντας ἐκ Σιδῶνος ἐπὶ τὸ τεῖχος ἀναβιβάσαντες,
ὅπως ἄποπτον εἴη ἀπὸ τοῦ στρατοπέδου, σφά-
4 ξαντες ἔρριψαν εἰς τὴν θάλασσαν. ἀπέθανον δὲ
τῶν μὲν Τυρίων ἐς ὀκτακισχιλίους, τῶν Μακεδόνων δὲ ἐν τῇ τότε προσβολῇ ῎Αδμητός τε ὁ
πρῶτος ἑλὼν τὸ τεῖχος, ἀνὴρ ἀγαθὸς γενόμενος,
καὶ ξὺν αὐτῷ εἴκοσι τῶν ὑπασπιστῶν· ἐν δὲ τῇ
πάσῃ πολιορκίᾳ μάλιστα ἐς τετρακοσίους.

5 Τοῖς δὲ ἐς τὸ ἱερὸν τοῦ ῾Ηρακλέους καταφυ-
γοῦσιν (ἦσαν δὲ αὐτῶν τε τῶν Τυρίων οἱ μάλιστα
ἐν τέλει καὶ ὁ βασιλεὺς ᾿Αζέμιλκος καὶ Καρχηδο-
νίων τινὲς θεωροὶ ἐς τιμὴν τοῦ ῾Ηρακλέους κατὰ
δή τι[να] νόμιμον παλαιὸν εἰς τὴν μητρόπολιν
ἀφικόμενοι) τούτοις ξύμπασιν ἄδειαν δίδωσιν
᾿Αλέξανδρος· τοὺς δὲ ἄλλους ἠνδραπόδισε, καὶ
ἐπράθησαν Τυρίων τε καὶ τῶν ξένων ὅσοι ἐγκατε-
6 λήφθησαν μάλιστα ἐς τρισμυρίους. ᾿Αλέξανδρος δὲ

---

[1] 6,000, QC. 4, 16, who makes Al. crucify 2,000 more (cf. D.
46, 3; all male survivors, not less than 2,000, J. xviii 3, 18).

[2] Called Straton by D. 46, 6–47, 6 (cf. J. xviii 3, 9 ff.), with
story of his being replaced by ' Ballonymus ' (' Abdalonymus '
in QC. iv 1, 15 ff., locating the incident at Sidon, cf. J. xi 10,
8).

[3] In QC. 4, 18 he only spares the envoys.

it was in enemy possession: but they massed together at what is called the Shrine of Agenor, and there turned to resist the Macedonians. Alexander with his hypaspists attacked them, killed some of them fighting there, and pursued the fugitives. The 3 slaughter was great, now that those coming from the harbour were already masters of the city and Coenus' battalion had passed inside. The rage of the Macedonians was indiscriminate, as they were embittered by the protracted nature of the siege and because the Tyrians had captured some of their men sailing from Sidon, made them mount the wall, so that they might be seen from the camp, cut them down and cast them into the sea. Some eight 4 thousand Tyrians fell;[1] in the actual attack the Macedonians lost Admetus, the first to mount on the wall, after he proved himself a brave man, with twenty of the hypaspists; in the entire siege the losses were about four hundred.

As for those who fled to the temple of Heracles, 5 including among the Tyrians themselves the men of most authority and King Azemilcus,[2] as well as some Carthaginian envoys who had come to their mother-city to pay honour to Heracles, according to an ancient custom, Alexander granted them all complete pardon;[3] he enslaved the rest; some 30,000[4] were sold, what with Tyrians and foreigners

---

[4] A conventional figure. D. 46, 4 has only the women and children enslaved (the men are massacred), but alleges (cf. 41, 2) that most had been shipped off to Carthage, whereas QC. 3, 20 with 4, 18 suggests a decision to send them off which was never (and presumably could not have been) carried out. (Early hopes of help from Carthage had been disappointed, D. 40, 3; QC. 3, 19; J. xi 10, 12.) QC. 4, 15 f. alleges that the Sidonians saved 15,000 Tyrians from the victor's cruelty. Repopulation of Tyre by Al., J. xviii 3, 19, cf. D. xviii 37.

τῷ Ἡρακλεῖ ἔθυσέ τε καὶ πομπὴν ἔστειλε ξὺν τῇ
δυνάμει ὡπλισμένῃ· καὶ αἱ νῆες ξυνεπόμπευσαν
τῷ Ἡρακλεῖ, καὶ ἀγῶνα γυμνικὸν ἐν τῷ ἱερῷ καὶ
λαμπάδα ἐποίησε· καὶ τὴν μηχανήν, ᾗ τὸ τεῖχος
κατεσείσθη, ἀνέθηκεν ἐς τὸν νεὼν καὶ τὴν ναῦν τὴν
Τυρίαν τὴν ἱερὰν τοῦ Ἡρακλέους, ἥντινα ἐν τῷ
ἐπίπλῳ ἔλαβε, καὶ ταύτην τῷ Ἡρακλεῖ ἀνέθηκεν
καὶ ἐπίγραμμα ἐπ' αὐτῇ, ἢ αὐτὸς ποιήσας ἢ ὅτου
δὴ ἄλλου ποιήσαντος, οὐκ ἄξιον μνήμης τὸ ἐπί-
γραμμα· διὰ τοῦτο καὶ ἐγὼ αὐτὸ ἀναγράψαι
ἀπηξίωσα. Τύρος μὲν δὴ οὕτως ἑάλω ἐπὶ ἄρχοντος
Νικήτου Ἀθήνησι μηνὸς Ἑκατομβαιῶνος.

25. Ἔτι δὲ ἐν τῇ πολιορκίᾳ τῆς Τύρου ξυν-
εχομένου Ἀλεξάνδρου ἀφίκοντο παρὰ Δαρείου
πρέσβεις ὡς αὐτὸν ἀπαγγέλλοντες μύρια μὲν
τάλαντα ὑπὲρ τῆς μητρός τε καὶ τῆς γυναικὸς καὶ
τῶν παίδων δοῦναι ἐθέλειν Ἀλεξάνδρῳ Δαρεῖον·
τὴν δὲ χώραν πᾶσαν τὴν ἐντὸς Εὐφράτου ποταμοῦ
ἔστε ἐπὶ θάλασσαν τὴν Ἑλληνικὴν Ἀλεξάνδρου
εἶναι· γήμαντα δὲ τὴν Δαρείου παῖδα Ἀλέξανδρον
2 φίλον τε εἶναι Δαρείῳ καὶ ξύμμαχον. καὶ τούτων
ἐν τῷ ξυλλόγῳ τῶν ἑταίρων ἀπαγγελθέντων
Παρμενίωνα μὲν λέγουσιν Ἀλεξάνδρῳ εἰπεῖν ὅτι
αὐτὸς ἂν Ἀλέξανδρος ὢν ἐπὶ τούτοις ἠγάπησε
καταλύσας τὸν πόλεμον μηκέτι τὸ πρόσω κινδυ-
νεύειν· Ἀλέξανδρον δὲ Παρμενίωνι ἀποκρίνασθαι
ὅτι καὶ αὐτὸς ἄν, εἴπερ Παρμενίων ἦν, οὕτως
ἔπραξεν, ἐπεὶ δὲ Ἀλέξανδρός ἐστιν, ἀποκρινεῖσθαι
3 Δαρείῳ ἅπερ δὴ καὶ ἀπεκρίνατο. ἔφη γὰρ οὔτε
χρημάτων δεῖσθαι παρὰ Δαρείου οὔτε τῆς χώρας
λαβεῖν ἀντὶ τῆς πάσης τὸ μέρος· εἶναι γὰρ τά τε
χρήματα καὶ τὴν χώραν αὐτοῦ πᾶσαν· γῆμαί τε εἰ

captured at Tyre.   Alexander sacrificed to Heracles [5]   6   332
and held a procession in his honour, with his forces   B.C.
under arms; there was a naval review too in honour
of Heracles, and Alexander held athletic games
in the temple enclosure and a relay torch-race; the
engine which battered down the wall was dedicated
to the temple; and the Tyrian sacred ship, consecrated to Heracles, which he captured in the attack,
was dedicated to Heracles with an inscription, either
of his own composition or of someone else's, not
worth recording; that is why I did not trouble to
copy it.[6]   It was in this way that Tyre was captured
in the archonship of Nicetus at Athens in the month
Hecatombaeon.[7]

25. While Alexander was still occupied in the
siege of Tyre, envoys came to him from Darius
announcing that Darius was ready to give Alexander
10,000 Talents for his mother, wife and children;
to cede all the country west of Euphrates to the
Greek sea, to give Alexander his daughter in marriage and be his friend and ally. When this was   2
reported in the council of the Companions, it is said
that Parmenio told Alexander that if he were
Alexander he would be glad to stop the war on these
terms without further risks, and that Alexander
answered Parmenio that he too would have done
this if he had been Parmenio, but as he was Alexander, he would make the reply to Darius he actually
made: he needed no money from Darius, nor a part   3
of the country instead of the whole; for the money
and country all belonged to him; if he chose to marry

[5] D. 46, 6.
[6] Presumably Pt. or Ar. did.
[7] July/Aug. 332 B.C.

ἐθέλοι τὴν Δαρείου παῖδα, γῆμαι ἂν καὶ οὐ
διδόντος Δαρείου· ἐκέλευέ τε αὐτὸν ἥκειν, εἴ τι
εὑρέσθαι ἐθέλοι φιλάνθρωπον παρ' αὐτοῦ. ταῦτα
ὡς ἤκουσε Δαρεῖος, τὰς μὲν ξυμβάσεις ἀπέγνω τὰς
πρὸς Ἀλέξανδρον, ἐν παρασκευῇ δὲ τοῦ πολέμου
αὖθις ἦν.

4   Ἀλέξανδρος δὲ ἐπ' Αἰγύπτου ἔγνω ποιεῖσθαι τὸν
στόλον. καὶ ἦν αὐτῷ τὰ μὲν ἄλλα τῆς Παλαι-
στίνης καλουμένης Συρίας προσκεχωρηκότα ἤδη,
εὐνοῦχος δέ τις, ᾧ ὄνομα ἦν Βάτις, κρατῶν τῆς
Γαζαίων πόλεως, οὐ προσεῖχεν Ἀλεξάνδρῳ, ἀλλὰ
Ἀραβάς τε μισθωτοὺς ἐπαγαγόμενος καὶ σῖτον ἐκ
πολλοῦ παρεσκευακὼς διαρκῆ ἐς χρόνιον πολιορκίαν καὶ τῷ χωρίῳ πιστεύων μήποτε ἂν βίᾳ
ἁλῶναι, ἔγνω μὴ δέχεσθαι τῇ πόλει Ἀλέξανδρον.

26. Ἀπέχει δὲ ἡ Γάζα τῆς μὲν θαλάσσης εἴκοσι
μάλιστα σταδίους, καὶ ἔστι ψαμμώδης καὶ βαθεῖα
ἐς αὐτὴν ἡ ἄνοδος καὶ ἡ θάλασσα ἡ κατὰ τὴν πόλιν
τεναγώδης πᾶσα. μεγάλη δὲ πόλις ἡ Γάζα ἦν καὶ
ἐπὶ χώματος ὑψηλοῦ ᾤκιστο καὶ τεῖχος περιεβέβλητο αὐτῇ ὀχυρόν. ἐσχάτη δὲ ᾤκεῖτο ὡς ἐπ'
Αἴγυπτον ἐκ Φοινίκης ἰόντι ἐπὶ τῇ ἀρχῇ τῆς ἐρήμου.

2   Ἀλέξανδρος δὲ ὡς ἀφίκετο πρὸς τὴν πόλιν, τῇ
μὲν πρώτῃ κατεστρατοπέδευσεν ᾗ μάλιστα ἐπίμα-
χον αὐτῷ ἐφαίνετο τὸ τεῖχος, καὶ μηχανὰς

---

[1] QC. 5, 1 ff. puts arrival of letter *after* siege, and *now* makes
Darius offer to surrender lands west of Halys, contrast D.,
cf. 14, 1 n.   J. xi 12, 3 f. is vague, but D. 54, 1–6; QC. iv 11;
J. xi 12, 5 ff. put the offer A. records here (but with 30,000
Talents) just before Gaugamela, along with the exchange

Darius' daughter, he would marry her, even if Darius did not give her; and Darius must come to him, if he wished for favourable treatment at his hands. When Darius received this reply he despaired of making terms with Alexander and began to prepare again for war.[1]

Alexander now determined to make his expedition 4 to Egypt.[2] Palestinian Syria (as it is called) had already come over to him, except for a eunuch named Batis, who was master of the city of Gaza; he procured a force of Arab mercenaries, and some time before had got ready grain for a long siege; trusting that the place could never be taken by assault, he decided not to admit Alexander into the city.

26. Gaza is about 20 stades from the sea, and the way up to it is over deep sand, while the sea by the city is nothing but shoals. Gaza was a large city, built on a high mound, with a strong wall round it. It was the last town on the edge of the desert on the way from Phoenicia to Egypt.[1]

When Alexander reached the city, he encamped 2 the first day where the wall seemed easiest to attack, and ordered siege engines to be fitted together.

(rhetorically amplified by QC.) between Al. and Parmenio. § 2 appears to be from the 'vulgate'.

[2] D. 48 here interpolates the activity of Agis and Amyntas (13, 2–6; App. VI) and a decree of the Greek *synedrion* to send envoys to congratulate Al. on Issus; perhaps they reached Al. at Tyre, as QC. 5, 11 dates the decree to the Isthmia (early summer), but cf. iii 5, 1 n. QC. 5, 13 ff. inserts an account of operations by sea (App. II 3) and in Asia Minor, cf. 5, 9 for surrender of Rhodes, and gives certain appointments, see Berve nos. 76, 732 (for error by QC.), 806, which were probably mentioned in A's source(s) and omitted by him.

[1] Siege of Gaza, D. 48, 7, two months long (Josephus, *Jewish Antiquities* xi 325), i.e. Sept.–Nov., cf. 24, 6 n.; QC. 5, 10; 6, 7 ff. (in many details different from A.); P. 25, 3 f. (Al's wound).

συμπηγνύναι ἐκέλευσεν. οἱ δὲ μηχανοποιοὶ γνώμην
ἀπεδείκνυντο ἄπορον εἶναι βίᾳ ἑλεῖν τὸ τεῖχος διὰ
3 ὕψος τοῦ χώματος. ἀλλὰ Ἀλεξάνδρῳ αἱρετέον
ἐδόκει εἶναι ὅσῳ ἀπορώτερον· ἐκπλήξειν γὰρ τοὺς
πολεμίους τὸ ἔργον τῷ παραλόγῳ ἐπὶ μέγα, καὶ τὸ
μὴ ἑλεῖν αἰσχρὸν εἶναί οἱ λεγόμενον ἔς τε τοὺς
Ἕλληνας καὶ ἐς Δαρεῖον. ἐδόκει δὴ χῶμα ἐν
κύκλῳ τῆς πόλεως χωννύναι, ὡς ἐξ ἴσου ἀπὸ τοῦ
χωσθέντος ἐπάγεσθαι τὰς μηχανὰς τοῖς τείχεσι.
καὶ ἐχώννυτο κατὰ τὸ νότιον μάλιστα τῆς πόλεως
4 τεῖχος, ἵνα ἐπιμαχώτερα ἐφαίνετο. ὡς δὲ ἐδόκει
ἐξῆρθαι συμμέτρως τὸ χῶμα, μηχανὰς ἐπιστήσαντες οἱ Μακεδόνες ἐπῆγον ὡς ἐπὶ τὸ τεῖχος τῶν
Γαζαίων. καὶ ἐν τούτῳ θύοντι Ἀλεξάνδρῳ καὶ
ἐστεφανωμένῳ τε καὶ κατάρχεσθαι μέλλοντι τοῦ
πρώτου ἱερείου κατὰ νόμον τῶν τις σαρκοφάγων
ὀρνίθων ὑπερπετόμενος ὑπὲρ τοῦ βωμοῦ λίθον
ἐμβάλλει ἐς τὴν κεφαλήν, ὅντινα τοῖν ποδοῖν
ἔφερε. καὶ Ἀλέξανδρος ἤρετο Ἀρίστανδρον τὸν
μάντιν, ὅ τι νοοῖ ὁ οἰωνός. ὁ δὲ ἀποκρίνεται ὅτι·
ὦ βασιλεῦ, τὴν μὲν πόλιν αἱρήσεις, αὐτῷ δέ σοι
φυλακτέα ἐστὶν ἐπὶ τῇδε τῇ ἡμέρᾳ.

27. Ταῦτα ἀκούσας Ἀλέξανδρος τέως μὲν πρὸς
ταῖς μηχαναῖς ἔξω βέλους αὐτὸν εἶχεν· ὡς δὲ
ἐκδρομή τε ἐκ τῆς πόλεως καρτερὰ ἐγίγνετο καὶ
πῦρ τε ἐπέφερον ταῖς μηχαναῖς οἱ Ἄραβες καὶ τοὺς
Μακεδόνας ἀμυνομένους κάτωθεν αὐτοὶ ἐξ ὑπερδεξίου τοῦ χωρίου ἔβαλλόν τε καὶ ὤθουν κατὰ τοῦ
ποιητοῦ χώματος, ἐνταῦθα ἢ ἑκὼν ἀπειθεῖ Ἀλέξανδρος τῷ μάντει ἢ ἐκπλαγεὶς ἐν τῷ ἔργῳ οὐκ
ἐμνημόνευσε τῆς μαντείας, ἀλλ' ἀναλαβὼν τοὺς

The engineers, however, suggested that it was impracticable to take the city by force owing to the height of the mound. Alexander thought, on the contrary, that the more impracticable it was, the more necessary was the capture; for the achievement would strike great terror into his enemies just because it was beyond calculation, while not to take it would be a blow to his prestige when reported to the Greeks and Darius.[2] It was decided to raise a mound all round the city, and so bring up the engines against the walls, at an equal height on the earth heaped up. The mound was built chiefly against the city's southern part of the wall, where the assault seemed most likely to succeed. When the Macedonians thought they had built the mound to the proper height, they set engines on it and brought them up against the city wall. Just at this time, as Alexander was sacrificing, wearing garlands, and just about to consecrate the first victim according to the ceremonial, a carnivorous bird, as it flew over the altar, dropped on his head a stone which it was carrying in its talons. Alexander asked Aristander the seer what the omen meant, and he answered, 'Sire, you will capture the city; but today you must take care of your own person.'

27. On hearing this Alexander kept himself for a time by the engines, out of range; but then there was a vigorous sally from the city, the Arabs tried to set fire to the engines, pelting the Macedonians, who were resisting below, from a commanding position, and pushing them down the artificial mound, and Alexander disobeyed the seer on purpose, unless he lost control of himself in the action and forgot the prophecy, for he brought up the hypaspists

[2] Cf. i 4, 3; 13, 6 f.; ii 4, 4; iv 21, 3; vi 16, 2; vii 15, 3.

ὑπασπιστὰς παρεβοήθει, ἵνα μάλιστα ἐπιέζοντο οἱ
2 Μακεδόνες. καὶ τούτους μὲν ἔσχε τὸ μὴ οὐκ
αἰσχρᾷ φυγῇ ὠσθῆναι κατὰ τοῦ χώματος, αὐτὸς δὲ
βάλλεται καταπέλτῃ διὰ τῆς ἀσπίδος διαμπὰξ καὶ
τοῦ θώρακος ἐς τὸν ὦμον. ὡς δὲ ἔγνω τὰ ἀμφὶ τὸ
τραῦμα ἀληθεύσαντα Ἀρίστανδρον, ἐχάρη, ὅτι καὶ
τὴν πόλιν δὴ αἱρήσειν ἐδόκει Ἀριστάνδρου ἕνεκα.
3 Καὶ αὐτὸς μὲν τὸ τραῦμα ἐθεραπεύετο χαλεπῶς·
ἀφικνοῦνται δ' αὐτῷ μετάπεμπτοι ἀπὸ θαλάσσης αἱ
μηχαναί, αἷς Τύρον εἷλε. καὶ χῶμα χωννύναι ἐν
κύκλῳ πάντοθεν τῆς πόλεως ἐκέλευσεν, εὖρος μὲν
ἐς δύο σταδίους, ὕψος δὲ ἐς πόδας πεντήκοντα καὶ
4 διακοσίους. ὡς δὲ αἵ τε μηχαναὶ αὐτῷ ἐποιήθησαν
καὶ ἐπαχθεῖσαι κατὰ τὸ χῶμα κατέσεισαν τοῦ
τείχους ἐπὶ πολύ, ὑπονόμων τε ἄλλῃ καὶ ἄλλῃ
ὀρυσσομένων καὶ τοῦ χοῦ ἀφανῶς ἐκφερομένου τὸ
τεῖχος πολλαχῇ ἠρείπετο ὑφιζάνον κατὰ τὸ κε-
νούμενον, τοῖς τε βέλεσιν ἐπὶ πολὺ κατεῖχον οἱ
Μακεδόνες ἀναστέλλοντες τοὺς προμαχομένους τῶν
πύργων, ἐς μὲν τρεῖς προσβολὰς οἱ ἐκ τῆς πόλεως
ἀποθνῃσκόντων τε αὐτοῖς πολλῶν καὶ τιτρωσκο-
5 μένων ὅμως ἀντεῖχον. τῇ τετάρτῃ δὲ τῶν Μακεδόνων τὴν φάλαγγα πάντοθεν προσαγαγὼν Ἀλέξανδρος τῇ μὲν ὑπορυσσόμενον τὸ τεῖχος
καταβάλλει, τῇ δὲ παιόμενον ταῖς μηχαναῖς κατα-
σείει ἐπὶ πολύ, ὡς μὴ χαλεπὴν ταῖς κλίμαξιν τὴν
6 προσβολὴν κατὰ τὰ ἐρηριμμένα ἐνδοῦναι. αἵ τε
οὖν κλίμακες προσήγοντο τῷ τείχει καὶ ἔρις πολλὴ
ἦν τῶν Μακεδόνων ὅσοι τι ἀρετῆς μετεποιοῦντο

---

¹ Though we could take the engines from Tyre to be
additional to those mentioned in 26, 2 f., this sentence suggests

and went to the help of the Macedonians where they
were most hardly pressed. He did, in fact, stay them
from being driven down the mound in ignominious
flight, but was himself hit by a shot from a catapult
right through his shield and corselet in the shoulder.
But his knowledge that Aristander had been right
about the wound made him glad, since on Aristander's account he thought that he would surely
take the city too.

Alexander was not easily treated of his wound.
However, the engines with which he had captured
Tyre now arrived; he had sent for them by sea.
He ordered a mound to be erected the whole way
round the city, two stades broad, two hundred and
fifty feet high.[1] When his engines had been constructed and brought up to the mound and had
battered down much of the wall, tunnels were driven
here and there and the earth below removed
secretly, till the wall collapsed in several places,
subsiding where the soil was emptied away, while
the Macedonians controlled a large space with their
volleys and drove back the defenders from the
towers. The defenders, though losing many dead
and wounded, held out against three onslaughts.
But in the fourth Alexander brought up his phalanx
of Macedonians on all sides, threw down the wall,
now undermined, at one place, and brought it down
for a great stretch in another, battered as it was with
his engines, so that it was not hard to make the
assault with ladders over the fallen parts. So the
ladders were set against the wall, and there was
much rivalry among those Macedonians who laid

2

3

4

5

6

---

that 26, 2-27, 2 and 27, 3 ff. are doublets, the first perhaps from
Ar., the second from Pt. So Wirth *RE* xxiii 2472.

ὅστις πρῶτος αἱρήσει τὸ τεῖχος· καὶ αἱρεῖ πρῶτος
Νεοπτόλεμος τῶν ἑταίρων τοῦ Αἰακιδῶν γένους·
ἐπὶ δὲ αὐτῷ ἄλλαι καὶ ἄλλαι τάξεις ὁμοῦ τοῖς
7 ἡγεμόσιν ἀνέβαινον. ὡς δὲ ἅπαξ παρῆλθόν τινες
ἐντὸς τοῦ τείχους τῶν Μακεδόνων, κατασχίσαντες
ἄλλας καὶ ἄλλας πύλας, ὅσαις ἕκαστοι ἐπετύγχανον,
δέχονται εἴσω τὴν στρατιὰν πᾶσαν. οἱ δὲ Γαζαῖοι
καὶ τῆς πόλεώς σφισιν ἤδη ἐχομένης ξυνεστηκότες
ὅμως ἐμάχοντο, καὶ ἀπέθανον πάντες αὐτοῦ μαχό-
μενοι ὡς ἕκαστοι ἐτάχθησαν· παῖδας δὲ καὶ
γυναῖκας ἐξηνδραπόδισεν αὐτῶν Ἀλέξανδρος. τὴν
πόλιν δὲ ξυνοικίσας ἐκ τῶν περιοίκων ἐχρῆτο ὅσα
φρουρίῳ ἐς τὸν πόλεμον.

332
B.C.

some claim to distinction for their courage, which would take the wall first; the first was Neoptolemus, one of the Companions and of the family of the Aeacidae. After him, battalion after battalion went up with their officers. As soon as some of the 7 Macedonians had got inside the wall they tore down gate after gate, as they came to them, and admitted the entire army. The Gazaeans held together and continued to resist, though their city was already in enemy hands; and all perished there, fighting each man at his post. Alexander sold their women and children into slavery, populated the city from the surrounding tribesmen and used it as a fortress town for the war.[2]

---

[2] For other ' native ' foundations by Al. cf. iv 28, 4; vi 17, 4; *Ind.* 40, 7 f.; perhaps vi 22, 3 (cf. QC. ix 10, 7); QC. ix 10, 3; n. on A. iii 24, 5. QC. iv 6, 31 here says that after the capture Al. despatched Amyntas to levy reinforcements in Macedon; for their arrival cf. A. iii 16, 10. Probably A. omitted this item, which would have been in his source.

BOOK III

ΒΙΒΛΙΟΝ ΤΡΙΤΟΝ

1. Ἀλέξανδρος δὲ ἐπ' Αἰγύπτου, ἵναπερ τὸ πρῶτον ὡρμήθη, ἐστέλλετο, καὶ ἑβδόμῃ ἡμέρᾳ ἀπό τῆς Γάζης ἐλαύνων ἧκεν εἰς Πηλούσιον τῆς Αἰγύπτου. ὁ δὲ ναυτικὸς στρατὸς παρέπλει αὐτῷ ἐκ Φοινίκης ὡς ἐπ' Αἴγυπτον· καὶ καταλαμβάνει

2 τὰς ναῦς ἐν Πηλουσίῳ ὁρμούσας. Μαζάκης δὲ ὁ Πέρσης, ὃς ἦν σατράπης Αἰγύπτου ἐκ Δαρείου καθεστηκώς, τήν τε ἐν Ἰσσῷ μάχην ὅπως συνέβη πεπυσμένος καὶ Δαρεῖον ὅτι αἰσχρᾷ φυγῇ ἔφυγεν, καὶ Φοινίκην τε καὶ Συρίαν καὶ τῆς Ἀραβίας τὰ πολλὰ ὑπὸ Ἀλεξάνδρου ἐχόμενα, αὐτῷ τε οὐκ οὔσης δυνάμεως Περσικῆς, ἐδέχετο ταῖς τε πόλεσι

3 φιλίως καὶ τῇ χώρᾳ Ἀλέξανδρον. ὁ δὲ εἰς μὲν Πηλούσιον φυλακὴν εἰσήγαγε, τοὺς δὲ ἐπὶ τῶν νεῶν ἀναπλεῖν κατὰ τὸν ποταμὸν κελεύσας ἔστε ἐπὶ Μέμφιν πόλιν αὐτὸς ἐφ' Ἡλιουπόλεως ᾔει, ἐν δεξιᾷ ἔχων τὸν ποταμὸν τὸν Νεῖλον, καὶ ὅσα καθ' ὁδὸν χωρία ἐνδιδόντων τῶν ἐνοικούντων κατασχὼν διὰ τῆς ἐρήμου ἀφίκετο ἐς Ἡλιούπολιν·

4 ἐκεῖθεν δὲ διαβὰς τὸν πόρον ἧκεν ἐς Μέμφιν· καὶ θύει ἐκεῖ τοῖς τε ἄλλοις θεοῖς καὶ τῷ Ἄπιδι καὶ ἀγῶνα ἐποίησε γυμνικόν τε καὶ μουσικόν· ἧκον δὲ αὐτῷ οἱ ἀμφὶ ταῦτα τεχνῖται ἐκ τῆς Ἑλλάδος οἱ

---

[1] Nov. 332 B.C., cf. ii 26, 1 n., the right season for invading Egypt.
[2] The Persian garrison had presumably been removed to fight at Issus under the satrap, Sauaces, ii 11, 8.

BOOK III

1. Alexander now set out for Egypt, his original goal, and marching from Gaza arrived after six days at Pelusium in Egypt.[1] His fleet coasted along with him from Phoenicia towards Egypt; and he found them already at anchor at Pelusium. Mazaces the 2 Persian, who had been appointed satrap of Egypt by Darius, on learning how the battle of Issus had gone, of the shameful flight of Darius, and that Phoenicia, Syria, and the greater part of Arabia were in Alexander's hands, and being without any Persian force,[2] received Alexander in a friendly way into the cities and the country.[3] Alexander put a garrison into 3 Pelusium, told the officers of his fleet to sail up the river as far as Memphis and went in person towards Heliopolis, with the river Nile on his right; he took over all the districts on his route through the surrender of the inhabitants, and traversed the desert to reach Heliopolis. Thence he crossed the river and 4 went to Memphis, where he sacrificed to the gods, especially Apis, and held athletic and musical games; the most famous performers in both athletics

---

[3] D. 49, 1 f. and QC. iv 7, 1 ff. rightly stress that the Egyptians, who had been independent of Persia between 405 B.C. and the imperfect reconquest by Artaxerxes Ochus in 343/2 B.C. and again in 338–6 B.C. (F. K. Kienitz, *Die politische Gesch. Aegyptens vom 7. bis zum 4. Jahrhundert* 102 ff.; A. T. Olmstead, *Hist. of Persian Empire* 440 f.; 491 ff.), welcomed the enemy of Persia (cf. also ii 13, 3 n.), especially no doubt as he, unlike Ochus, was careful to honour Egyptian gods (§ 4 f.).

δοκιμώτατοι. ἐκ δὲ Μέμφιος κατέπλει κατὰ τὸν
ποταμὸν ὡς ἐπὶ θάλασσαν τούς τε ὑπασπιστὰς ἐπὶ
τῶν νεῶν λαβὼν καὶ τοὺς τοξότας καὶ τοὺς
Ἀγριᾶνας καὶ τῶν ἱππέων τὴν βασιλικὴν ἴλην τὴν
5 τῶν ἑταίρων. ἐλθὼν δὲ ἐς Κάνωβον καὶ κατὰ τὴν
λίμνην τὴν Μαρίαν περιπλεύσας ἀποβαίνει, ὅπου
νῦν Ἀλεξάνδρεια πόλις ᾤκισται, Ἀλεξάνδρου
ἐπώνυμος. καὶ ἔδοξεν αὐτῷ ὁ χῶρος κάλλιστος
κτίσαι ἐν αὐτῷ πόλιν καὶ γενέσθαι ἂν εὐδαίμονα
τὴν πόλιν. πόθος οὖν λαμβάνει αὐτὸν τοῦ ἔργου,
καὶ αὐτὸς τὰ σημεῖα τῇ πόλει ἔθηκεν, ἵνα τε
ἀγορὰν ἐν αὐτῇ δείμασθαι ἔδει καὶ ἱερὰ ὅσα καὶ
θεῶν ὧντινων, τῶν μὲν Ἑλληνικῶν, Ἴσιδος δὲ
Αἰγυπτίας, καὶ τὸ τεῖχος ᾗ περιβεβλῆσθαι. καὶ
ἐπὶ τούτοις ἐθύετο, καὶ τὰ ἱερὰ καλὰ ἐφαίνετο.

2. Λέγεται δέ τις καὶ τοιόσδε λόγος, οὐκ ἄπιστος
ἔμοιγε· ἐθέλειν μὲν Ἀλέξανδρον καταλείπειν
αὐτὸν τὰ σημεῖα τοῦ τειχισμοῦ τοῖς τέκτοσιν, οὐκ
εἶναι δὲ ὅτῳ τὴν γῆν ἐπιγράψουσιν· τῶν δὴ τεκτό-
νων τινὰ ἐπιφρασθέντα, ὅσα ἐν τεύχεσιν ἄλφιτα οἱ
στρατιῶται ἐκόμιζον ξυναγαγόντα ἐπιβάλλειν τῇ
γῇ, ἵναπερ ὁ βασιλεὺς ὑφηγεῖτο, καὶ τὸν κύκλον
οὕτω περιγραφῆναι τοῦ περιτειχισμοῦ, ὅντινα τῇ
2 πόλει ἐποίει. τοῦτο δὲ ἐπιλεξαμένους τοὺς μάντεις
καὶ μάλιστα δὴ Ἀρίστανδρον τὸν Τελμισσέα, ὃς δὴ

---

[4] Cf. P. 26; D. 52, QC. iv 8, 1 f. and 5 f. and J. xi 11, 3
put the foundation of Alexandria after the visit to Siwah,
cf. App. V 1. Site: Strabo xvii 1, 6 f.; P. M. Fraser, *Ptolemaic
Alexandria* ch. 1. Strabo says that the settlers were natives
(cf. QC. iv 8, 5), mercenaries and Greeks; for parallels: A.

and music came to him there from Greece. From Memphis he sailed downstream towards the sea, taking on board the hypaspists, archers and Agrianians, and from the cavalry the royal squadron of the Companions. When he had reached Canobus and sailed round Lake Mareotis, he went ashore where the city of Alexandria, named after him, is now situated. It struck him that the position was admirable for founding a city there and that it would prosper.[4] A longing for the work therefore seized him;[5] he himself marked out where the city's marketplace was to be built, how many temples there were to be and the gods, some Greek, and Isis the Egyptian, for whom they were to be erected, and where the wall was to be built round it. With this in view he offered sacrifice, and the sacrifice proved favourable.

2. A story of the following sort is told,[1] and personally I do not disbelieve it; Alexander desired to leave the builders outlines of the fortification, but had no means of marking the ground. One of the builders, however, had the happy thought of collecting the meal which the soldiers carried in vessels, and of dropping it on the ground wherever the king indicated. In this way was the circle of the surrounding wall which he proposed to make for the city marked out. The soothsayers, and especially Aristander the Telmissian, who was reported to have

iv 4, 1; 22, 5; 24, 7; v 29, 3; vii 21, 7. Al's motives for founding cities: iv 1, 3 f.; 24, 7; vi 15, 2; 21, 5; 22, 3; vii 21, 7. He inherited from Philip the practice of commemorating his own name in such foundations, cf. Philippi, Philippopolis.

[5] App. V 3.

[1] ' Vulgate ', cf. QC. iv 8, 6; P. 26. For A's comment, cf. his preface.

πολλὰ μὲν καὶ ἄλλα ἀληθεῦσαι ἐλέγετο Ἀλεξάνδρῳ, φάναι εὐδαίμονα ἔσεσθαι τὴν πόλιν τά τε
ἄλλα καὶ τῶν ἐκ γῆς καρπῶν εἵνεκα.

3 Ἐν τούτῳ δὲ καὶ Ἡγέλοχος κατέπλευσεν εἰς
Αἴγυπτον καὶ ἀπαγγέλλει Ἀλεξάνδρῳ Τενεδίους τε
ἀποστάντας Περσῶν σφίσι προσθέσθαι (καὶ γὰρ
καὶ ἄκοντας Πέρσαις προσχωρῆσαι) καὶ Χίων ὅτι
δὴ ὁ δῆμος ἐπηγάγετο σφᾶς βίᾳ τῶν κατεχόντων
τὴν πόλιν, οὓς Αὐτοφραδάτης τε καὶ Φαρνάβαζος
4 ἐγκατέστησαν· ἁλῶναι δὲ αὐτόθι καὶ Φαρνάβαζον
ἐγκαταληφθέντα καὶ Ἀριστόνικον Μηθυμναῖον τὸν
τύραννον ἐσπλεύσαντα ἐς τὸν λιμένα τῆς Χίου ξὺν
ἡμιολίαις λῃστρικαῖς πέντε, ὑπὸ σφῶν ἐχόμενον
τὸν λιμένα οὐ γνόντα, ἀλλ' ἐξαπατηθέντα γὰρ πρὸς
τῶν τὰ κλεῖθρα ἐχόντων τοῦ λιμένος, ὅτι τὸ
5 Φαρναβάζου ἄρα ναυτικὸν ὁρμεῖ ἐν αὐτῷ· καὶ τοὺς
μὲν λῃστὰς πάντας αὐτοῦ κατακοπῆναι πρὸς σφῶν,
Ἀριστόνικον δὲ ἦγε παρὰ Ἀλέξανδρον καὶ
Ἀπολλωνίδην τὸν Χῖον καὶ Φησῖνον καὶ Μεγαρέα
καὶ τοὺς ἄλλους, ὅσοι τῆς τε ἀποστάσεως τῆς
Χίων ξυνεπελάβοντο καὶ ἐν τῷ τότε τὰ πράγματα
6 τῆς νήσου βίᾳ εἶχον· καὶ Μιτυλήνην δὲ Χάρητα
ἔχοντα ὅτι ἀφείλετο καὶ τὰς ἄλλας τὰς ἐν Λέσβῳ
πόλεις καὶ αὐτὰς ὁμολογίᾳ προσηγάγετο, Ἀμφοτερὸν δὲ σὺν ἑξήκοντα ναυσὶν ἐπὶ Κῶ ἔπεμψεν·
ἐπικαλεῖσθαι γὰρ σφᾶς τοὺς Κῴους· καὶ αὐτὸς
καταπλεύσας ὅτι εὗρε τὴν Κῶ πρὸς Ἀμφοτεροῦ
7 ἤδη ἐχομένην. καὶ τοὺς μὲν ἄλλους ὅσοι αἰχμάλωτοι ἦγεν Ἡγέλοχος, Φαρνάβαζος δὲ ἀπέδρα ἐν
Κῷ λαθὼν τοὺς φύλακας. Ἀλέξανδρος δὲ τοὺς
τυράννους μὲν τοὺς ἐκ τῶν πόλεων ἐς τὰς πόλεις
πέμπει χρήσασθαι ὅπως ἐθέλοιεν, τοὺς δὲ ἀμφὶ

332–1
B.C.

made many other correct prophecies to Alexander, reflecting upon this, said that the city would be prosperous in general, but particularly in the fruits of the earth.

Hegelochus now arrived by sea in Egypt and re- 3 ported to Alexander that the people of Tenedos had revolted from the Persians and come over to them (in fact they had joined the Persians against their will) and that the people of Chios had brought his forces into the city, in spite of the men occupying it, installed by Autophradates and Pharnabazus; Pharna- 4 bazus had been caught and captured there, with Aristonicus of Methymna, the tyrant, who had sailed into the harbour of Chios with five pirate frigates, unaware that the Macedonians were in possession of the harbour, for he had been misled by the assertion of the men in control of the boom to the harbour, that Pharnabazus' fleet was anchored there; the pirates 5 had all been cut down by his own men, but he had brought Aristonicus to Alexander, with Apollonides the Chian and Phesinus and Megareus and the rest of those who had assisted the revolt of the Chians, and who were for the time ruling the island by force. He 6 reported also that he had captured Mitylene from Chares, and had won over by agreement the other cities in Lesbos as well. He had sent Amphoterus with sixty ships to Cos on appeal from the people of Cos, and had sailed himself to Cos and found it already in the possession of Amphoterus. All the 7 remaining captives Hegelochus brought with him, except Pharnabazus, who had slipped his guards in Cos and escaped. Alexander sent the tyrants to the cities from which they came, to be treated as the citizens pleased; but the Chians with Apollonides

Ἀπολλωνίδην τοὺς Χίους ἐς Ἐλεφαντίνην πόλιν
Αἰγυπτίαν ξὺν φυλακῇ ἀκριβεῖ ἔπεμψεν.

3. Ἐπὶ τούτοις δὲ πόθος λαμβάνει αὐτὸν ἐλθεῖν
παρ' Ἄμμωνα ἐς Λιβύην, τὸ μέν τι τῷ θεῷ
χρησόμενον, ὅτι ἀτρεκὲς ἐλέγετο εἶναι τὸ μαντεῖον
τοῦ Ἄμμωνος καὶ χρήσασθαι αὐτῷ Περσέα καὶ
Ἡρακλέα, τὸν μὲν ἐπὶ τὴν Γοργόνα ὅτε πρὸς
Πολυδέκτου ἐστέλλετο, τὸν δὲ ὅτε παρ' Ἀνταῖον
ᾔει εἰς Λιβύην καὶ παρὰ Βούσιριν εἰς Αἴγυπτον.
2 Ἀλεξάνδρῳ δὲ φιλοτιμία ἦν πρὸς Περσέα καὶ
Ἡρακλέα, ἀπὸ γένους τε ὄντι τοῦ ἀμφοῖν καί τι
καὶ αὐτὸς τῆς γενέσεως τῆς ἑαυτοῦ ἐς Ἄμμωνα
ἀνέφερε, καθάπερ οἱ μῦθοι τὴν Ἡρακλέους τε καὶ
Περσέως ἐς Δία. καὶ οὖν παρ' Ἄμμωνα ταύτῃ τῇ
γνώμῃ ἐστέλλετο, ὡς καὶ τὰ αὑτοῦ ἀτρεκέστερον
εἰσόμενος ἢ φήσων γε ἐγνωκέναι.

3 Μέχρι μὲν δὴ Παραιτονίου παρὰ θάλασσαν ᾔει
δι' ἐρήμου, οὐ μέντοι δι' ἀνύδρου τῆς χώρας,
σταδίους ἐς χιλίους καὶ ἑξακοσίους, ὡς λέγει
Ἀριστόβουλος. ἐντεῦθεν δὲ ἐς τὴν μεσόγαιαν
ἐτράπετο, ἵνα τὸ μαντεῖον ἦν τοῦ Ἄμμωνος. ἔστι
δὲ ἐρήμη τε ἡ ὁδὸς καὶ ψάμμος ἡ πολλὴ αὐτῆς καὶ
4 ἄνυδρος. ὕδωρ δὲ ἐξ οὐρανοῦ πολὺ Ἀλεξάνδρῳ
ἐγένετο, καὶ τοῦτο ἐς τὸ θεῖον ἀνηνέχθη. ἀνηνέχθη
δὲ ἐς τὸ θεῖον καὶ τόδε· ἄνεμος νότος ἐπὰν πνεύσῃ
ἐν ἐκείνῳ τῷ χώρῳ, τῆς ψάμμου ἐπιφορεῖ κατὰ τῆς
ὁδοῦ ἐπὶ μέγα, καὶ ἀφανίζεται τῆς ὁδοῦ τὰ σημεῖα
οὐδὲ ἔστιν εἰδέναι ἵνα χρὴ πορεύεσθαι καθάπερ ἐν
πελάγει τῇ ψάμμῳ, ὅτι σημεῖα οὐκ ἔστι κατὰ τὴν

---

[2] A. returns to his main source(s), who normally recorded
actions in which Al. was not personally engaged, not when

were sent to the city of Elephantine in Egypt, with a strong guard.[2]

3. After this a longing seized Alexander to pay a visit to Ammon in Libya, for one reason to consult the god, since the oracle of Ammon was said to be infallible, and to have been consulted by Perseus, when he was sent by Polydectes against the Gorgon, and by Heracles when he was on his way into Libya to find Antaeus, and into Egypt to find Busiris. Alexander sought to rival Perseus and Heracles, as he was descended from them both; and in addition he himself traced his birth in part to Ammon, just as the legends traced that of Heracles and Perseus to Zeus. In any case he set out for Ammon with this idea, hoping to secure more exact knowledge of his affairs, or at least to say he had secured it.[1]

As far as Paraetonium [Mersah Matruh] he went along the coast through country which, though desert, is not wholly waterless, a distance of sixteen hundred stades, as Aristobulus tells us. There he turned into the interior, where the oracle of Ammon lay. The route is desolate; most of it is sand, and waterless. Alexander, however, had plenty of rain, and this was attributed to the divinity. And so was the following incident. Whenever a south wind blows in that country, it makes a great heap of sand on the route and obscures its marks, and one cannot get one's bearings in a sort of ocean of sand, since

they occurred but when they were reported to him. QC. iv 8, 11–13 (with other particulars) puts Al's decisions about the Greek islands after the visit to Siwah, cf. 5, 1 n. See also App. II. Al's imprisonment of the Chian oligarchs hardly gave effect to Chios' decree (Tod 192) that they should be tried by the Greek *synedrion*.

[1] For the visit to the oracle of Ammon in the oasis of Siwah see App. V; for Heracles and Perseus, App. IV.

ὁδὸν οὔτε που ὄρος οὔτε δένδρον οὔτε γήλοφοι
βέβαιοι ἀνεστηκότες, οἷστισιν οἱ ὁδῖται τεκμαίροιντο
ἂν τὴν πορείαν, καθάπερ οἱ ναῦται τοῖς ἄστροις·
ἀλλὰ ἐπλανᾶτο γὰρ ἡ στρατιὰ Ἀλεξάνδρῳ καὶ οἱ
5 ἡγεμόνες τῆς ὁδοῦ ἀμφίβολοι ἦσαν. Πτολεμαῖος
μὲν δὴ ὁ Λάγου λέγει δράκοντας δύο ἰέναι πρὸ τοῦ
στρατεύματος φωνὴν ἱέντας, καὶ τούτοις Ἀλέξανδρον κελεῦσαι ἔπεσθαι τοὺς ἡγεμόνας πιστεύ-
σαντας τῷ θείῳ, τοὺς δὲ ἡγήσασθαι τὴν ὁδὸν τήν
6 τε ἐς τὸ μαντεῖον καὶ ὀπίσω αὖθις· Ἀριστόβουλος
δέ, καὶ ὁ πλείων λόγος ταύτῃ κατέχει, κόρακας δύο
προπετομένους πρὸ τῆς στρατιᾶς, τούτους γενέσθαι
Ἀλεξάνδρῳ τοὺς ἡγεμόνας. καὶ ὅτι μὲν θεῖόν τι
ξυνεπέλαβεν αὐτῷ ἔχω ἰσχυρίσασθαι, ὅτι καὶ τὸ
εἰκὸς ταύτῃ ἔχει, τὸ δὲ ἀτρεκὲς τοῦ λόγου ἀφείλοντο οἱ ἄλλῃ καὶ ἄλλῃ ὑπὲρ αὐτοῦ ἐξηγησάμενοι.

4. Ὁ δὲ χῶρος, ἵναπερ τοῦ Ἄμμωνος τὸ ἱερόν
ἐστι, τὰ μὲν κύκλῳ πάντα ἔρημα καὶ ψάμμον τὸ
πᾶν ἔχει καὶ ἄνυδρον, αὐτὸς δὲ ἐν μέσῳ ὀλίγος ὢν
(ὅσον γὰρ πλεῖστον αὐτοῦ ἐς πλάτος διέχει ἐς
τεσσαράκοντα μάλιστα σταδίους ἔρχεται) κατά-
πλεώς ἐστιν ἡμέρων δένδρων, ἐλαιῶν καὶ φοινίκων,
2 καὶ ἔνδροσος μόνος τῶν πέριξ. καὶ πηγὴ ἐξ αὐτοῦ
ἀνίσχει οὐδέν τι ἐοικυῖα ταῖς πηγαῖς, ὅσαι ἄλλαι ἐκ
γῆς ἀνίσχουσιν. ἐν μὲν γὰρ μεσημβρίᾳ ψυχρὸν τὸ
ὕδωρ γευσαμένῳ τε καὶ ἔτι μᾶλλον ἁψαμένῳ οἷον
ψυχρότατον· ἐγκλίναντος δὲ τοῦ ἡλίου ἐς ἑσπέραν
θερμότερον, καὶ ἀπὸ τῆς ἑσπέρας ἔτι θερμότερον
ἔστε ἐπὶ μέσας τὰς νύκτας, μέσων δὲ νυκτῶν
ἑαυτοῦ θερμότατον· ἀπὸ δὲ μέσων νυκτῶν ψύχεται
ἐν τάξει, καὶ ἕωθεν ψυχρὸν ἤδη ἐστί, ψυχρότατον
δὲ μεσημβρίας· καὶ τοῦτο ἀμείβει ἐν τάξει ἐπὶ

there are no marks along the route, no mountain anywhere, no tree, no solid hillocks standing up, by
which the wayfarers might judge their proper course,
as sailors do from the stars; in fact Alexander's army
went astray, and the guides were in doubt as to the
route. Now Ptolemy son of Lagos says that two 5
serpents preceded the army giving voice, and Alexander told his leaders to follow them and trust the
divinity; and the serpents led the way to the oracle
and back again. But Aristobulus agrees with the 6
more common and prevalent version, that two crows,
flying in advance of the army, acted as guides to
Alexander. That some divine help was given him I
can confidently assert, because probability suggests it
too; but the exact truth of the story cannot be told;
that is precluded by the way in which different
writers about Alexander have given different accounts.

4. The district [Siwah] in which the Temple of Ammon lies is desert all round, covered with sand, and
without water. But the site in the centre, which is
small (for its broadest stretch only comes to about
forty stades), is full of garden trees, olives and palms,
and of all the surrounding country it alone catches
the dew. A spring, too, rises from it, not at all like 2
other springs which rise from the ground. For at
midday the water is cold to the taste and even more
to the touch, as cold as can be, but when the sun
sinks towards evening it is warmer, and from evening
on it grows warmer and warmer till midnight, and at
midnight it is at its warmest; but after midnight it
cools off in turn, and from dawn onwards it is already
cold, but coldest at midday. This change occurs

3 ἑκάστῃ [τῇ] ἡμέρᾳ. γίγνονται δὲ καὶ ἅλες
αὐτόματοι ἐν τῷ χωρίῳ τούτῳ ὀρυκτοί· καὶ
τούτων ἔστιν οὓς ἐς Αἴγυπτον φέρουσι τῶν ἱερέων
τινὲς τοῦ Ἄμμωνος. ἐπειδὰν γὰρ ἐπ' Αἰγύπτου
στέλλωνται, ἐς κοιτίδας πλεκτὰς ἐκ φοίνικος
ἐσβαλόντες δῶρον τῷ βασιλεῖ ἀποφέρουσιν ἢ εἴ τῳ
4 ἄλλῳ. ἔστι δὲ μακρός τε ὁ χόνδρος (ἤδη ⟨δέ⟩
τινες αὐτῶν καὶ ὑπὲρ τρεῖς δακτύλους) καὶ
καθαρὸς ὥσπερ κρύσταλλος· καὶ τούτῳ ἐπὶ ταῖς
θυσίαις χρῶνται, ὡς καθαρωτέρῳ τῶν ἀπὸ θαλάσσης ἁλῶν, Αἰγύπτιοί τε καὶ ὅσοι ἄλλοι τοῦ θείου
5 οὐκ ἀμελῶς ἔχουσιν. ἐνταῦθα Ἀλέξανδρος τόν τε
χῶρον ἐθαύμασε καὶ τῷ θεῷ ἐχρήσατο· καὶ
ἀκούσας ὅσα αὐτῷ πρὸς θυμοῦ ἦν, ὡς ἔλεγεν,
ἀνέζευξεν ἐπ' Αἰγύπτου, ὡς μὲν Ἀριστόβουλος
λέγει, τὴν αὐτὴν ὀπίσω ὁδόν, ὡς δὲ Πτολεμαῖος ὁ
Λάγου, ἄλλην εὐθεῖαν ὡς ἐπὶ Μέμφιν.

5. Εἰς Μέμφιν δὲ αὐτῷ πρεσβεῖαί τε πολλαὶ ἐκ
τῆς Ἑλλάδος ἧκον, καὶ οὐκ ἔστιν ὅντινα ἀτυχή-
σαντα ὧν ἐδεῖτο ἀπέπεμψε, καὶ στρατιὰ παραγί-
γνεται παρὰ μὲν Ἀντιπάτρου μισθοφόροι Ἕλληνες
ἐς τετρακοσίους, ὧν ἡγεῖτο Μενοίτας [1] ὁ Ἡγησάν-
δρου, ἐκ Θρᾴκης δὲ ἱππεῖς ἐς πεντακοσίους, ὧν
2 ἦρχεν Ἀσκληπιόδωρος ὁ Εὐνίκου. ἐνταῦθα θύει
τῷ Διὶ τῷ βασιλεῖ καὶ πομπεύει ξὺν τῇ στρατιᾷ ἐν
τοῖς ὅπλοις καὶ ἀγῶνα ποιεῖ γυμνικὸν καὶ μουσικόν.
καὶ τὰ κατὰ τὴν Αἴγυπτον ἐνταῦθα ἐκόμισε· δύο
μὲν νομάρχας Αἰγύπτου κατέστησεν Αἰγυπτίους,
Δολόασπιν καὶ Πέτισιν, καὶ τούτοις διένειμε τὴν

---

[1] Μενοίτας; some read Μενίδας (cf. iii 12, 3; 13, 3 etc).

regularly every day. Then there are natural salts in 3 331
this district, to be obtained by digging; some are   B.C.
taken by priests of Ammon to Egypt. Whenever
they are going off to Egypt, they pack the salt into
baskets woven of palm leaves, to be conveyed as a
present to the king or to someone else. The grains 4
of this salt are large, some of them have been known
to be more than three fingers' breadth, and clear as
crystal. Egyptians and others who are particular
about religious observance use this salt in their
sacrifices, as being purer than the sea-salts. Now 5
Alexander surveyed the site with wonder, and made
his enquiry of the god; he received the answer his
heart desired, as he said, and turned back for Egypt,
by the same route according to Aristobulus, but
according to Ptolemy son of Lagos, by a different
way, direct to Memphis.

5. At Memphis many embassies reached him from
Greece, and he sent away no one disappointed in his
request.[1] He was also joined by a force sent by
Antipater, Greek mercenaries four hundred strong,
under the command of Menoetas[2] son of Hegesander,
and about five hundred Thracian horse, under command of Asclepiodorus son of Eunicus. Then Alex- 2
ander sacrificed to Zeus the King and held a procession with his force under arms and celebrated athletic
and musical games. He then made his arrangements
for Egypt; he appointed two Egyptians, Doloaspis
and Petisis as nomarchs, dividing the whole country

---

[1] The embassies may include that mentioned in ii 25, 4 n.,
but QC. iv 8, 12 f. specifically names Athens, Rhodes, Chios
and Mitylene, and Al. perhaps deferred decisions recorded in
2, 7 till now, so QC. He also makes Al. go up the Nile to
Memphis and beyond, iv 8, 2 and 7 ff.

[2] Or Menidas, see critical note.

χώραν τὴν Αἰγυπτίαν· Πετίσιος δὲ ἀπειπαμένου
3 τὴν ἀρχὴν Δολόασπις ἐκδέχεται πᾶσαν. φρουρ-
άρχους δὲ τῶν ἑταίρων ἐν Μέμφει μὲν Πανταλέοντα
κατέστησε τὸν Πυδναῖον, ἐν Πηλουσίῳ δὲ Πολέμωνα τὸν Μεγακλέους Πελλαῖον· τῶν ξένων δὲ
ἄρχειν Λυκίδαν Αἰτωλόν, γραμματέα δὲ ἐπὶ τῶν
ξένων Εὔγνωστον τὸν Ξενοφάντου τῶν ἑταίρων·
ἐπισκόπους δὲ αὐτῶν Αἰσχύλον τε καὶ Ἔφιππον
4 τὸν Χαλκιδέως.[1] Λιβύης δὲ τῆς προσχώρου
ἄρχειν δίδωσιν Ἀπολλώνιον Χαρίνου, Ἀραβίας δὲ
τῆς πρὸς Ἡρώων πόλει Κλεομένην τὸν ἐκ Ναυ-
κράτιος· καὶ τούτῳ παρηγγέλλετο τοὺς μὲν
νομάρχας ἐᾶν ἄρχειν τῶν νομῶν τῶν κατὰ σφᾶς
καθάπερ ἐκ παλαιοῦ καθειστήκει, αὐτὸν δὲ ἐκλέγειν
παρ' αὐτῶν τοὺς φόρους· οἱ δὲ ἀποφέρειν αὐτῷ
5 ἐτάχθησαν. στρατηγοὺς δὲ τῇ στρατιᾷ κατέστησεν, ἥντινα ἐν Αἰγύπτῳ ὑπελείπετο, Πευκέσταν τε
τὸν Μακαρτάτου καὶ Βάλακρον τὸν Ἀμύντου,
ναύαρχον δὲ ἐπὶ τῶν νεῶν Πολέμωνα τὸν Θηραμέ-
νους· σωματοφύλακα δὲ ἀντὶ Ἀρρύβα[2] [τὸν]
Λεοννάτον τὸν †Ὀνάσου[3] ἔταξεν· Ἀρρύβας γὰρ
6 νόσῳ ἀπέθανεν. ἀπέθανε δὲ καὶ Ἀντίοχος ὁ
ἄρχων τῶν τοξοτῶν, καὶ ἀντὶ τοῦ⟨του⟩ ἄρχειν
ἐπέστησε τοῖς τοξόταις Ὀμβρίωνα Κρῆτα. ἐπὶ δὲ
τοὺς ξυμμάχους τοὺς πεζούς, ὧν Βάλακρος ἡγεῖτο,

---

[1] Χαλκιδέως: Χαλκιδέα Geier.
[2] Ἀρρύββας would be the right form.
[3] Leonnatus is son Ἀντέου (vi 28. 4): Ἄνθους (Arrian ed.
Roos vol. ii 254, 4), Εὔνου (*Ind.* 18. 3); the true name cannot
be determined.

---

[3] Or, with Geier's emendation, ' a Chalcidean '; he can then
be identified with Ephippus of Olynthus (since Olynthus had
been the centre of the Chalcidean federation), author of a work

of Egypt between them; Petisis, however, declined   331
the power, and Doloaspis took it all. As garrison 3 B.C.
commandants he appointed Companions, Pantaleon
of Pydna at Memphis, and Polemon, son of Megacles
of Pella at Pelusium; Lycidas, an Aetolian, was to
command the mercenaries and Eugnostos son of
Xenophantes, one of the Companions, to be secretary
in charge of the mercenaries, with Aeschylus and
Ephippus son of Chalcideus as their overseers.[3] The 4
government of the neighbouring country of Libya
was given to Apollonius son of Charinus; and that of
Arabia round Heroönpolis to Cleomenes from Nau-
cratis.[4] He was instructed to permit the nomarchs
to govern their own districts in accordance with the
ancient practices, but to exact the tribute from them
himself, while they were ordered to pay it over to
him. As generals of the army which he was leaving 5
behind in Egypt he appointed Peucestas son of
Macartatus and Balacrus son of Amyntas, and as
admiral of the fleet, Polemon son of Theramenes.
As bodyguard in place of Arrhybas, who had died of
disease, he appointed Leonnatus son of Anteas.
Antiochus, the commander of the archers, had also 6
died, and in his place Alexander appointed as commander of the archers Ombrion, a Cretan. The
allied infantry, of which Balacrus had been com-

' On the Death of Al. and Hephaestion ' (Jacoby no. 126),
very hostile to Al., as one might expect most of those who came
from a city Philip had destroyed to have been, though the
attitude is stranger if Ephippus, like Callisthenes, had taken
service with Al., and might, if the identification is right, be
more plausibly connected with Al's treatment of Callisthenes.
However, Chalcideus is attested as a personal name, and
emendation is not required.
    [4] See vii 23, 6 ff. with notes. The other officers named are
totally or almost unknown.

ἐπεὶ Βάλακρος ἐν Αἰγύπτῳ ὑπελείπετο, Κάλανον
7 κατέστησεν ἡγεμόνα. κατανεῖμαι δὲ λέγεται ἐς
πολλοὺς τὴν ἀρχὴν τῆς Αἰγύπτου τήν τε φύσιν τῆς
χώρας θαυμάσας καὶ τὴν ὀχυρότητα, ὅτι οὐκ
ἀσφαλές οἱ ἐφαίνετο ἑνὶ ἐπιτρέψαι ἄρχειν Αἰγύπτου
πάσης. καὶ Ῥωμαῖοί μοι δοκοῦσι παρ' Ἀλεξάνδρου μαθόντες ἐν φυλακῇ ἔχειν Αἴγυπτον καὶ
μηδένα τῶν ἀπὸ βουλῆς ἐπὶ τῷδε ἐκπέμπειν
ὕπαρχον Αἰγύπτου, ἀλλὰ τῶν εἰς τοὺς ἱππέας
σφίσι ξυντελούντων.

6. Ἀλέξανδρος δὲ ἅμα τῷ ἦρι ὑποφαίνοντι ἐκ
Μέμφιος ᾔει ἐπὶ Φοινίκης· καὶ ἐγεφυρώθη αὐτῷ ὅ
τε κατὰ Μέμφιν πόρος τοῦ Νείλου καὶ αἱ διώρυχες
αὐτοῦ πᾶσαι. ὡς δὲ ἀφίκετο ἐς Τύρον, καταλαμβάνει ἐνταῦθα ἧκον αὐτῷ ἤδη καὶ τὸ ναυτικόν.
ἐν Τύρῳ δὲ αὖθις θύει τῷ Ἡρακλεῖ καὶ ἀγῶνα
2 ποιεῖ γυμνικόν τε καὶ μουσικόν. ἐνταῦθα ἀφικνεῖται παρ' αὐτὸν ἐξ Ἀθηνῶν ἡ Πάραλος πρέσβεις
ἄγουσα Διόφαντον καὶ Ἀχιλλέα· ξυνεπρέσβευον δὲ
αὐτοῖς καὶ οἱ Πάραλοι ξύμπαντες. καὶ οὗτοι τῶν
τε ἄλλων ἔτυχον ὧν ἕνεκα ἐστάλησαν καὶ τοὺς
αἰχμαλώτους ἀφῆκεν Ἀθηναίοις ὅσοι ἐπὶ Γρανίκῳ

---

[5] QC. iv 8, 4 f. names only Aeschylus of Rhodes and Peucestas
the Macedonian, who were ' put in charge ' of Egypt with
4,000 soldiers, Apollonius ' put in charge ' of the adjoining
region of Africa, Cleomenes appointed to collect the taxes of
Egypt and Africa, and Polemon to protect the mouths of the
Nile with 30 triremes. Clearly Al. divided civil administration
from military command, and gave Cleomenes special fiscal
duties as well as other civil powers in ' Arabia '; for ' Arabia '
and ' Libya ' cf. Strabo xvii 1, 30, which does not make clear
their delimitation from Upper Egypt. The military arrangements are impenetrable. Berve distinguished the ' army ' of

mander, were placed under Calanus, since Balacrus 331
was being left behind in Egypt.[5] It is said that he 7 B.C.
divided the government of Egypt between many
officers, as he was strongly impressed by the character
and defensibility of the country and did not think it
safe to entrust the command of all Egypt to one man.[6]
The Romans, I think, learnt from Alexander to keep
a watch on Egypt, and never to send anyone from
the Senate as governor, but only those whom they
class as Knights.[7]

6. When spring began to show itself, Alexander
started from Memphis for Phoenicia; bridges were
made for him to cross over the river Nile at Memphis
and over all its canals. When he reached Tyre, he
found his fleet had already arrived there. At Tyre
he sacrificed a second time to Heracles and held
athletic and musical games.[1] There the *Paralus*[2] 2
from Athens reached him, bringing Diophantus and
Achilles as envoys; the entire crew of the *Paralus*
were associated with them in the embassy. They
achieved all the objects of their mission; in particular
Alexander gave up to the Athenians all the Athenians

Peucestas and Balacrus from the mercenaries: not convincing.
For a consortium of generals cf. the later arrangements in
Media (vi 27, 3). I doubt if A. or QC. gives a true picture.
Recent history suggested that the danger for Al. lay in native
revolt strengthened by Greek mercenaries: a wholly divided
command would have been least fitted to prevent this.

[6] Pt. in fact used the natural strength of Egypt to turn
himself from satrap into independent king. But I doubt for
that reason if the comment is his: more probably ' vulgate '.

[7] A's comment; in fact the circumstances and Roman
organization were different, cf. Tacitus, *Annals* ii 59; *Histories*
i 11; Dio Cassius li 17.

[1] QC iv 8, 16; P. 29.

[2] Athens' sacred galley, used to convey ambassadors.

3 Ἀθηναίων ἑάλωσαν. τὰ δὲ ἐν Πελοποννήσῳ ὅτι αὐτῷ νενεωτερίσθαι ἀπήγγελτο, Ἀμφοτερὸν πέμπει βοηθεῖν Πελοποννησίων ὅσοι ἔς τε τὸν Περσικὸν πόλεμον βέβαιοι ἦσαν καὶ Λακεδαιμονίων οὐ κατήκουον. Φοίνιξι δὲ καὶ Κυπρίοις προσετάχθη ἑκατὸν ναῦς ἄλλας πρὸς αἷς ἔχοντα Ἀμφοτερὸν ἔπεμπε στέλλειν ἐπὶ Πελοποννήσου.

4 Αὐτὸς δὲ ἤδη ἄνω ὡρμᾶτο ὡς ἐπὶ Θάψακόν τε καὶ τὸν Εὐφράτην ποταμόν, ἐν Φοινίκῃ μὲν ἐπὶ τῶν φόρων τῇ ξυλλογῇ καταστήσας Κοίρανον Βεροιαῖον, Φιλόξενον δὲ τῆς Ἀσίας τὰ ἐπὶ τάδε τοῦ Ταύρου ἐκλέγειν. τῶν ξὺν αὑτῷ δὲ χρημάτων τὴν φυλακὴν ἀντὶ τούτων ἐπέτρεψεν Ἁρπάλῳ τῷ Μαχάτα ἄρτι

5 ἐκ τῆς φυγῆς ἥκοντι. Ἅρπαλος γὰρ τὰ μὲν πρῶτα ἔφυγε, Φιλίππου ἔτι βασιλεύοντος, ὅτι πιστὸς ἦν ⟨Ἀλεξάνδρῳ [1]⟩, καὶ Πτολεμαῖος ὁ Λάγου ἐπὶ τῷ αὐτῷ ἔφυγε καὶ Νέαρχος ὁ Ἀνδροτίμου καὶ Ἐριγύϊος ὁ Λαρίχου καὶ Λαομέδων ὁ τούτου ἀδελφός, ὅτι ὕποπτα ἦν Ἀλεξάνδρῳ ἐς Φίλιππον, ἐπειδὴ Εὐρυδίκην γυναῖκα ἠγάγετο Φίλιππος, Ὀλυμπιάδα δὲ τὴν Ἀλεξάνδρου μητέρα

6 ἠτίμασε. τελευτήσαντος δὲ Φιλίππου κατελθόντας ἀπὸ τῆς φυγῆς ὅσοι δι' αὐτὸν ἔφευγον Πτολεμαῖον μὲν σωματοφύλακα κατέστησεν, Ἅρπαλον δὲ ἐπὶ τῶν χρημάτων, ὅτι αὐτῷ τὸ σῶμα ἐς τὰ πολέμια ἀχρεῖον ἦν, Ἐριγύϊον δὲ ἱππάρχην τῶν ξυμμάχων, Λαομέδοντα δὲ τὸν τούτου ἀδελφόν, ὅτι δίγλωσσος ἦν [ἐς τὰ βαρβαρικὰ γράμματα],[2] ἐπὶ τοῖς αἰχμαλώτοις βαρβάροις, Νέαρχον δὲ σατραπεύειν Λυκίας

---

[1] I have followed a suggestion of Roos and inserted Ἀλεξάνδρῳ. Arrian's style always favours absolute explicitness.

[2] [ἐς . . . γράμματα]. Surely a gloss.

captured at the Granicus.[3]   On learning that there   3   331
was a movement of revolt against him in the Pelopon-   B.C.
nese, he sent Amphoterus to help the Peloponnesians
who were loyal in regard to the Persian war and were
not giving ear to the Lacedaemonians.   Orders were
also given to the Phoenicians and Cyprians to send to
the Peloponnese a hundred ships in addition to those
he was despatching under command of Amphoterus.

Alexander himself was already starting inland   4
towards Thapsacus and the river Euphrates, after
appointing Coeranus, a Beroean, to collect taxes in
Phoenicia, and Philoxenus to be collector in Asia this
side of the Taurus.[4]   In their place he entrusted the
custody of the moneys with him to Harpalus son of
Machatas, who had just returned from exile;
Harpalus had first been sent into exile while Philip   5
was still on the throne, because he was loyal to
Alexander; Ptolemy son of Lagos was exiled on the
same account, with Nearchus son of Androtimus,
Erigyius son of Larichus and Laomedon his brother,
since there was a lack of confidence between Alexander and Philip after Philip took Eurydice to wife,
and disgraced Olympias the mother of Alexander.[5]
On Philip's death those who had been banished on   6
Alexander's account returned, Ptolemy was appointed one of the bodyguards, Harpalus treasurer,
since his physique made him unfit for fighting,
Erigyius commander of the allied cavalry, Laomedon
his brother, since he was bilingual,[6] officer in charge
of the barbarian captives, and Nearchus satrap of

---

[3] Cf. i 29, 5; on § 3 f. see App. VI.
[4] See Badian, *GR* 1965, 168 f.; *Ancient Society and Institutions (Studies presented to V. L. Ehrenberg)* 54 ff.
[5] Introd. § 47; for the name Eurydice cf. Berve no. 434.
[6] Presumably meaning that he knew Persian or Aramaic.

καὶ τῆς ἐχομένης Λυκίας χώρας ἔστε ἐπὶ τὸν
7 Ταῦρον τὸ ὄρος. ὀλίγον δὲ πρόσθεν τῆς μάχης τῆς
ἐν Ἰσσῷ γενομένης ἀναπεισθεὶς πρὸς Ταυρίσκου
ἀνδρὸς κακοῦ Ἅρπαλος φεύγει ξὺν Ταυρίσκῳ.
καὶ ὁ μὲν Ταυρίσκος παρ᾽ Ἀλέξανδρον τὸν
Ἠπειρώτην ἐς Ἰταλίαν σταλεὶς ἐκεῖ ἐτελεύτησεν,
Ἁρπάλῳ δὲ ἐν τῇ Μεγαρίδι ἡ φυγὴ ἦν. ἀλλὰ
Ἀλέξανδρος πείθει αὐτὸν κατελθεῖν πίστεις δοὺς
οὐδέν οἱ μεῖον ἔσεσθαι ἐπὶ τῇ φυγῇ· οὐδὲ ἐγένετο
ἐπανελθόντι, ἀλλὰ ἐπὶ τῶν χρημάτων αὖθις ἐτάχθη
Ἅρπαλος. ἐς Λυδίαν δὲ σατράπην Μένανδρον
8 ἐκπέμπει τῶν ἑταίρων· ἐπὶ δὲ τοῖς ξένοις, ὧν
ἡγεῖτο Μένανδρος, Κλέαρχος [1] αὐτῷ ἐτάχθη.
ἀντὶ δὲ Ἀρίμμα [1] σατράπην Συρίας Ἀσκληπιόδωρον τὸν Εὐνίκου ἀπέδειξεν, ὅτι Ἀρίμμας βλακεῦ-
σαι ἐδόκει αὐτῷ ἐν τῇ παρασκευῇ, ἥντινα ἐτάχθη
παρασκευάσαι τῇ στρατιᾷ κατὰ τὴν ὁδὸν τὴν ἄνω.

7. Καὶ ἀφίκετο ἐς Θάψακον Ἀλέξανδρος μηνὸς
Ἑκατομβαιῶνος ἐπὶ ἄρχοντος Ἀθήνησιν Ἀριστο-
φάνους· καὶ καταλαμβάνει δυοῖν γεφύραιν ἐζευγ-

---

[1] See historical note.

[7] Brother of Olympias, he was fighting for the Greek city of
Taras against her south Italian neighbours and perished in
331/30 B.C.
[8] Probably an error, A's or a scribe's, for Cleander, cf. iii
12, 2; 26, 3; vi 27, 4.
[9] Cf. ii 13, 7 n. If the text is right, Arimmas had succeeded
Menon for reasons unknown. Droysen, however, amended
'Arimmas' to 'Menon, son of Cerdimmas'. The conjecture
is bold. QC. states (a) that after his capture of Damascus (A.
ii 11, 10 n.) Parmenio (not Menon) was put in charge of Hollow
Syria (iv 1, 4); (b) that after the capture of Tyre, where he
presumably rejoined Al. (cf. A. ii 25), Parmenio handed over

Lycia and the country bordering on Lycia as far as
Mount Taurus. But not long before the battle of
Issus Harpalus was led astray by Tauriscus, a scoun-
drel, and fled with him. Tauriscus made his way to
Italy to Alexander (King) of Epirus,[7] and died there;
Harpalus took refuge in the Megarid. However,
Alexander persuaded him to return, giving him
assurances that he would not suffer for his flight; and
in fact on his return he was again set in charge of the
treasure. Alexander sent Menander, one of the
Companions, to Lydia as satrap, appointing Clearchus[8] to command the mercenaries of whom Menander had had charge. In place of Arimmas he made
Asclepiodorus son of Eunicus satrap of Syria, since
he considered Arimmas to have been slack in the
preparations he had been instructed to make for the
army in its march up country.[9]

7. Alexander arrived at Thapsacus in the month
Hecatombaeon [July–Aug.] of the year in which
Aristophanes was archon at Athens.[1] There he

Hollow Syria to Andromachus (iv 5, 9); (c) that Andromachus,
whom Al. had put in charge of Syria, was burned alive by
the Samaritans, that Al. personally avenged him by an expedition presumably from Tyre in 331, and appointed Memnon
(editors ' Menon ') in his place (iv 8, 9–11). As to (a) we can
suppose that Parmenio was in general control of Syria, so long
as he operated there with his expeditionary force (cf. his
operations in Phrygia, A. i 24, 3), without prejudice to the
appointment of Menon as permanent satrap and commander
in north Syria; as to (b) that Andromachus' province lay to the
south of Menon's province; as to (c) that Menon was transferred to this southern province on his death and himself replaced in the north by Arimmas. Cf. Bosworth, *CQ* 1975 with
valuable discussion of the varied meanings of Hollow Syria.
[1] Cf. for chs 7–10 D. 53–6; QC. iv 9–11 (analogies both
with A. and variant tradition in D.); P. 31; J. xi 12; chronology, App. VIII 4 f.; route, App. VII.

μένον τὸν πόρον. καὶ γὰρ καὶ Μαζαῖος, ὅτῳ ἡ
φυλακὴ τοῦ ποταμοῦ ἐκ Δαρείου ἐπετέτραπτο,
ἱππέας μὲν ἔχων περὶ τρισχιλίους, ⟨πεζοὺς
δὲ . . .⟩[1] καὶ τούτων Ἕλληνας μισθοφόρους
δισχιλίους, τέως μὲν αὐτοῦ ἐπὶ τῷ ποταμῷ
2 ἐφύλασσε, καὶ ἐπὶ τῷδε οὐ ξυνεχὴς ἡ γέφυρα
ἐζευγμένη ἦν ἔστε ἐπὶ τὴν ἀντιπέρας ὄχθην τοῖς
Μακεδόσι, δειμαίνουσι μὴ ἐπιθοῖντο οἱ ἀμφὶ
Μαζαῖον τῇ γεφύρᾳ ἵνα ἐπαύετο· Μαζαῖος δὲ ὡς
ἤκουσεν ἤδη προσάγοντα Ἀλέξανδρον, ᾤχετο
φεύγων ξὺν τῇ στρατιᾷ πάσῃ. καὶ εὐθὺς ὡς ἔφυγε
Μαζαῖος ἐπεβλήθησαν αἱ γέφυραι τῇ ὄχθῃ τῇ
πέραν καὶ διέβη ἐπ᾽ αὐτῶν ξὺν τῇ στρατιᾷ Ἀλέξανδρος.

3   Ἔνθεν δὲ ἐχώρει ἄνω, ἐν ἀριστερᾷ ἔχων τὸν
Εὐφράτην ποταμὸν καὶ τῆς Ἀρμενίας τὰ ὄρη, διὰ
τῆς Μεσοποταμίας καλουμένης χώρας. οὐκ εὐθεῖαν δὲ ἐπὶ Βαβυλῶνος ἦγεν ἀπὸ τοῦ Εὐφράτου
ὁρμηθείς, ὅτι τὴν ἑτέραν ἰόντι εὐπορώτερα τὰ
ξύμπαντα τῷ στρατῷ ἦν, καὶ χιλὸς τοῖς ἵπποις καὶ
τὰ ἐπιτήδεια ἐκ τῆς χώρας λαμβάνειν καὶ τὸ
4 καῦμα οὐχ ὡσαύτως ἐπιφλέγον. ἁλόντες δέ τινες
κατὰ τὴν ὁδὸν τῶν ἀπὸ τοῦ Δαρείου στρατεύματος
κατασκοπῆς ἕνεκα ἀπεσκεδασμένων ἐξήγγειλαν,
ὅτι Δαρεῖος ἐπὶ τοῦ Τίγρητος ποταμοῦ κάθηται
ἐγνωκὼς εἴργειν Ἀλέξανδρον, εἰ διαβαίνοι· καὶ
εἶναι αὐτῷ στρατιὰν πολὺ μείζονα ἢ ξὺν ᾗ ἐν
5 Κιλικίᾳ ἐμάχετο. ταῦτα ἀκούσας Ἀλέξανδρος ᾔει
σπουδῇ ὡς ἐπὶ τὸν Τίγρητα. ὡς δὲ ἀφίκετο, οὔτε
αὐτὸν Δαρεῖον καταλαμβάνει οὔτε τὴν φυλακήν,

---

[1] πεζοὺς δὲ ἴσους Roos.

found the river crossing secured by two bridges. The fact was that Mazaeus, to whom Darius had entrusted the defence of the river, with about three thousand cavalry and . . .[2] foot, including two thousand Greek mercenaries,[3] for some time kept guard over the river, and so the bridge had not been 2 completed by the Macedonians right up to the opposite bank, for fear that Mazaeus' troops would attack the bridge where it stopped short; but on learning that Alexander was already marching up, Mazaeus hurried off with all his forces. As soon as Mazaeus fled, the bridges were carried right over to the far bank and Alexander crossed over them with his army.

Thence he continued inland through the country 3 called Mesopotamia, keeping on his left the Euphrates and the mountains of Armenia. On setting out from the Euphrates he did not take the direct route for Babylon, since by going the other road all supplies were easier to obtain for the army, green fodder for the horses and provisions from the country, and the heat was less intense. Some of those who had been 4 sent out in different directions from Darius' army as scouts were captured, and reported that Darius was in position on the River Tigris, determined to check Alexander if he crossed, and that he had a much larger army than that with which he had fought in Cilicia. On hearing this Alexander hurried towards 5 the Tigris, but once he arrived there he found neither Darius himself nor the guard which Darius had left

---

[2] The figure is lost. QC. gives Mazaeus 6,000 horse, thinks he was to defend Euphrates and then Tigris (sometimes confused, cf. 9, 7 and 9), and to ' scorch the earth ' (9, 7 f. and 12-14; 10, 12-14), cf. D. 55, 1 relating only to Tigris.

[3] App. VI 2.

ἥντινα ἀπολελοίπει Δαρεῖος, ἀλλὰ διαβαίνει τὸν
πόρον, χαλεπῶς μὲν δι' ὀξύτητα τοῦ ῥοῦ, οὐδενὸς
δὲ εἴργοντος.

6 Ἐνταῦθα ἀναπαύει τὸν στρατόν· καὶ τῆς
σελήνης τὸ πολὺ ἐκλιπὲς ἐγένετο· καὶ Ἀλέξανδρος
ἔθυε τῇ τε σελήνῃ καὶ τῷ ἡλίῳ καὶ τῇ γῇ, ὅτων τὸ
ἔργον τοῦτο λόγος εἶναι κατέχει. καὶ ἐδόκει
Ἀριστάνδρῳ πρὸς Μακεδόνων καὶ Ἀλεξάνδρου
εἶναι τῆς σελήνης τὸ πάθημα καὶ ἐκείνου τοῦ μηνὸς
ἔσεσθαι ἡ μάχη, καὶ ἐκ τῶν ἱερῶν νίκην σημαίνε-
7 σθαι Ἀλεξάνδρῳ. ἄρας δὲ ἀπὸ τοῦ Τίγρητος ᾔει
διὰ τῆς Ἀσσυρίας χώρας, ἐν ἀριστερᾷ μὲν ἔχων τὰ
Γορδυηνῶν ὄρη, ἐν δεξιᾷ δὲ αὐτὸν τὸν Τίγρητα.
τετάρτῃ δὲ ἡμέρᾳ ἀπὸ τῆς διαβάσεως οἱ πρόδρομοι
αὐτῷ ἐξαγγέλλουσιν, ὅτι ἱππεῖς ἐστιν οἳ [1] πολέμιοι ἀνὰ τὸ πεδίον φαίνονται, ὅσοι δέ, οὐκ ἔχειν
εἰκάσαι. ξυντάξας οὖν τὴν στρατιὰν προὐχώρει
ὡς ἐς μάχην· καὶ ἄλλοι αὖ τῶν προδρόμων προσ-
ελάσαντες ἀκριβέστερον οὗτοι κατιδόντες ἔφασκον
δοκεῖν εἶναί σφισιν οὐ πλείους ἢ χιλίους τοὺς
ἱππέας.

8. Ἀναλαβὼν οὖν τήν τε βασιλικὴν ἴλην καὶ τῶν
ἑταίρων μίαν καὶ τῶν προδρόμων τοὺς Παίονας
ἤλαυνε σπουδῇ, τὴν δὲ ἄλλην στρατιὰν βάδην
ἔπεσθαι ἐκέλευσεν. οἱ δὲ τῶν Περσῶν ἱππεῖς
κατιδόντες τοὺς ἀμφ' Ἀλέξανδρον ὀξέως ἐπάγοντας
ἔφευγον ἀνὰ κράτος. καὶ Ἀλέξανδρος διώκων
2 ἐνέκειτο· καὶ οἱ μὲν πολλοὶ ἀπέφυγον, τοὺς δέ
τινας καὶ ἀπέκτειναν, ὅσοις οἱ ἵπποι ἐν τῇ φυγῇ
ἔκαμον, τοὺς δὲ καὶ ζῶντας αὐτοῖς ἵπποις ἔλαβον·

---

[1] ἐστιν οἳ Schmieder.   Roos kept the MS οὗτοι.

behind, and crossed the river; this was difficult because of the swiftness of the current, but there was no opposition.[4]

There he gave his army a rest. There was an almost total eclipse of the moon, and Alexander sacrificed to the Moon, Sun and Earth, who are all said to cause an eclipse. Aristander thought that the eclipse was favourable to the Macedonians and Alexander, that the battle would take place that month, and that the sacrifices portended victory to Alexander.[5] Starting from the Tigris, Alexander passed through the Assyrian land with the Gordyenian mountains on his left,[6] and the Tigris on his right. On the fourth day after the crossing,[7] the *prodromoi* reported that some enemy cavalry were to be seen over the plain, but they could not guess their numbers. So he drew up his force and advanced as to battle; then other *prodromoi* rode in, who had made a more accurate inspection, and reported that they estimated the cavalry at no more than a thousand.

8. Alexander then took with him the royal squadron, one squadron of Companions and the Paeonian *prodromoi* and moved on rapidly, ordering the rest of the army to follow at marching pace. But the Persian cavalry, observing the troops with Alexander coming up rapidly, lost no time in flight. Alexander pressed the pursuit, and though the greater number of them got away, some whose horses wearied in the flight were killed and others captured alive with their

2

---

[4] D. 55, 3 ff.; QC. 9, 15 ff. make much of the difficulty of fording the river; QC. 9, 23 has Mazaeus attack immediately afterwards.

[5] App. VIII 5. D. 55, 6 is worthless.

[6] QC. 10, 8.

[7] The place, not the day, of the crossing, to fit the time-table; the Greek word is ambiguous.

καὶ παρὰ τούτων ἔμαθον, ὅτι οὐ πόρρω εἴη
Δαρεῖος ξὺν δυνάμει πολλῇ.

3 Βεβοηθήκεσαν γὰρ Δαρείῳ Ἰνδῶν τε ὅσοι
Βακτρίοις ὅμοροι καὶ αὐτοὶ Βάκτριοι καὶ Σογδια-
νοί· τούτων μὲν πάντων ἡγεῖτο Βῆσσος ὁ τῆς
Βακτρίων χώρας σατράπης. εἵποντο δὲ αὐτοῖς καὶ
Σάκαι—Σκυθικὸν τοῦτο τὸ γένος τῶν τὴν Ἀσίαν
ἐποικούντων Σκυθῶν—οὐχ ὑπήκοοι οὗτοι Βήσσου,
ἀλλὰ κατὰ συμμαχίαν τὴν Δαρείου· ἡγεῖτο δὲ
αὐτῶν Μαυάκης· αὐτοὶ δὲ ἱπποτοξόται ἦσαν.
4 Βαρσαέ⟨ν⟩της δὲ Ἀραχωτῶν σατράπης Ἀρα-
χωτούς τε ἦγε καὶ τοὺς ὀρείους Ἰνδοὺς καλουμένους. Σατιβαρζάνης δὲ ὁ Ἀρείων σατράπης
Ἀρείους ἦγεν. Παρθυαίους δὲ καὶ Ὑρκανίους καὶ
Τοπείρους,[1] τοὺς πάντας ἱππέας, Φραταφέρνης
ἦγεν. Μήδων δὲ ἡγεῖτο Ἀτροπάτης· ξυνετάτ-
τοντο δὲ Μήδοις Καδούσιοί τε καὶ Ἀλβανοὶ καὶ
5 Σακεσῖναι. τοὺς δὲ προσοίκους τῇ ἐρυθρᾷ θαλάσσῃ
Ὀροντοβάτης καὶ Ἀριοβαρζάνης καὶ Ὀ⟨ρ⟩ξίνης
ἐκόσμουν. Οὔξιοι δὲ καὶ Σουσιανοὶ ἡγεμόνα
παρείχοντο Ὀξάθρην τὸν Ἀβουλίτου. Βουπάρης
δὲ Βαβυλωνίων ἡγεῖτο. οἱ ⟨δ'⟩ ἀνάσπαστοι
Κᾶρες καὶ Σιττακηνοὶ σὺν Βαβυλωνίοις ἐτετάχατο.
Ἀρμενίων δὲ Ὀρόντης καὶ Μιθραύστης ἦρχε, καὶ
6 Ἀριάκης Καππαδοκῶν. Σύρους δὲ τούς τε ἐκ τῆς

---

[1] Perhaps Ταπούρους; the spelling varies in different
passages.

---

[1] QC. iv 10, 9 ff.; in 9, 1–10 and D. 39, 3 f. and 53 we have
some account of Persian mobilization and army movements;
D. 53, 1 says that his troops were given longer swords and
lances to match the Macedonian (cf. A. i 15, 5); QC. 9, 3 refers
to better defensive armour. Perhaps all this applies only to

mounts. From these they learnt that Darius was
not far off with a large force.[1]

331
B.C.

It was large because Darius had obtained the help 3
of those Indians who bordered on the Bactrians,
together with the Bactrians and Sogdianians themselves, all under the command of Bessus, the satrap
of Bactria. They were joined by Sacae, a Scythian
people, belonging to the Scyths who inhabit Asia,
who came, not as subjects of Bessus, but on the
basis of an alliance with Darius; Mauaces was their
commander, and they were mounted archers.[2] Barsa- 4
entes, satrap of the Arachotians, led both the Arachotians and the Indian hillmen, as they were called,
Satibarzanes, their satrap, the Areians, Phrataphernes the Parthyaeans, Hyrcanians and Topeirians,
all cavalry, Atropates the Medes; along with the
Medes, Cadusians, Albanians and Sacesinians were
marshalled. The tribes bordering on the Red Sea 5
were directed by Orontobates, Ariobarzanes and
Orxines.[3] The Uxians and Susianians had Oxathres
son of Abulites as commander. Bupares was in command of the Babylonians. The Carians who had been
transplanted[4] and Sittacenians had been brigaded
with the Babylonians. The Armenians were under
Orontes and Mithraustes, the Cappadocians under
Ariaces. The Syrians of Hollow Syria[5] and all 6

some contingents, cf. A. iii 13, 4; vii 6, 5. For following list
cf. 11, 3 n. For troops from the eastern satrapies, separated
from west Iran by the Elburz mountains and central Persian
desert, and absent in 333 B.C. (QC. iii 2, 9) cf. D. 39, 3; QC.
iv 9, 2.

[2] Apparently from the Pamir highlands in Tadzhik,
U.S.S.R., not nomad Scyths (Herrmann, *RE* s.v. Sakai).

[3] QC. 12, 7 f. gives them different commands.

[4] The Persians sometimes transplanted rebellious subjects.

[5] Presumably men who had escaped from Issus.

κοίλης καὶ ὅσοι τῆς μεταξὺ τῶν ποταμῶν Συρίας
Μαζαῖος ἦγεν. ἐλέγετο δὲ ἡ πᾶσα στρατιὰ ἡ
Δαρείου ἱππεῖς μὲν ἐς τετρακισμυρίους, πεζοὶ δὲ ἐς
ἑκατὸν μυριάδας, καὶ ἅρματα δρεπανηφόρα διακόσια, ἐλέφαντες δὲ οὐ πολλοί, ἀλλὰ ἐς πεντεκαίδεκα μάλιστα Ἰνδοῖς τοῖς ἐπὶ τάδε τοῦ Ἰνδοῦ
ἦσαν.

7   Ξὺν ταύτῃ τῇ δυνάμει ἐστρατοπεδεύκει Δαρεῖος
ἐν Γαυγαμήλοις πρὸς ποταμῷ Βουμήλῳ, ἀπέχων
Ἀρβήλων τῆς πόλεως ὅσον ἑξακοσίους σταδίους,
ἐν χώρῳ ὁμαλῷ πάντῃ. καὶ γὰρ καὶ ὅσα ἀνώμαλα
αὐτοῦ ἐς ἱππασίαν, ταῦτα δὲ ἐκ πολλοῦ οἱ Πέρσαι
τοῖς τε ἅρμασιν ἐπελαύνειν εὐπετῆ πεποιήκεσαν καὶ
τῇ ἵππῳ ἱππάσιμα. ἦσαν γὰρ οἳ ἀνέπειθον
Δαρεῖον ὑπὲρ τῆς πρὸς Ἰσσῷ γενομένης μάχης,
ὅτι ἄρα ἐμειονέκτησε τῶν χωρίων τῇ στενότητι·
καὶ Δαρεῖος οὐ χαλεπῶς ἐπείθετο.

9. Ταῦτα ὡς ἐξηγγέλθη Ἀλεξάνδρῳ πρὸς τῶν
κατασκόπων τῶν Περσῶν ὅσοι ἑάλωσαν, ἔμεινεν
αὐτοῦ ἵνα ἐξηγγέλθη ἡμέρας τέσσαρας· καὶ τήν
[τε] στρατιὰν ἐκ τῆς ὁδοῦ ἀνέπαυσε, τὸ δὲ
στρατόπεδον τάφρῳ τε καὶ χάρακι ἐτείχισεν.
ἔγνω γὰρ τὰ μὲν σκευοφόρα ἀπολείπειν καὶ ὅσοι
τῶν στρατιωτῶν ἀπόμαχοι ἦσαν, αὐτὸς δὲ ξὺν τοῖς
μαχίμοις οὐδὲν ἄλλο ὅτι μὴ ὅπλα φέρουσιν ἰέναι ἐς
2   τὸν ἀγῶνα. ἀναλαβὼν οὖν τὴν δύναμιν νυκτὸς
ἦγεν ἀμφὶ δευτέραν φυλακὴν μάλιστα, ὡς ἅμ'
ἡμέρᾳ προσμίξαι τοῖς βαρβάροις. Δαρεῖος δέ, ὡς
προσηγγέλθη αὐτῷ προσάγων ἤδη Ἀλέξανδρος,
ἐκτάσσει τὴν στρατιὰν ὡς ἐς μάχην· καὶ Ἀλέξανδρος ἦγεν ὡσαύτως τεταγμένους. καὶ ἀπεῖχε μὲν

from Mesopotamian Syria were led by Mazaeus. 331
The number of Darius' forces was said to be 40,000 B.C.
horse, 1,000,000 foot, 200 chariots carrying scythes,[6]
and a few elephants; the Indians on this side of the
Indus had some fifteen.[7]

With this army Darius had encamped at Gauga- 7
mela by the River Bumelus, about six hundred stades
from the city of Arbela,[8] in a position level on all
sides. In fact where the ground was uneven for
cavalry, the Persians had for some time past been
making it easy for chariots to drive and for cavalry to
ride over;[9] for some argued that in the battle of Issus
Darius had really had the worst of it because of the
narrowness of the battlefield, and Darius very readily
assented.

9. On receiving this information from the captured
Persian scouts, Alexander stopped where he had
received it for four days; he rested his army after the
march and strengthened his camp by a ditch and
palisade, as he had decided to leave behind the
baggage animals and soldiers unfit for fighting, and
to advance to battle himself with his fit troops bur-
dened with nothing but their arms.[1] So taking his 2
force by night, he led them off just about the second
watch, so as to meet the enemy at dawn. Darius, on
hearing that Alexander was already advancing,
arrayed his army for battle, while Alexander was also
bringing up his army in battle array. The armies

[6] For description, D. 53, 2; QC. 9, 4 f.; previous use,
Xenophon, *Anabasis* i 6, 1; *Hellenica* iv 1, 17 ff.
[7] Appendix IX, 3.
[8] Cf. vi 11, 4 (Pt. and Ar.); P. 31, 3; Strabo xvi 1, 3.
QC. 9, 9 (unlike D. 53, 4) was perhaps aware of the truth.
[9] QC. 9, 10.
[1] QC. iv 10, 15. Yet some *impedimenta* were moved forward, cf. A. 12, 5; 14, 5; QC. 12, 3.

ἀλλήλων τὰ στρατόπεδα ὅσον ἑξήκοντα σταδίους,
οὐ μήν πω καθεώρων ἀλλήλους· γήλοφοι γὰρ ἐν
μέσῳ ἐπίπροσθεν ἀμφοῖν ἦσαν.

3 Ὡς δὲ ἀπεῖχεν Ἀλέξανδρος ὅσον ἐς τριάκοντα
σταδίους καὶ κατ' αὐτῶν ἤδη τῶν γηλόφων ᾔει
αὐτῷ ὁ στρατός, ἐνταῦθα, ὡς εἶδε τοὺς βαρβάρους,
ἔστησε τὴν αὑτοῦ φάλαγγα· καὶ ξυγκαλέσας αὖ
τούς τε ἑταίρους καὶ στρατηγοὺς καὶ ἰλάρχας καὶ
τῶν συμμάχων τε καὶ τῶν μισθοφόρων ξένων τοὺς
ἡγεμόνας ἐβουλεύετο, εἰ αὐτόθεν ἐπάγοι ἤδη τὴν
φάλαγγα, ὡς οἱ πλεῖστοι ἄγειν ἐκέλευον, ἢ καθάπερ
4 Παρμενίωνι [καλῶς] ἐδόκει, τότε μὲν αὐτοῦ
καταστρατοπεδεύειν, κατασκέψασθαι δὲ τόν τε
χῶρον ξύμπαντα, εἰ δή τι ὕποπτον αὐτοῦ ἢ ἄπορον,
ἢ εἴ πῃ τάφροι ἢ σκόλοπες καταπεπηγότες ἀφανεῖς,
καὶ τὰς τάξεις τῶν πολεμίων ἀκριβέστερον κατιδεῖν.
καὶ νικᾷ Παρμενίων τῇ γνώμῃ, καὶ καταστρατοπε-
δεύουσιν αὐτοῦ ὅπως τεταγμένοι ἔμελλον ἰέναι ἐς
τὴν μάχην.

5 Ἀλέξανδρος δὲ ἀναλαβὼν τοὺς ψιλοὺς καὶ τῶν
ἱππέων τοὺς ἑταίρους περιῄει ἐν κύκλῳ σκοπῶν τὴν
χώραν πᾶσαν, ἵνα τὸ ἔργον αὐτῷ ἔσεσθαι ἔμελλεν.
ἐπανελθὼν δὲ καὶ ξυγκαλέσας αὖθις τοὺς αὐτοὺς
ἡγεμόνας, αὐτοὺς μὲν οὐκ ἔφη χρῆναι παρακαλεῖ-
σθαι πρὸς οὗ ἐς τὸν ἀγῶνα· πάλαι γὰρ εἶναι δι'
ἀρετῆς τε τὴν σφῶν παρακεκλημένους καὶ ὑπὸ τῶν
6 πολλάκις ἤδη καλῶν ἔργων ἀποδεδειγμένων. τοὺς
κατὰ σφᾶς δὲ ἑκάστους ἐξορμᾶν ἠξίου, λοχαγόν τε
λοχίτας καὶ ἰλάρχην τὴν ἴλην τὴν αὑτοῦ ἕκαστον

---

² QC. makes them 150 stades apart (10, 15), interpolates
here an attempt by Darius to stir up disloyalty among Al's
Greek troops (10, 16 f.), the death of Darius' wife and the

331
B.C.

were about sixty stades apart, but had not yet
sighted one another, for there were hills intervening
in front of both.[2]

Alexander was about thirty stades away and his 3
army was already descending these hills, when he
sighted the enemy; he stopped his phalanx there, and
again summoned the Companions, generals, squadron
commanders and commanders of the allies and foreign
mercenary troops, and put the question whether he
should advance his phalanx at once from this point,
as most of them urged, or, as Parmenio thought best, 4
camp there for the time being, survey the whole of
the terrain, in case any part afforded ground for
suspicion or was impassable, or in case there were
ditches anywhere, or hidden stakes fixed in the soil,[3]
and make a thorough reconnaissance of the enemy's
dispositions. Parmenio's advice prevailed, and they
camped there, in the order in which they were to en-
gage in battle.

Taking with him the light-armed troops and the 5
Companion cavalry, Alexander rode all round, in-
specting the whole of the ground where his work was
to be done. Then he returned and again summoned
the same officers, and said that there was no need for
him to inspire them to the fight; they had long ago
been inspired by their own bravery and by their many
splendid exploits in the past; but he required each 6
of them to encourage his own men; the infantry
captains their companies, the squadron commanders

---

negotiations in A. ii 25, 1 (10, 18–12, 1; both before the Tigris
crossing in D. 54), and makes Persians as well as A. advance
and cause a panic in Al's army, which bivouacks; only on the
next day does Al. occupy the hills and call the council of
§ 3 (12, 14–24).

[3] For use of stakes, QC. 13, 36 f.

καὶ ταξιάρχους τὰς τάξεις, τούς τε ἡγεμόνας τῶν
πεζῶν τὴν φάλαγγα ἕκαστον τήν οἱ ἐπιτετραμ-
μένην, ὡς ἐν τῆδε τῇ μάχῃ οὐχ ὑπὲρ Κοίλης
Συρίας ἢ Φοινίκης, οὐδὲ ὑπὲρ Αἰγύπτου, ὡς πρόσθεν, μαχουμένους, ἀλλὰ ὑπὲρ τῆς ξυμπάσης
Ἀσίας, οὕστινας χρὴ ἄρχειν, ἐν τῷ τότε κρι-
7 θησόμενον. οὔκουν τὴν ἐς τὰ καλὰ ἐξόρμησιν διὰ
πολλῶν ἀναγκαίαν αὐτοῖς εἶναι οἴκοθεν τοῦτο
ἔχουσιν, ἀλλὰ κόσμου τε ἐν τῷ κινδύνῳ ὅπως τις
καθ᾽ αὑτὸν ἐπιμελήσεται καὶ σιγῆς ἀκριβοῦς,
ὁπότε σιγῶντας ἐπιέναι δέοι, καὶ αὖ λαμπρᾶς τῆς
βοῆς, ἵνα ἐμβοῆσαι καλόν, καὶ ἀλαλαγμοῦ ὡς
8 φοβερωτάτου, ὁπότε ἐπαλαλάξαι καιρός, αὐτοί τε
ὅπως ὀξέως κατακούοιεν τῶν [τε] παραγγελ-
λομένων καὶ παρ᾽ αὐτῶν αὖ ὅπως ἐς τὰς τάξεις
ὀξέως παραδιδῶνται τὰ παραγγέλματα· ἕν τε τῷ
καθ᾽ αὑτὸν ἕκαστον καὶ τὸ πᾶν μεμνῆσθαι ξυγκιν-
δυνεῦόν τε ἀμελουμένῳ καὶ δι᾽ ἐπιμελείας ἐκπο-
νουμένῳ ξυνορθούμενον.

10. Ταῦτα καὶ τοιαῦτα ἄλλα οὐ πολλὰ παρακαλέσας τε καὶ ἀντιπαρακληθεὶς πρὸς τῶν ἡγεμόνων
θαρρεῖν ἐπὶ σφίσι, δειπνοποιεῖσθαί τε καὶ ἀναπαύεσθαι ἐκέλευσε τὸν στρατόν. Παρμενίων δὲ λέγουσιν ὅτι ἀφικόμενος παρ᾽ αὐτὸν ἐπὶ τὴν σκηνήν,
νύκτωρ παρήνει ἐπιθέσθαι τοῖς Πέρσαις· ἀπροσδοκήτοις τε γὰρ καὶ ἀνατεταραγμένοις καὶ ἅμα ἐν
2 νυκτὶ φοβερωτέροις ἐπιθήσεσθαι. ὁ δὲ ἐκείνῳ μὲν
ἀποκρίνεται, ὅτι καὶ ἄλλοι κατήκουον τῶν λόγων,
αἰσχρὸν εἶναι κλέψαι τὴν νίκην, ἀλλὰ φανερῶς καὶ

---

⁴ Callisthenes imputed to Al. ' lengthy discourses ' with
the Greek allies just before the battle (P. 33, 1); at that point
D. 56, 4 and QC. 13, 38–14 *fin.* set speeches.

their own squadrons, the battalion commanders their
battalions, and the infantry commanders the phalanx
of which each was placed in charge. In this battle,
he pointed out, they were to fight, not as before, for
Hollow Syria or Phoenicia or Egypt: it was the
sovereignty of all Asia that was there and then to be
decided. There was then no need for them to employ 7
long speeches to make their men act with that sense
of honour which was born in them, but they were to
urge each man in the moment of danger to attend in
his own place in the line to the requirements of order,
to keep perfect silence when that was necessary in the
advance, and by contrast to give a ringing shout when
it was right to shout, and a howl to inspire the
greatest terror when the moment came to howl;
they themselves were to obey orders sharply and to 8
pass them on sharply to their regiments, and every
man should recall that neglect of his own duty
brought the whole cause into common danger, while
energetic attention to it contributed to the common
success.[4]

10. These and other such brief exhortations
brought in return assurances from the commanders
that he could rely on them. So he ordered his army
to take their meal and rest. They say [1] that Parmenio went to him in his tent and advised him to
attack the Persians at night; they would be surprised,
confused and more prone to panic in a night attack.
Alexander, however, replied, since others were 2
listening, that it was dishonourable to steal the vic-

---

[1] ' Vulgate ', or Pt. and Ar.? Unlike P. 31, 5 ff., QC. iv
13, 3 ff. transposes this to the council, where most (' the older
Companions ', P.) agreed with Parmenio.

ἄνευ σοφίσματος χρῆναι νικῆσαι Ἀλέξανδρον. καὶ τὸ μεγαλήγορον αὐτοῦ τοῦτο οὐχ ὑπέρογκον μᾶλλόν τι ἢ εὐθαρσὲς ἐν τοῖς κινδύνοις ἐφαίνετο· δοκεῖν δ' ἔμοιγε, καὶ λογισμῷ ἀκριβεῖ ἐχρήσατο ἐν

3 τῷ τοιῷδε· ἐν νυκτὶ γὰρ τοῖς τε ἀποχρώντως καὶ τοῖς ἐνδεῶς πρὸς τὰς μάχας παρεσκευασμένοις πολλὰ ἐκ τοῦ παραλόγου ξυμβάντα τοὺς μὲν ἔσφηλε, τοὺς κρείσσονας, τοῖς χείροσι δὲ παρὰ τὰ ἐξ ἀμφοῖν ἐλπισθέντα τὴν νίκην παρέδωκεν. αὐτῷ τε κινδυνεύοντι τὸ πολὺ ἐν ταῖς μάχαις σφαλερὰ ἡ νὺξ κατεφαίνετο, καὶ ἅμα ἡσσηθέντι τε αὖθις Δαρείῳ τὴν ξυγχώρησιν τοῦ χείρονι ὄντι χειρόνων ἡγεῖσθαι ἡ λαθραία τε καὶ νυκτερινὴ ἐκ

4 σφῶν ἐπίθεσις ἀφῃρεῖτο, εἴ τέ τι ἐκ τοῦ παραλόγου πταῖσμα σφίσι ξυμπέσοι, τοῖς μὲν πολεμίοις τὰ κύκλῳ φίλια καὶ αὐτοὶ τῆς χώρας ἔμπειροι, σφεῖς δὲ ἄπειροι ἐν πολεμίοις τοῖς πᾶσιν, ὧν οὐ μικρὰ μοῖρα οἱ αἰχμάλωτοι ἦσαν, ξυνεπιθησόμενοι ἐν νυκτὶ μὴ ὅτι πταίσασιν, ἀλλὰ καὶ εἰ μὴ παρὰ πολὺ νικῶντες φαίνοιντο. τούτων τε τῶν λογισμῶν ἕνεκα ἐπαινῶ Ἀλέξανδρον καὶ τοῦ ἐς τὸ φανερὸν ὑπερόγκου οὐ μεῖον.

11. Δαρεῖος δὲ καὶ ὁ ξὺν Δαρείῳ στρατὸς οὕτως ὅπως τὴν ἀρχὴν ἐτάξαντο ἔμειναν τῆς νυκτὸς ξυντεταγμένοι, ὅτι οὔτε στρατόπεδον αὐτοῖς περιεβέβλητο ἀκριβὲς καὶ ἅμα ἐφοβοῦντο μή σφισι

2 νύκτωρ ἐπιθοῖντο οἱ πολέμιοι. καὶ εἴπερ τι ἄλλο, καὶ τοῦτο ἐκάκωσε τοῖς Πέρσαις ἐν τῷ τότε τὰ πράγματα, ἡ στάσις ἡ πολλὴ ἡ ξὺν τοῖς ὅπλοις καὶ τὸ δέος, ὅ τι περ φιλεῖ πρὸ τῶν μεγάλων κινδύνων γίγνεσθαι, οὐκ ἐκ τοῦ παραυτίκα σχεδιασθέν, ἀλλ'

tory, and that Alexander had to win his victory openly
and without stratagem.[2] This grandiloquence looked
like confidence in danger rather than arrogance,[3] but
in my own view he made a careful calculation on some
such principle as this: at night, whether forces are
adequately or deficiently prepared for battle, things
have so often turned out contrary to rational ex-
pectation that the stronger side has been foiled and
victory gone to the weaker, contrary to the expecta-
tions of both. Though Alexander commonly ran
risks in battle, the hazards of the night were manifest
to him; moreover, if Darius were again defeated, the
fact that their attack had been covert and nocturnal
would prevent him conceding his inferiority and that
of the troops he commanded, but if his own Macedonian forces were to incur any incalculable reverse,
all the country round was friendly to the enemy and
familiar to them, while his own men had no knowledge of it, and enemies in everyone, no small part of
whom were the prisoners of war, and these would join
in attack by night, if the Macedonians should not be
clearly and decisively victorious, let alone if they were
to fail. These considerations, not less than the
arrogance he paraded, lead me to commend Alexander.

11. Darius and his army remained during the night
marshalled in their original order; for they had no
proper camp surrounding them, and they also feared
that the enemy would make a night attack. It did
more harm than anything else to the Persian cause at
this crisis, that they stood so long under arms and
that the fear, which usually precedes great dangers,

---

[2] So too QC. and P.
[3] A. probably means that the reply seemed arrogant, yet
really showed confidence, and in his own view prudence; his
comments were not original, cf. P. 31, 7 f.

ἐν πολλῷ χρόνῳ μελετηθέν τε καὶ τὰς γνώμας
αὐτοῖς δουλωσάμενον.

3 Ἐτάχθη δὲ αὐτῷ ἡ στρατιὰ ὧδε· ἑάλω γὰρ
ὕστερον ἡ τάξις, ἥντινα ἔταξε Δαρεῖος, γεγραμ-
μένη, ὡς λέγει Ἀριστόβουλος. τὸ μὲν εὐώνυμον
αὐτῷ κέρας οἵ τε Βάκτριοι ἱππεῖς εἶχον καὶ ξὺν
τούτοις Δάαι καὶ Ἀραχωτοί· ἐπὶ δὲ τούτοις
Πέρσαι ἐτετάχατο, ἱππεῖς τε ὁμοῦ καὶ πεζοὶ
ἀναμεμιγμένοι, καὶ Σούσιοι ἐπὶ Πέρσαις, ἐπὶ δὲ
4 Σουσίοις Καδούσιοι. αὕτη μὲν ἡ τοῦ εὐωνύμου
κέρως ἔστε ἐπὶ τὸ μέσον τῆς πάσης φάλαγγος
τάξις ἦν· κατὰ δὲ τὸ δεξιὸν οἵ τε ἐκ Κοίλης
Συρίας καὶ οἱ ἐκ τῆς μέσης τῶν ποταμῶν ἐτετάχατο, καὶ Μῆδοι ἔτι κατὰ τὸ δεξιόν, ἐπὶ δὲ
Παρθυαῖοι καὶ Σάκαι, ἐπὶ δὲ Τόπειροι καὶ
Ὑρκάνιοι, ἐπὶ δὲ Ἀλβανοὶ καὶ Σακεσ[ε]ῖναι,
οὗτοι μὲν ἔστε ἐπὶ τὸ μέσον τῆς πάσης φάλαγγος.
5 κατὰ τὸ μέσον δέ, ἵνα ἦν βασιλεὺς Δαρεῖος, οἵ τε
συγγενεῖς οἱ βασιλέως ἐτετάχατο καὶ οἱ μηλοφόροι
Πέρσαι καὶ Ἰνδοὶ καὶ Κᾶρες οἱ ἀνάσπαστοι
καλούμενοι καὶ οἱ Μάρδοι τοξόται· Οὔξιοι δὲ καὶ
Βαβυλώνιοι καὶ οἱ πρὸς τῇ ἐρυθρᾷ θαλάσσῃ καὶ
6 Σιττακηνοὶ εἰς βάθος ἐπιτεταγμένοι ἦσαν. προετετάχατο δὲ ἐπὶ μὲν τοῦ εὐωνύμου κατὰ τὸ δεξιὸν τοῦ
Ἀλεξάνδρου οἵ τε Σκύθαι ἱππεῖς καὶ τῶν Βακτριανῶν ἐς χιλίους καὶ ἅρματα δρεπανηφόρα ἑκατόν.

---

[1] Contra, QC. iv 13, 11–14.

[2] Perhaps from Callisthenes; where else? Pt. neglected
the information, but perhaps 8, 3 ff. represent his account;
Sogdianians and Areians only occur there, and Persians(!).
Dahae (= 'Scythians' of § 6; 13, 2; they lived in steppes east
of Caspian and north of the Parthyaeans) and Mardians only

was not produced suddenly by a crisis, but cultivated for a long period, till it mastered their minds.[1]

Darius' army was drawn up as follows (Aristobulus 3 tells us that a document giving the order as Darius drew it up was afterwards captured).[2] His left wing was held by the Bactrian cavalry with the Dahae and Arachotians; next to them Persians had been marshalled, cavalry and infantry mixed, and after the Persians Susians, and then Cadusians. This was the 4 disposition of the left wing up to the centre of the entire phalanx. On the right [3] had been marshalled the troops from Hollow Syria and Mesopotamia; and further to the right were Medes, then Parthyaeans and Sacians, then Topeirians and Hyrcanians, next Albanians and Sacesinians, right up to the centre of the entire phalanx. In the centre, with king Darius, 5 had been posted the king's kinsmen,[4] the Persians whose spears are fitted with golden apples,[5] the Indians, the 'transplanted' Carians, as they were called, and the Mardian bowmen.[6] The Uxians, Babylonians, Red Sea peoples and Sittacenians had been posted in deep formation behind them. Then, 6 in advance, on the left wing, facing Alexander's right, had been posted the Scythian cavalry, some thousand Bactrians, and a hundred chariots carrying scythes.

here; hence neither Ar. nor Pt. gave a full list, unless A. has excerpted carelessly. QC. 12, 5 ff. is different again.

[3] Commander, Mazaeus, D. 59, 5; by a slip QC. 15, 2 gives Bessus whom he correctly puts on the left in 12, 6.

[4] 1,000 strong, D. 59, 2; an honorific title, cf. 'Companions'.

[5] The royal bodyguard, 1,000 strong, with apples instead of spikes at butt-ends of spears, cf. Herodotus vii 40 f.

[6] D. 59, 2 ff. and QC. 14, 8, who divide the line into left and right, put Darius on the left, perhaps because in fact, the Persian line being longer, he was opposite Al. (A. 13, 1; 14, 2). Carians: 8, 5 n.

οἱ δὲ ἐλέφαντες ἔστησαν κατὰ τὴν [Δαρείου] [1]
ἴλην τὴν βασιλικὴν καὶ ἅρματα ἐς πεντήκοντα.
7 τοῦ δὲ δεξιοῦ οἵ τε Ἀρμενίων καὶ Καππαδοκῶν
ἱππεῖς προετετάχατο καὶ ἅρματα δρεπανηφόρα
πεντήκοντα. οἱ δὲ Ἕλληνες οἱ μισθοφόροι παρὰ
Δαρεῖόν τε αὐτὸν ἑκατέρωθεν καὶ τοὺς ἅμα αὐτῷ
Πέρσας κατὰ τὴν φάλαγγα αὐτὴν τῶν Μακεδόνων
ὡς μόνοι δὴ ἀντίρροποι τῇ φάλαγγι ἐτάχθησαν.
8 Ἀλεξάνδρῳ δὲ ἡ στρατιὰ ἐκοσμήθη ὧδε. τὸ
μὲν δεξιὸν αὐτῷ εἶχον τῶν ἱππέων οἱ ἑταῖροι, ὧν
προετέτακτο ἡ ἴλη ἡ βασιλική, ἧς Κλεῖτος ὁ
Δρωπίδου ἰλάρχης ἦν, ἐπὶ δὲ ταύτῃ Γλαυκίου ἴλη,
ἐχομένη δ' αὐτῆς ἡ Ἀρίστωνος, ἐπὶ δὲ ἡ Σωπόλιδος τοῦ Ἑρμοδώρου, ἐπὶ δὲ ἡ Ἡρακλείδου τοῦ
Ἀντιόχου, ἐπὶ ταύτῃ δὲ ἡ Δημητρίου τοῦ Ἀλθαι-
μένους, ταύτης δὲ ἐχομένη ἡ Μελεάγρου, τελευταία
δὲ τῶν [βασιλικῶν] [2] ἰλῶν ἧς Ἡγέλοχος ὁ
Ἱπποστράτου ἰλάρχης ἦν. ξυμπάσης δὲ τῆς ἵππου
9 τῶν ἑταίρων Φιλώτας ἦρχεν ὁ Παρμενίωνος. τῆς
δὲ φάλαγγος τῶν Μακεδόνων ἐχόμενον τῶν ἱππέων πρῶτον τὸ ἄγημα ἐτέτακτο τῶν ὑπασπιστῶν
καὶ ἐπὶ τούτῳ οἱ ἄλλοι ὑπασπισταί· ἡγεῖτο δὲ
αὐτῶν Νικάνωρ ὁ Παρμενίωνος· τούτων δὲ
ἐχομένη ἡ Κοίνου τοῦ Πολεμοκράτους τάξις ἦν,
μετὰ δὲ τούτους ἡ Περδίκκου τοῦ Ὀρόντου, ἔπειτα
ἡ Μελεάγρου τοῦ Νεοπτολέμου, ἐπὶ δὲ ἡ Πολυπέρχοντος τοῦ Σιμμίου, ἐπὶ δὲ ἡ Ἀμύντου τοῦ
Φιλίππου· ταύτης δὲ ἡγεῖτο Σιμμίας, ὅτι Ἀμύντας
ἐπὶ Μακεδονίας ἐς ξυλλογὴν στρατιᾶς ἐσταλμένος
10 ἦν. τὸ δὲ εὐώνυμον τῆς φάλαγγος τῶν Μακεδόνων

---

[1] Deleted by Gronovius.
[2] I have bracketed βασιλικῶν.

The elephants were posted ahead of [Darius'] royal
squadron, with fifty chariots. In front of the right
wing had been posted the Armenian and Cappadocian
cavalry and fifty chariots carrying scythes. The
Greek mercenaries [7] were stationed on either side of
Darius and of the Persian troops with him, exactly
opposite the Macedonian phalanx, as they were
considered the only troops capable of being a counter-
poise to it.

Alexander's army was marshalled as follows.[8] His
right wing was held by the Companion cavalry, the
royal squadron in front; it was commanded by
Clitus son of Dropides; in successive order came those
of Glaucias, Aristo, Sopolis son of Hermodorus,
Heraclides son of Antiochus, Demetrius son of Althae-
menes, Meleager and lastly that commanded by
Hegelochus son of Hippostratus. The Companion
cavalry as a whole was commanded by Philotas son of
Parmenio. As for the Macedonian infantry phalanx,
the *agema* of the hypaspists was stationed first next
the cavalry and then the rest of the hypaspists; they
were under Nicanor son of Parmenio; then came successively the battalions of Coenus son of Polemocrates, Perdiccas son of Orontes, Meleager son of
Neoptolemus, Polyperchon son of Simmias and
Amyntas son of Philip;[9] this was led by Simmias,
since Amyntas had been sent to Macedonia to collect
troops. The left of the Macedonian phalanx was

---

[7] Cf. 7, 1; never mentioned by D. and QC.

[8] Cf. D. 57, 1–4; QC. 13, 26 ff., incomplete extracts from a
common source which (i) gave the hypaspists the anachronistic
name of silver-shields; (ii) gave the ethnic composition of
phalanx battalions (cf. A. 16, 11); (iii) substituted Philip for
Simmias as taxiarch.

[9] An error for Andromenes, cf. 16, 10 and often.

ἡ Κρατεροῦ τοῦ Ἀλεξάνδρου τάξις εἶχε, καὶ αὐτὸς
Κρατερὸς ἐξῆρχε τοῦ εὐωνύμου τῶν πεζῶν· καὶ
ἱππεῖς ἐχόμενοι αὐτοῦ οἱ ξύμμαχοι, ὧν ἡγεῖτο
Ἐριγύϊος ὁ Λαρίχου· τούτων δὲ ἐχόμενοι ὡς ἐπὶ
τὸ εὐώνυμον κέρας οἱ Θεσσαλοὶ ἱππεῖς, ὧν ἦρχε
Φίλιππος ὁ Μενελάου. ξύμπαν δὲ τὸ εὐώνυμον
ἦγε Παρμενίων ὁ Φιλώτα, καὶ ἀμφ᾽ αὐτὸν οἱ τῶν
Φαρσαλίων ἱππεῖς οἱ κράτιστοί τε καὶ πλεῖστοι τῆς
Θεσσαλικῆς ἵππου ἀνεστρέφοντο.

12. Ἡ μὲν ἐπὶ μετώπου τάξις Ἀλεξάνδρῳ ὧδε
κεκόσμητο· ἐπέταξε δὲ καὶ δευτέραν τάξιν ὡς
εἶναι τὴν φάλαγγα ἀμφίστομον. καὶ παρηγγέλλετο
τοῖς ἡγεμόσι τῶν ἐπιτεταγμένων, εἰ κυκλουμένους
τοὺς σφῶν πρὸς τοῦ Περσικοῦ στρατεύματος
κατίδοιεν, ἐπιστρέψαντας ἐς τὸ ἔμπαλιν δέχεσθαι
2 τοὺς βαρβάρους· ἐς ἐπικαμπὴν δέ, εἴ που ἀνάγκη
καταλαμβάνοι ἢ ἀναπτύξαι ἢ ξυγκλεῖσαι τὴν
φάλαγγα, κατὰ μὲν τὸ δεξιὸν κέρας ἐχόμενοι τῆς
βασιλικῆς ἴλης τῶν Ἀγριάνων ἐτάχθησαν οἱ
ἡμίσεες, ὧν ἡγεῖτο Ἄτταλος, καὶ μετὰ τούτων οἱ
Μακεδόνες οἱ τοξόται, ὧν Βρίσων ἦρχεν, ἐχόμενοι
δὲ τῶν τοξοτῶν οἱ ἀρχαῖοι καλούμενοι ξένοι καὶ
3 ἄρχων τούτων Κλέανδρος. προετάχθησαν δὲ τῶν
τε Ἀγριάνων καὶ τῶν τοξοτῶν οἵ τε πρόδρομοι
ἱππεῖς καὶ οἱ Παίονες, ὧν Ἀρέτης καὶ Ἀρίστων
ἡγοῦντο. ξυμπάντων δὲ προτεταγμένοι ἦσαν οἱ
μισθοφόροι ἱππεῖς, ὧν Μενίδας ἦρχε. τῆς δὲ
βασιλικῆς ἴλης καὶ τῶν ἄλλων ἑταίρων προτεταγμένοι ἦσαν τῶν τε Ἀγριάνων καὶ τῶν τοξοτῶν οἱ

---

10 Part only, cf. 12, 4.
1 Clearly hoplites, i.e. Greek allies (not otherwise mentioned)

held by the battalion of Craterus son of Alexander, who also commanded the (entire) left of the infantry. Next to them came the allied cavalry,[10] under Erigyius son of Larichus; next them, on the left wing, were the Thessalian cavalry under Philippus son of Menelaus. The commander of the entire left was Parmenio son of Philotas, and round him rode the Pharsalian cavalry, the finest and most numerous of the Thessalian horsemen.

12. This was the order in which Alexander had marshalled his front, but he also posted a second line, so that his phalanx faced both ways.[1] The commanders of this reserve had instructions to face about and receive the barbarian attack, if they saw their own forces being surrounded by the Persian army. However, in case a need arose to extend or contract 2 the line, on the right wing but at an angle to it,[2] half the Agrianians under Attalus were posted next to the royal squadron, along with the Macedonian archers under Brison, and next to the archers the so-called old mercenaries under Cleander; in front of the 3 Agrianians and archers cavalry were stationed, consisting of the *prodromoi* and the Paeonians under the command of Aretas and Ariston, and in front of all these the mercenary cavalry[3] under Menidas. The royal squadron and the other Companions had half the Agrianians and archers[4] stationed in their front

and mercenaries other than Cleander's force, which comprised either (i) those who had crossed to Asia with Al. or (ii) those previously sent there by Philip, as against (iii) later reinforcements.
  [2] The translation is certain, but cf. App. IX 2.
  [3] Some only, cf. § 5.
  [4] Macedonians?

ἡμίσεες, καὶ οἱ Βαλάκρου ἀκοντισταί· οὗτοι κατὰ
4 ⟨τὰ⟩ ἅρματα τὰ δρεπανηφόρα ἐτετάχατο. Μενίδα
δὲ καὶ τοῖς ἀμφ' αὐτὸν παρήγγελτο, εἰ περιίπ-
πεύοιεν οἱ πολέμιοι τὸ κέρας σφῶν, ἐς πλαγίους
ἐμβάλλειν αὐτοὺς ἐπικάμψαντας. τὰ μὲν ἐπὶ τοῦ
δεξιοῦ κέρως οὕτως ἐτέτακτο Ἀλεξάνδρῳ· κατὰ
δὲ τὸ εὐώνυμον ἐς ἐπικαμπὴν οἵ τε Θρᾶκες
ἐτετάχατο, ὧν ἡγεῖτο Σιτάλκης, καὶ ἐπὶ τούτοις οἱ
ξύμμαχοι ἱππεῖς, ὧν ἦρχε Κοίρανος,[1] ἐπὶ δὲ οἱ
Ὀδρύσαι ἱππεῖς, ὧν ἡγεῖτο Ἀγάθων ὁ Τυρίμμα.
5 ξυμπάντων δὲ ταύτῃ προετάχθη ἡ ξενικὴ ἵππος ἡ
τῶν μισθοφόρων, ὧν Ἀνδρόμαχος ὁ Ἱέρωνος
ἦρχεν. ἐπὶ δὲ τοῖς σκευοφόροις οἱ ἀπὸ Θρᾴκης
πεζοὶ ἐς φυλακὴν ἐτάχθησαν. ⟨ἦν δὲ⟩ ἡ πᾶσα
στρατιὰ Ἀλεξάνδρου ἱππεῖς μὲν ἐς ἑπτακισχιλίους,
πεζοὶ δὲ ἀμφὶ τὰς τέσσαρας μυριάδας.

13. Ὡς δὲ ὁμοῦ ἤδη τὰ στρατόπεδα ἐγίγνετο,
ὤφθη Δαρεῖός τε καὶ οἱ ἀμφ' αὐτόν, οἵ τε μηλοφόροι Πέρσαι καὶ Ἰνδοὶ καὶ Ἀλβανοὶ καὶ Κᾶρες οἱ
ἀνάσπαστοι καὶ οἱ Μάρδοι τοξόται, κατ' αὐτὸν
Ἀλέξανδρον τεταγμένοι καὶ τὴν ἴλην τὴν βασιλικήν. ἦγε δὲ ὡς ἐπὶ τὸ δεξιὸν τὸ αὑτοῦ Ἀλέξανδρος μᾶλλον, καὶ οἱ Πέρσαι ἀντιπαρῆγον,
ὑπερφαλαγγοῦντες πολὺ ἐπὶ τῷ σφῶν εὐωνύμῳ.
2 ἤδη τε οἱ τῶν Σκυθῶν ἱππεῖς παριππεύοντες
ἥπτοντο τῶν προτεταγμένων τῆς Ἀλεξάνδρου
τάξεως καὶ Ἀλέξανδρος ἔτι ὅμως ἦγεν ἐπὶ δόρυ,
καὶ ἐγγὺς ἦν τοῦ ἐξαλλάσσειν τὸν ὡδοποιημένον

---

[1] Κοίρανος; perhaps rather Κάρανος (cf. iii 28, 2; iv 3, 7;
5, 7; 6, 2, but Berve nos. 412 and 442 distinguishes them).

[5] Probably Balkan troops.

with the javelin-men of Balacrus;[5] they were posted
opposite the chariots carrying scythes.   Menidas and   4
his men had instructions to wheel at an angle and
attack the enemy on the flank, if they rode round
their wing.   This was the disposition of Alexander's
right; on the left at an angle he posted the Thracians
under Sitalces' command,[6] and next them the allied
cavalry under Coeranus, and then the Odrysian horse
under Agathon, son of Tyrimmas.[7]   Here, in front of   5
the whole force, was stationed the foreign mercenary
cavalry under Andromachus, son of Hieron.   The
Thracian foot [8] were posted to guard the baggage
animals.   Alexander's entire army numbered some
7,000 cavalry and about 40,000 infantry.[9]

13. As the armies were now nearing one another,
Darius and his immediate followers were in full sight;
there were the Persians ' with the Golden Apples ',
Indians, Albanians, the ' transplanted ' Carians and
the Mardian archers, all ranged opposite Alexander
himself and the royal squadron.   But Alexander
moved his men rather in the direction of his right, on
which the Persians moved accordingly, their left far
outflanking Alexander's army.[1]   The Scythian cav-   2
alry, riding along Alexander's line, were already in
contact with the troops posted in front of it; but
Alexander still continued steadily his march towards
his right, and was nearly clear of the ground which

---

[6] Javelin-men, cf. i 28, 4.

[7] The Thracians of i 14, 3.   D. 57, 5 puts the Cretan archers
on the left, where they could have fulfilled the same function
as Brison's men on the right.   Another omission in A. or his
sources.

[8] Other than Sitalces' men.

[9] App. IX 3.

[1] Cf. perhaps D. 57, 6; QC. iv 15, 1.   For the battle cf.
App. IX.

ARRIAN

πρὸς τῶν Περσῶν χῶρον. ἔνθα δὴ δείσας Δαρεῖος
μὴ προχωρησάντων ἐς τὰ οὐχ ὁμαλὰ τῶν Μακεδόνων ἀχρεῖά σφισι γένηται τὰ ἅρματα, κελεύει
τοὺς προτεταγμένους τοῦ εὐωνύμου περιιππεύειν τὸ
κέρας τὸ δεξιόν, ᾗ Ἀλέξανδρος ἦγε, τοῦ μηκέτι
3 προσωτέρω αὐτοὺς ἐξάγειν τὸ κέρας. τούτου δὲ
γενομένου Ἀλέξανδρος ἐμβάλλειν κελεύει ἐς αὐτοὺς
τοὺς μισθοφόρους ἱππέας, ὧν Μενίδας ἡγεῖτο.
ἀντεκδραμόντες δὲ ἐπ' αὐτοὺς οἵ τε Σκύθαι ἱππεῖς
καὶ τῶν Βακτρίων οἱ ξυντεταγμένοι τοῖς Σκύθαις
τρέπουσιν ὀλίγους ὄντας πολλῷ πλείονες. Ἀλέξανδρος δὲ τοὺς περὶ Ἀρίστωνα[1] τε, τοὺς Παίονας,
καὶ τοὺς ξένους ἐμβαλεῖν τοῖς Σκύθαις ἐκέλευσε·
4 καὶ ἐγκλίνουσιν οἱ βάρβαροι. Βάκτριοι δὲ οἱ ἄλλοι
πελάσαντες τοῖς Παίοσί τε καὶ ξένοις τούς τε
σφῶν φεύγοντας ἤδη ἀνέστρεψαν ἐς τὴν μάχην καὶ
τὴν ἱππομαχίαν ξυστῆναι ἐποίησαν. καὶ ἔπιπτον
μὲν πλείονες τῶν Ἀλεξάνδρου, τῷ τε πλήθει τῶν
βαρβάρων βιαζόμενοι καὶ ὅτι αὐτοί τε οἱ Σκύθαι
καὶ οἱ ἵπποι αὐτοῖς ἀκριβέστερον εἰς φυλακὴν
πεφραγμένοι ἦσαν. ἀλλὰ καὶ ὣς τάς τε προσβολὰς
αὐτῶν ἐδέχοντο οἱ Μακεδόνες καὶ βίᾳ κατ' ἴλας
προσπίπτοντες ἐξώθουν ἐκ τῆς τάξεως.
5 Καὶ ἐν τούτῳ τὰ ἅρματα τὰ δρεπανηφόρα ἐφῆκαν
οἱ βάρβαροι κατ' αὐτὸν Ἀλέξανδρον, ὡς ἀναταρά-
ξοντες αὐτῷ τὴν φάλαγγα. καὶ ταύτῃ μάλιστα
ἐψεύσθησαν· τὰ μὲν γὰρ εὐθὺς ὡς προσεφέρετο
κατηκόντισαν οἵ τε Ἀγριᾶνες καὶ οἱ ξὺν Βαλάκρῳ

[1] Ἀρίστωνα Schmeider: Ἀρέτην codd.

[2] Aretas in the manuscripts, but the *prodromoi* are not
named, and cf. 14, 1, which, however, Schwartz (Introd. n. 24)
took to be Pt's version of 13, 1–4 (Ar.). And cf. §4 n. 4.

had been made a treadable level by the Persians.
This made Darius fear that if the Macedonians
reached the uneven ground his chariots would cease
to be of service, and he ordered the troops in advance
of his left wing to ride round the Macedonian right,
where Alexander was leading, so that they might not
prolong their wing any farther. In reply Alexander 3
ordered his mercenary cavalry under Menidas to
charge them. At once the Scythian cavalry and
those of the Bactrians brigaded with them rushed out
in a counter-charge, and drove them back, as they
were far more numerous than Menidas' small squadron. But Alexander ordered the Paeonians with
Ariston[2] and the mercenaries to charge the Scythians,
and the barbarians wavered. The rest of the Bac- 4
trians, however, came up against the Paeonians and
mercenaries, restored to the battle those on their own
side who were then turning to flight, and made the
cavalry engagement a close one. Alexander's men
fell in greater numbers, under pressure from the
number of the barbarians, and also because the
Scythians, riders and horses alike, were better protected by defensive armour. Yet even so the
Macedonians[3] stood up against their onsets, attacked
vigorously, squadron after squadron,[4] and broke their
formation.

At this point the Persians launched their scythe- 5
carrying chariots direct against Alexander, to throw
his line out of formation; but in this they were sig-
nally disappointed. For first, as they approached, the
Agrianians and the javelin-men under Balacrus, who

---

[3] i.e. Al's troops, cf. 14, 5 for lack of ethnic meaning.
[4] Odd, if only Menidas' and Ariston's squadrons were
engaged.

ἀκοντισταὶ οἱ προτεταγμένοι τῆς ἵππου τῶν
ἑταίρων· τὰ δὲ τῶν ῥυτήρων ἀντιλαμβανόμενοι
τούς τε ἀναβάτας κατέσπων καὶ τοὺς ἵππους
6 περιϊστάμενοι ἔκοπτον. ἔστι δὲ ἃ καὶ διεξέπεσε
διὰ τῶν τάξεων· διέσχον γάρ, ὥσπερ παρήγγελτο
αὐτοῖς, ἵνα προσέπιπτε τὰ ἅρματα· καὶ ταύτῃ
μάλιστα ξυνέβη αὐτά τε σῶα καὶ οἷς ἐπηλάθη
ἀβλαβῶς διελθεῖν· ἀλλὰ καὶ τούτων οἵ τε ἱπποκό-
μοι τῆς Ἀλεξάνδρου στρατιᾶς καὶ οἱ ὑπασπισταὶ οἱ
βασιλικοὶ ἐκράτησαν.

14. Ὡς δὲ Δαρεῖος ἐπῆγεν ἤδη τὴν φάλαγγα
πᾶσαν, ἐνταῦθα Ἀλέξανδρος Ἀρέτην μὲν κελεύει
ἐμβαλεῖν τοῖς περιϊππεύουσι τὸ κέρας σφῶν τὸ
2 δεξιὸν ὡς ἐς κύκλωσιν· αὐτὸς δὲ τέως μὲν ἐπὶ
κέρως τοὺς ἀμφ' αὐτὸν ἦγε, τῶν δὲ ἐκβοηθησά-
ντων ἱππέων τοῖς κυκλουμένοις τὸ κέρας τὸ δεξιὸν
παραρρηξάντων τι τῆς πρώτης φάλαγγος τῶν
βαρβάρων ἐπιστρέψας κατὰ τὸ διέχον καὶ ὥσπερ
ἔμβολον ποιήσας τῆς τε ἵππου τῆς ἑταιρικῆς καὶ
τῆς φάλαγγος τῆς ταύτῃ τεταγμένης ἦγε δρόμῳ τε
3 καὶ ἀλαλαγμῷ ὡς ἐπ' αὐτὸν Δαρεῖον. καὶ χρόνον
μέν τινα ὀλίγον ἐν χερσὶν ἡ μάχη ἐγένετο· ὡς δὲ οἵ
τε ἱππεῖς οἱ ἀμφὶ Ἀλέξανδρον καὶ αὐτὸς Ἀλέξανδρος εὐρώστως ἐνέκειντο ὠθισμοῖς τε χρώμενοι
καὶ τοῖς ξυστοῖς τὰ πρόσωπα· τῶν Περσῶν
κόπτοντες, ἥ τε φάλαγξ ἡ Μακεδονικὴ πυκνὴ καὶ
ταῖς σαρίσσαις πεφρικυῖα ἐμβεβλήκει ἤδη αὐτοῖς,
καὶ πάντα ὁμοῦ τὰ δεινὰ καὶ πάλαι ἤδη φοβερῷ
ὄντι Δαρείῳ ἐφαίνετο, πρῶτος αὐτὸς ἐπιστρέψας
ἔφευγεν· ἐφοβήθησαν δὲ καὶ οἱ περιϊππεύοντες τῶν

had been stationed in front of the Companion cavalry, met them with volleys; and then they snatched hold of the reins, pulled down the drivers, and crowding round the horses, cut them down. Some did pass 6 right through the Greek lines, which, as they had been ordered, parted where the chariots attacked; this was the main reason why the chariots passed through unscathed and the troops against which they were launched were unharmed. These chariots too were overpowered by the grooms of Alexander's army and the royal hypaspists.[5]

14. When Darius now attacked all along the line, Alexander ordered Aretas to charge the Persian cavalry which was riding round his right wing to encircle it; he himself for a short time led on his army 2 in column;[1] but when the cavalry, sent off to attack the Persians who were encircling the right wing, had in some degree broken the front of the Persian phalanx, he wheeled towards the gap, and making a wedge [2] of the Companion cavalry and the part of the phalanx stationed there, led them on at the double with a loud battle cry straight at Darius. Now for a 3 little time it became a hand-to-hand fight, but when the cavalry with Alexander, and Alexander himself, pressed vigorously, shoving the Persians and striking their faces with their spears, and the Macedonian phalanx, solid and bristling with its pikes, had got to close quarters with them, and Darius, who had now long been in a panic, saw nothing but terrors all around, he was himself the first to turn and flee. The Persians who were trying on horseback to

---

[5] Inexplicable, as 11, 9 puts them in the front line.
[1] Presumably referring to his oblique advance.
[2] Marsden, *Campaign of Gaugamela* 68 f., shows how this applies to the horse, but not to the foot.

Περσῶν τὸ κέρας ἐμβαλόντων ἐς αὐτοὺς εὐρώστως
τῶν ἀμφὶ Ἀρέτην.

4 Ταύτῃ μὲν δὴ τῶν Περσῶν φυγὴ καρτερὰ ἦν,
καὶ οἱ Μακεδόνες ἐφεπόμενοι ἐφόνευον τοὺς
φεύγοντας. οἱ δὲ ἀμφὶ Σιμμίαν καὶ ἡ τούτου τάξις
οὐκέτι ξυνεξορμῆσαι Ἀλεξάνδρῳ δυνατοὶ ἐγένοντο
ἐς τὴν δίωξιν, ἀλλ᾽ ἐπιστήσαντες τὴν φάλαγγα
αὐτοῦ ἠγωνίζοντο, ὅτι τὸ εὐώνυμον τῶν Μακε-
5 δόνων πονεῖσθαι ἠγγέλλετο. καὶ ταύτῃ παραρ-
ραγείσης αὐτοῖς τῆς τάξεως κατὰ τὸ διέχον
διεκπαίουσι τῶν τε Ἰνδῶν τινες καὶ τῆς Περσικῆς
ἵππου ὡς ἐπὶ τὰ σκευοφόρα τῶν Μακεδόνων· καὶ
τὸ ἔργον ἐκεῖ καρτερὸν ἐγίγνετο. οἵ τε γὰρ
Πέρσαι θρασέως προσέκειντο ἀνόπλοις τοῖς πολλοῖς
καὶ οὐ προσδοκήσασιν ἐπὶ σφᾶς διεκπεσεῖσθαί
τινας διακόψαντας διπλῆν τὴν φάλαγγα, καὶ οἱ
αἰχμάλωτοι βάρβαροι ἐμβαλόντων τῶν Περσῶν
ξυνεπέθεντο καὶ αὐτοὶ τοῖς Μακεδόσιν ἐν τῷ ἔργῳ.
6 τῶν δὲ ἐπιτεταγμένων τῇ πρώτῃ φάλαγγι οἱ
ἡγεμόνες ὀξέως μαθόντες τὸ γιγνόμενον μεταβα-
λόντες, ᾗπερ παρήγγελτο αὐτοῖς, τὴν τάξιν ἐπιγί-
γνονται κατὰ νώτου τοῖς Πέρσαις, καὶ πολλοὺς μὲν
αὐτῶν αὐτοῦ ἀμφὶ τοῖς σκευοφόροις ξυνεχομένους
ἀπέκτειναν, οἱ δὲ αὐτῶν ἐγκλίναντες ἔφευγον. οἱ
δ᾽ ἐπὶ τοῦ δεξιοῦ κέρως τῶν Περσῶν οὔπω τῆς
φυγῆς τῆς Δαρείου ᾐσθημένοι περιιππεύσαντες τὸ
Ἀλεξάνδρου εὐώνυμον κατὰ κέρας τοῖς ἀμφὶ τὸν
Παρμενίωνα ἐνέβαλλον.

15. Καὶ ἐν τούτῳ ἀμφιβόλων τὰ πρῶτα γενομένων τῶν Μακεδόνων πέμπει Παρμενίων παρ᾽
Ἀλέξανδρον σπουδῇ ἀγγελοῦντα, ὅτι ἐν ἀγῶνι
ξυνέχεται τὸ κατὰ σφᾶς καὶ βοηθεῖν δεῖ. ταῦτα

envelop the Macedonian right also took fright at the
vigorous charge of Aretas and his men.

At this place indeed the Persian rout was complete, 4
and the Macedonians in pursuit were slaughtering the
fugitives. But Simmias and his battalion were no
longer able to join Alexander in the pursuit, but had
halted their phalanx and were fighting where they
stood, since the Macedonian left was reported to be
in difficulties. At this point their line had been 5
broken, and into the gap some Indians and Persian
cavalry made a thrust right up to the Macedonians'
baggage animals. There the action was becoming
severe, for the Persians fell boldly on men who were
mostly unarmed and had never expected that anyone
would cut through the double line of the phalanx and
get right through to attack them; what is more, the
captive barbarians themselves, as the Persians broke
in, joined with them in the action and attacked the
Macedonians. However, the commanders of the 6
troops which formed the reserve to the first phalanx
quickly learned what had happened, turned about
face, according to previous orders, appeared in the
rear of the Persians, and killed large numbers of them
there, crowded together round the baggage animals.
Some, however, gave way and escaped. The Persians
of the right wing, who had not yet noticed Darius'
flight, wheeling round Alexander's left, were assailing
Parmenio's troops.

15. At this juncture, since at first the Macedonians
were between two fires, Parmenio sent a despatch
rider to Alexander to report with all haste that his
troops were in distress and needed help. On receiv-

ὡς ἐξηγγέλθη Ἀλεξάνδρῳ, τοῦ μὲν διώκειν ἔτι
ἀπετράπετο, ἐπιστρέψας δὲ ξὺν τῇ ἵππῳ τῶν
ἑταίρων ὡς ἐπὶ τὸ δεξιὸν τῶν βαρβάρων ἦγε
δρόμῳ. καὶ πρῶτα μὲν τοῖς φεύγουσι τῶν πολεμίων ἱππεῦσι, τοῖς τε Παρθυαίοις καὶ τῶν Ἰνδῶν
ἔστιν οἷς καὶ Πέρσαις τοῖς πλείστοις καὶ κρατίστοις
2 ἐμβάλλει. καὶ ἱππομαχία αὕτη καρτερωτάτη τοῦ
παντὸς ἔργου ξυνέστη. ἐς βάθος τε γὰρ οἷα δὴ
ἰληδὸν τεταγμένοι ἀνέστρεφον οἱ βάρβαροι καὶ
ἀντιμέτωποι τοῖς ἀμφ' Ἀλέξανδρον ξυμπεσόντες
οὔτε ἀκοντισμῷ ἔτι οὔτ' ἐξελιγμοῖς τῶν ἵππων,
ἥπερ ἱππομαχίας δίκη, ἐχρῶντο, ἀλλὰ διεκπαῖσαι
πᾶς τις τὸ καθ' αὑτόν, ὡς μόνην ταύτην σωτηρίαν
σφίσιν οὖσαν, ἐπειγόμενοι ἔκοπτόν τε καὶ ἐκόπτο-
ντο ἀφειδῶς, οἷα δὴ οὐχ ὑπὲρ νίκης ἀλλοτρίας ἔτι,
ἀλλ' ὑπὲρ σωτηρίας οἰκείας ἀγωνιζόμενοι. καὶ
ἐνταῦθα πίπτουσι μὲν ἀμφὶ ἑξήκοντα τῶν ἑταίρων
τοῦ Ἀλεξάνδρου, καὶ τιτρώσκεται Ἡφαιστίων τε
αὐτὸς καὶ Κοῖνος καὶ Μενίδας· ἀλλὰ ἐκράτησε καὶ
τούτων Ἀλέξανδρος.

3   Καὶ τούτων μὲν ὅσοι διεξέπαισαν διὰ τῶν ἀμφ'
Ἀλέξανδρον ἔφευγον ἀνὰ κράτος· Ἀλέξανδρος δὲ
ἐγγὺς ἦν προσμῖξαι ἤδη τῷ δεξιῷ κέρατι τῶν
πολεμίων. καὶ ἐν τούτῳ οἱ Θεσσαλοὶ ἱππεῖς
λαμπρῶς ἀγωνισάμενοι οὐχ ὑπελείποντο Ἀλεξάνδρῳ τοῦ ἔργου· ἀλλὰ ἔφευγον γὰρ ἤδη οἱ ἀπὸ
τοῦ δεξιοῦ κέρως τῶν βαρβάρων, ὁπότε Ἀλέξανδρος αὐτοῖς ξυνέμιξεν, ὥστε ἀποτραπόμενος
Ἀλέξανδρος ἐς τὸ διώκειν αὖθις Δαρεῖον ἐξώρμησε·
4 καὶ ἐδίωξεν ἔστε φάος ἦν· καὶ οἱ ἀμφὶ Παρμενίωνα τὸ καθ' αὑτοὺς διώκοντες εἵποντο. ἀλλὰ
Ἀλέξανδρος μὲν διαβὰς τὸν ποταμὸν τὸν Λύκον

ing this message, Alexander turned back from further pursuit, and wheeling round with the Companion cavalry, came galloping down on the Persian right and charged first the enemy cavalry in flight, the Parthyaeans, some Indians and the Persians, the most numerous and best of the enemy forces. This proved 2 the fiercest cavalry engagement of the whole action. The barbarians, who were drawn up in depth, since they were in squadrons, rallied, and clashed with Alexander's troops front to front: there was no more javelin-throwing and no manoeuvring of horses, as usual in a cavalry engagement, but each strove hard to break his own way through; they kept on giving and taking blows unsparingly, treating this as the one hope of safety, inasmuch as they were men now no longer fighting for another's victory, but for their own very lives. There about sixty of the Companions of Alexander fell, and Hephaestion himself, Coenus and Menidas were wounded. Still, Alexander overcame these enemies also.

Those of the Persians who broke their way through 3 Alexander's troops took to headlong flight, and Alexander was now ready to come to blows with the enemy's right wing. Meanwhile the Thessalian cavalry, who fought brilliantly, showed no inferiority to Alexander in the action; in fact the barbarian right were already in flight when Alexander encountered them. So Alexander turned away and resumed his pursuit of Darius, which lasted as long as the light held; and Parmenio's troops followed, 4 pursuing their opponents. However, when Alexander had crossed the river Lycus,[1] he encamped there,

---

[1] Greater Zab. Cf. D. 61, 1 f.; QC iv 16, 7 ff.; v 1, 3–10 for Darius' flight and the pursuit to Arbela.

κατεστρατοπέδευσεν αὐτοῦ, ὡς ἀναπαῦσαι ὀλίγον
τούς τε ἄνδρας καὶ τοὺς ἵππους· Παρμενίων δὲ τό
τε στρατόπεδον τῶν βαρβάρων εἷλε καὶ τὰ σκευοφόρα καὶ τοὺς ἐλέφαντας καὶ τὰς καμήλους.

5 Ἀλέξανδρος δὲ ἀναπαύσας τοὺς ἀμφ' αὑτὸν
ἱππέας ἔστε ἐπὶ μέσας νύκτας προὐχώρει αὖθις
κατὰ σπουδὴν ἐπ' Ἄρβηλα, ὡς Δαρεῖόν τε αἱρήσων
ἐκεῖ καὶ τὰ χρήματα καὶ τὴν ἄλλην κατασκευὴν
τὴν βασιλικήν. καὶ ἀφίκετο εἰς Ἄρβηλα τῇ
ὑστεραίᾳ διώξας τοὺς πάντας ἐκ τῆς μάχης σταδίους μάλιστα ἐς ἑξακοσίους. καὶ Δαρεῖον μὲν οὐ
καταλαμβάνει ἐν Ἀρβήλοις, ἀλλὰ ἔφευγεν οὐδέν τι
ἐλινύσας Δαρεῖος· τὰ χρήματα δὲ ἐγκατελήφθη καὶ
ἡ κατασκευὴ πᾶσα, καὶ τὸ ἅρμα τὸ Δαρείου αὖθις
ἐγκατελήφθη καὶ ἡ ἀσπὶς αὖθις καὶ τὰ τόξα ἑάλω.

6 Ἀπέθανον δὲ τῶν ἀμφ' Ἀλέξανδρον ἄνδρες μὲν
ἐς ἑκατὸν μάλιστα, ἵπποι δὲ ἔκ τε τῶν τραυμάτων
καὶ τῆς κακοπαθείας τῆς ἐν τῇ διώξει ὑπὲρ τοὺς
χιλίους, καὶ τούτων τῆς ἑταιρικῆς ἵππου σχεδόν τι
οἱ ἡμίσεες. τῶν βαρβάρων δὲ νεκρῶν μὲν ἐλέγοντο
ἐς τριάκοντα μυριάδας, ἑάλωσαν δὲ πολὺ πλείονες
τῶν ἀποθανόντων καὶ οἱ ἐλέφαντες καὶ τῶν
ἁρμάτων ὅσα μὴ κατεκόπη ἐν τῇ μάχῃ.

7 Τοῦτο ⟨τὸ⟩ τέλος τῇ μάχῃ ταύτῃ ἐγένετο ἐπὶ
ἄρχοντος Ἀθηναίοις Ἀριστοφάνους μηνὸς Πυανε-
ψιῶνος· καὶ Ἀριστάνδρῳ ξυνέβη ἡ μαντεία ἐν τῷ
αὐτῷ μηνί, ἐν ὅτῳ ἡ σελήνη ἐκλιπὴς ἐφάνη, τήν τε
μάχην Ἀλεξάνδρῳ καὶ τὴν νίκην γενέσθαι.

16. Δαρεῖος μὲν δὴ εὐθὺς ἐκ τῆς μάχης παρὰ τὰ
ὄρη τὰ Ἀρμενίων ἤλαυνεν ἐπὶ Μηδίας, καὶ ξὺν

---

[2] P. 34, 1 has Al. proclaimed king of Asia at Arbela, cf.
Introd. n. 64.

331
B.C.

to give his men and horses a little rest, while Parmenio took the Persian camp with the baggage train, elephants and camels.

Alexander rested his cavalry till towards midnight, 5 and hurried on again to Arbela, to seize Darius there with his treasure and the other royal belongings. He arrived at Arbela next day, having covered in all, since the battle, about six hundred stades in the pursuit. However, he did not catch Darius at Arbela, as he continued his flight without pause, though his treasure and all his equipment was captured and his chariot was seized then a second time, and his shield was taken a second time, and his bow and arrows too.[2]

Up to a hundred of Alexander's troops were lost, 6 with over a thousand horses from wounds and distress in the pursuit, of which about half belonged to the Companions. The barbarian corpses were said to number some three hundred thousand, but far more were made prisoner than killed, and the elephants and all the chariots which had not been cut down in the battle were also captured.[3]

So ended this battle in the month Pyanepsion of 7 the archonship at Athens of Aristophanes.[4] Aristander's prophecy came true, that Alexander's battle and victory would occur in the same month in which the moon was partially eclipsed.

16. Darius made straight from the battle by the Armenian mountains for Media, accompanied in

---

[3] D. 61: 90,000 Persians, 500 Macedonians (plus many wounded, who might well die later); QC. iv 16, 26: 40,000 Persians, under 300 Macedonians.

[4] An error (October/November); really 26 Boedromion = 1 Oct. (Plut., *Camillus* 19, 3), cf. App. VIII 5.

αὐτῷ οἵ τε Βάκτριοι ἱππεῖς, ὡς τότε ἐν τῇ μάχῃ
ξυνετάχθησαν, ἔφευγον καὶ Περσῶν οἵ τε συγγενεῖς οἱ βασιλέως καὶ τῶν μηλοφόρων καλουμένων
2 οὐ πολλοί. προσεγένοντο δὲ αὐτῷ κατὰ τὴν φυγὴν
καὶ τῶν μισθοφόρων ξένων ἐς δισχιλίους, οὓς
Πά⟨τ⟩ρων τε ὁ Φωκεὺς καὶ Γλαῦκος ὁ Αἰτωλὸς
ἦγον. ταύτῃ δὲ αὐτῷ ἡ φυγὴ ἐπὶ Μηδίας ἐγίγνετο,
ὅτι ἐδόκει τὴν ἐπὶ Σούσων τε καὶ Βαβυλῶνος ἥξειν
Ἀλέξανδρον ἐκ τῆς μάχης, ὅτι οἰκουμένη τε
ἐκείνη πᾶσα ἦν καὶ ὁδὸς τοῖς σκευοφόροις οὐ
χαλεπή, καὶ ἅμα τοῦ πολέμου τὸ ἆθλον ἡ Βαβυλὼν
καὶ τὰ Σοῦσα ἐφαίνετο· ἡ δὲ ἐπὶ Μηδίας μεγάλῳ
στρατεύματι οὐκ εὔπορος.
3   Καὶ οὐκ ἐψεύσθη Δαρεῖος. Ἀλέξανδρος γὰρ ἐξ
Ἀρβήλων ὁρμηθεὶς τὴν ἐπὶ Βαβυλῶνος εὐθὺς
προὐχώρει. ἤδη τε οὐ πόρρω Βαβυλῶνος ἦν καὶ
τὴν δύναμιν ξυντεταγμένην ὡς ἐς μάχην ἦγε, καὶ
οἱ Βαβυλώνιοι πανδημεὶ ἀπήντων αὐτῷ ξὺν ἱερεῦσί
τε σφῶν καὶ ἄρχουσι, δῶρά τε ὡς ἕκαστοι φέροντες
καὶ τὴν πόλιν ἐνδιδόντες καὶ τὴν ἄκραν καὶ τὰ
4 χρήματα. Ἀλέξανδρος δὲ παρελθὼν εἰς τὴν Βαβυ-
λῶνα τὰ ἱερά, ἃ Ξέρξης καθεῖλεν, ἀνοικοδομεῖν
προσέταξε Βαβυλωνίοις, τά τε ἄλλα καὶ τοῦ Βήλου
τὸ ἱερόν, ὃν μάλιστα θεῶν τιμῶσι Βαβυλώνιοι.
σατράπην δὲ κατέστησε Βαβυλῶνος Μαζαῖον,
Ἀπολλόδωρον δὲ τὸν Ἀμφιπολίτην στρατηγὸν
τῶν μετὰ Μαζαίου ὑπολειπομένων στρατιωτῶν,
καὶ Ἀσκληπιόδωρον τὸν Φίλωνος τοὺς φόρους
5 ἐκλέγειν. κατέπεμψε δὲ καὶ ἐς Ἀρμενίαν Μιθρή-

---

¹ D. 64, 1; QC. v 1, 3–9.
² D. 64, 3 f.; QC. v 1, 11–23 and 45 (also on donatives to
troops).

flight by the Bactrian cavalry, as they had been
posted with him in the battle on that occasion; he
also had an escort of Persians, the royal kinsmen and
a few of the 'spearmen of the Golden Apples'. He 2
was joined during the flight by some two thousand of
the foreign mercenaries led by Patron the Phocian
and Glaucus the Aetolian. The reason why he fled
towards Media was that he thought Alexander after
the battle would take the route to Susa and Babylon,
since all of it was inhabited and the road itself was
easy for the baggage trains, and besides, Babylon and
Susa were the obvious prize of the war, whereas the
route to Media was not easy for a large force.[1]

Darius was not mistaken, for on leaving Arbela 3
Alexander at once advanced on the road to Babylon.
He was already near Babylon, and was leading his
force in battle order, when the Babylonians came to
meet him in mass, with their priests and rulers,
each section of the inhabitants bringing gifts and
offering surrender of the city, the citadel and the
treasure.[2] On entering Babylon Alexander directed 4
the Babylonians to rebuild the temples Xerxes destroyed, and especially the temple of Baal, whom the
Babylonians honour more than any other god. He
appointed Mazaeus satrap of Babylon and Apollodorus of Amphipolis general of the troops left behind
with Mazaeus, and Asclepiodorus son of Philo to
collect the taxes.[3] He also sent as satrap to Armenia [4] 5

331
B.C.

[482–81
B.C.]

---

[3] Mazaeus (11, 4 n.) fled to Babylon (QC. iv 6, 17) and, as
satrap, surrendered it (v 1, 17); QC. v 1, 43 f. agrees on his
appointment and that of Apollodorus (cf. D. 64, 5), makes
Agathon commandant of citadel and gives numbers of garrison
forces.
[4] It never came under Al's control (D. xix 23, 3). Cf.
D. 64, 6; QC. v 1, 44.

νην σατράπην, ὃς τὴν ἐν Σάρδεσιν ἀκρόπολιν
Ἀλεξάνδρῳ ἐνέδωκεν. ἔνθα δὴ καὶ τοῖς Χαλδαίοις
ἐνέτυχεν, καὶ ὅσα ἐδόκει Χαλδαίοις ἀμφὶ τὰ ἱερὰ τὰ
ἐν Βαβυλῶνι ἔπραξε, τά τε ἄλλα καὶ τῷ Βήλῳ
καθ᾽ ἃ ἐκεῖνοι ἐξηγοῦντο ἔθυσεν.

6   Αὐτὸς δὲ ἐπὶ Σούσων ἐστέλλετο· καὶ ἐντυγχάνει
αὐτῷ κατὰ τὴν ὁδὸν ὅ τε παῖς τοῦ Σουσίων
σατράπου καὶ παρὰ Φιλοξένου ἐπιστολεύς. Φιλόξενον γὰρ εὐθὺς ἐκ τῆς μάχης ἐπὶ Σούσων ἐστάλκει
Ἀλέξανδρος. τῇ δὲ ἐπιστολῇ τῇ παρὰ Φιλοξένου
ἐνεγέγραπτο, ὅτι τήν τε πόλιν οἱ Σούσιοι παραδε-
δώκασιν καὶ τὰ χρήματα πάντα σῶά ἐστιν Ἀλε-
7 ξάνδρῳ. ἀφίκετο δὲ ἐς Σοῦσα Ἀλέξανδρος ἐκ
Βαβυλῶνος ἐν ἡμέραις εἴκοσι· καὶ παρελθὼν ἐς
τὴν πόλιν τά τε χρήματα παρέλαβεν ὄντα ἀργυρίου
τάλαντα ἐς πεντακισμύρια καὶ τὴν ἄλλην κατασκευὴν τὴν βασιλικήν. πολλὰ δὲ καὶ ἄλλα κατελήφθη αὐτοῦ, ὅσα Ξέρξης ἀπὸ τῆς Ἑλλάδος ἄγων
ἦλθε, τά τε ἄλλα καὶ Ἁρμοδίου καὶ Ἀριστογεί-
8 τονος χαλκαῖ εἰκόνες. καὶ ταύτας Ἀθηναίοις
ὀπίσω πέμπει Ἀλέξανδρος, καὶ νῦν κεῖνται Ἀθήνησιν ἐν Κεραμεικῷ αἱ εἰκόνες, ᾗ ἄνιμεν ἐς πόλιν,
καταντικρὺ μάλιστα τοῦ Μητρῴου, ⟨οὐ⟩ μακρὰν
τῶν Εὐδανέμων τοῦ βωμοῦ· ὅστις δὲ μεμύηται
ταῖν θεαῖν ἐν Ἐλευσῖνι, οἶδε τοῦ Εὐδανέμου τὸν
βωμὸν ἐπὶ τοῦ δαπέδου ὄντα.

9   Ἐνταῦθα θύσας τῷ πατρίῳ νόμῳ Ἀλέξανδρος
καὶ λαμπάδα ποιήσας καὶ ἀγῶνα γυμνικόν, καταλιπὼν σατράπην μὲν τῆς Σουσιανῆς Ἀβουλίτην
ἄνδρα Πέρσην, φρούραρχον δὲ ἐν τῇ ἄκρᾳ τῶν

---

⁵ Cf. i 17, 6; ii 24, 6; iii 1, 4 f.; vii 17.

Mithrenes, who had surrendered the acropolis of   331
Sardis to Alexander. At Babylon too he met the   B.C.
Chaldaeans, and carried out all their recommenda-
tions on the Babylonian temples, and in particular
sacrificed to Baal, according to their instructions.[5]

He himself set out for Susa.[6] On the way he was 6
met by the son of the satrap of Susa [7] and a letter-
carrier from Philoxenus, whom Alexander had sent
to Susa directly after the battle. In Philoxenus'
letter it was stated that the people of Susa had handed
over the city and that all the treasure was in safe-
keeping for Alexander. Alexander reached Susa in 7
twenty days from Babylon; he entered the city and
took over the treasure, up to fifty thousand Talents of
silver,[8] and all the rest of the royal belongings. A
good deal was captured there in addition, all that
Xerxes brought back from Greece, notably bronze   [480-79
statues of Harmodius and Aristogeiton, which Alex-   B.C.]
ander sent back to the Athenians; they are now set 8
up at Athens in the Cerameicus, on the way by which
we ascend the Acropolis, just opposite the Metroön,
not far from the altar of the Eudanemoi. Anyone
who has been initiated into the mysteries of the Two
Goddesses at Eleusis is aware that the altar of Euda-
nemos is in the plain.[9]

There Alexander sacrificed in accordance with 9
ancestral custom, and held a relay torch race and
athletic contest. He left behind Abulites, a Persian,
as satrap of Susiana, Mazarus one of the Companions
as garrison commandant in the citadel of Susa and

---

[6] D. 65; QC. v 2, 1 ff. See App. VIII 6.
[7] Abulites, vii 4, 1; D. 65, 5; QC. v 2, 8 ff; cf. §9 below.
[8] App. X 3.
[9] Contrast vii 19, 2 (' vulgate '). No proof here that A.
was yet domiciled at Athens.

Σούσων Μάζαρον τῶν ἑταίρων καὶ στρατηγὸν
᾿Αρχέλαον τὸν Θεοδώρου, προύχώρει ὡς ἐπὶ
Πέρσας· ἐπὶ θάλασσαν δὲ κατέπεμψεν ὕπαρχον
10 Συρίας καὶ Φοινίκης καὶ Κιλικίας Μένητα. καὶ
τούτῳ ἔδωκεν ἀργυρίου τάλαντα ἐς τρισχίλια
φέρειν ἐπὶ θάλασσαν, καὶ ἀπ᾽ αὐτῶν ἀποστεῖλαι
παρ᾽ ᾿Αντίπατρον ὅσων ἂν δέηται ᾿Αντίπατρος ἐς
τὸν πρὸς Λακεδαιμονίους πόλεμον. ἐνταῦθα καὶ
᾿Αμύντας ὁ ᾿Ανδρομένους ξὺν τῇ δυνάμει ἀφίκετο,
11 ἣν ἐκ Μακεδονίας ἦγε. καὶ τούτων τοὺς μὲν
ἱππέας ἐς τὴν ἵππον τὴν ἑταιρικὴν κατέταξεν
᾿Αλέξανδρος, τοὺς πεζοὺς δὲ προσέθηκεν ταῖς
τάξεσι ταῖς ἄλλαις, κατὰ ἔθνη ἑκάστους ξυντάξας.
κατέστησε δὲ καὶ λόχους δύο ἐν ἑκάστῃ ἴλῃ, οὐ
πρόσθεν ὄντας λόχους ἱππικούς, καὶ λοχαγοὺς
ἐπέστησε τοὺς κατ᾽ ἀρετὴν προκριθέντας ἐκ τῶν
ἑταίρων.

---

[10] Cf. QC. v 2, 16 f., replacing Mazarus by Xenophilus,
perhaps his successor (cf. D. xix 17, 3; 18, 1; 48, 6), naming
Callicrates as treasurer and giving garrison force of 3,000.

[11] D. 64, 5 makes Apollodorus and Menes 'generals' of
Babylon and of the other provinces as far as Cilicia; QC. v
1, 43 gives this with the names in reverse order, wrongly
since Apollodorus was certainly in Babylonia. A modern view
that Menes was a financial official has no support in the evidence. As a former bodyguard (ii 12, 2), he was certainly of
high rank. Hence 'hyparch' is most naturally construed as
'satrap', cf. i 12, 8 n. Did he then succeed Asclepiodorus
and perhaps Menon too in Syria (iii 6, 8 n)—the former
had certainly been superseded by 327 (iv 13, 4)—and Balacrus
in Cilicia (ii 12, 2), who was killed fighting there at some
unknown date in Al's lifetime (D. xviii 22, 1)? So Bosworth,
CQ 1975. Against this, in iv 7, 2 (see note) Asclepiodorus is
still described as a hyparch in 329/8 B.C., when he brought
reinforcements to Al. Perhaps Menes had a general control

Archelaus son of Theodorus as general; and then he advanced against the Persians.[10] He sent down Menes to the sea as hyparch of Syria, Phoenicia and Cilicia,[11] and gave him up to three thousand silver Talents to take to the sea, from which he was to despatch to Antipater whatever Antipater required for the Lacedaemonian war.[12] There too Amyntas son of Andromenes arrived with the troops he brought from Macedon.[13] Of these Alexander assigned the horsemen to the Companion cavalry, and attached the foot to the other battalions, assigning them in accordance with their national origins. He also formed two companies in each squadron of cavalry (there had formerly been no cavalry companies), and as company-captains he appointed men distinguished for courage among the Companions.[14]

over the satrapies of Syria, Phoenicia and Cilicia, especially as D. and QC. both say that he was given power (like Apollodorus) to levy troops, probably to provide the reinforcements for Al. that arrived from Cilicia and Syria in 330–328 B.C. (QC. v 7, 12; vii 10, 11 f., cf. A. iv 7, 2), as well as a special responsibility to send money to Antipater (D. and QC. give the sum entrusted to him as 1000 Talents). On Bosworth's own view Phoenicia did not lie in the satrapy of Asclepiodorus; QC. iv 7, 9 says that Philotas (Berve no. 806, otherwise unknown) was put in charge of the area round Tyre, cf. also the fiscal post of Coeranus (A. iii 6, 4). No more is heard of Menes unless in iv 7, 2. On Al's death new satraps were appointed in both Syria and Cilicia; their immediate predecessors are unknown (D. xviii 3).

[12] Appendix VI.

[13] Cf. ii 27 n. D. 65, 1 makes him arrive on the march to Susa, QC. v 1, 39 ff. at Babylon, with 6,000 foot and 500 horse from Macedon, 3,500 foot and 600 horse from Thrace, 4,000 foot and 380 horse from Peloponnese; some discrepancies in D., who adds 50 Macedonian pages.

[14] Different military changes *en route* Babylon–Susa in QC. v 2, 2–7, cf. D. 65, 2.

17. Ἄρας δὲ ἐκ Σούσων καὶ διαβὰς τὸν Πασιτι-
γριν ποταμὸν ἐμβάλλει εἰς τὴν Οὐξίων γῆν.
Οὐξίων δὲ οἱ μὲν τὰ πεδία οἰκοῦντες τοῦ τε
σατράπου τῶν Περσῶν ἤκουον καὶ τότε Ἀλεξάνδρῳ σφας ἐνέδοσαν· οἱ δὲ ὄρειοι καλούμενοι
Οὔξιοι Πέρσαις τε οὐχ ὑπήκοοι ἦσαν καὶ τότε
πέμψαντες παρ' Ἀλέξανδρον οὐκ ἄλλως παρήσειν
ἔφασαν τὴν ἐπὶ Πέρσας ἰόντα ξὺν τῇ δυνάμει ἢ
λαβεῖν ὅσα καὶ παρὰ τοῦ Περσῶν βασιλέως ἐπὶ τῇ
2 παρόδῳ ἐλάμβανον. καὶ τούτους ἀποπέμπει Ἀλέξανδρος, ἥκειν κελεύσας ἐπὶ τὰ στενά, ὧν κρατοῦν-
τες ἐπὶ σφίσιν ἐδόκουν τὴν πάροδον εἶναι τὴν ἐς
Πέρσας, ἵνα καὶ παρ' αὐτοῦ λάβοιεν ⟨τὰ⟩ τεταγμένα. αὐτὸς δὲ ἀναλαβὼν τοὺς σωματοφύλακας
τοὺς βασιλικοὺς καὶ τοὺς ὑπασπιστὰς καὶ τῆς
ἄλλης στρατιᾶς ἐς ὀκτακισχιλίους τῆς νυκτὸς ᾔει
ἄλλην ἢ τὴν φανερὰν ἡγησαμένων αὐτῷ τῶν
3 Σουσίων. καὶ διελθὼν ὁδὸν τραχεῖαν καὶ δύσπορον
ἐν μιᾷ ἡμέρᾳ ἐπιπίπτει ταῖς κώμαις τῶν Οὐξίων,
καὶ λείαν τε πολλὴν ἔλαβε καὶ αὐτῶν ἔτι ἐν ταῖς
εὐναῖς ὄντων πολλοὺς κατέκτεινεν· οἱ δὲ ἀπέφυγον
ἐς τὰ ὄρη. αὐτὸς δὲ ᾔει σπουδῇ ἐπὶ τὰ στενά, ἵνα
ἀπαντήσεσθαι οἱ Οὔξιοι πανδημεὶ ἐδόκουν ληψό-
4 μενοι τὰ τεταγμένα. Κρατερὸν δὲ ἔτι πρόσθεν
ἀπέστειλε τὰ ἄκρα καταληψόμενον, ἔνθα ᾤετο
βιαζομένους τοὺς Οὐξίους ἀποχωρήσειν. αὐτὸς δὲ
πολλῷ τάχει ᾔει· καὶ φθάνει τε κρατήσας τῶν
παρόδων καὶ ξυντεταγμένους τοὺς ἀμφ' αὐτὸν ἔχων
ἐξ ὑπερδεξίων χωρίων ἐπῆγεν ὡς ἐπὶ τοὺς βαρβά-
5 ρους. οἱ δὲ τῷ τε τάχει τῷ Ἀλεξάνδρου ἐκπλαγέντες καὶ τοῖς χωρίοις, οἷς μάλιστα δὴ ἐπεποί-
θεσαν, πλεονεκτούμενοι ἔφυγον οὐδὲ ἐς χεῖρας

17. Leaving Susa and crossing the river Pasitigris [Karun], Alexander invaded the land of the Uxians.[1] The Uxians who inhabited the plains had obeyed the Persian satrap, and now surrendered to Alexander; but the Uxian hillmen, as they were called, were not subject to Persia, and now sent a message to Alexander that they would only permit him to take the route towards Persia with his army if they received what they used to receive from the Persian king on his passage. Alexander sent them away, with orders to go to the pass, their control of which made them think that the way through to Persia was in their hands, in order to receive from him too what was prescribed. He took the royal bodyguards, the hypaspists and some eight thousand of the rest of the army, marched by night on a road different from the obvious way, with Susian guides, and passing along a rough and difficult path in one day, fell upon the Uxian villages, obtained a great deal of plunder, and killed many of them still in their beds; the rest escaped to the hills. Then he marched swiftly to the pass where the Uxians were likely to meet him in full force, to receive what was prescribed. He sent Craterus even further in advance, to seize the heights where he supposed the Uxians would retreat under pressure, but he himself came on very rapidly, got first to the pass and occupied it, and with his men in due battle order led them from a commanding position to attack the Uxians. Astounded at Alexander's speed of movement, and placed at a disadvantage by the very terrain in which they had put their chief trust, they fled without so much as coming to close quarters.

330
B.C.

2

3

4

5

---

[1] After 3 days march, D. 67; QC. v 3, 1 ff. There are various discrepancies from A. in their accounts.

ἐλθόντες· καὶ οἱ μὲν αὐτῶν ὑπὸ τῶν ἀμφ' Ἀλέξανδρον ἐν τῇ φυγῇ ἀπέθανον, πολλοὶ δὲ καὶ κατὰ
τὴν ὁδὸν κρημνώδη οὖσαν· οἱ πλεῖστοι δὲ ἐπὶ τὰ
ὄρη ἀναφεύγοντες ἐμπίπτουσιν ἐς τοὺς ἀμφὶ
6 Κρατερὸν καὶ ὑπὸ τούτων ἀπώλοντο. ταῦτα τὰ
γέρα παρ' Ἀλεξάνδρου λαβόντες χαλεπῶς εὕροντο
δεόμενοι παρ' αὐτοῦ τὴν χώραν τὴν σφῶν ἔχοντες
φόρους ὅσα ἔτη Ἀλεξάνδρῳ ἀποφέρειν. Πτολεμαῖος δὲ ὁ Λάγου λέγει τὴν Δαρείου μητέρα
δεηθῆναι ὑπὲρ αὐτῶν Ἀλεξάνδρου δοῦναί σφισι τὴν
χώραν οἰκεῖν. ὁ φόρος δὲ ὁ συνταχθεὶς ἦν ἵπποι ἐς
ἔτος ἑκατὸν καὶ ὑποζύγια πεντακόσια καὶ πρόβατα
τρισμύρια. χρήματα γὰρ οὐκ ἦν Οὐξίοις οὐδὲ ἡ γῆ
οἷα ἐργάζεσθαι, ἀλλὰ νομεῖς αὐτῶν οἱ πολλοὶ ἦσαν.
18. Ἐκ δὲ τούτου τὰ μὲν σκευοφόρα καὶ τοὺς
Θεσσαλοὺς ἱππέας καὶ τοὺς ξυμμάχους καὶ τοὺς
μισθοφόρους τοὺς ξένους καὶ ὅσοι ἄλλοι τοῦ
στρατεύματος βαρύτερον ὡπλισμένοι ξὺν Παρμενίωνι ἐκπέμπει ὡς ἐπὶ Πέρσας ἄγειν κατὰ τὴν
2 ἁμαξιτὸν τὴν ἐς Πέρσας φέρουσαν. αὐτὸς δὲ τούς
τε Μακεδόνας τοὺς πεζοὺς ἀναλαβὼν καὶ τὴν ἵππον
τὴν ἑταιρικὴν καὶ τοὺς προδρόμους ἱππέας καὶ τοὺς
Ἀγριᾶνας καὶ τοὺς τοξότας ᾔει σπουδῇ τὴν διὰ
τῶν ὀρῶν. ὡς δὲ ἐπὶ τὰς πύλας τὰς Περσίδας
ἀφίκετο, καταλαμβάνει αὐτοῦ Ἀριοβαρζάνην τὸν
Περσῶν σατράπην πεζοὺς μὲν ἐς τετρακισμυρίους
ἔχοντα, ἱππέας δὲ ἐς ἑπτακοσίους, διατετειχικότα
τὰς πύλας καὶ αὐτοῦ πρὸς τῷ τείχει ἐστρατοπε-
δευκότα, ὡς εἴργειν τῆς παρόδου Ἀλέξανδρον.

---

[2] A's specific reference to Pt. may suggest that this detail,
unlike others, was not in Ar.

Some of them were killed by Alexander's troops in the flight, and many too perished on the precipitous path. The greater number escaped to the hills, only to encounter Craterus' forces and be destroyed by them. These were the gifts of honour they received from Alexander; and it was only with difficulty that they obtained from him their request to retain their own territory, paying annual tribute to Alexander. Ptolemy son of Lagus says that the mother of Darius implored Alexander on their behalf to give them their territory to dwell in.[2] The tribute assessed was a hundred horses every year with five hundred transport animals and thirty thousand from their flocks and herds. For the Uxians had no money or arable land, but were mostly herdsmen.

18. After this,[1] Alexander sent off the baggage train, the Thessalian cavalry, the allies, the foreign mercenaries, and all the other heavier-armed troops of his army with Parmenio, who was to lead them against the Persians by the carriage way that goes into their country. He himself took with him the Macedonian foot, the Companion cavalry and *prodromoi*, the Agrianians and the archers, and marched at full speed over the mountain route. When he arrived at the Persian Gates,[2] he found there Ariobarzanes, the satrap of Persia,[3] with some forty thousand infantry and seven hundred horse;[4] he had built a wall across the Gates and was encamped there by the wall, to bar Alexander's passage.

330
B.C.

6

2

---

[1] D. 68; QC. v 3, 16–4, 34 differ on various points from A. on this campaign, for which see Fuller 228 ff., with map; Al's route is not certain. Cf. Strabo xv 3, 6.

[2] On the fifth day (D. and QC.).

[3] The province of Persia proper.

[4] D. gives 25,000 (so QC.) + 300.

3 Τότε μὲν δὴ αὐτοῦ κατεστρατοπεδεύσατο· τῇ δὲ
ὑστεραίᾳ ξυντάξας τὴν στρατιὰν ἐπῆγε τῷ τείχει.
ὡς δὲ ἄπορόν τε διὰ δυσχωρίαν ἐφαίνετο αἱρεθῆναι
καὶ πολλὰς πληγὰς οἱ ἀμφ' αὐτὸν ἐλάμβανον ἐξ
ὑπερδεξίου τε χωρίου καὶ ἀπὸ μηχανῶν βαλλόμε-
4 νοι, τότε μὲν ἀποχωρεῖ ἐς τὸ στρατόπεδον· τῶν δὲ
αἰχμαλώτων φρασάντων ἄλλην ὁδὸν περιάξειν
αὐτόν, ὡς εἴσω παρελθεῖν τῶν πυλῶν, ἐπεὶ
τραχεῖαν τὴν ὁδὸν καὶ στενὴν ἐπύθετο, Κρατερὸν
μὲν αὐτοῦ καταλείπει ἐπὶ στρατοπέδου τήν τε
αὐτοῦ τάξιν ἔχοντα καὶ τὴν Μελεάγρου καὶ τῶν
τοξοτῶν ὀλίγους καὶ τῶν ἱππέων ἐς πεντακοσίους,
5 καὶ προστάττει αὐτῷ, ἐπειδὰν ἐκπεριεληλυθότα
αὐτὸν αἴσθηται καὶ προσάγοντα ἤδη τῷ στρατοπέδῳ τῶν Περσῶν (αἰσθήσεσθαι δὲ οὐ χαλεπῶς,
σημανεῖν γὰρ αὐτῷ τὰς σάλπιγγας), τότε δὲ
προσβαλεῖν τῷ τείχει· αὐτὸς δὲ προυχώρει νύκτωρ
καὶ διελθὼν ὅσον ἑκατὸν σταδίους ἀναλαμβάνει
τοὺς ὑπασπιστὰς καὶ τὴν Περδίκκου τάξιν καὶ τῶν
τοξοτῶν τοὺς κουφοτάτους καὶ τοὺς Ἀγριᾶνας καὶ
τῶν ἑταίρων τὴν ἵλην τὴν βασιλικὴν καὶ τετραρ-
χίαν πρὸς ταύτῃ μίαν ἱππικήν, καὶ ξὺν τούτοις
ᾔει ἐπικάμψας ὡς ἐπὶ τὰς πύλας, ἵν' οἱ αἰχμάλωτοι
6 ἦγον. Ἀμύνταν δὲ καὶ Φιλώταν καὶ Κοῖνον τὴν
ἄλλην στρατιὰν ὡς ἐπὶ τὸ πεδίον ἄγειν καὶ τὸν
ποταμόν, ὃν ἐχρῆν περᾶσαι ἰόντα ἐπὶ Πέρσας,
γεφυροῦν ἐκέλευσεν· αὐτὸς δὲ ᾔει ὁδὸν χαλεπὴν καὶ
τραχεῖαν καὶ ταύτην δρόμῳ τὸ πολὺ ᾖγε. τὴν μὲν
δὴ πρώτην φυλακὴν τῶν βαρβάρων πρὶν φάους
ἐπιπεσὼν διέφθειρε καὶ τῶν δευτέρων τοὺς πολ-
7 λούς· τῆς τρίτης δὲ οἱ πλείους διέφυγον, καὶ οὐδὲ

For the moment Alexander encamped there, but **3** 330 B.C.
next day he marshalled his troops and led them to the
assault of the wall. But as it appeared impregnable
from the difficulty of the ground, and as his troops
were suffering many blows from fire directed from
commanding heights and from catapults, for the
moment he fell back on the camp. His prisoners [5] **4**
undertook to lead him round by a different road, so
that he would make his way within the gates; but as
he gathered from enquiry that this road was rough
and narrow, he left Craterus there in charge of the
camp with his own battalion and Meleager's, a few of
the archers, and about five hundred horse, and in- **5**
structed him to attack the wall, as soon as he observed
that Alexander himself had managed to get right
round and was nearing the Persian camp (Craterus
would easily observe this from a bugle signal). So
he himself advanced by night, and after traversing
about a hundred stades, took the hypaspists, with
Perdiccas' battalion, the lightest armed of the archers,
the Agrianians, the royal squadron of the Companions, and a tetrarchy [6] of cavalry in addition, and with
them made a turning movement towards the gates,
guided thither by the prisoners. Amyntas, Philotas **6**
and Coenus were instructed to march the remainder
of the army to the plain, and to bridge the river [7]
which he had to cross to enter Persia. He himself
traversed a difficult and rough path, and most of it at
full speed. He fell upon the first barbarian guard
before dawn and destroyed it together with the
greater part of the second; most of the third escaped, **7**

[5] A bilingual Lycian in D. and QC., and P. **37**, 1.
[6] Obscure: evidently more than one squadron, cf. Introd.
58–60.
[7] Araxes (Palvar), D. 69, 2; QC 5, 2. The plain is Ardakan.

οὗτοι ἐς τὸ στρατόπεδον τὸ ᾿Αριοβαρζάνου ἔφυγον,
ἀλλ᾽ αὐτόθεν ὡς εἶχον ἐς τὰ ὄρη πεφοβημένοι,
ὥστε ἔλαθεν ὑπὸ τὴν ἕω ἐπιπεσὼν τῷ στρατοπέδῳ
τῶν πολεμίων. καὶ ἅμα μὲν προσέβαλλε τῇ τάφρῳ,
ἅμα δὲ αἱ σάλπιγγες ἐσήμαινον τοῖς ἀμφὶ Κρατε-
8 ρόν, καὶ Κρατερὸς προσῆγε τῷ προτειχίσματι. οἱ
πολέμιοι δὲ πάντοθεν ἀμφίβολοι γιγνόμενοι οὐδὲ ἐς
χεῖρας ἐλθόντες ἔφυγον, ἀλλὰ πανταχόθεν γὰρ
εἴργοντο, τῇ μὲν ᾿Αλεξάνδρου ἐπικειμένου, ἄλλῃ δὲ
τῶν ἀμφὶ Κρατερὸν παραθεόντων, ὥστε ἠναγκά-
σθησαν οἱ πολλοὶ αὐτῶν ἐς τὰ τείχη ἀποστρέψαντες
φεύγειν· εἴχετο δὲ καὶ τὰ τείχη πρὸς τῶν Μακε-
9 δόνων ἤδη. ᾿Αλέξανδρος γὰρ τοῦτο αὐτὸ ὅπερ
ξυνέβη ὑποτοπήσας Πτολεμαῖον ἀπολελοίπει αὐτοῦ,
ἔχοντα τῶν πεζῶν ἐς τρισχιλίους, ὥστε οἱ μὲν
πλεῖστοι τῶν βαρβάρων ἐν χερσὶ πρὸς τῶν Μακεδόνων κατεκόπησαν, οἱ δὲ καὶ ἐν τῇ φυγῇ φοβερᾷ
γενομένῃ κατὰ τῶν κρημνῶν ῥίψαντες ἀπώλοντο·
αὐτὸς δὲ ὁ ᾿Αριοβαρζάνης ξὺν ὀλίγοις ἱππεῦσιν ἐς
τὰ ὄρη ἀπέφυγεν.

10 ᾿Αλέξανδρος δὲ σπουδῇ αὖθις ἦγεν ὡς ἐπὶ τὸν
ποταμὸν καὶ καταλαμβάνει ἤδη πεποιημένην ἐπ᾽
αὐτοῦ γέφυραν καὶ διαβαίνει ξὺν τῇ στρατιᾷ
εὐπετῶς. ἐντεῦθεν δὲ αὖθις σπουδῇ ἤλαυνεν ἐς
Πέρσας, ὥ⟨σ⟩τε ἔφθη ἀφικέσθαι πρὶν τὰ χρήματα
διαρπάσασθαι τοὺς φύλακας. ἔλαβε δὲ καὶ τὰ ἐν
Πασαργάδαις χρήματα ἐν τοῖς Κύρου τοῦ πρώτου
11 θησαυροῖς. σατράπην μὲν δὴ Περσῶν κατέστησε
Φρασαόρτην τὸν ῾Ρεομίθρου παῖδα· τὰ βασίλεια δὲ
τὰ Περσικὰ ἐνέπρησε, Παρμενίωνος σώζειν ξυμ-

---

[8] See iii 29, 6 n.

yet even they did not flee to Ariobarzanes' camp, but
ran in terror from the spot just as they were to the
mountains, so that he had not been observed by the
time he assaulted the enemy's camp about dawn.
At the same moment as he attacked the trench, the
bugles sounded, notifying Craterus' troops, and
Craterus assaulted the wall. So the enemy were 8
caught on all sides, never so much as came to blows,
and took to flight; but as they were hemmed in from
all quarters, Alexander pressing on one side, Craterus'
troops hastening up on the other, most of them were
forced to turn back to the walls for refuge. However,
by this time the walls themselves were in Macedonian
hands, for Alexander had surmised what actually 9
happened, and had left Ptolemy [8] there with some
three thousand infantry, so that most of the Persians
were cut down by the Macedonians at close quarters,
while the others threw themselves over the cliffs in
their flight, when it became a panic, and perished;
Ariobarzanes himself escaped with a handful of horsemen to the hills.[9]

Once again Alexander marched at full speed to the 10
river, found the bridge there already constructed and
crossed with his army without difficulty. Thence he
hurried on again towards Persia [10] and arrived there
before the garrison had plundered the treasure. He
also captured the treasure which had been at Pasargadae in the treasury of Cyrus the First.[11] He ap- 11
pointed Phrasaortes the son of Rheomithras satrap of
Persia. He set the Persian palace on fire, though
Parmenio urged him to preserve it, arguing, among

[9] QC. 4, 33 ff. gives him 5,000 men and makes him try to
seize Persepolis and die fighting its garrison, but cf. A. iii 23, 7.
[10] Persepolis. See App. X for what follows.
[11] 559–529 B.C.

βουλεύοντος, τά τε ἄλλα καὶ ὅτι οὐ καλὸν αὐτοῦ
κτήματα ἤδη ἀπολλύναι καὶ ὅτι οὐχ ὡσαύτως
προσέξουσιν αὐτῷ οἱ κατὰ τὴν Ἀσίαν ἄνθρωποι,
ὡς οὐδὲ αὐτῷ ἐγνωκότι κατέχειν τῆς Ἀσίας τὴν
12 ἀρχήν, ἀλλὰ ἐπελθεῖν μόνον νικῶντα. ὁ δὲ τιμω-
ρήσασθαι ἐθέλειν Πέρσας ἔφασκεν ἀνθ᾽ ὧν ἐπὶ τὴν
Ἑλλάδα ἐλάσαντες τάς τε Ἀθήνας κατέσκαψαν καὶ
τὰ ἱερὰ ἐνέπρησαν, καὶ ὅσα ἄλλα κακὰ τοὺς
Ἕλληνας εἰργάσαντο, ὑπὲρ τούτων δίκας λαβεῖν.
ἀλλ᾽ οὐδ᾽ ἐμοὶ δοκεῖ σὺν νῷ δρᾶσαι τοῦτό γε
Ἀλέξανδρος οὐδὲ εἶναί τις αὕτη Περσῶν τῶν πάλαι
τιμωρία.

19. Ταῦτα δὲ διαπραξάμενος προὐχώρει ἐπὶ
Μηδίας· ἐκεῖ γὰρ ἐπυνθάνετο εἶναι Δαρεῖον.
γνώμην δὲ πεποίητο Δαρεῖος, εἰ μὲν ἐπὶ Σούσων
καὶ Βαβυλῶνος μένοι Ἀλέξανδρος, αὐτοῦ προσμένειν καὶ αὐτὸς ἐν Μήδοις, εἰ δή τι νεωτερισθείη
τῶν ἀμφ᾽ Ἀλέξανδρον· εἰ δ᾽ ἐλαύνοι ἐπ᾽ αὐτόν,
αὐτὸς δὲ ἄνω ἰέναι τὴν ἐπὶ Παρθυαίους τε καὶ
Ὑρκανίαν ἔστε ἐπὶ Βάκτρα, τήν τε χώραν φθείρων
πᾶσαν καὶ ἄπορον ποιῶν Ἀλεξάνδρῳ τὴν πρόσω
2 ὁδόν. τὰς μὲν δὴ γυναῖκας καὶ τὴν ἄλλην τὴν ἔτι
ἀμφ᾽ αὑτὸν κατασκευὴν καὶ τὰς ἁρμαμάξας ἐπὶ
τὰς Κασπίας καλουμένας πύλας πέμπει, αὐτὸς δὲ
ξὺν τῇ δυνάμει, ἥτις ἐκ τῶν παρόντων ξυνείλεκτο
αὐτῷ, προσέμενεν ἐν Ἐκβατάνοις. ταῦτα ἀκούων
Ἀλέξανδρος προὐχώρει ἐπὶ Μηδίας. καὶ Πα-
ρ⟨α⟩ιτάκας μὲν εἰς τὴν χώραν αὐτῶν ἐμβαλὼν
κατεστρέψατο καὶ σατραπεύειν ἔταξεν αὐτῶν
Ὀξ[ο]άθρην τὸν Ἀβουλίτου τοῦ [πρότερον]
3 Σούσων σατράπου παῖδα. αὐτὸς δὲ ὡς ἠγγέλθη
κατὰ τὴν ὁδόν, ὅτι ἐγνωκὼς εἴη Δαρεῖος ἀπαντᾶν

other things, that it was not good to destroy what was now his own property, and that the Asians would not so readily adhere to him, but would suppose that even he had not decided to retain the empire of Asia but only to conquer and pass on.   Alexander said that he 12 wished to punish the Persians for sacking Athens and burning the temples when they invaded Greece, and to exact retribution for all the other injuries they had done to the Greeks.   I too do not think that Alexander showed good sense in this action nor that he could punish Persians of a long past age.

330
B.C.

[480
B.C.]

19. After these measures Alexander went on towards Media, for he was getting information that Darius was there.   Darius had determined, if Alexander were to remain at Susa and Babylon, to wait himself where he was in Media, in case there were any new developments on Alexander's side, but if Alexander were to march straight against him, he proposed to go up country to the Parthyaeans and Hyrcania, as far as Bactra, ravaging all the country and making further progress impossible for Alexander.   He sent the women, all the belongings he had 2 still with him and the closed waggons to what are called the Caspian gates, while he stayed himself in Ecbatana with the force he had collected from available resources.   On hearing this, Alexander went on towards Media, and subdued the Paraetacae by invading their territory, and appointed Oxathres, son of Abulites the satrap of Susa, as satrap over them. As he was informed on the road that Darius had 3 decided to meet him in battle and fight it out again,

τε αὐτῷ ὡς ἐς μάχην καὶ αὖθις διακινδυνεύειν,
Σκύθας τε γὰρ αὐτῷ ἥκειν καὶ Καδουσίους συμμάχους, τὰ μὲν ὑποζύγια καὶ τοὺς τούτων φύλακας
καὶ τὴν ἄλλην κατασκευὴν ἕπεσθαι ἐκέλευσε, τὴν
στρατιὰν δὲ τὴν ἄλλην ἀναλαβὼν ἦγεν ἐσταλμένους
ὡς ἐς μάχην. καὶ ἀφικνεῖται δωδεκάτῃ ἡμέρᾳ ἐς
4 Μηδίαν. ἔνθα ἔμαθεν οὐκ οὖσαν ἀξιόμαχον δύναμιν Δαρείῳ οὐδὲ Καδουσίους ἢ Σκύθας αὐτῷ
συμμάχους ἥκοντας, ἀλλ' ὅτι φεύγειν ἐγνωκὼς εἴη
Δαρεῖος· ὁ δὲ ἔτι μᾶλλον ἦγε σπουδῇ. ὡς δὲ
ἀπεῖχεν Ἐκβατάνων ὅσον τριῶν ἡμερῶν ὁδόν,
ἐνταῦθα ἀπήντα αὐτῷ Βισθάνης ὁ Ὤχου παῖς τοῦ
5 πρὸ Δαρείου βασιλεύσαντος Περσῶν· καὶ οὗτος
ἀπήγγειλεν, ὅτι Δαρεῖος ἐς πέμπτην ἡμέραν εἴη
πεφευγὼς ἔχων τά τε κρήματα ⟨τὰ⟩ ἐκ Μήδων ἐς
ἑπτακισχίλια τάλαντα καὶ στρατιὰν ἱππέας μὲν ἐς
τρισχιλίους, πεζοὺς δὲ ἐς ἑξακισχιλίους.

Ἐλθὼν δὲ ἐς Ἐκβάτανα Ἀλέξανδρος τοὺς μὲν
Θετταλοὺς ἱππέας καὶ τοὺς ἄλλους ξυμμάχους
ἀποπέμπει ὀπίσω ἐπὶ θάλασσαν, τόν τε μισθὸν
ἀποδοὺς αὐτοῖς ἐντελῆ τὸν ξυντεταγμένον καὶ
6 δισχίλια παρ' αὐτοῦ τάλαντα ἐπιδούς· ὅστις δὲ
ἰδίᾳ βούλοιτο ἔτι μισθοφορεῖν παρ' αὐτῷ, ἀπογρά-
φεσθαι ἐκέλευσε· καὶ ἐγένοντο οἱ ἀπογραψάμενοι
οὐκ ὀλίγοι. Ἐπόκιλλον δὲ τὸν Πολυειδοῦς ἔταξε
καταγαγεῖν αὐτοὺς ὡς ἐπὶ θάλασσαν, ἱππέας
ἄλλους ἔχοντα ἐς φυλακὴν αὐτῶν· οἱ γὰρ Θεσσαλοὶ
τοὺς ἵππους αὐτοῦ ἀπέδοντο. ἐπέστειλε δὲ καὶ

---

[1] For Darius' plans and movements from Gaugamela to
arrest by Bessus see D. 64, 1; 73, 1; QC. v 1, (3-9); 8-12.
The Cadusii lived in mountains SW. of Caspian (Strabo xi 7, 1)
and the Scythians of §3 presumably W. of Caspian, as Ecbatana

since he had been joined by Scythian and Cadusian 303
allies, he ordered the draught animals with their B.C.
keepers and all the rest of the stores to follow, while
he took the rest of the army with him ready for battle.
He reached Media on the twelfth day. There he 4
learned that Darius' force was not capable of fighting
and that the Cadusians and Scythians had not arrived
to help him, but that Darius had resolved on flight.
Alexander marched on all the more rapidly. But
when he was about three days' journey from Ecbatana
he was met by Bisthanes son of Ochus, the predecessor
of Darius as King of Persia, who reported that Darius 5
had fled four days before, with his treasure from
Media of seven thousand Talents and with about
three thousand cavalry and about six thousand infantry.[1]

On arriving at Ecbatana, Alexander sent back the
Thessalian cavalry and the rest of the allies to the sea,
giving the agreed pay in full, and adding as a personal
gift two thousand Talents; on his orders any individual 6
who wanted to continue serving in his army as a
mercenary was to enrol, and a great number did so
enrol.[2] He appointed Epocillus son of Polyides to
conduct them to the sea, with other cavalry to escort
them, for the Thessalians sold their horses on the spot.

is the intended mobilization centre; Darius finally decided to
carry on the war in east Iran (QC. v 9, 5 ff.); D. 73, 2 gives him
30,000 Persians and Greek mercenaries, QC. 8, 3 f. 34,000 foot
(including 4,000 mercenaries, but cf. 23, 9 n.) and 4,000 horse.
See App. VIII.
    [2] Cf. iii 25, 4; 29, 4; v 27, 5; D. 74, 3 and QC. vi 2, 17
(dismissal at Hecatompylos, cf. 23, 1 n.); P. 42, 3 (after *news*
of Darius' arrest); A. v 27, 5 n. QC. v 7, 12 records arrival in
Media of reinforcements for Al. from Cilicia of 5000 foot and
1000 horse—under 'Plato' of Athens (Berve no. 732)! For
Alexander's army after Ecbatana (Hamadan) see App. XIII.

Μένητι, ἐπειδὰν ἀφίκωνται ἐπὶ θάλασσαν, ἐπιμε-
ληθῆναι ὅπως ἐπὶ τριήρων κομισθήσονται ἐς
7 Εὔβοιαν. Παρμενίωνα δὲ προσέταξε τὰ χρήματα
τὰ ἐκ Περσῶν κομιζόμενα εἰς τὴν ἄκραν τὴν ἐν
Ἐκβατάνοις καταθέσθαι καὶ Ἁρπάλῳ παραδοῦναι·
Ἅρπαλον γὰρ ἐπὶ τῶν χρημάτων ἀπέλιπε καὶ
φυλακὴν τῶν χρημάτων Μακεδόνας ἐς ἑξακισχιλίους καὶ ἱππέας καὶ ψιλοὺς ὀλίγους· αὐτὸν δὲ
Παρμενίωνα τοὺς ξένους ἀναλαβόντα καὶ τοὺς
Θρᾷκας καὶ ὅσοι ἄλλοι ἱππεῖς ἔξω τῆς ἵππου τῆς
ἑταιρικῆς παρὰ τὴν χώραν τὴν Καδουσίων ἐλαύνειν
8 ἐς Ὑρκανίαν. Κλείτῳ δὲ τῷ τῆς βασιλικῆς ἴλης
ἡγεμόνι ἐπέστειλεν, ἐπειδὰν ἐκ Σούσων εἰς
Ἐκβάτανα ἀφίκηται, κατελέλειπτο γὰρ ἐν Σούσοις
ἀρρωστῶν, ἀναλαβόντα τοὺς Μακεδόνας τοὺς ἐπὶ
τῶν χρημάτων τότε ὑπολειφθέντας ἰέναι τὴν ἐπὶ
Παρθυαίους, ἵνα καὶ αὐτὸς ἥξειν ἔμελλεν.

20. Αὐτὸς δὲ ἀναλαβὼν τήν τε ἵππον τῶν
ἑταίρων καὶ τοὺς προδρόμους καὶ τοὺς μισθοφόρους
ἱππέας, ὧν Ἐριγύϊος ἡγεῖτο, καὶ τὴν φάλαγγα τὴν
Μακεδονικὴν ἔξω τῶν ἐπὶ τοῖς χρήμασι ταχθέντων
καὶ τοὺς τοξότας καὶ τοὺς Ἀγριᾶνας ἤλαυνεν ὡς
ἐπὶ Δαρεῖον. καὶ αὐτῷ κατὰ τὴν ὁδὸν σπουδῇ
γιγνομένῃ τῶν τε στρατιωτῶν πολλοὶ κάμνοντες
2 ὑπελείποντο καὶ ἵπποι ἀπέθνησκον· ἀλλὰ καὶ ὣς
ἦγε, καὶ ἀφικνεῖται ἐς Ῥάγας ἑνδεκάτῃ ἡμέρᾳ.
διέχει δὲ ὁ χῶρος οὗτος ἀπὸ τῶν Κασπίων πυλῶν
ὁδὸν ἡμέρας μιᾶς ἐλαύνοντι ὡς Ἀλέξανδρος ἦγε.
Δαρεῖος δὲ ἐφθάκει ἤδη παρεληλυθὼς εἴσω τῶν

---

³ Cf. 16, 9.
⁴ See Appendixes X 3, XI 4, XIII 5 (we do not know why

He instructed Menes [3] too, when they reached the coast, to see to their being conveyed on triremes to Euboea. Parmenio was ordered to deposit in the citadel of Ecbatana the treasure conveyed from Persia and to hand it over to Harpalus; for he left Harpalus in charge of the treasure, with some six thousand Macedonians, cavalry and a few light troops to protect it. Parmenio himself was instructed to take the mercenaries, Thracians and any cavalry other than the Companion cavalry past the land of the Cadusians and march into Hyrcania. [4] Clitus the commander of the royal squadron was ordered, on reaching Ecbatana from Susa, where he had been left sick, to take the Macedonians who had been left for the time being to protect the treasure and proceed on the road for Parthyaea, where he himself also proposed to go.

20. Alexander then taking the cavalry, Companions and *prodromoi*, and the mercenary horse under Erigyius, and the Macedonian phalanx (except for those detailed to protect the treasure) along with the archers and the Agrianians, began his march against Darius. [1] By reason of the speed of his march many of his troops were left behind worn out, while the horses were dying. Still Alexander went on and reached Rhagae on the eleventh day. This place is one day's journey from the Caspian gates for anyone marching like Alexander. Darius, however, was too

7

8

2

Parmenio remained in Media, 26, 3). Harpalus: iii 6, 4–7; vii 12, 7 n.; E. Badian, *Historia* 1960, 245 ff.; *JHS* 1961, 16 ff.

[1] App. VIII 7. D. compresses the pursuit of Darius into one sentence, P. 42 f. is anecdotal, QC. v 13 often discordant with A.

πυλῶν τῶν Κασπίων. τῶν δὲ συμφευγόντων
Δαρείῳ πολλοὶ μὲν ἀπολιπόντες αὐτὸν ἐν τῇ φυγῇ
ἐπὶ τὰ αὑτῶν ἕκαστοι ἀπεχώρουν, οὐκ ὀλίγοι δὲ
3 καὶ Ἀλεξάνδρῳ σφᾶς ἐνεδίδοσαν. Ἀλέξανδρος δὲ
ὡς ἀπέγνω κατὰ πόδας αἱρήσειν Δαρεῖον, μείνας
αὐτοῦ πέντε ἡμέρας καὶ ἀναπαύσας τὸν στρατὸν
Μηδίας μὲν σατράπην ἀπέδειξεν Ὀξυδάτην Πέρσην
ἄνδρα, ὃς ἐτύγχανε πρὸς Δαρείου ξυνειλημμένος καὶ
ἐν Σούσοις εἰργόμενος· τοῦτο αὐτῷ ἐς πίστιν ἦν
πρὸς Ἀλέξανδρον· αὐτὸς δὲ ὡς ἐπὶ Παρθυαίους
4 ἦγε. καὶ τῇ μὲν πρώτῃ πρὸς ταῖς Κασπίαις
πύλαις ἐστρατοπέδευσε, τῇ δευτέρᾳ δὲ εἴσω παρῆλθε τῶν πυλῶν ἔστε οἰκούμενα ἦν. ἐπισιτισόμενος [1] δὲ αὐτόθεν, ὅτι ἔρημον τὴν πρόσω χώραν
ἤκουεν, ἐς προνομὴν ἐκπέμπει Κοῖνον ξὺν ἱππεῦσί
τε καὶ τῶν πεζῶν ὀλίγοις.

21. Καὶ ἐν τούτῳ ἀφικνεῖται παρ' αὐτὸν ἀπὸ τοῦ
Δαρείου στρατοπέδου Βαγιστάνης Βαβυλώνιος
ἀνὴρ τῶν γνωρίμων καὶ ξὺν τούτῳ Ἀντίβηλος τῶν
Μαζαίου παίδων. οὗτοι ἀπήγγειλαν ὅτι Ναβαρζάνης τε, χιλιάρχης τῶν ξὺν Δαρείῳ φευγόντων
ἱππέων, καὶ Βῆσσος ὁ Βακτρίων σατράπης καὶ
Βαρσαέντης ὁ Ἀραχωτῶν καὶ Δραγγῶν σατράπης
2 ξυνειληφότες εἶεν Δαρεῖον. ταῦτα ἀκούσας Ἀλέξανδρος ἔτι μᾶλλον ἦγε σπουδῇ, τοὺς ἑταίρους
μόνους ἔχων ἀμφ' αὑτὸν καὶ τοὺς προδρόμους
ἱππέας καὶ τῶν πεζῶν τοὺς εὐρωστοτάτους τε καὶ
κουφοτάτους ἐπιλεξάμενος, οὐδὲ τοὺς ἀμφὶ Κοῖνον
προσμείνας ἐκ τῆς προνομῆς ἐπανελθεῖν. τοῖς δὲ
ὑπολειπομένοις ἐπιστήσας Κρατερὸν προστάττει

---

[1] ἐπισιτισόμενος Krüger; ἐπισιτισάμενος codd.

330
B.C.

quick and had already passed the Caspian gates.
Many of those who shared his flight deserted him
during its course, and went off to their homes, and a
good number had surrendered to Alexander. Des- 3
pairing of capturing Darius by close pursuit, Alexander remained there five days and rested his force;
he appointed Oxydates satrap of Media, a Persian
who had been arrested by Darius and imprisoned at
Susa;[2] this made Alexander trust him. Alexander
then marched towards the Parthyaeans. The first 4
day he encamped by the Caspian gates, on the second
he passed within the gates to the limit of the inhabited
country. In order to get provisions there, since he
heard that the country beyond was desert, he sent
Coenus to forage with cavalry and a few foot-soldiers.

21. At this point Bagistanes came to him from
Darius' camp, a Babylonian and a noble, with Anti-
belus, one of Mazaeus' sons. They reported that
Nabarzanes, chiliarch of the cavalry which had shared
Darius' flight, Bessus satrap of Bactria and Barsaentes
satrap of the Arachotians and the Drangians [1] had
arrested Darius. On learning this Alexander pressed 2
on faster than ever, with only the Companions, the
mounted *prodromoi*, and the strongest and lightest of
the infantry, carefully selected, without even waiting
for Coenus and his men to return from foraging. He
put Craterus in command of those left behind and
ordered him to follow, but not by forced marches.

---

[2] QC. vi 2, 11 puts this after Darius' death.
[1] Elsewhere called Zarangians.

3 ⟨ἕπεσθαι⟩ μὴ μακρὰς ὁδοὺς ἄγοντα. οἱ δὲ ἀμφ'
αὐτὸν τὰ ὅπλα εἶχον μόνον καὶ δύο ἡμερῶν σιτία.
ἐλθὼν δὲ τήν τε νύκτα ὅλην καὶ τῆς ἐπιούσης
ἡμέρας μέχρι μεσημβρίας ὀλίγον χρόνον ἀναπαύσας
τὸν στρατὸν αὖθις ἦει ὅλην νύκτα, καὶ ἅμα ἡμέρᾳ
ὑποφαινούσῃ παρῆν εἰς τὸ στρατόπεδον, ὅθεν
4 ἀφωρμήκει ὀπίσω Βαγιστάνης. καὶ τοὺς μὲν πολεμίους οὐ κατέλαβε, Δαρείου δὲ πέρι ἐπύθετο
αὐτὸν μὲν συνειλημμένον ἄγεσθαι ἐφ' ἁρμαμάξης,
Βήσσῳ δὲ ἀντὶ Δαρείου εἶναι τὸ κράτος καὶ
ἡγεμόνα ὠνομάσθαι Βῆσσον πρός τε τῶν Βακτρίων
ἱππέων καὶ τῶν ἄλλων ὅσοι βάρβαροι ξυνέφευγον
Δαρείῳ, πλὴν Ἀρταβάζου καὶ τῶν Ἀρταβάζου
παίδων καὶ τῶν Ἑλλήνων τῶν μισθοφόρων·
τούτους δὲ πιστοὺς εἶναι Δαρείῳ, καὶ εἴργειν μὲν τὰ
γιγνόμενα οὐ δυνατοὺς εἶναι, ἐκτραπέντας δὲ ἔξω
τῆς λεωφόρου ὁδοῦ ὡς ἐπὶ τὰ ὄρη ἰέναι κατὰ σφᾶς,
οὐ μετέχοντας τοῖς ἀμφὶ Βῆσσον τοῦ ἔργου.
5 γνώμην δὲ πεποιῆσθαι τοὺς ξυλλαβόντας Δαρεῖον,
εἰ μὲν διώκοντα σφᾶς Ἀλέξανδρον πυνθάνοιντο,
παραδοῦναι Δαρεῖον Ἀλεξάνδρῳ καὶ σφίσι τι
ἀγαθὸν εὑρίσκεσθαι· εἰ δὲ τὸ ἔμπαλιν ἐπανε-
ληλυθότα μάθοιεν, τοὺς δὲ στρατιάν τε ξυλλέγειν
ὅσην πλείστην δύναιντο καὶ διασώζειν ἐς τὸ κοινὸν
τὴν ἀρχήν. Βῆσσον δὲ ἐν τῷ παρόντι ἐξηγεῖσθαι
κατ' οἰκειότητά τε τὴν Δαρείου καὶ ὅτι ἐν τῇ αὐτοῦ
σατραπείᾳ τὸ ἔργον ἐγίγνετο.
6 Ταῦτα ἀκούσαντι Ἀλεξάνδρῳ ἀνὰ κράτος διω-
κτέα ἐφαίνετο. καὶ ἤδη μὲν ἐξέκαμνον οἵ τε
ἄνδρες καὶ οἱ ἵπποι ὑπὸ τῇ ταλαιπωρίᾳ τῇ ξυνεχεῖ·
ἀλλὰ καὶ ὡς ἦγε, καὶ διελθὼν ὁδὸν πολλὴν τῆς τε

His own men had nothing but their arms and two days' rations. Travelling all night and the next day till noon, he rested his troops a short time and then went on again all night, and at dawn he reached the camp, from which Bagistanes had started back. But he did not overtake the enemy, though he learnt that Darius was being carried in a closed waggon under arrest, that Bessus had the sovereignty in place of Darius and had been saluted as leader by the Bactrian cavalry and the other barbarians who had fled with Darius, except by Artabazus [2] and his sons and the Greek mercenaries, that they were loyal to Darius, and as they were unable to prevent what was taking place, had turned off the main road and were making for the mountains [3] by themselves, taking no part in the action of Bessus and his followers, while those who had seized Darius had decided, if they learned that Alexander was pursuing them, to give him up to Alexander and make good terms for themselves, but if they learned that he had turned back, to collect as large an army as they could and preserve their power in common; Bessus was in command for the time because of his relationship to Darius and because the act was done in his satrapy.[4]

On hearing this, Alexander decided that he must pursue with the utmost vigour. Already his men and horses were growing utterly wearied under the continued hardship; none the less, he pressed on, and

[2] Connected by marriage with Darius, and also with Memnon (i 12, 9 n.), he had spent some years in exile at Philip's court, and was loyal first to Darius, then to Al.

[3] Of Tapuria (23, 1), i.e. Elburz.

[4] A mistake; Bessus' satrapy was not Parthyaea but Bactria.

νυκτὸς καὶ τῆς ἐπὶ ταύτῃ ἡμέρας ἔστε ἐπὶ μεσημβρίαν ἀφικνεῖται ἔς τινα κώμην, ἵνα τῇ προτεραίᾳ
7 ἐστρατοπεδεύκεσαν οἱ Δαρεῖον ἄγοντες. ἐνταῦθα
ἀκούσας ὅτι νυκτὸς ποιεῖσθαι τὴν πορείαν ἐγνωσμένον εἴη τοῖς βαρβάροις, ἤλεγχε τοὺς προσχώρους, εἰ δή τινα εἰδεῖεν ἐπιτομωτέραν ὁδὸν ἐπὶ τοὺς
φεύγοντας. οἱ δὲ εἰδέναι μὲν ἔφασαν, ἐρήμην δὲ
εἶναι τὴν ὁδὸν δι᾽ ἀνυδρίαν. ὁ δὲ ταύτην ἄγειν
ἐκέλευσε· καὶ γνοὺς ὅτι οὐχ ἕψονται οἱ πεζοὶ αὐτῷ
σπουδῇ ἐλαύνοντι τῶν μὲν ἱππέων ἐς πεντακοσίους
κατεβίβασεν ἀπὸ τῶν ἵππων, τοὺς ἡγεμόνας δὲ
τῶν πεζῶν καὶ τῶν ἄλλων ἐπιλεξάμενος τοὺς
κρατιστεύοντας ἐπιβῆναι τῶν ἵππων ἐκέλευσεν
8 οὕτως ὅπως οἱ πεζοὶ ὡπλισμένοι ἦσαν. Νικάνορα
δὲ τὸν τῶν ὑπασπιστῶν ἡγεμόνα καὶ Ἄτταλον τὸν
τῶν Ἀγριάνων κατὰ τὴν ὁδόν, ἥντινα οἱ ἀμφὶ
Βῆσσον προὐκεχωρήκεσαν, τοὺς ὑπολειφθέντας
ἄγειν ἐκέλευσε, καὶ τούτους ὡς κουφότατα ἐσταλμένους, τοὺς δὲ ἄλλους πεζοὺς ἐν τάξει ἔπεσθαι.
9 αὐτὸς δὲ ἀμφὶ δείλην ἄγειν ἀρξάμενος δρόμῳ
ἡγεῖτο· διελθὼν δὲ τῆς νυκτὸς σταδίους ἐς τετρακοσίους ὑπὸ τὴν ἕω ἐπιτυγχάνει τοῖς βαρβάροις
ἀτάκτως ἰοῦσι καὶ ἀνόπλοις, ὥστε ὀλίγοι μέν τινες
αὐτῶν ὡς ἀμυνούμενοι ὥρμησαν, οἱ δὲ πολλοὶ εὐθὺς
ὡς Ἀλέξανδρον αὐτὸν κατεῖδον οὐδὲ ἐς χεῖρας
ἐλθόντες ἔφευγον· καὶ οἱ τραπέντες ἐς ἀλκὴν
10 ὀλίγων πεσόντων καὶ οὗτοι ἔφυγον. Βῆσσος δὲ
καὶ οἱ ξὺν αὐτῷ τέως μὲν ἐφ᾽ ἁρμαμάξης Δαρεῖον
μετὰ σφῶν ἐκόμιζον· ὡς δὲ ὁμοῦ ἤδη ἦν Ἀλέξανδρος, Δαρεῖον μὲν Σατιβαρζάνης καὶ Βαρσαέντης κατατρώσαντες αὐτοῦ ἀπέλιπον, αὐτοὶ δὲ
ἔφυγον ξὺν ἱππεῦσιν ἑξακοσίοις. Δαρεῖος δὲ ἀπο-

accomplishing a great distance during the night and
the following day till noon, he reached a village
where the party with Darius had bivouacked the day
before. As he heard there that the barbarians had 7
determined to travel by night, he asked the inhabitants whether they knew of any short cut to get to
the fugitives. They replied that they did, but that
the road was desolate for lack of water. He told
them to guide him along this road, and seeing that
his infantry would not keep up with him if he pushed
on at full speed, he dismounted some five hundred
horsemen, selected from the officers of the infantry
and the rest those who had best kept up their
strength, and ordered them to mount the horses,
carrying their usual infantry arms. Nicanor the 8
commander of the hypaspists, and Attalus commander of the Agrianians, were ordered to lead the
men who were left behind along the road already
taken by Bessus and his party with the lightest possible
equipment, and the rest of the infantry were to
follow in ordinary formation. Alexander then 9
started off himself at evening, and led his troops on
at full speed; during the night he covered up to four
hundred stades, and just at dawn came upon the
Persians marching in disorder without arms, so that
only a few of them attempted resistance; as soon as
they saw Alexander himself, most of them did not
even wait to come to close quarters but took to flight;
those who did turn to make a fight of it also fled on
losing a few of their number. For a time Bessus and 10
his immediate followers continued to convey Darius
with them in the closed waggon; but when Alexander was right upon them, Satibarzanes and Barsaentes wounded Darius, left him where he was and
escaped themselves with six hundred horsemen.

θνήσκει ὀλίγον ὕστερον ἐκ τῶν τραυμάτων πρὶν
ὀφθῆναι Ἀλεξάνδρῳ.

22. Ἀλέξανδρος δὲ τὸ μὲν σῶμα τοῦ Δαρείου ἐς
Πέρσας ἀπέπεμψε, θάψαι κελεύσας ἐν ταῖς βασιλικαῖς θήκαις, καθάπερ καὶ οἱ ἄλλοι οἱ πρὸ
Δαρείου βασιλεῖς· σατράπην δὲ ἀπέδειξε Παρθυαίων καὶ Ὑρκανίων Ἀμμινάπην Παρθυαῖον·
ἦν δὲ οὗτος τῶν Αἴγυπτον ἐνδόντων Ἀλεξάνδρῳ
μετὰ Μαζάκου. Τληπόλεμος δὲ Πυθοφάνους τῶν
ἑταίρων ξυνετάχθη αὐτῷ σκοπεῖν τὰ ἐν Παρθυαίοις
τε καὶ Ὑρκανίοις.

2   Τοῦτο τὸ τέλος Δαρείῳ ἐγένετο ἐπὶ ἄρχοντος
Ἀθηναίοις Ἀριστοφῶντος μηνὸς Ἑκατομβαιῶνος,
ἀνδρὶ τὰ μὲν πολέμια, εἴπερ τινὶ ἄλλῳ, μαλθακῷ τε
καὶ οὐ φρενήρει, εἰς δὲ τἆλλα οὐδὲν ἀνεπιεικὲς
ἔργον ἀποδειξαμένῳ ἢ οὐδὲ ἐγγενόμενον αὐτῷ
ἀποδείξασθαι, ὅτι ὁμοῦ μὲν ἐς τὴν βασιλείαν παρελθεῖν, ὁμοῦ δὲ προσπολεμεῖσθαι πρός τε Μακεδόνων καὶ τῶν Ἑλλήνων ξυνέβη. οὔκουν οὐδὲ
ἐθέλοντι ἐξῆν ἔτι ὑβρίζειν ἐς τοὺς ὑπηκόους ἐν
μείζονι κινδύνῳ ἤπερ ἐκεῖνοι καθεστηκότι. ζῶντι
μὲν δὴ ξυμφοραὶ αὐτῷ ἄλλαι ἐπ' ἄλλαις ξυνηνέ-
3   χθησαν, οὐδέ τις ἀνακωχὴ ἐγένετο ἐπειδὴ πρῶτον
ἐς τὴν ἀρχὴν παρῆλθεν· ἀλλὰ εὐθὺς μὲν τὸ τῶν
σατραπῶν ἐπὶ Γρανίκῳ πταῖσμα ξυνέβη τὸ ἱππικόν,
εὐθὺς δὲ Ἰωνία τε καὶ Αἰολὶς εἴχοντο καὶ Φρύγες
ἀμφότεροι καὶ Λυδία καὶ Κᾶρες πλὴν Ἁλικαρνασ-
4   σέων· ὀλίγον δὲ ὕστερον καὶ Ἁλικαρνασσὸς
ἐξῄρητο, ἐπὶ δὲ ἡ παραλία πᾶσα ἔστε ἐπὶ Κιλικίαν·
ἔνθεν δὲ ἡ αὐτοῦ ἐπ' Ἰσσῷ ἧσσα, ἵνα τήν τε μητέρα

---

5 In the 'vulgate' Darius was still alive when found by

Darius died of his wound soon after, before Alexander had seen him.[5]

22. Alexander sent Darius' body to Persepolis, ordering it to be buried in the royal tomb, like the other kings who ruled before him.[1]   He appointed as satrap of the Parthyaeans and Hyrcanians Amminapes, a Parthyaean; he was one of those with Mazacus, who had surrendered Egypt to Alexander.[2]   Tlepolemus son of Pythophanes, one of the Companions, was associated in the appointment with him, to superintend Parthyaea and Hyrcania.

This was the end of Darius, when Aristophon was 2 archon at Athens in the month Hecatombaeon.[3]   No man showed less spirit or sense in warfare; but in other matters he committed no offence, perhaps for lack of opportunity, since the moment of his accession was also the moment of the attack on him by the Macedonians and Greeks.   So even if he had had the will, he was no longer free to play the tyrant to his subjects, as his position was more dangerous than theirs.   His life was one series of disasters, with no 3 respite, after his accession.   The cavalry disaster of his satraps on the Granicus happened at once, and at once Ionia and Aeolis were in the enemy's hands, with both Phrygias, Lydia and all Caria except Halicarnassus; the loss of Halicarnassus, and then of all 4 the coast-line as far as Cilicia soon followed.   Next came his defeat at Issus, where he saw his mother

the Macedonians, QC. v 13, 24 f. (broken by lacuna); P. 43; J. xi 15.

  [1] Cf. vi 29.
  [2] QC. vi 4, 25 puts this in Hyrcania, ignoring Tlepolemus. Amminapes was eventually replaced by Phrataphernes (iii 23, 4) at least by 326 B.C. (v 20, 7) but perhaps not as early as autumn 330 B.C. (cf. iii 28, 2).
  [3] July 330, cf. App. VIII 6–10.   A's reflections follow.

αἰχμαλωτισθεῖσαν καὶ τὴν γυναῖκα καὶ τοὺς παῖδας
ἐπεῖδεν· ἐπὶ τῷδε Φοινίκη τε ἀπώλετο καὶ
Αἴγυπτος πᾶσα· ἐπὶ δὲ αὐτὸς ἐν Ἀρβήλοις ἔφυγέ
τε ἐν πρώτοις αἰσχρῶς καὶ στρατιὰν πλείστην
5 παντὸς τοῦ βαρβαρικοῦ γένους ἀπώλεσε· φυγάς τε
ἐκ τούτου τῆς αὑτοῦ ἀρχῆς πλανώμενος καὶ τελευτῶν πρὸς τῶν ἀμφ' αὐτὸν ἐς τὰ ἔσχατα προδοθείς,
βασιλεύς τε ἐν τῷ αὐτῷ καὶ δεσμώτης ξὺν ἀτιμίᾳ
ἀγόμενος, τέλος δὲ πρὸς τῶν οἰκειοτάτων ἐπιβου-
λευθεὶς ἀπώλετο. ζῶντι μὲν Δαρείῳ τοιαῦτα
6 ξυνηνέχθη, τελευτήσαντι δὲ ταφή τε ἡ βασιλικὴ καὶ
τῶν παίδων ὁποῖα καὶ βασιλεύοντος αὐτοῦ τροφή
τε ⟨παρ'⟩ Ἀλεξάνδρου καὶ παίδευσις, καὶ γαμβρὸς
Ἀλέξανδρος. ὁπότε δὲ ἐτελεύτα, ἐγεγόνει ἀμφὶ τὰ
πεντήκοντα ἔτη.

23. Ἀλέξανδρος δὲ τοὺς ὑπολειφθέντας ἐν τῇ
διώξει τῆς στρατιᾶς ἀναλαβὼν ἐς Ὑρκανίαν προύχώρει. κεῖται δὲ ἡ Ὑρκανία χώρα ἐν ἀριστερᾷ
τῆς ὁδοῦ τῆς ἐπὶ Βάκτρα φερούσης· καὶ τῇ μὲν
ὄρεσιν ἀπείργεται δασέσι καὶ ὑψηλοῖς, τὸ πεδίον δὲ
αὐτῆς καθήκει ἔστε ἐπὶ τὴν μεγάλην τὴν ταύτῃ
θάλασσαν. ταύτην δὲ ἦγεν, ὅτι ταύτῃ τοὺς ξένους
τοὺς ἀμφὶ Δαρεῖον διαπεφευγέναι ἐς τὰ τῶν
Ταπούρων ὄρη ἐπύθετο καὶ αὐτοὺς ἅμα τοὺς
2 Ταπούρους χειρωσόμενος. τριχῇ δὴ διελὼν τὸν
στρατὸν αὐτὸς μὲν τὴν ἐπιτομωτάτην καὶ χαλε-
πωτάτην ἡγήσατο, τὸ πλεῖστον καὶ ἅμα τὸ κουφό-
τατον τῆς δυνάμεως ἄγων· Κρατερὸν δὲ τήν τε
αὑτοῦ τάξιν ἔχοντα καὶ τὴν Ἀμύντου καὶ τῶν
τοξοτῶν ἔστιν οὓς καὶ ὀλίγους τῶν ἱππέων ἐπὶ
Ταπούρων ἔστειλεν· Ἐριγύϊον δὲ τούς τε ξένους

with his wife and children taken prisoners; then
Phoenicia and all Egypt were lost; and then he himself was among the first to flee dishonourably at
Arbela, and lost the greatest army of the whole
barbarian race; a fugitive from his own kingdom and 5
a wanderer, he was at last betrayed by his own escort
to the worst of fates, to be at once a king and prisoner
carried off in dishonour; finally he perished by a conspiracy of his closest connections. These were the
tragedies of Darius' life. After death he had a royal 6
burial and his children were brought up and educated
by Alexander as if he were still on the throne, and
Alexander married his daughter.[4] At his death he
was about fifty years old.

23. Alexander, taking over the troops left behind
in the pursuit, advanced into Hyrcania, which lies on
the left of the road leading to Bactria;[1] on one side
it is bounded by high, wooded mountains, but its
plain stretches to the Great Sea [Caspian] in those
parts. Alexander marched this way because he had
learned that the mercenaries with Darius had escaped to the Tapurian mountains [Elburz]; besides,
he intended to subdue the Tapurians themselves. He 2
divided his army into three parts, and himself took the
shortest and hardest road with the largest part and
lightest armed of his force; he sent Craterus with his
own battalion and that of Amyntas, some of the
archers, and a few horsemen, against the Tapurians,
and Erigyius was ordered to take the mercenaries and

---

[4] In 324, vii 4, 4; she was murdered after Al's death by
Roxane (P. 77). Education: D. 67, 1; QC. v 2, 18 ff.
[1] Hyrcanian campaign: App. VIII 10; D. 75 f.; QC. vi 4 f.;
P. 44; 46 f.; Strabo xi 7 (cf ii 1, 14) with citations from Ar.
F 19 f., whose topographical material A. ignores. QC. vi 2,
15 ff (at Hecatompylos, cf. D. 74) and P. 47 (in Hyrcania) tell
that Al. had to persuade the Macedonians to march on.

καὶ τὴν λοιπὴν ἵππον ἀναλαβόντα τὴν λεωφόρον τε
καὶ μακροτέραν ἡγεῖσθαι ἐκέλευσε, τὰς ἁμάξας καὶ
τὰ σκευοφόρα καὶ τὸν ἄλλον ὅμιλον ἄγοντα.

3 Ὑπερβαλὼν δὲ τὰ πρῶτα ὄρη καὶ καταστρατοπεδεύσας αὐτοῦ ἀναλαβὼν τούς τε ὑπασπιστὰς καὶ
τῆς Μακεδονικῆς φάλαγγος τοὺς κουφοτάτους καὶ
τῶν τοξοτῶν ἔστιν οὓς ᾔει χαλεπὴν ὁδὸν καὶ
δύσπορον, φύλακας τῶν ὁδῶν καταλιπών, ἵνα
σφαλερόν τι αὐτῷ ἐφαίνετο, ὡς μὴ τοῖς ἑπομένοις
κατ' ἐκεῖνα ἐπιθοῖντο οἱ τὰ ὄρη ἔχοντες τῶν βαρβά-
4 ρων. αὐτὸς δὲ μετὰ τῶν τοξοτῶν διελθὼν τὰ
στενὰ ἐν τῷ πεδίῳ κατεστρατοπέδευσε πρὸς
ποταμῷ οὐ μεγάλῳ. καὶ ἐνταῦθα ὄντος αὐτοῦ
Ναβαρζάνης τε ὁ Δαρείου χιλιάρχης καὶ Φραταφέρνης ὁ Ὑρκανίας τε καὶ Παρθυαίων σατράπης
καὶ ἄλλοι τῶν ἀμφὶ Δαρεῖον Περσῶν οἱ ἐπιφανέ-
5 στατοι ἀφικόμενοι παρέδοσαν σφᾶς αὐτούς. ὑπομείνας δὲ ἐν τῷ στρατοπέδῳ τέσσαρας ἡμέρας
ἀνέλαβε τοὺς ὑπολειφθέντας κατὰ τὴν ὁδόν, τοὺς
μὲν ἄλλους ἀσφαλῶς διελθόντας, τοῖς δὲ Ἀγριᾶσιν
ὀπισθοφυλακοῦσιν ἐπέθεντο οἱ ὄρειοι τῶν βαρβάρων, καὶ μεῖον ἔχοντες τῷ ἀκροβολισμῷ ἀπηλλάγησαν.

6 Ἄρας δὲ ἐντεῦθεν προῄει ὡς ἐφ' Ὑρκανίαν εἰς
Ζαδράκαρτα πόλιν Ὑρκανίων. καὶ ἐν τούτῳ οἱ
περὶ Κρατερὸν ξυνέμιξαν αὐτῷ, τοῖς μὲν ξένοις τοῖς
Δαρείου οὐκ ἐντετυχηκότες, τὴν χώραν δὲ ὅσην
διαπεπορευμένοι ἦσαν τὴν μὲν βίᾳ, τὴν δὲ ἐνδιδό-

---

[2] Al. had only 3 phalanx battalions with him at this time
(Introd. 61), the third being that of Coenus (24, 1).   Contra

the rest of the cavalry and bring them along the high-road, which was longer, convoying the waggons, the baggage train and the rest of his people.[2]

After he had crossed the first mountains and had 3 encamped there, Alexander took the hypaspists and the lightest armed of the Macedonian phalanx and some of the archers, and marched along a rough and difficult road, leaving troops behind to guard the roads where he thought there was danger, so that the barbarians in possession of the heights might not attack the forces coming after at those points. He 4 himself with the archers crossed the pass and camped in the plain by a small river. While he was there, Nabarzanes, Darius' chiliarch, Phrataphernes the satrap of Hyrcania and Parthyaea and other very highly placed Persian officers of Darius came and gave themselves up.[3] After waiting four days in the 5 camp, he picked up those who had been left behind on the march, most of whom had got through with safety; the native hillmen had attacked the Agrianians, guarding the rear, but had the worst of a long range skirmish and withdrew.

Starting off again, Alexander advanced towards 6 Hyrcania to Zadracarta, a city of the Hyrcanians.[4] At this point Craterus and his troops joined him; they had not fallen in with Darius' mercenaries, but partly by force and partly by the surrender of the

Lane Fox (cf. Introd. n. 99) A's words do not imply that Coenus' battalion was less heavily armoured than the rest; Al. took not only the lightest armed (e.g. the hypaspists) but the largest part of the force.

[3] Phrataphernes (henceforth unswervingly loyal), QC. vi 4, 23; he puts Nabarzanes' surrender later, after prior negotiations, 4, 8 ff.; 5, 22.

[4] App. VIII 10.

ντων τῶν κατοικούντων προσπεποιημένοι. ἐνταῦθα
καὶ Ἐριγύϊος ἧκε σὺν τοῖς σκευοφόροις καὶ ταῖς
7 ἁμάξαις. ὀλίγον δὲ ὕστερον Ἀρτάβαζος ἀφίκετο
παρ᾽ Ἀλέξανδρον καὶ τῶν παίδων αὐτοῦ Κωφὴν
καὶ Ἀριοβαρζάνης καὶ Ἀρσάμης καὶ ξὺν τούτοις
παρὰ τῶν ξένων τῶν ξὺν Δαρείῳ πρέσβεις καὶ
Αὐτοφραδάτης ὁ Ταπούρων σατράπης. Αὐτοφραδάτῃ μὲν δὴ τὴν σατραπείαν ἀπέδωκεν,
Ἀρτάβαζον δὲ καὶ τοὺς παῖδας ἅμα οἷ ἐν τιμῇ ἦγε,
τά τε ἄλλα ἐν τοῖς πρώτοις Περσῶν ὄντας καὶ τῆς
8 ἐς Δαρεῖον πίστεως ἕνεκα. τοῖς πρέσβεσι δὲ τῶν
Ἑλλήνων δεομένοις σπείσασθαί σφισιν ὑπὲρ τοῦ
παντὸς ξενικοῦ ἀπεκρίνατο ὁμολογίαν μὲν οὐκ ἂν
ποιήσασθαι πρὸς αὐτοὺς οὐδεμίαν· ἀδικεῖν γὰρ
μεγάλα τοὺς στρατευομένους ἐναντία τῇ Ἑλλάδι
παρὰ τοῖς βαρβάροις παρὰ τὰ δόγματα τῶν Ἑλ-
λήνων· ἐκέλευσε δὲ ἥκειν ξύμπαντας καὶ παραδιδόναι σφᾶς αὐτοὺς ἐπιτρέποντας Ἀλεξάνδρῳ
χρῆσθαι ὅ τι βούλοιτο, ἢ σώζεσθαι ὅπῃ δύναιντο.
9 οἱ δὲ ἐπιτρέπειν ἔφασαν σφᾶς τε αὐτοὺς καὶ τοὺς
ἄλλους Ἀλεξάνδρῳ· ξυμπέμπειν τε ἐκέλευον τὸν
ἡγησόμενον αὐτοῖς, ὡς ἀσφαλῶς διακομισθεῖεν
παρ᾽ αὐτόν· εἶναι δὲ ἐλέγοντο ἐς χιλίους καὶ
πεντακοσίους. καὶ Ἀλέξανδρος πέμπει Ἀνδρόνικον τὸν Ἀγέρρου καὶ Ἀρτάβαζον παρ᾽ αὐτούς.

24. Αὐτὸς δὲ προῆγεν ὡς ἐπὶ Μάρδους, ἀναλαβὼν τούς τε ὑπασπιστὰς καὶ τοὺς τοξότας καὶ τοὺς
Ἀγριᾶνας καὶ τὴν Κοίνου καὶ Ἀμύντου τάξιν καὶ
τῶν ἑταίρων ἱππέων τοὺς ἡμίσεας καὶ τοὺς ἱπ-

---

⁵ QC. 4, 24 and 5, 1 ff. puts Autophradates' surrender before
Artabazus'. Al. rewards or punishes men for their conduct
to Darius as it suits him; the motivation in A. is naive.

inhabitants, they had taken over all the territory they had traversed. Erigyius too arrived there with the baggage trains and the waggons. Soon after, 7 Artabazus came to join Alexander with Cophen, Ariobarzanes and Arsames among his sons and Autophradates, satrap of the Tapurians, and envoys from the mercenaries who had been with Darius. Alexander gave the satrapy back to Autophradates, while he kept Artabazus and his sons by him in an honourable position, as they were among the most eminent Persians and especially because of their loyalty to Darius.[5] To the envoys of the Greeks, however, who 8 begged him to grant them terms for the whole mercenary force, he replied that he would make no compact with them whatever; men who fought with the barbarians against Greece against the decrees of the Greeks were guilty of grave wrongs.[6] He ordered them to come in a body and surrender, leaving it to him to do what he would with them; if not, they must take what steps they could for their own safety. They replied that they placed themselves and the rest 9 in Alexander's hands, and urged him to send an officer to lead them under safe conduct to his camp. They were said to be about one thousand five hundred.[7] Alexander sent Andronicus, son of Agerrus, and Artabazus to them.

24. He himself proceeded against the Mardians,[1] taking the hypaspists, archers, Agrianians, the battalions of Coenus and Amyntas, half the Com-

---

[6] See Introd. 38 and 40.

[7] Cf. 19, 5 n. QC. 5, 6–10 (cf. D. 76, 2) now also gives 1500; 500 had evidently been lost since 331.

[1] Or Amardi, west of Hyrcanian coastal plain (Strabo xi 8. 8; 13. 3). Cf. D. 76, 3 f.; QC. 5, 11 ff.

πακοντιστάς· ἤδη γὰρ αὐτῷ καὶ ἱππακοντισταὶ
2 τάξις ἦσαν. ἐπελθὼν δὲ τὸ πολὺ μέρος τῆς χώρας
τῶν Μάρδων πολλοὺς μὲν ἀπέκτεινεν αὐτῶν
φεύγοντας, οὓς δέ τινας ἐς ἀλκὴν τετραμμένους,
πολλοὺς δὲ ζῶντας ἔλαβεν. οὐ γὰρ ἔστιν ὅστις
χρόνου ἐμβεβλήκει ἐς τὴν γῆν αὐτῶν ἐπὶ πολέμῳ
διά τε δυσχωρίαν καὶ ὅτι πένητες οἱ Μάρδοι καὶ
μάχιμοι ἐπὶ τῇ πενίᾳ ἦσαν. οὔκουν οὐδὲ ᾿Αλέ-
ξανδρον ἐμβαλεῖν ἄν ποτε δείσαντες, ἄλλως τε καὶ
προκεχωρηκότα ἤδη ἐς τὸ πρόσω, ταύτῃ μᾶλλόν τι
3 ἀφύλακτοι ἡλίσκοντο. πολλοὶ δὲ αὐτῶν καὶ ἐς τὰ
ὄρη κατέφυγον, ἃ δὴ ὑπερύψηλά τε καὶ ἀπότομα
αὐτοῖς ἐν τῇ χώρᾳ ἐστίν, ὡς πρὸς ταῦτά γε οὐχ
ἥξοντα ᾿Αλέξανδρον. ἐπεὶ δὲ καὶ ταύτῃ προσῆγεν,
οἱ δὲ πέμψαντες πρέσβεις σφᾶς τε αὐτοὺς ἐνέδοσαν
καὶ τὴν χώραν· καὶ ᾿Αλέξανδρος αὐτοὺς μὲν
ἀφῆκεν, σατράπην δὲ ἀπέδειξεν αὐτῶν Αὐτοφραδάτην, ὅνπερ καὶ Ταπούρων.

4   Αὐτὸς δὲ ἐπανελθὼν εἰς τὸ στρατόπεδον, ἔνθενπερ ὡρμήθη ἐς τῶν Μάρδων τὴν γῆν, κατέλαβε
τοὺς ῞Ελληνας τοὺς μισθοφόρους ἥκοντας καὶ τοὺς
Λακεδαιμονίων πρέσβεις, οἳ παρὰ βασιλέα Δαρεῖον
ἐπρέσβευον, Καλλιστρατίδαν τε καὶ Παύσιππον καὶ
Μόνιμον καὶ ᾿Ονόμαντα, καὶ ᾿Αθηναίων Δρωπίδην.
τούτους μὲν δὴ ξυλλαβὼν ἐν φυλακῇ εἶχε, τοὺς
Σινωπέων δὲ ἀφῆκεν, ὅτι Σινωπεῖς οὔτε τοῦ
κοινοῦ τῶν ῾Ελλήνων μετεῖχον, ὑπὸ Πέρσαις τε
τεταγμένοι οὐκ ἀπεικότα ποιεῖν ἐδόκουν παρὰ τὸν
5 βασιλέα σφῶν πρεσβεύοντες. ἀφῆκεν δὲ καὶ τῶν
ἄλλων ῾Ελλήνων, ὅσοι πρὸ τῆς εἰρήνης τε καὶ τῆς
ξυμμαχίας τῆς πρὸς Μακεδόνας γενομένης παρὰ

panion cavalry and the mounted javelin-men, for by
this time they formed a battalion. Passing through 2
the greater part of the Mardian country, he killed
many of them in flight, and some who had offered
resistance; a great number were captured alive.
Now, no one had invaded their country for a long
time, owing to the difficulty of the terrain, and
because the Mardians were not only poor, but warlike. So they could never have had any apprehen-
sion that Alexander would invade their country,
especially as he had already marched so far beyond
it, and for this reason they were taken more off their
guard. But many of them also took refuge in the 3
mountains, which are very high and precipitous in
their country, feeling sure that Alexander would not
penetrate so far. But when he actually reached this
refuge, they sent envoys and surrendered themselves
and their country; and Alexander released them, and
appointed as their satrap Autophradates, whom he
had also made satrap of the Tapurians.

He himself returned to the camp from which he 4
had set out for the Mardian land, and found that the
mercenary Greeks had arrived with the Lacedaemonian envoys who were on an embassy to king
Darius, Callistratidas, Pausippus, Monimus and Ono-
mas, with Dropides from Athens. He arrested these
men and kept them in custody, but released envoys
from Sinope, since the Sinopeans were not part of the
Greek league but subject to Persia, and he did not
think they were acting unreasonably in sending an
embassy to their own king.[2] He released the other 5
Greeks too who served the Persians as mercenaries
before the peace and alliance made (by the Greeks)

---

[2] QC. 5, 6 ff.; cf. Introd. 40; App. VI. QC. says the
Athenian Democrates fell on his sword.

Πέρσαις ἐμισθοφόρουν, καὶ Καλχηδονίων Ἡρακλείδην. τὸν πρεσβευτὴν ἀφῆκεν· τοὺς δὲ ἄλλους
ξυστρατεύεσθαί οἱ ἐπὶ μισθῷ τῷ αὐτῷ ἐκέλευσε·
καὶ ἐπέταξεν αὐτοῖς Ἀνδρόνικον, ὅσπερ ἤγαγέ τε
αὐτοὺς καὶ ἔνδηλος γεγόνει οὐ φαῦλον ποιούμενος
σῶσαι τοὺς ἄνδρας.

25. Ταῦτα δὲ διαπραξάμενος ἦγεν ὡς ἐπὶ Ζαδράκαρτα, τὴν μεγίστην πόλιν τῆς Ὑρκανίας, ἵνα
καὶ τὰ βασίλεια τοῖς Ὑρκανίοις ἦν. καὶ ἐνταῦθα
διατρίψας ἡμέρας πεντεκαίδεκα καὶ θύσας τοῖς
θεοῖς ὡς νόμος καὶ ἀγῶνα γυμνικὸν ποιήσας ὡς
ἐπὶ Παρθυαίους ἦγεν· ἐκεῖθεν δὲ ἐπὶ τὰ τῆς
Ἀρείας ὅρια καὶ Σουσίαν, πόλιν τῆς Ἀρείας, ἵνα
καὶ Σατιβαρζάνης ἧκε παρ' αὐτὸν ὁ τῶν Ἀρείων
2 σατράπης. τούτῳ μὲν δὴ τὴν σατραπείαν ἀποδοὺς
ξυμπέμπει αὐτῷ Ἀνάξιππον τῶν ἑταίρων δοὺς
αὐτῷ τῶν ἱππακοντιστῶν ἐς τεσσαράκοντα, ὡς
ἔχοι φύλακας καθιστάναι τῶν τόπων, τοῦ μὴ
ἀδικεῖσθαι τοὺς Ἀρείους πρὸς τῆς στρατιᾶς κατὰ
τὴν πάροδον.

3 Ἐν τούτῳ δὲ ἀφικνοῦνται παρ' αὐτὸν Περσῶν
τινες, οἳ ἤγγελλον Βῆσσον τήν τε τιάραν ὀρθὴν
ἔχειν καὶ τὴν Περσικὴν στολὴν φοροῦντα Ἀρτοξέρξην τε καλεῖσθαι ἀντὶ Βήσσου καὶ βασιλέα
φάσκειν εἶναι τῆς Ἀσίας· ἔχειν τε ἀμφ' αὐτὸν
Περσῶν τε τοὺς ἐς Βάκτρα διαφυγόντας καὶ αὐτῶν
Βακτριανῶν πολλούς· προσδοκᾶσθαι δὲ ἥξειν
αὐτῷ καὶ Σκύθας ξυμμάχους.

---

[3] Cf. Introd. 38.

[4] QC. v 9, 15 (cf. A. 16, 2) makes Patron their leader.
Andronicus, a Macedonian, replaced him.

with the Macedonians,[3] as well as Heraclides, the
envoy from Calchedon, and ordered the other Greeks
to join his army for the same pay as they had been
receiving, under the command of Andronicus, who
had been their leader and had shown his anxiety to
save their lives.[4]

25. After carrying all this out, he made for Zadracarta, the greatest city of Hyrcania, the place where
the Hyrcanian palace was. There he spent fifteen
days, and sacrificed to the gods as custom directed,
and held an athletic contest,[1] and then marched
towards the Parthyaeans, and thence to the borders
of Areia and to Susia, a city of Areia, where he was
also met by Satibarzanes, the satrap of the Areians.
Alexander confirmed him in his satrapy,[2] and sent 2
with him Anaxippus, one of the Companions, with
about forty mounted javelin-men, so that he might
have guards to set for various places, to prevent the
Areians being injured by the army on its passage.

Meanwhile some Persians met Alexander and 3
reported that Bessus was wearing his cap upright,
dressing in Persian royal garb,[3] calling himself
Artaxerxes instead of Bessus, and giving out that he
was King of Asia; he was attended by the Persians
who had escaped to Bactria and by many of the
Bactrians themselves; and he was expecting Scythian
allies as well to join him.

[1] D. 77; QC. vi 5, 24 ff.; J. xii 3 put here (P. 46 beyond
Jaxartes) a visit from the queen of the Amazons, cf. Introd.
12. A. omits the denials of Pt. and Ar. Cf. iv 15, 4; vii 13.
See also App. XII 1 f.
[2] QC. 6, 13 makes him give Al. the news about Bessus; no
mention of Anaxippus, but cf. D. 78, 1. For Al's route, and
for dates, covering chs 25-28 see App. VIII 11-14; his army,
App. XIII.
[3] App. XIV 2.

4 Ἀλέξανδρος δὲ ὁμοῦ ἤδη ἔχων τὴν πᾶσαν
δύναμιν ᾖει ἐπὶ Βάκτρων, ἵνα καὶ Φίλιππος ὁ
Μενελάου παρ' αὐτὸν ἀφίκετο ἐκ Μηδίας, ἔχων
τούς τε μισθοφόρους ἱππέας, ὧν ἡγεῖτο αὐτός, καὶ
Θεσσαλῶν τοὺς ἐθελοντὰς ὑπομείναντας καὶ τοὺς
ξένους τοὺς Ἀνδρομάχου. Νικάνωρ δὲ ὁ Παρμενίωνος ὁ τῶν ὑπασπιστῶν ἄρχων τετελευτήκει ἤδη
5 νόσῳ. ἰόντι δὲ Ἀλεξάνδρῳ τὴν ἐπὶ Βάκτρα
ἐξηγγέλθη Σατιβαρζάνης ὁ Ἀρείων σατράπης
Ἀνάξιππον μὲν καὶ τοὺς ἱππακοντιστὰς τοὺς ξὺν
αὐτῷ ἀπεκτονώς, ὁπλίζων δὲ τοὺς Ἀρείους καὶ
ξυνάγων εἰς Ἀρτακόανα πόλιν, ἵνα τὸ βασίλειον ἦν
τῶν Ἀρείων· ἐκεῖθεν δὲ ὅτι ἔγνωκεν, ἐπειδὰν
προκεχωρηκότα Ἀλέξανδρον πύθηται, ἰέναι ξὺν τῇ
δυνάμει παρὰ Βῆσσον, ὡς ξὺν ἐκείνῳ ἐπιθησό-
6 μενος ὅπῃ ἂν τύχῃ τοῖς Μακεδόσι. ταῦτα ὡς
ἐξηγγέλθη αὐτῷ, τὴν μὲν ἐπὶ Βάκτρα ὁδὸν οὐκ
ἦγεν, ἀναλαβὼν δὲ τούς τε ἑταίρους ἱππέας καὶ τοὺς
ἱππακοντιστὰς καὶ τοὺς τοξότας καὶ τοὺς Ἀγριᾶνας
καὶ τὴν Ἀμύντου τε καὶ Κοίνου τάξιν, τὴν δὲ
ἄλλην δύναμιν αὐτοῦ καταλιπὼν καὶ ἐπ' αὐτῇ
Κρατερὸν ἡγεμόνα, σπουδῇ ἦγεν ὡς ἐπὶ Σατιβαρζάνην τε καὶ τοὺς Ἀρείους καὶ διελθὼν ἐν δυσὶν
ἡμέραις σταδίους ἐς ἑξακοσίους πρὸς Ἀρτακόανα
ἦκεν.

7 Σατιβαρζάνης μὲν οὖν, ὡς ἔγνω ἐγγὺς ὄντα
Ἀλέξανδρον, τῇ ὀξύτητι τῆς ἐφόδου ἐκπλαγεὶς ξὺν
ὀλίγοις ἱππεῦσι τῶν Ἀρείων ἔφυγε· πρὸς γὰρ τῶν
πολλῶν στρατιωτῶν κατελείφθη ἐν τῇ φυγῇ, ὡς
κἀκεῖνοι ἔμαθον προσάγοντα Ἀλέξανδρον. Ἀλέξανδρος δέ, ὅσους ξυναιτίους τῆς ἀποστάσεως
κατέμαθε καὶ ἐν τῷ τότε ἀπολελοιπότας τὰς κώμας,

With his whole force now reassembled Alexander **4** 330
was on his way towards Bactra when Philip son of   B.C.
Menelaus joined him from Media with the mercenary
cavalry under his own command, the Thessalian
volunteers who had remained in the army and
Andromachus' foreign corps. Nicanor son of Parmenio, commander of the hypaspists, had already
died of sickness.[4] While Alexander was on his way 5
to Bactra, news was brought that Satibarzanes, satrap
of Areia, had massacred Anaxippus and his mounted
javelin-men, was arming the Areians and leading
them in a body to the city of Artacoana, where the
Areian palace was, and that he had decided, on
learning of Alexander's advance, to go from there
with his troops to Bessus and join him in attacking the
Macedonians wherever opportunity offered. When 6
this was reported to Alexander he did not continue
on the road to Bactra, but took the Companion
cavalry, the mounted javelin-men, archers, Agrianians,
and Amyntas' and Coenus' battalions, and leaving
behind there the rest of the army with Craterus in
charge, advanced swiftly against Satibarzanes and the
Areians; after covering about six hundred stades in
two days, he arrived at Artacoana.[5]

Satibarzanes, on learning of Alexander's proximity, 7
was astounded at the speed of his approach, and fled
with a few Areian horsemen; for in his flight he was
deserted by most of his soldiers, as they too learnt
that Alexander was approaching. Alexander pursued sharply all those he found to have had a hand

---

[4] QC. vi 6, 18 f., making Philip and others join Al. at Artacoana and with different forces, cf. App. XIII 4 f.

[5] At or near Herat, App. VIII 11. Other tales in D. 78;
QC. 6, 20–34.

τούτους δὲ ἄλλη καὶ ἄλλη, ὀξείας τὰς διώξεις
ποιησάμενος, τοὺς μὲν ἀπέκτεινε, τοὺς δὲ ἠνδραπό-
δισε· σατράπην δὲ Ἀρείων ἀπέδειξεν Ἀρσάκην,
8 ἄνδρα Πέρσην. αὐτὸς δὲ ξὺν τοῖς ἀμφὶ Κρατερὸν
ὑπολελειμμένοις, ὁμοῦ οὖσιν ἤδη, ὡς ἐπὶ τὴν
Ζαραγγαίων χώραν ἦγε· καὶ ἀφικνεῖται ἵνα τὰ
βασίλεια τῶν Ζαραγγαίων ἦν. Βαρσαέντης δέ, ὃς
τότε κατεῖχε τὴν χώραν, εἷς ὢν τῶν ξυνεπιθεμένων
Δαρείῳ ἐν τῇ φυγῇ, προσιόντα Ἀλέξανδρον μαθὼν
ἐς Ἰνδοὺς τοὺς ἐπὶ τάδε τοῦ Ἰνδοῦ ποταμοῦ ἔφυγε.
ξυλλαβόντες δὲ αὐτὸν οἱ Ἰνδοὶ παρ᾽ Ἀλέξανδρον
ἀπέστειλαν, καὶ ἀποθνήσκει πρὸς Ἀλεξάνδρου τῆς
ἐς Δαρεῖον ἀδικίας ἕνεκα.

26. Ἐνταῦθα καὶ τὴν Φιλώτα ἐπιβουλὴν τοῦ
Παρμενίωνος ἔμαθεν Ἀλέξανδρος, καὶ λέγει Πτολεμαῖος καὶ Ἀριστόβουλος, ὅτι προσηγγελμένη
⟨μὲν ἦν⟩ ἤδη οἱ καὶ πρότερον ἐν Αἰγύπτῳ, οὐ
μέντοι πιστή γε ἐφάνη τῆς τε φιλίας τῆς πάλαι
ἕνεκα καὶ τῆς ἐξ αὐτοῦ ἐς Παρμενίωνά τε τὸν
πατέρα τὸν Φιλώτα τιμῆς καὶ ἐς αὐτὸν Φιλώταν
2 πίστεως. Πτολεμαῖος δὲ ὁ Λάγου λέγει εἰσα-
χθῆναι εἰς Μακεδόνας Φιλώταν καὶ κατηγορῆσαι
μὲν αὐτοῦ ἰσχυρῶς Ἀλέξανδρον, ἀπολογήσασθαι δὲ
αὐτὸν Φιλώταν· καὶ τοὺς ἐπιμηνυτὰς τοῦ ἔργου
παρελθόντας ἐξελέγξαι Φιλώταν τε καὶ τοὺς ἀμφ᾽
αὐτὸν ἄλλοις τε ἐλέγχοις οὐκ ἀφανέσι καὶ μάλιστα
δὴ ὅτι αὐτὸς Φιλώτας πεπύσθαι μὲν ἐπιβουλήν τινα
Ἀλεξάνδρῳ παρασκευαζομένην συνέφη, ἐξηλέγχετο
δὲ κατασιωπήσας ταύτην πρὸς Ἀλέξανδρον, καίτοι
δὶς ἐπὶ τὴν σκηνὴν ὁσημέραι τὴν Ἀλεξάνδρου

in the revolt, who had at the time deserted their villages, and going in different directions, he killed some and enslaved the rest. As satrap of Areia he appointed Arsaces, a Persian.[6] With the force left 8 under Craterus, which had now joined him, he marched towards the territory of the Zarangaeans, and arrived at the place where their palace was.[7] Barsaentes, who was then in occupation of the country, and was one of those who had joined in attacking Darius on his flight, on learning that Alexander was approaching, fled to the Indians on this side of the river Indus; but they seized him and sent him to Alexander, who put him to death for the wrong he had done Darius.

26. It was there too that Alexander learnt of the conspiracy of Philotas son of Parmenio.[1] Ptolemy and Aristobulus say that it had already been reported to him earlier in Egypt, but he did not think it credible because of their long friendship, the honour he had shown to Parmenio, Philotas' father, and the trust he had reposed in Philotas himself. Ptolemy 2 son of Lagus gives the following account. Philotas was summoned before the Macedonians, Alexander vigorously accused him, Philotas made his defence; then those who had denounced the plot came forward and convicted Philotas and his associates with clear proofs; in particular, they showed that while Philotas himself admitted that he had heard of some sort of plot being laid against Alexander, he was convicted of having said nothing of it to Alexander, though he

[6] Presumably 'Arsames', made satrap of the Zarangaeans after Philotas' death in QC. vii 3, 1.

[7] The Zarangaean capital should be at or near Farah, App. VIII 12 f. Cf. D. 78, 4; QC. vi 6, 36; 7, 1.

[1] See App. XI on 26–27, 4.

3 φοιτῶν. καὶ Φιλώταν μὲν κατακοντισθῆναι πρὸς
τῶν Μακεδόνων καὶ ὅσοι ἄλλοι μετέσχον αὐτῷ τῆς
ἐπιβουλῆς ἐπὶ Παρμενίωνα δὲ σταλῆναι Πολυδά-
μαντα, ἕνα τῶν ἑταίρων, γράμματα φέροντα παρ'
Ἀλεξάνδρου πρὸς τοὺς στρατηγοὺς τοὺς ἐν Μηδίᾳ,
Κλέανδρόν τε καὶ Σιτάλκην καὶ Μεν[ν]ίδαν· οὗτοι
γὰρ ἐπὶ τῆς στρατιᾶς, ἧς Παρμενίων ἦρχε, τεταγ-
4 μένοι ἦσαν· καὶ πρὸς τούτων ἀποθανεῖν Παρμενίωνα, τυχὸν μὲν ὅτι οὐ πιστὸν ἐδόκει εἶναι Ἀλέξανδρος Φιλώτα ἐπιβουλεύοντος μὴ ξυμμετασχεῖν
Παρμενίωνα τῷ παιδὶ τοῦ βουλεύματος, τυχὸν δὲ
ὅτι, εἰ καὶ μὴ ξυμμετέσχε, σφαλερὸς ἤδη ἦν περιὼν
Παρμενίων τοῦ παιδὸς αὐτοῦ ἀνῃρημένου, ἐν
τοσαύτῃ ὢν ἀξιώσει παρά τε αὐτῷ Ἀλεξάνδρῳ
καὶ ἐς τὸ ἄλλο στράτευμα, μὴ ὅτι τὸ Μακεδονικόν,
ἀλλὰ καὶ τῶν ἄλλων ξένων, ὧν πολλάκις καὶ ἐν
μέρει καὶ παρὰ τὸ μέρος κατὰ πρόσταξιν τὴν
Ἀλεξάνδρου ξὺν χάριτι ἐξηγεῖτο.

27. Λέγουσι δὲ καὶ Ἀμύνταν τὸν Ἀνδρομένους
κατὰ τὸν αὐτὸν χρόνον ὑπαχθῆναι ἐς κρίσιν καὶ
Πολέμωνα καὶ Ἄτταλον καὶ Σιμμίαν τοὺς
Ἀμύντου ἀδελφούς, ὡς ξυμμετασχόντας καὶ
αὐτοὺς τῆς ἐπιβουλῆς τῆς κατ' Ἀλεξάνδρου κατὰ
2 πίστιν τε καὶ ἑταιρίαν τὴν Φιλώτα. καὶ ἐδόκει
πιστοτέρα ἡ ἐπιβουλὴ ἐς τὸ πλῆθος, ὅτι Πολέμων,
εἷς τῶν ἀδελφῶν τῶν Ἀμύντου, ξυλληφθέντος
Φιλώτα ἔφυγεν ἐς τοὺς πολεμίους. ἀλλ' Ἀμύντας
γε ξὺν τοῖς ἀδελφοῖς ὑπομείνας τὴν δίκην καὶ
ἀπολογησάμενος ἐν Μακεδόσι καρτερῶς ἀφίεται
τῆς αἰτίας· καὶ εὐθὺς ὡς ἀπέφυγεν ἐν τῇ ἐκκλησίᾳ
ἠξίωσεν ἐφεθῆναί οἱ ἐλθεῖν παρὰ τὸν ἀδελφὸν καὶ
3 ἐπαναγαγεῖν αὐτὸν παρ' Ἀλέξανδρον· καὶ οἱ

visited Alexander's tent twice daily. Philotas was 3 330
shot down with javelins by the Macedonians, along B.C.
with all his accomplices. As for action against Parmenio, Polydamas, one of the Companions, was sent
with a letter from Alexander to the generals in
Media, Cleander and Sitalces and Menidas, who had
been posted to the force under Parmenio's command.[2]
At their hands Parmenio perished, possibly because 4
Alexander could not believe that when Philotas was
conspiring, Parmenio had no share in his own son's
design, possibly because, even supposing he had no
such share, it had now become a danger for Parmenio
to survive his son's execution, on account of the high
honour which he enjoyed with Alexander himself and
in the view of the army too—not only the Macedonian
but the foreign troops also, whom he had often commanded with popularity both in and out of turn by
Alexander's order.

27. They also say that Amyntas son of Andromenes
was brought to trial at the same time, together with
Polemon, Attalus and Simmias, his brothers, on the
charge that they too had joined in the conspiracy
against Alexander as loyal comrades of Philotas.
Moreover the conspiracy seemed more credible to the 2
masses, because Polemon, one of Amyntas' brothers,
deserted to the enemy as soon as Philotas was arrested. However, Amyntas at least with his (other)
brothers stood his trial, made a vigorous defence
before the Macedonians, and was acquitted of the
charge; and the moment he was acquitted, he asked
leave to go and bring Polemon back again to Alexander; the Macedonians agreed. He departed that 3

---

[2] For the ride across the central Persian desert Strabo xv
2, 10; D. 80, 3; QC. vii 2, 18.

Μακεδόνες ξυγχωροῦσιν. ὁ δὲ ἀπελθὼν αὐτῇ τῇ ἡμέρᾳ τὸν Πολέμωνα ἐπανήγαγε. καὶ ταύτῃ πολὺ ἔτι μᾶλλον ἢ πρόσθεν ἔξω αἰτίας ἐφάνη Ἀμύντας. ἀλλὰ ὀλίγον γὰρ ὕστερον κώμην τινὰ πολιορκῶν τοξευθεὶς ἐκ τῆς πληγῆς ἐτελεύτησεν, ὥστε οὐδὲν πλέον αὐτῷ γίγνεται τὴν κρίσιν ἀποφυγόντι ὅτι μὴ ἀγαθῷ νομιζομένῳ ἀποθανεῖν.

4 Ἀλέξανδρος δέ, καταστήσας ἐπὶ τοὺς ἑταίρους ἱππάρχας δύο, Ἡφαιστίωνά τε τὸν Ἀμύντορος καὶ Κλεῖτον τὸν Δρωπίδου, καὶ δίχα διελὼν τὴν τάξιν τῶν ἑταίρων, ὅτι οὐδὲ φίλτατον ἂν ἠβούλετο ἕνα τοσούτων ἱππέων, ἄλλως τε καὶ τῶν κρατίστων τοῦ παντὸς ἱππικοῦ κατά τε ἀξίωσιν καὶ τὴν ἄλλην ἀρετήν, ἐξηγεῖσθαι, ἀφικνεῖται ἐς τοὺς πάλαι μὲν Ἀριάσπας καλουμένους, ὕστερον δὲ Εὐεργέτας ἐπονομασθέντας, ὅτι Κύρῳ τῷ Καμβύσου ξυνεπε-

5 λάβοντο τῆς ἐς Σκύθας ἐλάσεως. καὶ τούτους Ἀλέξανδρος ὧν τε ἐς Κῦρον ὑπῆρξαν οἱ πρόγονοι αὐτῶν τιμήσας καὶ αὐτοὺς καταμαθὼν ἄνδρας οὐ κατὰ τοὺς ἄλλους τοὺς ταύτῃ βαρβάρους πολιτεύοντας, ἀλλὰ τοῦ δικαίου ἴσα καὶ τοῖς κρατίστοις τῶν Ἑλλήνων μεταποιουμένους, ἐλευθέρους τε ἀφῆκεν καὶ χώραν τῆς ὁμόρου ὅσην αὐτοὶ σφίσιν ᾔτησαν, οὐ πολλὴν δὲ οὐδ' αὐτοὶ ᾔτησαν, προσέθηκεν. ἐνταῦθα θύσας τῷ Ἀπόλλωνι Δημήτριον μὲν ἕνα τῶν σωματοφυλάκων ὑποπτεύσας μετασχεῖν Φιλώτᾳ τῆς ἐπιβουλῆς ξυνέλαβε· σωματοφύλακα δὲ ἀντὶ Δημητρίου ἀπέδειξε Πτολεμαῖον τὸν Λάγου.

28. Ταῦτα δὲ διαπραξάμενος προῄει ὡς ἐπὶ

---

[1] i.e. not even Hephaestion.

very day and brought him back; and thus his own innocence appeared much clearer than before. Soon after, however, when besieging a village, he received an arrow wound of which he died; so that all he gained from his acquittal was that he died with his good name unsmirched.

Alexander now put two hipparchs in charge of the Companions, Hephaestion son of Amyntor and Clitus son of Dropides, and after dividing the Companions' brigade into two parts, since he would not have wished a single man, though his closest friend,[1] to command so large a body of cavalry, especially as it was the best of all his mounted force in reputation and valour, he arrived among the people formerly called Ariaspians, but later also nicknamed Benefactors, because they assisted Cyrus son of Cambyses in his Scythian expedition. Alexander honoured this people for the services their ancestors had done to Cyrus and from his own observation that they were not governed like the other barbarians of these parts, but also claimed to follow justice as much as the best of the Greeks; he therefore granted them freedom and added to their territory as much as they asked for themselves of the neighbouring country, though they only asked for a modest portion.[2] There he sacrificed to Apollo, arrested Demetrius, one of the bodyguards, suspecting that he had a hand in Philotas' conspiracy,[3] and appointed as bodyguard Ptolemy son of Lagus in his place.

28. After carrying out all these measures, Alex-

---

[2] D. 81; QC. vii 3, 1 f. make Al. appoint a governor with different names, five days out of the Zarangaean capital (QC.). Cf. App. VIII 11 f.

[3] QC. vi 11, 35 ff. makes him die with Philotas.

Βάκτρα τε καὶ Βῆσσον, Δράγγας τε καὶ Γαδρω-
σοὺς ἐν τῇ παρόδῳ παραστησάμενος. παρεστήσατο
δὲ καὶ τοὺς Ἀραχώτας καὶ σατράπην κατέστησεν
ἐπ' αὐτοῖς Μένωνα. ἐπῆλθε δὲ καὶ τῶν Ἰνδῶν
τοὺς προσχώρους Ἀραχώταις. ξύμπαντα δὲ ταῦτα
τὰ ἔθνη διὰ χιόνος τε πολλῆς καὶ ξὺν ἀπορίᾳ τῶν
ἐπιτηδείων καὶ τῶν στρατιωτῶν ταλαιπωρίᾳ
2 ἐπῆλθε. μαθὼν δὲ τοὺς Ἀρείους αὖθις ἀφεστάναι,
Σατιβαρζάνου ἐς τὴν χώραν αὐτῶν ἐμβαλόντος σὺν
ἱππεῦσι δισχιλίοις, οὓς παρὰ Βήσσου ἔλαβεν,
ἀποστέλλει παρ' αὐτοὺς Ἀρτάβαζόν τε τὸν
Πέρσην καὶ Ἐριγύιον καὶ Κάρανον τῶν ἑταίρων.
προσέταξε δὲ καὶ Φραταφέρνην τὸν τῶν Παρθυαίων
σατράπην ξυνεμβαλεῖν αὐτοῖς ἐς τοὺς Ἀρείους.
3 καὶ γίγνεται μάχη τοῖς ἀμφὶ Ἐριγύϊον καὶ
Κάρανον πρὸς Σατιβαρζάνην καρτερά, οὐδὲ πρόσθεν οἱ βάρβαροι ἐνέκλιναν πρὶν Σατιβαρζάνην
ξυμπεσόντα Ἐριγυΐῳ πρὸς Ἐριγυῖου πληγέντα
δόρατι ἐς τὸ πρόσωπον ἀποθανεῖν. τότε δὲ
ἐγκλίναντες οἱ βάρβαροι προτροπάδην ἔφευγον.
4 Ἐν τούτῳ δὲ Ἀλέξανδρος πρὸς τὸν Καύκασον τὸ
ὄρος ἦγεν, ἵνα καὶ πόλιν ἔκτισε καὶ ὠνόμασεν
Ἀλεξάνδρειαν· καὶ θύσας ἐνταῦθα τοῖς θεοῖς ὅσοις
νόμος αὐτῷ ὑπερέβαλε τὸ ὄρος τὸν Καύκασον,
σατράπην μὲν τῇ χώρᾳ ἐπιτάξας Προέξην, ἄνδρα
Πέρσην, τῶν δὲ ἑταίρων Νειλόξενον τὸν Σατύρου
ἐπίσκοπον ξὺν στρατιᾷ ἀπολιπών.

---

[1] App. VIII 9.
[2] QC. vi 3, 5 gives him 4,000 foot and 600 horse. For
arrival of reinforcements ib. 2 and 4.
[3] D. 81, 3; QC. vii 3, 2 (in Ariaspia).

ander proceeded towards Bactra and against Bessus   330
and on the way won over the Drangians and Gadro-   B.C.
sians,¹ and the Arachotians as well, appointing Menon
as satrap to govern them.² He also came upon the
Indians nearest the Arachotians. He came on all
these tribes through deep snow, with provisions
wanting and his men in distress. On learning that   2
the Areians had again revolted, since Satibarzanes
had invaded their country with two thousand horse,
whom he had received from Bessus, he sent Artabazus
the Persian and two Companions, Erigyius and Caranus to their country and also ordered Phrataphernes,
the satrap of Parthyaea, to help them in their attack
on the Areians.³ A fierce battle took place between   3
the troops of Erigyius and Caranus and Satibarzanes;
indeed, the Persians did not give way till in single
combat with Erigyius Satibarzanes was struck in the
face with a spear and killed. Then the barbarians
turned and fled headlong.⁴

Meanwhile Alexander led his army to Mount   4 330-29
Caucasus,⁵ where he founded a city he called Alexan-   B.C.
dria.⁶ There he sacrificed to the gods to whom he
customarily sacrificed, and then crossed Mount   329
Caucasus, appointing as satrap of the district Proexes,   B.C.
a Persian, with Niloxenes son of Satyrus, one of the
Companions, as overseer in command of troops.⁷

---

⁴ D. 83; QC. 4, 33 ff. (embellished), who makes Erigyius
rejoin Al. at Bactra, in 329 B.C.

⁵ Hindu-Kush, cf. App. XII. March: App. VIII 10 f.

⁶ Cf. iv 22 4; Strabo xv 2, 10; D. 83, 2, (mentioning other
(or another) settlements nearby, e.g. perhaps Nicaea (iv
22, 6)); QC. vii 3, 23. The settlers in Alexandria (QC.) or
all the cities (D.) were 7,000 natives; D. adds 3,000 camp-
followers and some volunteers among mercenaries, QC. unfit
soldiers. Cf. App. VIII 14-16 for march.

⁷ QC. ignores these appointments. Cf. iv 22, 5.

5 Τὸ δὲ ὄρος ὁ Καύκασος ὑψηλὸν μέν ἐστιν ὥσπερ
τι ἄλλο τῆς Ἀσίας, ὡς λέγει Ἀριστόβουλος, ψιλὸν
δὲ τὸ πολὺ αὐτοῦ τό γε ταύτῃ. μακρὸν γὰρ ὄρος
παρατέταται ὁ Καύκασος, ὥστε καὶ τὸν Ταῦρον τὸ
ὄρος, ὃς δὴ τὴν Κιλικίαν τε καὶ Παμφυλίαν ἀπείρ-
γει, ἀπὸ τοῦ Καυκάσου εἶναι λέγουσι καὶ ἄλλα
ὄρη μεγάλα, ἀπὸ τοῦ Καυκάσου διακεκριμένα ἄλλῃ

6 καὶ ἄλλῃ ἐπωνυμίᾳ κατὰ ἤθη τὰ ἑκάστων. ἀλλὰ
ἕν γε τούτῳ τῷ Καυκάσῳ οὐδὲν ἄλλο ὅτι μὴ
τέρμινθοι πεφύκασι καὶ σίλφιον, ὡς λέγει Ἀριστό-
βουλος· ἀλλὰ καὶ ὡς ἐπῳκεῖτο πολλοῖς ἀνθρώποις
καὶ πρόβατα πολλὰ καὶ κτήνη ἐνέμοντο, ὅτι καὶ
χαίρουσι τῷ σιλφίῳ τὰ πρόβατα, καὶ εἰ ἐκ πολλοῦ
πρόβατον σιλφίου αἴσθοιτο, καὶ θεῖ ἐπ᾽ αὐτὸ καὶ τό
τε ἄνθος ἐπινέμεται καὶ τὴν ῥίζαν ἀνορύττον καὶ

7 ταύτην κατεσθίει. ἐπὶ τῷδε ἐν Κυρήνῃ ὡς μακρο-
τάτω ἀπελαύνουσι τὰς ποίμνας τῶν χωρίων, ἵνα
αὐτοῖς τὸ σίλφιον φύεται. οἱ δὲ καὶ περιφράσσουσι
τὸν χῶρον, τοῦ μηδὲ εἰ πελάσειεν αὐτῷ πρόβατα,
δυνατὰ γενέσθαι εἴσω παρελθεῖν, ὅτι πολλοῦ ἄξιον
Κυρηναίοις τὸ σίλφιον.

8 Βῆσσος δὲ ἔχων ἀμφ᾽ αὑτὸν Περσῶν τε τοὺς
μετασχόντας αὐτῷ τῆς Δαρείου συλλήψεως καὶ
αὐτῶν Βακτρίων ἐς ἑπτακισχιλίους καὶ Δάας τοὺς
ἐπὶ τάδε τοῦ Ταναΐδος ποταμοῦ ἐποικοῦντας
ἔφθειρε τὴν ὑπὸ τῷ ὄρει τῷ Καυκάσῳ, ὡς ἐρημίᾳ
τε τῆς χώρας τῆς ἐν μέσῳ αὐτοῦ τε καὶ Ἀλεξάνδρου καὶ ἀπορίᾳ τῶν ἐπιτηδείων ἀπείρξων Ἀλέ-

9 ξανδρον τοῦ μὴ ἐλαύνειν πρόσω. ἀλλὰ Ἀλέξανδρος
ἤλαυνεν οὐδὲν μεῖον, χαλεπῶς μὲν διά τε χιόνος
πολλῆς καὶ ἐνδείᾳ τῶν ἀναγκαίων, ᾔει δὲ ὅμως.
Βῆσσος δέ, ἐπεὶ ἐξηγγέλλετο αὐτῷ οὐ πόρρω ἤδη

Mount Caucasus, according to Aristobulus, is as
high as any mountain in Asia; most of it is bare, at
least on this side.   In fact it is a long mountain range,
so that they say that even Mount Taurus, which forms
the boundary of Cilicia and Pamphylia, is really a part
of Mount Caucasus as well as other great mountains
which have been distinguished from Mount Caucasus
by various names traditional among the different
peoples.[8]   In this particular Mount Caucasus, how- 6
ever, nothing grows save terebinths and silphium
according to Aristobulus.   But even so it was inhabited by a large number of people and many flocks
and herds grazed there, since the flocks like the
silphium, and if they notice it ever so far away they
run to it, nibble its flower, and dig up and eat the 7
root.   For this reason in Cyrene they drive their
flocks as far as possible from the places where their
silphium grows; some even hurdle off the area, so
that even if the flocks approach they cannot get in,
since silphium is very valuable to the Cyrenaeans.

Bessus, attended by the Persians who had joined in 8
the arrest of Darius, by some seven thousand of the
Bactrians themselves, and by the Dahae who live on
this side of the river Tanais [Syr-darya], was ravaging
the land lying under Mount Caucasus, hoping that this
desolation of the country lying between himself and
Alexander and want of provisions would stop Alexander from proceeding farther.   But Alexander ad- 9
vanced none the less, with difficulty indeed, through
thick snow and with necessaries lacking, but still he
came on.   As soon as Bessus was told that Alexander

---

   [8] A. inserts his own comment, from Eratosthenes (App.
XII 3), between two citations from Ar.

ὧν Ἀλέξανδρος, διαβὰς τὸν Ὦξον ποταμὸν τὰ μὲν
πλοῖα ἐφ᾽ ὧν διέβη κατέκαυσεν, αὐτὸς δὲ ἐς
10 Ναύτακα τῆς Σογδιανῆς χώρας ἀπεχώρει. εἵποντο
δὲ αὐτῷ οἵ τε ἀμφὶ Σπιταμένην καὶ Ὀξυάρτην,
ἔχοντες τοὺς ἐκ τῆς Σογδιανῆς ἱππέας, καὶ Δάαι οἱ
ἀπὸ τοῦ Ταναΐδος. οἱ δὲ τῶν Βακτρίων ἱππεῖς ὡς
φεύγειν ἐγνωκότα ἔμαθον Βῆσσον, ἄλλος ἄλλῃ ἐπὶ
τὰ σφῶν ἕκαστοι ἀπηλλάγησαν.

29. Ἀλέξανδρος δὲ ἐς Δράψακα ἀφικόμενος καὶ
ἀναπαύσας τὴν στρατιὰν ἐς Ἄορνόν τε ἦγε καὶ
Βάκτρα, αἳ δὴ μέγισταί εἰσι πόλεις ἐν τῇ Βακτρίων
χώρᾳ. καὶ ταύτας τε ἐξ ἐφόδου ἔλαβε καὶ
φυλακὴν ἐν τῇ ἄκρᾳ τῆς Ἀόρνου ἀπέλιπε καὶ ἐπὶ
ταύτης Ἀρχέλαον τὸν Ἀνδρόκλου τῶν ἑταίρων·
τοῖς δὲ ἄλλοις Βακτρίοις οὐ χαλεπῶς προσχω-
ρήσασιν ἐπέταξε σατράπην Ἀρτάβαζον τὸν Πέρσην.

2 Αὐτὸς δὲ ἦγεν ὡς ἐπὶ τὸν Ὦξον ποταμόν. ὁ δὲ
Ὦξος ῥέει μὲν ἐκ τοῦ ὄρους τοῦ Καυκάσου, ἔστι δὲ
ποταμῶν μέγιστος τῶν ἐν τῇ Ἀσίᾳ, ὅσους γε δὴ
Ἀλέξανδρος καὶ οἱ ξὺν Ἀλεξάνδρῳ ἐπῆλθον, πλὴν
τῶν Ἰνδῶν ποταμῶν· οἱ δὲ Ἰνδοὶ πάντων ποταμῶν
μέγιστοί εἰσιν. ἐξίησι δὲ ὁ Ὦξος ἐς τὴν μεγάλην
3 θάλασσαν τὴν κατὰ Ὑρκανίαν. διαβάλλειν δὲ
ἐπιχειροῦντι αὐτῷ τὸν ποταμὸν πάντῃ ἄπορον
ἐφαίνετο· τὸ μὲν γὰρ εὖρος ἦν ἐς ἓξ μάλιστα
σταδίους, βάθος δὲ οὐ πρὸς λόγον τοῦ εὔρους, ἀλλὰ
πολὺ δή τι βαθύτερος καὶ ψαμμώδης καὶ ῥεῦμα
ὀξύ⟨ς⟩, ὡς τὰ καταπηγνύμενα πρὸς αὐτοῦ τοῦ ῥοῦ
ἐκστρέφεσθαι ἐκ τῆς γῆς οὐ χαλεπῶς, οἷα δὴ οὐδὲ
4 βεβαίως κατὰ τῆς ψάμμου ἱδρυμένα. ἄλλως τε καὶ
ἀπορία ὕλης ἐν τοῖς πόνοις ἦν καὶ τριβὴ πολλὴ

was now not far off, he crossed the river Oxus [Amu-darya], burned the boats on which he had crossed, and himself retreated towards Nautaca in the Sogdianian country, accompanied by the followers of Spitamenes 10 and Oxyartes with the horsemen from Sogdiana, and by the Dahae from the Tanais, though the Bactrian cavalry, when they learnt that he had determined on flight, dispersed in different directions to their homes.[9]

29. Alexander arrived at Drapsaca, and after resting his army led them on to Aornos and Bactra, the greatest cities of Bactria, which he took at his first attempt. He left a garrison in the citadel of Aornos under command of Archelaus son of Androcles, one of the Companions. To govern the rest of the Bactrians, who readily adhered to him, he appointed Artabazus the Persian as satrap.[1]

He himself marched towards the river Oxus, which 2 flows from Mount Caucasus and is the greatest of the Asian rivers Alexander and his followers reached, except the rivers of India; they are the greatest of all rivers. The Oxus flows into the Great Sea in its Hyrcanian part.[2] When Alexander attempted to 3 cross the river it appeared impossible at every point. It was about six stades broad, but disproportionately deeper, in fact far deeper, sandy and fast-flowing, so that piles fixed into the bed were easily twisted out of the ground by the stream alone, not getting a firm hold in the sand. Apart from this, want of timber 4 was another difficulty, and it was clear that there

[9] Cf. D. 83; QC. vii 3, 22-4, 25.
[1] QC. vii 5, 1. (For operations against Bessus, D. 83; QC. vii 5; App. VIII 16.)
[2] App. XII.

ἐφαίνετο, εἰ μακρόθεν μετίοιεν ὅσα ἐς γεφύρωσιν
τοῦ πόρου. ξυναγαγὼν οὖν τὰς διφθέρας, ὑφ' αἷς
ἐσκήνουν οἱ στρατιῶται, φορυτοῦ ἐμπλῆσαι ἐκέλευσεν ὡς ξηροτάτου καὶ καταδῆσαί τε καὶ
ξυρράψαι ἀκριβῶς, τοῦ μὴ ἐσδύεσθαι ἐς αὐτὰς τοῦ
ὕδατος. ἐμπλησθεῖσαι δὲ καὶ ξυρραφεῖσαι ἱκαναὶ
ἐγένοντο διαβιβάσαι τὴν στρατιὰν ἐν πέντε ἡμέραις.

5 Πρὶν δὲ διαβαίνειν τὸν ποταμὸν τῶν τε Μακεδόνων ἐπιλέξας τοὺς πρεσβυτάτους καὶ ἤδη ἀπολέ-
μους καὶ τῶν Θεσσαλῶν τοὺς ἐθελοντὰς καταμεί-
ναντας ἐπ' οἴκου ἀπέστειλεν. ἐκπέμπει δὲ καὶ
Στασάνορα, ἕνα τῶν ἑταίρων, ἐς Ἀρείους, προστάξας Ἀρσάκην μὲν τὸν σατράπην τῶν Ἀρείων
ξυλλαβεῖν, ὅτι ἐθελοκακεῖν αὐτῷ Ἀρσάκης ἔδοξεν,
αὐτὸν δὲ σατράπην εἶναι ἀντ' ἐκείνου Ἀρείων.

6 Περάσας δὲ τὸν Ὄξον ποταμὸν ἦγε κατὰ
σπουδήν, ἵνα Βῆσσον εἶναι ξὺν τῇ δυνάμει ἐπυνθάνετο. καὶ ἐν τούτῳ ἀφικνοῦνται παρὰ Σπιταμένους καὶ Δαταφέρνου πρὸς αὐτὸν ἀγγέλλοντες,
ὅτι Σπιταμένης καὶ Δαταφέρνης, εἰ πεμφθείη
αὐτοῖς καὶ ὀλίγη στρατιὰ καὶ ἡγεμὼν τῇ στρατιᾷ,
ξυλλήψονται Βῆσσον καὶ παραδώσουσιν Ἀλεξάν-
δρῳ· ἐπεὶ καὶ νῦν ἀδέσμῳ φυλακῇ φυλάσσεσθαι
7 πρὸς αὐτῶν Βῆσσον. ταῦτα ὡς ἤκουσεν Ἀλέξανδρος, αὐτὸς μὲν ἀναπαύων ἦγε τὴν στρατιὰν
σχολαίτερον ἢ πρόσθεν, Πτολεμαῖον δὲ τὸν Λάγου
ἀποστέλλει τῶν τε ἑταίρων ἱππαρχίας τρεῖς ἄγοντα
καὶ τοὺς ἱππακοντιστὰς ξύμπαντας, πεζῶν δὲ τήν

---

³ So QC. vii 5, 17.
⁴ QC. 5, 27 makes Al. send home 900 men a little later.
⁵ In QC. viii 3, 17 Stasanor replaces ' Arsames ' only in 328.
⁶ Pt. is clearly the source down to 30, 5 at least; he is not

would be long delay if they were to fetch from a distance enough to bridge the stream. So he collected the hides the troops used for tent covers and ordered them to be filled with the driest possible chaff, and then to be tied down and stitched neatly together so as to be watertight. When they were filled and stitched together they were efficient enough to take the army across in five days.[3]

Before crossing the river Alexander selected from the Macedonians the oldest men who were no longer fit for service and the Thessalian volunteers who had remained behind and sent them on their way home.[4] He also sent Stasanor, one of the Companions, to Areia, with instructions to arrest Arsaces, satrap of the Areians, because he thought him guilty of treason to himself; Stasanor was to take his place as satrap of Areia.[5]

After crossing the river Oxus he marched rapidly to the place where according to his information Bessus and his force were to be found. At this time men came to him from Spitamenes and Dataphernes with the message that if quite a small force were sent them, and a man to command it, they would seize Bessus and hand him over to Alexander; in fact they already had him under open arrest. On hearing this, Alexander for his own part rested his army and led it on more leisurely than before, but sent Ptolemy son of Lagus [6] with three hipparchies of the Companion cavalry, all the mounted javelin-men and of

named in QC's different story, and C. B. Welles (*Miscellanea Rostagni* 1963, 101 ff.) questions if he had the commands reported here and in 18, 9; iv 29, 1; vi 11, 8, or tells credible stories of them; I agree with the refutation of his criticisms of Pt. by J. Seibert, *Untersuchungen zur Geschichte Ptolemaios I*, 4 ff. Hipparchies: Introd. 58 ff.

ARRIAN

τε Φιλώτα τάξιν καὶ τῶν ὑπασπιστῶν χιλιαρχίαν μίαν καὶ τοὺς Ἀγριᾶνας πάντας καὶ τῶν τοξοτῶν τοὺς ἡμίσεας, σπουδῇ ἐλαύνειν κελεύσας ὡς Σπιταμένην τε καὶ Δαταφέρνην. καὶ Πτολεμαῖος ᾔει ὡς ἐτέτακτο, καὶ διελθὼν ἐν ἡμέραις τέτταρσι σταθμοὺς δέκα ἀφικνεῖται ἐς τὸ στρατόπεδον, οὗ τῇ προτεραίᾳ ηὐλισμένοι ἦσαν οἱ ἀμφὶ τὸν Σπιταμένην βάρβαροι.

30. Ἐνταῦθα ἔμαθε Πτολεμαῖος ὅτι οὐ βεβαία τῷ Σπιταμένει καὶ Δαταφέρνῃ ἡ γνώμη ἐστὶν ἀμφὶ τῇ παραδόσει τοῦ Βήσσου. τοὺς μὲν δὴ πεζοὺς κατέλιπε, προστάξας ἕπεσθαι ἐν τάξει, αὐτὸς δὲ ξὺν τοῖς ἱππεῦσιν ἐλάσας ἀφίκετο πρὸς κώμην τινά, ἵνα ὁ Βήσσος ἦν ξὺν ὀλίγοις στρατιώ-
2 ταις. οἱ γὰρ ἀμφὶ τὸν Σπιταμένην μετακεχω-ρήκεσαν ἤδη ἐκεῖθεν, καταιδεσθέντες αὐτοὶ παρα-δοῦναι τὸν Βήσσον. Πτολεμαῖος δὲ περιστήσας ἐν κύκλῳ τῆς κώμης τοὺς ἱππέας (ἦν γάρ τι καὶ τεῖχος περιβεβλημένον καὶ πύλαι κατ' αὐτὸ) ἐπεκηρυκεύετο τοῖς ἐν τῇ κώμῃ βαρβάροις ἀπαθεῖς σφᾶς ἀπαλλάσσεσθαι παραδόντας Βήσσον. οἱ δὲ
3 ἐδέχοντο τοὺς ξὺν Πτολεμαίῳ ἐς τὴν κώμην. καὶ Πτολεμαῖος ξυλλαβὼν Βήσσον ὀπίσω ἐπανῄει. προπέμψας δὲ ἤρετο Ἀλέξανδρον, ὅπως χρὴ ἐς ὄψιν ἄγειν Ἀλεξάνδρου Βήσσον. καὶ Ἀλέξανδρος γυμνὸν ἐν κλοιῷ δήσαντα οὕτως ἄγειν ἐκέλευσε καὶ καταστήσαντα ἐν δεξιᾷ τῆς ὁδοῦ, ᾗ αὐτός τε καὶ ἡ στρατιὰ παρελεύσεσθαι ἔμελλε. καὶ Πτολεμαῖος οὕτως ἐποίησεν.
4 Ἀλέξανδρος δὲ ἰδὼν τὸν Βήσσον ἐπιστήσας τὸ ἅρμα ἤρετο ἀνθ' ὅτου τὸν βασιλέα τὸν αὐτοῦ καὶ ἅμα καὶ οἰκεῖον καὶ εὐεργέτην γενόμενον Δαρεῖον τὰ

the infantry the battalion of Philotas, one chiliarchy of the hypaspists, all the Agrianes, and half the archers, with orders to proceed by forced marches to Spitamenes and Dataphernes. Ptolemy went as directed, and traversing ten days' marches in four days arrived at the camp where the barbarians with Spitamenes had bivouacked the previous day.

30. There he learnt that Spitamenes and Dataphernes had not quite made up their mind about the surrender of Bessus. He therefore left the infantry behind, with instructions to follow in formation, and rode on himself with the cavalry, and arrived at a village where Bessus was with a few soldiers. Spita- 2 menes and his men had already withdrawn, as they were ashamed to hand Bessus over personally. Ptolemy stationed the cavalry in a cordon round the village—it had some sort of wall thrown round it, and gates in the wall—and made a proclamation to the barbarians in the village that they would depart unscathed if they handed Bessus over. They admitted Ptolemy and his troops into the village, and after 3 seizing Bessus he retired. Then he sent a messenger ahead and asked Alexander in what way he should bring Bessus into his presence. Alexander ordered him to bring Bessus bound, naked, and wearing a wooden collar, and set him on the right of the road by which Alexander and his army were to pass. Ptolemy did so.

On seeing Bessus Alexander stopped his car and 4 asked him why he had first seized Darius, who had been his king, and in addition his relative and bene-

μὲν πρῶτα ξυνέλαβε καὶ δήσας ἦγεν, ἔπειτα
ἀπέκτεινε. καὶ ὁ Βῆσσος οὐ μόνῳ οἷ ταῦτα δόξαντα πρᾶξαι ἔφη, ἀλλὰ ξὺν τοῖς τότε ἀμφὶ
Δαρεῖον οὖσιν, ὡς σωτηρίαν σφίσιν εὑρέσθαι παρ᾽
5 Ἀλεξάνδρου. Ἀλέξανδρος δὲ ἐπὶ τοῖσδε μαστιγοῦν
ἐκέλευεν αὐτὸν καὶ ἐπιλέγειν τὸν κήρυκα ταὐτὰ
ἐκεῖνα ὅσα αὐτὸς τῷ Βήσσῳ ἐν τῇ πύστει ὠνείδισε.
Βῆσσος μὲν δὴ οὕτως αἰκισθεὶς ἀποπέμπεται ἐς
Βάκτρα ἀποθανούμενος. καὶ ταῦτα Πτολεμαῖος
ὑπὲρ Βήσσου ἀνέγραψεν· Ἀριστόβουλος δὲ τοὺς
ἀμφὶ Σπιταμένην τε καὶ Δαταφέρνην Πτολεμαίῳ
ἀγαγεῖν Βῆσσον καὶ παραδοῦναι Ἀλεξάνδρῳ γυμνὸν
ἐν κλοιῷ δήσαντας.

6 Ἀλέξανδρος δὲ ἀναπληρώσας τὸ ἱππικὸν ἐκ τῶν
αὐτόθεν ἵππων (πολλοὶ γὰρ αὐτῷ ἵπποι ἔν τε τῇ
ὑπερβολῇ τοῦ Καυκάσου καὶ ἐν τῇ ἐπὶ τὸν Ὄξον τε
καὶ ἀπὸ τοῦ Ὄξου πορείᾳ ἐξέλιπον) ὡς ἐπὶ
Μαράκανδα ἦγε· τὰ δέ ἐστι βασίλεια τῆς Σογδια-
7 νῶν χώρας. ἔνθεν δὲ ἐπὶ τὸν Τάναϊν ποταμὸν
προῄει. τῷ δὲ Τανάϊδι τούτῳ, ὃν δὴ καὶ Ἰαξάρτην [1] ἄλλῳ ὀνόματι πρὸς τῶν ἐπιχωρίων βαρβάρων καλεῖσθαι λέγει Ἀριστόβουλος, αἱ πηγαὶ μὲν
ἐκ τοῦ Καυκάσου ὄρους καὶ αὐτῷ εἰσιν· ἐξίησι δὲ
καὶ οὗτος ὁ ποταμὸς εἰς τὴν Ὑρκανίαν θάλασσαν.
8 ἄλλος δὲ ἂν εἴη Τάναϊς ὑπὲρ ὅτου λέγει Ἡρόδοτος
ὁ λογοποιὸς ὄγδοον εἶναι τῶν ποταμῶν τῶν

---

[1] Ἰαξάρτην, Palmarius: Ὀρξάντην codd. See historical note.

[1] Cf. iv 7, 3, giving the sequel, not a variant story from
another source. Different versions: D. 83, 8 (followed by
long lacuna); QC. vii 5, 40 ff.; 10, 10.
[2] The minor discrepancy (Pearson *LH* 166) suggests that
Ar. had not read Pt. or was correcting him silently.

factor, led him about in chains, and then murdered
him. Bessus replied that he had acted not by any
private decision of his own but in concert with all then
attending on Darius, to obtain immunity from Alexander. At this Alexander ordered him to be whipped 5
and the herald to announce during the whipping the
crimes for which he himself had blamed Bessus in his
question. After this torture Bessus was sent to
Bactra to be put to death.[1] This is Ptolemy's account of Bessus: Aristobulus, however, says that it
was the followers of Spitamenes and Dataphernes who
took Bessus to Ptolemy and handed him over to Alexander naked and bound, wearing a wooden collar.[2]

Alexander brought his cavalry to full strength with 6
horses from the vicinity, for a good many horses had
been lost in the crossing of Mount Caucasus and on
the marches both to and from the Oxus, and led his
troops towards Maracanda [Samarcand], a royal
residence of the Sogdianian land. Thence he ad- 7
vanced to the river Tanais [Syr-darya]. The springs
of this Tanais too, which Aristobulus says is called by
the natives a different name, Jaxartes,[3] rise in Mount
Caucasus; and this river also flows out into the
Hyrcanian Sea. The Tanais [Don], which the 8
historian Herodotus describes as the eighth of the Scy-

---

[3] The Syr-darya, which in fact rises in the Kirgiz, not the
'Caucasus' (here Hindu-Kush), and flows into the Aral Sea,
not the 'Hyrcanian' (Caspian); cf. App. XII for these and
other geographical confusions. Greek writers normally give
the Iranian name for the Syr-darya as Jaxartes; here the
manuscripts read 'Orxantes', and in vii 16, 3 (the only other
place where A. does not use 'Tanais') 'Oxyartes'; P. 45 has
'Orexartes'. It is thus doubtful what A. (or Ar.) actually
wrote: I have hesitantly adopted emendations in both places
in the *Anabasis*.

Σκυθικῶν Τάναϊν, καὶ ῥέειν μὲν ἐκ λίμνης μεγάλης
ἀνίσχοντα, ἐκδιδόναι δὲ ἐς μείζω ἔτι λίμνην, τὴν
καλουμένην Μαιῶτιν· καὶ τὸν Τάναϊν τοῦτον εἰσὶν
9 οἳ ὅρον ποιοῦσι τῆς Ἀσίας καὶ τῆς Εὐρώπης, οἷς
δὴ ἀπὸ τοῦ μυχοῦ τοῦ πόντου τοῦ Εὐξείνου ἡ λίμνη
τε ἡ Μαιῶτις καὶ ὁ ἐς ταύτην ἐξιεὶς ποταμὸς ὁ
Τάναϊς οὗτος διείργει τὴν Ἀσίαν καὶ τὴν Εὐρώπην,
καθάπερ ἡ κατὰ Γάδειρά τε καὶ τοὺς ἀντιπέρας
Γαδείρων Λίβυας τοὺς Νομάδας θάλασσα τὴν
Λιβύην αὖ καὶ τὴν Εὐρώπην διείργει, οἷς γε δὴ ἡ
Λιβύη ἀπὸ τῆς Ἀσίας τῆς ἄλλης τῷ Νείλῳ ποταμῷ
διακέκριται.

10 Ἐνταῦθα ἀποσκεδασθέντες τινὲς τῶν Μακεδόνων ἐς προνομὴν κατακόπτονται πρὸς τῶν
βαρβάρων· οἱ δὲ δράσαντες τὸ ἔργον ἀπέφυγον ἐς
ὄρος τραχύτατον καὶ πάντη ἀπότομον· ἦσαν δὲ τὸ
πλῆθος ἐς τρισμυρίους. καὶ ἐπὶ τούτους Ἀλέξανδρος τοὺς κουφοτάτους τῆς στρατιᾶς ἀναλαβὼν
11 ἦγεν. ἔνθα δὴ προσβολαὶ πολλαὶ ἐγίγνοντο τοῖς
Μακεδόσιν ἐς τὸ ὄρος· καὶ τὰ μὲν πρῶτα ἀπε-
κρούοντο βαλλόμενοι ἐκ τῶν βαρβάρων, καὶ ἄλλοι
τε πολλοὶ τραυματίαι ἐγένοντο καὶ αὐτὸς Ἀλέξανδρος ἐς τὴν κνήμην τοξεύεται διαμπὰξ καὶ τῆς
περόνης τι ἀποθραύεται αὐτῷ ἐκ τοῦ τοξεύματος.
ἀλλὰ καὶ ὡς ἔλαβέ τε τὸ χωρίον, καὶ τῶν βαρβάρων
οἱ μὲν αὐτοῦ κατεκόπησαν πρὸς τῶν Μακεδόνων,
πολλοὶ δὲ καὶ κατὰ τῶν πετρῶν ῥίψαντες σφᾶς
ἀπέθανον, ὥστε ἐκ τρισμυρίων οὐ πλείους ἀποσωθῆναι ὀκτακισχιλίων.

thian rivers, rising and flowing out of a great lake, and running into a greater lake, called Maeotis [Sea of Azov], will be a different Tanaïs. Some make this Tanaïs the boundary between Asia and Europe; in their view, from the corner of the Euxine Sea Lake Maeotis and this river Tanaïs, which flows into it, separate Asia and Europe, just as the sea between Gadeira [Cadiz] and the nomad Libyans opposite separates Libya in turn from Europe; in their view Libya is divided from the rest of Asia by the river Nile.[4]

Here some of the Macedonians who had scattered for foraging were cut down by the barbarians. The authors of the deed took refuge in a very rugged and completely precipitous mountain; they numbered about thirty thousand. Alexander took his lightest troops and led them to attack the fugitives. Then the Macedonians attempted many assaults upon the mountain; at first they were driven back by volleys from the barbarians, and a great many were wounded; notably, Alexander himself was shot right through the leg with an arrow, and a part of his fibula-bone was broken. But even so he captured the position, and some of the barbarians were cut down there and then by the Macedonians, while many perished by throwing themselves down the rocks, so that out of thirty thousand not more than eight thousand saved their lives.[5]

---

[4] In antiquity the division between Asia and 'Libya' (Africa) was sometimes placed at the Suez isthmus (e.g. Herodotus ii 16 f.), sometimes at the Nile (e.g. Strabo ii 5, 26); before Herodotus Libya was often included in Asia, but those who regarded it as separate would treat Arrian as meaning that 'Libya is parted from the rest that is Asia . . .'

[5] With §6–11 cf. QC. vii 6, 1–10; App. VIII 12.

BOOK IV

ΒΙΒΛΙΟΝ ΤΕΤΑΡΤΟΝ

1. Οὐ πολλαῖς δὲ ἡμέραις ὕστερον ἀφικνοῦνται παρ' Ἀλέξανδρον πρέσβεις παρά τε Σκυθῶν τῶν Ἀβίων καλουμένων (οὓς καὶ Ὅμηρος δικαιοτάτους ἀνθρώπους εἰπὼν ἐν τῇ ποιήσει ἐπήνεσεν· οἰκοῦσι δὲ ἐν τῇ Ἀσίᾳ οὗτοι αὐτόνομοι, οὐχ ἥκιστα διὰ πενίαν τε καὶ δικαιότητα) καὶ παρὰ τῶν ἐκ τῆς Εὐρώπης Σκυθῶν, οἳ δὴ τὸ μέγιστον 2 ἔθνος [Σκυθικὸν] ἐν τῇ Εὐρώπῃ ἐποικοῦσιν. καὶ τούτοις ξυμπέμπει Ἀλέξανδρος τῶν ἑταίρων, πρόφασιν μὲν κατὰ πρεσβείαν φιλίαν ξυνθησομένους, ὁ δὲ νοῦς τῆς πομπῆς ἐς κατασκοπήν τι μᾶλλον ἔφερε φύσεώς τε τῆς χώρας τῆς Σκυθικῆς καὶ πλήθους αὐτῶν καὶ νομαίων καὶ ὁπλίσεως, ἥντινα ἔχοντες στέλλονται ἐς τὰς μάχας.

3 Αὐτὸς δὲ πρὸς τῷ Τανάϊδι ποταμῷ ἐπενόει πόλιν οἰκίσαι, καὶ ταύτην ἑαυτοῦ ἐπώνυμον. ὅ τε γὰρ χῶρος ἐπιτήδειος αὐτῷ ἐφαίνετο αὐξῆσαι ἐπὶ μέγα τὴν πόλιν καὶ ἐν καλῷ οἰκισθήσεσθαι τῆς ἐπὶ Σκύθας, εἴποτε ξυμβαίνοι, ἐλάσεως καὶ τῆς προφυλακῆς τῆς χώρας πρὸς τὰς καταδρομὰς τῶν 4 πέραν τοῦ ποταμοῦ ἐποικούντων βαρβάρων. ἐδόκει δ' ἂν καὶ μεγάλη γενέσθαι ἡ πόλις πλήθει τε τῶν ἐς αὐτὴν ξυνοικιζομένων καὶ τοῦ ὀνόματος τῇ λαμπρότητι. καὶ ἐν τούτῳ οἱ πρόσχωροι τῷ ποταμῷ βάρβαροι τούς τε τὰ φρούρια ἐν ταῖς πόλεσι σφῶν ἔχοντας στρατιώτας τῶν Μακεδόνων ξυλλαβόντες ἀπέκτειναν καὶ τὰς πόλεις ἐς ἀσφάλειάν

BOOK IV

1. Not many days later, envoys came to Alexander from the Abian Scythians, as they are called, whom Homer praised in his epic by calling them ' most just of men '; they live in Asia, and are independent, chiefly through their poverty and their sense of justice. Envoys came too from the European Scythians, the largest nation dwelling in Europe. Alexander sent some of the Companions with them, pretending it was an embassy to conclude a friendly agreement; but the idea of the mission was rather to spy out the nature of the Scythians' land, their numbers, their customs and the arms they use on their warlike expeditions.[1]

He was himself planning to found a city on the Tanais, and to give it his own name. For in his view the site was suitable for the city to rise to greatness, and it would be well placed for any eventual invasion of Scythia and as a defence bastion of the country against the raids of the barbarians dwelling on the other side of the river. He thought that the city would actually rise to greatness because of the number of settlers and the splendour of its name.[2] At this point the barbarians near the river seized and killed the Macedonian troops garrisoning their cities, and then began to strengthen the defences of the

2

3

4

---

[1] QC. vii 6, 11 f. Scyths: App. XII. Cf. i 3, 1 n.; iii 8, 3 n.; iv 3, 6 n.

[2] QC. 6, 13. Motivation: iii 1, 5 n. Cf. App. VIII for all topographical matters in this book.

5 τινα μᾶλλον ὠχύρουν. ξυνεπελάβοντο δὲ αὐτοῖς
τῆς ἀποστάσεως καὶ τῶν Σογδιανῶν οἱ πολλοί,
ἐπαρθέντες πρὸς τῶν ξυλλαβόντων Βῆσσον, ὥστε
καὶ τῶν Βακτριανῶν ἔστιν οὓς σφισιν οὗτοι
ξυναπέστησαν, εἴτε δὴ καὶ δείσαντες Ἀλέξανδρον,
εἴτε καὶ λόγον ἐπὶ τῇ ἀποστάσει διδόντες, ὅτι ἐς
ἕνα ξύλλογον ἐπηγγέλκει Ἀλέξανδρος ξυνελθεῖν
τοὺς ὑπάρχους τῆς χώρας ἐκείνης εἰς Ζαρίασπα,
τὴν μεγίστην πόλιν, ὡς ἐπ' ἀγαθῷ οὐδενὶ τοῦ ξυλ-
λόγου γιγνομένου.

2. Ταῦτα ὡς ἀπηγγέλθη Ἀλεξάνδρῳ, παραγγείλας τοῖς πεζοῖς κατὰ λόχους κλίμακας ποιεῖσθαι
ὅσα⟨ι⟩ ἑκάστῳ λόχῳ ἐπηγγέλθησαν, αὐτὸς μὲν ἐπὶ
τὴν πρώτην ἀπὸ τοῦ στρατοπέδου ὁρμηθεὶς πόλιν
προὐχώρει, ᾗ ὄνομα ἦν Γάζα· ἐς γὰρ ἑπτὰ πόλεις
ξυμπεφευγέναι ἐλέγοντο οἱ ἐκ τῆς χώρας βάρβαροι·
2 Κρατερὸν δὲ ἐκπέμπει πρὸς τὴν καλουμένην
Κυρούπολιν, ἥπερ μεγίστη πασῶν καὶ ἐς αὐτὴν οἱ
πλεῖστοι ξυνειλεγμένοι ἦσαν τῶν βαρβάρων. παρήγγελτο δὲ αὐτῷ στρατοπεδεῦσαι πλησίον τῆς
πόλεως καὶ τάφρον τε ἐν κύκλῳ αὐτῆς ὀρύξαι καὶ
χάρακα περιβαλέσθαι καὶ τὰς μηχανὰς ὅσαις
χρῆσθαι ξυμπηγνύναι, ὡς πρὸς τοὺς ἀμφὶ Κρατερὸν
τὴν γνώμην τετραμμένοι οἱ ἐκ τῆς πόλεως ταύτης
ἀδύνατοι ὦσι ταῖς ἄλλαις πόλεσιν ἐπωφελεῖν.
3 αὐτὸς δὲ ἐπὶ τὴν Γάζαν ἐπεὶ ἀφίκετο, ὡς εἶχεν ἐξ
ἐφόδου σημαίνει προσβάλλειν τῷ τείχει γηΐνῳ τε
καὶ οὐχ ὑψηλῷ ὄντι, προσθέντας ἐν κύκλῳ πάντοθεν
τὰς κλίμακας· οἱ δὲ σφενδονῆται αὐτῷ καὶ οἱ
τοξόται τε καὶ ἀκοντισταὶ ὁμοῦ τῇ ἐφόδῳ τῶν
πεζῶν ἐσηκόντιζον ἐς τοὺς προμαχομένους ἀπὸ τοῦ

cities for their security. They were joined in the
revolt by most of the Sogdianians, stirred up by the
party which had arrested Bessus, so that they also
drew into their revolt some of the Bactrians; it may
be that they were really terrified of Alexander, or
that it was a pretext they gave for revolt that Alexander had instructed the hyparchs of that country to
come to a joint conference at Zariaspa, the greatest
city, and that this conference was not for their benefit.[3]

2. When this was reported to Alexander, he
ordered the infantry, company by company, to make
ladders, each company a certain number; and he
advanced himself to the first city on leaving the camp,
called Gaza; the barbarians of the district were said
to have taken refuge in seven cities. He sent 2
Craterus to that called Cyropolis, the largest of them
all, where the greatest number of barbarians had
collected. Craterus was ordered to encamp near the
city, to dig a ditch and throw a stockade round it, and
to fit together as many siege engines as he required,
so that the defenders of this city might have their
minds fully occupied with Craterus and his troops and
be unable to help those in the other cities. When 3
Alexander himself arrived at Gaza, on his first
approach without more ado he ordered his men to
attack the wall, which was made of earth and of no
great height, and to place their ladders against it on
all sides; at the moment of the infantry attack his
slingers, archers and javelin-men showered volleys

[3] For capture of rebel cities, QC. vii 6, 13–23.

τείχους καὶ βέλη ἀπὸ μηχανῶν ἠφίετο, ὥστε ὀξέως
μὲν ὑπὸ τοῦ πλήθους τῶν βελῶν ἐγυμνώθη τὸ
τεῖχος τῶν προμαχομένων, ταχεῖα δὲ ἡ πρόσθεσις
τῶν κλιμάκων καὶ ἡ ἀνάβασις τῶν Μακεδόνων ἡ
4 ἐπὶ τὸ τεῖχος ἐγίγνετο. τοὺς μὲν δὴ ἄνδρας πάντας
ἀπέκτειναν, οὕτως ἐξ Ἀλεξάνδρου προστεταγμέ-
νον, γυναῖκας δὲ καὶ παῖδας καὶ τὴν ἄλλην λείαν
διήρπασαν. ἔνθεν δὲ εὐθὺς ἦγεν ἐπὶ τὴν δευτέραν
ἀπ᾽ ἐκείνης πόλιν ᾠκισμένην, καὶ ταύτην τῷ αὐτῷ
τε τρόπῳ καὶ τῇ αὐτῇ ἡμέρᾳ λαμβάνει καὶ τοὺς
ἁλόντας τὰ αὐτὰ ἔπραξεν. ὁ δὲ ἦγεν ἐπὶ τὴν τρίτην
πόλιν, καὶ ταύτην τῇ ὑστεραίᾳ ἐπὶ τῇ πρώτῃ
προσβολῇ εἷλεν.

5   Ἐν ᾧ δὲ αὐτὸς ξὺν τοῖς πεζοῖς ἀμφὶ ταῦτα εἶχε,
τοὺς ἱππέας ἐκπέμπει ἐς τὰς δύο τὰς πλησίον
πόλεις προστάξας παραφυλάττειν τοὺς ἀνθρώπους
τοὺς ἔνδον, μήποτε τὴν ἅλωσιν αἰσθόμενοι τῶν
πλησίον πόλεων καὶ ἅμα τὴν αὐτοῦ οὐ διὰ μακροῦ
ἔφοδον οἱ δὲ ἐς φυγὴν τραπέντες ἄποροι αὐτῷ
διώκειν γένωνται. καὶ ξυνέβη τε οὕτως ὅπως
εἴκασε, καὶ ἐν δέοντι ἐγένετο αὐτῷ ἡ πομπὴ τῶν
6 ἱππέων. οἱ γὰρ τὰς δύο τὰς οὔπω ἑαλωκυίας
πόλεις ἔχοντες τῶν βαρβάρων, ὡς καπνόν τε εἶδον
ἀπὸ τῆς πρὸ[ς] σφῶν πόλεως ἐμπιπραμένης καί
τινες καὶ ἀπὸ τοῦ πάθους αὐτοῦ διαφυγόντες
αὐτάγγελοι τῆς ἁλώσεως ἐγένοντο, ὡς τάχους
ἕκαστοι εἶχον ἀθρόοι ἐκ τῶν πόλεως φεύγοντες
ἐμπίπτουσιν ἐς τὸ στῖφος τῶν ἱππέων ξυντεταγμένον καὶ κατεκόπησαν οἱ πλεῖστοι αὐτῶν.

3. Οὕτω δὴ τὰς πέντε πόλεις ἐν δυσὶν ἡμέραις
ἑλών τε καὶ ἐξανδραποδισάμενος ᾔει ἐπὶ τὴν
μεγίστην αὐτῶν τὴν Κύρου πόλιν. ἡ δὲ τετειχι-

upon the defenders on the walls, and missiles were
hurled from the catapults, so that the wall was soon
cleared of defenders by the great shower of missiles,
and it was quick work for the Macedonians to set up
the ladders and ascend the wall. They put all the 4
men to the sword according to Alexander's orders and
seized as plunder the women, children and other
spoils. Thence Alexander marched at once to the
second city, which lay next to this one, captured it
too in the same fashion on the same day, and gave his
captives the same treatment. He advanced then to
the third city, and took it next day at the first
assault.

While he himself was thus busied with his infantry, 5
he despatched the cavalry to the two next cities, with
instructions to watch the men within carefully, in
case they learned of the capture of the neighbouring
cities and also of his own impending approach, and
took to flight, and then pursuit might be impracticable. Things turned out just as he guessed, and the
despatch of the cavalry came none too soon. For the 6
barbarians who held the two yet untaken cities saw
the smoke rising, as the city next in front of them was
ablaze, and when a few who escaped the catastrophe
itself gave first-hand information of the capture, they
attempted as fast as they could to escape from these
cities in a mass, but ran straight into the close array
of cavalry, and most of them were cut down.

3. After thus capturing the five cities in two days
and enslaving the survivors, Alexander marched
against the largest of them, Cyropolis [Ura-Tyube].

σμένη τε ἦν ὑψηλοτέρῳ τείχει ἤπερ αἱ ἄλλαι, οἷα
δὴ ὑπὸ Κύρου οἰκισθεῖσα, καὶ τοῦ πλείστου καὶ
μαχιμωτάτου τῶν ταύτῃ βαρβάρων ἐς ταύτην
συμπεφευγότος οὐχ ὡσαύτως ῥᾳδία ἐξ ἐφόδου
ἑλεῖν τοῖς Μακεδόσιν ἐγίγνετο. ἀλλὰ μηχανὰς γὰρ
προσάγων τῷ τείχει Ἀλέξανδρος ταύτῃ μὲν κατασείειν ἐπενόει τὸ τεῖχος καὶ κατὰ τὸ ἀεὶ παραρ-
2 ρηγνύμενον αὐτοῦ τὰς προσβολὰς ποιεῖσθαι. αὐτὸς
δὲ ὡς κατεῖδε τοὺς ἔκρους τοῦ ποταμοῦ, ὃς διὰ τῆς
πόλεως χείμαρρους ὢν διέρχεται, ξηροὺς ἐν τῷ
τότε ὕδατος καὶ οὐ ξυνεχεῖς τοῖς τείχεσιν, ἀλλ’
οἵους παρασχεῖν πάροδον τοῖς στρατιώταις διαδῦναι
ἐς τὴν πόλιν, ἀναλαβὼν τούς τε σωματοφύλακας
καὶ τοὺς ὑπασπιστὰς καὶ τοὺς τοξότας καὶ τοὺς
Ἀγριᾶνας τετραμμένων τῶν βαρβάρων πρὸς τὰς
μηχανὰς καὶ τοὺς ταύτῃ προσμαχομένους λανθάνει
κατὰ τοὺς ἔκρους ξὺν ὀλίγοις τὸ πρῶτον παρελθὼν
3 ἐς τὴν πόλιν· ἀναρρήξας δὲ ἔνδοθεν τῶν πυλῶν, αἳ
κατὰ τοῦτο τὸ χωρίον ἦσαν, δέχεται καὶ τοὺς
ἄλλους στρατιώτας εὐπετῶς. ἔνθα δὴ οἱ βάρβαροι
ἐχομένην ἤδη τὴν πόλιν αἰσθόμενοι ἐπὶ τοὺς ἀμφὶ
Ἀλέξανδρον ὅμως ἐτράπησαν· καὶ γίνεται προσβολὴ αὐτῶν καρτερά, καὶ βάλλεται λίθῳ αὐτὸς
Ἀλέξανδρος βιαίως τήν τε κεφαλὴν καὶ τὸν αὐχένα
καὶ Κρατερὸς τοξεύματι καὶ πολλοὶ ἄλλοι τῶν
ἡγεμόνων· ἀλλὰ καὶ ὣς ἐξέωσαν ἐκ τῆς ἀγορᾶς
4 τοὺς βαρβάρους. καὶ ἐν τούτῳ οἱ κατὰ τὸ τεῖχος
προσβεβληκότες ἔρημον ἤδη τὸ τεῖχος τῶν προμαχομένων αἱροῦσιν. ἐν μὲν δὴ τῇ πρώτῃ καταλήψει
τῆς πόλεως ἀπέθανον τῶν πολεμίων μάλιστα ἐς
ὀκτακισχιλίους· οἱ δὲ λοιποὶ (ἦσαν γὰρ οἱ πάντες
ἐς μυρίους καὶ πεντακισχιλίους μαχίμους οἱ

This was fortified with a higher wall than the rest, since Cyrus had founded it; and as the greatest number and the best fighters of the barbarians round about had taken refuge in it, it was not so easy for the Macedonians to capture it straight off. However, Alexander brought up engines to the wall and proposed to batter it down in this way and to make assaults wherever breaches occurred. But when he 2 personally observed that the outlets of the river, a winter torrent which runs through the city, were dry at the time, and did not reach up to the wall, but were low enough to permit a passage by which soldiers could pass into the city, he took the bodyguards, hypaspists, archers and Agrianes, and while the tribesmen were engaged with the siege-engines and the troops attacking there, he slipped unobserved along the channels, penetrated the city at first with only a few men, and broke open the gates from within 3 which were at that point and easily admitted the rest of the troops. Then the barbarians, seeing that their city was already in the enemy's hands, none the less turned upon Alexander and his force. They made a vigorous onslaught; Alexander himself was struck violently with a stone on his head and neck, and Craterus was wounded by an arrow, as were many other officers. None the less they cleared the market-place of the tribesmen. Meanwhile those 4 who had assaulted the wall captured it, now that it was denuded of defenders. In the first occupation of the city about eight thousand of the enemy perished; the rest (the whole number gathered together there

ξυνεληλυθότες) καταφεύγουσιν ἐς τὴν ἄκραν. καὶ
τούτους περιστρατοπεδεύσας Ἀλέξανδρος ἡμέραν
μίαν ἐφρούρησεν· οἱ δὲ ἐνδείᾳ ὕδατος ἐνεχείρισαν
σφᾶς Ἀλεξάνδρῳ.

5   Τὴν δὲ ἑβδόμην πόλιν ἐξ ἐφόδου ἔλαβε, Πτολεμαῖος μὲν λέγει, ὅτι αὐτοὺς σφᾶς ἐνδόντας, Ἀριστόβουλος δέ, ὅτι βίᾳ καὶ ταύτην ἐξεῖλεν καὶ ὅτι
πάντας τοὺς καταληφθέντας ἐν αὐτῇ ἀπέκτεινε.
Πτολεμαῖος δὲ κατανεῖμαι λέγει αὐτὸν τοὺς ἀνθρώπους τῇ στρατιᾷ καὶ δεδεμένους κελεῦσαι φυλάσσεσθαι ἔστ' ἂν ἐκ τῆς χώρας ἀπαλλάττηται αὐτός,
ὡς μηδένα ἀπολείπεσθαι τῶν τὴν ἀπόστασιν πραξ-
άντων.

6   Ἐν τούτῳ δὲ τῶν τε ἐκ τῆς Ἀσίας Σκυθῶν
στρατιὰ ἀφικνεῖται πρὸς τὰς ὄχθας τοῦ ποταμοῦ
τοῦ Τανάιδος, ἀκούσαντες οἱ πολλοὶ αὐτῶν, ὅτι
ἔστιν οἳ καὶ τῶν ἐπέκεινα τοῦ ποταμοῦ βαρβάρων
ἀπ' Ἀλεξάνδρου ἀφεστᾶσιν, ὡς, εἰ δή τι λόγου ὂν
ἄξιον νεωτερίζοιτο, καὶ αὐτοὶ ἐπιθησόμενοι τοῖς
Μακεδόσι. καὶ οἱ ἀμφὶ Σπιταμένην δὲ ἀπηγ-
γέλθησαν ὅτι τοὺς ἐν Μαρακάνδοις καταλειφθέντας
7 ἐν τῇ ἄκρᾳ πολιορκοῦσιν. ἔνθα δὴ Ἀλέξανδρος
ἐπὶ μὲν τοὺς ἀμφὶ Σπιταμένην Ἀνδρόμαχόν τε
ἀποστέλλει καὶ Μενέδημον καὶ Κάρανον, ἱππέας
μὲν ἔχοντας τῶν ἑταίρων ἐς ἑξήκοντα καὶ τῶν
μισθοφόρων ὀκτακοσίους, ὧν Κάρανος ἡγεῖτο,
πεζοὺς δὲ μισθοφόρους ἐς χιλίους πεντακοσίους·
ἐπιτάσσει δὲ αὐτοῖς Φαρνούχην τὸν ἑρμηνέα, τὸ μὲν
γένος Λύκιον τὸν Φαρνούχην, ἐμπείρως δὲ τῆς τε
φωνῆς τῶν ταύτῃ βαρβάρων ἔχοντα καὶ τὰ ἄλλα
ὁμιλῆσαι αὐτοῖς δεξιὸν φαινόμενον.

329
B.C.

came to some fifteen thousand fighting men) took refuge in the citadel: Alexander blockaded and kept guard on them for a day, and because of want of water they surrendered to him.

The seventh city he took at first assault. Ptolemy 5 says that they surrendered, Aristobulus that Alexander captured this city too by force, and killed all he found within; Ptolemy also says that he distributed the men among his army and ordered them to be kept bound and under guard till he left their country, so that none of those responsible for the revolt should be left behind.

Meanwhile an army of the Asian Scythians arrived 6 on the banks of the river Tanais; most of them had heard that some of the barbarians on that side of the river had revolted from Alexander, and they intended, should any important rising occur, to join in attacking the Macedonians.[1] News was also brought that Spitamenes and his troops were besieging those who had been left behind at Maracanda in the citadel. On this Alexander sent against the troops of Spitamenes, Andromachus, Menedemus, and Caranus, with cavalry comprising some sixty Companions and eight hundred of the mercenaries under Caranus, and with about fifteen hundred mercenary infantry; and he placed these forces under command of Pharnuches the interpreter, a Lycian by birth who was expert in the language of the barbarians of these parts and seemed in general to be skilful in dealings with them.[2]

---

[1] QC. vii 7, 1 thinks they were menaced by the new city. 'Asia': there is a muddle here. On any view Al. was in Asia, but if the 'Tanais' was the frontier between Europe and Asia (App. XII 4), Scythians across the river were in Europe!

[2] QC. 6, 24 names only Menedemus and gives him 3,000 foot and 800 horse.

4. Αὐτὸς δὲ τὴν πόλιν, ἣν ἐπενόει, τειχίσας ἐν
ἡμέραις εἴκοσι καὶ ξυνοικίσας ἐς αὐτὴν τῶν τε
Ἑλλήνων μισθοφόρων καὶ ὅστις τῶν προσοικού-
ντων βαρβάρων ἐθελοντὴς μετέσχε τῆς ξυνοικήσεως
καί τινας καὶ τῶν ἐκ τοῦ στρατοπέδου Μακεδόνων,
ὅσοι ἀπόμαχοι ἤδη ἦσαν, θύσας τοῖς θεοῖς ὡς
νόμος αὐτῷ καὶ ἀγῶνα ἱππικόν τε καὶ γυμνικὸν
ποιήσας, ὡς οὐκ ἀπαλλασσομένους ἑώρα τοὺς
2 Σκύθας ἀπὸ τῆς ὄχθης τοῦ ποταμοῦ, ἀλλ' ἐκτοξεύοντες ἐς τὸν ποταμὸν ἑωρῶντο οὐ πλατὺν ταύτῃ
ὄντα, καί τινα καὶ πρὸς ὕβριν τοῦ Ἀλεξάνδρου
βαρβαρικῶς ἐθρασύναντο, ὡς οὐκ ἂν τολμήσαντα
Ἀλέξανδρον ἅψασθαι Σκυθῶν ἢ μαθόντα ἂν ὅτι
περ τὸ διάφορον Σκύθαις τε καὶ τοῖς Ἀσιανοῖς
βαρβάροις, — ὑπὸ τούτων παροξυνόμενος ἐπενόει
διαβαίνειν ἐπ' αὐτοὺς καὶ τὰς διφθέρας παρε-
3 σκεύαζεν ἐπὶ τῷ πόρῳ. θυμουμένῳ δὲ ἐπὶ τῇ διαβάσει τὰ ἱερὰ οὐκ ἐγίγνετο· ὁ δὲ βαρέως μὲν
ἔφερεν οὐ γιγνομένων, ὅμως δὲ ἐκαρτέρει καὶ
ἔμενεν. ὡς δὲ οὐκ ἀνίεσαν οἱ Σκύθαι, αὖθις ἐπὶ τῇ
διαβάσει ἐθύετο, καὶ αὖθις [1] κίνδυνον αὐτῷ σημαίνεσθαι Ἀρίστανδρος ὁ μάντις ἔφραζεν· ὁ δὲ
κρεῖσσον ἔφη ἐς ἔσχατον κινδύνου ἐλθεῖν ἢ κατε-
στραμμένον ξύμπασαν ὀλίγου δεῖν τὴν Ἀσίαν
γέλωτα εἶναι Σκύθαις, καθάπερ Δαρεῖος ὁ Ξέρξου
πατὴρ πάλαι ἐγένετο. Ἀρίστανδρος δὲ οὐκ ἔφη
παρὰ τὰ ἐκ τοῦ θείου σημαινόμενα ἄλλα ἀποδεί-
ξεσθαι, ὅτι ἄλλα ἐθέλει ἀκοῦσαι Ἀλέξανδρος.
4   Ὁ δέ, ὡς αἵ τε διφθέραι αὐτῷ παρεσκευασμέναι
ἦσαν ἐπὶ τῷ πόρῳ καὶ ὁ στρατὸς ἐξωπλισμένος

---

[1] αὖθις Castiglioni: αὖ ἐς codd.

4. Alexander himself now spent twenty days in building the wall of the city he proposed to found, and settling there some Greek mercenaries, any of the neighbouring barbarians who shared in the settlement as volunteers, and also some Macedonians from the army who were no longer fit for active service.[1] He then sacrificed to the gods in accordance with his custom and held a cavalry and athletic contest. As he saw that the Scythians were not leaving the river bank but were observed shooting 2 from it arrows into the river, which was not very broad here, and were also insulting Alexander with barbaric boasts that he would not dare to touch Scythians or he would learn the difference between Scythians and the barbarians of Asia, his irritation made him plan to cross and attack them, and he began to get ready the hides for the crossing. But when he sacrificed with 3 a view to crossing, the omens were not favourable. Though much annoyed by this, still he restrained himself and stayed where he was. But as the Scythians did not give up, he sacrificed again with a view to crossing, and Aristander the prophet again said that danger to him was portended. Alexander replied that it was better to go to any extremity of danger than, after subduing almost the whole of Asia, to be a laughing-stock to Scythians, as Darius the father of Xerxes had been long ago. Yet Aristander refused to interpret the sacrifices in any way contrary to the signs from heaven because Alexander desired to hear something different.

As soon as the hides had been got ready for his 4 crossing, and the army was stationed on the bank

---

[1] App. VIII 16.   Types of settlers: iii 1, 5n.

ἐφειστήκει τῷ ποταμῷ, αἵ τε μηχαναὶ ἀπὸ
ξυνθήματος ἐξηκόντιζον ἐς τοὺς Σκύθας παριπ-
πεύοντας ἐπὶ τῇ ὄχθῃ καὶ ἔστιν οἳ αὐτῶν ἐτιτρώσκοντο ἐκ τῶν βελῶν, εἷς δὲ δὴ διὰ τοῦ γέρρου τε
καὶ τοῦ θώρακος διαμπὰξ πληγεὶς πίπτει ἀπὸ τοῦ
ἵππου, οἱ μὲν ἐξεπλάγησαν πρός τε τῶν βελῶν τὴν
διὰ μακροῦ ἄφεσιν καὶ ὅτι ἀνὴρ ἀγαθὸς αὐτοῖς
τετελευτήκει, καὶ ὀλίγον ἀνεχώρησαν ἀπὸ τῆς
5 ὄχθης· Ἀλέξανδρος δὲ τεταραγμένους πρὸς τὰ
βέλη ἰδὼν ὑπὸ σαλπίγγων ἐπέρα τὸν ποταμὸν
αὐτὸς ἡγούμενος· εἵπετο δὲ αὐτῷ καὶ ἡ ἄλλη
στρατιά. πρῶτον μὲν δὴ τοὺς τοξότας καὶ σφενδονήτας ἀποβιβάσας σφενδονᾶν τε καὶ ἐκτοξεύειν
ἐκέλευσεν ἐς τοὺς Σκύθας, ὡς μὴ πελάζειν αὐτοὺς
τῇ φάλαγγι τῶν πεζῶν ἐκβαινούσῃ, πρὶν τὴν ἵππον
6 αὐτῷ διαβῆναι πᾶσαν. ὡς δὲ ἀθρόοι ἐπὶ τῇ ὄχθῃ
ἐγένοντο, ἐφῆκεν ἐπὶ τοὺς Σκύθας τὸ μὲν πρῶτον
μίαν ἱππαρχίαν τῶν ξένων καὶ τῶν σαρισσοφόρων
ἴλας τέσσαρας· καὶ τούτους δεξάμενοι οἱ Σκύθαι
καὶ ἐς κύκλους περιιππεύοντες ἔβαλλόν τε πολλοὶ
ὀλίγους ⟨καὶ⟩ αὐτοὶ οὐ χαλεπῶς διεφύγγανον.
Ἀλέξανδρος δὲ τούς τε τοξότας καὶ τοὺς Ἀγριᾶνας
καὶ τοὺς ἄλλους ψιλούς, ὧν Βάλακρος ἦρχεν,
ἀναμίξας τοῖς ἱππεῦσιν ἐπῆγεν ἐπὶ τοὺς Σκύθας.
7 ὡς δὲ ὁμοῦ ἤδη ἐγίγνοντο, ἐλάσαι ἐκέλευσεν ἐς
αὐτοὺς τῶν τε ἑταίρων τρεῖς ἱππαρχίας καὶ τοὺς
ἱππακοντιστὰς ξύμπαντας· καὶ αὐτὸς δὲ τὴν
λοιπὴν ἵππον ἄγων σπουδῇ ἐνέβαλεν ὀρθίαις ταῖς
ἴλαις. οὔκουν ἔτι οἷοί τε ἦσαν ἐξελίσσειν τὴν ἱπ-

fully armed, the catapults on a signal hurled their
volleys at the Scythians riding along the bank, and
some were wounded by the missiles; one was actually
pierced right through his shield and corslet, and fell
from his horse. The Scythians were dismayed at the
long-range discharge of the missiles and at the loss of
a brave man and retreated a little from the bank.
Seeing them in disorder because of the missiles, 5
Alexander sounded his bugles and began the crossing
of the river, himself in the van; the rest of the army
followed him. He first disembarked the archers and
slingers, and told them to shoot their bullets and
arrows at the Scythians, to keep them from approaching the phalanx of the infantry as it disembarked,
before his cavalry had fully crossed. When they were 6
all in a body on the bank, he launched at the Scythians
first a hipparchy of the mercenaries and four squadrons of the lancers.[2] The Scythians awaited their
onslaught, riding round in circles and shooting at
them; they were many against few, and easily evaded
their attack. Alexander then mixed up his archers,
the Agrianians and the other light troops under
Balacrus, with the cavalry, and led them against the
Scythians. Once they were quite close, he ordered 7
three hipparchies [3] of the Companions and all the
mounted javelin-men to charge at them; and he
himself brought up the rest of the cavalry at full
speed and went in with his squadrons in column. So
the Scythians were no longer able to wheel round in

---

[2] Introd. n. 84.   [3] Introd. 59 f.

πασίαν ἐς κύκλους, ὡς πρόσθεν ἔτι· ὁμοῦ μὲν γὰρ
ἡ ἵππος προσέκειτο αὐτοῖς, ὁμοῦ δὲ οἱ ψιλοὶ
ἀναμεμιγμένοι τοῖς ἱππεῦσιν οὐκ εἴων τὰς ἐπι-
στροφὰς ἀσφαλεῖς ποιεῖσθαι. ἔνθα λαμπρὰ ἤδη
8 φυγὴ τῶν Σκυθῶν ἦν· καὶ πίπτουσι μὲν αὐτῶν ἐς
χιλίους καὶ εἷς τῶν ἡγεμόνων, Σατράκης, ἑάλωσαν
δὲ ἐς ἑκατὸν καὶ πεντήκοντα. ὡς δὲ ἡ δίωξις
ὀξεῖά τε καὶ διὰ καύματος πολλοῦ ταλαιπώρως
ἐγίνετο, δίψει τε ἡ στρατιὰ πᾶσα εἴχετο καὶ αὐτὸς
Ἀλέξανδρος ἐλαύνων πίνει ὁποῖον ἦν ὕδωρ ἐν τῇ γῇ
9 ἐκείνῃ. καὶ ἦν γὰρ πονηρὸν τὸ ὕδωρ, ῥεῦμα
ἀθρόον κατασκήπτει αὐτῷ ἐς τὴν γαστέρα· καὶ
ἐπὶ τῷδε ἡ δίωξις οὐκ ἐπὶ πάντων Σκυθῶν ἐγένετο·
εἰ δὲ μή, δοκοῦσιν ἄν μοι καὶ πάντες διαφθαρῆναι
ἐν τῇ φυγῇ, εἰ μὴ Ἀλεξάνδρῳ τὸ σῶμα ἔκαμεν.
καὶ αὐτὸς ἐς ἔσχατον κινδύνου ἐλθὼν ἐκομίσθη
ὀπίσω ἐς τὸ στρατόπεδον. καὶ οὕτω ξυνέβη ἡ
μαντεία Ἀριστάνδρῳ.

5. Ὀλίγον δὲ ὕστερον παρὰ τοῦ Σκυθῶν βασιλέως ἀφικνοῦνται παρ᾽ Ἀλέξανδρον πρέσβεις, ὑπὲρ
τῶν πραχθέντων ἐς ἀπολογίαν ἐκπεμφθέντες, ὅτι
οὐκ ἀπὸ ⟨τοῦ⟩ κοινοῦ τῶν Σκυθῶν ἐπράχθη,
ἀλλὰ καθ᾽ ἁρπαγὴν λῃστρικῷ τρόπῳ σταλέντων,
καὶ αὐτὸς ὅτι ἐθέλοι ποιεῖν τὰ ἐπαγγελλόμενα.
καὶ τούτῳ φιλάνθρωπα ἐπιστέλλει Ἀλέξανδρος,
ὅτι οὔτε ἀπιστοῦντα μὴ ἐπεξιέναι καλὸν αὐτῷ
ἐφαίνετο, οὔτε κατὰ καιρὸν ἦν ἐν τῷ τότε
ἐπεξιέναι.

2 Οἱ δὲ ἐν Μαρακάνδοις ἐν τῇ ἄκρᾳ φρουρούμενοι
Μακεδόνες προσβολῆς γενομένης τῇ ἄκρᾳ ἐκ Σπιταμένους τε καὶ τῶν ἀμφ᾽ αὐτὸν ἐπεκδραμόντες
ἀπέκτεινάν τε τῶν πολεμίων ἔστιν οὓς καὶ ἀπώ-

circles as they had been doing up till then; for the
cavalry was now pressing them, and at the same
moment the light troops, mingled with the cavalry,
prevented their turning about safely. The Scythians
were by now in open flight; about a thousand fell, 8
with one of their commanders, Satraces, while about a
hundred and fifty were captured. The pursuit was
sharp and distressing because of the great heat, so
that all the army was consumed by thirst, and Alexander himself, as he rode on, drank whatever kind of
water there was in that country. The water was in 9
fact bad, and so sudden diarrhoea attacked his
stomach; for this reason the pursuit did not extend
to all the Scythians. Otherwise I think they would
all have perished in their flight, had not Alexander
been taken ill. Personally he fell into serious
danger, and was carried back into the camp. In this
way Aristander's prophecy came true.[4]

5. Soon afterwards envoys reached Alexander from
the Scythian king;[1] they had been sent to excuse
what had occurred, on the ground that it had not been
the action of the Scythian community, but only that
of raiders and freebooters; the king himself was
ready to do what was required of him. Alexander
gave a kindly answer, since he thought it dishonourable not to press the attack, if he distrusted the king,
and not the right moment to press it.[2]

The Macedonians who were blockaded in the 2
citadel at Maracanda, when an assault was made on
the citadel by Spitamenes and his troops, sallied out,
killed some of the enemy, drove off the whole body,

---

[4] See Fuller 236 ff. QC. vii 7, 1–9, 16 has many divergencies. Cf. also Marsden (i 20, 8 n.) 97, 165 f.

[1] QC. vii 9, 17 ff.

[2] What follows is clearly from Pt. (cf. 6, 1). See App.
VIII 12.

σαντο ξύμπαντας, καὶ αὐτοὶ ἀπαθεῖς ἀπεχώρησαν
3 ἐς τὴν ἄκραν. ὡς δὲ καὶ οἱ ὑπ᾽ Ἀλεξάνδρου
ἐσταλμένοι ἐς Μαράκανδα ἤδη προσάγοντες Σπιταμένει ἐξηγγέλλοντο, τὴν μὲν πολιορκίαν ἐκλείπει
τῆς ἄκρας, αὐτὸς δὲ ὡς ἐς τὰ βασίλεια [1] τῆς
Σογδιανῆς ἀνεχώρει. Φαρνούχης δὲ καὶ οἱ ξὺν
αὐτῷ στρατηγοὶ σπεύδοντες ἐξελάσαι αὐτὸν παντάπασιν ἐπί τε τὰ ὅρια τῆς Σογδιανῆς ξυνείποντο
ὑποχωροῦντι καὶ εἰς τοὺς Νομάδας τοὺς Σκύθας
4 οὐδενὶ λογισμῷ ξυνεσβάλλουσιν. ἔνθα δὴ προσλα-
βὼν ὁ Σπιταμένης τῶν Σκυθῶν ἱππέων ἐς ἑξακοσίους προσεπήρθη ὑπὸ τῆς ξυμμαχίας τῆς Σκυθικῆς
δέξασθαι ἐπιόντας τοὺς Μακεδόνας· παρατα-
ξάμενος δὲ ἐν χωρίῳ ὁμαλῷ πρὸς τῇ ἐρήμῳ τῆς
Σκυθικῆς ὑπομεῖναι μὲν τοὺς πολεμίους ἢ αὐτὸς ἐς
αὐτοὺς ἐμβαλεῖν οὐκ ἤθελε, περιϊππεύων δὲ ἐτό-
5 ξευεν ἐς τὴν φάλαγγα τῶν πεζῶν. καὶ ἐπελαυ-
νόντων μὲν αὐτοῖς τῶν ἀμφὶ Φαρνούχην ἔφευγεν
εὐπετῶς, οἷα δὴ ὠκυτέρων τε αὐτοῖς καὶ ἐν τῷ
τότε ἀκμαιοτέρων ὄντων τῶν ἵππων, τοῖς δὲ ἀμφὶ
Ἀνδρόμαχον ὑπό τε τῆς ξυνεχοῦς πορείας καὶ ἅμα
χιλοῦ ἀπορίᾳ κεκάκωτο ἡ ἵππος· μένουσι δὲ ἢ
ὑποχωροῦσιν ἐπέκειντο εὐρώστως οἱ Σκύθαι.
6 ἔνθα δὴ πολλῶν μὲν τιτρωσκομένων ἐκ τῶν
τοξευμάτων, ἔστι δὲ ὧν καὶ πιπτόντων, ἐς πλαίσιον
ἰσόπλευρον τάξαντες τοὺς στρατιώτας ἀνεχώρουν
ὡς ἐπὶ τὸν ποταμὸν τὸν Πολυτίμητον, ὅτι νάπος
ταύτῃ ἦν, ὡς μήτε τοῖς βαρβάροις εὐπετὲς ἔτι
εἶναι ἐκτοξεύειν ἐς αὐτούς, σφίσι τε οἱ πεζοὶ
ὠφελιμώτεροι ὦσι.

[1] βασίλεια codd: βόρεια Polak, Roos etc, but see App.
VIII 16.

and retired unharmed themselves to the citadel. As
soon as Spitamenes heard that the force sent by
Alexander to Maracanda was already drawing near,
he abandoned the siege of the citadel and retreated
himself towards the royal residence of Sogdiana.[3]
Pharnuches and the officers with him, hurrying on to
drive him out altogether, pursued as he withdrew to
the frontiers of Sogdiana, and without calculating the
risk came into conflict with the nomad Scythians as
well. On this Spitamenes, adding some six hundred
Scythian horse to his force, was encouraged by the
Scythian reinforcement to await the Macedonian
attack; he drew up his men on a level space near the
Scythian desert, but his plan was not merely to await
the enemy, or to charge them himself; wheeling
round and round, he shot volleys of arrows into
the infantry phalanx. When Pharnuches' troops
charged them, he had no difficulty in riding off, as
his horses were swifter and at the moment fresher,
while the horses of Andromachus' troops had suffered
from the forced march and want of fodder. But when
they stood their ground or withdrew, the Scythians
swooped vigorously upon them. By now many were
being wounded by the arrows, and some actually
falling, and the officers formed their men into a square
and withdrew towards the river Polytimetus [Zerav-
shan], as there was a wooded glen near by, so that the
Scythians could no longer easily shoot at them, and
their infantry might be of more use to them.

[3] See App. VIII 16.

7   Κάρανος δὲ ὁ ἱππάρχης οὐκ ἀνακοινώσας Ἀνδρομάχῳ διαβαίνειν ἐπεχείρησε τὸν ποταμὸν ὡς ἐς
ἀσφαλὲς ταύτῃ καταστήσων τὴν ἵππον· καὶ οἱ
πεζοὶ αὐτῷ ἐπηκολούθησαν, οὐκ ἐκ παραγγέλματος,
ἀλλὰ φοβερά τε καὶ οὐδενὶ κόσμῳ ἐγένετο αὐτοῖς ἡ
ἔσβασις ἡ ἐς τὸν ποταμὸν κατὰ κρημνώδεις τὰς
8 ὄχθας. καὶ οἱ βάρβαροι αἰσθόμενοι τὴν ἁμαρτίαν
τῶν Μακεδόνων αὐτοῖς ἵπποις ἔνθεν καὶ ἔνθεν
ἐσβάλλουσιν ἐς τὸν πόρον. καὶ οἱ μὲν τῶν ἤδη
διαβεβηκότων καὶ ἀποχωρούντων εἴχοντο, οἱ δὲ
τοὺς διαβαίνοντας ἀντιμέτωποι ταχθέντες ἀνεῖλουν
9 ἐς τὸν ποταμόν, οἱ δὲ ἀπὸ τῶν πλαγίων ἐξετόξευον
ἐς αὐτούς, οἱ δὲ τοῖς ἔτι ἐσβαίνουσιν ἐπέκειντο,
ὥστε ἀπορίᾳ πάντοθεν ξυνεχόμενοι οἱ Μακεδόνες
ἐς νῆσόν τινα τῶν ἐν τῷ ποταμῷ ξυμφεύγουσιν οὐ
μεγάλην. καὶ περιστάντες αὐτοὺς οἱ Σκύθαι τε καὶ
οἱ ξὺν Σπιταμένει ἱππεῖς ἐν κύκλῳ πάντας κατετό-
ξευσαν· ὀλίγους δὲ ἠνδραποδίσαντο αὐτῶν, καὶ
τούτους πάντας ἀπέκτειναν.

6. Ἀριστόβουλος δὲ ἐνέδρᾳ τὸ πολὺ τῆς στρατιᾶς
διαφθαρῆναι λέγει, τῶν Σκυθῶν ἐν παραδείσῳ
κρυφθέντων, οἳ ἐκ τοῦ ἀφανοῦς ἐπεγένοντο τοῖς
Μακεδόσιν ἐν αὐτῷ τῷ ἔργῳ· ἵνα τὸν μὲν Φαρνούχην παραχωρεῖν τῆς ἡγεμονίας τοῖς ξυμπεμφθεῖσι
Μακεδόσιν, ὡς οὐκ ἐμπείρως ἔχοντα ἔργων
πολεμικῶν, ἀλλ' ἐπὶ τῷ καθομιλῆσαι τοὺς βαρβάρους μᾶλλόν τι πρὸς Ἀλεξάνδρου ἢ ἐπὶ τῷ ἐν ταῖς
μάχαις ἐξηγεῖσθαι ἐσταλμένον, τοὺς δὲ Μακεδόνας
2 τε εἶναι καὶ ἑταίρους βασιλέως. Ἀνδρόμαχον δὲ

Caranus, the commander of the cavalry, without 7 329 B.C. notifying Andromachus attempted to cross the river, hoping to get his cavalry into safety there, and the infantry followed him, without any instructions, in a panic-stricken and disorderly descent into the river from the banks which were precipitous. The barbar- 8 ians on seeing the error of the Macedonians dashed, mounted as they were, from all directions into the stream. Some pressed on after those who had already crossed and were in retreat, others were ranged in front of the men crossing and penned them back into the river, or showered arrows at them from 9 the flanks, or attacked those still entering the river. Then the Macedonians, helpless and pressed on every side, took refuge in a body on one of the small islands in the river. The Scythians and Spitamenes' cavalry stationed themselves round in a circle and shot them all down; a few were made prisoners but they too were all killed.

6. Aristobulus, however, states that the greater part of this force was destroyed by an ambush; the Scythians, having hidden themselves in a park, attacked the Macedonians from their concealment in the very course of the action, at the moment when Pharnuches was retiring from his command in favour of the Macedonians who had been sent with him, on the ground that he had no military experience, but had been sent by Alexander to treat with the barbarians rather than to command in battles, while they were both Macedonians and Companions of the king. However, Andromachus, Caranus and Mene- 2

355

καὶ Κάρανον καὶ Μενέδημον οὐ δέξασθαι τὴν
ἡγεμονίαν, τὸ μέν τι ὡς μὴ δοκεῖν παρὰ τὰ ἐπηγ-
γελμένα ὑπὸ Ἀλεξάνδρου αὐτούς τι κατὰ σφᾶς
νεωτερίζειν, τὸ δὲ καὶ ἐν αὐτῷ τῷ δεινῷ οὐκ
ἐθελήσαντας, εἰ δή τι πταίσειαν, μὴ ὅσον κατ'
ἄνδρα μόνον μετέχειν αὐτοῦ, ἀλλὰ καὶ ὡς τὸ πᾶν
αὐτοὺς κακῶς ἐξηγησαμένους. ἐν τούτῳ δὴ τῷ
θορύβῳ τε καὶ τῇ ἀταξίᾳ ἐπιθεμένους αὐτοῖς τοὺς
βαρβάρους κατακόψαι πάντας, ὥστε ἱππέας μὲν μὴ
πλείονας τῶν τεσσαράκοντα ἀποσωθῆναι, πεζοὺς δὲ
ἐς τριακοσίους.

3 Ταῦτα δὲ ὡς ἠγγέλθη Ἀλεξάνδρῳ, ἤλγησέ τε τῷ
πάθει τῶν στρατιωτῶν καὶ ἔγνω σπουδῇ ἐλαύνειν
ὡς ἐπὶ Σπιταμένην τε καὶ τοὺς ἀμφ' αὐτὸν βαρβάρους. ἀναλαβὼν οὖν τῶν τε ἑταίρων ἱππέων τοὺς
ἡμίσεας καὶ τοὺς ὑπασπιστὰς ξύμπαντας καὶ τοὺς
τοξότας καὶ τοὺς Ἀγριᾶνας καὶ τῆς φάλαγγος τοὺς
κουφοτάτους ᾔει ὡς ἐπὶ Μαράκανδα, ἵνα ἐπανήκειν
Σπιταμένην ἐπυνθάνετο καὶ αὖθις πολιορκεῖν τοὺς
4 ἐν τῇ ἄκρᾳ. καὶ αὐτὸς μὲν ἐν τρισὶν ἡμέραις
διελθὼν χιλίους καὶ πεντακοσίους σταδίους τῇ
τετάρτῃ ὑπὸ τὴν ἕω προσῆγε τῇ πόλει. Σπιταμένης δὲ καὶ οἱ ἀμφ' αὐτόν, ὡς ἐξηγγέλθη προσάγων Ἀλέξανδρος, οὐκ ἔμειναν, ἀλλ' ἐκλιπόντες τὴν
5 πόλιν φεύγουσιν. ὁ δὲ ἐχόμενος αὐτῶν ἐδίωκεν·
ὡς δὲ ἐπὶ ⟨τὸν⟩ χῶρον ἧκεν, οὗ ἡ μάχη ἐγένετο,
θάψας τοὺς στρατιώτας ὡς ἐκ τῶν παρόντων
εἵπετο ἔστε ἐπὶ τὴν ἔρημον τοῖς φεύγουσιν.
ἐκεῖθεν δὲ ἀναστρέφων ἐπόρθει τὴν χώραν καὶ τοὺς

---

[1] QC. vii 7, 30 ff. also has an ambuscade but does not

demus did not accept the command, partly to avoid
the appearance of taking any initiative of their own
contrary to the commands of Alexander, and partly
because in the very moment of crisis they were not
disposed, in case of a disaster, to be involved in it not
simply as individuals but as men who had themselves
directed the whole enterprise badly. It was in this
confusion and disorder that the barbarians charged
and cut them all to pieces, so that not more than
forty cavalry and about three hundred foot-soldiers
escaped.[1]

When this was reported to Alexander he was 3
distressed at the disaster to his men and decided to
march at full speed against Spitamenes and the
barbarians with him.[2] He therefore took half the
Companion cavalry, the archers and Agrianians, and
the lightest-armed of the phalanx and marched to
Maracanda, where he learnt Spitamenes had returned
and was again besieging the garrison in the citadel.
Alexander covered fifteen hundred stades in three 4
days,[3] and approached the city on the fourth about
dawn. Spitamenes and his troops did not stay on
learning that Alexander was drawing near, but left
the city and fled. Alexander pursued them closely, 5
and when he reached the place of the battle, he buried
the soldiers as best he could and followed the fugitives
right up to the desert. Thence he turned back,

---

much resemble Ar. Losses: 2,000 foot and 300 horse, cf.
3, 7 n.
   [2] In QC. 7, 39 Al. hears the news before crossing the Syr-
darya and conceals it. For his operations against Spitamenes
cf. QC. 9, 20-10, 9; App. VIII 12.
   [3] From Ar., cf. Strabo xi 11, 5. He knew that Polytimetus
was a Macedonian name and may have given Ochus as the
native name, cf. Pearson *LH* 168 f.

ἐς τὰ ἐρύματα καταπεφευγότας τῶν βαρβάρων
ἔκτεινεν, ὅτι ξυνεπιθέσθαι ἐξηγγέλλοντο καὶ αὐτοὶ
τοῖς Μακεδόσι· καὶ ἐπῆλθε πᾶσαν τὴν χώραν ὅσην
ὁ ποταμὸς ὁ Πολυτίμητος ἐπάρδων ἐπέρχεται.
6 ἵνα δὲ ἀφανίζεται τῷ ποταμῷ τὸ ὕδωρ, ἐντεῦθεν
ἤδη τὸ ἐπέκεινα ἔρημος ἡ χώρα ἐστίν· ἀφανίζεται
δὲ καίπερ πολλοῦ ὢν ὕδατος ἐς τὴν ψάμμον. καὶ
ἄλλοι ποταμοὶ ὡσαύτως ἐκεῖ ἀφανίζονται μεγάλοι
καὶ ἀέ[ν]ναοι, ὅ τε Ἔπαρδος, ὃς ῥέει διὰ Μάρδων
τῆς χώρας, καὶ Ἄρειος, ὅτου ἐπώνυμος ἡ τῶν
Ἀρείων γῆ ἐστιν, καὶ Ἐτύμανδρος, ὃς δι᾽ Εὐεργε-
7 τῶν ῥέει. καὶ εἰσὶ ξύμπαντες οὗτοι τηλικοῦτοι
ποταμοὶ ὥστε οὐδεὶς αὐτῶν μείων ἐστὶ τοῦ
Πηνειοῦ τοῦ Θεσσαλικοῦ ποταμοῦ, ὃς διὰ τῶν
Τεμπῶν ῥέων ἐκδιδοῖ ἐς θάλασσαν· ὁ δὲ Πολυτίμητος πολὺ ἔτι μείζων ἢ κατὰ τὸν Πηνειὸν ποταμόν ἐστι.

7. Ταῦτα δὲ διαπραξάμενος ἐς Ζαρίασπα ἀφί-
κετο· καὶ αὐτοῦ κατέμενεν ἔστε παρελθεῖν τὸ
ἀκμαῖον τοῦ χειμῶνος. ἐν τούτῳ δὲ ἀφίκοντο παρ᾽
αὐτὸν Φραταφέρνης τε ὁ Παρθυαίων σατράπης καὶ
Στασάνωρ ὁ ἐς Ἀρείους ἀποπεμφθεὶς ὡς Ἀρσάκην
ξυλληψόμενος, τόν τε Ἀρσάκην δεδεμένον ἄγοντες
καὶ Βραζάνην, ὅντινα Βῆσσος τῆς Παρθυαίων
σατράπην κατέστησε, καί τινας ἄλλους τῶν τότε
2 ξὺν Βήσσῳ ἀποστάντων. ἧκον δὲ ἐν τῷ αὐτῷ
Ἐπόκιλλος καὶ Μελαμνίδας καὶ Πτολεμαῖος ὁ τῶν
Θρακῶν στρατηγὸς ἀπὸ θαλάσσης, οἳ τά τε
χρήματα ⟨τὰ⟩ ξὺν Μένητι πεμφθέντα καὶ τοὺς
ξυμμάχους ὡς ἐπὶ θάλασσαν κατήγαγον. καὶ
Ἄσανδρος δὲ ἐν τούτῳ ἧκεν καὶ Νέαρχος, στρατιὰν
Ἑλλήνων μισθοφόρων ἄγοντες, καὶ †Βῆσσός τε ὁ

ravaged the country and killed the barbarians who   329
had taken refuge in the forts, because they too were   B.C.
reported to have joined in the attack on the Macedonians. He traversed the entire country the river   6
Polytimetus [Zeravshan] waters; at the very point
where the stream disappears there is nothing but
desert: the stream, though it carries much water,
disappears into the sand. Other rivers, though great
and perennial, disappear there in the same way; the
Epardus, which runs through the Mardian country,
the Areius, which gives its name to the country Areia,
and the Etymandrus, which runs through the country
of the Euergetae. All these rivers are so great that   7
none is inferior to the Peneius, the river of Thessaly
which runs through Tempe and then discharges into
the sea; the Polytimetus is out of all comparison
larger than the river Peneius.

7. After Alexander had carried out these measures,   329–8
he arrived at Zariaspa, and remained there till the   B.C.
depth of winter was past.[1] At this time Phrataphernes the satrap of Parthyaea came to him with
Stasanor who had been sent to Areia to arrest
Arsaces, bringing him in chains along with Brazanes,
whom Bessus had made satrap of Parthyaea, and
others who had revolted with Bessus.[2] He was   2
joined at the same time from the seacoast by Epocillus, Melamnidas and Ptolemaeus the commander of
the Thracians who had escorted the treasure sent
with Menes and the allies down to the sea. Asander
and Nearchus also arrived at this time with a Greek
mercenary force, as did ' Bessus ', the satrap of Syria,

---

[1] Winter 329/8 B.C. Zariaspa: App. VIII 13. Cf. QC.
vii 10, 10 for his leaving Peucolaus with 3,000 men in Sogdiana.
[2] Ignored in QC., perhaps rightly, cf. 18, 3 n.

Συρίας σατράπης καὶ Ἀσκληπιόδωρος ὁ ὕπαρχος,
ἀπὸ θαλάσσης καὶ οὗτοι στρατιὰν ἄγοντες.

3 Ἔνθα δὴ ξύλλογον ἐκ τῶν παρόντων ξυναγαγὼν
Ἀλέξανδρος παρήγαγεν ἐς αὐτοὺς Βῆσσον· καὶ
κατηγορήσας τὴν Δαρείου προδοσίαν τήν τε ῥῖνα
Βήσσου ἀποτμηθῆναι καὶ τὰ ὦτα ἄκρα ἐκέλευσεν,
αὐτὸν δὲ ἐς Ἐκβάτανα ἄγεσθαι, ὡς ἐκεῖ ἐν τῷ
Μήδων τε καὶ Περσῶν ξυλλόγῳ ἀποθανούμενον.

4 καὶ ἐγὼ οὔτε τὴν ἄγαν ταύτην τιμωρίαν Βήσσου
ἐπαινῶ, ἀλλὰ βαρβαρικὴν εἶναι τίθεμαι τῶν ἀκρω-
τηρίων τὴν λώβην καὶ ὑπαχθῆναι Ἀλέξανδρον
ξύμφημι ἐς ζῆλον τοῦ Μηδικοῦ τε καὶ Περσικοῦ
πλούτου καὶ τῆς κατὰ τοὺς βαρβάρους βασιλέας
οὐκ ἴσης ἐς τοὺς ὑπηκόους ξυνδιαιτήσεως, ἐσθῆτά
τε ὅτι Μηδικὴν ἀντὶ τῆς Μακεδονικῆς τε καὶ
πατρίου Ἡρακλείδης ὢν μετέλαβεν, οὐδαμῇ
ἐπαινῶ, καὶ τὴν κίταριν τὴν Περσικὴν τῶν νενι-
κημένων ἀντὶ ὧν αὐτὸς ὁ νικῶν πάλαι ἐφόρει

5 ἀμεῖψαι οὐκ ἐπῃδέσθη, οὐδὲν τούτων ἐπαινῶ, ἀλλ'
εἴπερ τι ἄλλο, καὶ τὰ Ἀλεξάνδρου μεγάλα πράγματα ἐς τεκμηρίωσιν τίθεμαι ὡς οὔτε τὸ σῶμα
ὅτῳ εἴη καρτερόν, οὔτε ὅστις γένει ἐπιφανής, οὔτε

---

[3] ' Bessus ' is corrupt. QC. 10, 12 makes Asclepiodorus
bring him 4,500 troops from Syria, while Antipater sends 8,000
Greeks, including 600 horse; these might be the men brought
by the ' hyparch from the coast '; Schmieder proposed to
substitute Asclepiodorus for ' Bessus ' and Menes for Asclepiodorus, but while we must suppose that a scribe wrote ' Bessus '
for some other name, because his mind was still preoccupied
with the true Bessus of § 1, the additional error of trans-
position is less easy to accept. Bosworth, *CQ* 1975, would
read ' Menon ' (cf. iii 6, 8 n.); on his view of iii 16, 9 (see n.),
Menes had replaced both Menon and Asclepiodorus in the

and Asclepiodorus the hyparch from the coast, also
bringing troops.[3]

Then Alexander summoned a council of those 3
present, brought Bessus before them, and accusing
him of treachery towards Darius, commanded that his
nose and ear-laps should be cut off, and that he
should be taken to Ecbatana, to be put to death there
in the assembly of Medes and Persians.[4] For my 4
part, I do not approve of this excessive punishment of
Bessus; I regard the mutilation of the extremities as
barbaric, and I agree that Alexander was carried away
into imitation of Median and Persian opulence and of
the custom of barbarian kings not to countenance
equality with subjects in their daily lives. Nor do I
at all approve the facts that, though a descendant of
Heracles, he substituted the dress of Medes for that
traditional with Macedonians and that he exchanged
the tiara of the Persians, whom he himself had
conquered, for the head-dress he had long worn,[5] but 5
I take it that nothing is clearer proof than Alexander's
great successes of the truth that neither bodily
strength in anyone nor distinction of birth nor

satrapies of north and south Syria, and they were freed to
bring on troops he had raised to Al. But if this were right,
both men should have been designated as former satraps and
the circumscription of each should have been given. I should
prefer to read ' Menes ', even though this means that he did not
stay long in his large province (which on my hypothesis em-
braced more than Syria), and to take ' hyparch ' here to indicate Asclepiodorus' subordination to him; this is its proper
sense, even though it is sometimes equivalent to satrap. QC.
gives other details of the reinforcements, amounting to 19,400
foot and 2,600 horse.

[4] QC. vii 10, 10. For what follows to end of ch. 14 see App.
XV.

[5] But cf. vii 29, 4.

κατὰ πόλεμον εἰ δή τις διευτυχοίη ἔτι μᾶλλον ἢ
Ἀλέξανδρος, οὐδὲ εἰ τὴν Λιβύην τις πρὸς τῇ
Ἀσίᾳ, καθάπερ οὖν ἐπενόει ἐκεῖνος, ἐκπεριπλεύσας
κατάσχοι, οὐδὲ εἰ τὴν Εὐρώπην ἐπὶ τῇ Ἀσίᾳ τε καὶ
Λιβύῃ τρίτην, τούτων πάντων οὐδέν τι ὄφελος ἐς
εὐδαιμονίαν ἀνθρώπου, εἰ μὴ σωφρονεῖν ἐν ταὐτῷ
ὑπάρχοι τούτῳ τῷ ἀνθρώπῳ τῷ τὰ μεγάλα, ὡς
δοκεῖ, πράγματα πράξαντι.

8. Ἔνθα δὴ καὶ τὸ Κλείτου τοῦ Δρωπίδου
πάθημα καὶ τὴν Ἀλεξάνδρου ἐπ' αὐτῷ ξυμφοράν,
εἰ καὶ ὀλίγον ὕστερον ἐπράχθη, οὐκ ἔξω τοῦ καιροῦ
ἀφηγήσομαι. εἶναι μὲν γὰρ ἡμέραν ἱερὰν τοῦ
Διονύσου Μακεδόσι καὶ θύειν Διονύσῳ ὅσα ἔτη ἐν
2 αὐτῇ Ἀλέξανδρον· τὸν δὲ τοῦ Διονύσου μὲν ἐν τῷ
τότε ἀμελῆσαι λέγουσι, Διοσκούροιν δὲ θῦσαι, ἐξ
ὅτου δὴ ἐπιφρασθέντα τοῖν Διοσκούροιν τὴν θυσίαν·
πόρρω δὲ τοῦ πότου προϊόντος (καὶ γὰρ καὶ τὰ τῶν
πότων ἤδη Ἀλεξάνδρῳ ἐς τὸ βαρβαρικώτερον
νενεώτεριστο) ἀλλ' ἔν γε τῷ πότῳ τότε ὑπὲρ τοῖν
Διοσκούροιν λόγους γίγνεσθαι, ὅπως ἐς Δία
ἀνηνέχθη αὐτοῖν ἡ γένεσις ἀφαιρεθεῖσα Τυνδάρεω.
3 καί τινας τῶν παρόντων κολακείᾳ τῇ Ἀλεξάνδρου,
οἷοι δὴ ἄνδρες διέφθειράν τε ἀεὶ καὶ οὔποτε
παύσονται ἐπιτρίβοντες τὰ τῶν ἀεὶ βασιλέων
πράγματα, κατ' οὐδὲν ἀξιοῦν συμβάλλειν Ἀλεξάνδρῳ τε καὶ τοῖς Ἀλεξάνδρου ἔργοις τὸν Πολυδεύ-
κην καὶ τὸν Κάστορα. οἱ δὲ οὐδὲ τοῦ Ἡρακλέους
ἀπείχοντο ἐν τῷ πότῳ· ἀλλὰ τὸν φθόνον γὰρ
ἐμποδὼν ἵστασθαι τοῖς ζῶσι τὸ μὴ οὐ τὰς δικαίας
τιμὰς αὐτοῖς ἐκ τῶν ξυνόντων γίγνεσθαι.

---

[1] Chronologically this comes after 16, 3.

continuous good fortune in war, greater even than Alexander's—no matter if a man were to sail out right round Libya as well as Asia and subdue them, as Alexander actually thought of doing, or were to make Europe, with Asia and Libya, a third part of his empire—that not one of all these things is any contribution to man's happiness, unless the man whose achievements are apparently so great were to possess at the same time command of his own passions.

8. At this point it will be the moment for me to relate the tragedy of Clitus son of Dropides and the suffering it caused to Alexander, even though it actually occurred later.[1] The story goes as follows. The Macedonians kept a day sacred to Dionysus and Alexander sacrificed to him yearly on that day; only on this particular occasion he neglected Dionysus but sacrificed to the Dioscuri; some reason had made him think of sacrificing to them. The drinking was prolonged (and, in fact, Alexander had already taken to new and more barbaric ways in drinking), and in the course of the drinking-bout talk occurred about the Dioscuri and how Tyndareus was robbed of their fatherhood which was now referred to Zeus. Some of the company (that type of men who have always and will always continue to injure the interests of kings) [2] out of flattery to Alexander claimed that there was no comparison between Castor and Pollux and Alexander and Alexander's achievements. In the bout others did not even leave Heracles untouched; it was only envy, they said, which stood in the way of living men and kept them from receiving their due honours from their fellows.

2

3

---

[2] Cf. ii 6, 4 and 6; vii 12, 5; 29, 1.

4 Κλεῖτον δὲ δῆλον μὲν εἶναι πάλαι ἤδη ἀχθόμενον τοῦ τε Ἀλεξάνδρου τῇ ἐς τὸ βαρβαρικώτερον μετακινήσει καὶ τῶν κολακευόντων αὐτὸν τοῖς λόγοις· τότε δὲ καὶ αὐτὸν πρὸς τοῦ οἴνου παροξυνόμενον οὐκ ἐᾶν οὔτε ἐς τὸ θεῖον ὑβρίζειν, οὔτε [ἐς] τὰ τῶν πάλαι ἡρώων ἔργα ἐκφαυλίζοντας χάριν ταύτην ἄχαριν προστιθέναι Ἀλεξάνδρῳ.

5 εἶναι γὰρ οὖν οὐδὲ τὰ Ἀλεξάνδρου οὕτω τι μεγάλα καὶ θαυμαστὰ ὡς ἐκεῖνοι ἐπαίρουσιν· οὔκουν μόνον καταπρᾶξαι αὐτά, ἀλλὰ τὸ πολὺ γὰρ μέρος Μακεδόνων εἶναι τὰ ἔργα. καὶ τοῦτον τὸν λόγον ἀνιᾶσαι Ἀλέξανδρον λεχθέντα. οὐδὲ ἐγὼ ἐπαινῶ τὸν λόγον, ἀλλὰ ἱκανὸν γὰρ εἶναι τίθεμαι ἐν τοιᾷδε παροινίᾳ τὸ καθ᾽ αὑτὸν σιγῶντα ἔχειν μηδὲ τὰ

6 αὐτὰ τοῖς ἄλλοις ἐς κολακείαν πλημμελεῖν. ὡς δὲ καὶ τῶν Φιλίππου τινὲς ἔργων, ὅτι οὐ μεγάλα οὐδὲ θαυμαστὰ Φιλίππῳ κατεπράχθη, οὐδεμιᾷ ξὺν δίκῃ ἐπεμνήσθησαν, χαριζόμενοι καὶ οὗτοι Ἀλεξάνδρῳ, τὸν Κλεῖτον ἤδη οὐκέτι ἐν ἑαυτοῦ ὄντα πρεσβεύειν μὲν τὰ τοῦ Φιλίππου, καταβάλλειν δὲ Ἀλέξανδρόν τε καὶ τὰ τούτου ἔργα, παροινοῦντα ἤδη τὸν Κλεῖτον, τά τε ἄλλα καὶ πολὺν εἶναι ἐξονειδίζοντα Ἀλεξάνδρῳ, ὅτι πρὸς αὑτοῦ ἄρα ἐσώθη, ὁπότε ἡ ἱππομαχία ἡ ἐπὶ Γρανίκῳ ξυνειστήκει πρὸς Πέρσας·

7 καὶ δὴ καὶ τὴν δεξιὰν τὴν αὑτοῦ σοβαρῶς ἀνατείναντα, αὕτη σε ἡ χείρ, φάναι, ὦ Ἀλέξανδρε, ἐν τῷ τότε ἔσωσε. καὶ Ἀλέξανδρον οὐκέτι φέρειν τοῦ Κλείτου τὴν παροινίαν τε καὶ ὕβριν, ἀλλὰ ἀναπηδᾶν γὰρ ξὺν ὀργῇ ἐπ᾽ αὐτόν, κατέχεσθαι δὲ ὑπὸ τῶν ξυμπινόντων. Κλεῖτον δὲ οὐκ ἀνιέναι ὑβρίζοντα.

8 Ἀλέξανδρος δὲ ἐβόα ἄρα καλῶν τοὺς ὑπασπιστάς· οὐδενὸς δὲ ὑπακούοντος ἐς ταὐτὰ ἔφη καθεστη-

Clitus, however, had made it plain for some time 4 328
past that he was aggrieved both by Alexander's B.C.
change-over to the more barbaric style and by the
expressions of his flatterers; and now under the
stimulus of wine he would not let them show dis-
respect for the divine power, or belittle the deeds of
the heroes of old, to do Alexander a favour that was
none. Nor in his view were Alexander's achieve- 5
ments so great and wonderful as they cried them up
to be; and Alexander had not achieved them by himself, but they were in great part Macedonian achievements. Alexander was deeply hurt by his words.
Nor do I approve them; I think it enough, amid such
drunkenness, for a man to keep his own views to
himself without committing the same errors of
flattery as the rest. But when some even referred 6
to Philip's achievements, quite unjustly suggesting
that his achievements were not great or remarkable,
again trying to gratify Alexander, Clitus could no
longer control himself but spoke up in favour of
Philip's achievements, making little of Alexander and
his; he was now heated with wine and heaped re-
proaches on Alexander; after all Alexander owed his
life to him, when the cavalry battle on the Granicus
had been joined with the Persians; what is more, he 7
actually raised his right hand with an insolent gesture
and cried, ' This very hand, Alexander, saved you
then! ' [3] Alexander could no longer bear Clitus'
drunken arrogance and leapt up in anger to strike
him, but was held back by his fellow drinkers. Still
Clitus did not restrain his insults and Alexander 8
shouted out for the hypaspists; but as no one obeyed,

[3] Cf. i 15, 8.

κέναι Δαρείῳ, ὁπότε πρὸς Βήσσου τε καὶ τῶν ἀμφὶ
Βῆσσον ξυλληφθεὶς ἤγετο οὐδὲν ἄλλο ὅτι μὴ ὄνομα
ὢν βασιλέως. οὔκουν ἔτι οἵους τε εἶναι κατέχειν
αὐτὸν τοὺς ἑταίρους, ἀλλ' ἀναπηδήσαντα γὰρ οἱ μὲν
λόγχην ἁρπάσαι λέγουσι τῶν σωματοφυλάκων
9 τινὸς καὶ ταύτῃ παίσαντα Κλεῖτον ἀποκτεῖναι, οἱ δὲ
σάρισσαν παρὰ τῶν φυλάκων τινὸς [καὶ ταύτῃ].¹
Ἀριστόβουλος δὲ ὅθεν μὲν ἡ παροινία ὡρμήθη οὐ
λέγει, Κλείτου δὲ γενέσθαι μόνου τὴν ἁμαρτίαν, ὅν
γε ὠργισμένου Ἀλεξάνδρου καὶ ἀναπηδήσαντος ἐπ'
αὐτὸν ὡς διαχρησομένου ἀπαχθῆναι μὲν διὰ
θυρῶν ἔξω ὑπὲρ τὸ τεῖχός τε καὶ τὴν τάφρον τῆς
ἄκρας, ἵνα ἐγίνετο, πρὸς Πτολεμαίου τοῦ Λάγου
τοῦ σωματοφύλακος· οὐ καρτερήσαντα δὲ ἀνα-
στρέψαι αὖθις καὶ περιπετῆ Ἀλεξάνδρῳ γενέσθαι
Κλεῖτον ἀνακαλοῦντι, καὶ φάναι ὅτι· οὗτός τοι ἐγὼ
ὁ Κλεῖτος, ὦ Ἀλέξανδρε· καὶ ἐν τούτῳ πληγέντα
τῇ σαρίσσῃ ἀποθανεῖν.

9. Καὶ ἐγὼ Κλεῖτον μὲν τῆς ὕβρεως τῆς ἐς τὸν
βασιλέα τὸν αὑτοῦ μεγαλωστὶ μέμφομαι· Ἀλέξανδρον δὲ τῆς συμφορᾶς οἰκτείρω, ὅτι δυοῖν κακοῖν
ἐν τῷ τότε ἡττημένον ἐπέδειξεν αὑτόν, ὑφ' ὅτων
δὴ καὶ τοῦ ἑτέρου οὐκ ἐπέοικεν ἄνδρα σωφρονοῦντα
2 ἐξηττᾶσθαι, ὀργῆς τε καὶ παροινίας. ἀλλὰ τὰ ἐπὶ
τοῖσδε αὖ ἐπαινῶ Ἀλεξάνδρου, ὅτι παραυτίκα ἔγνω
σχέτλιον ἔργον ἐργασάμενος. καὶ λέγουσιν εἰσὶν οἳ
[τὰ Ἀλεξάνδρου] ὅτι ἐρείσας τὴν σάρισσαν πρὸς
τὸν τοῖχον ἐπιπίπτειν ἐγνώκει αὐτῇ, ὡς οὐ καλὸν
3 αὑτῷ ζῆν ἀποκτείναντι φίλον αὑτοῦ ἐν οἴνῳ. οἱ
πολλοὶ δὲ ξυγγραφεῖς τοῦτο μὲν οὐ λέγουσιν,

---

¹ Deleted by Castiglioni.

328
B.C.

he cried that he had come to the same pass as Darius, when he was led prisoner by Bessus and his confederates, and that he had nothing now left but the name of king. No longer could the Companions hold him back; he leapt up and, as some say, snatched a spear from one of the bodyguards and struck Clitus a mortal blow with it; according to others, it was a long pike 9 from one of the guards he used. But Aristobulus, while not telling the origin of this drinking bout, holds that the entire fault lay with Clitus, since when Alexander leapt up in passion to kill him, Clitus was hurried away outside through the doors over the wall and ditch of the citadel (where all this happened) by Ptolemy son of Lagus, one of the bodyguards, but could not control himself, and turned back; he met with Alexander just as Alexander was calling out ' Clitus! ' and cried, ' Here I am, Clitus, Alexander !' and there and then was struck with the pike and died.

9. I myself strongly blame Clitus for his insolence towards his king, and pity Alexander for his misfortune, since he then showed himself the slave of two vices, by neither of which is it fitting for a man of sense to be overcome, namely, anger and drunkenness. But for the sequel I commend Alexander, in that he 2 immediately recognized the savagery of his action. Some say that Alexander leaned the pike against the wall, intending to fall upon it himself, as it was not honourable for him to live after killing a friend in his cups. But most historians have a different story: 3

ἀπελθόντα δὲ ἐς τὴν εὐνὴν κεῖσθαι ὀδυρόμενον,
αὐτόν τε τὸν Κλεῖτον ὀνομαστὶ ἀνακαλοῦντα καὶ
τὴν Κλείτου μὲν ἀδελφήν, αὐτὸν δὲ ἀναθρεψαμένην,
Λανίκην τὴν Δρωπίδου παῖδα, ὡς καλὰ ἄρα αὐτῇ
4 τροφεῖα ἀποτετικὼς εἴη ἀνδρωθείς, ἥ γε τοὺς μὲν
παῖδας τοὺς ἑαυτῆς ὑπὲρ αὐτοῦ μαχομένους ἐπεῖδεν
ἀποθανόντας, τὸν ἀδελφὸν δὲ αὐτῆς αὐτὸς αὐτο-
χειρίᾳ ἔκτεινε· φονέα τε τῶν φίλων οὐ διαλείπειν
αὐτὸν ἀνακαλοῦντα, ἄσιτόν τε καὶ ἄποτον καρτε-
ρεῖν ἔστε ἐπὶ τρεῖς ἡμέρας, οὐδέ τινα ἄλλην
θεραπείαν θεραπεῦσαι τὸ σῶμα.

5 Καὶ ἐπὶ τούτοις τῶν μάντεών τινες μῆνιν ἐκ
Διονύσου ᾖδον, ὅτι ἡ θυσία ἐξελείφθη Ἀλεξάνδρῳ
ἡ τοῦ Διονύσου. καὶ Ἀλέξανδρος μόγις πρὸς τῶν
ἑταίρων πεισθεὶς σίτου τε ἥψατο καὶ τὸ σῶμα
κακῶς ἐθεράπευσε· καὶ τῷ Διονύσῳ τὴν θυσίαν
ἀπέδωκεν, ἐπεὶ οὐδὲ αὐτῷ ἄκοντι ἦν ἐς μῆνιν τοῦ
θείου μᾶλλόν τι ἢ τὴν αὐτοῦ κακότητα ἀναφέρεσθαι
6 τὴν ξυμφοράν. ταῦτα μεγαλωστὶ ἐπαινῶ Ἀλεξάνδρου, τὸ μήτε ἀπαυθαδιάσασθαι ἐπὶ κακῷ, μήτε
προστάτην τε καὶ ξυνήγορον κακίονα ἔτι γενέσθαι
τοῦ ἁμαρτηθέντος, ἀλλὰ ξυμφῆσαι γὰρ ἐπταικέναι
ἄνθρωπόν γε ὄντα.

7 Εἰσὶ δὲ οἳ λέγουσιν Ἀνάξαρχον τὸν σοφιστὴν
ἐλθεῖν μὲν παρ' Ἀλέξανδρον κληθέντα, ὡς παρα-
μυθησόμενον· εὑρόντα δὲ κείμενον καὶ ἐπιστέ-
νοντα, ἀγνοεῖν, φάναι ἐπιγελάσαντα, διότι ἐπὶ
τῷδε οἱ πάλαι σοφοὶ ἄνδρες τὴν Δίκην πάρεδρον τῷ
Διὶ ἐποίησαν ὡς ὅ τι ἂν πρὸς τοῦ Διὸς κυρωθῇ,
τοῦτο ξὺν δίκῃ πεπραγμένον. καὶ οὖν καὶ τὰ ἐκ
βασιλέως μεγάλου γιγνόμενα δίκαια χρῆναι νομί-
ζεσθαι, πρῶτα μὲν πρὸς αὐτοῦ βασιλέως, ἔπειτα

they say that Alexander took to his bed and lay there
mourning, crying out the name of Clitus and of Clitus'
sister, Lanice,[1] daughter of Dropides, who had nursed
him: what a fine return for her nursing had he given
her, now that he was a man! She had seen her sons
die fighting for him, and now with his own hand he
had killed her brother. He kept again and again
calling himself the murderer of his friends, refused
firmly all food or drink for three days, and neglected
all other bodily needs.

In these circumstances some of the prophets ' sang
the wrath ' of Dionysus, because Alexander had
neglected the sacrifice to him. With some difficulty
Alexander was persuaded by his friends to eat, and
take some slight care of his person; and he paid the
due sacrifice to Dionysus, since it was not uncongenial
to him that the disaster should be referred to divine
wrath rather than to his own evil nature. In this I
highly commend Alexander; he did not brazen out
his evil act, nor degenerate further by becoming
champion and advocate of his error; he admitted that
he had erred, as a man may.[2]

Some say that Anaxarchus the Sophist[3] came by
summons to Alexander to offer consolation, and
finding him groaning on his bed, laughed at him and
said that he had not learnt why the old philosophers
made Justice sit by the throne of Zeus, because
whatever is determined by Zeus is done with Justice;
so too the acts of a great King should be held just,
first by the king himself and then by the rest of man-

328
B.C.

4

5

6

7

---

[1] Hellanice .QC. viii 1, 21.

[2] Cf. vii 29, 2.

[3] For his life and works see Diels, *Fragmente der Vorsokratiker*
no. 72. Here and in ch. 11 he may be traduced.

8 πρὸς τῶν ἄλλων ἀνθρώπων. ταῦτα εἰπόντα παρα-
μυθήσασθαι μὲν Ἀλέξανδρον ἐν τῷ τότε, κακὸν δὲ
μέγα, ὡς ἐγώ φημι, ἐξεργάσασθαι Ἀλεξάνδρῳ καὶ
μεῖζον ἔτι ἢ ὅτῳ τότε ξυνείχετο, εἴπερ οὖν σοφοῦ
ἀνδρὸς τήνδε ἔγνω τὴν δόξαν, ὡς οὐ τὰ δίκαια ἄρα
χρὴ σπουδῇ ἐπιλεγόμενον πράττειν τὸν βασιλέα,
ἀλλὰ ὅ τι ἂν καὶ ὅπως οὖν ἐκ βασιλέως πραχθῇ,
9 τοῦτο δίκαιον νομίζειν. ἐπεὶ καὶ προσκυνεῖσθαι
ἐθέλειν Ἀλέξανδρον λόγος κατέχει, ὑπούσης μὲν
αὐτῷ καὶ τῆς ἀμφὶ τοῦ Ἄμμωνος πατρὸς μᾶλλόν τι
ἢ Φιλίππου δόξης, θαυμάζοντα δὲ ἤδη τὰ Περσῶν
καὶ Μήδων τῆς τε ἐσθῆτος τῇ ἀμείψει καὶ τῆς
ἄλλης θεραπείας τῇ μετακοσμήσει. οὐκ ἐνδεῆσαι
δὲ οὐδὲ πρὸς τοῦτο αὐτῷ τοὺς κολακείᾳ ἐς αὐτὸ
ἐνδιδόντας, ἄλλους τέ τινας καὶ δὴ καὶ τῶν σοφι-
στῶν τῶν ἀμφ᾽ αὐτὸν Ἀνάξαρχόν τε καὶ Ἆγιν
Ἀργεῖον, ἐποποιόν.

10. Καλλισθένην δὲ τὸν Ὀλύνθιον Ἀριστοτέλους
τε τῶν λόγων διακηκοότα καὶ τὸν τρόπον ὄντα
ὑπαγροικότερον οὐκ ἐπαινεῖν ταῦτα. τούτου μὲν
δὴ ἕνεκα καὶ αὐτὸς Καλλισθένει ξυμφέρομαι, ἐκεῖνα
δὲ οὐκέτι ἐπιεικῆ δοκῶ τοῦ Καλλισθένους, εἴπερ
ἀληθῆ ξυγγέγραπται, ὅτι ὑφ᾽ αὑτῷ εἶναι ἀπέφαινε
καὶ τῇ αὑτοῦ ξυγγραφῇ Ἀλέξανδρόν τε καὶ τὰ
2 Ἀλεξάνδρου ἔργα, οὔκουν αὐτὸς ἀφῖχθαι ἐξ Ἀλεξάνδρου δόξαν κτησόμενος, ἀλλὰ ἐκεῖνον εὐκλεᾶ ἐς
ἀνθρώπους ποιήσων· καὶ οὖν καὶ τοῦ θείου τὴν
μετουσίαν Ἀλεξάνδρῳ οὐκ ἐξ ὧν Ὀλυμπιὰς ὑπὲρ
τῆς γενέσεως αὐτοῦ ψεύδεται ἀνηρτῆσθαι, ἀλλὰ ἐξ
ὧν ἂν αὐτὸς ὑπὲρ Ἀλεξάνδρου ξυγγράψας ἐξενέγκῃ
3 ἐς ἀνθρώπους. εἰσὶ δὲ οἳ καὶ τάδε ἀνέγραψαν, ὡς
ἄρα ἤρετο αὐτόν ποτε Φιλώτας ὅντινα οἴοιτο

kind. These words are said to have consoled Alexander 8 328
for the time, but I say that he did Alexander even   B.C.
greater harm than the affliction he then suffered from,
if indeed he gave this opinion as that of a sage, that
the duty of the king is not to act justly after earnest
consideration, but that anything done by a king in
any form is to be accounted just. The fact is that the 9
report prevails that Alexander desired people actually
to do him obeisance, from the underlying idea that
his father was Ammon and not Philip,[4] and as he was
now expressing his admiration for the ways of the
Persians and Medes, both in his change of dress and
in addition by the altered arrangements for his
attendance, and that even as to obeisance there was
no lack of flatterers to give him his wish, among whom
the most prominent were Anaxarchus and Agis of
Argos, an epic poet, two of the sophists at his court.

10. It is said that Callisthenes of Olynthus, a past
pupil of Aristotle, and with something of the boor in
his character, did not approve of this, and here I myself agree with Callisthenes; on the other hand I
think Callisthenes went beyond reason, if the record
is true, in declaring that Alexander and his exploits
depended on him and his history; it was not he who 2
had come to win fame from Alexander, but it would
be his work to make Alexander renowned among
men; and again, that Alexander's share in divinity
did not depend on Olympias' invention about his
birth, but on the account he would write and publish
in Alexander's interest. Some too have recorded 3
that Philotas once asked him whom he thought to be

[4] App. V. Cf. vii 29, 3; 30, 2.

μάλιστα τιμηθῆναι πρὸς τῆς Ἀθηναίων πόλεως·
τὸν δὲ ἀποκρίνασθαι Ἁρμόδιον καὶ Ἀριστογείτονα,
ὅτι τὸν ἕτερον τοῖν τυράννοιν ἔκτειναν καὶ τυραν-
4 νίδα ὅτι κατέλυσαν. ἐρέσθαι δὲ αὖθις τὸν Φιλώταν
εἰ τῷ τύραννον κτείναντι ὑπάρχοι παρ᾽ οὕστινας
ἐθέλει τῶν Ἑλλήνων φυγόντα σώζεσθαι· καὶ
ἀποκρίνασθαι αὖθις Καλλισθένην, εἰ καὶ μὴ παρ᾽
ἄλλους, παρά γε Ἀθηναίους ὅτι φυγόντι ὑπάρχοι
σώζεσθαι. τούτους γὰρ καὶ πρὸς Εὐρυσθέα πολε-
μῆσαι ὑπὲρ τῶν παίδων τῶν Ἡρακλέους, τυραν-
νοῦντα ἐν τῷ τότε τῆς Ἑλλάδος.
5   Ὑπὲρ δὲ τῆς προσκυνήσεως ὅπως ἠναντιώθη
Ἀλεξάνδρῳ, καὶ τοιόσδε κατέχει λόγος. ξυγκεῖ-
σθαι μὲν γὰρ τῷ Ἀλεξάνδρῳ πρὸς τοὺς σοφιστάς
τε καὶ τοὺς ἀμφ᾽ αὐτὸν Περσῶν καὶ Μήδων τοὺς
δοκιμωτάτους μνήμην τοῦ λόγου τοῦδε ἐν πότῳ
6 ἐμβαλεῖν· ἄρξαι δὲ τοῦ λόγου Ἀνάξαρχον, ὡς πολὺ
δικαιότερον ἂν θεὸν νομιζόμενον Ἀλέξανδρον
Διονύσου τε καὶ Ἡρακλέους, μὴ ὅτι τῶν ἔργων
ἕνεκα ὅσα καὶ ἡλίκα καταπέπρακται Ἀλεξάνδρῳ,
ἀλλὰ καὶ ὅτι Διόνυσος μὲν Θηβαῖος ἦν, οὐδέν τι
προσήκων Μακεδόσι, καὶ Ἡρακλῆς Ἀργεῖος,
οὐδὲ οὗτος προσήκων ὅτι μὴ κατὰ γένος τὸ Ἀλε-
ξάνδρου· Ἡρακλείδην γὰρ εἶναι Ἀλέξανδρον·
7 Μακεδόνας δὲ ἂν τὸν σφῶν βασιλέα δικαιότερον
θείαις τιμαῖς κοσμοῦντας. καὶ γὰρ οὐδὲ ἐκεῖνο
εἶναι ἀμφίλογον ὅτι ἀπελθόντα γε ἐξ ἀνθρώπων ὡς
θεὸν τιμήσουσι· πόσῳ δὴ δικαιότερον ζῶντα

---

[1] The two joint tyrants were Hippias and his brother
Hipparchus. By killing Hipparchus only, Harmodius and
Aristogiton did not destroy the tyranny, but in fact caused
Hippias to become a severe despot.

held in highest honour by the Athenians; and he
replied, Harmodius and Aristogiton, because they
slew one of the two tyrants, and destroyed the
tyranny,[1] and that when Philotas asked him again if 4
a tyrannicide could find a safe refuge among any of
the Greeks he wished, Callisthenes again answered
that he would find a safe refuge in Athens at least;
the Athenians had even fought on behalf of the children of Heracles against Eurystheus, who was tyrant
then over Greece.

As to Callisthenes' opposition to Alexander 5
regarding obeisance, the following story is also
prevalent. It had been agreed between Alexander
and the Sophists and the most illustrious of the
Persians and Medes at his court that mention of this
topic should be introduced at a wine-party.[2] Anaxar- 6
chus began the subject, saying that it would be far
more just to reckon Alexander a god than Dionysus
and Heracles, not so much because of the magnitude
and nature of Alexander's achievements, but also
because Dionysus was a Theban, and had no connection with Macedon, and Heracles an Argive, also
unconnected with Macedon, except for Alexander's
family, for he was descended from Heracles; but that 7
Macedonians in their turn would be more justified in
paying the respect of divine honours to their own
king; in any case there was no doubt that when
Alexander had departed from men they would
honour him as a god; how much more just, then,
that they should give him his due in life rather than

---

[2] This story, though surely false, may reflect early contro-
versies on the propriety of deifying Al. QC. viii 5, 8 substitutes
the poets Agis and Cleo for Anaxarchus. Besides App. XIV
see App. IV.

γεραίρειν ἤπερ τελευτήσαντα ἐς οὐδὲν ὄφελος τῷ
τιμωμένῳ.

11. Λεχθέντων δὲ τούτων τε καὶ τοιούτων
λόγων πρὸς Ἀναξάρχου τοὺς μὲν μετεσχηκότας
τῆς βουλῆς ἐπαινεῖν τὸν λόγον καὶ δὴ ἐθέλειν
ἄρχεσθαι τῆς προσκυνήσεως, τοὺς Μακεδόνας δὲ
τοὺς πολλοὺς ἀχθομένους τῷ λόγῳ σιγῇ ἔχειν.
2 Καλλισθένην δὲ ὑπολαβόντα, Ἀλέξανδρον μὲν,
εἰπεῖν, ὦ Ἀνάξαρχε, οὐδεμιᾶς ἀνάξιον ἀποφαίνω
τιμῆς ὅσαι ξύμμετροι ἀνθρώπῳ· ἀλλὰ διακεκρίσθαι
γὰρ τοῖς ἀνθρώποις ὅσαι τε ἀνθρώπιναι τιμαὶ καὶ
ὅσαι θεῖαι πολλοῖς μὲν καὶ ἄλλοις, καθάπερ ναῶν τε
οἰκοδομήσει καὶ ἀγαλμάτων ἀναστάσει καὶ τεμένη
ὅτι τοῖς θεοῖς ἐξαιρεῖται καὶ θύεται ἐκείνοις καὶ
σπένδεται, καὶ ὕμνοι μὲν ἐς τοὺς θεοὺς ποιοῦνται,
ἔπαινοι δὲ ἐς ἀνθρώπους—ἀτὰρ οὐχ ἥκιστα τῷ τῆς
3 προσκυνήσεως νόμῳ. τοὺς μὲν γὰρ ἀνθρώπους
φιλεῖσθαι πρὸς τῶν ἀσπαζομένων, τὸ θεῖον δέ, ὅτι
ἄνω που ἱδρυμένον καὶ οὐδὲ ψαῦσαι αὐτοῦ θέμις,
ἐπὶ τῷδε ἄρα τῇ προσκυνήσει γεραίρεται, καὶ χοροὶ
τοῖς θεοῖς ἵστανται καὶ παιᾶνες ἐπὶ τοῖς θεοῖς
ᾄδονται. καὶ οὐδὲν θαυμαστόν, ὁπότε γε καὶ
αὐτῶν τῶν θεῶν ἄλλοις ἄλλαι τιμαὶ πρόσκεινται,
καὶ ναὶ μὰ Δία ἥρωσιν ἄλλαι, καὶ αὗται ἀποκεκρι-
4 μέναι τοῦ θείου. οὔκουν εἰκὸς ξύμπαντα ταῦτα
ἀναταράσσοντας τοὺς μὲν ἀνθρώπους ἐς σχῆμα
ὑπέρογκον καθιστάναι τῶν τιμῶν ταῖς ὑπερβολαῖς,
τοὺς θεοὺς δὲ τό γε ἐπὶ σφίσιν ἐς ταπεινότητα οὐ
πρέπουσαν καταβάλλειν τὰ ἴσα ἀνθρώποις τιμῶν-
τας. οὔκουν οὐδὲ Ἀλέξανδρον ἀνασχέσθαι ἄν, εἰ
τῶν ἰδιωτῶν τις εἰσποιοῖτο ταῖς βασιλικαῖς τιμαῖς
5 χειροτονίᾳ ἢ ψήφῳ οὐ δικαίᾳ. πολὺ ἂν οὖν

when he was dead and the honour would profit him nothing.

11. When Anaxarchus had said this and the like, those who shared in the scheme approved his argument and were actually ready to begin doing obeisance, but the Macedonians for the most part were opposed to it, though silent. Callisthenes broke in 2 and said: 'Anaxarchus, I declare Alexander unworthy of no honour appropriate for a man; but men have used numerous ways of distinguishing all the honours which are appropriate for men and for gods; thus we build temples and erect images and set aside precincts for the gods, and we offer them sacrifices and libations and compose hymns to them, while eulogies are for men; but the most important distinction concerns the matter of obeisance. At 3 greeting men receive a kiss, but what is divine, I suppose because it is seated above us and we are forbidden even to touch it, is for that very reason honoured by obeisance; dances, too, are held for the gods, and paeans sung in their praise. In this distinction there is nothing surprising, since among the gods themselves all are not honoured in the same way; and what is more, there are different honours for the heroes, distinct again from those paid to gods. It is not, therefore, proper to confuse all this, by rais- 4 ing mortals to extravagant proportions by excesses of honour, while bringing the gods, as far as men can, down to a demeaning and unfitting level by honouring them in the same way as men. So Alexander himself would not endure it for a moment, if some private person were to thrust himself into the royal honours by unjust election or vote, and the gods would have 5

ARRIAN

δικαιότερον τοὺς θεοὺς δυσχεραίνειν ὅσοι ἄνθρωποι
ἐς τὰς θείας τιμὰς σφᾶς εἰσποιοῦσιν ἢ πρὸς ἄλλων
εἰσποιούμενοι ἀνέχονται. Ἀλέξανδρον δὲ πόρρω
τοῦ ἱκανοῦ ἀνδρῶν ἀγαθῶν τὸν ἄριστον εἶναί τε καὶ
δοκεῖν, καὶ βασιλέων τὸν βασιλικώτατον καὶ στρα-
6 τηγῶν τὸν ἀξιοστρατηγότατον. καὶ σέ, εἴπερ τινὰ
ἄλλον, ὦ Ἀνάξαρχε, εἰσηγητήν τε τούτων τῶν
λόγων ἐχρῆν γίγνεσθαι καὶ κωλυτὴν τῶν ἐναντίων,
ἐπὶ σοφίᾳ τε καὶ παιδεύσει Ἀλεξάνδρῳ ξυνόντα.
οὔκουν ἄρχειν γε τοῦδε τοῦ λόγου πρέπον ἦν, ἀλλὰ
μεμνῆσθαι γὰρ οὐ Καμβύσῃ οὐδὲ Ξέρξῃ ξυνόντα ἢ
ξυμβουλεύοντα, ἀλλὰ Φιλίππου μὲν παιδί, Ἡρα-
κλείδῃ δὲ ἀπὸ γένους καὶ Αἰακίδῃ, ὅτου οἱ
πρόγονοι ἐξ Ἄργους ἐς Μακεδονίαν ἦλθον, οὐδὲ
βίᾳ, ἀλλὰ νόμῳ Μακεδόνων ἄρχοντες διετέλεσαν.
7 οὔκουν οὐδὲ αὐτῷ τῷ Ἡρακλεῖ ζῶντι ἔτι θεῖαι
τιμαὶ παρ' Ἑλλήνων ἐγένοντο, ἀλλ' οὐδὲ τελευτήσαντι πρόσθεν ἢ πρὸς τοῦ θεοῦ τοῦ ἐς Δελφοῖς
ἐπιθεσπισθῆναι ὡς θεὸν τιμᾶν Ἡρακλέα. εἰ δέ,
ὅτι ἐν τῇ βαρβάρῳ γῇ οἱ λόγοι γίγνονται, βαρβαρικὰ χρὴ ἔχειν τὰ φρονήματα, καὶ ἐγὼ τῆς Ἑλλάδος μεμνῆσθαί σε ἀξιῶ, ὦ Ἀλέξανδρε, ἧς ἕνεκα
ὁ πᾶς στόλος σοι ἐγένετο, προσθεῖναι τὴν Ἀσίαν τῇ
8 Ἑλλάδι. καὶ οὖν ἐνθυμήθητι, ἐκεῖσε ἐπανελθὼν
ἆρά γε καὶ τοὺς Ἕλληνας τοὺς ἐλευθερωτάτους
προσαναγκάσεις ἐς τὴν προσκύνησιν, ἢ Ἑλλήνων
μὲν ἀφέξῃ, Μακεδόσι δὲ προσθήσεις τήνδε τὴν
ἀτιμίαν, ἢ διακεκριμένα ἔσται σοι αὐτῷ τὰ τῶν
τιμῶν ἐς ἅπαν, ὡς πρὸς Ἑλλήνων μὲν καὶ Μακεδόνων ἀνθρωπίνως τε καὶ Ἑλληνικῶς τιμᾶσθαι,
9 πρὸς δὲ τῶν βαρβάρων μόνων βαρβαρικῶς; εἰ δὲ
ὑπὲρ Κύρου τοῦ Καμβύσου λέγεται πρῶτον προσ-

far better cause to be displeased with any men who
thrust themselves or permit others to thrust them
into divine honours. Alexander both is and is
thought to be above all measure the bravest of the
brave, most kingly of kings, most worthy to command
of all commanders. As for you, Anaxarchus, you 6
above all should have expounded these arguments
and stopped those on the other side, as you are
attending on Alexander as philosopher and instructor.
It was improper for you to take the lead in this topic;
you should rather have remembered that you are not
attending nor advising a Cambyses [1] or Xerxes, but
a son of Philip, a descendant of Heracles and of
Aeacus, whose forefathers came from Argos to
Macedonia, and have continued to rule the Macedonians not by force but in accordance with custom.
Even Heracles himself did not receive divine honours 7
from the Greeks in his own lifetime, nor even after
his death till the god of Delphi gave his sanction to
honouring him as a god. If, however, we must think
like barbarians, as we are speaking in their country,
even so I appeal personally to you, Alexander, to
remember Greece, on whose behalf you made your
whole expedition, to annex Asia to Greece. Consider 8
this too; when you return there, will you actually
compel the Greeks as well, the freest of mankind, to
do you obeisance, or will you keep away from the
Greeks, but put this dishonour on the Macedonians,
or will you yourself make a distinction once for all in
this matter of honours and receive from Greeks and
Macedonians honours of a human and Greek style,
and barbarian honours only from barbarians? But 9
if it is said of Cyrus son of Cambyses that he was the

[1] King of Persia 528–522 B.C.

κυνηθῆναι ἀνθρώπων Κῦρον καὶ ἐπὶ τῷδε ἐμ-
μεῖναι Πέρσαις τε καὶ Μήδοις τήνδε τὴν ταπεινότητα, χρὴ ἐνθυμεῖσθαι ὅτι τὸν Κῦρον ἐκεῖνον
Σκύθαι ἐσωφρόνισαν, πένητες ἄνδρες καὶ αὐτόνομοι, καὶ Δαρεῖον ἄλλοι αὖ Σκύθαι, καὶ Ξέρξην
Ἀθηναῖοι καὶ Λακεδαιμόνιοι, καὶ Ἀρτοξέρξην
Κλέαρχος καὶ Ξενοφῶν καὶ οἱ ξὺν τούτοις μύριοι,
καὶ Δαρεῖον τοῦτον Ἀλέξανδρος μὴ προσκυνού-
μενος.

12. Ταῦτα δὴ καὶ τοιαῦτα εἰπόντα Καλλισθένην
ἀνιᾶσαι μὲν μεγαλωστὶ Ἀλέξανδρον, Μακεδόσι δὲ
πρὸς θυμοῦ εἰπεῖν. καὶ τοῦτο γνόντα Ἀλέξανδρον
πέμψαντα κωλῦσαι Μακεδόνας [1] μεμνῆσθαι ἔτι τῆς
2 προσκυνήσεως. ἀλλὰ σιγῆς γὰρ γενομένης ἐπὶ
τοῖς λόγοις ἀναστάντας Περσῶν τοὺς πρεσβυτάτους ἐφεξῆς προσκυνεῖν. Λεοννάτου δέ, ἕνα τῶν
ἑταίρων, ἐπειδή τις ἐδόκει τῶν Περσῶν αὐτῷ οὐκ
ἐν κόσμῳ προσκυνῆσαι, τὸν δὲ ἐπιγελάσαι τῷ
σχήματι τοῦ Περσοῦ ὡς ταπεινῷ· καὶ τούτῳ
χαλεπήναντα τότε Ἀλέξανδρον ξυναλλαγῆναι αὖθις.
3 ἀναγέγραπται δὲ δὴ καὶ τοιόσδε λόγος. προπίνειν
φιάλην χρυσῆν ἐν κύκλῳ Ἀλέξανδρον πρώτοις μὲν
τούτοις πρὸς οὕστινας ξυνέκειτο αὐτῷ τὰ τῆς
προσκυνήσεως, τὸν δὲ πρῶτον ἐκπιόντα τὴν φιάλην
προσκυνῆσαί τε ἀναστάντα καὶ φιληθῆναι πρὸς
αὐτοῦ, καὶ τοῦτο ἐφεξῆς διὰ πάντων χωρῆσαι.
4 ὡς δὲ ἐς Καλλισθένην ἧκεν ἡ πρόποσις, ἀναστῆναι
μὲν Καλλισθένην καὶ ἐκπιεῖν τὴν φιάλην, καὶ
προσελθόντα ἐθέλειν φιλῆσαι οὐ προσκυνήσαντα.
τὸν δὲ τυχεῖν μὲν τότε διαλεγόμενον Ἡφαιστίωνι·

---

[1] Roos bracketed this word.

first of men to receive obeisance and that therefore
this humiliation became traditional with Persians and
Medes, you must remember that this very Cyrus was
brought to his senses by Scythians, a people poor but
free, Darius too by other Scythians,[2] Xerxes by
Athenians and Lacedaemonians,[3] and Artaxerxes by
Clearchus, Xenophon and their Ten Thousand,[4] and
Darius by Alexander here, who does not receive
obeisance.'

12. By these and the like words Callisthenes greatly
provoked Alexander, but pleased the Macedonians,
and realizing this, Alexander sent and told the
Macedonians to think no more of obeisance. When,
however, a silence fell after these words, the senior
Persians arose and did obeisance one by one. Leonnatus, one of the Companions, thinking that one of
the Persians made his obeisance ungracefully,
mocked his posture as abject; Alexander was angry
with him at the time, though reconciled later. The
following story has also been recorded. Alexander
sent round a loving cup of gold, first to those with
whom he had made an agreement about obeisance;
the first who drank from it rose, did obeisance, and
received a kiss from Alexander, and this went round
all in turn. But when the pledge came to Callisthenes, he rose, drank from the cup, went up to
Alexander and made to kiss him without having done
obeisance. At the moment Alexander was talking to
Hephaestion, and therefore was not attending to see

2

3

4

---

[2] For the defeat and death of Cyrus, the founder of the
Persian empire, in 529 B.C. by the Scythian Massagetae see
Herodotus i 208–214; for the defeat of Darius I by the Euro-
pean Scythians c. 513 B.C., ib. iv 1, 83–142.

[3] 480–479 B.C.

[4] 401–400 B.C.

οὔκουν προσέχειν τὸν νοῦν, εἰ καὶ τὰ τῆς προσκυ-
5 νήσεως ἐπιτελῆ τῷ Καλλισθένει ἐγένετο. ἀλλὰ
Δημήτριον γὰρ τὸν Πυθώνακτος, ἕνα τῶν ἑταίρων,
ὡς προσῄει αὐτῷ ὁ Καλλισθένης φιλήσων, φάναι
ὅτι οὐ προσκυνήσας πρόσεισιν. καὶ τὸν Ἀλέξανδρον οὐ παρασχεῖν φιλῆσαι ἑαυτόν· τὸν δὲ Καλλισθένην, φιλήματι, φάναι, ἔλαττον ἔχων ἄπειμι.

6 Καὶ τούτων ἐγώ, ὅσα ἐς ὕβριν τε τὴν Ἀλεξάνδρου τὴν ἐν τῷ παραυτίκα καὶ ἐς σκαιότητα τὴν
Καλλισθένους φέροντα, οὐδὲν οὐδαμῇ ἐπαινῶ, ἀλλὰ
τὸ καθ' αὑτὸν γὰρ κοσμίως τίθεσθαι ἐξαρκεῖν
φημί, αὔξοντα ὡς ἀνυστὸν τὰ βασιλέως πράγματα
7 ὅτῳ τις ξυνεῖναι οὐκ ἀπηξίωσεν. οὔκουν ἀπει-
κότως δι' ἀπεχθείας γενέσθαι Ἀλεξάνδρῳ Καλλισθένην τίθεμαι ἐπὶ τῇ ἀκαίρῳ τε παρρησίᾳ καὶ
ὑπερόγκῳ ἀβελτερίᾳ. ἐφ' ὅτῳ τεκμαίρομαι μὴ
χαλεπῶς πιστευθῆναι τοὺς κατειπόντας Καλλισθένους, ὅτι μετέσχε τῆς ἐπιβουλῆς τῆς γενομένης
Ἀλεξάνδρῳ ἐκ τῶν παίδων, τοὺς δέ, ὅτι καὶ ἐπῆρεν
αὐτὸς ἐς τὸ ἐπιβουλεῦσαι. ξυνέβη δὲ τὰ τῆς
ἐπιβουλῆς ὧδε.

13. Ἐκ Φιλίππου ἦν ἤδη καθεστηκὸς τῶν ἐν
τέλει Μακεδόνων τοὺς παῖδας ὅσοι ἐς ἡλικίαν
ἐμειρακιεύοντο καταλέγεσθαι ἐς θεραπείαν τοῦ
βασιλέως, τά τε περὶ τὴν ἄλλην δίαιταν τοῦ
σώματος διακονεῖσθαι βασιλεῖ καὶ κοιμώμενον
φυλάσσειν τούτοις ἐπετέτραπτο. καὶ ὁπότε ἐξ-
ελαύνοι βασιλεύς, τοὺς ἵππους παρὰ τῶν ἱπποκόμων
δεχόμενοι ἐκεῖνοι προσῆγον καὶ ἀνέβαλλον οὗτοι
βασιλέα τὸν Περσικὸν τρόπον καὶ τῆς ἐπὶ θήρᾳ
2 φιλοτιμίας βασιλεῖ κοινωνοὶ ἦσαν. τούτων καὶ
Ἑρμόλαος ἦν, Σωπόλιδος μὲν παῖς, φιλοσοφίᾳ δὲ

whether the ceremony of obeisance had been carried
out by Callisthenes himself. But as Callisthenes
approached to kiss Alexander, Demetrius son of
Pythonax, one of the Companions, remarked that he
was coming without having done obeisance. Alexander did not permit Callisthenes to kiss him; and
Callisthenes remarked, ' I shall go away short of a
kiss.'

In these incidents I do not at all approve either of
Alexander's arrogance at the time or of Callisthenes'
tactlessness, but in fact I think it enough for a man
to show moderation in his own individual conduct,
and that he should be ready to exalt royalty as far as
practicable, once he has consented to attend on a
king. So I think that Alexander's hostility to
Callisthenes was not unreasonable in view of his
untimely freedom of speech and arrogant folly, and
on this account I infer that Callisthenes' detractors
were readily believed that he had a part in the plot
laid against Alexander by his pages, some of them
even saying that Callisthenes had incited them to the
plot. The plot occurred as follows.[1]

13. It was a practice going back to Philip's time
that the sons of Macedonian notables who had
reached adolescence should be enlisted for the service
of the king; and besides general attendance on his
person the duty of guarding him when asleep had
been entrusted to them. Again, whenever the king
rode out, they received the horses from the grooms
and led them up, and they mounted the king in
Persian fashion, and were his companions in the
rivalry of the chase. One of them was Hermolaus
son of Sopolis; he was reputed to be a zealous student

---

[1] Cf. 22, 1 for the date.

ἐδόκει προσέχειν τὸν νοῦν καὶ Καλλισθένην θεραπεύειν ἐπὶ τῷδε. ὑπὲρ τούτου λόγος κατέχει, ὅτι ἐν θήρᾳ προσφερομένου Ἀλεξάνδρῳ συὸς ἔφθη βαλὼν τὸν σῦν ὁ Ἑρμόλαος· καὶ ὁ μὲν σῦς πίπτει βληθείς, Ἀλέξανδρος δὲ τοῦ καιροῦ ὑστερήσας ἐχαλέπηνε τῷ Ἑρμολάῳ καὶ κελεύει αὐτὸν πρὸς ὀργὴν πληγὰς λαβεῖν ὁρώντων τῶν ἄλλων παίδων, καὶ τὸν ἵππον αὐτοῦ ἀφείλετο.

3 Τοῦτον τὸν Ἑρμόλαον ἀλγήσαντα τῇ ὕβρει φράσαι πρὸς Σώστρατον τὸν Ἀμύντου, ἡλικιώτην τε ἑαυτοῦ καὶ ἐραστὴν ὄντα, ὅτι οὐ βιωτὸν οἷ ἐστι μὴ τιμωρησαμένῳ Ἀλέξανδρον τῆς ὕβρεως, καὶ τὸν Σώστρατον οὐ χαλεπῶς συμπεῖσαι μετασχεῖν τοῦ
4 ἔργου, ἅτε ἐρῶντα. ὑπὸ τούτων δὲ ἀναπεισθῆναι Ἀντίπατρόν τε τὸν Ἀσκληπιοδώρου τοῦ Συρίας σατραπεύσαντος καὶ Ἐπιμένην τὸν Ἀρσαίου καὶ Ἀντικλέα τὸν Θεοκρίτου καὶ Φιλώταν τὸν Κάρσιδος τοῦ Θρᾳκός. ὡς οὖν περιῆκεν ἐς Ἀντίπατρον ἡ νυκτερινὴ φυλακή, ταύτῃ τῇ νυκτὶ ξυγκείμενον εἶναι ἀποκτεῖναι Ἀλέξανδρον, κοιμωμένῳ ἐπιπεσόντας.

5 Ξυμβῆναι δὲ οἱ μὲν αὐτομάτως λέγουσιν ἔστε ⟨ἐφ'⟩ ἡμέραν πίνειν Ἀλέξανδρον, Ἀριστόβουλος δὲ ὧδε ἀνέγραψε. Σύραν γυναῖκα ἐφομαρτεῖν Ἀλεξάνδρῳ κάτοχον ἐκ τοῦ θείου γιγνομένην καὶ ταύτην τὸ μὲν πρῶτον γέλωτα εἶναι Ἀλεξάνδρῳ τε καὶ τοῖς ἀμφ' αὐτόν· ὡς δὲ τὰ πάντα ἐν τῇ κατοχῇ ἀληθεύουσα ἐφαίνετο, οὐκέτι ἀμελεῖσθαι ὑπ' Ἀλεξάνδρου, ἀλλ' εἶναι γὰρ τῇ Σύρᾳ πρόσοδον πρὸς τὸν βασιλέα καὶ νύκτωρ καὶ μεθ' ἡμέραν, καὶ καθεύ
6 δοντι πολλάκις ἤδη ἐπιστῆναι. καὶ δὴ καὶ τότε ἀπαλλασσομένου ἐκ τοῦ πότου κατεχομένην ἐκ τοῦ

of philosophy and to be a follower of Callisthenes for
this purpose. The story is prevalent about him that
in a hunt a wild boar charged Alexander and that
Hermolaus struck it before Alexander could; it fell
from his stroke, and Alexander, too late for his
chance, was angry with Hermolaus and in his passion
ordered him to be whipped in the presence of the
other pages, and took his horse from him.

According to the story, this Hermolaus felt the 3
outrage bitterly and told Sostratus son of Amyntas,
a boy of the same age and his lover, that he found
life no longer worth living until he had avenged himself on Alexander for the outrage, and easily persuaded Sostratus as his lover to join in the enterprise;
they won over Antipater son of Asclepiodorus, who 4
had been satrap of Syria, Epimenes son of Arseus,
Anticles son of Theocritus, and Philotas son of Carsis
the Thracian, and so when the turn of keeping guard
by night fell to Antipater, it was agreed to kill Alexander that night by attacking him in his sleep.

But it so happened according to some writers that 5
Alexander went on drinking unprompted till daybreak, whereas Aristobulus tells this story. A Syrian
woman possessed by the divine spirit followed Alexander constantly; at first she was a laughing-stock
both to Alexander and his court; but when it became
clear that everything she uttered when possessed
came true, Alexander no longer treated her with
contempt but gave her access to his person day and
night and she now often watched over him as he
slept. So on this occasion, when Alexander ceased 6
from his potations, she met him, while possessed by

θείου ἐντυχεῖν, καὶ δεῖσθαι ἐπανελθόντα πίνειν ὅλην
τὴν νύκτα· καὶ ᾿Αλέξανδρον θεῖόν τι εἶναι νομί-
σαντα ἐπανελθεῖν τε καὶ πίνειν, καὶ οὕτως τοῖς
παισὶ διαπεσεῖν τὸ ἔργον.

7 Τῇ δὲ ὑστεραίᾳ ᾿Επιμένης ὁ ᾿Αρσαίου τῶν
μετεχόντων τῆς ἐπιβουλῆς φράζει τὴν πρᾶξιν
Χαρικλεῖ τῷ Μενάνδρου, ἐραστῇ ἑαυτοῦ γεγονότι·
Χαρικλῆς δὲ φράζει Εὐρυλόχῳ τῷ ἀδελφῷ τῷ
᾿Επιμένους. καὶ ὁ Εὐρύλοχος ἐλθὼν ἐπὶ τὴν
σκηνὴν τὴν ᾿Αλεξάνδρου Πτολεμαίῳ τῷ Λάγου τῷ
σωματοφύλακι καταλέγει ἅπαν τὸ πρᾶγμα· ὁ δὲ
᾿Αλεξάνδρῳ ἔφρασε. καὶ ὁ ᾿Αλέξανδρος ξυλλαβεῖν
κελεύει ὧν τὰ ὀνόματα εἶπεν ὁ Εὐρύλοχος· καὶ
οὗτοι στρεβλούμενοι σφῶν τε αὐτῶν κατεῖπον τὴν
ἐπιβουλὴν καί τινας καὶ ἄλλους ὠνόμασαν.

14. ᾿Αριστόβουλος μὲν λέγει ὅτι καὶ Καλλισθένην
ἐπᾶραι σφᾶς ἔφασαν ἐς τὸ τόλμημα· καὶ Πτολεμαῖος ὡσαύτως λέγει. οἱ δὲ πολλοὶ οὐ ταύτῃ
λέγουσιν, ἀλλὰ διὰ μῖσος γὰρ τὸ ἤδη ὂν πρὸς Καλλισθένην ἐξ ᾿Αλεξάνδρου καὶ ὅτι ὁ ῾Ερμόλαος ἐς τὰ
μάλιστα ἐπιτήδειος ἦν τῷ Καλλισθένει, οὐ χαλεπῶς
πιστεῦσαι τὰ χείρω ὑπὲρ Καλλισθένους ᾿Αλέ-
2 ξανδρον. ἤδη δέ τινες καὶ τάδε ἀνέγραψαν, τὸν
῾Ερμόλαον προαχθέντα ἐς τοὺς Μακεδόνας ὁμολο-
γεῖν τε ἐπιβουλεῦσαι—καὶ γὰρ οὐκ εἶναι ἔτι
ἐλευθέρῳ ἀνδρὶ φέρειν τὴν ὕβριν τὴν ᾿Αλεξάνδρου—
πάντα καταλέγοντα, τήν τε Φιλώτα οὐκ ἔνδικον
τελευτὴν καὶ ⟨τὴν⟩ τοῦ πατρὸς αὐτοῦ Παρμενίωνος
ἔτι ἐκνομωτέραν καὶ τῶν ἄλλων τῶν τότε ἀποθανόντων, καὶ τὴν Κλείτου ἐν μέθῃ ἀναίρεσιν, καὶ τὴν
ἐσθῆτα τὴν Μηδικήν, καὶ τὴν προσκύνησιν τὴν
βουλευθεῖσαν καὶ οὔπω πεπαυμένην, καὶ πότους τε

the divine spirit, and begged him to return and
continue drinking all night long; Alexander believed
this to be a divine sign, returned to his cups, and so
the boys' plot came to nothing.

Next day Epimenes son of Arseus, one of the 7
conspirators, told Charicles son of Menander, his
lover, of the plot, Charicles told Eurylochus brother
of Epimenes, and Eurylochus went to Alexander's
tent, and revealed the whole affair to Ptolemy son of
Lagus who told Alexander, and Alexander ordered
the arrest of all whose names Eurylochus had given;
they were put on the rack, revealed their own plot
and implicated others as well.

14. Aristobulus tells that they said Callisthenes had
urged them on to the attempt, and Ptolemy agrees.
But most authorities have a different version, that it
was only because he had already come to hate Callisthenes and because Hermolaus was particularly close
to Callisthenes, that Alexander readily believed the
worst of Callisthenes. Some have also recorded that 2
Hermolaus, when summoned before the Macedonians,
confessed his plot, for (he said) no free man could
longer endure Alexander's arrogance, and went over
the whole story, the unjust end of Philotas, and the
still more illegal death of Parmenio and of the others
who perished at that time, the drunken murder of
Clitus, the Median dress, the plan not yet abandoned

καὶ ὕπνους τοὺς Ἀλεξάνδρου· ταῦτα οὐ φέροντα
ἔτι ἐλευθερῶσαι ἐθελῆσαι ἑαυτόν τε καὶ τοὺς
3 ἄλλους Μακεδόνας. τοῦτον μὲν δὴ αὐτόν τε καὶ
τοὺς ξὺν αὐτῷ ξυλληφθέντας καταλευσθῆναι πρὸς
τῶν παρόντων. Καλλισθένην δὲ Ἀριστόβουλος
μὲν λέγει δεδεμένον ἐν πέδαις ξυμπεριάγεσθαι τῇ
στρατιᾷ, ἔπειτα νόσῳ τελευτῆσαι, Πτολεμαῖος δὲ
ὁ Λάγου στρεβλωθέντα καὶ κρεμασθέντα ἀποθανεῖν. οὕτως οὐδὲ οἱ πάνυ πιστοὶ ἐς τὴν ἀφήγησιν
καὶ ξυγγενόμενοι ἐν τῷ τότε Ἀλεξάνδρῳ ὑπὲρ τῶν
γνωρίμων τε καὶ οὐ λαθόντων σφᾶς ὅπως ἐπράχθη
4 ξύμφωνα ἀνέγραψαν. πολλὰ δὲ καὶ ἄλλα ὑπὲρ
τούτων αὐτῶν ἄλλοι ἄλλως ἀφηγήσαντο, ἀλλ' ἐμοὶ
ταῦτα ἀποχρῶντα ἔστω ἀναγεγραμμένα. ταῦτα
μὲν δὴ οὐ πολλῷ ὕστερον πραχθέντα ἐγὼ ἐν τοῖσδε
τοῖς ἀμφὶ Κλεῖτον ξυνενεχθεῖσιν Ἀλεξάνδρου
ἀνέγραψα, τούτοις μᾶλλόν τι οἰκεῖα ὑπολαβὼν ἐς
τὴν ἀφήγησιν.

15. Παρ' Ἀλέξανδρον δὲ ἧκεν καὶ αὖθις Σκυθῶν
τῶν ἐκ τῆς Εὐρώπης πρεσβεία ξὺν τοῖς πρέσβεσιν
οἷς αὐτὸς ἐς Σκύθας ἔστειλεν. ὁ μὲν δὴ τότε
βασιλεὺς τῶν Σκυθῶν ὅτε οὗτοι ὑπὸ Ἀλεξάνδρου
ἐπέμποντο τετελευτηκὼς ἐτύγχανεν, ἀδελφὸς δὲ
2 ἐκείνου ἐβασίλευεν. ἦν δὲ ὁ νοῦς τῆς πρεσβείας
ἐθέλειν ποιεῖν πᾶν τὸ ἐξ Ἀλεξάνδρου ἐπαγγελ-
λόμενον Σκύθας· καὶ δῶρα ἔφερον Ἀλεξάνδρῳ
παρὰ τοῦ βασιλέως τῶν Σκυθῶν ὅσα μέγιστα
νομίζεται ἐν Σκύθαις· καὶ τὴν θυγατέρα ὅτι ἐθέλει
Ἀλεξάνδρῳ δοῦναι γυναῖκα βεβαιότητος οὕνεκα
3 τῆς πρὸς Ἀλέξανδρον φιλίας τε καὶ ξυμμαχίας. εἰ
δὲ ἀπαξιοῖ τὴν Σκυθῶν βασίλισσαν γῆμαι Ἀλέ-

to introduce obeisance, and Alexander's drinking and sleeping habits; it was all this he would bear no longer and sought to liberate himself and the other Macedonians; he was then stoned to death by the 3 assemblage, along with his fellow prisoners. As for Callisthenes, Aristobulus says he was bound with fetters and carried round with the army, but at length died of sickness, Ptolemy son of Lagus that he was racked and put to death by hanging. Thus not even those whose narratives are entirely trustworthy and who actually accompanied Alexander at that time agree in their accounts of events which were public and within their own knowledge. There are many 4 other varying accounts of the same events in different histories, but I must be content with what I have recorded. They occurred a little later, but I have recorded them in connection with the affair between Clitus and Alexander, thinking them to be more relevant here to my narrative.

15. Envoys came to Alexander[1] a second time from the European Scythians, together with the envoys he himself had sent to Scythia, for the king of the Scythians at the time when they were being sent by Alexander had died; and his brother was reigning. The purpose of the embassy was to express the 2 readiness of the Scythians to do whatever Alexander commanded; they brought gifts for Alexander from the king of Scythia which are most highly regarded in Scythia, and said that the king was willing to give Alexander his daughter in marriage, to confirm his friendship and alliance. If, however, Alexander 3 should not think fit to marry the Scythian princess,

---

[1] Presumably at winter-quarters at Zariaspa (7, 1), whence his departure is recorded in 15, 7; QC. vii 1, 7 ff. gives an account parallel to 1–4 (omitting 5 f.) in midsummer 328.

ξανδρος, ἀλλὰ τῶν γε σατραπῶν τῶν τῆς Σκυθικῆς
χώρας καὶ ὅσοι ἄλλοι δυνάσται κατὰ τὴν γῆν τὴν
Σκυθίδα, τούτων τὰς παῖδας ἐθέλειν δοῦναι τοῖς
πιστοτάτοις τῶν ἀμφ' Ἀλέξανδρον· ἥξειν δὲ καὶ
αὐτὸς ἔφασκεν, εἰ κελεύοιτο, ὡς παρ' αὐτοῦ Ἀλε-
4 ξάνδρου ἀκοῦσαι ὅσα ἐπαγγέλλοι. ἀφίκετο δ' ἐν
τούτῳ παρ' Ἀλέξανδρον καὶ Φαρασμάνης ὁ
Χορασμίων βασιλεὺς ξὺν ἱππεῦσι χιλίοις καὶ
πεντακοσίοις. ἔφασκεν δὲ ὁ Φαρασμάνης ὅμορος
οἰκεῖν τῷ τε Κόλχων γένει καὶ ταῖς γυναιξὶ ταῖς
Ἀμαζόσι, καὶ εἰ θέλοι Ἀλέξανδρος ἐπὶ Κόλχους τε
καὶ Ἀμαζόνας ἐλάσας καταστρέψασθαι τὰ ἐπὶ τὸν
πόντον τὸν Εὔξεινον ταύτῃ καθήκοντα γένη, ὁδῶν
τε ἡγεμὼν ἔσεσθαι ἐπηγγέλλετο καὶ τὰ ἐπιτήδεια
τῇ στρατιᾷ παρασκευάσειν.
5   Τοῖς τε οὖν παρὰ τῶν Σκυθῶν ἥκουσι φιλάνθρωπα ἀποκρίνεται Ἀλέξανδρος καὶ ἐς τὸν τότε
καιρὸν ξύμφορα, γάμου δὲ οὐδὲν δεῖσθαι Σκυθικοῦ,
καὶ Φαρασμάνην ἐπαινέσας τε καὶ φιλίαν καὶ
ξυμμαχίαν πρὸς αὐτὸν ξυνθέμενος αὐτῷ μὲν τότε
οὐκ ἔφη ἐν καιρῷ εἶναι ἐλαύνειν ἐπὶ τὸν Πόντον·
Ἀρταβάζῳ δὲ τῷ Πέρσῃ, ὅτῳ τὰ Βακτρίων ἐξ
Ἀλεξάνδρου ἐπετέτακτο, καὶ ὅσοι ἄλλοι πρόσχωροι
τούτῳ σατράπαι ξυστήσας Φαρασμάνην ἀποπέμπει
6 ἐς τὰ ἤθη τὰ αὐτοῦ. αὐτῷ δὲ τὰ Ἰνδῶν ἔφη ἐν
τῷ τότε μέλειν. τούτους γὰρ καταστρεψάμενος
πᾶσαν ἂν ἤδη ἔχειν τὴν Ἀσίαν· ἐχομένης δὲ τῆς
Ἀσίας ἐπανιέναι ἂν ἐς τὴν Ἑλλάδα, ἐκεῖθεν δ' ἐφ'
Ἑλλησπόντου τε καὶ τῆς Προποντίδος ξὺν τῇ
δυνάμει πάσῃ τῇ τε ναυτικῇ καὶ τῇ πεζικῇ ἐλάσειν
εἴσω τοῦ Πόντου· καὶ ἐς τὸ τότε ἠξίου ἀποθέσθαι
Φαρασμάνην ὅσα ἐν τῷ παραυτίκα ἐπηγγέλλετο.

he was still willing to give the daughters of the
satraps of the Scythian territory and of the chief
personages in Scythia to Alexander's most trusted
followers; he would also come to visit Alexander, if
summoned, and hear Alexander's commands from
Alexander himself. At the same time Pharasmanes, 4
king of the Chorasmians, came to Alexander with
fifteen hundred horsemen; he said that he lived on
the borders of the Colchians and the Amazons, and if
Alexander desired to attack Colchis and the Amazons
and subdue all the races that extended in these regions
to the Euxine Sea, he promised to act as guide and
to provide supplies for the army.[2]

Alexander then replied to the Scythian envoys 5
graciously and as his interest at the time demanded,
that he had no need of a Scythian marriage. He
commended Pharasmanes and entered into friendship
and alliance with him, but said that for him it was
not then the moment to march to Pontus. But he
recommended Pharasmanes to Artabazus the Persian, to whom he had entrusted affairs in Bactria, and
to all the other neighbouring satraps, and sent him
back to his own abode. He said that for the time 6
being his own concern was India; for by subduing
India he would at once be in possession of Asia as a
whole, and with Asia in his possession he would return
to Greece, and march thence by the Hellespont and
Propontis to Pontus with all his naval and land forces;
he expected Pharasmanes to save up the promises he
made now till that time.[3]

---

[2] App. XII.
[3] For subsequent operations QC. vii 10, 13 ff. (very different);
App. VIII 14.

7   Αὐτὸς δὲ ἐπὶ τὸν Ὦξον τε ποταμὸν ᾔει αὖθις καὶ
εἰς τὴν Σογδιανὴν προχωρεῖν ἐγνώκει, ὅτι πολλοὺς
τῶν Σογδιανῶν ἐς τὰ ἐρύματα ξυμπεφευγέναι
ἠγγέλλετο οὐδὲ ἐθέλειν κατακούειν τοῦ σατράπου,
ὅστις αὐτοῖς ἐξ Ἀλεξάνδρου ἐπετέτακτο. στρατο-
πεδεύοντος δὲ αὐτοῦ ἐπὶ τῷ ποταμῷ τῷ Ὦξῳ οὐ
μακρὰν τῆς σκηνῆς τῆς αὐτοῦ Ἀλεξάνδρου πηγὴ
ὕδατος καὶ ἄλλη ἐλαίου πηγὴ πλησίον αὐτῆς
8   ἀνέσχε. καὶ Πτολεμαίῳ τῷ Λάγου τῷ σωματοφύλακι ἐπειδὴ ἐσηγγέλθη τὸ τέρας, Πτολεμαῖος
Ἀλεξάνδρῳ ἔφρασεν. Ἀλέξανδρος δὲ ἔθυεν ἐπὶ
τῷ φάσματι ὅσα οἱ μάντεις ἐξηγοῦντο. Ἀρίστανδρος δὲ πόνων εἶναι σημεῖον τοῦ ἐλαίου τὴν πηγὴν
ἔφασκεν, ἀλλὰ καὶ νίκην ἐπὶ τοῖς πόνοις σημαίνειν.

16. Διαβὰς οὖν ξὺν μέρει τῆς στρατιᾶς ἐς τὴν
Σογδιανήν, Πολυπέρχοντα δὲ καὶ Ἄτταλον καὶ
Γοργίαν καὶ Μελέαγρον αὐτοῦ ἐν Βάκτροις ὑπολι-
πόμενος τούτοις μὲν παρήγγειλεν τήν τε χώραν ἐν
φυλακῇ ἔχειν, ὡς μή τι νεωτερίσωσιν οἱ ταύτῃ
βάρβαροι, καὶ τοὺς ἔτι ἀφεστηκότας αὐτῶν ἐξαι-
2   ρεῖν· αὐτὸς δὲ ἐς πέντε μέρη διελὼν τὴν ἅμα οἷ
στρατιὰν τῶν μὲν Ἡφαιστίωνα ἄρχειν ἔταξε, τῶν
δὲ Πτολεμαῖον τὸν Λάγου τὸν σωματοφύλακα·
τοῖς τρίτοις δὲ Περδίκκαν ἐπέταξε· τῆς δὲ τετάρ-
της τάξεως Κοῖνος καὶ Ἀρτάβαζος ἡγοῦντο
αὐτῷ· τὴν δὲ πέμπτην μοῖραν ἀναλαβὼν αὐτὸς
3   ἐπῄει τὴν χώραν ὡς ἐπὶ Μαράκανδα. καὶ οἱ ἄλλοι
ὡς ἑκάστοις προὐχώρει ἐπῄεσαν, τοὺς μέν τινας
τῶν ἐς τὰ ἐρύματα ξυμπεφευγότων βίᾳ ἐξαιροῦντες,
τοὺς δὲ καὶ ὁμολογίᾳ προσχωροῦντάς σφισιν
ἀναλαμβάνοντες. ὡς δὲ ξύμπασα αὐτῷ ἡ δύναμις
ἐπελθοῦσα τῶν Σογδιανῶν τῆς χώρας τὴν πολλὴν

He himself returned to the river Oxus; he had
determined to move into Sogdiana, since it was
reported that many of the Sogdianians had taken
refuge in their forts and would not obey the satrap
set over them by Alexander. While he was encamped on the river Oxus, not far from his own tent
a spring of water, and another of oil near by, came up
from the ground. When this prodigy was notified
to Ptolemy son of Lagus, the royal bodyguard, he told
Alexander, and Alexander sacrificed on account of
this portent as the soothsayers directed. Aristander
said that the spring of oil was a sign of tribulations to
come, but that it portended victory after the tribulations.[4]

16. Passing with part of his force into Sogdiana,
he left behind Polyperchon, Attalus, Gorgias and
Meleager there in Bactra and told them to protect
the country, prevent the barbarians there giving
trouble and destroy those still in revolt. He himself divided the force with him into five parts, and
appointed Hephaestion to command one, Ptolemy
son of Lagus, the bodyguard, another; the third was
put under Perdiccas, and the fourth brigade was
commanded by Coenus and Artabazus; he took the
fifth himself and invaded the country in the direction
of Maracanda. Each of the other divisions carried
out such attacks as its success allowed, violently
destroying some of those who had taken refuge in
the forts, and accepting the surrender of others by
agreement. But when his whole force, after traversing the greater part of Sogdiana, arrived at Mara-

7   Spring
328
B.C.

8

2

3

---

[4] Presumably from Pt. Cf. P. 57, 4 f. (with no mention of
Pt.). Strabo xi 7, 3 puts the discovery of petroleum on the
Ochus, perhaps following Ar., cf. Pearson, *LH* 169.

ἐς Μαράκανδα ἀφίκετο, Ἡφαιστίωνα μὲν ἐκπέμπει
τὰς ἐν τῇ Σογδιανῇ πόλεις συνοικίζειν, Κοῖνον δὲ
καὶ Ἀρτάβαζον ὡς ἐς Σκύθας, ὅτι ἐς Σκύθας
καταπεφευγέναι Σπιταμένης αὐτῷ ἐξηγγέλλετο,
αὐτὸς δὲ ξὺν τῇ λοιπῇ στρατιᾷ ἐπιὼν τῆς Σογδιανῆς
ὅσα ἔτι πρὸς τῶν ἀφεστηκότων κατείχετο ταῦτα οὐ
χαλεπῶς ἐξῄρει.

4   Ἐν τούτοις δὲ Ἀλεξάνδρου ὄντος Σπιταμένης τε
καὶ σὺν αὐτῷ τῶν Σογδιανῶν τινες φυγάδων ἐς
τῶν Σκυθῶν τῶν Μασσαγετῶν καλουμένων τὴν
χώραν ξυμπεφευγότες ξυναγαγόντες τῶν Μασσαγετῶν ἱππέας ἑξακοσίους ἀφίκοντο πρός τι
5 φρούριον τῶν κατὰ τὴν Βακτριανήν. καὶ τῷ τε
φρουράρχῳ οὐδὲν πολέμιον προσδεχομένῳ ἐπιπεσόντες καὶ τοῖς ξὺν τούτῳ τὴν φυλακὴν ἔχουσιν
τοὺς μὲν στρατιώτας διέφθειραν, τὸν φρούραρχον
δὲ ἑλόντες ἐν φυλακῇ εἶχον. θαρσήσαντες δὲ ἐπὶ
τοῦ φρουρίου τῇ καταλήψει ὀλίγαις ἡμέραις ὕστερον
Ζαριάσποις πελάσαντες τῇ μὲν πόλει προσβαλεῖν
ἀπέγνωσαν, λείαν δὲ πολλὴν περιβαλλόμενοι ἤλαυ-
νον.

6   Ἦσαν δὲ ἐν τοῖς Ζαριάσποις νόσῳ ὑπολελειμμένοι τῶν ἑταίρων ἱππέων οὐ πολλοὶ καὶ ξὺν
τούτοις Πείθων τε ὁ Σωσικλέους, ἐπὶ τῆς βασιλικῆς θεραπείας τῆς ἐν Ζαριάσποις τεταγμένος, καὶ
Ἀριστόνικος ὁ κιθαρῳδός. καὶ οὗτοι αἰσθόμενοι
τῶν Σκυθῶν τὴν καταδρομήν (ἤδη γὰρ ἐκ τῆς
νόσου ἀναρρωσθέντες ὅπλα τε ἔφερον καὶ τῶν
ἵππων ἐπέβαινον) ξυναγαγόντες τούς τε μισθοφόρους ἱππέας ἐς ὀγδοήκοντα, οἳ ἐπὶ φυλακῇ τῶν
Ζαριάσπων ὑπολελειμμένοι ἦσαν, καὶ τῶν παίδων
τινὰς τῶν βασιλικῶν ἐκβοηθοῦσιν ἐπὶ τοὺς Μασ-

328
B.C.

canda, he sent Hephaestion to settle people in cities in Sogdiana, and Coenus and Artabazus in the direction of Scythia, since news came that Spitamenes had taken refuge there, while he himself with the rest of the troops went on to parts of Sogdiana still held by the rebels, and destroyed them without trouble.

While Alexander was thus engaged, Spitamenes 4 and some fugitives from Sogdiana in his company had fled for refuge to the land of the Scythians called Massagetae[1]; there they collected six hundred horsemen of the Massagetae and arrived at one of the forts in the Bactrian region. Attacking the com- 5 mandant of the fort, who was not expecting enemy action, and his garrison, they destroyed the soldiers, took the commandant prisoner and kept him in custody. Emboldened by capturing the fort, they approached Zariaspa a few days later, and though they decided not to assault the city, they surrounded it and carried off much booty.

In the city of Zariaspa there were a few of the 6 Companion cavalry, left there as invalids with Pithon son of Sosicles, who had been put in charge of the royal retinue at Zariaspa, and Aristonicus the harpist. On learning of the Scythian raid, as they had now recovered and could bear arms and mount horseback, they assembled about eighty mercenary cavalry, who had been left behind to garrison Zariaspa, and some of the King's pages, and sallied out against the

---

[1] Probably between Oxus and Caspian. QC. viii 1, 3 ff. tells another story, also featuring Craterus (A. 17, 1), whose command is not recorded.

7 σαγέτας. καὶ τῇ μὲν πρώτῃ προσβολῇ οὐδὲν ὑποτοπήσασι τοῖς Σκύθαις ἐπιπεσόντες τήν τε λείαν ξύμπασαν ἀφείλοντο αὐτοὺς καὶ τῶν ἀγόντων τὴν λείαν οὐκ ὀλίγους ἀπέκτειναν. ἐπανιόντες δὲ αὐτοὶ ἀτάκτως, ἅτε οὐδενὸς ἐξηγουμένου, ἐνεδρευθέντες πρὸς Σπιταμένους καὶ τῶν Σκυθῶν τῶν μὲν ἑταίρων ἀποβάλλουσιν ἑπτά, τῶν δὲ μισθοφόρων ἱππέων ἑξήκοντα. καὶ Ἀριστόνικος ὁ κιθαρῳδὸς αὐτοῦ ἀποθνήσκει, οὐ κατὰ κιθαρῳδὸν ἀνὴρ ἀγαθὸς γενόμενος. Πείθων δὲ τρωθεὶς ζῶν λαμβάνεται πρὸς τῶν Σκυθῶν.

17. Καὶ ταῦτα ὡς Κρατερῷ ἐξηγγέλθη, σπουδῇ ἐπὶ τοὺς Μασσαγέτας ἤλαυνεν. οἱ δὲ ὡς ἐπύθοντο πλησίον ἐπελαύνοντά σφισι Κρατερόν, ἔφευγον ἀνὰ κράτος ὡς εἰς τὴν ἐρήμην. καὶ Κρατερὸς ἐχόμενος αὐτῶν αὐτοῖς τε ἐκείνοις περιπίπτει οὐ πόρρω τῆς ἐρήμου καὶ ἄλλοις ἱππεῦσι Μασσαγετῶν ὑπὲρ τοὺς 2 χιλίους. καὶ μάχη γίγνεται τῶν τε Μακεδόνων καὶ τῶν Σκυθῶν καρτερά· καὶ ἐνίκων οἱ Μακεδόνες. τῶν δὲ Σκυθῶν ἀπέθανον μὲν ἑκατὸν καὶ πεντήκοντα ἱππεῖς· οἱ δὲ ἄλλοι οὐ χαλεπῶς ἐς τὴν ἐρήμην διεσώθησαν, ὅτι ἄπορον ἦν προσωτέρω τοῖς Μακεδόσι διώκειν.

3 Καὶ ἐν τούτῳ Ἀλέξανδρος Ἀρτάβαζον μὲν τῆς σατραπείας τῆς Βακτρίων ἀπαλλάττει δεηθέντα διὰ γήρας, Ἀμύνταν δὲ τὸν Νικολάου σατράπην ἀντ' αὐτοῦ καθίστησι. Κοῖνον δὲ ἀπολείπει αὐτοῦ τήν τε αὐτοῦ τάξιν καὶ τὴν Μελεάγρου ἔχοντα καὶ τῶν ἑταίρων ἱππέων ἐς τετρακοσίους καὶ τοὺς ἱππακοντιστὰς πάντας καὶ τῶν Βακτρίων τε καὶ

---

[1] QC. viii 1, 19 and 2, 14 has first Clitus, then Amyntas,

Massagetae. At the first charge, falling on the
Scythians when they suspected nothing, they robbed
them of their entire plunder, and killed many who
were driving it off, but when they were returning, in
some disorder since there was no one in command,
Spitamenes and the Scythians caught them in an
ambush, where they lost seven Companions, and
sixty mercenary cavalry. Aristonicus the harpist
died there, with more courage than a harpist might
have. Pithon was wounded and taken alive by the
Scythians.

17. When this was reported to Craterus, he
marched at all speed against the Massagetae, and
when they learned that he was coming up close to
them, they fled headlong towards the desert. Craterus pressed upon and overtook them not far from
the desert with over a thousand other Massagetaean
horsemen. A fierce battle took place between the   2
Macedonians and the Scythians, which the Macedonians won. Of the Scythians a hundred and fifty
horsemen perished, but the rest easily got away into
the desert, since it was impracticable for the Macedonians to pursue further.

Meanwhile Alexander relieved Artabazus of the   3
satrapy of Bactria at his own request on account of
old age and appointed Amyntas son of Nicolaus in
his place.[1] He left Coenus there with his own
battalion and Meleager's, about four hundred of the
Companion cavalry, all the mounted javelin-men, and

---

succeed Artabazus, whom he makes out to be 95 (he could not
have been over 57, Berve no. 152); place, Maracanda. Al.
sends Hephaestion to winter in Bactria, and after further
operations, marches to Nautaca, 2, 13–9, leaving winter
quarters there after 2 months, 4, 1, cf. A. 18, 1; 19, 4; 21, 10;
22, 3.

Σογδιανῶν καὶ ὅσοι ἄλλοι μετὰ ᾿Αμύντου ἐτάχθησαν, προστάξας ἅπασιν ἀκούειν Κοίνου καὶ
διαχειμάζειν αὐτοῦ ἐν τῇ Σογδιανῇ, τῆς τε χώρας
ἕνεκα τῆς φυλακῆς καὶ εἴ πη ἄρα Σπιταμένην
περιφερόμενον κατὰ τὸν χειμῶνα ἐνεδρεύσαντας
ξυλλαβεῖν.

4 Σπιταμένης δὲ καὶ οἱ ἀμφ᾿ αὐτὸν ὡς φρουραῖς
τε πάντα κατειλημμένα ἑώρων ἐκ τῶν Μακεδόνων
καί σφιν ἄπορα πάντῃ τὰ τῆς φυγῆς ἐγίγνετο, ὡς
ἐπὶ Κοῖνόν τε καὶ τὴν ξὺν τούτῳ στρατιὰν ἐτρά-
ποντο, ὡς ταύτῃ μᾶλλόν τι ἀξιόμαχοι ἐσόμενοι.
ἀφικόμενοι δὲ ἐς Γαβάς, χωρίον τῆς Σογδιανῆς
ὀχυρὸν ἐν μεθορίῳ τῆς τε Σογδιανῶν γῆς καὶ τῆς
Μασσαγετῶν Σκυθῶν ᾠκισμένον, ἀναπείθουσιν οὐ
χαλεπῶς τῶν Σκυθῶν ἱππέας ἐς τρισχιλίους
5 συνεμβάλλειν σφίσιν ἐς τὴν Σογδιανήν. οἱ δὲ
Σκύθαι οὗτοι ἀπορίᾳ τε πολλῇ ἔχονται καὶ ἅμα ὅτι
οὔτε πόλεις εἰσὶν αὐτοῖς οὔτε ἑδραῖοι οἰκοῦσιν, ὡς
δειμαίνειν ἂν περὶ τῶν φιλτάτων, οὐ χαλεποὶ
ἀναπεισθῆναί εἰσιν ἐς ἄλλον καὶ ἄλλον πόλεμον.
ὡς δὲ Κοῖνός τε καὶ οἱ ἀμφ᾿ αὐτὸν ἔμαθον προσ-
ιόντας τοὺς ξὺν Σπιταμένει ἱππέας, ἀπήντων καὶ
6 αὐτοὶ μετὰ τῆς στρατιᾶς. καὶ γίγνεται αὐτῶν
μάχη καρτερά, καὶ νικῶσιν οἱ Μακεδόνες, ὥστε
τῶν μὲν βαρβάρων ἱππέων ὑπὲρ τοὺς ὀκτακοσίους
πεσεῖν ἐν τῇ μάχῃ, τῶν δὲ ξὺν Κοίνῳ ἱππέας μὲν ἐς
εἴκοσι καὶ πέντε, πεζοὺς δὲ δώδεκα. οἵ τε οὖν
Σογδιανοὶ οἱ ἔτι ὑπολειπόμενοι ξὺν Σπιταμένει καὶ
τῶν Βακτρίων οἱ πολλοὶ ἀπολείπουσιν ἐν τῇ φυγῇ
Σπιταμένην καὶ ἀφικόμενοι παρὰ Κοῖνον παρέδοσαν
7 σφᾶς αὐτοὺς Κοίνῳ, οἵ τε Μασσαγέται οἱ Σκύθαι
κακῶς πεπραγότες τὰ μὲν σκευοφόρα τῶν ξυμπα-

the Bactrians and Sogdianians attached to Amyntas, commanding them all to take their orders from Coenus, and to winter there in Sogdiana, to protect the region and to try to ambush and capture Spitamenes, if he moved around anywhere in the winter.[2]

4 Spitamenes and his troops, seeing every place occupied by Macedonian garrisons and no means of escape anywhere for themselves, turned against Coenus and his troops, on the basis that they would be rather more equal to fighting there. On arriving at Gabae, a stronghold of Sogdiana, lying on the border of Sogdiana and the land of the Massagetaean Scythians, they easily induced about three thousand Scythian horsemen to join them in a raid on Sogdiana. 5 These Scythians are in the grip of dire poverty, and, since they have no cities and no settled habitations, and hence no fear for their loved ones, they are easy to inveigle into one war after another. When Coenus and his colleagues learned that the cavalry with Spitamenes was approaching, they went to meet them with their troops. There was a fierce battle, which 6 the Macedonians won, so that over eight hundred of the barbarian cavalry fell in the battle, but of Coenus' troops only about twenty-five horsemen and twelve foot-soldiers. At this the Sogdianians still left with Spitamenes and the greater number of the Bactrians deserted Spitamenes in the flight, came to Coenus and surrendered to him. The Massagetaean Scy- 7 thians after this disaster plundered the baggage

---

[2] In winter 329/8 B.C. Al. had almost evacuated Sogdiana and had then to reconquer it.

ραταξαμένων σφίσι Βακτρίων τε καὶ Σογδιανῶν
διήρπασαν, αὐτοὶ δὲ ξὺν Σπιταμένει ἐς τὴν ἔρημον
ἔφευγον. ὡς δὲ ἐξηγγέλλετο αὐτοῖς Ἀλέξανδρος
ἐν ὁρμῇ ὢν ἐπὶ τὴν ἔρημον ἐλαύνειν ἀποτεμόντες
τοῦ Σπιταμένους τὴν κεφαλὴν παρὰ Ἀλέξανδρον
πέμπουσιν, ὡς ἀποτρέψοντες ἀπὸ σφῶν αὐτῶν
τούτῳ τῷ ἔργῳ.

18. Καὶ ἐν τούτῳ Κοῖνός τε ἐς Ναύτακα παρ'
Ἀλέξανδρον ἐπανέρχεται καὶ οἱ ἀμφὶ Κρατερόν τε
καὶ Φραταφέρνην τὸν τῶν Παρθυαίων σατράπην
καὶ Στασάνωρ ὁ Ἀρείων, πεπραγμένων σφίσι
2 πάντων ὅσα ἐξ Ἀλεξάνδρου ἐτέτακτο. Ἀλέξανδρος δὲ περὶ Ναύτακα ἀναπαύων τὴν στρατιὰν
ὅ τι περ ἀκμαῖον τοῦ χειμῶνος, Φραταφέρνην μὲν
ἀποστέλλει ἐς Μάρδους καὶ Ταπ⟨ο⟩ύρους ⟨Αὐτο⟩-
φραδάτην ἐπανάξοντα τὸν σατράπην, ὅτι πολλάκις
ἤδη μετάπεμπτος ἐξ Ἀλεξάνδρου γιγνόμενος οὐχ
3 ὑπήκουε καλοῦντι. Στασάνορα δὲ ἐς Δράγγας
σατράπην ἐκπέμπει, ἐς Μήδους δὲ Ἀτροπάτην ἐπὶ
σατραπείᾳ καὶ τοῦτον τῇ Μήδων, ὅτι Ὀξυδάτης
ἐθελοκακεῖν αὐτῷ ἐφαίνετο. Σταμένην δὲ ἐπὶ
Βαβυλῶνος στέλλει, ὅτι Μαζαῖος ὁ Βαβυλώνιος
ὕπαρχος τετελευτηκέναι αὐτῷ ἐξηγγέλλετο. Σώπολιν δὲ καὶ Ἐπόκιλλον καὶ Μεν[ν]ίδαν ἐς Μακεδονίαν ἐκπέμπει, τὴν στρατιὰν τὴν ἐκ Μακεδονίας
αὐτῷ ἀνάξοντας.

4 Ἅμα δὲ τῷ ἦρι ὑποφαίνοντι προὐχώρει ὡς ἐπὶ
τὴν ἐν τῇ Σογδιανῇ πέτραν, ἐς ἣν πολλοὺς μὲν τῶν

---

[3] QC. viii 3, 1 ff. has Spitamenes killed by his wife, with no
record of these operations; the ' Dahae ' then submit.

trains of the Bactrians and Sogdianians who had been with them in line of battle, and fled themselves with Spitamenes to the desert. When they learnt that Alexander was already on the move and marching towards the desert, they cut off Spitamenes' head and sent it to Alexander, to keep him away from themselves by this action.[3]

18. Meantime Coenus had returned to Alexander at Nautaca as had Craterus, Phrataphernes the satrap of Parthyaea, and Stasanor satrap of Areia, after carrying out all Alexander's orders. Alexander, [2] while resting his force at Nautaca, since it was the depth of winter, despatched Phrataphernes to the Mardians and Tapurians, to bring back the satrap Autophradates, as he had often before been sent for by Alexander but ignored the summons. He sent [3] Stasanor to the Drangians as satrap, and Atropates to the Medes as satrap of Media, since he thought Oxydates was wilfully neglecting his duty to him. He despatched Stamenes to Babylon, since Mazaeus the hyparch of Babylon was reported to him to be dead.[1] Sopolis and Epocillus and Menidas were sent to Macedonia, to bring up for him the force from Macedonia.[2]

With the first appearance of spring Alexander [4] [327 B.C.] marched forward towards the Rock of Sogdiana[3]

---

[1] Cf. QC. viii 3, 17 (Arsaces for Atropates; nothing on Sopolis, Hermolaus' father (!) etc). 'Hyparch': 12, 8 n. A. seems to be partly duplicating 7, 1; probably Pt. and Ar. put the return of Phrataphernes and Stasanor (cf. iii 29, 5) at different times; 18, 1 is likely to be correct.

[2] Introd. n. 90.

[3] Early spring 327 B.C., cf. 17, 3 n. QC. vii 11, 1 ff. calls this the rock of 'Ariamazes', puts its capture early in 328 B.C. and has Al. execute the leading men.

ARRIAN

Σογδιανῶν ξυμπεφευγέναι αὐτῷ ἐξηγγέλλετο· καὶ
ἡ Ὀξυάρτου δὲ γυνὴ τοῦ Βακτρίου καὶ αἱ παῖδες αἱ
Ὀξυάρτου ἐς τὴν πέτραν ταύτην ξυμπεφευγέναι
ἐλέγοντο, Ὀξυάρτου αὐτὰς ὡς ἐς ἀνάλωτον δῆθεν
τὸ χωρίον ἐκεῖνο ὑπεκθεμένου, ὅτι καὶ αὐτὸς
ἀφειστήκει ἀπ' Ἀλεξάνδρου. ταύτης γὰρ ἐξαιρεθείσης οὐκέτι οὐδὲν ὑπολειφθήσεσθαι ἐδόκει τῶν
5 Σογδιανῶν τοῖς νεωτερίζειν ἐθέλουσιν. ὡς δὲ
ἐπέλασαν τῇ πέτρᾳ, καταλαμβάνει πάντῃ ἀπότομον
ἐς τὴν προσβολὴν σιτία τε ξυγκεκομισμένους τοὺς
βαρβάρους ὡς ἐς χρόνιον πολιορκίαν. καὶ χιὼν
πολλὴ ἐπιπεσοῦσα τήν τε πρόσβασιν ἀπορωτέραν
ἐποίει τοῖς Μακεδόσι καὶ ἅμα ἐν ἀφθονίᾳ ὕδατος
τοὺς βαρβάρους διῆγεν. ἀλλὰ καὶ ὣς προσβάλλειν
6 ἐδόκει τῷ χωρίῳ. καὶ γάρ τι καὶ ὑπέρογκον ὑπὸ
τῶν βαρβάρων λεχθὲν ἐς φιλοτιμίαν ξὺν ὀργῇ
ἐμβεβλήκει Ἀλέξανδρον. προκληθέντες γὰρ ἐς
ξύμβασιν καὶ προτεινομένου σφίσιν, ὅτι σώοις
ὑπάρξει ἐπὶ τὰ σφέτερα ἀπαλλαγῆναι παραδοῦσι τὸ
χωρίον, οἱ δὲ σὺν γέλωτι βαρβαρίζοντες πτηνοὺς
ἐκέλευον ζητεῖν στρατιώτας Ἀλέξανδρον, οἵτινες
αὐτῷ ἐξαιρήσουσι τὸ ὄρος, ὡς τῶν γε ἄλλων
7 ἀνθρώπων οὐδεμίαν ὥραν σφίσιν οὖσαν. ἔνθα δὴ
ἐκήρυξεν Ἀλέξανδρος τῷ μὲν πρώτῳ ἀναβάντι
δώδεκα τάλαντα εἶναι τὸ γέρας, δευτέρῳ δὲ ἐπὶ
τούτῳ τὰ δεύτερα καὶ τρίτῳ τὰ ἐφεξῆς, ὡς τελευ-
ταῖον εἶναι τῷ τελευταίῳ ἀνελθόντι τριακοσίους
δαρεικοὺς τὸ γέρας. καὶ τοῦτο τὸ κήρυγμα
παρώξυνεν ἔτι μᾶλλον καὶ ἄλλως τοὺς Μακεδόνας
ὡρμημένους.

19. Ξυνταξάμενοι δὴ ὅσοι πετροβατεῖν ἐν ταῖς
πολιορκίαις αὐτῷ μεμελετήκεσαν, ἐς τριακοσίους

where, he was told, many of the Sogdianians had fled
for refuge; the wife of Oxyartes the Bactrian and his
daughters were also said to have taken refuge on this
rock, Oxyartes having put them there out of the way
in a place he thought impregnable at the time of his
own revolt from Alexander. Once this rock had been
taken, Alexander thought that the Sogdianians who
were ready to revolt would have no further recourse
left. But when they approached the rock, Alexander 5
found that it was sheer on all sides against attack,
and that the tribesmen had stored provisions there
for a long siege; a deep fall of snow made the
approach more impracticable for the Macedonians,
while it assured the tribesmen of abundant water.
Yet even so Alexander decided to assault the place.
A boastful remark by the barbarians had contributed 6
to Alexander's passionate pursuit of the glory of
success; when summoned to make terms, which were
offered on the basis that they would be allowed to go
safe to their homes if they gave up the position, they
told Alexander with barbaric laughter to look for
soldiers with wings to capture the mountain for him,
since no other men would give them any concern.
Then Alexander proclaimed that the first to scale the 7
height should have a prize of twelve Talents, the
second a second prize, the third another prize and so
on, the last to reach the top to have three hundred
darics.[4] Eager as the Macedonians already were,
this proclamation still further increased their ardour.

19. So then when all had mustered who had
practised rock-climbing in their previous sieges,

[4] Persian gold coins.

τὸν ἀριθμόν, καὶ πασσάλους μικροὺς σιδηροῦς, οἷς
αἱ σκηναὶ καταπεπήγεσαν αὐτοῖς, παρασκευάσα-
ντες, τοῦ καταπηγνύναι αὐτοὺς ἔς τε τὴν χιόνα
ὅπου πεπηγυῖα φανείη καὶ εἴ πού τι τῆς χώρας
ἔρημον χιόνος ὑποφαίνοιτο, καὶ τούτους καλωδίοις
ἐκ λίνου ἰσχυροῖς ἐκδήσαντες τῆς νυκτὸς πρού-
χώρουν κατὰ τὸ ἀποτομώτατόν τε τῆς πέτρας καὶ
2 ταύτῃ ἀφυλακτότατον. καὶ τούτους τοὺς πασσάλους καταπηγνύντες τοὺς μὲν ἐς τὴν γῆν, ὅπου
διεφαίνετο, τοὺς δὲ καὶ τῆς χιόνος ἐς τὰ μάλιστα οὐ
θρυφθησόμενα, ἀνεῖλκον σφᾶς αὐτοὺς ἄλλοι ἄλλῃ
τῆς πέτρας. καὶ τούτων ἐς τριάκοντα μὲν ἐν τῇ
ἀναβάσει διεφθάρησαν, ὥστε οὐδὲ τὰ σώματα
αὐτῶν ἐς ταφὴν εὑρέθη ἐμπεσόντα ἄλλῃ καὶ ἄλλῃ
3 τῆς χιόνος. οἱ δὲ λοιποὶ ἀναβάντες ὑπὸ τὴν ἔω καὶ
τὸ ἄκρον τοῦ ὄρους καταλαβόντες σινδόνας κατέ-
σειον ὡς ἐπὶ τὸ στρατόπεδον τῶν Μακεδόνων,
οὕτως αὐτοῖς ἐξ Ἀλεξάνδρου παρηγγελμένον.
πέμψας δὴ κήρυκα ἐμβοῆσαι ἐκέλευσε τοῖς προφυ-
λάσσουσι τῶν βαρβάρων μὴ διατρίβειν ἔτι, ἀλλὰ
παραδιδόναι σφᾶς· ἐξευρῆσθαι γὰρ δὴ τοὺς
πτηνοὺς ἀνθρώπους καὶ ἔχεσθαι ὑπὸ αὐτῶν τοῦ
ὄρους τὰ ἄκρα· καὶ ἅμα ἐδείκνυεν τοὺς ὑπὲρ τῆς
κορυφῆς στρατιώτας.
4 Οἱ δὲ βάρβαροι ἐκπλαγέντες τῷ παραλόγῳ τῆς
ὄψεως καὶ πλείονάς τε ὑποτοπήσαντες εἶναι τοὺς
κατέχοντας τὰ ἄκρα καὶ ἀκριβῶς ὡπλισμένους
ἐνέδοσαν σφᾶς αὐτούς· οὕτω πρὸς τὴν ὄψιν τῶν
ὀλίγων ἐκείνων Μακεδόνων φοβεροὶ ἐγένοντο.
ἔνθα δὴ ἄλλων τε πολλῶν γυναῖκες καὶ παῖδες
ἐλήφθησαν καὶ ἡ γυνὴ ἡ Ὀξυάρτου καὶ οἱ παῖδες.
5 καὶ ἦν γὰρ Ὀξυάρτῃ παῖς παρθένος ἐν ὥρᾳ γάμου,

327
B.C.

numbering about three hundred, and had got ready small iron pegs, with which their tents had been pegged down, to fix them into the snow where it appeared to be frozen firm and also in any space bare of snow which might show through, and had bound the pegs to strong linen ropes, they set out at night to the part of the rock which was least guarded, because most precipitous. They fixed the pegs into 2 the ground where it was visible, or in the snow where it seemed least likely to give way, and each in a different place, hauled themselves up the rock. About thirty of them perished in the ascent, in such a way that their bodies were not even found for burial, having fallen in different parts of the snow. The rest, 3 however, climbed up about dawn, seized the summit of the mound, and waved linen flags to the Macedonian camp, in accordance with Alexander's instructions to them. Then Alexander sent a herald and told him to shout to the front line of the barbarians, not to delay further but to give themselves up, for he had actually found the men with wings, and the summit of their mound was in their hands, pointing at the same time to the soldiers on the peak.

The barbarians were astounded at a sight they had 4 never reckoned on, and suspecting that the soldiers occupying the heights were more numerous and fully armed, they surrendered; such was their panic at seeing those few Macedonians. Here were captured the wives and children of many men, notably the wife and daughters of Oxyartes. Now Oxyartes had a maiden 5

Ῥωξάνη ὀνόματι, ἣν δὴ καλλίστην τῶν Ἀσιανῶν γυναικῶν λέγουσιν ὀφθῆναι οἱ ξὺν Ἀλεξάνδρῳ στρατεύσαντες μετά γε τὴν Δαρείου γυναῖκα. καὶ ταύτην ἰδόντα Ἀλέξανδρον ἐς ἔρωτα ἐλθεῖν αὐτῆς· ἐρασθέντα δὲ οὐκ ἐθελῆσαι ὑβρίσαι καθάπερ

6 αἰχμάλωτον, ἀλλὰ γῆμαι γὰρ οὐκ ἀπαξιῶσαι. καὶ τοῦτο ἐγὼ Ἀλεξάνδρου τὸ ἔργον ἐπαινῶ μᾶλλόν τι ἢ μέμφομαι. καίτοι τῆς γε Δαρείου γυναικός, ἣ καλλίστη δὴ ἐλέγετο τῶν ἐν τῇ Ἀσίᾳ γυναικῶν, ἢ οὐκ ἦλθεν ἐς ἐπιθυμίαν ἢ καρτερὸς αὐτὸς αὑτοῦ ἐγένετο, νέος τε ὢν καὶ τὰ μάλιστα ἐν ἀκμῇ τῆς εὐτυχίας, ὁπότε ὑβρίζουσιν οἱ ἄνθρωποι· ὁ δὲ κατῃδέσθη τε καὶ ἐφείσατο, σωφροσύνῃ τε πολλῇ διαχρώμενος καὶ δόξης ἅμα ἀγαθῆς οὐκ ἀτόπῳ ἐφέσει.

20. Καὶ τοίνυν καὶ λόγος κατέχει ὀλίγον μετὰ τὴν μάχην, ἣ πρὸς Ἰσσῷ Δαρείῳ τε καὶ Ἀλεξάνδρῳ ξυνέβη, ἀποδράντα ἐλθεῖν παρὰ Δαρεῖον τὸν εὐνοῦχον τὸν φύλακα αὐτῷ τῆς γυναικός. καὶ τοῦτον ὡς εἶδε Δαρεῖος, πρῶτα μὲν πυθέσθαι εἰ ζῶσιν αὐτῷ αἱ παῖδες [καὶ οἱ υἱοί] καὶ ἡ γυνή τε

2 καὶ ἡ μήτηρ. ὡς δὲ ζώσας τε ἐπύθετο καὶ βασίλισσαι ὅτι καλοῦνται καὶ ἡ θεραπεία ὅτι ἀμφ᾽ αὐτάς ἐστιν, ἥντινα καὶ ἐπὶ Δαρείου ἐθεραπεύοντο, ἐπὶ τῷδε αὖ πυθέσθαι εἰ σωφρονεῖ αὐτῷ ἡ γυνὴ ἔτι. ὡς δὲ σωφρονοῦσαν ἐπύθετο, αὖθις ἐρέσθαι μή τι βίαιον ἐξ Ἀλεξάνδρου αὐτῇ ἐς ὕβριν ξυνέβη· καὶ τὸν εὐνοῦχον ἐπομόσαντα φάναι ὅτι· ὦ βασιλεῦ, οὕτω τοι ὡς ἀπέλιπες ἔχει ἡ σὴ γυνή, καὶ Ἀλέξανδρος ἀνδρῶν ἄριστός τέ ἐστι καὶ σωφρονέσ-

3 τατος. ἐπὶ τοῖσδε ἀνατεῖναι Δαρεῖον ἐς τὸν

daughter of age to marry called Roxane,[1] and those
who served with Alexander [2] said that she was the
loveliest woman they had seen in Asia next to Darius'
wife, and that when Alexander saw her he fell in love
with her; despite his passion he was not ready to
violate her as a war captive, but did not think it
beneath him to take her in marriage. This was an 6
action of Alexander that I approve and do not censure.
As for Darius' wife, who was said to be the most
beautiful woman in Asia, either he felt no desire for
her or he controlled himself, young as he was and at
the very height of good fortune, when men act
violently: he respected and spared her, showing much
restraint as well as an ambition for good repute
which was not misplaced.[3]

20. There is indeed a story prevalent [1] that soon
after the battle of Issus between Darius and Alexander the eunuch in charge of Darius' wife escaped to
Darius. When Darius saw him, he first asked if his
daughters, wife and mother were alive. When he 2
learnt that they were, and had the title of queens,
and the same attendance as in Darius' court, he next
asked if his wife remained true to him. On learning
that she was, he enquired again whether she had been
outraged by Alexander. The eunuch replied on
his oath, ' Your wife, sir, is as you left her, and Alexander is the noblest and most self-controlled of men.'
Darius then stretched his hands to the heavens and 3

---

[1] QC. viii 4, 19 ff. (cf. P. 47, 4) does not connect the marriage
with Roxane and the capture of this rock (cf. 18, 4 n.), while
Strabo xi 11, 4 connects it with that of the rock of Sisimithres
(A. 21). The marriage may in fact be later, after Oxyartes'
submission, 20, 4, perhaps recorded by QC. in its due time.

[2] ' Vulgate '? More probably Pt./Ar.

[3] Cf. ii 12, 8 n.

[1] ' Vulgate '. Main sources again from § 4.

οὐρανὸν τὰς χεῖρας καὶ εὔξασθαι ὧδε· ἀλλ' ὦ Ζεῦ
βασιλεῦ, ὅτῳ ἐπιτέτραπται νέμειν τὰ βασιλέων
πράγματα ἐν ἀνθρώποις, σὺ νῦν μάλιστα μὲν ἐμοὶ
φύλαξον Περσῶν τε καὶ Μήδων τὴν ἀρχήν, ὥσπερ
οὖν καὶ ἔδωκας· εἰ δὲ δὴ ἐγὼ οὐκέτι σοι βασιλεὺς
τῆς Ἀσίας, σὺ δὲ μηδενὶ ἄλλῳ ὅτι μὴ Ἀλεξάνδρῳ
παραδοῦναι τὸ ἐμὸν κράτος. οὕτως οὐδὲ πρὸς τῶν
πολεμίων ἄρα ἀμελεῖται ὅσα σώφρονα ἔργα.

4   Ὀξυάρτης δὲ ἀκούσας τοὺς παῖδας ἐχομένους,
ἀκούσας δὲ καὶ ὑπὲρ Ῥωξάνης τῆς θυγατρὸς ὅτι
μέλει αὐτῆς Ἀλεξάνδρῳ, θαρσήσας ἀφίκετο παρὰ
Ἀλέξανδρον, καὶ ἦν ἐν τιμῇ παρ' αὐτῷ, ᾗπερ εἰκὸς
ἐπὶ ξυντυχίᾳ τοιαύτῃ.

21. Ἀλέξανδρος δέ, ὡς τὰ ἐν Σογδιανοῖς αὐτῷ
διεπέπρακτο, ἐχομένης ἤδη καὶ τῆς πέτρας ἐς
Παρειτάκας προὐχώρει, ὅτι καὶ ἐν Παρειτάκαις
χωρίον τι ὀχυρόν, ἄλλην πέτραν, κατέχειν ἐλέγοντο
πολλοὶ τῶν βαρβάρων. ἐκαλεῖτο δὲ αὕτη Χοριήνου
ἡ πέτρα· καὶ ἐς αὐτὴν αὐτός τε ὁ Χοριήνης
ξυμπεφεύγει καὶ ἄλλοι τῶν ὑπάρχων οὐκ ὀλίγοι.
2   ἦν δὲ τὸ μὲν ὕψος τῆς πέτρας ἐς σταδίους εἴκοσι,
κύκλος δὲ ἐς ἑξήκοντα· αὐτὴ δὲ ἀπότομος πάντοθεν, ἄνοδος δὲ ἐς αὐτὴν μία καὶ αὐτὴ στενή τε καὶ
οὐκ εὔπορος, οἷα δὴ παρὰ τὴν φύσιν τοῦ χωρίου
πεποιημένη, ὡς χαλεπὴ εἶναι καὶ μηδενὸς εἴργοντος
καὶ καθ' ἕνα ἀνελθεῖν, φάραγξ τε κύκλῳ περιεῖργε
τὴν πέτραν βαθεῖα, ὥστε ὅστις προσάξειν στρατιὰν
τῇ πέτρᾳ ἔμελλε, πολὺ πρόσθεν αὐτῷ τὴν φάραγγα
εἶναι χωστέον, ὡς ἐξ ὁμαλοῦ ὁρμᾶσθαι προσάγοντα
ἐς προσβολὴν τὸν στρατόν.

prayed in these terms: ' O Zeus the King, to whom
it has been given to order the affairs of Kings among
men, I beseech thee most of all to preserve my
sovereignty over Persians and Medes, as thou didst
grant it me; but if I am by your wish no longer to be
king of Asia, to give my power to none but Alexander.'
Thus even enemies are not indifferent to virtuous
acts.

When Oxyartes heard that his daughters were 4
captives, but also that Alexander was showing solici-
tude for his daughter Roxane, he ventured to come
to Alexander and was honourably treated by him, as
was appropriate on so happy an event.

21. After completing his work in Sogdiana, with
the rock now in his possession, Alexander advanced
to the Pareitacae, since many of the barbarians were
reported to be holding a strong place in their country,
another rock, called the Rock of Chorienes; Chorienes
himself and many other hyparchs had taken refuge
there.[1] The height of this rock was about twenty 2
stades,[2] its circuit about sixty; it was sheer on all
sides; there was only one way up to it, and this was
narrow and difficult, since it had been constructed
in defiance of the nature of the place, so that it was
hard, even without opposition, to ascend even in
single file. A deep ravine also protected the rock all
round, hence anyone who was going to bring an army
up to the rock would be obliged first to do much
filling up of the ravine, so as to start from level
ground when bringing up his force to the assault.

[1] Sisimithres in QC. viii 2, 19 ff. (who puts the episode late
in 328) and Strabo xi 11, 4; Chorienes was perhaps the official
title of this local chief (' hyparch '). P. 58 has an allusion.
[2] This can only mean 20 stades from foot to peak; it is not a
measurement of height (von Schwarz, App. VIII 2).

3 Ἀλλὰ καὶ ὡς Ἀλέξανδρος ἥπτετο τοῦ ἔργου·
οὕτως πάντα ᾤετο χρῆναι βατά τε αὐτῷ καὶ
ἐξαιρετέα εἶναι, ἐς τοσόνδε τόλμης τε καὶ εὐτυχίας
προκεχωρήκει. τέμνων δὴ τὰς ἐλάτας (πολλαὶ γὰρ
καὶ ὑπερύψηλοι ἐλάται ἦσαν ἐν κύκλῳ τοῦ ὄρους)
κλίμακας ἐκ τούτων ἐποίει, ὡς κάθοδον εἶναι ἐς τὴν
φάραγγα τῇ στρατιᾷ· οὐ γὰρ ἦν ἄλλως κατελθεῖν
4 ἐς αὐτήν. καὶ τὰς μὲν ἡμέρας αὐτὸς Ἀλέξανδρος
ἐφειστήκει τῷ ἔργῳ τὸ ἥμισυ τοῦ στρατοῦ ἔχων
ἐργαζόμενον, τὰς δὲ νύκτας ἐν μέρει οἱ σωματο-
φύλακες αὐτῷ εἰργάζοντο, Περδίκκας τε καὶ Λεοννάτος καὶ Πτολεμαῖος ὁ Λάγου, τῷ λοιπῷ μέρει
τῆς στρατιᾶς τριχῇ διανενεμημένῳ, ὅπερ αὐτῷ ἐς
τὴν νύκτα ἀπετέτακτο. ἤνυτον δὲ τῆς ἡμέρας οὐ
πλέον ἤπερ εἴκοσι πήχεις καὶ τῆς νυκτὸς ὀλίγον
ἀποδέον, καίτοι ξυμπάσης τῆς στρατιᾶς ἐργαζο-
μένης· οὕτω τό τε χωρίον ἄπορον ἦν καὶ τὸ ἔργον
5 ἐν αὐτῷ χαλεπόν. κατιόντες δ' ἐς τὴν φάραγγα
πασσάλους κατεπήγνυον ἐς τὸ ὀξύτατον τῆς
φάραγγος, διέχοντας ἀλλήλων ὅσον ξύμμετρον πρὸς
ἰσχύν τε καὶ ξυνοχὴν τῶν ἐπιβαλλομένων. ἐπέβαλ-
λον δὲ πλέγματα ἐκ λύγων εἰς γεφύρας μάλιστα
ἰδέαν, καὶ ταῦτα ξυνδοῦντες χοῦν ἄνωθεν ἐπεφόρουν, ὡς ἐξ ὁμαλοῦ γίγνεσθαι τῇ στρατιᾷ τὴν
πρόσοδον τὴν πρὸς τὴν πέτραν.
6 Οἱ δὲ βάρβαροι τὰ μὲν πρῶτα κατεφρόνουν ὡς
ἀπόρου πάντῃ τοῦ ἐγχειρήματος· ὡς δὲ τοξεύματα
ἤδη ἐς τὴν πέτραν ἐξικνεῖτο καὶ αὐτοὶ ἀδύνατοι
ἦσαν ἄνωθεν ἐξείργειν τοὺς Μακεδόνας (ἐπεποίητο
γὰρ αὐτοῖς προκαλύμματα πρὸς τὰ βέλη, ὡς ὑπ'
αὐτοῖς ἀβλαβῶς ἐργάζεσθαι) ἐκπλαγεὶς ὁ Χοριήνης
πρὸς τὰ γιγνόμενα κήρυκα πέμπει πρὸς Ἀλέ-

Even so, Alexander took the work in hand, as he 3 327
thought that no place should be beyond him to get B.C.
up to and capture, to such a point of daring and
success had he advanced.[3] So he felled the pines
(for there were many tall pines all round the mountain) and made ladders of them, to enable the army
to descend into the ravine, as there was no other
means to get down. By day Alexander himself 4
superintended the operations, keeping half his army
at work; by night his bodyguards worked in relays,
Perdiccas, Leonnatus and Ptolemy son of Lagus,
with the rest of the army, divided into three sections,
which he had assigned for the night work. By day-
time they could not complete more than twenty
cubits, at night rather less, even though all the army
was at work; so difficult was the ground, and so hard
the work there. They would first descend into the 5
ravine and fix stakes in its narrowest part, just so far
apart from one another that they could be strong
enough to bear and hold together the loads piled upon
them. They would then fix upon the stakes withies
plaited into wicker-work, very much in the shape of
a bridge, bind these closely together and heap earth
on them from above, so that the approach for the
troops to the rock might be on the level.

At first the tribesmen treated the enterprise with 6
contempt as wholly impracticable; but when at
length arrows began to find the range of the rock,
while they proved unable from above to interfere with
the Macedonians who had made screens against the
missiles, so as to work beneath them unharmed,
Chorienes was aghast at what was happening and
sent a herald to Alexander begging him to send

----

[3] Cf. ii 26, 3 n.   No doubt A. follows Pt. (cf. § 4).

ξανδρον, δεόμενος Ὀξυάρτην οἱ ἀναπέμψαι. καὶ
7 πέμπει Ὀξυάρτην Ἀλέξανδρος. ὁ δὲ ἀφικόμενος
πείθει Χοριήνην ἐπιτρέψαι Ἀλεξάνδρῳ αὑτόν τε
καὶ τὸ χωρίον. βίᾳ μὲν γὰρ οὐδὲν ὅ τι οὐχ ἁλωτὸν
εἶναι Ἀλεξάνδρῳ καὶ τῇ στρατιᾷ τῇ ἐκείνου, ἐς
πίστιν δὲ ἐλθόντος καὶ φιλίαν, . . .[1] τὴν πίστιν τε
καὶ δικαιότητα μεγαλωστὶ ἐπῄνει τοῦ βασιλέως, τά
τε ἄλλα καὶ τὸ αὐτοῦ ἐν πρώτοις ἐς βεβαίωσιν τοῦ
8 λόγου προφέρων. τούτοις πεισθεὶς ὁ Χοριήνης
αὐτός τε ἧκε παρ' Ἀλέξανδρον καὶ τῶν οἰκείων
τινὲς καὶ ἑταίρων αὐτοῦ. ἐλθόντι δὲ τῷ Χοριήνῃ
φιλάνθρωπά τε ἀποκρινάμενος καὶ πίστιν ἐς φιλίαν
δοὺς αὐτὸν μὲν κατέχει, πέμψαι δὲ κελεύει τῶν
συγκατελθόντων τινὰς αὐτῷ ἐς τὴν πέτραν τοὺς
9 κελεύσοντας ἐνδοῦναι τὸ χωρίον. καὶ ἐνδίδοται
ὑπὸ τῶν ξυμπεφευγότων, ὥστε καὶ αὐτὸς Ἀλέξανδρος ἀναλαβὼν τῶν ὑπασπιστῶν ἐς πεντακοσίους ἀνέβη κατὰ θέαν τῆς πέτρας, καὶ τοσούτου
ἐδέησεν ἀνεπιεικές τι ἐς τὸν Χοριήνην ἔργον
ἀποδείξασθαι, ὥστε καὶ αὐτὸ τὸ χωρίον ἐκεῖνο
ἐπιτρέπει Χοριήνῃ καὶ ὕπαρχον εἶναι ὅσωνπερ καὶ
πρόσθεν ἔδωκεν.
10 Ξυνέβη δὲ χειμῶνί τε κακοπαθῆσαι αὐτῷ τὴν
στρατιὰν πολλῆς χιόνος ἐπιπεσούσης ἐν τῇ πολιορκίᾳ καὶ ἅμα ἀπορίᾳ τῶν ἐπιτηδείων ἐπιέσθησαν.
ἀλλὰ Χοριήνης ἐς δίμηνον σιτία ἔφη δώσειν τῇ
στρατιᾷ καὶ ἔδωκεν σῖτόν τε καὶ οἶνον τῶν ἐν τῇ
πέτρᾳ ἀποθέτων κρέα τε ταριχηρὰ κατὰ σκηνήν.
καὶ ταῦτα δοὺς οὐκ ἔφασκεν ἀναλῶσαι τῶν παρε-
σκευασμένων ἐς τὴν πολιορκίαν οὐδὲ τὴν δεκάτην
μοῖραν. ἔνθεν ἐν τιμῇ μᾶλλον τῷ Ἀλεξάνδρῳ ἦν

[1] I agree with Krüger that there is a lacuna after φιλίαν.

Oxyartes [4] to him. Alexander complied, and when   7   327
Oxyartes arrived, he urged Chorienes to surrender   B.C.
himself and the stronghold to Alexander; there was
not a place in the world Alexander and his army
could not take by force, but if Chorienes tried his
good faith and friendship . . . He commended highly
the good faith and justice of the King, chiefly adducing his own treatment as proof of his contention.
Chorienes was persuaded by his words, and presented   8
himself to Alexander with some of his kinsfolk and
friends.   On his arrival Alexander gave him a
friendly reply and an assurance of his friendship,
retaining Chorienes himself, but telling him to send
some of those who came down with him to the rock
to order the stronghold to be given up.   And it was   9
surrendered by the refugees, so that Alexander
himself could actually take five hundred of the
hypaspists and go up to view the rock.   Far from
maltreating Chorienes, he even entrusted this very
stronghold to him and made him hyparch of the people
he had previously administered.

The army, as it happened, had suffered much in the   10
winter, a great deal of snow having fallen during the
siege, and they were also distressed by want of
provisions.   But Chorienes said he would furnish the
army with provisions for two months, gave them corn
and wine from the stores in the rock, and distributed
dried meat among the tents.[5]   After all these gifts
he said he had not used up even a tenth of what they
had laid in for the siege.   This made Alexander
regard him with the greater respect as a man who

[4] QC., ' Oxartes ', Oxyartes having not yet submitted!
[5] Cf. anecdote in QC. viii 4, 18 ff. in different context.

ὡς οὐ πρὸς βίαν μᾶλλον ἢ κατὰ γνώμην ἐνδοὺς τὴν πέτραν.

22. Ταῦτα δὲ καταπραξάμενος Ἀλέξανδρος αὐτὸς μὲν ἐς Βάκτρα ᾔει, Κρατερὸν δὲ τῶν ἑταίρων ἱππέας ἔχοντα ἑξακοσίους καὶ τῶν πεζῶν τήν τε αὐτοῦ τάξιν καὶ τὴν Πολυπέρχοντος καὶ Ἀττάλου καὶ τὴν Ἀλκέτα ἐπὶ Κατάνην τε καὶ Αὐστάνην ἐκπέμπει, οἳ δὴ μόνοι ἔτι ὑπελείποντο ἐν τῇ
2 Παρειτακηνῶν χώρᾳ ἀφεστηκότες. καὶ μάχης γενομένης πρὸς αὐτοὺς καρτερᾶς νικῶσιν οἱ ἀμφὶ Κρατερὸν τῇ μάχῃ· καὶ Κατάνης μὲν ἀποθνήσκει αὐτοῦ μαχόμενος, Αὐστάνης δὲ ξυλληφθεὶς ἀνήχθη παρ᾽ Ἀλέξανδρον· τῶν δὲ ξὺν αὐτοῖς βαρβάρων ἱππεῖς μὲν ἀπέθανον ἑκατὸν καὶ εἴκοσι, πεζοὶ δὲ ἀμφὶ τοὺς χιλίους πεντακοσίους. ταῦτα δὲ ὡς ἐπράχθη τοῖς ἀμφὶ Κρατερόν, καὶ οὗτοι ἐς Βάκτρα ἦσαν. καὶ ἐν Βάκτροις τὸ ἀμφὶ Καλλισθένην τε καὶ τοὺς παῖδας πάθημα Ἀλεξάνδρῳ ξυνηνέχθη.
3 Ἐκ Βάκτρων δὲ ἐξήκοντος ἤδη τοῦ ἦρος [1] ἀναλαβὼν τὴν στρατιὰν προὐχώρει ὡς ἐπ᾽ Ἰνδούς, Ἀμύνταν ἀπολιπὼν ἐν τῇ χώρᾳ τῶν Βακτρίων καὶ ξὺν αὐτῷ ἱππέας μὲν τρισχιλίους καὶ πεντακο-
4 σίους, πεζοὺς δὲ μυρίους. ὑπερβαλὼν δὲ τὸν Καύκασον ἐν δέκα ἡμέραις ἀφίκετο εἰς Ἀλεξάνδρειαν πόλιν τὴν κτισθεῖσαν ἐν Παραπαμισάδαις, ὅτε τὸ πρῶτον ἐπὶ Βάκτρων ἐστέλλετο. καὶ τὸν μὲν ὕπαρχον, ὅστις αὐτῷ ἐπὶ τῆς πόλεως τότε ἐτάχθη, παραλύει τῆς ἀρχῆς, ὅτι οὐ καλῶς ἐξηγεῖ-
5 σθαι ἔδοξε· προσκατοικίσας δὲ καὶ ἄλλους τῶν

---

[1] codd.: θέρους A. Fränkel. See historical note.

had given up the stronghold not so much under force as from free will.

22. After this achievement Alexander himself took the road to Bactra, but sent Craterus with six hundred of the Companion cavalry, his own battalion of the infantry and those of Polyperchon, Attalus and Alcetas against Catanes and Austanes, the only rebels left in Pareitacene. In a fierce battle with 2 them Craterus' troops won the day; Catanes perished on the field, Austanes was captured and brought before Alexander; of the barbarians who fought with them a hundred and twenty cavalry and about fifteen hundred foot perished.[1] After their success Craterus' force too made for Bactra, where Alexander's misfortune with Callisthenes and the pages occurred.[2]

Now that spring was ending, Alexander took his 3 force from Bactra and advanced towards India, leaving Amyntas in Bactria with three thousand and five hundred cavalry and ten thousand infantry.[3] Cross- 4 ing the Caucasus in ten days,[4] he arrived at Alexandria, the city he had founded in the district of the Parapamisadae during his first expedition to Bactra. The hyparch whom he had then put in charge of the city was now dismissed from his office, as he appeared to have governed badly. He settled in Alexandria 5

[1] QC. VIII 5, 1 f., giving Polyperchon (cf. 27, 5 n.) a separate mission.

[2] Strabo xi 11, 4 says that Callisthenes was ' arrested and imprisoned ' at Caryatae in Bactria.

[3] QC. does not mention the garrison. A. in turn is silent on the great revolt of this presumably mercenary force in 325 (D. 99, 5 f.; QC. ix 7); Amyntas is not mentioned in this connection and had been replaced as satrap at Al's death by Philippus (D. xviii 3, 3 etc.). Chronology: App. VIII 19. Emendation (reading ' summer ' for ' spring ') would remove a puzzle, but seems palaeographically too daring.

[4] Not by the same pass as in 329, Strabo xv 1, 26.

περιοίκων τε καὶ ὅσοι τῶν στρατιωτῶν ἀπόμαχοι
ἦσαν ἐς τὴν Ἀλεξάνδρειαν Νικάνορα μέν, ἕνα τῶν
ἑταίρων, τὴν πόλιν αὐτὴν κοσμεῖν ἐκέλευσε, σατράπην δὲ Τυρίεσπιν κατέστησε τῆς τε χώρας τῆς
Παραπαμισαδῶν καὶ τῆς ἄλλης ἔστε ἐπὶ τὸν
6 Κωφῆνα ποταμόν. ἀφικόμενος δὲ ἐς Νίκαιαν
πόλιν καὶ τῇ Ἀθηνᾷ θύσας προὐχώρει ὡς ἐπὶ τὸν
Κωφῆνα, προπέμψας κήρυκα ὡς Ταξίλην τε καὶ
τοὺς ἐπὶ τάδε τοῦ Ἰνδοῦ ποταμοῦ, κελεύσας
ἀπαντᾶν ὅπως ἂν ἑκάστοις προχωρῇ. καὶ Ταξίλης
τε καὶ οἱ ἄλλοι ὕπαρχοι ἀπήντων, δῶρα τὰ μέγιστα
παρ' Ἰνδοῖς νομιζόμενα κομίζοντες, καὶ τοὺς
ἐλέφαντας δώσειν ἔφασκον τοὺς παρὰ σφίσιν
ὄντας, ἀριθμὸν ἐς πέντε καὶ εἴκοσιν.
7 Ἔνθα δὴ διελὼν τὴν στρατιὰν Ἡφαιστίωνα μὲν
καὶ Περδίκκαν ἐκπέμπει ἐς τὴν Πευκελαῶτιν
χώραν ὡς ἐπὶ τὸν Ἰνδὸν ποταμόν, ἔχοντας τήν τε
Γοργίου τάξιν καὶ Κλείτου καὶ Μελεάγρου καὶ τῶν
ἑταίρων ἱππέων τοὺς ἡμίσεας καὶ τοὺς μισθοφόρους ἱππέας ξύμπαντας, προστάξας τά τε κατὰ
τὴν ὁδὸν χωρία ἢ βίᾳ ἐξαιρεῖν ἢ ὁμολογίᾳ παρ-
ίστασθαι καὶ ἐπὶ τὸν Ἰνδὸν ποταμὸν ἀφικομένους
παρασκευάζειν ὅσα ἐς τὴν διάβασιν τοῦ ποταμοῦ
ξύμφορα. ξὺν τούτοις δὲ καὶ Ταξίλης καὶ οἱ ἄλλοι
8 ὕπαρχοι στέλλονται. καὶ οὗτοι ὡς ἀφίκοντο πρὸς
τὸν Ἰνδὸν ποταμόν, ἔπρασσον ὅσα ἐξ Ἀλεξάνδρου
ἦν τεταγμένα. Ἄστις δὲ ὁ τῆς Πευκελαώτιδος
ὕπαρχος νεωτερίσας αὐτός τε ἀπόλλυται καὶ τὴν
πόλιν προσαπώλεσεν, ἐς ἥντινα ξυμπεφεύγει.

---

[5] For Alexandria and Nicaea see iii 28, 4 n.
[6] The river Kabul. See App. VIII 19 f. on chronology and
geography of all operations in the rest of this book.

more people from the neighbourhood together with all the soldiers unfit for fighting and ordered Nicanor, one of the Companions, to govern the city itself, while he appointed Tyriespis satrap of the country both of the Parapamisadae and of the land as far as the river Cophen.   Then after reaching Nicaea [5] and sacrificing to Athena, he advanced towards the Cophen,[6] having sent a herald in advance to Taxilas and the Indians on this side of the river Indus with orders to meet him, each at their earliest convenience; Taxilas and the other hyparchs [7] complied, bringing the gifts the Indians prize most, and promised to give him the elephants they had, twenty-five in number.

Here he divided his army, and sent Hephaestion and Perdiccas to the territory of Peucelaotis towards the river Indus, with the battalions of Gorgias, Clitus and Meleager, half of the Companion cavalry and all the mercenary cavalry, with instructions to take by storm or receive in surrender all towns on their march; when they had reached the Indus, they were to get everything ready for the crossing of the river.[8] Taxilas and the other hyparchs were sent with them. They arrived at the river Indus and carried out Alexander's instructions.   But Astis, the hyparch of the district of Peucelaotis, attempted revolt, and perished himself, besides involving in ruin the city to

[7] App. XV 2. Taxilas had submitted to Al. while in Sogdiana (D. 86, 4, cf. QC. viii 12, 5), probably in hope of aid against Porus, his old enemy (v 18, 7); he ruled at Taxila near Rawalpindi, Porus between Hydaspes (Jhelum) and Acesines (Chenab).   § 8 shows that Taxilas was supporting a rebel against the ruler of the Astaceni (capital, Charsadda), whose own ' revolt ' against Al. was probably provoked by fear of Taxilas.

[8] QC. viii 10, 2.   A. does not mention the mercenary foot, most Balkan troops and the mounted archers in either army.

6

8

ARRIAN

ἐξεῖλον γὰρ αὐτὴν ἐν τριάκοντα ἡμέραις προσκα-
θήμενοι οἱ ξὺν Ἡφαιστίωνι. καὶ αὐτὸς μὲν
Ἄστις ἀποθνήσκει, τῆς πόλεως δὲ ἐπιμελεῖσθαι
ἐτάχθη Σαγγαῖος, ὃς ἔτι πρόσθεν πεφευγὼς
Ἄστιν παρὰ Ταξίλην ηὐτομολήκει· καὶ τοῦτο ἦν
αὐτῷ τὸ πιστὸν πρὸς Ἀλέξανδρον.

23. Ἀλέξανδρος δέ, ἄγων τοὺς ὑπασπιστὰς καὶ
τῶν ἑταίρων ἱππέων ὅσοι μὴ σὺν Ἡφαιστίωνι
ἐτετάχατο καὶ τῶν ἀσθεταίρων [1] καλουμένων τὰς
τάξεις καὶ τοὺς τοξότας καὶ τοὺς Ἀγριᾶνας καὶ
τοὺς ἱππακοντιστάς, προὐχώρει ἐς τὴν Ἀσπ-
⟨ασ⟩ίων τε καὶ Γουραίων χώραν καὶ Ἀσσακηνῶν.
2 πορευθεὶς δὲ παρὰ τὸν Χόην καλούμενον ποταμὸν
ὀρεινήν τε ὁδὸν καὶ τραχεῖαν καὶ τοῦτον διαβὰς
χαλεπῶς τῶν μὲν πεζῶν τὸ πλῆθος βάδην ἔπεσθαί
οἱ ἐκέλευσεν, αὐτὸς δὲ ἀναλαβὼν τοὺς ἱππέας
ξύμπαντας καὶ τῶν πεζῶν τῶν Μακεδόνων ἐς
ὀκτακοσίους ἐπιβιβάσας τῶν ἵππων ξὺν ταῖς ἀσπίσι
ταῖς πεζικαῖς σπουδῇ ἦγεν, ὅτι τοὺς ταύτῃ οἰκοῦν-
τας βαρβάρους ξυμπεφευγέναι ἔς τε τὰ ὄρη τὰ
κατὰ τὴν χώραν ἐξηγγέλλετο αὐτῷ καὶ ἐς τὰς
3 πόλεις ὅσαι ὀχυραὶ αὐτῶν ἐς τὸ ἀπομάχεσθαι. καὶ
τούτων τῇ πρώτῃ καθ' ὁδὸν πόλει ᾠκισμένῃ
προσβαλὼν τοὺς μὲν πρὸ τῆς πόλεως τεταγμένους
ὡς εἶχεν ἐξ ἐφόδου ἐτρέψατο καὶ κατέκλεισεν ἐς
τὴν πόλιν, αὐτὸς δὲ τιτρώσκεται βέλει διὰ τοῦ
θώρακος ἐς τὸν ὦμον· τὸ δὲ τραῦμα οὐ χαλεπὸν
αὐτῷ ἐγένετο· ὁ γὰρ θώραξ ἔσχε τὸ μὴ οὐ διαμπὰξ
διὰ τοῦ ὤμου ἐλθεῖν τὸ βέλος· καὶ Πτολεμαῖος ὁ
Λάγου ἐτρώθη καὶ Λεοννάτος.

---

[1] πεϡεταίρων editors, but cf. Introd. n. 99.

327–6
B.C.

which he had fled for refuge; for Hephaestion and
his troops captured it after a siege of thirty days.
Astis himself was put to death and Sangaeus appointed to govern the city; he had previously escaped
from Astis and gone over to Taxilas; this guaranteed
his loyalty to Alexander.

23. Taking the hypaspists, all the Companion
cavalry not detailed with Hephaestion, and the
battalions of the so-called *asthetairoi*,[1] with the
archers, Agrianians, and mounted javelin-men,[2]
Alexander advanced to the district of the Aspasians,
Guraeans and Assacenians.[3] After marching along 2
the river called Cheos by a mountainous, rough route,
and crossing the river with some difficulty, he ordered
the infantry force to follow him at marching pace,
while he took all the cavalry himself with about eight
hundred of the Macedonian foot-soldiers, whom he
had mounted, with their infantry shields, and moved
at full speed, as he had learnt that the barbarians
living here had fled for refuge to the hills of the district and to the cities which were their defensive
strongholds. Attacking the first of these cities 3
which was built on his route without making preparations, he put to flight the forces drawn up in front of
the city and at the first onslaught shut them up in the
city, though he himself received an arrow wound
through the corselet in his shoulder. (The wound
caused him little trouble, for the breastplate prevented the dart passing right through the shoulder.)
Ptolemy son of Lagus and Leonnatus were also
wounded.

[1] Introd. n. 99
[2] Introd. § 59.
[3] QC. viii 10 f. recounts operations described in rest of
this book, with variants, mostly of small value.

4 Τότε μὲν δὴ ἵνα ἐπιμαχώτατον τοῦ τείχους
ἐφαίνετο ἐστρατοπεδεύσατο πρὸς τῇ πόλει· τῇ δὲ
ὑστεραίᾳ ὑπὸ τὴν ἕω, διπλοῦν γὰρ τεῖχος περιεβέβλητο τῇ πόλει, ἐς μὲν τὸ πρῶτον ἅτε οὐκ
ἀκριβῶς τετειχισμένον οὐ χαλεπῶς ἐβιάσαντο οἱ
Μακεδόνες, πρὸς δὲ τῷ δευτέρῳ ὀλίγον ἀντισχόντες
οἱ βάρβαροι, ὡς αἵ τε κλίμακες προσέκειντο ἤδη
καὶ ὑπὸ τῶν βελῶν πάντοθεν ἐτιτρώσκοντο οἱ
προμαχόμενοι, οὐκ ἔμειναν, ἀλλὰ κατὰ τὰς πύλας
5 ὡς ἐπὶ τὰ ὄρη ἐκπίπτουσιν ἐκ τῆς πόλεως. καὶ
τούτων οἱ μὲν ἐν τῇ φυγῇ ἀποθνήσκουσιν, ὅσους δὲ
ζῶντας ἔλαβον αὐτῶν, ξύμπαντας ἀποκτείνουσιν οἱ
Μακεδόνες, ὅτι ἐτρώθη ὑπ' αὐτῶν 'Αλέξανδρος
ὀργιζόμενοι· οἱ πολλοὶ δὲ ἐς τὰ ὄρη, ὅτι οὐ
μακρὰν τῆς πόλεως τὰ ὄρη ἦν, ἀπέφυγον. τὴν
πόλιν δὲ κατασκάψας ἐς "Ανδακα ἄλλην πόλιν ἦγε.
ταύτην δὲ ὁμολογίᾳ ἐνδοθεῖσαν κατασχὼν Κρατερὸν
μὲν ξὺν τοῖς ἄλλοις ἡγεμόσι τῶν πεζῶν καταλείπει
αὐτοῦ ἐξαιρεῖν ὅσαι ἂν ἄλλαι πόλεις μὴ ἑκοῦσαι
προσχωρῶσι καὶ τὰ κατὰ τὴν χώραν ὅπως ξυμφο-
ρώτατον ἐς τὰ παρόντα κοσμεῖν.

24. Αὐτὸς δὲ ἄγων τοὺς ὑπασπιστάς τε καὶ τοὺς
τοξότας καὶ τοὺς 'Αγριᾶνας καὶ τὴν Κοίνου τε καὶ
'Αττάλου τάξιν καὶ τῶν ἱππέων τὸ ἄγημα καὶ τῶν
ἄλλων ἑταίρων ἐς τέσσαρας μάλιστα ἱππαρχίας καὶ
τῶν ἱπποτοξοτῶν τοὺς ἡμίσεας ὡς ἐπὶ τὸν ποταμὸν
τὸν † Εὔασ . . . πόλεως προὐχώρει, ἵνα ὁ τῶν
'Ασπασίων ὕπαρχος ἦν· καὶ διελθὼν πολλὴν ὁδὸν
2 δευτεραῖος ἀφίκετο πρὸς τὴν πόλιν. οἱ δὲ βάρβαροι

---

⁴ QC. 10, 3–6 makes Al. defer attack till Craterus arrived
with the foot, and order the massacre. He then inserts the
surrender of Nysa, see A. v 1 ff.

Alexander then placed his camp by the city where 4   327–6 the wall appeared easiest to assault, and next day B.C. about dawn, there being a double wall about the city, the Macedonians easily forced their way through the first, as it had not been built with care; at the second wall the barbarians made a short stand, yet once the ladders had been put up and the defenders were being wounded on all sides by the missiles, they did not stand their ground, but came tumbling out of the city by the gates in the direction of the hills. Some 5 of them perished in the flight, and the Macedonians killed all they captured alive, out of anger that they had wounded Alexander; however, most of them escaped to the hills, as they were not far from the city.[4] Alexander razed the city to the ground and went on to another named Andaca. When it had surrendered on terms and was in his possession, he left Craterus there with the other infantry commanders to destroy any other cities that did not come over of their free will, and to make the arrangements in the country most advantageous for the time being.

24. He himself took the hypaspists, archers, and Agrianians, with Coenus' and Attalus' battalions, the *agêma* of cavalry and other Companions up to about four hipparchies[1] and half the mounted archers, and advanced towards the river . . . a city[2] where the hyparch of the Aspasians was; after a long road-march, he reached the city on the second day. When the barbarians learned of Alexander's 2

[1] Introd. 58–60.
[2] In the lacuna the letters ' Euas . . .' may belong to the name of a river or a city.

προσάγοντα αἰσθόμενοι Ἀλέξανδρον ἐμπρήσαντες
τὴν πόλιν ἔφευγον πρὸς τὰ ὄρη. οἱ δ' ἀμφ'
Ἀλέξανδρον εἴχοντο τῶν φευγόντων ἔστε ἐπὶ τὰ
ὄρη, καὶ φόνος πολὺς γίγνεται τῶν βαρβάρων, πρὶν
ἐς τὰς δυσχωρίας φθάσαι ἀπελθόντας.

3 Τὸν δὲ ἡγεμόνα αὐτὸν τῶν ταύτῃ Ἰνδῶν Πτολεμαῖος ὁ Λάγου πρός τινι ἤδη γηλόφῳ ὄντα κατιδὼν
καὶ τῶν ὑπασπιστῶν ἔστιν οὓς ἀμφ' αὐτὸν ξὺν πολὺ
ἐλάττοσιν αὐτὸς ὢν ὅμως ἐδίωκεν ἔτι ἐκ τοῦ ἵππου·
ὡς δὲ χαλεπὸς ὁ γήλοφος τῷ ἵππῳ ἀναδραμεῖν ἦν,
τοῦτον μὲν αὐτοῦ καταλείπει παραδούς τινι τῶν
ὑπασπιστῶν ἄγειν, αὐτὸς δὲ ὡς εἶχε πεζὸς τῷ
4 Ἰνδῷ εἵπετο. ὁ δὲ ὡς πελάζοντα ἤδη κατεῖδε τὸν
Πτολεμαῖον, αὐτός τε μεταβάλλει ἐς τὸ ἔμπαλιν καὶ
οἱ ὑπασπισταὶ ξὺν αὐτῷ. καὶ ὁ μὲν Ἰνδὸς τοῦ
Πτολεμαίου διὰ τοῦ θώρακος παίει ἐκ χειρὸς ἐς τὸ
στῆθος ξυστῷ μακρῷ, καὶ ὁ θώραξ ἔσχε τὴν
πληγήν· Πτολεμαῖος δὲ τὸν μηρὸν διαμπὰξ βαλὼν
5 τοῦ Ἰνδοῦ καταβάλλει τε καὶ σκυλεύει αὐτόν. ὡς
δὲ τὸν ἡγεμόνα σφῶν κείμενον οἱ ἀμφ' αὐτὸν εἶδον,
οὗτοι μὲν οὐκέτι ἔμενον, οἱ δὲ ἐκ τῶν ὀρῶν αἱρό-
μενον τὸν νεκρὸν τοῦ ὑπάρχου ἰδόντες πρὸς τῶν
πολεμίων ἤλγησάν τε καὶ καταδραμόντες ξυν-
άπτουσιν ἐπ' αὐτῷ μάχην καρτερὰν πρὸς τῷ
γηλόφῳ. ἤδη γὰρ καὶ Ἀλέξανδρος ἔχων τοὺς ἀπὸ
τῶν ἵππων καταβεβηκότας πεζοὺς πρὸς τῷ γηλόφῳ
ἦν. καὶ οὗτοι ἐπιγενόμενοι μόγις ἐξέωσαν τοὺς
Ἰνδοὺς ἐς τὰ ὄρη καὶ τοῦ νεκροῦ ἐκράτησαν.

6 Ὑπερβαλὼν δὲ τὰ ὄρη Ἀλέξανδρος ἐς πόλιν
κατῆλθεν, ᾗ ὄνομα ἦν Ἀριγαῖον· καὶ ταύτην καταλαμβάνει ἐμπεπρησμένην ὑπὸ τῶν ἐνοικούντων καὶ
τοὺς ἀνθρώπους πεφευγότας. ἐνταῦθα δὲ ἀφίκοντο

approach, they burned the city and fled to the
mountains.   Alexander's troops followed close on the
fugitives as far as the mountains, and there was a
great slaughter of the barbarians, until they got away
first into the rough country.[3]

The actual leader of the Indians of this district was 3
observed by Ptolemy son of Lagus, already close to
a foothill; Ptolemy had with him some of the hypaspists, and though far inferior in numbers, he still
continued to pursue him on horse, but as the hill was
hard for his horse to go up, he left his mount there,
handing it to one of the hypaspists to lead, and in
person followed the Indian on foot, just as he was.
When the Indian saw Ptolemy drawing near, he him- 4
self turned round at bay, and his hypaspists with him,
and with his long spear struck at close quarters
through Ptolemy's corselet to his breast; the corselet
checked the blow.   But Ptolemy drove right through
the Indian's thigh, and felled and despoiled him.
While his followers, on seeing their leader lying there, 5
did not continue to stand their ground, others from
the hills, seeing the enemy carrying off their hyparch's
body, rushed down in their distress and joined in a
fierce battle near the hill.   Now Alexander was already near the hill with his infantry dismounted.
When they came on the scene they pushed the
Indians back to the mountains, though with difficulty,
and got possession of the body.

After crossing the hills, Alexander descended at a 6
city called Arigaeum and found that it had been set
on fire by its inhabitants; and that the people had

[3] At least the following story must be from Pt.

αὐτῷ καὶ οἱ ἀμφὶ Κρατερὸν ξὺν τῇ στρατιᾷ πεπραγμένων σφίσι ξυμπάντων ὅσα ὑπὸ τοῦ βασιλέως
7 ἐτέτακτο. ταύτην μὲν δὴ τὴν πόλιν, ὅτι ἐν
ἐπικαίρῳ χωρίῳ ἐδόκει ᾠκίσθαι, ἐκτειχίσαι τε
προστάσσει Κρατερῷ καὶ ξυνοικίσαι ἐς αὐτὴν τούς
τε προσχώρους ὅσοι ἐθελονταί καὶ εἰ δή τινες
ἀπόμαχοι τῆς στρατιᾶς. αὐτὸς δὲ προὐχώρει ἵνα
ξυμπεφευγέναι ἐπυνθάνετο τοὺς πολλοὺς τῶν ταύτῃ
βαρβάρων. ἐλθὼν δὲ πρός τι ὄρος κατεστρατοπέδευσεν ὑπὸ ταῖς ὑπωρείαις τοῦ ὄρους.

8 Καὶ ἐν τούτῳ Πτολεμαῖος ὁ Λάγου ἐκπεμφθεὶς
μὲν ὑπὸ Ἀλεξάνδρου ἐς προνομήν, προελθὼν δὲ
προσωτέρω αὐτὸς ξὺν ὀλίγοις ὡς ἐς κατασκοπήν,
ἀπαγγέλλει Ἀλεξάνδρῳ πυρὰ κατιδεῖν τῶν βαρβάρων πλείονα ἢ ἐν τῷ Ἀλεξάνδρου στρατοπέδῳ.
9 καὶ Ἀλέξανδρος τῷ μὲν πλήθει τῶν πυρῶν ἠπί-
στησεν, εἶναι δέ τι ξυνεστηκὸς τῶν ταύτῃ βαρβάρων αἰσθόμενος μέρος μὲν τῆς στρατιᾶς αὐτοῦ
καταλείπει πρὸς τῷ ὄρει ὡς εἶχον ἐστρατοπεδευ-
μένους· αὐτὸς δὲ ἀναλαβὼν ὅσοι ἀποχρῶντες ἐς τὰ
ἀπηγγελμένα ἐφαίνοντο, ὡς πλησίον ἤδη ἀφεώρων
10 τὰ πυρά, τρίχα διανέμει τὴν στρατιάν. καὶ τῷ μὲν
ἑνὶ ἐπέταξε Λεοννάτον τὸν σωματοφύλακα, ξυντάξας αὐτῷ τήν τε Ἀττάλου καὶ τὴν Βαλάκρου
τάξιν· τὴν δευτέραν δὲ μοῖραν Πτολεμαίῳ τῷ
Λάγου ἄγειν ἔδωκε, τῶν τε ὑπασπιστῶν τῶν βασιλικῶν τὸ τρίτον μέρος καὶ τὴν Φιλίππου καὶ
Φιλώτα τάξιν καὶ δύο χιλιαρχίας τῶν τοξοτῶν καὶ
τοὺς Ἀγριᾶνας καὶ τῶν ἱππέων τοὺς ἡμίσεας· τὴν
δὲ τρίτην μοῖραν αὐτὸς ἦγεν ἵνα οἱ πλεῖστοι τῶν
βαρβάρων ἐφαίνοντο.

25. Οἱ δὲ ὡς ᾔσθοντο προσάγοντας τοὺς Μακε-

327–6
B.C.

fled.   Here he was met by Craterus and his colleagues
with the army, after they had carried out all Alexander's instructions.[4]   As this city seemed to be on 7
a favourable site for a settlement, he instructed
Craterus to fortify it and to bring into the place as
settlers any volunteers from the neighbouring people
and any soldiers unfit for service.[5]   He himself
advanced where he was told most of the barbarians
of the region had taken refuge; and reaching the
mountain he camped there at its foot.

At this time Ptolemy son of Lagus,[6] who had been 8
sent foraging by Alexander, and had himself advanced further ahead with a few others to scout,
reported to Alexander that he had sighted barbarian
fires more numerous than in Alexander's camp.
Alexander was incredulous about the number of the 9
fires, but realizing that there was a concentration of
barbarians who belonged to this region, he left part
of his army behind, encamped as they were by the
hill, and himself taking what appeared to be a
number sufficient in view of this report, divided his
men into three parts as soon as they saw the fires
close at hand.   He put Leonnatus the bodyguard in 10
command of one, assigning him the battalions of
Attalus and Balacrus; the second, consisting of a
third of the hypaspists, the battalions of Philip and
Philotas, and two chiliarchies of archers, the Agrianians
and half the cavalry, was placed under Ptolemy son
of Lagus, while he himself led the third division,
where the greatest number of the barbarians appeared to be.

25. When they saw the Macedonians approach,

---

[4] Cf. 23, 5.
[5] Cf. iii 1, 5 n.   Tarn ii 248 is perverse.
[6] Pt. again the source at least till 25, 4.

δόνας, κατεῖχον γὰρ χωρία ὑπερδέξια, τῷ τε
πλήθει σφῶν θαρσήσαντες καὶ τῶν Μακεδόνων, ὅτι
ὀλίγοι ἐφαίνοντο, καταφρονήσαντες ἐς τὸ πεδίον
ὑποκατέβησαν· καὶ μάχη γίγνεται καρτερά. ἀλλὰ
2 τούτους μὲν οὐ ξὺν πόνῳ ἐνίκα ᾿Αλέξανδρος· οἱ δὲ
ἀμφὶ Πτολεμαῖον οὐκ ἐν τῷ ὁμαλῷ παρετάξαντο,
ἀλλὰ γήλοφον γὰρ κατεῖχον οἱ βάρβαροι, ὀρθίους
ποιήσαντας¹ τοὺς λόχους Πτολεμαῖος προσῆγεν
ᾗπερ ἐπιμαχ[ιμ]ώτατον τοῦ λόφου ἐφαίνετο, οὐ
πάντη τὸν λόφον κυκλωσάμενος, ἀλλ᾿ ἀπολιπών, εἰ
φεύγειν ἐθέλοιεν οἱ βάρβαροι, χώραν αὐτοῖς ἐς τὴν
3 φυγήν. καὶ γίγνεται καὶ τούτοις μάχη καρτερὰ
τοῦ χωρίου τῇ χαλεπότητι καὶ ὅτι οὐ κατὰ τοὺς
ἄλλους τοὺς ταύτῃ βαρβάρους οἱ ᾿Ινδοί, ἀλλὰ πολὺ
δή τι ἀλκιμώτατοι τῶν προσχώρων εἰσίν. ἐξώ-
σθησαν δὲ καὶ οὗτοι ἀπὸ τοῦ ὄρους ὑπὸ τῶν
Μακεδόνων· καὶ οἱ ἀμφὶ Λεοννάτον τῇ τρίτῃ μοίρᾳ
τῆς στρατιᾶς ὡσαύτως ἔπραξαν· ἐνίκων γὰρ καὶ
4 οὗτοι τοὺς κατὰ σφᾶς. καὶ λέγει Πτολεμαῖος
ἀνθρώπους μὲν ληφθῆναι τοὺς πάντας ὑπὲρ τετρακισμυρίους, βοῶν δὲ ὑπὲρ τὰς τρεῖς καὶ εἴκοσι
μυριάδας· καὶ τούτων τὰς καλλίστας ἐπιλεξάμενον
᾿Αλέξανδρον, ὅτι διαφέρουσαι αὐτῷ κάλλει τε καὶ
μεγέθει ἐφαίνοντο, πέμψαι ἐθέλειν ἐς Μακεδονίαν
ἐργάζεσθαι τὴν χώραν.
5   ᾿Εντεῦθεν ἐπὶ τὴν τῶν ᾿Ασσακηνῶν χώραν ἦγεν·
τούτους γὰρ ἐξηγγέλλετο παρεσκευάσθαι ὡς μαχουμένους, ἱππέας μὲν ἐς δισχιλίους ἔχοντας,
πεζοὺς δὲ ὑπὲρ τοὺς τρισμυρίους, τριάκοντα δὲ
ἐλέφαντας. Κρατερὸς μὲν δὴ ἐκτετειχικὼς ἤδη

¹ Reiske: ποιήσαντες codd.; Roos.

for they were occupying a commanding position, confident in their numbers and despising the Macedonians, as they appeared to be few, they descended below to the plain; a fierce battle followed. Still Alexander defeated them without much difficulty. Ptolemy's troops marshalled themselves on uneven 2 ground, but as the barbarians were holding a hill, they formed into columns, and Ptolemy led them up to the point where the hill seemed most open to assault, not surrounding it on all sides, but leaving a space for flight, in case the barbarians chose to flee. Here too the battle was fierce, both because of the 3 difficulty of the position and because these Indians were not like the other barbarians of these parts but much the most warlike people of the region. But even they were pushed off the hill by the Macedonians. Leonnatus and his troops in the third division of the army were equally successful; they too defeated their opponents. Ptolemy says that over 4 forty thousand men in all and over two hundred and thirty thousand oxen were captured and that Alexander selected the finest oxen because he thought them of unusual beauty and size and wished to send them into Macedonia to work the soil.

Thence he proceeded to the territory of the 5 Assacenians,[1] who were reported to have prepared for battle with some two thousand horsemen, over thirty thousand infantry, and thirty elephants. Craterus,

---

[1] By implication previous operations had been against the Aspasians (23, 1), no opposition being recorded from Guraeans.

τὴν πόλιν, ἐφ' ἧς τῷ οἰκισμῷ κατελέλειπτο, τούς τε
βαρύτερον ὡπλισμένους τῆς στρατιᾶς Ἀλεξάνδρῳ
ἦγεν καὶ τὰς μηχανάς, εἴ που πολιορκίας δεήσειεν.
6 αὐτὸς δὲ Ἀλέξανδρος τούς τε ἑταίρους ἱππέας
ἄγων καὶ τοὺς ἱππακοντιστὰς καὶ τὴν Κοίνου καὶ
Πολυπέρχοντος τάξιν καὶ τοὺς Ἀγριᾶνας τοὺς
χιλίους [1] καὶ τοὺς τοξότας ᾔει ὡς ἐπὶ τοὺς Ἀσ-
7 σακηνούς· ἦγε δὲ διὰ τῆς Γουραίων χώρας. καὶ
τὸν ποταμὸν τὸν ἐπώνυμον τῆς χώρας τὸν Γουραῖον
χαλεπῶς διέβη, διὰ βαθύτητά τε καὶ ὅτι ὀξὺς ὁ
ῥοῦς ἦν αὐτῷ καὶ οἱ λίθοι στρογγύλοι ἐν τῷ
ποταμῷ ὄντες σφαλεροὶ τοῖς ἐπιβαίνουσιν ἐγίγνοντο. οἱ δὲ βάρβαροι ὡς προσάγοντα ᾔσθοντο
Ἀλέξανδρον, ἀθρόοι μὲν ἐς μάχην καταστῆναι οὐκ
ἐτόλμησαν, διαλυθέντες δὲ ὡς ἕκαστοι κατὰ πόλεις
ταύτας ἐπενόουν ἀπομαχόμενοι διασώζειν.

26. Καὶ Ἀλέξανδρος πρῶτα μὲν ἐπὶ Μάσσαγα
ἦγε, τὴν μεγίστην τῶν ταύτῃ πόλεων. ὡς δὲ
προσῆγεν ἤδη τοῖς τείχεσι, θαρρήσαντες οἱ βάρβαροι τοῖς μισθοφόροις τοῖς ἐκ τῶν πρόσω Ἰνδῶν,
ἦσαν γὰρ οὗτοι ἐς ἑπτακισχιλίους, ὡς στρατοπε-
δευομένους εἶδον τοὺς Μακεδόνας, δρόμῳ ἐπ'
2 αὐτοὺς ᾔεσαν. καὶ Ἀλέξανδρος ἰδὼν πλησίον τῆς
πόλεως ἐσομένην τὴν μάχην προσωτέρω ἐκκαλέ-
σασθαι αὐτοὺς βουληθεὶς τῶν τειχῶν, ὡς εἰ τροπὴ
γίγνοιτο, ἐγίγνωσκεν γὰρ ἐσομένην, μὴ δι' ὀλίγου
ἐς τὴν πόλιν καταφυγόντες εὐμαρῶς διασώζοιντο,
ὡς ἐκθέοντας εἶδε τοὺς βαρβάρους, μεταβαλλομέ-
νους κελεύει τοὺς Μακεδόνας ὀπίσω ἀποχωρεῖν ὡς

---

[1] codd.; Roos. Others write καὶ τοὺς ψιλοὺς (cf. IV 30, 6)
or ἐς χιλίους. See historical note.

who had finished fortifying the city of whose settlement he had been left in charge, brought Alexander
the heavier armed troops of the army with the siege
engines, in case a siege proved necessary. Alexander **6**
marched himself with the Companion cavalry, the
mounted javelin-men, the battalions of Coenus and
Polyperchon, the thousand Agrianians,[2] and the
archers, towards the Assacenians through the country
of the Guraeans. He crossed the river Guraeus[3] **7**
(which shares its name with the country) with difficulty, because of its depth and rapid current, and the
rounded stones in the river proved slippery to step
on. But when the barbarians became aware of his
approach, they dared not take their stand in mass
for a battle, but dispersed to their own cities with the
intention of securing the defence and safety of each.

26. Alexander marched first against Massaga, the
greatest city of the region. When he was already
close to the walls, the barbarians, relying on mercenary Indians brought from further India, about seven
thousand men,[1] charged the Macedonians at the
double as soon as they saw them pitching camp.
Alexander who had seen that the battle would be **2**
near the city, wished to entice them out further from
their walls, so that if a rout took place (and he was
sure it would) they should not have their city close at
hand for refuge and easily escape, and as soon as he
saw the barbarians sallying out, he ordered the

---

[2] Hardly more than 500 in 334 B.C. (Introd. 56), but 1,000
in 331/30 B.C. (QC. v 3, 6), they must have been reinforced by
'Thracians' (Berve i 137 ff.). Cf. Introd. 65. But the text is
suspect (see critical note).

[3] Panjkora or Landai (united Panjkora-Swat river).

[1] QC. viii 10, 23 gives 38,000 foot, probably referring to
the whole Assacenian force, cf. 24, 5–7 above; his story of the
siege, 10, 26–36, is incompatible with A's.

πρὸς γήλοφόν τινα ἀπέχοντα ἀπὸ τοῦ χωρίου,
ἵναπερ στρατοπεδεύειν ἐγνώκει, ἑπτά που μάλιστα
3 σταδίους. καὶ οἱ πολέμιοι ἀναθαρσήσαντες, ὡς
ἐγκεκλικότων ἤδη τῶν Μακεδόνων, δρόμῳ τε καὶ
ξὺν οὐδενὶ κόσμῳ ἐφέροντο ἐς αὐτούς. ὡς δὲ
ἐξικνεῖτο ἤδη τὰ τοξεύματα, ἐνταῦθα Ἀλέξανδρος
ἀπὸ ξυνθήματος ἐπιστρέψας ἐς αὐτοὺς τὴν φάλαγγα
4 δρόμῳ ἀντεπῆγε. πρῶτοι δὲ οἱ ἱππακοντισταί τε
αὐτῷ καὶ οἱ Ἀγριᾶνες καὶ οἱ τοξόται ἐκδραμόντες
ξυνέμιξαν τοῖς βαρβάροις· αὐτὸς δὲ τὴν φάλαγγα
ἐν τάξει ἦγεν. οἱ δὲ Ἰνδοὶ τῷ τε παραλόγῳ
ἐκπλαγέντες καὶ ἅμα ἐν χερσὶ γεγενημένης τῆς
μάχης ἐγκλίναντες ἔφευγον ἐς τὴν πόλιν. καὶ
ἀπέθανον μὲν αὐτῶν ἀμφὶ τοὺς διακοσίους, οἱ δὲ
λοιποὶ ἐς τὰ τείχη κατεκλείσθησαν. καὶ Ἀλέξανδρος προσῆγε τῷ τείχει τὴν φάλαγγα, καὶ ἐντεῦθεν
τοξεύεται μὲν ἀπὸ τοῦ τείχους ἐς τὸ σφυρὸν οὐ
5 χαλεπῶς. ἐπαγαγὼν δὲ τὰς μηχανὰς τῇ ὑστεραίᾳ
τῶν μὲν τειχῶν τι εὐμαρῶς κατέσεισε, βιαζομένους
δὲ ταύτῃ τοὺς Μακεδόνας ᾗ παρέρρηκτο τοῦ τείχους οὐκ ἀτόλμως οἱ Ἰνδοὶ ἠμύνοντο, ὥστε ταύτῃ
μὲν τῇ ἡμέρᾳ ἀνεκαλέσατο τὴν στρατιάν. τῇ δὲ
ὑστεραίᾳ τῶν τε Μακεδόνων αὐτῶν ἡ προσβολὴ
καρτερωτέρα ἐγίγνετο καὶ πύργος ἐπήχθη ξύλινος
τοῖς τείχεσιν, ὅθεν ἐκτοξεύοντες οἱ τοξόται καὶ
βέλη ἀπὸ μηχανῶν ἀφιέμενα ἀνέστελλεν ἐπὶ πολὺ
τοὺς Ἰνδούς. ἀλλ' οὐδὲ ὡς βιάσασθαι εἴσω τοῦ
τείχους οἷοί τε ἐγένοντο.

6 Τῇ δὲ τρίτῃ προσαγαγὼν αὖθις τὴν φάλαγγα καὶ
ἀπὸ μηχανῆς γέφυραν ἐπιβαλὼν τοῦ τείχους ᾗ
παρερρωγὸς ἦν, ταύτῃ ἐπῆγε τοὺς ὑπασπιστάς,
οἵπερ αὐτῷ καὶ Τύρον ὡσαύτως ἐξεῖλον. πολλῶν

327–6
B.C.

Macedonians to turn right about and withdraw
towards a hill, just about seven stades away from the
place where he had decided to camp. Emboldened 3
by the belief that the Macedonians had already given
way, the enemy rushed on them at full speed and in
disorder. When the arrows were just reaching his
troops, Alexander wheeled his phalanx towards them
by a signal and led it on at the double. The mounted 4
javelin-men, the Agrianians and the archers first
dashed forward and joined battle with the barbarians,
while Alexander himself kept the phalanx in formation. The Indians were appalled at what they had
never reckoned on, and as soon as it had come to
hand to hand fighting, they turned and fled to the
city. Some two hundred perished, but the rest were
shut up inside their walls. Alexander brought up
his phalanx to the wall, and was then wounded in his
ankle by an arrow from the wall, but not seriously.
Next day he brought up the engines and easily 5
destroyed a part of the walls; the Macedonians
pressed in at the breach made, but the Indians resisted bravely, and so that day Alexander recalled his
troops. On the next the Macedonian attack was
stronger, and a wooden tower was brought up against
the walls, from which the archers shot volleys, while
the engines hurled missiles; they pushed the Indians
a long way back, but even so they could not force
their way inside the wall.

However, on the third day Alexander brought up 6
the phalanx and threw a bridge from an engine on to
the breach in the wall, over which he led the hypaspists, who had helped him in the same way to capture

δὲ ὑπὸ προθυμίας ὠθουμένων ἄχθος λαβοῦσα μεῖζον
ἢ γέφυρα κατερράγη καὶ πίπτουσι ξὺν αὐτῇ οἱ
7 Μακεδόνες. οἱ δὲ βάρβαροι ἰδόντες τὸ γιγνόμενον
λίθοις τε ξὺν βοῇ ἀπὸ τῶν τειχῶν καὶ τοξεύμασι
καὶ ἄλλῳ ὅτῳ τις μετὰ χεῖρας ἔχων ἐτύγχανεν ἢ
ὅτῳ τις ἐν τῷ τότε ἔλαβεν ἐξηκόντιζον ἐς τοὺς
Μακεδόνας· οἱ δὲ καὶ κατὰ θύρας, αἵτινες αὐτοῖς
κατὰ τὰ μεσοπύργια μικραὶ ἦσαν, ἐκθέοντες ἐκ
χειρὸς ἔπαιον τεταραγμένους.

27. Ἀλέξανδρος δὲ πέμπει Ἀλκέταν ξὺν τῇ
αὐτοῦ τάξει τούς τε κατατετρωμένους ἀναλαβεῖν
καὶ ὅσοι προσεμάχοντο ἐπανακαλέσασθαι ὡς ἐπὶ τὸ
στρατόπεδον. καὶ τῇ τετάρτῃ ὡσαύτως ἀπ᾽ ἄλλης
μηχανῆς ἄλλη ἐπιβάθρα αὐτῷ προσήγετο πρὸς τὸ
τεῖχος.

2 Καὶ οἱ Ἰνδοί, ἕως μὲν αὐτοῖς ὁ ἡγεμὼν τοῦ
χωρίου περιῆν, ἀπεμάχοντο καρτερῶς· ὡς δὲ βέλει
ἀπὸ μηχανῆς τυπεὶς ἀποθνήσκει ἐκεῖνος, αὐτῶν τε
οἱ μέν τινες πεπτωκότες ἐν τῇ ξυνεχεῖ πολιορκίᾳ,
οἱ πολλοὶ δὲ τραυματίαι τε καὶ ἄπομαχοι ἦσαν,
3 ἐπεκηρυκεύοντο πρὸς Ἀλέξανδρον. τῷ δὲ ἀσμένῳ
γίνεται ἄνδρας ἀγαθοὺς διασῶσαι· καὶ ξυμβαίνει
ἐπὶ τῷδε Ἀλέξανδρος τοῖς μισθοφόροις Ἰνδοῖς ὡς
καταχθέντας ἐς τὴν ἄλλην στρατιὰν ξὺν αὐτῷ
στρατεύεσθαι. οἱ μὲν δὴ ἐξῆλθον ξὺν τοῖς ὅπλοις,
καὶ κατεστρατοπέδευσαν κατὰ σφᾶς ἐπὶ γηλόφῳ,
ὃς ἦν ἀντίπορος τοῦ τῶν Μακεδόνων στρατοπέδου.
νυκτὸς δὲ ἐπενόουν δρασμῷ διαχρησάμενοι ἐς τὰ
σφέτερα ἤθη ἀπαναστῆναι οὐκ ἐθέλοντες ἐναντία
4 αἴρεσθαι τοῖς ἄλλοις Ἰνδοῖς ὅπλα. καὶ ταῦτα ὡς
ἐξηγγέλθη Ἀλεξάνδρῳ, περιστήσας τῆς νυκτὸς τῷ
γηλόφῳ τὴν στρατιὰν πᾶσαν κατακόπτει τοὺς

Tyre.   Many were shoved forward in eagerness, the 327–6 B.C.
bridge received too great a weight and broke, and the
Macedonians fell with it.   Seeing what was happen- 7
ing, the barbarians shouted and volleyed stones on
the Macedonians from the walls, and arrows and
anything else anyone happened to have in his hands
or could seize at the moment, while others ran out at
the small gates in the curtain walls and struck at them
in their confusion at close quarters.

27. Alexander sent Alcetas with his battalion to
pick up the wounded and to recall to the camp all who
were still offering resistance.   On the fourth day
another step-ladder was brought up to the wall in
the same way by another engine.

The Indians resisted strongly as long as the com- 2
mander of the place survived, but when he was hit
by a missile from a catapult and killed, with part of
their number already fallen in continuous siege and
most of them wounded and unfit for service, they
sent a herald to Alexander.   He was glad to be able 3
to save the lives of brave men, granted terms to the
mercenary Indians on the basis that they should join
the rest of his army and take the field with him.
They came out with their arms, and encamped by
themselves on a hill facing the Macedonian camp;
however, they intended to slip away at night and
escape to their own homes, as they had no wish to
bear arms against the rest of the Indians.   When 4
this was reported to Alexander, he threw his whole
force round the hill in the night, and cut down the

Ἰνδοὺς ἐν μέσῳ ἀπολαβών, τήν τε πόλιν αἱρεῖ κατὰ κράτος ἐρημωθεῖσαν τῶν προμαχομένων, καὶ τὴν μητέρα τὴν Ἀσσακάνου καὶ τὴν παῖδα ἔλαβεν. ἀπέθανον δὲ ἐν τῇ πάσῃ πολιορκίᾳ τῶν ξὺν Ἀλεξάνδρῳ ἐς πέντε καὶ εἴκοσιν.

5 Ἔνθεν δὲ Κοῖνον μὲν ὡς ἐπὶ Βάζιρα ἐκπέμπει, γνώμην ποιησάμενος ὅτι μαθόντες τῶν Μασσακανῶν τὴν ἅλωσιν ἐνδώσουσι σφᾶς αὐτούς. Ἄτταλον δὲ καὶ Ἀλκέταν καὶ Δημήτριον τὸν ἱππάρχην ἐπὶ Ὦρα στέλλει, ἄλλην πόλιν, παραγγείλας περιτει-
6 χίζειν τὴν πόλιν ἔστ' ἂν ἀφίκηται αὐτός. καὶ γίγνεται ἐκδρομὴ τῶν ἐκ τῆς πόλεως ἐπὶ τοὺς ἀμφὶ Ἀλκέταν. οὐ χαλεπῶς δὲ τρεψάμενοι αὐτοὺς οἱ Μακεδόνες εἴσω τοῦ τείχους ἐς τὴν πόλιν ἀποστρέφουσι. καὶ Κοίνῳ οὐ προχωρεῖ τὰ ἐν τοῖς Βαζίροις, ἀλλὰ πιστεύοντες γὰρ τοῦ χωρίου τῇ ὀχυρότητι, ὅτι ὑπερύψηλόν τε ἦν καὶ πάντῃ ἀκριβῶς τετειχισμένον, οὐδὲν ξυμβατικὸν ἐνεδίδοσαν.

7 Ταῦτα μαθὼν Ἀλέξανδρος ὥρμητο μὲν ὡς ἐπὶ Βάζιρα, γνοὺς δὲ ὅτι τῶν προσοίκων τινὲς βαρβάρων παριέναι ἐς τὰ Ὦρα τὴν πόλιν λαθόντες μέλλουσι, πρὸς Ἀβισάρου ἐπὶ τῷδε ἐσταλμένοι, ἐπὶ τὰ Ὦρα πρῶτον ἦγε· Κοῖνον δὲ ἐπιτειχίσαι τῇ πόλει τῶν Βαζιρέων καρτερόν τι χωρίον προτέταξε, καὶ ἐν τούτῳ φυλακὴν καταλιπόντα ἀποχρῶσαν, ὡς μὴ ἄδεια εἴη τοῖς ἐν τῇ πόλει χρῆσθαι τῇ χώρᾳ, αὐτὸν ἄγοντα τῆς στρατιᾶς τὴν λοιπὴν παρ' αὐτὸν
8 ἰέναι. οἱ δὲ ἐκ τῶν Βαζίρων ὡς εἶδον ἀπιόντα ξὺν

---

[1] D. 84 (after long lacuna), cf. QC. viii 10, 34 ff, tells of surrender of the 'queen'; QC. and J. xii 7 suggest that Al. had a son by her. The massacre, ignored by QC. and differently described by D., is condemned by P. 59, 3 f.; not all

Indians whom he had thus enclosed, took their city by assault, deprived as it was of its defenders, and captured Assacenus' mother and daughter.[1] In the entire siege some twenty-five of Alexander's men perished.[2]

From this place he sent Coenus to Bazira, having 5 formed the belief that on learning of the capture of Massaga it would surrender, while Attalus, Alcetas and Demetrius the hipparch [3] were sent against another city, Ora, and directed to throw a wall round it pending his own arrival. The townsmen made a 6 sally against Alcetas' forces, but the Macedonians easily repulsed them and drove them back into the city within the wall. Coenus was not successful at Bazira, where the townspeople, trusting in the strength of their site, since it was very high and fortified carefully all round, gave no signs of surrendering on terms.

On learning this, Alexander started towards 7 Bazira; but knowing that some of the neighbouring barbarians were preparing to slip unseen into the city of Ora, as Abisares [4] had despatched them for this purpose, he advanced first against Ora, and commanded Coenus to fortify a strong position near the city of Bazira and leave a sufficient garrison in it, to prevent the townsmen having the use of the country without risk, and then himself to bring the rest of the army to join him. The men in Bazira, on seeing 8

ancients need have shared his view, cf. Caesar, *Gallic Wars* iv 13–15.

[2] QC. viii 10, 22 wrongly makes the siege begin before that of Massaga.

[3] QC. viii 11, 1 makes Polyperchon sole commander (cf. 22, 1 n.).

[4] He ruled in Hazara; for his covert hostility cf. iv 30, 7; v 8, 3; 20, 5; 22, 2; 29, 4 f.

τῷ πλείστῳ τῆς στρατιᾶς τὸν Κοῖνον, καταφρονήσαντες τῶν Μακεδόνων, ὡς οὐ γενομένων ἂν
σφισιν ἀξιομάχων, ἐπεκθέουσιν ἐς τὸ πεδίον· καὶ
γίγνεται αὐτῶν μάχη καρτερά. καὶ ἐν ταύτῃ
πίπτουσι μὲν τῶν βαρβάρων ἐς πεντακοσίους,
ζῶντες δὲ ἐλήφθησαν ὑπὲρ τοὺς ἑβδομήκοντα· οἱ
δὲ λοιποὶ ἐν τῇ πόλει ξυμφυγόντες βεβαιότερον ἤδη
εἴργοντο τῆς χώρας ὑπὸ τῶν ἐκ τοῦ ἐπιτειχίσματος.
9 καὶ Ἀλεξάνδρῳ δὲ τῶν Ὤρων ἡ πολιορκία οὐ
χαλεπὴ ἐγένετο, ἀλλ' εὐθὺς ἐξ ἐφόδου προσβαλὼν
τοῖς τείχεσι τῆς πόλεως ἐκράτησε, καὶ τοὺς
ἐλέφαντας τοὺς ἐγκαταλειφθέντας ἔλαβε.

28. Καὶ ταῦτα οἱ ἐν τοῖς Βαζίροις ὡς ἔμαθον,
ἀπογνόντες τὰ σφέτερα πράγματα ἀμφὶ μέσας
νύκτας τὴν πόλιν ἐκλείπουσιν, ἔφυγον δὲ ἐς τὴν
πέτραν. ὡς δὲ καὶ οἱ ἄλλοι βάρβαροι ἔπραττον·
ἀπολιπόντες τὰς πόλεις ξύμπαντες ἔφευγον ἐς τὴν
πέτραν τὴν ἐν τῇ χώρᾳ τὴν Ἄορνον καλουμένην.
μέγα γάρ τι τοῦτο χρῆμα πέτρας ἐν τῇ χώρᾳ
ταύτῃ ἐστί, καὶ λόγος ὑπὲρ αὐτῆς κατέχει οὐδὲ
Ἡρακλεῖ τῷ Διὸς ἁλωτὸν γενέσθαι τὴν πέτραν.
2 εἰ μὲν δὴ καὶ ἐς Ἰνδοὺς ἀφίκετο ὁ Ἡρακλῆς ὁ
Θηβαῖος ἢ ὁ Τύριος ἢ ὁ Αἰγύπτιος ἐς οὐδέτερα ἔχω
ἰσχυρίσασθαι· μᾶλλον δὲ δοκῶ ὅτι οὐκ ἀφίκετο,
ἀλλὰ πάντα γὰρ ὅσα χαλεπὰ οἱ ἄνθρωποι ἐς
τοσόνδε ἄρα αὔξουσιν αὐτῶν τὴν χαλεπότητα, ὡς
καὶ τῷ Ἡρακλεῖ ἂν ἄπορα γενέσθαι μυθεύειν.
κἀγὼ ὑπὲρ τῆς πέτρας ταύτης οὕτω γιγνώσκω, τὸν
Ἡρακλέα ἐς κόμπον τοῦ λόγου ἐπιφημίζεσθαι.

---

[1] A's comment cf. App. IV 4. § 4, if not also 30, 4, shows
that the story stood in one of A's main sources, perhaps Ar.

327–6
B.C.

Coenus depart with most of the army, made light of
the Macedonians, supposing that they would not be
their equals in the field, and sallied out into the plain;
there was a fierce battle, in which about five hundred
of the barbarians fell, and over seventy were taken
alive; the rest took refuge in the city, where they
were now more firmly barred from the country by
those who held the stronghold facing the wall. The 9
siege of Ora caused Alexander no difficulty; he
attacked the walls at once, seized the city at the first
attempt, and captured the elephants left there.

28. When the inhabitants of Bazira learnt this,
they despaired of their position, and about midnight
deserted the city and fled to the rock, as did the other
barbarians; leaving their cities they all fled to the
rock in this neighbourhood called Aornos. It is an
enormous sort of rock in this country, and the prevalent story about it is that even Heracles the son of
Zeus was unable to capture it. In fact I cannot 2
assert with confidence if Heracles, whether the
Theban or the Tyrian or the Egyptian Heracles,[1] ever
actually reached India; I incline to think that he
did not, but that men will magnify difficulties they
meet, so far as to make up a story that even Heracles
would not have overcome them. So it is my own
view about this rock, that the name of Heracles is

rather than Pt., cf. App. XVI in vol ii.; A. first gives it with
reserve, because of his own disbelief that the Greek Heracles
had come to Aornos, but then treats it as a fact that Al.
believed it. The story of the dimensions of Aornos (Pt/Ar?)
is certainly well-founded, cf. Sir A. Stein (App. VIII 2) pp.
128 ff. D. 85, 2; QC. viii 11, 2 tell that Heracles was thwarted
by an earthquake, Strabo (incredulous of the whole tale) that
he was thrice repulsed (xv 1, 8). No doubt there were many
variants. Fuller 245 ff. supplies plan and photographs of
Aornos = Pir-Sar.

3 τὸν μὲν δὴ κύκλον τῆς πέτρας λέγουσιν ἐς διακοσίους σταδίους μάλιστα εἶναι, ὕψος δὲ αὐτῆς,
ἵναπερ χθαμαλώτατον, σταδίων ἕνδεκα, καὶ ἀνά-
βασιν χειροποίητον μίαν χαλεπήν· εἶναι δὲ καὶ
ὕδωρ ἐν ἄκρᾳ τῇ πέτρᾳ πολὺ καὶ καθαρόν, πηγὴν
ἀνίσχουσαν, ὡς καὶ ἀπορρεῖν ἀπὸ τῆς πηγῆς ὕδωρ,
καὶ ὕλην καὶ γῆν ἀγαθὴν ἐργάσιμον ὅσην καὶ
χιλίοις ἀνθρώποις ἀποχρῶσαν ἂν εἶναι ἐργάζεσθαι.

4 Καὶ ταῦτα ἀκούοντα Ἀλέξανδρον πόθος λαμβάνει ἐξελεῖν καὶ τοῦτο τὸ ὄρος, οὐχ ἥκιστα ἐπὶ τῷ
ἀμφὶ τὸν Ἡρακλέα μύθῳ πεφημισμένῳ. τὰ μὲν
δὴ Ὦρα καὶ τὰ Μάσσαγα φρούρια ἐποίησεν ἐπὶ τῇ

5 χώρᾳ, τὰ Βάζιρα δὲ πόλιν[1] ἐξετείχισε. καὶ οἱ
ἀμφὶ Ἡφαιστίωνά τε καὶ Περδίκκαν αὐτῷ ἄλλην
πόλιν ἐκτειχίσαντες, Ὀροβάτις ὄνομα τῇ πόλει
ἦν, καὶ φρουρὰν καταλιπόντες ὡς ἐπὶ τὸν Ἰνδὸν
ποταμὸν ᾔεσαν· ὡς δὲ ἀφίκοντο, ἔπρασσον ἤδη
ὅσα ἐς τὸ ζεῦξαι τὸν Ἰνδὸν ὑπὸ Ἀλεξάνδρου
ἐτέτακτο.

6 Ἀλέξανδρος δὲ τῆς μὲν χώρας τῆς ἐπὶ τάδε τοῦ
Ἰνδοῦ ποταμοῦ σατράπην κατέστησε Νικάνορα τῶν
ἑταίρων. αὐτὸς δὲ τὰ μὲν πρῶτα ὡς ἐπὶ τὸν
Ἰνδὸν ποταμὸν ἦγε, καὶ πόλιν τε Πευκελαῶτιν οὐ
πόρρω τοῦ Ἰνδοῦ ᾠκισμένην ὁμολογίᾳ παρεστήσατο καὶ ἐν αὐτῇ φρουρὰν καταστήσας τῶν
Μακεδόνων καὶ Φίλιππον ἐπὶ τῇ φρουρᾷ ἡγεμόνα,
ὁ δὲ καὶ ἄλλα προσηγάγετο μικρὰ πολίσματα πρὸς
τῷ Ἰνδῷ ποταμῷ ᾠκισμένα. ξυνείποντο δὲ αὐτῷ
Κωφαῖός τε καὶ Ἀσσαγέτης οἱ ὕπαρχοι τῆς

7 χώρας. ἀφικόμενος δὲ ἐς Ἐμβόλιμα πόλιν, ἢ

---

[1] Roos inserted ⟨τὴν⟩ before πόλιν.

brought into the tale as a boast. The circumference 3 327-6
of the rock, it is said, is about two hundred stades, its   B.C.
height at its lowest part eleven stades,[2] with only one
way up, made by hand and rough. On the top of the
rock there is said to be plenty of pure water which
comes from a perennial spring, from which water
actually pours out, as well as wood and good arable
land which would be enough for a thousand men to
till.

As soon as Alexander heard this, he was seized with 4
a longing to capture this mountain too, not least
because of the legend about Heracles.[3] He made
Ora and Massaga into forts to control the district, and
fortified Bazira as a city. Hephaestion, Perdiccas 5
and their men fortified another city for him, called
Orobatis, and leaving a garrison there went on towards the river Indus; on arrival, they were engaged
in following all Alexander's instructions for bridging
the Indus.

Alexander appointed Nicanor, one of the Com- 6 326
panions, satrap of the region this side of the river   B.C.
Indus. He himself first went towards the river Indus
and took over by surrender the city of Peucelaotis,
situated not far from it, and set a Macedonian
garrison there with Philippus as commandant; he
also took over various small towns lying near the river
Indus. Cophaeus and Assagetes, the hyparchs of the
country, were in attendance on him. Then on reach- 7

---

[2] Cf. iv 21, 2 n.   [3] App. IV 3.

ξύνεγγυς τῆς πέτρας τῆς Ἀόρνου ᾠκεῖτο, Κρατερὸν μὲν ξὺν μέρει τῆς στρατιᾶς καταλείπει αὐτοῦ,
σῖτόν τε ἐς τὴν πόλιν ὡς πλεῖστον ξυνάγειν ⟨κε-
λεύσας⟩ [1] καὶ ὅσα ἄλλα ἐς χρόνιον τριβήν, ὡς
ἐντεῦθεν ὁρμωμένους τοὺς Μακεδόνας χρονίῳ
πολιορκίᾳ ἐκτρυχῶσαι τοὺς κατέχοντας τὴν πέτραν,
8 εἰ μὴ ἐξ ἐφόδου ληφθείη. αὐτὸς δὲ τοὺς τοξότας τε
ἀναλαβὼν καὶ τοὺς Ἀγριᾶνας καὶ τὴν Κοίνου
τάξιν καὶ ἀπὸ τῆς ἄλλης φάλαγγος ἐπιλέξας τοὺς
κουφοτάτους τε καὶ ἅμα εὐοπλοτάτους καὶ τῶν
ἑταίρων ἱππέων ἐς διακοσίους καὶ ἱπποτοξότας ἐς
ἑκατὸν προσῆγε τῇ πέτρᾳ. καὶ ταύτῃ μὲν τῇ
ἡμέρᾳ κατεστρατοπεδεύσατο, ἵνα ἐπιτήδειον αὐτῷ
ἐφαίνετο, τῇ δὲ ὑστεραίᾳ ὀλίγον προελθὼν ὡς πρὸς
τὴν πέτραν αὖθις ἐστρατοπεδεύσατο.

29. Καὶ ἐν τούτῳ ἧκον παρ' αὐτὸν τῶν προσχώρων τινές, σφᾶς τε αὐτοὺς ἐνδιδόντες καὶ
ἡγήσεσθαι φάσκοντες ἐς τῆς πέτρας τὸ ἐπιμαχώτατον, ὅθεν οὐ χαλεπὸν αὐτῷ ἔσεσθαι ἑλεῖν τὸ
χωρίον. καὶ ξὺν τούτοις πέμπει Πτολεμαῖον τὸν
Λάγου τὸν σωματοφύλακα τούς τε Ἀγριᾶνας
ἄγοντα καὶ τοὺς ψιλοὺς τοὺς ἄλλους καὶ τῶν
ὑπασπιστῶν ἐπιλέκτους, προστάξας, ἐπειδὰν κατα-
λάβῃ τὸ χωρίον, κατέχειν μὲν αὐτὸ ἰσχυρᾷ φυλακῇ,
2 οἷ δὲ σημαίνειν ὅτι ἔχεται. καὶ Πτολεμαῖος
ἐλθὼν ὁδὸν τραχεῖάν τε καὶ δύσπορον λανθάνει τοὺς
βαρβάρους κατασχὼν τὸν τόπον· καὶ τοῦτον
χάρακι ἐν κύκλῳ καὶ τάφρῳ ὀχυρώσας πυρσὸν

[1] Some such word must have been omitted (Polak).

---

[1] See also D. 85 f.; QC. viii 11. Pt. is evidently A's source
(even if the allusions to Heracles are inserted from Ar.).

ing the city of Embolima, which lay near the rock of 326
Aornos, he left Craterus there with part of the army B.C.
with instructions to get as much grain as possible into
the city and everything else a long delay would make
necessary, so that the Macedonians might use the city
as a base, and wear out the holders of the rock by a
long blockade, if it were not captured by first assault.
He himself took the archers, the Agrianians and 8
Coenus' battalion and, selecting the most nimble but
at the same time the best armed men from the rest
of the phalanx, about two hundred of the Companion
cavalry and a hundred mounted archers, approached
the rock. That day he encamped in a place he
thought convenient; on the next he advanced a little
nearer the rock and camped again.

29. At this point some of the neighbouring people
came to Alexander and surrendered, promising to
lead him to the part of the rock which could best be
assaulted, from which he could capture the position
without difficulty.[1] With these men he sent Ptolemy
son of Lagus, the bodyguard, in command of the
Agrianians, the light troops including men chosen
from the hypaspists,[2] ordering him as soon as he
captured the position to occupy it with a strong
garrison, and signal to him that it was in his hands.
Ptolemy pursued a rough and difficult track and 2
seized the place, unobserved by the barbarians; he
strengthened it with a stockade all round and a
trench, and raised a fire-signal from the height where

---

[1] See iii 29, 7 n. Note that Pt. records an implied criticism of
himself in § 4. Chares (Jacoby no. 125 F. 16) has an anecdote
that may relate to this siege and date it c. April 326 B.C., cf.
Stein pp. 152 f.
[2] Introd. 62.

αἴρει ἀπὸ τοῦ ὄρους ἔνθεν ὀφθήσεσθαι ὑπὸ ᾿Αλε-
ξάνδρου ἔμελλεν. καὶ ὤφθη τε ἅμα ἡ φλὸξ καὶ
᾿Αλέξανδρος ἐπῆγε τῇ ὑστεραίᾳ τὴν στρατιάν·
ἀμυνομένων δὲ τῶν βαρβάρων οὐδὲν πλέον αὐτῷ
3 ὑπὸ δυσχωρίας ἐγίγνετο. ὡς δὲ ᾿Αλεξάνδρῳ
ἄπορον τὴν προσβολὴν κατέμαθον οἱ βάρβαροι,
ἀναστρέψαντες τοῖς ἀμφὶ Πτολεμαῖον αὐτοὶ προσ-
έβαλλον· καὶ γίγνεται αὐτῶν τε καὶ τῶν Μακεδόνων μάχη καρτερά, τῶν μὲν διασπάσαι τὸν
χάρακα σπουδὴν ποιουμένων, τῶν ᾿Ινδῶν, Πτολεμαίου δὲ διαφυλάξαι τὸ χωρίον· καὶ μεῖον
σχόντες οἱ βάρβαροι ἐν τῷ ἀκροβολισμῷ νυκτὸς
ἐπιγενομένης ἀπεχώρησαν.

4   ᾿Αλέξανδρος δὲ τῶν ᾿Ινδῶν τινα τῶν αὐτομόλων
πιστόν τε ἄλλως καὶ τῶν χωρίων δαήμονα ἐπιλεξάμενος πέμπει παρὰ Πτολεμαῖον τῆς νυκτός,
γράμματα φέροντα [τὸν ᾿Ινδόν],[1] ἵνα ἐνεγέγραπτο,
ἐπειδὰν αὐτὸς προσβάλλῃ τῇ πέτρᾳ, τὸν δὲ ἐπιέναι
τοῖς βαρβάροις κατὰ τὸ ὄρος μηδὲ ἀγαπᾶν ἐν
φυλακῇ ἔχοντα τὸ χωρίον, ὡς ἀμφοτέρωθεν βαλ-
5 λομένους τοὺς ᾿Ινδοὺς ἀμφιβόλους γίγνεσθαι. καὶ
αὐτὸς ἅμα τῇ ἡμέρᾳ ἄρας ἐκ τοῦ στρατοπέδου
προσῆγε τὴν στρατιὰν κατὰ τὴν πρόσβασιν, ᾗ
Πτολεμαῖος λαθὼν ἀνέβη, γνώμην ποιούμενος,
ὡς, εἰ ταύτῃ βιασάμενος ξυμμίξει τοῖς ἀμφὶ
Πτολεμαῖον, οὐ χαλεπὸν ἔτι ἐσόμενον αὐτῷ τὸ
6 ἔργον. καὶ ξυνέβη οὕτως. ἔστε μὲν γὰρ ἐπὶ
μεσημβρίαν ξυνειστήκει καρτερὰ μάχη τοῖς τε
᾿Ινδοῖς καὶ τοῖς Μακεδόσιν, τῶν μὲν ἐκβιαζομένων
ἐς τὴν πρόσβασιν, τῶν δὲ βαλλόντων ἀνιόντας· ὡς
δὲ οὐκ ἀνίεσαν οἱ Μακεδόνες, ἄλλοι ἐπ᾿ ἄλλοις

[1] Deleted by Polak.

Alexander was likely to see it. The flare was seen at once, and next day Alexander brought up his army; the barbarians offered opposition and he had no success, owing to difficulties of terrain. But as 3 soon as the barbarians realized that Alexander's advance was impracticable, they turned and attacked Ptolemy and his troops, and a fierce battle took place between them and the Macedonians, the Indians trying strenuously to pull down the stockade, Ptolemy to keep his hold on the position; the barbarians had the worst of the exchange of missiles, and withdrew at nightfall.

Alexander selected a deserter from the Indians, 4 whom he trusted and who also had exact knowledge of the locality, and sent him by night to Ptolemy with a letter directing him, as soon as Alexander himself approached the rock, to attack the barbarians from the height and not to content himself with merely defending the position; the Indians would then not know which way to turn, when they were fired on from both sides. At dawn Alexander himself 5 moved from his camp and brought his army to the approach by which Ptolemy had secretly ascended, reckoning that if he could force his way in this direction and join Ptolemy's force, he would have no more difficulty in the task. That was what happened. Until midday there was a fierce battle between the 6 Indians and the Macedonians, who tried to force the approach, while the Indians volleyed at them as they climbed up. But as the Macedonians kept constantly coming up, one detachment after another, while their

ἐπιόντες, οἱ δὲ πρόσθεν ἀναπαυόμενοι, μόγις δὴ
ἀμφὶ δείλην ἐκράτησαν τῆς παρόδου καὶ ξυνέμιξαν
τοῖς ξὺν Πτολεμαίῳ. ἐκεῖθεν δὲ ὁμοῦ ἤδη γενομένη ἡ στρατιὰ πᾶσα ἐπήγετο αὖθις ὡς ἐπ' αὐτὴν
τὴν πέτραν· ἀλλὰ γὰρ ἔτι ἄπορος ἦν αὐτῇ ἡ
προσβολή, ταύτῃ μὲν δὴ τῇ ἡμέρᾳ τοῦτο τὸ τέλος
γίγνεται.

7   Ὑπὸ δὲ τὴν ἕω παραγγέλλει στρατιώτῃ ἑκάστῳ
κόπτειν χάρακας ἑκατὸν κατ' ἄνδρα. καὶ οὗτοι
κεκομμένοι ἦσαν καὶ αὐτὸς ἐχώννυεν ἀρξάμενος
ἀπὸ τῆς κορυφῆς τοῦ λόφου, ἵνα ἐστρατοπεδευκότες
ἦσαν, ὡς ἐπὶ τὴν πέτραν χῶμα μέγα, ἔνθεν τοξεύ-
ματά τε ἂν ἐξικνεῖσθαι ἐς τοὺς προμαχομένους
[δυνατὰ] αὐτῷ ἐφαίνετο καὶ ἀπὸ μηχανῶν βέλη
ἀφιέμενα· καὶ ἐχώννυον αὐτῷ πᾶς τις ἀντιλαμ-
βανόμενος τοῦ ἔργου· καὶ αὐτὸς ἐφειστήκει
θεατὴς καὶ ἐπαινέτης τοῦ ξὺν προθυμίᾳ περαινο-
μένου, κολαστὴς δὲ τοῦ ἐν τῷ παραχρῆμα ἐκλιποῦς.

30. Τῇ μὲν δὴ πρώτῃ ἡμέρᾳ ὡς ἐπὶ στάδιον
ἔχωσεν αὐτῷ ὁ στρατός. ἐς δὲ τὴν ὑστεραίαν οἵ
τε σφενδονῆται σφενδονῶντες ἐς τοὺς Ἰνδοὺς ἐκ
τοῦ ἤδη κεχωσμένου καὶ ἀπὸ τῶν μηχανῶν βέλη
ἀφιέμενα ἀνέστελλε τῶν Ἰνδῶν τὰς ἐκδρομὰς τὰς
ἐπὶ τοὺς χωννύοντας. καὶ ἐχώννυτο αὐτῷ ἐς τρεῖς
ἡμέρας ξυνεχῶς τὸ χωρίον. τῇ τετάρτῃ δὲ βιασάμενοι τῶν Μακεδόνων οὐ πολλοὶ κατέσχον
ὀλίγον γήλοφον ἰσόπεδον τῇ πέτρᾳ. καὶ Ἀλέξανδρος οὐδέν τι ἐλινύων ἐπῆγε τὸ χῶμα ξυνάψαι
ἐθέλων τὸ χωννύμενον τῷ γηλόφῳ, ὅντινα οἱ ὀλίγοι
αὐτῷ ἤδη κατεῖχον.

2   Οἱ δὲ Ἰνδοὶ πρός τε τὴν ἀδιήγητον τόλμαν τῶν
ἐς τὸν γήλοφον βιασαμένων Μακεδόνων ἐκπλα-

326
B.C.

predecessors rested from the attack, with much difficulty they mastered the ascent in the afternoon and joined up with Ptolemy's force. From that moment the army, now united, made a renewed onslaught as a whole on the rock itself. But the attack there still proved impracticable. This was the close of operations that day.

At dawn Alexander told each soldier to cut a 7 hundred stakes; when they had all been cut, he himself started to raise a great mound, beginning from the top of the crest of the hill on which they had encamped and extending up to the rock; from this he thought arrows and missiles hurled from the engines would reach the defenders. All hands took part in the work of building the mound; Alexander himself stood by, watching and approving where it proceeded with vigour, and punishing failures to make immediate progress.

30. On the first day the army built the mound to about a stade in length. On the next, the slingers fired on the Indians from the mound so far as it had been built, and missiles were flung from the engines; this checked the sallies the Indians made against the builders of the mound. The pile went on growing for three days continuously on the chosen spot. On the fourth a few Macedonians made a rush and held a small hill on the same level as the rock, and Alexander without a moment's delay extended the mound, anxious to connect it with the hill this small party was already holding for him

The Indians were astounded at the indescribable 2 boldness of the Macedonians who had forced their

443

γέντες καὶ τὸ χῶμα ξυνάπτον ἤδη ὁρῶντες, τοῦ
μὲν ἀπομάχεσθαι ἔτι ἀπείχοντο, πέμψαντες δὲ
κήρυκας σφῶν παρὰ Ἀλέξανδρον ἐθέλειν ἔφασκον
ἐνδοῦναι τὴν πέτραν, εἴ σφισι σπένδοιτο. γνώμην
δὲ ἐπεποίηντο ἐν τῷ ἔτι διαμέλλοντι τῶν σπονδῶν
διαγαγόντες τὴν ἡμέραν νυκτὸς ὡς ἕκαστοι δια-
3 σκεδάννυσθαι ἐπὶ τὰ σφέτερα ἤθη. καὶ τοῦτο ὡς
ἐπύθετο Ἀλέξανδρος, ἐνδίδωσιν αὐτοῖς χρόνον τε
ἐς τὴν ἀποχώρησιν καὶ τῆς φυλακῆς τὴν κύκλωσιν
τὴν πάντη ἀφελεῖν. καὶ αὐτὸς ἔμενεν ἔστε ἤρξαντο
τῆς ἀποχωρήσεως· καὶ ἐν τούτῳ ἀναλαβὼν τῶν
σωματοφυλάκων καὶ τῶν ὑπασπιστῶν ἐς ἑπτακοσίους
κατὰ τὸ ἐκλελειμμένον τῆς πέτρας ἀνέρχεται ἐς
αὐτὴν πρῶτος, καὶ οἱ Μακεδόνες ἄλλος ἄλλῃ
4 ἀνιμῶντες ἀλλήλους ἀνῄεσαν. καὶ οὗτοι ἐπὶ τοὺς
ἀποχωροῦντας τῶν βαρβάρων τραπόμενοι ἀπὸ
ξυνθήματος, πολλοὺς μὲν αὐτῶν ἐν τῇ φυγῇ ἀπέκτειναν, οἱ δὲ καὶ πεφοβημένως ἀποχωροῦντες κατὰ
τῶν κρημνῶν ῥίψαντες σφᾶς ἀπέθανον. εἴχετό τε
Ἀλεξάνδρῳ ἡ πέτρα ἡ τῷ Ἡρακλεῖ ἄπορος
γενομένη καὶ ἔθυεν ἐπ' αὐτῇ Ἀλέξανδρος καὶ
κατεσκεύασε φρούριον, παραδοὺς Σισικόττῳ ἐπιμελεῖσθαι τῆς φρουρᾶς, ὃς ἐξ Ἰνδῶν μὲν πάλαι
ηὐτομολήκει ἐς Βάκτρα παρὰ Βῆσσον, Ἀλεξάνδρου δὲ κατασχόντος τὴν χώραν τὴν Βακτρίαν
ξυνεστράτευέ τε αὐτῷ καὶ πιστὸς ἐς τὰ μάλιστα
ἐφαίνετο.
5 Ἄρας δ' ἐκ τῆς πέτρας ἐς τὴν Ἀσσακηνῶν
χώραν ἐμβάλλει. Τὸν γὰρ ἀδελφὸν τὸν Ἀσσακάνου ἐξηγγέλλετο τούς τε ἐλέφαντας ἔχοντα καὶ τῶν
προσχώρων βαρβάρων πολλοὺς ξυμπεφευγέναι ἐς
τὰ ταύτῃ ὄρη. καὶ ἀφικόμενος ἐς Δύρτα πόλιν

way to the hill, and seeing the mound already connected with it, began to desist from any defence, and
sent a herald on their behalf to Alexander, saying
they were willing to surrender the rock, on terms
being granted them. They had formed a plan of
spending the day in the delays incident to the treaty
and scattering at night to their various homes. But 3
when Alexander discovered this, he gave them time
to withdraw and to remove the round of sentries
who guarded all points, waited himself till they began
their withdrawal and then took some seven hundred
of the bodyguards and hypaspists to the deserted part
of the rock. He was himself the first to scale it and
the Macedonians followed, pulling each other up at
different points. At a signal they turned on the 4
retreating barbarians and killed many of them in
flight; in the panic of their escape some threw
themselves down the cliffs and perished. Alexander
was now in possession of the rock Heracles could not
take, sacrificed on it, and set a garrison there,
appointing to command the guard Sisicottus,[1] who had
long ago deserted from the Indians and joined Bessus
at Bactra, but taken service under Alexander when
he became master of Bactria and shown himself
especially trustworthy.

On leaving the rock, Alexander invaded the district 5
of the Assacenians,[2] for it was reported that Assa-
canus' brother with the elephants and many of the
neighbouring barbarians had taken refuge in the
hills there. When he arrived at a city called Dyrta,

---

[1] ' Sisicostus ', QC. viii 11, 25, recording his appointment.
[2] D. 86, 2; QC. viii 12, 1 ff. record different operations
against ' Aphrices ' or ' Erices '.

τῶν μὲν ⟨ἐν⟩οικούντων οὐδένα καταλαμβάνει οὐδὲ
ἐν τῇ χώρᾳ τῇ πρὸς τῇ πόλει· ἐς δὲ τὴν ὑστεραίαν
Νέαρχόν τε καὶ ᾿Αντίοχον τοὺς χιλιάρχους τῶν
6 ὑπασπιστῶν ἐκπέμπει· καὶ Νεάρχῳ μὲν τοὺς
᾿Αγριᾶνας ⟨καὶ⟩[1] τοὺς ψιλοὺς ἄγειν ἔδωκεν,
᾿Αντιόχῳ δὲ τήν τε αὐτοῦ χιλιαρχίαν καὶ δύο ἐπὶ
ταύτῃ ἄλλας. ἐστέλλοντο δὲ τά τε χωρία κατ-
οψόμενοι καὶ εἴ πού τινας τῶν βαρβάρων ξυλλαβεῖν
ἐς ἔλεγχον τῶν κατὰ τὴν χώραν, τῶν τε ἄλλων καὶ
μάλιστα δὴ τὰ ἀμφὶ τοὺς ἐλέφαντας ἔμελεν αὐτῷ
μαθεῖν.

7 Αὐτὸς δὲ ὡς ἐπὶ τὸν ᾿Ινδὸν ποταμὸν ἤδη ἦγε, καὶ
ἡ στρατιὰ αὐτῷ ὡδοποίει τὸ πρόσω ἰοῦσα ἄπορα
ἄλλως ὄντα τὰ ταύτῃ χωρία. ἐνταῦθα ξυλλαμβά-
νει ὀλίγους τῶν βαρβάρων, καὶ παρὰ τούτων
ἔμαθεν, ὅτι οἱ μὲν ἐν τῇ χώρᾳ ᾿Ινδοὶ παρὰ ᾿Αβι-
σάρῃ ἀποπεφευγότες εἶεν, τοὺς δὲ ἐλέφαντας ὅτι
αὐτοῦ κατέλιπον νέμεσθαι πρὸς τῷ ποταμῷ τῷ
᾿Ινδῷ· καὶ τούτους ἡγήσασθαί οἱ τὴν ὁδὸν ἐκέ-
8 λευσεν ὡς ἐπὶ τοὺς ἐλέφαντας. εἰσὶ δὲ ᾿Ινδῶν
πολλοὶ κυνηγέται τῶν ἐλεφάντων, καὶ τούτους
σπουδῇ ἀμφ᾽ αὑτὸν εἶχεν ᾿Αλέξανδρος, καὶ τότε
ἐθήρα ξὺν τούτοις τοὺς ἐλέφαντας· καὶ δύο μὲν
αὐτῶν ἀπόλλυνται κατὰ κρημνοῦ σφᾶς ῥίψαντες ἐν
τῇ διώξει, οἱ δὲ ἄλλοι ξυλληφθέντες ἔφερόν τε τοὺς
9 ἀμβάτας καὶ τῇ στρατιᾷ ξυνετάσσοντο. ἐπεὶ δὲ
καὶ ὕλῃ ἐργασίμῳ ἐνέτυχε παρὰ τὸν ποταμόν, καὶ
αὕτη ἐκόπη αὐτῷ ὑπὸ τῆς στρατιᾶς καὶ ναῦς
ἐποιήθησαν. καὶ αὗται κατὰ τὸν ᾿Ινδὸν ποταμὸν
ἤγοντο ὡς ἐπὶ τὴν γέφυραν, ἥντινα ῾Ηφαιστίων καὶ
Περδίκκας αὐτῷ ἐξῳκοδομηκότες πάλαι ἦσαν.

[1] Added by Gronovius.

he found none of the inhabitants there, nor in the neighbourhood; but next day he sent out Nearchus and Antiochus, the chiliarchs of the hypaspists[3]; Nearchus was given the Agrianians and the light 6 troops, and Antiochus his own chiliarchy and two more. They were sent to spy out the land and to seize any of the barbarians they might find for interrogation about details of the district; he was especially anxious to find out about the elephants.

He was himself now on the way to the river Indus, 7 and his army as it went forward made a road, since the country here was otherwise impracticable. Here he seized a few barbarians and learnt from them that the Indians of the district had fled to Abisares,[4] but that they had left their elephants grazing there near the river Indus. He commanded them to guide him on the way to the elephants. Many Indians are 8 hunters of elephants, and Alexander took pains to have them among his attendants, and at this time had their help in elephant hunts. Two of the beasts threw themselves over cliffs in the pursuit and perished; the rest were captured, permitted riders to mount them, and were put on the strength of the army. He also found a wood good for felling near the 9 river, and had it cut down by his troops, and ships built, which went down the river Indus to the bridge Hephaestion and Perdiccas had built for Alexander long before.[5]

3 Introd. 61.   4 iv 27, 7 n.   5 v 7, 1 n.

APPENDIX 1

THE BATTLE OF THE GRANICUS

1. Memnon proposed a strategy (on which see
Introd. 54) that implied that the Persian forces were
weaker than Al's (A. i 12; D. 18). According to
A. his army numbered about 30,000 foot and 5,000
horse; more probably, he had 43,000 foot and 6,100
horse (Introd. 56). A. gives the Persians at the
Granicus 20,000 horse and nearly as many mercenary foot; he mentions no other infantry (i 14, 4).
D. reduces the cavalry to over 10,000, but makes
their foot at least 100,000 strong; he never mentions
mercenaries (19, 4 f.). J. xi 6 (brief and worthless)
gives 600,000 as the Persian total. All these
estimates of their forces are doubtless exaggerated,
though A. 15, 5 could explain why the Macedonian
cavalry were superior, even if outnumbered. They
evidently consisted of local levies and mercenaries at
the disposal of the satraps in Anatolia who were in
command. According to D. 19, 4 the cavalry
included not only Paphlagonians but even Medes,
Hyrcanians and Bactrians. If this is true, we may
suppose that these troopers had not been sent from
Iran, but were settlers in Anatolia with a hereditary
obligation to military service. Lane Fox p. 516
acutely adduces evidence (especially Strabo xiii
4, 13) for such a Hyrcanian settlement in Lydia
established by Cyrus the Great.

2. P. 16 is in close accord with A. on the battle.
D. 19–21 is in fundamental disagreement. He omits
the debate between Al. and Parmenio and makes
Al. adopt the plan A. ascribes to Parmenio; he
encamps for the night and crosses at dawn, unopposed. If this is correct, 14, 5–15, 5 is all sheer
fiction. Of the cavalry engagement D. has somewhat different details (cf. Welles' notes), though
like A. he too concentrates on Al's heroic deeds;
his source was no less laudatory of Al. In his
account the Persian foot are not surrounded or,
except for some 2,000 prisoners, massacred; most
of them fled, though 10,000 were killed (as were
2,000 of the cavalry—A. 16, 2 gives over 1,000),
and the prisoners, horse and foot, numbered 20,000.
P. too differs from A. in saying that 2,500 Persian
cavalry and 20,000 footmen fell; in the very next
sentence (16, 8) he cites Ar., and this may suggest
that Ar. is the source of all his figures; in that case
it is natural to think that A. followed Pt. at least
on this point, cf. i 16, 4 n.

3. D's descriptions of Al's other battles are patently
unreliable; his account of the Granicus is too vague
to be rejected, if it stood by itself, but on general
grounds it is natural to prefer A's, since A. appears
to be following one or both of his main sources with
no reference to the ' vulgate '. Many modern
scholars, none the less, adopt D's story (or arbitrarily
combine it with A's, e.g. by accepting A's account of
the destruction of the mercenaries) on the ground
that it is unthinkable that Al. could have crossed
the stream in the face of enemy opposition and that
he must have deferred the attack and surprised the
Persians at dawn (cf. Lane Fox ch. 8). General

APPENDIX I

Fuller, a practised soldier, accepted A. without demur (147 ff.).

4. H. Strasburger (*Gnomon* 1937, 483 ff.) held that A's story was so absurd that it could not come from Pt., although he was among those who have held that A. normally followed Pt. alone, especially on the incidents of war. Yet we should then have no right to assume that Pt. was A's source for any statement, unless he is actually cited or there is some other positive argument for attribution. Surely, had A. adopted an account of Al's first battle totally at variance with that given by Pt., even if it came from Ar., he would have noted such a major discrepancy (cf. v 14, 3 ff.). We should also be obliged to form the lowest estimate of A's own judgement, in preferring a story that was less well authenticated and (so it is claimed) utterly incredible. I have no doubt that in fact A's version derived not only from Ar. (as the citation of Ar. in P's similar account suggests) but also from Pt.

5. The earliest account of the battle was no doubt that given by Callisthenes, whom A's sources seem to follow on Issus (App. III). Writing for eye-witnesses, Callisthenes cannot have falsified his account to the extent of making Al. cross the stream at once in the face of opposition, if he really crossed at dawn, unopposed. If Pt. and Ar. departed from the truest and earliest narrative, it must be that they themselves had forgotten what actually occurred or that they told a deliberate lie, which many others still alive would have recognized for what it was. In either case their authority would be vitiated, not only for this event but for every other that they re-counted. The truth of A's account of the battle of

the Granicus is crucial for the whole value of his history of Alexander.

6. Certainly Pt. and Ar. were apologists for Al. and capable of disguising or distorting the truth. Sheer mendacity on matters of common knowledge was surely not in their manner. What purpose would it have served here? They were not averse to telling that Al. could show caution (i 18; 20, 1; iii 9, 4) and craft (i 20, 5 f.; 27, 7; iv 3, 2; 26, 3); the suggestion by Lane Fox that 'cunning at dawn seemed less dashing in retrospect' can thus not explain the wilful perversion of the truth with which he taxes them. In fact, P. shows that Al's decision to attack at once was criticized as foolhardy. The writer whom D. followed, who was no less of an admirer of Al., perhaps thought it best to meet the charge by denying the facts on which it was based; since the 'vulgate' is full of fictions, it is not surprising to find another here. Pt. or Ar. or both met the criticism by inserting Al's own justification of his conduct in the debate with Parmenio. Now this debate may well have been private, and here invention could have had free scope. Parmenio is often traduced in our sources, perhaps by the malignity of Callisthenes (App. IX; X 2; XI 4). We may, if we choose, believe that the debate is unhistoric (which is not to say that Pt. and Ar. knew it to be such). But it would have been very maladroit for its inventor both to claim falsely that Alexander attacked without delay and that Parmenio advised the course that in reality Al. took. Those who knew the truth about the battle could then easily accept the debate and infer that Al. was saved by Parmenio from his own imprudence. It would have

been better to have suppressed Parmenio's advice
(cf. D's account) or even to have made Parmenio
advise instant attack and give Al. the credit for
waiting, cf. i 18.

APPENDIX II

NAVAL OPERATIONS 334–332

1. In 334 Al. had 160 ships (A. i 11, 6); the manuscripts of D. 17, 2 give 60, which may be amended
to 160; J. xi 6, 2 has 182, presumably in error.
QC. iv 5, 14 gives the same number of 160 for the
fleet when reassembled in 332. Al. was able to
cross the Hellespont unopposed, as the Persian fleet
had not mobilized in time. When it appeared off
Miletus, A. i 18, 5 says that it comprised about 400
ships. This may be an over-estimate. D. (29, 2;
31, 3) gives 300 in 333, not contradicted by A. ii
13, 4 which refers to the 100 best sailers. In 332 at
Tyre Al. was joined by 120 Cypriote and 80 Phoenician ships (ii 20, 1–3), while Tyre is plausibly said to
have had 80 (D. 41, 1). A Persian total of 300
ships is reasonable. In any event it is clear that in
334 it was vastly superior to Al's. We are told that
partly on this account, partly for lack of money to
pay the crews (cf. i 11, 3 n.), Al. disbanded his fleet
(A. i 20; D. 22, 5), except for a few, including 20
from Athens, which he kept to transport siege-
engines (D. 1.c.). The last point seems absurd;
how could he venture to send artillery by sea, when
the ships might be sunk or captured by the superior
Persian forces? Surely the Athenian ships were

kept as hostages. Al's ships were mainly Greek (Introd. 44), and to judge from Tod 192, league members should have borne the cost themselves of their naval contingents. However, they may have failed to provide enough funds; Al. lacked money for the time, and ships manned by mutinous crews would have been of little use. Probably his financial shortage was the vital cause of his decision, since even an inferior fleet, if it could have been kept at sea at all, would have hampered Persian naval activity, preventing the enemy admirals from sending out squadrons simultaneously to the Hellespont, the Macedonian coast and Greece. In 333 Al. saw that it was necessary to provide some naval force, though it would still be outnumbered. For other consequences of his decision see Introd. 44.

2. As A. always tends to concentrate on Al's own actions, we have to turn for supplementary information about Persian naval operations to D. and QC. According to D. Memnon (= M.), who had received large funds from Darius, mobilized 300 ships early in 333, with a substantial mercenary force, won over Chios and all the Lesbian cities except Mitylene which he took by force (29, 1 f.; A. ii 1 makes Chios fall by treachery, and Mitylene surrender but after M's death); most of the Cyclades sent envoys to him, and among the Greeks who favoured Persia (the majority, 31, 3), especially the Spartans, his successes raised hopes which he fomented by paying subsidies; at this point he died (29, 2–4). QC. iii 1, 19–21 tells that at Gordium Al., who had not yet heard of M's death, appointed Amphoterus as admiral and Hegelochus as general to recover Lesbos, Chios and Cos and provided

money and instructions for Antipater to defend the
homeland and Hellespont. Like D., he probably
put the fall of Mitylene (his ' Lesbos ') in M's lifetime. (For Cos cf. A. ii 5, 7; 13, 4; iii 2, 6.)
In ii 1 f. A. does not give a full account of Persian
naval successes before or after M's death; ii 13, 6
implies that the lower town of Halicarnassus was lost;
so was Miletus, QC. iv 1, 37; 5, 13, and the land
forces of the Persians in Caria ventured on a battle
with the Macedonians there, in which they were
indeed decisively beaten; both A. ii 5, 7 and QC.
iii 7, 4 recount this only indirectly by telling how Al.
heard of it at Soli. From A. ii 2, 3; iii 2, 6 we can
see that Amphoterus was subordinate to Hegelochus;
ii 2, 3 also shows that he received his commission
early in 333, and presumably, as QC. says, before
Al. moved east from Gordium. But as he was still
there in May (i 29, 4 n.), M's operations must have
begun in March or April, earlier and not later than
the arrival of ' the newly-wed ' at Gordium from
Macedon. D. 31, 3 ff. also says that Al. heard of the
loss of Chios and Lesbos and of the danger to Macedon and Greece before M. died; he dates the news
of the last event, which greatly relieved Al., just
before he fell ill; this must be his illness at Tarsus
(ii 4)—and D. 27, 7 has already brought Al. to
Cilicia in 334! If M. died in May, or even June,
Darius had ample time after hearing the news
(surely at Babylon, QC. iii 2, 1, and not earlier at
Susa, D. 30, 1; 31, 1) to recall the mercenaries who
were to fight at Issus under Thymondas (ii 2, 1;
13, 2, etc.), having joined the Grand Army in Syria
shortly before the battle (QC. iii 8, 1).

3. A's account of the Persian naval operations does

not make clear the full extent of their success and minimizes Greek support; while he is no doubt right in making out that island cities went over to them only as a result of treachery or *force majeure*, too little is said of the effects in Greece, cf. App. VI. Presumably the Spartan and Athenian envoys to Darius captured after Issus (ii 15, 2) had been sent off at this time. The Persian admirals would surely have done better to waste no time in the islands, and to have kept Antipater pre-occupied by threatening the Macedonian coast with part of their fleet, while taking the rest at once to Greece and raising revolts there; this criticism affects M., whose merits are commonly exaggerated, no less than his successors. Of course it was Darius who made the major error in withdrawing the mercenaries and putting everything to the test of battle with Al.

4. As no reliance could be placed on Athens, Hegelochus was able to do no more in 333 than defeat a Persian squadron in the Hellespont (QC. iv 1, 36) and perhaps then regain Tenedos (A. iii 2, 3); only after Issus, when Greek cities despaired of Persian victory, could he once more mobilize 160 ships; his successes contemporary with the siege of Tyre (perhaps Feb.–Aug. 332) are described in some detail by QC. iv 5, 14 ff., cf. A. iii 2, who characteristically relates them in connection with the report he made in person to Al. in Egypt (cf. iii 2, 3 n.), and with decisions Al. then took, cf. QC. iv 8, 11–14. Here again A. stresses that the Greeks of the islands really favoured Macedon throughout, and says nothing of sentiments on the mainland. No doubt this represents the line taken by Pt. and Ar. For Eresus and Chios Tod 191 f. supply further data.

APPENDIX III

ISSUS

1. This appendix is concerned principally with the relation of A's account to that of Callisthenes (henceforth C.), which in my judgement was the basis of those A. found in his sources. For an account of the battle and previous manoeuvres see Fuller 154 f. Like most other modern discussions this rests on the topographical investigations of Col. Janke (*Auf Alexanders des Grossen Pfaden*, 1904, cf. *Klio* X 137 ff.), whose findings are summarized by F. W. Walbank in his commentary on Polybius XII 17–22; they are rejected by Lane Fox. Maps are supplied by e.g. Fuller and Walbank.

2. In describing military operations ancient writers were in a difficulty in that they and their readers normally had no relevant maps. The best they could do was to provide a verbal description of the terrain. This was what C. attempted, but in some points his description was false or misleading. We do not know if Pt. or Ar. repeated or corrected his topographical account; certainly A. failed to do so; likewise QC., whose story seems in part to derive from the same ultimate source and sometimes supplements what A. tells us, at any rate for events before the battle itself. Probably neither of them understood the topography better than P., who thought that the two armies 'missed one another in the night' (20, 3). Certainly their accounts of the marches before the battle must have been obscure to any reader not possessed of the kind of information Janke supplied.

APPENDIX III

3. All our authorities except J., whose account is totally vague, agree that Darius placed himself in Al's rear. A. tells that at Tarsus, before marching west to Soli, Al. sent Parmenio east to seize the ' Gates ' dividing Cilicia from Syria (ii 5, 1). These comprise (a) a sandy defile between mount Amanus and the sea, through which runs the river Merkes Su; (b) the Jonah Pass, immediately to the south, a path zigzagging up an outrunner of Amanus; (c) the Beilan Pass a few kilometres south-east. QC. iii 7, 6 f. suggests that Parmenio got no further than Issus, through the Kara Kapu coastal pass between Mallus and Issus, on the route to the Syrian Gates, but this may not be true. It was after Al. had himself returned to Tarsus and moved east to Mallus that he heard from Parmenio that Darius was at Sochi (unidentified), two days march from the Syrian Gates, and evidently in the wide plain of the Melas or Kara Su (6, 1 cf. 6, 3); he then marched from Mallus, whose precise site on the Pyramus is not established, to Myriandros, which must have been south of the Jonah Pass near Alexandretta, since he had to descend on his return march to the Merkes Su plain (cf. 8, 2). These places can hardly have been less than about 105 km apart. A. seems to say that he covered this distance in two days, only to return and fight Darius, after a further march of 18.5 km according to C., but more probably of 31 km. Fuller (156) reports that a French corps in 1797 marched 72 miles and fought a battle in 48 hours, but this was in the north Italian plain, not in rough Cilician terrain. I doubt if Al. had any need to exhaust his men in this way, and suspect that as in other cases (App. VIII 3) an intermediate stage has been omitted; probably he paused at Issus, where

the sick were left, and reached Myriandrus on the second day thereafter. Meanwhile Darius had marched via the Arslan Boghaz through the Toprak Kalessi pass over the interior of Amanus (the Amanian Gates of 7, 1) and encamped just north of the mouth of the Pinarus; this must have taken rather over a week. Janke identified the Pinarus with the Deli Chai; Lane Fox revives the view that it was the Payas further south. This fits C's statement that Al. at Myriandrus was 100 stades away, i.e. about 18.5 km (the Deli Chai is 31 km from Alexandretta); moreover, C. gave the breadth of the Pinarus plain where the battle was to be fought as 14 stades, i.e. 2·59 km, whereas that of the Deli Chai is 6·7 km; the plain of the Payas, 4·4 km wide, is at least nearer to his estimate. However, the banks of the Payas are too steep to fit the course of the battle, and the deployment of Al's army, as described by C., could only have taken place between the Payas and the Deli Chai. Again, although A. (8, 1) supposed that Al's ' whole army ' had reached Myriandrus, it may well be that much of it was really still north of the Jonah Pass at the time when he turned to meet Darius, and this may account for C's figure of 100 stades, while his estimate of the breadth of the battle plain is on any view too low. Janke's judgement should be accepted.

4. Thus, starting at nightfall from Myriandros, when he had heard of Darius' presence behind him, i.e. about 6.30 p.m., Al. had to cover 31 km before the battle; he rested his men on the heights north of the Merkes-Su plain; the battle cannot have begun till the afternoon. Polybius criticizes C's account of the evolutions of both armies, on the ground that

they could not be reconciled with his statements about numbers and terrain. It was those statements that he should have challenged; C. exaggerated the Persian numbers at least, and his estimates of distances were much less likely to be reliable than his record of manoeuvres. In any event it is significant that Polybius plainly thought that his account, however absurd, was generally accepted (in vi 45, 1 he names him among the most learned of the old historians), and the summary Polybius gives of his story suggests that A's main sources largely agreed with and could have drawn on C.; we have no right to suppose that Pt. provided a more accurate account. As to (a) the distance between Myriandrus and the Pinarus and (b) the extent of the Pinarus plain (§ 3) A. indeed gives no estimates; the true extent of the Deli Chai plain allows ample room for even the excessive number of men that he, like all other sources, places in the front lines. (c) Both C. and A. (8, 5) have 30,000 Persian cavalry on the right and 30,000 mercenaries in the centre; C. puts an unstated number of peltasts on the left with ' the phalanx behind ', whereas A. (8, 6–8) makes the left consist of 60,000 hoplite Cardaces with other troops in the rear and mentions a flanking force of 20,000. The Cardaces cannot have been hoplites (Tarn ii 180 ff.); here the advantage lies with C. Polybius may simply have omitted what C. too had on the flanking force (cf. (f) below), as well as a parallel to A's statement that Darius threw troops over the Pinarus, which were withdrawn before the battle (8, 5 and 10); it is always important to remember that C's account must have been very detailed, and that little of it is preserved. (d) Both C. (Pol. 18, 9 f.) and A. (8, 6 and 11) placed

Darius in the centre with the mercenaries. (e) According to C. Al. marched north with the foot in front and horse behind (cf. A. 8, 3), but on reaching more open country deployed the foot in line of battle, at first 32 deep, then 16, then 8 (19, 6; 21, 1); A. 8, 2 f. has different but congruent details. (It was not to Polybius' purpose to mention the different regiments, as no doubt C., like A., did.) The deployment could have begun just north of the Kurudere ravine, about 40 stades from the battlefield; C. did not necessarily mean, as Polybius thought (20, 1), that it was complete at that point; the line could only have been thinned in stages as the country opened out. On the battlefield itself there was room for the 42,000 foot and 5,000 horse whose presence was in Polybius' view implied in C's history (19, 2); but P's own words show that in fact C. did not actually state how many men were engaged. (f) Like A. 8, 7; 9, 2 C. referred to the force Al. posted at an angle to his line to prevent outflanking (21, 5); this surely implies that he also mentioned the Persian flanking movement. (g) Whereas A. 8, 9 puts Al. (as always) on the right, C. allegedly said that he took care to be opposite Darius in the centre; but probably Polybius (22) has abbreviated; no doubt it was Al's plan to turn against Darius after smashing the Persian left, and the invention of the contemporary, Chares (11, 4 n.), cf. D. 33, 5 ff. and QC. iii 11, 7 ff., may suggest that his attack did reach the Persian centre before Darius fled, though this is not made clear by A. Polybius' contention that Al. could not have known where Darius would be posted betrays his own ignorance. (h) Polybius ridicules a manoeuvre recorded only by C., which Walbank explains (18, 9 n.); it is not inconsistent with A. (i) He urges that if the banks of the Pinarus were as steep as C. says, neither the Persian cavalry nor the Macedonian phalanx could have crossed the stream. Evidently C. exaggerated the steepness; so does A. 10, 1 (see note). (It follows that the Pinarus cannot be the Payas, cf. supra.) (j) Polybius taxes C. with other absurdities. His criticisms would have been just as apposite to the manoeuvres A. describes in 8, 11 and 9, 1 and 3; he would surely have pronounced them impracticable on broken ground in face of the enemy. Hence, if we believe that Polybius demonstrates that C. had no understanding of war, we must on the same reasoning convict A. and presumably Pt. If on the other hand Callisthenes' errors are confined to mistakes on numbers (shared by A's sources) and on estimates of distances (which they may not have given), there is no reason to deny that he was the prime source used by Pt. and Ar. themselves both for Issus and presumably for other military operations described in his history. (There is no evidence here or elsewhere that A. himself consulted C.)

5. A's topographical vagueness would have been for Polybius (xii 25 g) another and fully deserved ground for censure. Of course we can conjecture that Pt. or Ar. gave topographical details as detailed as C. and more exact, and that A. has omitted them, just as he commonly fails to excerpt anything from the geographical excursuses in Ar., which Strabo used, although they must have assisted a better understanding of Al's campaigns. But it does Pt. or Ar. or both no credit that they gave absurd estimates of the size of the Persian army, 600,000 men, and of its front line, 140,000, equalling or outdoing not only

APPENDIX III

C. but the estimates in D. 31, 2 (500,000 in all) and
QC. iii 2 (310,000 in total) and 9 (160,000 in the front
line); it is little excuse that this exaggeration of
Persian numbers was traditional; even Xenophon,
though an eye-witness, had reported one million in
the Persian army at Cunaxa (*Anab.* i 7, 12). The
conversion of the Cardaces into hoplites was also a
lie. At most we can say that Al's tactical dispositions, like the advice of Amyntas (6, 3), imply that
he must have been outnumbered and therefore in
danger of being outflanked. The exaggerations
tended to his greater glory, which Pt. and Ar., no
less than C., sought to enhance at the cost of truth.

6. As to D. and QC., once the armies were joined in
battle, their accounts, which suggest a common
source, are incompatible with A. But QC. (unlike
D. 33, 1) roughly agrees with A. about the Macedonian array, though not about the Persian, and
there are many affinities in his narrative of the previous manoeuvres, on which D. is extremely vague.
It would seem that QC. drew ultimately on the same
tradition as A. (as well as on one followed by D. that
diverged markedly), though he is much less full and
clear, even at his best. One point is of special
interest. In 7, 8 ff. he makes Al. accept Parmenio's
advice not to advance beyond Issus but fight in a
narrow space. In fact (as he too shows) Al. did advance, with the evident intention of facing Darius
in Syria. Thus he did not accept Parmenio's advice.
The result was that Darius took Issus and massacred
the Macedonians there. Al's decision cost them their
lives. Two modes of apology, if QC. is right that
the advice was tendered, were open. One was to
suppress the fact: thus A's sources. The second

was to make out that Al. adopted the advice in the hope that the reader, knowing that in the end (thanks to Darius) Al. did fight in Cilicia, would not notice that so far as in him lay Al. had disregarded it.

APPENDIX IV

ALEXANDER AND THE HEROES

1. As an Argead, Al. was reputed a descendant in the male line from Heracles and through Heracles' mother, Alcmene, from Perseus; through his own mother, Olympias, he claimed descent from Achilles by his son, Neoptolemus. In general the Greek world did not distinguish legend from history, and there is no reason to think that such genealogies, which were actually used to justify territorial claims in the fourth century, were not believed. Almost certainly, to Al., Heracles, Perseus and Achilles were real persons and his actual ancestors.

2. He was also strongly influenced by Homer, cf. P. 8; 26; Strabo xiii 1, 26 f.; Lane Fox ch. 3. A. had read in the 'vulgate' that he sought from childhood to emulate Achilles (vii 14, 4, cf. i 12, 1). He was ostensibly engaged in a Panhellenic crusade (cf. Introd. 40). Herodotus (i 3 f.) had represented the Trojan war as an incident in the struggle between Greeks and Asians continued in the Persian invasions of Greece in the fifth century, which he was to avenge. Isocrates had more than once touched on this theme (iv 154; 181; x 67; xii 42; 189), and had

urged Philip to emulate his ancestor, Heracles, who had shown his beneficence in uniting the Greeks for an earlier expedition against Troy (v 109 ff.). By his sacrifice at the tomb of Protesilaus, (i 11, 5, from Pt./Ar.), Al. symbolized that he was, like his ancestors, fighting for Greece against the barbarians. The account of his acts immediately after he crossed to Asia in A. i 11, 6 ff. seems to come from the 'vulgate', but is perfectly credible, and is confirmed at one point, his taking arms supposedly dedicated in the Trojan war, by a later allusion from the main sources (vi 10, 2). We are told that he sacrificed to Heracles (cf. i 4, 5; *Ind.* 36, 3), and sought to placate Priam for his death at the hands of Neoptolemus. Fragments of Callisthenes indicate that that historian sought to connect Al's advance through Asia with Homeric and other heroic stories (Pearson 39 ff.). Even the version of the Granicus A. follows depicts Al's *aristeia* in the Homeric style. Al. may well, then and later, have risked his life so recklessly, not only because this set his troops an example, but because such conduct was required by the heroic model he adopted.

3. It is no surprise then that we hear of Al. seeking to rival Heracles and Perseus by his visit to Siwah (iii 3, 2), or to outdo Heracles at Aornos (iv 28, 4 cf. 30, 4), or to follow in Dionysus' footsteps at Nysa (v 2, 5). At least one of A's main sources, perhaps Ar., lies behind these statements, and the *motiv* of his emulation of Heracles and Dionysus, though more prominent in the 'vulgate', is not confined to an inferior tradition, cf. further App. XVI in vol. II. Its credibility is supported by Nearchus' statement that he wished to outdo Cyrus and Semiramis

in marching through Gadrosia (Strabo xv i, 15), which also appeared in the ' vulgate ' (A. vi 24, 2).

4. It seems that in Afghanistan and India Al. and his men came across legends of figures they identified with Heracles and Dionysus (App. XVI). Similarly Al. had equated the Tyrian Melkarth with Heracles (ii 15, 7; 24, 5 f.; iii 6, 1), just as he had assumed that a Phrygian god was ' Zeus the king ' (ii 3, 6), and (on my view) identified Ammon with Zeus (App. V, cf. also vii 20, 1). It is A., following Herodotus (ii 43–5), who differentiates between the Greek, Tyrian and Egyptian Heracles and later distinguishes the Indian Heracles from these (ii 16, 1–6; iv 28, 2; *Ind.* 5 13), just as he doubts (v 1) if the Indian Dionysus is the Theban or Lydian; it is somewhat misleading when he says (ii 16, 7) that Al. wished to sacrifice to ' this Heracles ', i.e. the Tyrian; the very special honour Al. paid to the god at Tyre shows that Al. must have taken the Tyrian god to be his own ancestor.

5. ' After quitting this life, Heracles became a god instead of a mortal ' (Isocrates vi 17); he owed this exaltation to his ' virtue ' (ib. i 50; v 132), i.e. to noble and beneficent acts. We can only speculate whether a belief that he had equalled or excelled Heracles led Al. to expect a similar reward, and whether the fictitious debate in iv 10 reflects contemporary opinions and a prevalent view that deification should be at least deferred till death.

APPENDIX V

THE VISIT TO SIWAH (iii 3-4)

1. Though aware of other accounts (3, 5), A. seems to
rely entirely on Pt. or Ar. or both. Ar. is his source
for the distance, roughly correct, from Paraetonium
(Mersah-Matruh) to the oasis (3, 3), and since he was
more interested than Pt. in geographical matters,
probably for the description of the oasis (4, 1-4); if
so, the allusion to ' the king ' in 4, 3 suggests that he
wrote after Ptolemy assumed that title in 304.
(However that may be, A's use of the present tense
about dues paid to the king shows that he was mech-
anically copying his source.) A. twice records
discrepancies between Pt. and Ar. (3, 5 f.; 4, 5) and
evinces some incredulity in the reported miracles,
which appeared in some form in all accounts (D.
49-51; QC. iv 7; P. 26-8; J. xi 11); Strabo too
observed that the Alexander-historians were guilty
of many flatteries in describing the visit to Siwah,
though he held that something (just what he does not
say) in their stories deserved acceptance (xvii 1, 43).
On 4, 5 C. B. Welles (*Historia* 1962, 274 ff.) argues that
Pt. gave an impracticable route for Al's return; this
is refuted by P. M. Fraser, *Opuscula Atheniensia*
1967, 23 ff. He also contends that Ar. brought Al.
back to the site of Alexandria and agreed with the
' vulgate ' that the foundation of that city was later
than the visit to Siwah. But A. would surely have
noted this divergency from Pt. in a context in which
he records others. Welles thinks the vulgate's
chronology right, since Ps-Callisthenes, an Alexandrian writer who may be trusted on this point, says

the city was founded on 25 Tybi = 7 April. But 25 Tybi is probably 20 January, as in the Roman period when Ps-Callisthenes wrote (P. M. Fraser, *Ptolemaic Alexandria* ii p. 3). Welles supposes that Al. wished to consult the oracle about the foundation, but he had already ascertained the divine will on this matter (1, 5), and felt no need for oracular sanction when founding other cities. Finally, 6, 1 shows that he left Egypt before 7 April.

2. Strabo (l.c.) summarizes the account of Callisthenes (C.). Of course C. gave much more detail (cf. P. 27, 3); Strabo preserves only the following points.

(a) Al. wished to visit Siwah from ' love of glory ', to emulate Perseus and Heracles (cf. 3, 1).

(b) He went by Paraetonium (cf. 3, 3).

(c) The army was assisted by rain but impeded by a sandstorm (cf. 3, 3 f.).

(d) It was guided by two crows. (So Ar. and most writers, 3, 4; QC. has a flock of birds appearing near the oasis—where their presence would be natural; Pt's serpents are his own fabrication, perhaps somehow related to their association with the cult of Ammon.)

(e) Al. entered the inner shrine alone in his customary garb, whereas his entourage had to change their clothes and remain outside, where they could, none the less, hear what was said.

(f) The god gave his responses mainly by nods and signs.

(g) However, the prophet ' acted the part of Zeus ' or ' interpreted Zeus ' (τὸν Δία ὑποκριναμένου) and told Al. expressly that he was ' son of Zeus '. (He clearly spoke Greek, being accustomed to Greek enquirers.)

APPENDIX V

(h) Subsequently envoys arrived at Memphis from the oracle of Branchidae near Miletus with oracles ' about the *genesis* (cf. 5 below) of Al. from Zeus, the future victory near Arbela, the death of Darius and the Spartan revolt ', and the Sibyl of Erythrae also spoke about Al's noble birth. *Contra* Tarn (ii 357) C. cannot simply have invented these oracular responses. No doubt they were ambiguous in the usual manner, and were interpreted *post eventum* in C.'s sense; it follows that C. at least amended his history of Al. in Egypt after Gaugamela. ' Arbela ' is not the correct name for the battle (cf. iii 8, 7 n.; vi 11, 4), as Strabo also knew (xvi 1, 3 f.); but despite his own polemic on the topic, A. could use it himself (iii 22, 4), and Strabo may have preferred to give the name most easily intelligible to his readers; we are not to infer that C. was unreliable in his location of the battle, and therefore in other ways.

3. In (a)–(d) C. seems to have told a story substantially similar to A's (apart from Pt's serpents). Both connect the expedition with Al's romantic emulation of heroes (cf. App. IV). The difficulties of the journey were probably magnified in all sources, to make it seem more heroic; the journey was in fact often performed by Greeks and others, and it was the right season, winter, when rain could be expected; at most it may have been harder for Al., if he had a considerable force with him (its size is not recorded). Strabo's summary is so brief that we should not infer that C. mentioned no other motive for the expedition but Al's love of glory (A. 3, 2) nor that he neglected to record that Al. ' was possessed by a longing (*pothos*) to go to Ammon ' (ib.). For *pothos* cf. i 3, 5; ii 3, 1; iii 1, 5; iv 28, 4; v 2, 5;

vii 1, 1; 2, 2; 16, 2; in *Ind.* 20, 1, Nearchus para-
phrases it (20, 2) as ' a desire (*epithymia*) to do something always new and extraordinary '; for *epithymia*
cf. also v 25, 2. (The use of *pothos* and its related
verb in invented speeches in v 26, 1 and 27, 6 cannot
be regarded as of much significance.) The ' ingens
cupido ' in QC. iv 7, 8 (cf. iv 8, 3; vii 11, 4) probably
represents *pothos*; in ix 2, 2 he writes: ' vicit cupido
rationem '. Ehrenberg (*Al. and the Greeks* ch. II)
conjectured that Al. himself used to speak of his
pothos and that this illustrates an irrational part of his
character which led him to undertake extraordinary
enterprises. K. Kraft, *Der ' rationale ' Alexander*,
ch. IV treats it in each case as either representing a
desire that was *per se* reasonable for a general and
statesman, or more often as referring to a natural
curiosity, which still did not interfere with his
political and military objectives; apart from the
remarks of Nearchus, which he does not discuss, the
texts fit this interpretation well enough, and better
than the most high-flown interpretations which he
contests. On this occasion it was reasonable enough
for Al. to wish to consult an oracle reputed infallible,
given that he had no need to leave Egypt for the
Euphrates till the spring. As Kraft observes, he
seems to have abandoned as untimely his desire to
see Upper Egypt and Ethiopia (QC. iv 8, 3).

4. As to the journey, all accounts broadly agree and,
miracles apart, are credible. Whether or not present
in person, C., Pt. and Ar. could all have come by
reliable reports. But once Al. reaches the shrine,
C. disagrees with the vulgate, though not with A.,
who provides virtually no explicit information at all.
(a) In the ' vulgate ' (D. 51; QC. iv 7, 25; P. 27, 3;

APPENDIX V

J. xi 11, 7) Al. is first *greeted* by the priest as son of
' God ' or ' Zeus '; P. 27, 5 also reports a tale that his
words ' O paidion ' (' My son ') were misheard as
' O pai Dios ' (' Son of Zeus '). In answer to his
enquiries he was then told (all versions in varying
order) that (b) he had punished all the assassins of
Philip (Introd. § 46), though Philip was not his father,
and (c) that he would rule the whole world, as an
unconquerable god; J. alone adds that his companions were bidden by the oracle to honour him as a
god. It is clear that C. cannot have had (c); the
oracle from Branchidae, which he did report, would
have been an anti-climax, if Ammon had already
predicted world-rule. This being so, it is imprudent
to use the vulgate to establish what C. said or meant,
even though the details given by D. and QC. of the
oracular procedure amplify Strabo's allusion to the
god's ' nods and signs ' and may also derive from C.
(The details accord with the known ritual in Egyptian
oracles, cf. Lane Fox 208 f.; 523 f.) It is generally
held that C., like the vulgate, told that Al. was
greeted as son of Zeus by the priest, and not that the
sonship was revealed in an oracular response, since
the responses were heard by Al. alone and not made
known by him nor reported by C., Pt. or Ar. It would
probably have made little difference to Al's later
view of his relation to Ammon, if this interpretation
of the evidence were correct, but it is at least open to
question. (i) C., according to Strabo, directly stated
that Al's companions could hear what went on inside
the temple, though they remained without, and he is
naturally taken to mean that it was within the temple
that he heard that he was son of Zeus, nor does the
vulgate, for what it is worth, contradict this. (ii)
Strabo's summary of C. naturally suggests, by giving

first an account of the oracular procedure, that the priest's statement that Al. was son of Zeus was his verbal interpretation of the nods and signs by which the god announced a question put by Al. (iii) The authenticity of a letter from Al. to Olympias (P. 27, 5), in which he referred to certain responses that he would reveal only to her on his return, should not be admitted (Introd. 16); but even if it were genuine, it would not show that he kept all the responses secret, and in fact he did make it public that the oracle had instructed him on the gods to whom he should sacrifice (vi 19, 4; *Ind.* 18, 11), perhaps in answer to an enquiry about his best hope of achieving victory (cf. Xen., *Anabasis* iii 1, 6). Al. naturally wanted guidance on his future actions and would not have kept silent on any responses that might encourage his men. (iv) It cannot be inferred from Strabo that C. recorded none of the responses; as to Pt. and Ar. see 5 below. (The argument from their silence proves too much, as they did not report here the response on sacrifices.) It should at least be clear that C. made out that the priest recognized Al. as son of Zeus, and he cannot have written what was either displeasing to Al. or susceptible of ready disproof.

5. According to A. one reason why Al. went to Siwah was that ' he was tracing (ἀνέφερε) his *genesis* in part to Ammon, as the myths traced that of Heracles and Perseus to Zeus.' The word ' genesis ' naturally means ' birth ' and not descent (Lane Fox 524), and in the myths Heracles and Perseus were *sons* of Zeus. On becoming Pharaoh (as such, he sacrificed to the Egyptian gods, iii 1, 4), Al. was officially son of Amun-Ra, whom Al. would naturally have identified with Zeus (*infra*). To the new

APPENDIX V

Achilles the divine filiation must have been a congenial and plausible notion, of which he was seeking confirmation from the oracle that could give him more accurate information about his ' own affairs '. Kraft indeed has argued that that vague phrase does not refer to his sonship, for he went to Siwah in the conviction (Überzeugung) that he was son of Ammon. But this interpretation violates the logic of the Greek; the imperfect ἀνέφερε must mean that he was ' seeking to trace his birth to Ammon ' and γνώμη must be rendered ' purpose ' and not ' conviction '; for it would make no sense to say that Al. knew he was son of Ammon and *therefore* went to Siwah to find out about his (other) concerns. Thus A's authorities imply that he intended to enquire about his paternity, and they also say that he himself claimed that he had heard what was to his heart's desire (4, 5). This is oblique confirmation of C's story. Al. was evidently fortified in the belief that he wished to hold that he was son of Ammon. Now, if the assurance were couched in the usual dark ambiguities of an oracle, the construction C. and Al. himself preferred may not have been equally clear to everyone. One or both of A's sources may have had this obscurity in mind when stating Al's purpose as ' to acquire more accurate information or to say that he had acquired it ' (3, 4), and the same attitude is shown, no doubt by the same writer, when he notes the king's satisfaction with what he had heard, without telling us what this was. Both Pt. and Ar. were evidently reluctant to concede that Al. ever claimed to be son of a god with the alleged sanction of the oracle (cf. 10 f. below). As on other occasions (App. XIV), they resorted to deceptive reticence.

473

6. After 332 we hear of Al's real or alleged claim to be son alternatively of Ammon (iv 9, 9; vii 8, 3; P. 27. 5; 50, 6) or of Zeus (iv 8, 2; vii 2, 2; 29, 3; P. 27, 5; 28, 2; cf. C. in P. 33, 1) or of a god (vi 14, 2); QC. consistently writes ' son of Jupiter ', i.e. Zeus, but then he also equates Jupiter and ' Hammon ' (iv 7, 5), a common Latin practice. The equation of Ammon and Zeus was normal, both for Amun of Egyptian Thebes, and for the god at Siwah, whose cult was held to be derived from Thebes (Hdt. ii 42, 54–7), rightly in the view of many modern scholars (F. Chamoux, *Cyrène sous la Monarchie des Battiades* 56). The coins of Cyrene clearly identify Ammon and Zeus (ib. 329 ff.), just as Pindar (*Pythians* iv 28; fr. 36) and Herodotus (ii 55; iii 25) had done. Under the Ptolemies Thebes itself was renamed Diospolis, the city of Zeus (cf. *RE. s.v.* Ammon; Diod. i 15; Fraser, *Ptolemaic Alexandria* ch. v n. 24; for other such equations of Greek and Egyptian gods ib. nn. 30, 36, 50, 56, 150, 173 and in particular for that of Osiris or Serapis with Dionysus, ib. vol. i pp. 206, 255 f.; cf. also App. IV 4 above). Callisthenes, reported without demur by Strabo, makes the priest at Siwah impersonate or interpret Zeus (§ 2 f.). It would have been perfectly natural for Al. too to identify Ammon with Zeus.

7. It is true that Greeks referred to Ammon at times in ways which might suggest that they distinguished two gods. (a) The god worshipped at Siwah is normally called Ammon, not Zeus. But the Greeks had no name for Siwah; the oracle there is ' that in Ammon ' (Strabo xvii 1, 43), and just as they would speak of men going to Delphi or Dodona for oracular

help, so they spoke of going to Ammon. (b) Ammon as such had his cults in Athens and elsewhere in Greece by Alexander's time (C. J. Classen, *Historia* 1959, 349 ff.). That does not prove that the votaries distinguished Ammon from Zeus. Men could not be sure of a god's true name, cf. Aeschylus, *Agamemnon* 160 ff. with Fraenkel's note *ad loc.*, and E. Norden, *Agnostos Theos* 144 ff., nor whether other peoples might not have surer access to him; hence in religious acts it might be prudent to address him by more than one name, or to worship him with foreign rites, using his foreign name. Hence Al. himself swore both by Zeus of the Greeks and by Ammon of the Libyans (Nearchus, *Ind.* 35, 8) and regularly sacrificed to Ammon (vi 3, 1). To Al. the Greek and Macedonian god, Zeus, was ruler of gods and men, the supreme god, as doubtless was Ammon to the people of Siwah, and he means to invoke the supreme god who is at once Zeus to Greeks and Ammon to Libyans. Even writers like Herodotus, who expressly identified Zeus and Ammon, could speak at times of Ammon (especially when they refer to the oracle) and at times of Zeus.

8. Al. prayed the gods for aid, εἴπερ ὄντως Διόθεν ἐστι γεγονώς (P. 33, 1). This statement in the official history cannot have been false (*contra* Tarn ii 352, cf. App. IX 5). But what does it mean? The word εἴπερ can signify either ' if ' or ' since ', but as the formulation resembles such a Homeric prayer as we have in *Odyssey* IX 529, and Al. was influenced by Homer, I think that ' since ' is to be preferred, and we should not infer that Al. had any doubt about the relation to Zeus he referred to. The words Διόθεν γεγονώς are more naturally construed to mean ' son

475

of Zeus ' than ' descendent of Zeus ' (which Al. was officially, through Heracles), and in the light of C's own account of what the prophet at Siwah had said, that is surely what C. intended to convey. Thus he represents Al. as accepting that he was a son of Zeus. Doubts may still arise: Al's true formulation in the prayer may have been more ambiguous. There is no clear confirmation of the statements of QC. iv 7, 30 and vi 11, 23 (implicitly contradicted in viii 5, 5) that he officially *ordered* his divine filiation to be acknowledged, while still in Egypt, or at any time. His *wish* for such recognition, however, consistently appears in ' vulgate ' accounts of opposition to Al. among his own followers, in the trial of Philotas (QC. vi 10, 26 f.), in connection with Clitus' murder (A iv 8, 2; QC. viii 1, 42; P. 50, 6) and with *proscynesis* (A. iv 9, 9; QC. viii 5, 5) and in the trial of Hermolaus (QC. viii 7, 12; 8, 14; 10, 1 and 29). Ephippus of Olynthus, a contemporary (Pearson, *LH* 61), albeit hostile, averred that he dressed up as Ammon (but also as Artemis and Hermes) and that Gorgos, who was at least a historic person (Pearson 64), crowned him as son of Ammon. More important, A. tells on the authority of one or both of his main sources that the Oxydracae had heard that Al. was son of a god (vi 14, 2, reading θεοῦ; see note *ad loc.*) and that at Opis the mutinous troops gibed at his supposed claim to be son of Ammon (vii 8, 3). The story in vii 2, 3 and Strabo xv 1, 68 also presupposes that Al. was claiming in 326 to be son of Zeus; Strabo's version comes from Megasthenes, a contemporary who was familiar with Sibyrtius, one of Al's satraps, but A's may perhaps be derived from Nearchus (cf. note *ad loc.*); in any event the authority is good. At Athens in 324 Demosthenes could allude contemptuously to Al.'s desire to be son of Zeus or Posidon (Hyperides, *contra Dem.* 31).

9. Tarn and others hold that as Pharaoh Al. was son of Amun-Ra in a mystic sense that did not exclude Philip's paternity, and that the meaning of his mystic relation to the god was privately explained to him by the prophet at Siwah. Such a private interview remains possible, even if there were other responses which his companions overheard, and this theory gives a good sense to ' in part ' in 3, 2. Yet, as on Tarn's view Al. never divulged what he had been told (*supra*), there is necessarily no direct evidence for his hypothesis. Equally, it cannot be refuted by Al.'s supposed denial in a letter to the Samians that Philip was his father (P. 28); the fact that this letter corresponds in other respects to what we know to be true does not prove its authenticity, and it should be rejected, not because it does not fit Tarn's case, but on general grounds (Introd. 15). It is only one of many texts that show how men took Al. to be claiming that he was son of Zeus in the same sense as Heracles. A. himself clearly adopted this view (vii 29, 3). So presumably did the mutineers at Opis (vii 8, 3). Tarn concedes this and says that the misunderstanding provoked Al. to fury. But his indignation is equally easy to explain, if the men understood him perfectly well: he was angry because they were ridiculing its absurdity. On the other hand we cannot call in as proof that they were right the stories (possibly true) that Olympias herself put it about that she had been impregnated by a snake, sacred to Ammon and disguising the god (P. 2 etc., cf. A. iv 10, 2 from the ' vulgate '), for we do not know that Al. himself favoured them.

10. Tarn found indirect confirmation of his hypothesis in the fact that at Opis Al. is said to have referred to Philip as his father (vii 9, 2). But as I hope to show when discussing speeches in A. in vol. II (cf. also F. R. Wüst, *Historia* 1953/54, 177 ff.), this speech is A's invention. Admittedly, A. is here implicitly contradicting his own conception of Al's claim (vii 29, 3), no doubt without being conscious of inconsistency; and this makes it likely that he is using material from one of his main sources. It was again one of these sources that recorded how on one occasion Al. sacrificed to Heracles *as his ancestor* (vi 3, 1); in another speech, which Tarn himself regarded as fictitious, and rightly, even though not all his arguments are acceptable (ii 286 ff.), Al. himself is made to describe Heracles in this way (v 26, 5). But Heracles was his ancestor, only if he still acknowledged Philip as his father. Thus Pt. or Ar. or both not only failed to report that Al. claimed to be son of Zeus-Ammon (in any sense, even Tarn's), except indirectly in an account of the gibes of the mutineers, but implicitly denied, at least in vi 3, 1, that he ever disowned Philip as his father.

11. Pt. at least may have had a reason for suppressing Al's claim to be son of Zeus. Pt. himself was officially descended through his mother, Arsinoe, from king Amyntas I and was thus a Heraclid and cousin of Al.; as Theocritus put it (xvii 27), both numbered Heracles as their furthest ancestor (Satyrus, Jacoby no. 631). There was also a story that he was really a bastard son of Philip (QC. ix 8, 22, etc.); this cannot be true, nor even have seemed plausible, if he was born (Ps-Lucian, *Macrobioi* 12) in 367/6 B.C. when Philip was only 16 and in captivity at

Thebes, but perhaps he was born later, and himself propagated the tale, to give him an even closer connection with the Argead line than rival dynasts in the struggle for power within Al's empire could assert. (See Volkmann, *RE* xxiii 1603 f.) Pt's affinity with Al. would have been dissolved in either case, if Al. were regarded as son of Zeus-Ammon and not of Philip: yet to admit that Al. had made the claim and to impugn its veracity would have marred the ideal picture that Pt. clearly wished to draw of his former friend and king, a picture that inevitably had political overtones, since Pt. was in possession of Al's body and benefited from the prestige derived from the cult at his tomb. The safer course was thus to omit any direct reference to an inconvenient historical fact. No doubt the claim that Al. was son of a god helped to prepare the way for his deification, which took place in Egypt under the rule of Pt. himself, but perhaps only at a time after Pt. wrote his history (Fraser, *Ptolemaic Alexandria* 215 f. with Introd. § 11 above). It is less easy to see why Ar. should have concealed the truth, if such it was. One possibility is that he had read Pt. and on this, as on many other matters, deferred to his authority. But this is not a necessary explanation. The Macedonian high nobility in general can hardly have relished the suggestion that Al. was of divine birth and not, therefore, a member of the old reigning dynasty, to which many must have been related by marriage or descent. Domiciled in Macedon, Ar. may have been influenced by the feelings of many of Al's old Companions, whose admiration for their leader was perhaps commonly mixed with distaste for some of his more extravagant pretensions, his assumption of Oriental state and his claims to be son of

479

a god. If a connexion is to be seen between Al's divine filiation and his own apotheosis, it is also relevant that in Macedon the ruler-cult never took hold.

12. For the enormous bibliography see Seibert (Introd. n. 108).

APPENDIX VI

THE REVOLT OF AGIS

1. In 331 B.C. (cf. *infra*) king Agis of Sparta raised a formidable revolt against Macedon in Greece; to this, and to Agis' earlier activities, Arrian makes only brief allusions; and his reticence demands an explanation. Our chief sources are D. 62 f.; QC. vi 1 (though most of his account is lost); J. xxi 1; Aeschines iii 165 and Dinarchus i 34. Athens stood aloof, but in the Peloponnese Sparta was joined by her traditional allies, the Arcadians (except Megalopolis), the Achaeans (except Pellene) and Elis; Agis is said by D. to have mustered 20,000 foot and 2,000 horse; he defeated a Macedonian force under Corragus and besieged Megalopolis, while Antipater was long in collecting an army to meet him (Aeschines), no doubt because he was at first pre-occupied by a revolt in Thrace (D., who makes Memnon, the governor, its leader; this is mysterious and not easily believed, as Memnon later took reinforcements to Al., cf. QC. ix 3, 21, and Al. was not one to pardon disloyalty). Ultimately, Antipater mobilized 40,000 men, including Greek allies (D.), and defeated and

killed Agis near Megalopolis. The strength of his army is remarkable; in 334 he had been left only 12,000 Macedonian foot and 1,500 horse (D. 17, 5), and more Macedonians had been later sent east (Introd. 57, cf. §3 below), but probably available manpower was growing every year (cf. Griffith, *G. & R.* 1965, 129 ff.), and of course we do not know how many allies joined him. After his victory Antipater referred the punishment of Sparta to the allied *synedrion*, and that body in turn left the decision to Al. (D. 73, 5 f.). Aeschines tells that Spartan representatives were about to go up to Al. and plead their case, when he was speaking; that was in July/Aug. 330 (cf. iii 254). By then the revolt was over, but Aeschines does not show just when it was suppressed. If the decisive battle be placed in autumn 331, we can readily assume that the *synedrion* did not meet till the Isthmian festival in late spring or early summer 330 and that the Spartans were slow in despatching their emissaries. The date of the revolt's outbreak is also disputed, and here A's allusions are crucial.

2. A. ii 13, 4 ff. tells how Agis met the Persian admirals on Siphnos just when the news of Issus came through (Oct. 333), that he received 30 Talents and 10 triremes from them, which he gave his brother to use in Crete, and that he later rejoined Autophradates at Halicarnassus, but he neglects his later activity in Crete, where in 332 he was winning over cities (D. 48, 1; QC. iv 1, 39 f.), and probably securing mercenaries; in the war he allegedly had 10,000 (Dinarchus), and according to D. and QC. 8,000 survivors of Issus had joined him in Crete. This estimate is incompatible with A's statement that

only 8,000 in all escaped from Issus (H. W. Parke, *Greek Mercenary Soldiers* 199 thinks even this figure too high); moreover, A. seems to make them all go with Amyntas to Egypt (whereas D. and QC. iv 1, 27 give Amyntas only 4,000); there they must have sustained further losses (A. ii 13, 2 f.), and it is not recorded that any from this party ultimately went to Crete. However, A. is probably wrong in thinking that all the survivors from Issus were with Amyntas; the 2,000 still in Darius' service in 331 (iii 7, 1; 16, 2; in QC. iv 1, 3 they number 4,000) may be another remnant. All that we can say is that some who had fought at Issus found their way to Agis.

3. A. says that at Tyre in 331, perhaps as late as early July (App. VIII 4), Al. sent Amphoterus with ships to help the loyal Peloponnesians against a movement of revolt in the Peloponnese led by Sparta; he also ordered 100 Phoenician and Cypriote ships to Greece (iii 6, 2 f.). By contrast QC. iv 8, 15 makes him despatch Amphoterus from Egypt to free Crete and clear the seas of piracy, whereas A. iii 2, 6 does not suggest that Amphoterus, as well as Hegelochus, came to Egypt at all. Perhaps we can partially reconcile their evidence by assuming that Amphoterus' original instructions, given in Egypt, were amended when it was clear that the prime danger was no longer in Crete but in Greece. *Prima facie* A. seems to imply that Al. had already heard at latest in early July of Agis' success in raising other Peloponnesians in revolt. It is no objection that he sent only ships when troops were most needed to defeat the rebels. Al. could not spare troops without postponing his offensive in Mesopotamia. He could reckon that Antipater could outmatch Agis by land

without reinforcements. On the other hand a fleet, which he was free to send, could provide Antipater, in case of need, with the means of rapidly transporting forces by sea; it could cut off Agis, who was now presumably back at Sparta, from further supplies of soldiers from Crete, and it could help to neutralize Athens; at the very same time Al. at last ordered the release of Athenian prisoners taken in 334 (contrast i 29, 5), to conciliate that city (iii 6, 2). And, though our accounts of the revolt say nothing of the part played by Al's ships, they may in fact have served at least the last two purposes. It is more puzzling that in December 331 (iii 16, 10) Al. was to be joined by Amyntas, son of Andromenes, whom he had despatched home to bring him reinforcements late in 332 (D. 49, 1; QC. iv 6, 30) and who now brought him 6,500 Macedonians, 4,100 Thracians and 4,000–5,000 Peloponnesians (D. 65, 1; QC. v 1, 40 f.); these men can hardly have started later than July, if they marched all the way, but if they were shipped to Syria, they would have set out even later, and it seems strange that Antipater should have let them go, if he was then aware of the full dimensions of the revolt. That may suggest that in July, though the situation in the Peloponnese was already menacing, Sparta's allies were not yet committed to war and that Antipater did not feel justified in delaying compliance with Al's orders for reinforcements. It was perhaps from Amyntas that Al. himself first learned in December that the seditious movement in the Peloponnese had culminated in war, and as he then sent Antipater money for his operations, he did not yet know that the revolt had been repressed (iii 16, 10). All this must cast some doubt on the statement in QC. vi 1, 21 that the revolt broke out

suddenly and was ended before Gaugamela, i.e. 1
October. It had been preparing for some time, and
if Antipater's victory occurred so early, we might
expect a courier to have brought the news to Al. by
December, when he was at Susa or (see n. *ad loc.*)
approaching it. Aeschines actually says that Antipater was long in mustering his forces; but conceivably he is counting from the time when the
Spartans were in arms and not from the later point
when they had secured allies, and his testimony
need not prove that the revolt was not put down till
spring 330; we might prefer a date in October if
we need to give QC. any credence; he would then be
guilty of only a small chronological error.

4. QC. chose to describe the revolt after his narrative
of Darius' death, perhaps because one of his sources
recorded that it was then that Al. heard of its suppression; so J. (whose account is, however, full of
errors). In fact QC. himself says that the report
reached Al. only when he was at Bactra (vii 4, 32) in
spring 329; this is far too late, and perhaps he
garbled a statement in his source that it was there
that the Spartans sent to plead for their city overtook Al. (Earlier, in summer 330, Al. had captured
Spartan emissaries sent to Darius, A. iii 24, 4; we
can suppose that they had left in 332, before it was
known at Sparta that Al. was master of the seas and
the Syrian ports and that they had to make their way
via Egypt and the Red Sea, reaching Darius by a
long, slow detour.) D. recorded the revolt immediately after Gaugamela and absurdly makes it a
consequence of that battle; he also dates it to the
next Athenian archon year, 330/329, which is refuted by Aeschines as well as by A. D's dates are

notoriously unreliable; in 40, 1 and 64, 3 he makes Al. bury his dead after Issus and Gaugamela in the next archon year! If he, QC. and J. all drew ultimately on a common source for the revolt, it is plain that each took a different way of relating the story to Al's operations (cf. R. A. Lock, *Antichthon* 1972, 10 ff.), and thus fell into various chronological errors.

5. See also E. Badian, *Hermes* 1967, 170 ff., though I do not accept his conjecture that Al. tarried at Persepolis, because he was anxiously awaiting news from Greece, see App. VIII 6 for another explanation); G. L. Cawkwell, *CQ* 1969, 163 ff. (dating the revolt to 330); G. E. M. de Ste Croix, *Origins of the Peloponnesian War* 376 ff.

6. Why did A. and presumably his sources almost ignore these events? Perhaps because of their persistent tendency to minimize discontent in Greece, which made nonsense of Al's Panhellenic claims; they were equally silent about the events that led up to the Lamian war that broke out in autumn 323 (unless much is crammed into the lacuna in A. vii 12), for which Al's own actions were partly responsible, though they were careful to record the insincere congratulations of Greek envoys in vii 23, 2. But they were mainly concerned with Al's own campaigns and perhaps did not see it as their task to write a general history of his reign. And Al. did not allow the revolt to disturb his own strategy in 331; he assumed that somehow Antipater could cope with Agis, and he was proved right.

APPENDIX VII

THE SITE OF THAPSACUS

E. W. Marsden, *Campaign of Gaugamela* 81, with map and bibliographical references, observes that Thapsacus has been located anywhere between Jerablus and Deir ez Zor on the Euphrates; he prefers Sura without excluding somewhere near Meskene (which Strabo xvi 1, 13 might naturally suggest), but *contra* W. J. Farrell, *JHS* 1961, 153 ff., rejects Jerablus as inconsistent with our information about Al's march. I can see no inconsistency; the railway from the coast of Phoenicia to Mosul crosses the Euphrates at Jerablus, and if Al., having presumably read the account in Xen. *Anab.* i 5 of the difficulty of marching towards Babylon down the left bank of the Euphrates, had decided in advance to take the Tigris route (cf. A. iii 7, 3), it would have been rational to march north as far as Jerablus. On this hypothesis it is much easier to see why A. could say (ibid.) that from the time he crossed the river he had on his left the Euphrates (sc. after its eastward bend to the north) and the Armenian mountains. Furthermore, after Issus, Darius was in a hurry to put the river between Al. and himself, but he crossed at Thapsacus, coming south from the Amanid Pass (ii 13, 1). It is hard to see why he should have deferred a crossing not only until the bend of the river near Meskene but for another 60 miles thereafter. Similarly in 401 Jerablus was the nearest crossing for Cyrus to make for from the Syrian Gates, and it also fits well with the information in Ar. *ap.* A. vii 19, 3; Strabo xvi 3, 3 that shipbuilding materials and other cargoes could be shipped down- or up-stream to Thapsacus whence they were conveyed by portage to or from the coast. However the bend of the river near Meskene cannot be ruled out; Sura by contrast seems too far east.

APPENDIX VIII

GEOGRAPHICAL AND CHRONOLOGICAL QUESTIONS 333–326 B.C.

1. A., and sometimes QC. and D., may tell us that Al. marched from one point to another in so many days, or that he covered so many stades. These bits of information are recorded irregularly, and one bit is sometimes in one author, one in another. It is apparent that they are unmethodically excerpting from a much fuller body of material in their own sources, such as Pt. If we reject the hypothesis that Pt. or other historians writing after Al's death had access to 'royal journals' (Introd. 14), data of this kind must have come to them in turn from some other contemporary source. Callisthenes may have recorded such data, but his history broke off early. Probably they used the records of the 'bematists', who accompanied Al. (cf. Tod 188), measured routes by *bemata* or paces (Pliny, *Natural History* vi 61), and published reports under the title of *Stathmoi* (Stages), which also contained descriptions of lands that Al. visited or merely heard of. These descriptions were not free from inventions and fables, but no doubt the *Stathmoi* were fairly accurate about Al's actual

marches; Pliny (l.c., cf. vi 44 f.) cites them for distances, and they were apparently also used by Eratosthenes (c. 285–194 B.C.) for his great geographical work; see Jacoby nos. 119–23 with bibliography (cf. L. Pearson, *Historia* iii 439 ff.) Figures are particularly liable to corruption by copyists, and Pliny (vi 62) noticed that there were already variants in manuscripts at his disposal; some discrepancies between the totals produced by adding up the individual figures in Pliny or Strabo and those which each author supplies himself, and perhaps between particular figures in Pliny and Strabo, may be due to manuscript corruption. Pliny gives figures in Roman miles, but shows in vi 45 that he has converted stades into miles at 8:1. Unfortunately the stade is itself a unit of measurement based on the foot, and the length of the ' foot ' varied in different Greek systems, but in general the stade seems to be ·185 km for our purposes. To some extent such data can be controlled by the distances on modern routes, though the modern route need not correspond exactly to the ancient. For a day's march we can also adduce the experience of modern unmechanized armies. Clausewitz (cf. Marsden, *Campaign of Gaugamela* 19) set the average at 16 km a day, see J. Kromayer, *Hermes* 1896, 96 ff., for a wealth of comparative material; this applies indeed only to large armies, of the size Al. had at least until he left Ecbatana (cf. 7 below), and to significant distances; for several days even a large army can move faster, but it must then pause, to rest and let stragglers come up. In hard mountain country or intense heat or cold such a rate will be less easy to maintain. And Al. often had to pause for another reason: to collect provisions for further advance, especially when he had little information about the country ahead, or knew it to be desolate as well as potentially hostile.

2. Some works I have consulted for what follows are cited only by the author's name, viz:

E. Borza, *Classical Philology* 1972 (for the stay at Persepolis)

J. G. Droysen, *Geschichte des Hellenismus* [2], 1877

K. Fischer, *Bonner Jahrbücher* 1967, 129 ff. (Afghanistan)

A. Foucher (and E. Bazin-Foucher), *Mémoires de la Délégation archéologique française en Afghanistan*, I-II, 1942, 1947

J. Hansman, *Journal of Royal Asiatic Society* 1968, 111 ff. (cf. Hansman and D. Stronach, ib. 1970, 29 ff.)

S. J. Marquardt, *Philologus, Supplementband* X, 1905, 19 ff.

G. Radet, *Mélanges Glotz* II, 1932, 765 ff.

F. von Schwarz, *Alexanders des Grossen Feldzüge in Turkestan*, 1893 (second edition, 1906, not accessible)

A. F. von Stahl, *Geographical Journal* 1924, 312 ff.

Sir Aurel Stein, *On Alexander's Track to the Indus*, 1929

R. M. Wheeler, *Charsadda*, 1962

Further, W. W. Tarn, *GBI—Greeks in Bactria and India* [2], 1951

3. On the basis of mileage we may calculate that starting from Gordium in May 333 (i 29, 4 n.) Al. should have reached Tarsus early in July; nearly three months elapsed before Issus (ii 11, 10 n.), and though part of this interval was filled by his long illness (P. 19, 1), about a fortnight was spent on the visit to Soli, west of Tarsus, and in operations based

on that city before he began to move east. It is characteristic that A. records that he took a day to reach Anchialus on the route to Soli, and seven days in subduing the highlanders to the north (ii 5, 2 and 6), yet gives no other indication of the passage of time except for the statement that he reached Myriandrus ' on the second day ' *prima facie* from Mallus: one instance of the way in which only some of the bematists' records get into his narrative; in fact it seems probable that the ' second ' day is counted from a place between Mallus and Myriandrus (cf. ii 6, 2 n.). Perhaps the long delay and diversion to Soli can be explained: Al. may have hoped that Darius would put his army at risk in the Cilician hills and narrow plains; if so, he lost patience and began to advance into Syria at the very moment when his hope was fulfilled. A. provides no explanation and is not even conscious that there was anything to explain.

4. We find exactly the same phenomenon in the campaign of 331. Al. left Egypt at the very beginning of spring (iii 6, 1), presumably in March, but was not at Thapsacus on the Euphrates until some date between 10 July and 8 August (7, 1), and probably at the end of that period (*infra*), after pausing for an unspecified period at Tyre. QC. iv 9, 12 says that he reached the Euphrates ' in his eleventh camp '; this is another instance of (at best) unintelligent reportage from the bematists' records, for it naturally suggests that he took 11 days from Tyre to the river, and this is impossible; some intermediate and unrecorded halt is implied. Now the site of Thapsacus is unknown (App. VII), but Eratosthenes said that it was 2,400 stades from the

point at which Al. crossed the Tigris (Strabo ii 1, 38), and wherever either of these places may be located, his estimate of about 440 km is not widely different from those which Marsden 22 gives for the distance between his Thapsacus or mine (App. VII) and any of the probable crossing places of the Tigris. To cover this distance A. needed not 13 days (QC. iv 9, 14), but about 4 weeks; once again, QC. has (at best) omitted some intermediate stage. In fact not less than 43 days elapsed between Al's arrival at Thapsacus and the lunar eclipse of 20/21 September, which occurred after he had crossed the Tigris and rested his army (7, 6); no doubt several days were occupied in crossing each river, and Al. may himself have reached the Euphrates before most of his army had come up. Thus the time between 8 August and 20 September can readily be filled. But if Al. had marched without delay from the Nile to Thapsacus, he would have been there in June. The campaign in Samaria (QC. iv 8, 9–11) and the alleged inefficiency in making preparations (i.e. collecting supplies) on the part of the satrap of Syria (iii 6, 8) may be relevant, but once again he may have hoped that Darius would leave the broad plains of Mesopotamia and come to meet him in the hilly country of Syria. And once again, A. attempts no explanation of his strategical problems or plans.

5. P. 31, 4 makes the night preceding the battle of Gaugamela the eleventh after the eclipse; thus the battle occurred, if we reckon inclusively, on 1 October; this date is confirmed in his life of Camillus (19; cf. iii 15, 7 n.; Beloch, III, 2, 304 ff., 315), and there is no reason to reject it, especially as it agrees with the detailed time-table in A., given the as-

sumption that the day of 21 September was occupied with sacrifices (and no doubt with allaying alarm caused by the eclipse), cf. iii 7, 6.

Sept. 21	Sacrifices
	22–24	Three days' advance (7, 7)
	25	Contact with enemy (7, 7–9, 1)
	26–9	Four days' rest (9, 1)
	30	Renewed advance (night of 29th, 9, 2)
Oct. 1	Battle (for night of 30 Sept./1 Oct., 10–11).

Here, for once, we have a full record derived ultimately from the bematists. QC. also had information from the same source; he too knew of the four days' rest after contact had been made (iv 10, 10–15) and of the postponement of the battle by a day (iv 13), but he makes Al. set out from the Tigris at the second watch of 20/21 Sept., the eclipse having occurred at the first(!), and make contact with the enemy at daybreak of the 21st (10, 1–9). We must not interpret A's time-table from him, especially in view of the fiction of 10, 18–12, 2.

6. Al. took 20 days to cover 370 easy km from Babylon to Susa (A. iii 16, 7); we might allow as many for c. 400 km from Gaugamela to Babylon; there he stayed 34 days (QC. v 1, 36–9, cf. D. 64, 5). But conceivably he moved very fast to Babylon and stayed so long, partly to let his rear come up; even so, he can hardly have reached Susa before c. 5 December. After perhaps a short pause he crossed the mountains to Persepolis about 70 km NE of Shiraz; Eratosthenes' estimate of 4,200 stades from Susa (Strabo xv 3, 1) is grossly excessive, if correctly recorded, but the true distance is c. 590 km and he cannot have

arrived, even though he eventually had with him only a relatively small and quick moving force (iii 18, 2), before early January 330 (cf. § 7). QC. v 6, 11 ff. records a punitive expedition in the surrounding country with snow still on the ground ' about the setting of the Pleiads ', visible perhaps in late March rather than in late April (Borza n. 29). P. 37, 3 says that he remained at Persepolis for 4 months; if that means (parts of) 4 calendar months, he can have left in late April. The need to procure supplies (in winter) and to await the time when snow or mud would less impede his marching can account for so long a delay. It is a hard march of 700 km from Persepolis to Ecbatana (Hamadan), where he can hardly have arrived till early June; A. iii 19 supplies incomplete data, but till he was 3 days' march from Hamadan, he did not know that he would have no battle to fight, and could not risk dividing his army or wearying it by forced marches. QC. v 13, 2 makes him by-pass Hamadan, pursuing Darius on the direct route from Arak to Teheran, but A. shows that this is an error; Radet guesses that at this point he did divide his army, which would now have been safe, and that part took that route. Al. himself certainly went to Hamadan. If Darius had already gathered in supplies and then left them behind in hurried flight, he will not have needed to stay there long to collect provisions, and if he left Persepolis on (say) 25 April and Hamadan on 9 June, the average rate of progress would be 16 km a day.

7. Al. left Hamadan with a much smaller army, and probably beyond Rhagae he regularly divided it into detachments (App. XIII), as he no longer had to

contemplate a major battle, and this eased the problem of procuring food and water. He was thus able to make more rapid progress. Herodotus iv 201 reckons a day's journey as 200 stades, about 37 km, but he was not thinking of even a small army with its *impedimenta*. Kromayer (para. 1) shows that in the late nineteenth century a division of about 12,000 men could march on average 25–30 km a day; 33 was thought extraordinary. As Al. was often moving in difficult country or in harsh weather, and had to pause to gather supplies when he reached fertile districts, we should not expect an average rate of progress over the immense distances he covered in 330–329 above 30 km, though for many days together he must have marched at 35. See also § 21.

8. He reached Rhagae, 8 km S.E. of Teheran (its modern counterpart), on the 11th day from Hamadan (iii 20, 1), and the speed of his march forced him to pause there for 5 days. By the most direct route the distance is about 310 km (von Stahl), an average of about 28 km. Both von Stahl and Radet suppose that he took a more circuitous route, since Arrian *l.c.* says that at his rate of progress the Caspian Gates were only one day's march away, and the distance is about 70 km. But Arrian was surely judging by the rate of his pursuit of Darius on the last day, which was quite exceptional (*infra*). A pause at Rhagae was required no doubt for supplies. At any rate if he reached Hamadan in early June, he probably did not reach Rhagae till *c.* 20 June nor set out again till *c.* 25 June. The earlier we can date these movements, the better it will suit subsequent chronology.

9. He then got through the Caspian Gates, 82 km to the end of the defiles of Sialek and Sardar south of the Elburz mountains, at breakneck speed on the second day, and paused in the fertile plain of Choarene to obtain provisions, as he knew that the country ahead was desolate (iii 20, 4); von Stahl takes him to Aradan, 124 km from Teheran on the modern road, Radet not quite so far. Both assume that it was on this same day that he heard of Darius' arrest and resumed his advance that night, before the return of a foraging party (iii 21, 1 f.). But the text of A. does not require that assumption: A. was quite capable of omitting to record one or more days' rest in Choarene, and the speed of his pursuit of Darius in the next four days is more credible, if we accept that there had been such a rest. Von Stahl and Radet offer rival and conjectural reconstructions of that pursuit, which is said to have culminated in a final march of up to 400 stades or 70 km in the last night and part of the last day, perhaps 18 hours (21, 9), the only distance A. records. Until this last stage Al. had had foot as well as horse with him, and the distances he had covered were no doubt shorter. Radet ends the pursuit at Kharian not far from Shahrud, makes him cover 400 km in all from Rhagae and 270 from Choarene and cites the opinions of French military experts that this rate of marching is just, but only just, within the bounds of credibility (it was all in broiling heat). Von Stahl put the end of the pursuit near Damghan, only 344 km from Teheran on the modern road. Now after the pursuit Al. waited for the rest of his army to come up (23, 1), and QC. (vi 2, 15) puts the pause at the city later called Hecatompylos; nothing suggests that Al. turned back to meet the rest of his troops. Excava-

tions have revealed a city 32 km west of Damghan, not far from the main road, which has been identified with Hecatompylos by Hansman, on the very site where von Stahl guessed it would be found. If Hansman is right, Al's pursuit would seem to have covered not much more than 300 km in six days, or more if a pause is admitted in Choarene. This is easier to credit. However, Hansman's identification is based partly on the statements of Apollodorus of Artemita (first century B.C.) *ap.* Strabo xi 9, 1 that Rhagae was 500 stades from the Caspian Gates and Hecatompylos 1,260 further on; Hansman suggested that the stade must be taken as ·163 km here, since the true distance from Rhagae to the end of the defiles is 82 km, and that Hecatompylos had to be roughly where he was to find it. He wrongly invoked as well Pliny's estimate of 133 miles from the Gates, which at 8 stades to the mile is only 1,064 stades; this does not fit Hansman's site, and must be an error on any view, like Ammianus' 1,040 (xxxiii 6, 43). Marquardt would read 233 miles (= 1,860 stades) and this would then nearly agree with Eratosthenes' figure of 1960 in our manuscripts of Strabo xi 8, 9 (also amended by Marquardt to 1860); Strabo gives no indication that the distance was in dispute. Eratosthenes is also reported there to have given the distance of Hecatompylos to Alexandria in Areia (Herat) as 4,530 (Pliny vi 61 gives 4,600) and of the Caspian Gates to Alexandria as 6,400. Hecatompylos lay on the route, and the sum of the distances is really 6,490, if the figures are correct; on Marquardt's emendation, which gives 6,390, Strabo's 6,400 is closer as a round sum and, being equivalent to 1,182 km with the stade at ·185 km, nearer to the distance by the modern road (about 1,130 km). All this suggests that the figure of 1,260 km is a copyist's error, that Hansman's city is not Hecatompylos, which should have lain further east, and that it is unjustified to take the stade as ·163 km, an equation which does not yield possible results elsewhere (§ 13) and which is not necessary to account for the 500 stades, a round figure, from Rhagae to the Caspian Gates; even if Apollodorus' stade is ·185 km it is only 10 km too high. Thus Radet may be right on the length of the pursuit of Darius, though not about the number of days it occupied; we should add two or three of rest in Choarene.

10. On any view Darius' death falls early in July, and by mid-July, after a rest at Hecatompylos, Al. should have been ready to march into Hyrcania. A. (iii 23, 4; 25, 1) mentions a four-day wait in one camp, and a rest for 15 days at Zadracarta, the capital, which has been variously and uncertainly identified with Sari (which would fit best as base for the Mardian campaign, but cf. § 11) or Astrabad; QC. (vi 4, 8) confirms the first wait, gives additional topographical details, which von Stahl held to be accurate, and makes the Mardian campaign end on the fifth day (5, 22); this well illustrates how each writer is excerpting from much fuller data. Neither tells how much time in all was spent in Hyrcania, but it cannot have been less than a month. The country is exceptionally rich (iii 23, 1 n.), and once again Al. must have been provisioning himself for his march ' to Bactria ' (24, 4). He cannot have started before mid-August.

11. His route took him within about 600 stades from Artacoana, the capital of Areia (25, 6). No one doubts that this town, like the city of Alexandria he

founded in Areia, lay on or near the site of the modern Herat. It therefore follows that he did not mean to go by the oasis of Merv, surrounded by deserts; this was a place he never visited, though a city was founded there by his orders (Tarn ii 234). He must have joined the modern (and ancient) highroad from Teheran (Rhagae) via Meshed to Herat. Meshed is 840 km beyond the Caspian Gates and 709 from Astrabad by modern roads, but further from Sari (Strabo reckons roughly 6,000 stades from the Caspian sea to Areia (xi 8, 1; 10, 1) against 6,490 from the Gates to Alexandria in Areia). Hereabouts in a fertile oasis we should expect Al. to pause, and in fact he 're-assembled' his force at Susia (25, 1–4), surely the modern Tus near Meshed, and once the centre of that area. From Meshed to Herat is another 390 km by the modern road. QC. vi 6, 19 says that he marched fast because of shortage of supplies. A. (25, 6) suggests that he would never have visited Herat but for Satibarzanes' revolt, but this is implausible: Herat with 200,000 cultivated acres has been called 'a green island in a lifeless sea', and Al. would have had little choice but to pause here again for rest and supplies, before proceeding on what Strabo (xv 2, 8) calls the most direct route to Bactra (Balkh or Wazirabad), skirting the north side of the Hindu-Kush by Maimana and Mezar-i-Sharif for about 600 km (Foucher I 10 f.). Satibarzanes' revolt induced him to take Strabo's more circuitous southern route (below), 1,138 km by the modern road to Kabul with the Hindu-Kush still to cross. No doubt he wished to complete the subjugation of Areia, though the time-table forbids us to accept D's statement that he spent 30 days doing so (78, 4)—perhaps that was the time the march to the border of Areia occupied—just as he cannot have taken 60 days to settle Ariaspian affairs (QC. vii 3, 3)—perhaps the time of his march as far as the border of Arachosia. But other considerations may have made him change his original plan. He can hardly have arrived at Herat before late September, nor left until early October. The northern road is harder than the southern, and the climate more severe. It would have been rash to enter a hostile country with no guarantee of supplies and winter coming on, far from any secure base such as Al. had for other winter operations.

12. His march (we are told) lay through the lands of the Zarangaeans (or Drangaeans), Ariaspians, Arachotians and Parapamisadae (A. iii 25–8; Strabo xv 2, 10). In the first of these he rested (for 9 days, according to QC. vi 6, 36) at the ancient capital of Phra or Phrada, where a city was founded by his directions under the name of Prophthasia in memory of the detection there of Philotas' plot. Two cities, Alexandria and Alexandropolis, also commemorated him in Arachosia. His historians do not mention these foundations, and he certainly had no time to attend to them personally in autumn 330; like Alexandria-Merv and even Alexandria in Areia, they were doubtless founded later by his orders. (Droysen, iii² 193 ff. remains the clearest account, with evidence, for Al's colonies.) Strabo (xi 8, 9) and Pliny (vi 61), both apparently following the *Stathmoi*, give distances between Alexandria in Areia, Prophthasia, ' the Arachotian town ' and Ortospana near the modern Kabul. The modern road, which must always have been in use, since it is fairly easy, takes 1,138 km from Herat to Kabul via Farah (270), Girishk,

Kandahar (647), Kalat-i-Ghilzai (785) and Ghazni (1,010); figures in brackets show distances in km from Herat. I believe that Kiepert in his atlas rightly marked this as Al's route. Strabo (xv 2, 10) says that he reached the territory of the Parapamisadae, then covered in snow, *about* the setting of the Pleiads, i.e. in mid or late November (cf. § 21), and wintered in the place where he founded Alexandria ' under Caucasus ' (§ 14); A. iii 28, 1–4 refers more vaguely to deep snow, and fails to mention his winter quarters. Deep snow is most likely round Ghazni, where the climate is far harsher than either to the south or to the north. Ghazni may have been in the satrapy of Arachosia rather than of Parapamisus, but Strabo could have been thinking in geographical, not administrative terms; here Al. was in the heart of the mountains so named. Leaving Herat in early October, he could have reached Ghazni at the season named by Strabo, if he had taken the direct route and (to allow for rests) marched at the remarkably fast average rate of 35 km a day. But Strabo's statement must be false, if we take him by the kind of detour south of Farah which most scholars since Kiepert prefer, extending to near the Seistan or Helmund lake; for instance, Fischer makes him traverse 810 km. between Farah and Kandahar instead of 377. Moreover this detour seems without purpose, and I cannot discover good reasons for assuming it. Nothing prevents us from supposing that Drangiane then extended as far north as Farah and that the Ariaspians lived round about the Farah–Kandahar road; if they did not, then it would be best to hold that Al. never entered their land, and that they sent ambassadors with their submission, as the Gadrosians (A. iii 28, 1) must have done.

APPENDIX VIII

13. Turn now to the distances given by Strabo and Pliny. With a stade of ·185 km, Strabo's 6,490 stades from the Caspian Gates to Herat are 70 km too many by modern measurements, though the excess falls to 50, if we emend to 6,390 (§ 9). With a stade of ·163 km, the distance is about 70 km too small. Since ancient routes may well have taken slightly different courses, either discrepancy is acceptable. But, though our manuscripts of Pliny give a larger distance between Hecatompylos and Herat than Strabo, this does not compensate for the lower figure from the Gates to Hecatompylos; the sum of the figures (708 miles = 5,664 stades) is much too low, another reason for Marquardt's emendation (§ 9). From Herat to Prophthasia we have variants, 1,500, 1,592 or 1,600 stades, i.e. 280–296 km. (If the stade were ·163 km, the equation would be 245–260 km.) This clearly points to Prophthasia being at or near Farah, 270 km from Herat, *contra* Droysen 216 with wrong distance. These correspondences encourage us to expect light on Al's later route. But difficulties appear. I give Strabo's figures, with Pliny's (converted into stades) in brackets, and equivalents in km for Strabo's, taking the stade under A to be ·185 km and under B to be ·163 km. (It will emerge that the second equivalent is impossible.)

	Stades		Km	
			A	B
Prophthasia to Arachotian town	4,120	(4,520)	762	671
Arachotian town to Ortospana	2,000	(1,400)	370	326
Total	6,120	(5,920)	1,132	997

But by the direct modern road it is only 892 km from

Farah to Kabul. And where is the Arachotian
town? It should be at or near some modern centre,
as town sites are within limits determined by permanent geographical factors. Under A Ghazni is the
right distance from Farah, Kalat right from Kabul;
under B nothing offers. (Pliny gives no help; his
mileage from Prophthasia to the Arachotian town
may easily be emended to produce Strabo's 4,120
stades, but the distance thence to Ortospana remains too far from Ghazni, whatever the length of
the stade; this figure too must be corrupt.) However, Strabo's data will make sense if we suppose that
his source, also followed by Pliny, was guilty of
taking the distance from Herat to Farah to be an
additional item when it should really have been included in the distance from Herat to the Arachotian
town. If Strabo's total under A. really represents
the whole distance from Herat (Artacoana or Alexandria in Areia), and not just that from Farah (Prophthasia) to Kabul (near Ortospana), it is only 6 km.
too short. The Arachotian town would now be near
Kalat, long regarded as a candidate; by the modern
road it is only 23 km. further from Herat and 17
nearer to Kabul than Strabo's figures would now suggest, discrepancies that are perfectly acceptable.
Fischer indeed argues powerfully that Alexandria in
Arachosia is Kandahar; that is suggested by the fer-
tility of its plain, its importance on the route to the
lower Indus (cf. vi 17, 3 n.) and evidence that it was a
Hellenized centre in the early third century. Let
this be so: the very fact that Strabo and Pliny speak
of the Arachotian town and not of Alexandria in
Arachosia (whereas they do refer to Alexandria in
Areia and Prophthasia) suggests that the two
places were not identical, and that Fischer's hypo-

thesis does not oblige us to equate the Arachotian town with Kandahar rather than with a site near Kalat.

14. The new city (A. iii 28, 4) from which Al. crossed the Hindu-Kush to Bactra in spring 329 (cf. Strabo xv 2, 10) and to which he returned in late spring 326 (iv 22, 3 f.), wrongly placed by D. 83, 2 and QC. vii 3, 23 north of the range, was founded ' sub ipso Caucaso ' (Pliny vi 62) and ' in radicibus montis ' (QC.); Pliny puts it 400 stades (c. 70 km) from Ortospana; though its exact site has not been found, it was evidently near Begram and Charikar, perhaps at the junction of the Ghorband and Panjshir rivers in what Foucher (I 29) describes as the largest, richest and most populous basin of north Afghanistan, and close to the ancient Kapica, then more important than Kabul; for further speculation see Tarn, *GBI* 460 ff. The true distance from Kabul is c. 50 km. QC. vii 3, 18 plausibly tells that the army was revived after its march on reaching cultivated lands with abundant supplies; this valley, like that of Kabul (where perhaps some of the troops bivouacked, to ease the supply problem), enjoys a milder climate than the region of Ghazni which the army had traversed.

15. The topography of the campaigns of 329–327 is explained with exemplary conciseness and clarity by von Schwarz; though he wrongly denied the traditional equation of Bactra with Zariaspa (Reuss, *Rheinisches Museum* lxii, 591 ff; Kaerst, *Geschichte des Hellenismus* I ² 438), I follow him in general. A. makes little use of the descriptive material Ar. provided, but see iii 28, 5 f. (cf. Strabo xv 2, 10); 30, 7; iv 6, 6 (cf. Strabo xi 11, 5); perhaps 29, 2 ff.

There is often more in QC., esp. vii 5, 1 ff.; 6, 1 ff.
(better than A. iii 30, 10); 11, 1 ff. (better than A.
iv 18, 4 ff.); viii 2, 19 ff. Von Schwarz shows that
here again he must be following a good first hand
source. Except by allusion in iii 30, 6, A. has nothing
on the fearful hardships of the crossing of the Hindu-
Kush (QC. vii 4, 22–5) and of the waterless route from
Balkh to the Oxus (ib. 5, 1 ff.). In general (but cf.
iii 28, 8 f.; iv 21, 10) he tends to suppress evidence of
the risks Al. took with his men, see commentary on
vi 22 ff.

16. In spring 329 Al. with the snow still thick (A.
iii 28, 8) crossed the Hindu-Kush in 15 (Strabo xv
2, 10), 16 (D. 83, 1) or 17 (QC. vii 3, 21) days; perhaps
the whole march took longer, and different writers
took different views of the time spent in the actual
pass. The usual descent lay via Chulum or Tash-
kurgan (Aornos), but perhaps because Bessus expected Al. here and had ravaged the country (A.
iii 28, 7), Al. came down at Drapsaca (Adrapsa in
Strabo), i.e. Kunduz, and then proceeded to Bactra,
a great trading centre and in the heart of a fertile
land (Strabo ii 1, 14; xv 1, 18; QC. 3, 26 ff.), where
he must have stayed some time, resting his men and
getting in supplies, as it was high summer when he
advanced to the Oxus (Amu-Darya) at Khelif;
QC's distance, c. 74 km at a stade of ·185 km, is about
right and his description admirable (5, 1 ff.). A.
iii 29, 3 is accurate on the breadth of the Oxus; it is
100 m. deep, runs at 8–10 km a hour; the region
lacks timber, and Al. crossed it by a local method
known to von Schwarz. Bessus fled to Nautaca, conjecturally Shahr-i-Sabz, and then probably towards
Maracanda (Samarkand); the place where he was

captured cannot be identified. Al. must have
replaced his horses at Karshi (iii 30, 6), still the great
centre for horse-trading *c.* 1900, and the fort where
he was wounded (30, 10) will be Kungur-tau nearby.
Karshi is 142 km from Samarkand, which Al. reached
on the 4th day (QC. 6, 10), i.e. at about 35 km a day.
Thence he must have marched along the foot of the
Alai range to the Syr-Darya at a point von Schwarz
decisively identified with Khodjend near Lenina-
bad. His new city here, Alexandria Eschate, was
built in 20 days (A. iv 4, 1) or 17 (QC. 6, 26 f.); in
von Schwarz' day all buildings in this region were still
of mud. Of the rebel cities in iv 3 von Schwarz
conclusively identified Cyropolis with Ura-Tyube
from A's description, and on the ground that town
sites here are unalterably fixed by geographical
factors gave more conjectural identities to the
others. In iv 5, 3 we read that on Pharnuches'
approach Spitamenes withdrew from the siege of
Samarkand to the ' royal residence ($\beta\alpha\sigma i\lambda\epsilon\iota\alpha$) ' of
Sogdiana. Since Samarkand itself was the capital
of Sogdiana, editors have emended, with little
palaeographical plausibility, to ' the north ($\beta\acute{o}\rho\epsilon\iota\alpha$) '
of Sogdiana. The emendation should be rejected:
von Schwarz observed that the emirs, and presumably
the satraps, needed both winter and summer capi-
tals, Bukhara and Samarkand; here the former is
meant. Pharnuches' force was destroyed by the
river Zeravshan on the road to Bukhara. According
to iv 6, 3 Al. covered 1,500 stades or 278 km in his
march to relieve Samarkand; by the modern road
the distance is 290. But A. makes him cover this
mileage in 3 days; this is surely incredible (with
infantry). QC. vii 9, 21 reports that he reached the
scene of Pharnuches' defeat on the 4th day out of

Samarkand, and I suspect that A. has confused the two marches.

17. After extensive devastations Al. withdrew to Bactra for the winter 329/8 (iv 7, 1), returning in spring (15, 7) for systematic pacification with five separate forces (16, 2), whose movements cannot be traced. QC. vii 10, 14 ff. takes him on a waterless march of 330 km from the Oxus to Merv, which A. ignores and of which QC. gives no details, though the hardships would have been appalling. Von Schwarz rightly rejects it (like most historians), but makes Al. visit Merv in 330, which is also impossible; he never went there (§ 11). Spitamenes attacked Bactra while A. was in Sogdiana (16, 4 ff.); the desert of 17, 1 (*contra* von Schwarz) must be that between Balkh and the Oxus. After his attack failed, Spitamenes must have withdrawn to the Turkestan steppes west of the Oxus, where the Massagetae may be located, though Gabae cannot be identified (17, 4).

18. In 328/327 Al. wintered in Sogdiana, himself at Nautaca (17, 3; 18, 2), but started operations very early in spring 327 (18, 4), with deep snow still on the mountains (18, 5; 21, 10). He must have taken the road leading towards Termez from Shahr-i-Sabz, for von Schwarz locates the Rock of Sogdiana at Baisun-tau, some 20 km east of Derbend, more on the basis of QC's than of A's description. Thence he moved further east, for A's Rock of Chorienes (QC's Rock of Sisimithres) can be certainly identified with Koh-i-Nor at a point where the road from Dushambe (Stalinabad) to Boldzhuan crosses the river Vachsh about 80 km SE of Stalinabad; von

Schwarz shows that it was in fact impregnable. Once again QC. has an excellent description; the emendation in viii 2, 19 of an unknown place-name to Nautaca is the product of editorial ignorance. From this rock Al. must have returned to the Oxus at Termez via Stalinabad and roughly the modern railway route down the Surkhan valley; thence to Balkh.

19. It was late spring 327 when he recrossed the Hindu-Kush in 10 days by a different pass to his city under the ' Caucasus ' (iv 22, 4 n.). Thence he will have descended to Jellalabad in the Kabul valley (22, 6) via the Laghman route (Foucher). Here he divided his forces. Hephaestion and Perdiccas were sent direct to Peucelaotis, i.e. Charsadda (Wheeler) and the Indus (22, 7), not by the Khyber pass which leads to Peshawar but by the Michni pass further north (Foucher I 36 ff.). He himself proceeded to pacify the peoples in the hills and valleys north of the Kabul river. Strabo xv 1, 17, summarizing Ar's account of the climate in N.W. India, which A. omits, says on his authority that the march from Alexandria began only after the setting of the Pleiads, i.e. in November. Here again we have a long pause in Al's operations which A. does not mention, still less explain. Perhaps he had sent envoys to Taxilas and other Indian princes and was awaiting news of their attitudes. Taxilas in fact came to offer him allegiance, presumably at Jellalabad (22, 6 n.). The delay meant that the operations recounted by A. iv 23 ff. took place in winter and early spring 327/326. Stein thinks Aornos may have fallen in April (iv 29, 1 n.). Al. reached Taxila in spring 326 (Ar. *ap.* Strabo l.c.). This made it impossible for

the hostile tribes to take refuge in snow-clad mountains; Aornos, with a large, flat and cultivated surface on the summit, was an exceptional stronghold. A. ignores these conditions, though they were described by Ar.

20. Al's own route cannot be followed in any detail until his arrival in Swat. The river Choes (23, 2) must be the Kūnar; after marching up this valley, he crossed the mountains into Bajaur (24, 6); the passage of the Guraios (Sanskrit, Gaurī) or Panjkora (25, 7) brought him into the land of the Assaceni, which must be Swat and Bunēr. Sir Aurel Stein held on good grounds that Bazira (27, 5, etc.) or Beira (QC. viii 10, 22) is Bir-Kot in Upper Swat and Ora, evidently higher up the Swat valley, probably Ude-Gram; the capital of the Assaceni, Massaga (26, 1, cf. Strabo xv 1, 27), must be in Lower Swat, where there is more rich land; moreover, Al. reached it first, moving up the valley. All this fits the fact that at Ora there was hope of aid from Abisares (27, 7), ruling in Hazara (round Abbottabad) across the Indus; moreover the people in these parts took refuge at Aornos, which Stein proved was Pir-Sar, overlooking the Indus (this detail in QC. viii 11, 7 was vital for Stein's discovery, though in general A's description is better); easy passes lead from Upper Swat to the right bank of the Indus. Before assailing Aornos, Al. had thus to descend to the Indus via Charsadda (28, 6). Embolima (28, 7) or Ecbolima (QC.) cannot be identified. The final operations against the Assaceni are thought to have been in Bunēr (30, 5 f.; the site of Dyrta is not known). Fuller's account (245 ff.) makes Stein's discoveries more accessible, see also map, p. 125.

21. We hear of catapults in use in Sogdiana (iv 2, 3; 4, 4) and of perhaps other siege-engines there (3, 1) and at Massaga (26, 5) and Aornos (30, 1). In India sailors from the Mediterranean were available to man Al's river-flotilla (vi 1, 6; *Ind.* 18, 1). These allusions suggest that Al. had with him on his marches considerable *impedimenta* and many camp-followers, adding to the number of his men, as estimated in Appendix XIII (cf. 7 above), and making it harder to see how he could have kept up the rate of advance in 330 which the evidence seems to require. On certain occasions we are told that the baggage was despatched by easier and presumably longer routes than those he took himself (iii 18, 1; 23, 2). I would suppose that this was usual, and that in the long march from Hyrcania to Parapamisus the baggage train must have followed in the rear. The *whole* army need not have reached Ghazni in Nov. 330, nor have crossed the Hindu-Kush in early spring 329; note the long wait at Bactra before the march to the Syr-Darya, where we first hear again of engines.

APPENDIX IX

GAUGAMELA

1. The diversity of modern accounts (e.g. Tarn ii 182 ff., G. T. Griffith, *JHS* 1947, 77 ff., A. R. Burn, ib. 1952, 84 f., N. G. L. Hammond, *Hist. of Greece*, 615 ff., Fuller, 163 ff. and E. W. Marsden, *Campaign of Gaugamela*) shows that agreement among scholars on

the problems has not been attained and suggests that it is unattainable.

2. Not even the *site* has been securely identified, but this hardly matters, since it is clear that the battle was fought in a wide plain, advantageous to Darius' numerical superiority. That superiority is proved by Al's dispositions of his forces with a reserve phalanx which could face about, if the Persian got to his rear, and with mixed forces of cavalry and infantry (see Marsden 50, citing Xenophon, *Hipparchicus* 5, 13) set at an angle to his right and left flanks, to impede envelopment. This arrangement cannot be questioned, since D. 57 and QC. iv 13, 26 ff., drawing on a common source which is not A's, from which each gives incomplete extracts, broadly agree with A's account, and while the actual confusion in the fighting may help to explain the confusion in all descriptions of it, there was no like reason why historians should have been unable to ascertain the prior dispositions of the commanders. Unfortunately ' at an angle ' can be interpreted in various ways (see the works and plans of the scholars cited above), between which I cannot decide.

3. All the sources also give the Persian infantry, ill-armed and ill-trained, no important part in the battle. Hence, their numbers do not matter; the figures given (1,000,000 with some reserve by A's sources, 800,000 by D. 53, 3, 400,000 by J. xi 12, 5 and 200,000 by QC. iv 12, 13, though inconsistently in 9, 3 he makes Darius' army half as large again as in 333, for which see iii 2, 2), like those for the cavalry, were of course intended to show Al. as a David destroying a Goliath, whereas in fact he had a decisive superiority in quality. As to the cavalry,

we can disregard D's 200,000 and J's 100,000, but A's 40,000 and QC's 45,000 are more reasonable; perhaps the document used by Ar. gave their number (in which case QC's figure must be invention). Marsden estimates their strength at 34,000, on the assumptions that the lines of the two armies were approximately equal and that the length of the Macedonian line can be calculated; of these the first seems to be false (cf. para. 2), and the second far too optimistic. We do not know if A's figure for Al's numbers (40,000 foot and 7,000 horse) is accurate (App. XIII 1), and indeed Marsden himself reaches a new estimate, not much different, on the basis of the original size of Al's army in 334 (forgetting the forces he took over in Asia), plus attested reinforcements (not all of which may be recorded) and less garrisons and casualties, which he minimizes. He also assumes that the phalanx was drawn up 16 deep, and not 8 deep, as at Issus (App. III 3), though at Gaugamela Al. had every reason to extend rather than deepen his line. For other objections see Hammond's review in *JHS* 1966, 252 f. All that we can safely say is that the Macedonian cavalry were substantially outnumbered.

4. Of the actual battle A's account is not wholly clear (as shown especially by Griffith) and has too little about fighting under Parmenio on the left, not perhaps because Ptolemy, fighting on the right, knew little of it (he could surely have found out), but because all historians wished to attribute the glory to Al., if not to depreciate Parmenio. Nor does A. harmonize with D. 57–61, still less with the muddled story (evidently from D's source) in QC., who can even confuse left and right wings. Neither does

more than allude (D. 59, 8; QC. 15, 1–2) to the initial
fighting on Al's extreme right (A. 13), and though
both put the chariot charge early, allowing it rather
more effect than A., and have the decisive conflict
between Al. and Darius (who behaves with more
courage in their narratives, cf. ii 11, 3 n.), they
wholly differ about the break-through to the baggage.
In A. this is effected by Persian cavalry in the centre
coming through a gap in the Macedonian phalanx
after the attack by Al. on the right (14, 4 ff.), but D.
and QC. know nothing of this, nor consequently of the
fierce fighting described by A. 15, 2. D. makes
Mazaeus on the Persian right send cavalry round
Al's flank to the camp; unfortunately the units he
names are known to have been on the Persian left.
P. 32, 3 f., who also records this movement, makes a
similar mistake, and QC. actually transposes to the
camp the fighting between Bessus' forces on the
Persian left and Alexander's troops on his right
flank, described in A. 13 and 14, 3. As for the
romantic story in D. and QC. that Darius' mother
refused to be freed by the Persians who took the
camp, would not she, and the other captive women,
have been left behind in the rear camp (A. 9, 1)?

5. P's account is anecdotal and unintelligible. He
twice refers to Callisthenes, once for Al's prayer to
Zeus (App. V 7) and again on the lack of energy
allegedly shown by Parmenio (33, 1 and 6). It is not
clear to me that P. ever cites Callisthenes from
personal inspection, but be that as it may, he was
quite capable of muddling his account, especially as
it was not even his purpose to provide a full historical record but only to bring out the characteristics
of his hero (P. 1). Callisthenes evidently depreciated

Parmenio's services on this and probably other occasions, and glorified Al. It is quite another matter to suppose that he placed Persian units on the wrong wing, especially if his work is the source of Aristobulus' document (iii 11, 3 n.), or that he distorted the story except for flattery, or even for that purpose to an extent that was *patently* untrue. In particular, we cannot tax him with the absurdity of telling that Parmenio was heavily engaged at a time when he sent a message to Alexander, stationed on the other wing (as P's account implies) and still not fully armed and horsed for action, and that Al. then made a long speech—to the men under Parmenio's command; *contra* Tarn ii 352 f., this nonsense can only be P's.

6. Yet here we may have a substratum of truth. Parmenio is made to warn Al. of an outflanking movement round his left, threatening the baggage (so also QC. 15, 6 ff.); Al. refuses to take any action (for good reasons). Suppose that such a movement was made, probably before rather than after Parmenio (or Al.) was engaged; this could explain the 'vulgate' story that the camp was actually taken by Mazaeus' men. It was clearly proper, and at this stage practicable, for Parmenio to notify Al. Now contrast the other message Parmenio is reported by A. 15, 1 and all other sources (D. 60, 7; QC. 16, 1 ff.; P. 33, 6) to have sent to Al., when he was in hot pursuit of Darius, imploring his help against the Persian right. How could Parmenio know where Al. was then to be found amid all the dust (D. 60, 4; 61, 1; QC. 15, 32, cf. Fuller 178)? How could the messenger overtake him? D. in fact says that the message never got through, and in A. Parmenio

defeats the Persian right without help in the end.
It does more credit too to Al. as a general to suppose
that he turned back from his initial pursuit, *in case*
Parmenio were in danger. However, in retrospect it
appeared a misfortune that Darius had escaped, and
as the facts were that Parmenio had more difficulty
in overcoming the enemy and that Al. did turn back
to help him, those who sought to depreciate Parmenio
(perhaps with Al's encouragement) made out that
he was to blame for the incompleteness of the victory.
If it were also a fact that he had sent a message to
Al. early in the battle, or rather before it had
started, pointing out that he needed reinforcement if
he were to block an outflanking movement, it was
easier perhaps to fabricate a second message in
support of the contention that his failings had hampered Al's success. And since P. cites Callisthenes
on these failings in the context in which he mentions
the second message, the story, whether true or false,
may probably be his, and invented after Parmenio's
death; note that he did not describe an event of
winter 332/1 till after summer 330 (App. V 3), so
that his record was in substantial arrears. I have
indeed little doubt that Al's official version of the
battle largely springs from Callisthenes.

APPENDIX X

PERSEPOLIS

1. Though D. 69 and QC. v 5, 1 ff. (unlike A.) say
that Persepolis was surrendered to Al. by the Persian
officer, Tiridates, to whom Al. allegedly confided

the Persian treasury (QC. 6, 11), they also hold that
Al. sacked the *city* on entry (D. 70; QC. 6, 1–9), and
P. 37, 2 cites one of Al's supposed letters as evidence
that he ordered the massacre of the inhabitants.
A's account is so misleadingly brief, considering that
Al. stayed at Persepolis from January to May 330
(App. VIII 6), that these stories cannot be discounted.
The burning of the *palace* (iii 18, 11 f.) (confirmed by
excavations, see E. Schmidt, *Persepolis* I 78) is
plausibly set by QC. 7 and P. 38, 1 on the eve of his
departure for Ecbatana, though D. 72 puts it before
Al's campaign against neighbouring ' cities ', which
occurred in March-April (App. VIII 6) and in QC's
account (6, 11 ff.) before the fire; it is at least probable
that he deferred the act till he had ceased to require
it as a residence. A. clearly gives the official view,
adopted by Pt. and Ar. (also in Strabo xv 3, 6, who
often uses Ar.), that it was deliberate retribution for
the burning of Greek temples by the Persians in
480; it accords with this that Al. disbanded the
Greek allies, even the Thessalians, at Ecbatana
(iii 19, 5 and note); this was nearer home than
Persepolis, and moreover Al. had then learned that
Darius had been unable to mobilize another powerful
army (iii 19, 4); the Panhellenic aims of the war had
now been realized (Introd. 39 ff.), and all that remained was to fulfil Al's personal or Macedonian
designs of conquest. (This is brought out in D. 74, 3;
QC. vi 2, 15–4, 1; P. 47, 1 and J. xii 3 with variations.)
However, the arson was inconsistent with the role
he was about to assume as the rightful successor of
Darius; hence, it was officially admitted that he
regretted it later, not at once (P. 38, 4) but on his
return to Persepolis in 324 (vi 30, 1). By contrast,
in the ' vulgate ', going back to Clitarchus (Jacoby

no. 137) F. 11 (Athenaeus xiii 576 DE), Al. acted after
a drunken party at the instigation of the courtesan,
Thais (D., QC. and ' some accounts ' in P.). If this
was true, Pt. had a special reason (apart from his
partiality to Al.) to conceal it; Thais was his mistress
by whom he had three children, one of whom, Lagus,
was old enough to win a chariot race in 308/7 (Athenaeus l.c., cf. Dittenberger, *Sylloge Inscriptionum
Graecarum* [3] 314). QC 7, 10 f. says that the official
version was invented to cover up the truth.

2. However this may be, it must be admitted that in
this instance A's sources did justice to the good sense
of Parmenio. The reference to his disagreement with
Al., like all others, may go back to Callisthenes, who
probably traduced him (App. VI 6). Callisthenes
could well have fully approved of retribution on the
Persians, and he wrote before Al. himself had repented; his design would not have been to set Parmenio in a favourable light. There is some reason
to think that his history went down to 329 (Jacoby on
F. 38); the argument that he cannot have recorded
Al's Scythian campaign (iv 1 ff.), because he did not
mention or deny Al's meeting with the queen of the
Amazons (iv 15, 4 n.), is absurd; he would not have
recorded what did not happen, and he had no occasion
to refute a fiction that had not yet been invented.
If he did tell of Parmenio's advice here, it was hard
for later writers to expunge it from the record.

3. A's account in iii 18 has various omissions.
Nothing of the appointment of a Macedonian general
alongside the Persian satrap, which we should
expect, cf. QC. v 6, 11 (Nicarchides with 3,000 men).
Nothing of Tiridates (§ 1), and no details of the
Persian treasure. Here our sources are discordant

and untrustworthy. Cf. for treasure seized at Arbela, A. iii 15, 5 (no figure); D. 64, 3 (3,000 Talents of silver); QC. v 1, 10 (4,000); at Babylon, A. iii 16, 3; QC. v 1, 23 (no figures); at Susa, A. iii 16, 7 (*c.* 50,000, cf. QC. 2, 11); D. 66, 1 (40,000 plus 9,000 of gold, i.e. perhaps gold bullion worth 9,000 T.); P. 36, 1 (40,000 in coin); Strabo xv 3, 9 (50,000 or 40,000); at Persepolis, A. iii 18, 10 (no figure); D. 71, 1 (gold bullion worth 120,000, cf. QC. 6, 9 adding 6,000 at Pasargadae); P. 37, 2 (as much in coins as at Susa, i.e. 40,000). Strabo *l.c.* says that all were brought together at Ecbatana (A. iii 20, 7) and amounted to 180,000, perhaps implying 10,000–20,000 at Babylon, but much more if P. 37, 2 is right. Darius left Ecbatana with 7,000 T. (A. 19, 5) or 8,000 (Strabo), all taken by his murderers (Strabo), but D. makes Al. receive 8,000 from the royal treasurers after his death (74, 4) and QC. vi 2, 10 26,000 from recent booty.

APPENDIX XI

THE DEATHS OF PHILOTAS AND PARMENIO

1. A. cites Ar. as well as Pt. at iii 26, 1, but thereafter for reasons unknown relies solely on Pt's account of the trial of Philotas and murder of Parmenio. At 27, 1 he then proceeds: ' they say that Amyntas too ...'; the ' they ' are certainly Pt. and Ar. once more. QC. (vi 7-vii 2) has rhetorically embellished the story, especially with fictitious speeches, but no one thinks that the ' vulgate ' can here be totally neglected, cf. also D. 79 f.; P. 48 f.; J. xii 5.

APPENDIX XI

2. The obscure allusion in 26, 1 to previous charges made against Philotas is probably illuminated by P. 48, 3–49, 2, telling that Philotas' mistress conveyed through Craterus to Al. his criticisms of Al. and boasts that Al's successes were due to him and his father. (QC. vi 8, 1 also makes Craterus' rivalry with Philotas a cause of his ruin.) QC. 9, 18; 10, 26 ff.; 11, 5 and 23 f. makes out that Philotas showed disapproval of Al's claim to be son of Zeus-Ammon; this will not be credited by those who deny that Al. made any such claim, but if true, it would help to explain why delations against Philotas began in Egypt (Pt. and Ar.). Cf. also iv 10, 3 (' vulgate ').

3. D., QC. and P. all give details of the plot of Dymnus which Philotas admittedly failed to reveal to Al. and here again credibly supplement Pt's story. Pt. allows that there was other ' evidence ' of Philotas' guilt, but regards his failure to reveal the plot as the clearest proof; from this we may judge (a) that the other evidence was still more contemptible and (b) that there may be truth in what P. tells (§ 2 above) and perhaps in QC. vi 9, 14 (an ambiguous letter intercepted from Parmenio to his son). In QC. vi 11, 8 ff. the trial before the army is adjourned for a day; Philotas confesses in fear of torture, but is none the less barbarously tortured (cf. D. and P.) and then amplifies his confession, implicating Parmenio. It could be suggested that Pt. had nothing of this, because he disapproved of the torture of a noble or put no faith in a confession obtained under duress, but cf. iv 13, 7 and 14, 3; moreover, in antiquity such confessions were commonly treated as decisive. However, QC's story of Philotas' extorted confession and implication of Parmenio

cannot be true, as Pt. had to allow that against Parmenio there was no evidence. Nor is it any proof of Philotas' guilt that the army convicted him: we know how feeble was the best evidence against him, and they were faced with the alternative of disbelieving Al. With good reason D. 79, 1 and P. 50, 1, cf. 49, 7, condemn the killing of both Philotas and Parmenio. Al. himself may indeed have been persuaded of Philotas' guilt, however unjustifiably, but the murder of Parmenio is a different matter. Pt. did not profess to know his mind and suggests that he either believed in Parmenio's complicity or simply thought it unsafe to leave him alive after the execution of his son. The second explanation is pure *raison d'état*. Though given to moralizing, A. makes no comment.

4. The claims Philotas may have made (§ 2 above) that Parmenio and his sons were really responsible for Al's success were met by the Alexander-historians by stressing the occasions when Al. rejected Parmenio's advice, cf. i 13 and 18 from A's main sources, though ii 4; 25; iii 10 come from the ' vulgate ', cf. also i 11, 1 n.; App. III 6; X 2; at Gaugamela his conduct was deprecated, App. IX 7. All this may go back to Callisthenes; it is not peculiar to Pt. and Ar. and indeed not prominent in their accounts; note also in contrast iii 9, 4. If they say little of Parmenio's actions in the great battles, where he always commanded the left, or in the important tasks confided to him (i 24, 3; ii 5, 1; 11, 10: more here in QC.), this is perhaps because they always concentrate on Al's own doings: Pt. seems merely to have mentioned the expedition that kept him personally away from Mallus (vi 11, 8). There is

no sign that Al. himself had lost his trust in Parmenio, though he was now about 70 (QC. vi 11, 32; vii 2, 33), before Philotas' ' plot ' was denounced; his command in Media was important (App. XIII).

5. What A. (and QC.) say of the trial of Amyntas and his brothers tends to give the impression that Al. was more fair minded than the critical reader of ch. 26 might infer. Here too A. draws on Pt. and Ar. He says nothing of the execution of Alexander the Lyncestian after the semblance of a trial, but as our authorities for this event, D. (80, 2) and QC. (vii 1, 5–9, cf. viii 8, 6), betray no uneasiness about his guilt, this is more likely to be an omission by A. than a suppression by Pt. and Ar. of what they thought did Al. no credit. They had presumably told, as A. does (i 25), that Alexander (for whom cf. Introd. 46) had been arrested in winter 334/333 on the ground that Darius had made overtures to him through Sisines. (No words need be wasted here on the fantasy of Lane Fox ch. 10 that Ar. fr. 2 shows that Ar. had killed the man off at Thebes in 335.) Of course this was no better evidence against Alexander than that which Pt. held to be decisive against Philotas; it is not suggested that Alexander had even received, much less responded to Darius' letter, though QC. viii 8, 6 may mean that he had; this was probably fiction to justify the king's conduct to the incredulous. D. 32, 1 f. indeed makes out that the Lyncestian was only arrested in 332 in Cilicia on a warning from Olympias; and the same date is implied by QC's statements that he was kept in bonds for 3 years before trial; on the other hand, QC. evidently mentioned the arrest in one of his first two books (vii 1, 6) before he had brought Al. to Cilicia. Per-

haps he combined two versions, as Berve later did in supposing that the Lyncestian was deposed in 334/333 and arrested only in Cilicia; QC's two informers against him would then be Sisines (whom he places in a different story in iii 7, 11 f.) and Olympias. Berve argued that Al. would not have arrested the man and still employed his nephew, Amyntas son of Arrhabaeus, in a high command (i 28, 4); he explains Amyntas' later disappearance from the record by his connection with the Lyncestian. But the identification of Amyntas' father with the Arrhabaeus Al. had put to death in 336 is unattested and implausible; would Al. have ever trusted the son of one he had done to death? And would he have continued to trust him after deposing, but not after arresting, his uncle? Berve's view involves rejection of A. i 25, 10, presumably of Pt. Lane Fox does not hesitate to say that Pt's story in i 25 is fabrication. But Pt. surely had a reason when he concealed or distorted the truth, and here none can be seen. The arrest of the Lyncestian on evidence Olympias supplied would have been easier to justify than the imputation of guilt from Darius' letter to him. I do not doubt that to Al. and his friends the Lyncestian had always seemed ' unreliable ' (i 25, 5), to be removed at the first chance. Anything could be believed against a man with good cause for treason. So too his final execution required neither concealment nor apology.

6. See further the important article of E. Badian, *Transactions of the American Philological Association* 1960, 324 ff.

APPENDIX XII

CASPIAN, CAUCASUS, TANAIS

1. In both Al's day and A's it was believed that the known landmass of Europe, Asia and Africa was encircled by the Ocean or ' great sea ' to which A. often refers. Before Al. little was known in Greece of Iran and India. Much was discovered on the expedition; however, Al. and those who recorded his journeys were dependent on mere reports of country they did not see for themselves, which they could easily misinterpret; moreover, Strabo, following Eratosthenes (cf. A. v 3), castigates their contradictions and geographical falsifications, designed in his view to magnify Al's exploits (ii 1, 9; xi 5, 5; 6, 4; 7, 4; xv 1 *passim*, especially § 2, 9 and 28; xvi 1, 3); in reality some at least of the errors were due to genuine misunderstandings. Much more became known of Iran and India under Al's successors, but even this increase of knowledge did not save Eratosthenes (*c.* 275–194) and later geographers from serious mistakes.

2. Thus before Al. it had been disputed whether the Caspian sea (vii 16, 3), sometimes called the Hyrcanian sea (A. iii 29, 2; v 5, 4 and 26, 1) or ' the Caspian and Hycanian sea ' (vii 16, 2), was a gulf of the Ocean or, as Herodotus held (i 202 f.), a lake (cf. P. 44, 1 f.); on the latter view, Al. thought that it might be connected with the Black Sea, or more precisely with the Sea of Azov (the Maeotic lake), whose size Herodotus grossly exaggerated (iv 86), and at the end of his life he was preparing an exploratory expedition

to ascertain the truth (A. vii 16). Thus he was not as
certain of this hypothesis as, according to Strabo xi
7, 4, his historians were. Polyclitus (who, to judge
from this last text, accompanied Al.) took the
Caspian to be a lake, as it had sea-serpents (uncon-
firmed) and as the water was sweetish (in fact salinity
is low, especially by river mouths); he held it was
connected by an underground passage with the Sea
of Azov. This may be reconcileable with Ar's account (Strabo v 26, 1) of a trade route from Oxus to
Caspian and then overland to the Black Sea (on which
see Pearson 163), but a ' speech of Al.' (written up
by A.) treats the Caspian as a gulf of Ocean (v 26, 1).
Patrocles' explorations, c. 284/283, were to convince
Eratosthenes and Strabo (ii, 5, 18, cf. A. v 3, 4) that
this was true, and A. iii 29 follows suit by making
the Oxus flow into the ' great sea in its Hyrcanian
part '. Here, in giving the Oxus (Amu Darya) an
outlet into the Caspian, he agrees with Ar. (Strabo
xi 7, 3), nor did he doubt (vii, 16, 3) that Ar. (iii 30, 7)
was right in making the Jaxartes (Syr Darya) have
the same outlet. Today both rivers flow into the
Aral Sea, and the Syr Darya has always done so,
though there is some evidence that the Oxus did
once flow into the Caspian; the Aral, however, was
apparently not known in antiquity (J. O. Thomson,
Hist. of Anc. Geography 128; *contra* but unconvin-
cingly, J. R. Hamilton, *CQ* 1971, 110 ff.). Ar. was
also wrong in making the Jaxartes rise in the Hindu-
Kush, and not 700 miles north-west in the modern
Kirgiz.

3. A. iii 28, 4 f. and 30, 7 show that Caucasus was
Ar's name for the Hindu-Kush. The followers of
Alexander thus identified the true (' Scythian ')

523

APPENDIX XII

Caucasus between the Black Sea and the Caspian with the Hindu-Kush. Eratosthenes exposed this error (cf. v 3, 2 f.; 5, 3 ff.; *Ind.* 2, 2 ff.; 5, 10), substituting a highly simplified picture of a continuous range of mountains extending eastwards from Pamphylia to the northern border of India (i.e. the Himalayas), which he chose to call Taurus (cf. Strabo xi 8, 1), though acknowledging that they had various local names and that the true name for Ar's Caucasus was Parapamisus (or the like; there are various spellings); he argued (cf. also Strabo xi 5, 5) that the Alexander-historians misnamed Parapamisus, in order to bring Al. to the regions where Heracles had performed exploits (D. 83, 1; QC. vii 3, 22), where Prometheus had suffered at the ends of the earth and where Jason had penetrated; for such motivation cf. App. IV. Though aware of the facts, A. prefers to use the nomenclature of his sources.

4. It had long been known that the Tanais (Don) flowed into the Sea of Azov (Herodotus iv 57) and some thought it rose in the true Caucasus (Strabo xi 2, 2). Having identified the Hindu-Kush with the Caucasus, the Alexander-historians then supposed that the Iaxartes, which in their view rose in that mountain and had its outlet in a lake connected perhaps with the Sea of Azov, must be the Tanais; it is clear from A. iii 30, 7 f. that this error was not founded on a local name resembling Tanais, and iv 5, 6 (cf. Ar. F. 28 = Strabo xi 11, 5) shows how the Macedonians could impose their own names on rivers. Again, Strabo xi 7, 4 (from Eratosthenes) suggests that as it was agreed that the Tanais (Don) separated Asia from Europe (cf. A. iii 30, 8; QC. vii 7, 2), and as the region between the Don and the Caspian, ' a

considerable part of Asia ', had not been conquered by Al., the false equation was a deliberate attempt to obscure the truth; this explanation makes little sense, and again genuine misunderstanding seems more likely. It explains why on the Jaxartes Al. supposed himself to be in contact with both Asian and European Scythians (iv 1, 1; 3, 6); similarly he must have misinterpreted what he was told by Pharasmanes, king of the Chorasmians, who were domiciled east of the Caspian and south of the Aral (Tarn, *Greeks in Bactria and India*[2] 478 ff.); he no doubt mentioned a great lake, which was taken to be the Caspian/Black Sea, and other things he said, doubtless jumbled in translation, were referred by his hearers to peoples they knew by report or legend to be near the Black Sea, the Colchians and Amazons (iv 15). It is at least clear that Al. thought it possible for a people to be not far from both Bactria and the Black Sea. Compare his conjecture that the Indus was the upper Nile (vi. 1, 2; Nearchus *ap.* Strabo xv 1, 25) and the estimate that the Black Sea was not far from the Persian Gulf (*Ind.* 40, 5). The confusions found in A's main sources were of course shared by the ' vulgate ' (in D. etc), which I forbear to analyse. Once again A. obscures the geography by normally using Tanais for the Jaxartes (iv 1; 3; v 25; vii 10, 6), though aware of the truth (cf. iii 30, 8 and vii 16, 3, as emended).

APPENDIX XIII

ALEXANDER'S ARMY 331–326

1. At Gaugamela the Grand Army consisted of (at most) about 40,000 foot and 7,000 horse, cf. Introd. 56 f. The Macedonians included in these totals were the survivors of 15,000 foot (archers excluded) and 2,100 Companions and perhaps 800 *prodromoi*, who had been with Alexander since 334 or joined him in 333.

2. Both before and after Gaugamela the numbers of reinforcements and garrisons are more often reported by QC., or even D., than by A. There is no reason in principle to distrust their data, since they seem to preserve ' documentary ' material of other kinds (appointments and marches), though in detail they may be in error, and they too are not necessarily more complete in this kind of documentation than in any other. The size of the garrison A. records in Bactria (iv 22, 3) in itself shows that Al. must have received considerable reinforcements between 331 and 327, especially as he must also have left troops behind in other parts of Iran (§ 3); so much is implied by A. himself, when he names provincial generals or commandants of citadels, and is stated in iii 19, 7 (Media). Al's foundations of cities in Iran are also relevant; for the best collection of evidence cf. Droysen (App. VIII 12). A. mentions only the Alexandrias in Parapamisus and on the Jaxartes (iii 28, 4; iv 1, 3; 4, 1; 22, 5), perhaps because they alone were founded under Al's personal superintendence, but other such cities in Areia, Drangiane, Arachosia and

Bactria were evidently founded on his orders, and (it is natural to suppose) in 330–327, since he was never in these parts again; presumably all had a nucleus of soldiers drawn from the local garrisons, including Macedonians unfit for further campaigns, but predominantly mercenaries.

3. The following garrisons and detachments are actually attested outside Media (for which see § 5 below):

Babylon	1,000 (including 700 Macedonians, QC. v 1, 43; D. 64, 5)
Syria and Babylonia	2,000 (QC. l.c.)
Persepolis	3,000 (Macedonians, QC. v 6, 11)
Arachosia	4,600 (QC. vii 3, 5)
Bactria	13,500 (A. iv 22, 3)
Total	24,100

The force in Bactria was no doubt intended to hold down Sogdiane and perhaps Parapamisus too; it would be unwise to assume that Media, Hyrcania, Areia and Drangiane did not also require substantial forces, who were probably found from the troops Al. left in Media in June 330.

4. In the same period reinforcements are attested, amounting to 45,500 foot and perhaps over 6,000 horse.

331–330 (up to Alexander's arrival at Ecbatana); see A. iii 16, 10; D. 65, 1; QC. v 1, 40 f.; 7, 12.

Macedonians	6,000 foot, 500 horse
Thracians	3,500 foot, 600 horse
Mercenaries	9,000 foot, 2,000 (?) horse

330 (after Darius' death); A. iii 23, 8 f.; D 76, 2; QC. vi 5, 10; 6, 35.

Mercenaries (Greek) 2,000 foot, 130 horse
       (Others)   5,600 foot, 300 horse

329/328 (Bactria); see A. iv 7, 2; QC. vii 10, 11 f.

Mercenaries   19,400 foot, 2,600 horse.

5. A. iii 19, 5 ff. says that at Ecbatana Al. (a) dismissed all the Greek allies, except those who would take service as mercenaries, i.e. the survivors of 7,000 foot and 2,750 horse, mainly Thessalian (Introd. 56 f.); (b) detached up to 6,000 Macedonians, apparently foot (Introd. 61), with a few horse and light troops under Harpalus to guard the treasures; the 6,000 seem to have rejoined him later; (c) left Parmenio in command of the mercenaries, Thracians and all cavalry except the Companions. This last statement is not correct, since Al. still had the *prodromoi* with him in his pursuit of Darius (cf. also iv 4, 6), as well as Erigyius' mercenary horse (iii 20, 1; 23, 2), and he could give Erigyius and others 6,000 Greek foot and 600 horse against Satibarzanes (QC. vii 3, 2, cf. A. iii 28, 2), at a time when Greek reinforcements received earlier in the summer numbered only 2,000 foot and 130 horse, and before any troops left with Parmenio had yet rejoined him (*infra*). However, we should probably assume that Parmenio had command of *most* of the forces A. names, while Al. had all the Macedonians except those detached with Harpalus (*supra*) together with the Balkan contingents (e.g. the Agrianians, iii 20, 1) other than the Thracians. With no allowance for losses, the Macedonians numbered 17,900 (§ 1) — 3,700 (§ 3) + 6,500 (§ 4) — 6,000 (§ 5) = 14,700; the Balkan troops can

never have exceeded *c.* 4,000; and though the strength of the other units with Al. cannot be determined, it is clear that with losses taken into account, his army is unlikely to have numbered 25,000 men. The larger part of his forces, *c.* 47,000 less losses at Gaugamela, detachments of 6,000 (§ 3) and Greek allies sent home but plus reinforcements of up to 21,600 (§ 4), must have been left with Parmenio and Harpalus. Parmenio was intended to invade Hyrcania from the west (iii 19, 7), a task he never performed, we do not know why. As for Harpalus' 6,000 Macedonians, Black Clitus had instructions to bring them on to Parthyaea after the treasure had been deposited at Ecbatana (iii 19, 8), and they were evidently the 6,000 who joined Al. on the road to Arachosia along with 200 ' nobiles ' (probably Companion cavalry also left behind) and 5,000 Greek foot and 500 horse (QC. vii 3, 4); these men had apparently been sent forward by Parmenio and are not included in my figures for reinforcements.

6. Media lay on the most direct route to the Mediterranean, via Babylon but by-passing Susa and Persepolis, and it would not be surprising if an exceptionally large garrison remained there, perhaps larger than the 5,000 foot and 1,000 horse with which its generals rejoined Al. in Carmania later in 325 (QC. x 1, 2, cf. A. vi 27, 3). But probably some of Parmenio's men were moved forward into Hyrcania (where Thracians were serving in 327/326, cf. A. iv 18, 2; v 20, 7) and Parthyaea. It would be consistent with the known data if the total of troops left in these regions were about 12,000, and that figure would also correspond to the garrisons in Areia-Arachosia and Bactria.

7. By autumn 330 Al's field army had been increased by over 8,000 new mercenaries (§ 4) and by nearly 12,000 men sent on from Ecbatana (§ 5). This would have brought up its strength to perhaps over 40,000. However, it was immediately reduced by 11,200. First, Al. detached 6,600 men to repress Satibarzanes (§ 5); Erigyius, the commander, rejoined him at Bactra in summer 329 (QC. vii 4, 40, cf. A. iii 28, 2), but surely without his whole army, since shortly afterwards Stasanor was despatched to deal with new trouble in Areia (iii 29, 5), with no mention of troops, and Al. would hardly have left Areia and Drangiane ungarrisoned. Secondly, he left 4,600 men in Arachosia (§ 3) and surely some troops in Parapamisus, the jumping off ground for the Indian campaign he meditated in 328 (iv 15) and probably earlier; perhaps it is enough to point to the Alexandria founded there. A fair balance between casualties and detachments on the one side, and reinforcements on the other, might suggest that he invaded Bactria in spring 329 with some 25,000 European troops. Erigyius doubtless brought up part of his army, and in 329/328 he received 22,000 more men from Europe (§ 4). But casualties from hardships in the fighting of 329–327 cannot have been light; 2,000 men were lost in his one disaster here (iv 6, 2 cf. 3, 7), and he left 13,500 men at Bactra (iv 22, 3). He must have had no more than 35,000 European troops with him at the outset of the Indian campaign.

8. Curtius, however, alleges that he had 120,000 men for this expedition (viii 5, 4). If this were the truth, we should have to suppose that two thirds of his army consisted of Orientals. Some were undoubtedly now in his army (Introd. 59), but the proportion must be

vastly too high. Now Nearchus estimated that he had 120,000 ' fighting men ' with him on the Hydaspes in 326 (*Ind.* 19, 5), explicitly including Orientals, and Plutarch (66, 2) makes this the maximum of his foot in the Indian campaigns, adding 15,000 horse. But by 326 he had received further reinforcements from the west, over 30,000 foot and nearly 6,000 horse according to D. 95, 4, though only 7,000 foot and 5,000 horse according to QC. ix 3, 21. Moreover Taxilas, Porus and other Indian princes had provided over 10,000 men (v 8, 5; 24, 4). These figures alone show that Curtius is wrong; perhaps he has retrojected to the outset of the expedition the total given in his source for the largest army Al. commanded in India. But that total, despite the authority of Nearchus, is surely too high. For his operations in India, especially after Porus' defeat, Al. did not need forces so much greater than those with which he had conquered the Persian empire, and how could he have supplied them? One may suspect that as in the past his historians inflated Persian numbers to make his victories appear more astounding, so they now inflated the size of his own army, to impress readers with the magnitude of his power. In any event his real strength still lay in his European and especially in his Macedonian troops.

9. The relatively small size of Al.'s army after Ecbatana helps to explain the increased rapidity of his movements (cf. App. VIII 7); a still smaller force, like the 11,000 men who caught him up in Arachosia, could make still greater speed. (It might seem from iii 19, 7 that the 6,000 Macedonians among them had had to march from Ecbatana to Persepolis and back before coming on to Al., of course without any

deviation into Hyrcania; this is hard to credit, and the truth may be that these men formed a rearguard who had not reached Ecbatana when Al. left, but were still bringing up the treasures from Persepolis.) Indeed his own army was at times divided, and perhaps more often than is recorded; iii 25, 2 implies that he expected it to march through Areia in detachments, not all under his own eye; 25, 4 refers to their reunion; 27, 3 to minor operations that he did not direct himself. A's account is not precise or complete; it is a grave defect that he leaves us in constant ignorance of the forces at Al.'s disposal, ignorance that we can remedy only in part from the record, also incomplete, in D. and QC.

APPENDIX XIV

ARRIAN IV 7, 4–14, 4

1. The barbarity with which Al. treated Bessus evokes from A. disapproval of his adoption of Persian royal dress (contrast vii 29, 4). He evidently thought the matter important (cf. 9, 9), but does not say when Al. began the practice. D. 77, 4 ff.; QC. vi 6, 2 ff. and J. xii 3, 8 date it to his stay in Hyrcania, P. 45 in Parthyaea; the discrepancy is the less significant, if D. is right that he adopted Persian customs rather sparingly, to conciliate the Macedonians; in any case according to all these writers the date was summer 330, yet A. refers to it first in connection with an incident of summer 329. It seems evident that his main sources were silent as to the first occasion, though later they were bound to refer to Al's

' medism ' as a cause of the mutiny at Opis in 324, saying inexactly that it had offended the troops ' during the whole expedition ' (vii 8, 2 f., cf. 6, 2 with notes); in addition Pt. alludes to it indirectly in vi 30, 2 f. (see note), and Ar. mentions the diadem *ap.* vii 22, 4. But clearly it embarrassed them that their hero had abandoned the style of a Macedonian king, and what they could not deny they did their best to veil, cf. App. V 9 f. A. had to turn to the ' vulgate ', as we must, for fuller information.

2. The most complete descriptions of Persian royal dress, which was of Median origin (Herodotus i 135; vii 61 f.; Strabo xi 13, 9), are given by Xenophon, *Cyropaedia* viii 3, 13 and QC. iii 3, 17 ff.; see H-W. Ritter, *Diadem und Königsherrschaft* for much of what follows. Eratosthenes (Jacoby no. 241, F. 30 = P. 330 A) says that Al. did not assume the *tiara*, i.e. the stiff or ' upright ' peaked cap which was the sole prerogative of the king (A. iii 25, 3; Xenophon, *Anabasis* ii 5, 23), and must be identified with the *kitaris* or *kidaris*, nor the *kandys* (a cloak of purple and gold) or the (scarlet) trousers, cf. also P. 45 and D. (with no mention of the *tiara*), while D. says that he did wear the diadem (cf. A. vii 22, 4), the *chiton*, a tunic of purple and white, and the belt (of gold). Ephippus, who was certainly a contemporary (Pearson 61), mentions the *chiton*, purple mantle and diadem bound round the *kausia*, a traditional Macedonian hat (Jacoby no. 126, F. 5). Writing from memory, A. iv 7, 4 is apparently mistaken about the *tiara*.

3. A's excursus on dress leads him to describe out of chronological order (iv 8, 1; 14, 4) first the death of Clitus, second the *proscynesis* affair, and third the

pages' conspiracy. The first event is placed by QC. viii 1, 19 ff. at Maracanda just after the retirement of Artabazus (cf. A. 16, 3; 17, 3), to whom in his account Clitus was designated successor, and before Al. wintered at Nautaca (viii 2, 13–19, cf. A. 13, 3; 18, 1), sc. in 328/327, i.e. over a year after the point at which A. chooses to recount it. The second and third he puts after the measures described by A. in 22, 1 (cf. QC. viii 5, 2); and in fact A. 22, 2 confirms that the pages' conspiracy occurred then, i.e. at Bactra in the later part of that winter, 328—327. In QC. too (viii 5 ff.) the pages' conspiracy follows immediately on Callisthenes' objection to *proscynesis*, but Clitus' murder was clearly several months earlier. Adopting (as usual) a logical rather than a temporal order, P. connects the three incidents not only with each other but also with the prior execution of Philotas, for his purpose is to illustrate the king's tendency to behave despotically and the resistance it aroused; the Philotas affair itself is recounted immediately after particulars have been given of Al's Orientalizing measures, even including his later marriage to Roxane (47, 4). The table of contents of D. xvii shows that he too described the death of Callisthenes immediately after that of Clitus and before other incidents which intervened temporally. And A. makes roughly the same kind of links. Yet his order is normally chronological. Why did he change it?

4. Little in these chapters comes from his main sources. Ar's account of the death of Clitus is cited (8, 9), but it was clearly unsatisfactory, as it did not make clear ' the origin of the drinking bout ', naturally enough, as Ar. was at pains to deny that

Al. was given to hard drinking, quite implausibly
(vii 29, 4 n.), and to explain away another all-night
sitting (iv 13, 5). Ar. gave a part in the affair to
Ptolemy (different from that in QC. viii 1, 48), but
A. does not cite Pt. to confirm or refute it, and
presumably found nothing of it in Pt. Indeed the
main account in 8, 1–8, is in *oratio obliqua* throughout
after λέγουσι in 8, 2. Now it is evident that the
writers in question do not include Ar., in view of the
reference to Al's ' barbaric ' drinking habits (ibid.),
and the suggestion that when he writes ' *they* say '
Arrian means ' Pt. says ' ought not to receive any
consideration. The whole account in 8, 1–8, like
that of A's conduct after the murder (9, 2–4, 7 ff.),
must then come from the ' vulgate '; at most 9, 5
should be from Pt. or Ar. or both, and if from Pt., he
may simply have reported that Clitus was killed
with no circumstantial details, except that it was the
result of Al's failure to pay Dionysus due reverence,
a failure he duly made good; for a similar reticence
cf. ii 3, 8 n. (Ephippus fr. 3, in a quite different
context, traced the wrath of Dionysus back to the
destruction of Thebes; that shows how the same
motiv could be adapted by different writers.) For an
apologist the best course was to say as little as
possible. Again, A's whole account of *proscynesis* is
certainly from the ' vulgate '. Even when we come
to the pages' plot (para 11 f.), its origin (in Al's
arbitrary behaviour) is taken from ' a prevalent story ';
what the main sources told was simply that the conspirators, including Callisthenes, were detected and
punished; they did not record Hermolaus' defence
(14, 2), which in the ' vulgate ' contained bitter criticisms of Al., and by their silence on Callisthenes'
resistance to *proscynesis*, they obviously hoped to

conceal that part of his conduct which could command sympathy even among Macedonians. A. himself was worried by the disagreement of Pt. and Ar. on his fate (14, 4), and was not certain about his guilt (12, 7; 14, 1). But it was not such disquiet that obliged him to forsake his chief authorities; here they had too little, or nothing, to say about stories that 'were notable and not wholly incredible', and he had to turn to some other writer or writers, who probably did not follow a strictly chronological plan; it was then beyond A's skill to insert their account or accounts at the right temporal point.

5. The story in 12, 3–5 comes from the contemporary, Chares (cf. P. 54); the slight differences in the two versions, in particular the mention of the hearth in P., omitted by A., illustrates how in transmission details could be added or subtracted. We do not know of course that either A. or P. read Chares for himself, nor (as often assumed) that Chares was an eye-witness. However, his account may well be true, whereas the story of the debate in 10, 5–12, 2, told with significant variations in QC. viii 5, 5 ff., where Agis and Cleo replace Anaxarchus, must be false (cf. § 7 ff. below). Not even the statement in 12, 1 (cf. QC. viii 5, 21), that Al. gave up the attempt to impose *proscynesis* on the Macedonians can be trusted in itself; it is incompatible with another tale from the 'vulgate' in 14, 2. The anecdote about Leonnatus in 12, 2 finds parallels (and differences) in stories of Polyperchon in QC. viii 5, 22 and (in a later context) of Cassander in P. 74, 1; whether true or false, all have some value in illustrating the repugnance Macedonians felt for *proscynesis*, but for which they would not even have been invented; it is noteworthy

that it does not feature among the Oriental practices
of which the Macedonians complained at Opis in 324
(vii 6, 3 ff.; 8, 2 f.); and this does make it probable
that Al. had ceased to demand it of his western
followers.   It is plain that the ' vulgate ', whether or
not the term be used to include Chares, of whose
general reliability we may have our doubts (cf. § 13
below and ii 11, 4 n.), consists of a variety of traditions
or fictions, cf. also 9, 2; 14, 4.

6. A's account of the murder of Clitus can be compared with those of QC. vii 1, 19 ff. and P. 50 f.   All
know of the official version that the neglect of Dionysus' rites was to blame (cf. also the table of contents
in D.).   A. has it that the quarrel started with men
talking in a way that implied that Al. was son of
Zeus (8, 2 cf. 9, 9), and QC. 1, 42 and P. 50, 5 make
Clitus gibe at his claim to be son of Ammon (cf. App.
V 6).   P. 51, 1–3 makes him complain of A's Orientalizing, and one would guess that this was in A's source,
to explain his inserting the story after 7, 4 ff., though
he forgets to bring the point out in his own narrative.
In all accounts Clitus depreciates Al's achievements
in comparison with those of Philip and the Macedonians.   There are also many minor divergencies.
It would be unrewarding to analyse them.   Even if
all our sources went back to one basically reliable
witness, his testimony could easily have been carelessly transmitted or deliberately altered by later
writers; or equally, if there was more than one such
witness, we could expect confused and contradictory
recollections of a drunken brawl.   The exact truth
cannot be recovered.   For the sequel QC. viii 2, 1–12
and P. 52 again show both similarities with and differences from the ' vulgate ' in A., one of many

illustrations of the way in which that ' tradition ' varied, partly no doubt because of its mutations in successive writers.

7. Of the two stories about *proscynesis* that told by Chares, which may repose on knowledge he acquired as a court usher (P. 46), is credible and does not suggest that it was claimed as an honour due to a god. That interpretation is presupposed in the tale of the debate, and it is certainly false. For what follows see Lane Fox ch. 23 with bibliography, especially E. J. Bickermann, *Parola del Passato* 1963, 241 ff., correcting in some points J. P. V. D. Balsdon, *Historia* 1950, 363 ff.

8. ' Obeisance ' is a rather misleading translation of *proscynesis*, used *faute de mieux*. It was performed by kissing one's fingers towards the person honoured, perhaps by blowing a kiss. Greeks and presumably Macedonians rendered the honour only to the image that represented a god; it was a mark of the ' superstitious man ' that he would perform it only on his knees (Theophrastus, *Characters* 16, 5). But in Persia it was a mark of respect paid to superiors in rank, and therefore by all to the king (cf. Herodotus i 134). Herodotus suggests that the inferior fell on his knees, and QC. viii 5, 6 suggests that prostration always accompanied *proscynesis* to the king; it was certainly expected of Greek ambassadors (e.g. Herodotus vii 136). But in Persian eyes they were doubtless very lowly beings; the Persepolis reliefs (cf. Olmstead, *History of the Persian Empire* Plate XXX) show that Persian dignitaries did no more than make a half-bow in obeisance to the king. In Chares' story there is no place for prostration at

Alexander's banquet. Thus the Persian ceremony was, at least when performed by men of rank, no different in principle from the Greek, except that it was rendered to men. Greeks who forgot or did not know that in Persia all superiors received it believed that it betokened that the Persians worshipped the king as a god (cf. Isocrates iv 151); in fact the Persian king was not a god (*contra* QC. viii 5, 11), though he ruled by the grace of the supreme god, Ahura-Mazda.

9. Since Greeks and Macedonians in Alexander's court must have seen Persians performing *proscynesis* to superiors other than the king, they can hardly have shared the illusions of Isocrates. But that did not dispel the prejudices in which they had been reared. Greeks boasted that they ' did obeisance to no man as a master but only to the gods ' (Xenophon, *Anabasis* iii 2, 13, cf. iv 1, 35). To Aristotle it was an honour that only barbarians paid to men (*Rhetoric* 1367a 27). It is plausible to suppose that Al. sought to introduce the practice among all his courtiers, only in order to create a greater measure of equality between Persian and western notables and thus to conciliate the Persians. But that was not a motive with which the Macedonians would have sympathized. Their aversion to a ceremony they thought demeaning probably led Alexander to abandon this attempt at assimilation —with more prudence than he had made it. Callisthenes may have had a leading part in the resistance, and paid the price for it.

10. It is indeed evident that neither A. nor his source was aware that *proscynesis* did not import deification. It follows that the substance of Callis-

thenes' speech (11, 2 ff.) must have been invented by
a writer who had no contact with persons then at Al's
court or else misunderstood what they told him.
Part of it reads like an attack on any deification of a
mere human (11, 2–6), but it may also suggest that
deification is only inappropriate in a man's own lifetime (11, 7). Neither of these contentions is likely
to have been original to A. himself. He lived in a
time when for centuries past people in the Greek
world had been accustomed to deify the living ruler,
king or emperor. Admittedly at Rome itself official
apotheosis of the Caesars was deferred till after
death, and it might be suggested that A., writing
when already a highly placed senator (but cf. Introd.
1 and Appendix in vol. II), composed the speech
under the influence of such Roman ideas. But
though the words are surely his, I doubt if he would
himself have consciously invented the substance of
the speech or have imputed to Callisthenes a purely
Roman conception, which had no currency in the
contemporary Greek world where he had been
brought up. It is far more likely that the invention
belongs to the late fourth or early third century when
ruler cults still attracted objections (C. Habicht,
Gottmenschentum und griechische Städte, 213 ff.); in
Macedonia, on whose customs the speech lays
weight, it was never introduced, and in other Hellen-
istic kingdoms Al's immediate successors were not
officially recognized as gods in their own lifetime.
The fact that A. gives so much space to the contentions ascribed to Callisthenes may suggest that
when he read them he was favourably impressed;
certainly he explicitly commends Callisthenes for his
disapproval of Al's claim to *proscynesis* and adoption
of Persian dress and ceremonies (10, 1). In vii 29 he

was to take a different view. It looks as if he was readily influenced by what he had last perused.

11. By contrast he condemns Callisthenes for his alleged boastfulness (10, 2) and, unlike P. (54, 2), for his insolence to Al. at the banquet scene (12, 6), which in his view made it natural for Al. to suspect him of treason (12, 7). His comments on the conduct appropriate to a king's servant (12, 6) may recall Tacitus' preference for a middle path between ' abruptam contumaciam et deforme obsequium ' (*Annals* iv 20) and be taken as giving some support to the hypothesis that he wrote when he had known from his experience the practical conditions of life at a court; this would not, however, imply that the *Anabasis* was composed after his legateship in Cappadocia. The attitude revealed betrays no affinity with the admiration his old teacher, Epictetus, had expressed for the outspoken Helvidius Priscus (Epict. i 2 *passim*, esp. 19 ff.). True, Epictetus is advocating the principle that a man must be true to his own personality, and the personality of Helvidius was very different from that of Callisthenes, who was accused in antiquity of ' deifying ' Al. in his history, though making him into a son of Zeus (App. V) hardly amounted to that, and of whom Timaeus said that he deserved his fate for corrupting Al. with his flattery (Jacoby no. 124 T. 20 f., cf. F 31). Neither A. nor P., who has other anecdotes about Callisthenes' rift with Al. which illustrate his lack of tact (52 ff.), explains or even notices the seemingly flagrant contradiction between the character of his history and his conduct at court. One might think that if they had read the history for themselves that problem must have impinged on them too forcibly to be ig-

nored, and that even P.'s citations from it must be
second-hand. A. alludes to it only once (10, 1, from
which we are not to infer that it was actually in the
history that Callisthenes claimed that Al's fame
would depend on what he wrote), and not in such a
way as to indicate that he had read it. It seems clear
to me that he had not; otherwise we should expect
a different account of the visit to Siwah, nor would
Ar. have been cited in iii 11, 3, if he was himself
drawing on Callisthenes; indeed we should expect
explicit citations elsewhere, even if A. preferred other
authorities. Probably he had assumed that the work
was too adulatory because written in Al's lifetime
(*pref.* 2).

12. In his account of the pages' conspiracy A. draws
13, 1—4 from the ' vulgate ' (cf. QC. viii 6, 1–11) and
contrasts Ar. with the ' vulgate ' in 13, 5 f. (QC. 6,
12 ff. combines their versions), whereas Pt. is probably
used in 13, 7, as he is named as an agent in the discovery of the plot. (I see no reason to think that he
concealed the role played by Leonnatus, QC. 6, 22,
as he had no known quarrel with Leonnatus, and A.
probably derives from Pt. honourable mentions of
Leonnatus in other places; if QC. is right, we may
tax A. himself with a careless omission.) Pt. also
recorded that the conspirators under torture implicated Callisthenes (Ar. concurring) and that he was
racked and hanged (14, 1 and 3). However for Hermolaus' speech to the army justifying his conduct, A.
turns again to the ' vulgate '; the speech is embellished in QC. viii 7 f., who also gives Al. a reply. So
it would seem that Pt. and Ar. adopted the same
laconic style for this affair as for the fall of Philotas,
merely recording that a plot was discovered and the

authors punished by the army (what they said of the
fate of the pages has dropped out in A's version), and
passing over in silence those aspects of Al's behaviour
which provoked Macedonian discontent.

13. A. himself was disconcerted by the discrepancy
in their stories of Callisthenes' fate (14, 3 f.); he does
not notice Chares' statement (P. 55, 5) that Callisthenes died after seven months in fetters, but in 325!
As Jacoby observed, ' Pt. denied Callisthenes' innocence, Chares his execution, and Ar. both.' A.
failed to see that what Pt. and Ar. said and omitted
required a more critical assessment than he attempts.
For QC. Callisthenes is ' in caput regis innoxius, sed
haudquaquam aulae et assentantium accommodatus
ingenio ', and Al. himself repented of his death,
another device for exculpation (viii 8, 20 ff.); in his
story the pages confessed, but not under torture and
without implicating Callisthenes (6, 24 ff.; 7, 10), and
it was only after trial that they were all tortured to
death.   P. too cites as proof of Callisthenes' innocence
a letter of Al. to Craterus, Attalus and Alcetas (55, 3),
which gives a somewhat different account: the pages
did not denounce Callisthenes even under torture.
J. R. Hamilton (see his Commentary *ad loc.*) supposes
this letter to be genuine, since the addressees were
in fact absent on mission at the time (A. iv 22, 1, cf.
QC. viii 5, 2), and that would have been unknown to
a forger; but this argument ignores the obvious
possibility that a forger used a current history in
which such true information could have been found;
in my view (Introd. 15) all such letters stand, or
rather fall, together, and this letter does no more
than attest yet another variant in the ' vulgate '.   (It
must have purported to give *some* justification,

omitted by P., for the execution, even if it coheres
with the story of Al's later repentance, which the
continued assertion of Callisthenes' guilt by Pt. and
Ar. makes improbable.) Once again we find that
the ' vulgate ' is not an unified, ' Clitarchean '
tradition. Faced with all these irreconcilable divergencies in his sources, A. himself left the question of
Callisthenes' complicity open, while suggesting that
even if he were innocent he had brought his own fate
on himself (12, 6 f.). At all costs Al. had to be
excused.

APPENDIX XV

INDIA AND THE PERSIAN EMPIRE

1. In *Ind.* 1 A. says that the Assaceni (who lived in
Swat and Bunēr, App. VIII 20) and the Astaceni,
whose centre was Peucelaotis or Charsadda (ib. 19),
were subject to Cyrus (559–29 BC). Herodotus (iv.
44) tells how Darius I (521–486) sent Scylax on a
voyage down the Indus to its mouth and thence
round by sea to Egypt and how he shortly afterwards
subdued the ' Indians ', i.e. peoples in the Indus
valley, and ' made use of the sea '. Darius' inscriptions and Herodotus' lists of Persian army contingents
and tributaries (see vii 65; iii 94, 97 ff.) present
further evidence, lucidly discussed in *Cambridge
History of India* I ch. XIV, for Persian power in India
in the late sixth and fifth centuries. Its original
extent is not to be defined with certitude. In the
south the desert east of the Indus formed the frontier
(Herodotus iii 98), but it is less clear how much of the

plain between the Indus and Hyphasis ever belonged to Persia.

2. A. constantly refers to the local rulers in India on both sides of the Indus as hyparchs or under-governors (iv 22, 8; 24, 1; 28, 6; v 8, 5; 20, 6; 29, 4) or nomarchs, i.e. district governors (v 8, 3; 18, 2; vi 16, 1). If these Greek terms translate Indian or Persian titles, it might be inferred that their holders had once received authority from Persia and had, at least in theory, been subject to satraps. They also commonly bear the name of the people or city they rule, e.g. Abisares of the Abhisara, Assacenus (iv 27, 4), Astis, i.e. Astacenus (iv 22, 8, Porus of the Paurava, Taxilas of Taxila; his personal name was Omphis or Mophis (QC. viii 12, 4; D. 86, 4). Evidently they are native rajahs. A. also calls Porus a king (vi 2, 1, cf. v 19, 2), a title other writers accord to Taxilas, Abisares, the bad Porus, Sopithes (e.g. D. 86, 4; 90, 4; 91, 1 and 7). Even if this is correct, it does not imply that they, or their predecessors, had not been Persian vassals; compare the kings in Cyprus and Phoenicia. Similarly the ' self-governing ' cities may be communities which like some Greek cities in Asia enjoyed republican forms of local government under Persian suzerainty. Nor is it surprising that A's narrative does not explicitly refer to Persian rule beyond the Indus. There is not even any indication in book iv that Darius III had been in control of the peoples Al. conquered in 327–326 before crossing that river. Yet Indians who were ' neighbours of the Bactrians ' (iii, 8, 3), or lived ' this side of Indus ' (8, 6), or ' mountain Indians ' (8, 4) whose satrap was delivered up to Al. by Indians ' on this side of Indus ' (25, 8), had served in his armies. If Al. had con-

quered the Persian empire from the east, there would have been as little trace of Persian authority after Darius' death on the Mediterranean coast as there was in the valleys of the Indus and its tributaries.

3. However, just as frequent revolts in the west had at times reduced Persian dominion in the fourth century, so it could have contracted in India. Local rajahs could have made themselves independent, while retaining the official titles conferred by Persia, like later Nizams and Nabobs, or Dukes and Counts in mediaeval Europe. The facts that Al. was at first unaware that the Indus was not the upper Nile, knew nothing of the sea-route to Egypt and gave Nearchus a less venturesome task than Scylax suggest that the Persian nobility at his court were also ignorant of the lower Indus and that the maritime trade between its mouth and Egypt had ceased (cf. vi 1; *Ind.* 20, 1 and 5; 32). This implies that Sind had been lost since the fifth century. (It is immaterial that Aristotle, *Politics* 1332b 23 ff., knew about Scylax; we should not suppose that before leaving Macedon Al. took geographical lessons from him about a land he probably never then thought of entering or that he perused Herodotus, and that the stories of his ignorance must be mere inventions.) Again, ' India ', though the name must have first denoted the Indus plain, had come to mean the country beyond the river, and Eratosthenes held that in Al's time the Indus was the boundary between India and the Persian empire (Strabo xv 1, 10), while Megasthenes could aver that Alexander was the first to invade India, so defined, since Dionysus and Heracles (*Ind.* 5, 1–8; 9, 10 f.). This view was certainly propagated

to glorify Al., but it surely implies that there was no memory of Persian dominion beyond the Indus. It seems to me a mere fantasy to think that Al's men mutinied on the Hyphasis, because they did not wish to proceed beyond the Persian frontiers, and consented to return home by the mouth of the Indus, because they would still be within its confines: they were war-weary, and probably deluded into thinking this the easiest route; legalistic considerations would not have operated. And it flouts all the evidence to assume that Al. himself now merely sought to complete the conquest of the Persian empire. Beyond the Indus, in his own estimation, he was already going further.

Printed in Great Britain
by Richard Clay (The Chaucer Press), Ltd,
Bungay, Suffolk

THE LOEB CLASSICAL LIBRARY

VOLUMES ALREADY PUBLISHED

Latin Authors

AMMIANUS MARCELLINUS. Translated by J. C. Rolfe. 3 Vols.

APULEIUS: THE GOLDEN ASS (METAMORPHOSES). W. Adlington (1566). Revised by S. Gaselee.

ST. AUGUSTINE: CITY OF GOD. 7 Vols. Vol. I. G. E. McCracken. Vols. II and VII. W. M. Green. Vol. III. D. Wiesen. Vol. IV. P. Levine. Vol. V. E. M. Sanford and W. M. Green. Vol. VI. W. C. Greene.

ST. AUGUSTINE, CONFESSIONS OF. W. Watts (1631). 2 Vols.

ST. AUGUSTINE, SELECT LETTERS. J. H. Baxter.

AUSONIUS. H. G. Evelyn White. 2 Vols.

BEDE. J. E. King. 2 Vols.

BOETHIUS: TRACTS and DE CONSOLATIONE PHILOSOPHIAE. Rev. H. F. Stewart and E. K. Rand. Revised by S. J. Tester.

CAESAR: ALEXANDRIAN, AFRICAN and SPANISH WARS. A. G. Way.

CAESAR: CIVIL WARS. A. G. Peskett.

CAESAR: GALLIC WAR. H. J. Edwards.

CATO: DE RE RUSTICA. VARRO: DE RE RUSTICA. H. B. Ash and W. D. Hooper.

CATULLUS. F. W. Cornish. TIBULLUS. J. B. Postgate. PERVIGILIUM VENERIS. J. W. Mackail.

CELSUS: DE MEDICINA. W. G. Spencer. 3 Vols.

CICERO: BRUTUS and ORATOR. G. L. Hendrickson and H. M. Hubbell.

[CICERO]: AD HERENNIUM. H. Caplan.

CICERO: DE ORATORE, etc. 2 Vols. Vol. I. DE ORATORE, Books I and II. E. W. Sutton and H. Rackham. Vol. II. DE ORATORE, Book III. DE FATO; PARADOXA STOICORUM; DE PARTITIONE ORATORIA. H. Rackham.

CICERO: DE FINIBUS. H. Rackham.

CICERO: DE INVENTIONE, etc. H. M. Hubbell.

CICERO: DE NATURA DEORUM and ACADEMICA. H. Rackham.

CICERO: DE OFFICIIS. Walter Miller.

CICERO: DE REPUBLICA and DE LEGIBUS. Clinton W. Keyes.

Ovid: Heroides and Amores. Grant Showerman.
Ovid: Metamorphoses. F. J. Miller. 2 Vols.
Ovid: Tristia and Ex Ponto. A. L. Wheeler.
Persius. Cf. Juvenal.
Petronius. M. Heseltine. Seneca: Apocolocyntosis. W. H. D. Rouse.
Phaedrus and Babrius (Greek). B. E. Perry.
Plautus. Paul Nixon. 5 Vols.
Pliny: Letters, Panegyricus. Betty Radice. 2 Vols.
Pliny: Natural History. 10 Vols. Vols. I–V and IX. H. Rackham. VI.–VIII. W. H. S. Jones. X. D. E. Eichholz.
Propertius. H. E. Butler.
Prudentius. H. J. Thomson. 2 Vols.
Quintilian. H. E. Butler. 4 Vols.
Remains of Old Latin. E. H. Warmington. 4 Vols. Vol. I. (Ennius and Caecilius) Vol. II. (Livius, Naevius Pacuvius, Accius) Vol. III. (Lucilius and Laws of XII Tables) Vol. IV. (Archaic Inscriptions)
Sallust. J. C. Rolfe.
Scriptores Historiae Augustae. D. Magie. 3 Vols.
Seneca, The Elder: Controversiae, Suasoriae. M. Winterbottom. 2 Vols.
Seneca: Apocolocyntosis. Cf. Petronius.
Seneca: Epistulae Morales. R. M. Gummere. 3 Vols.
Seneca: Moral Essays. J. W. Basore. 3 Vols.
Seneca: Tragedies. F. J. Miller. 2 Vols.
Seneca: Naturales Quaestiones. T. H. Corcoran. 2 Vols.
Sidonius: Poems and Letters. W. B. Anderson. 2 Vols.
Silius Italicus. J. D. Duff. 2 Vols.
Statius. J. H. Mozley. 2 Vols.
Suetonius. J. C. Rolfe. 2 Vols.
Tacitus: Dialogus. Sir Wm. Peterson. Agricola and Germania. Maurice Hutton. Revised by M. Winterbottom, R. M. Ogilvie, E. H. Warmington.
Tacitus: Histories and Annals. C. H. Moore and J. Jackson. 4 Vols.
Terence. John Sargeaunt. 2 Vols.
Tertullian: Apologia and De Spectaculis. T. R. Glover. Minucius Felix. G. H. Rendall.
Valerius Flaccus. J. H. Mozley.
Varro: De Lingua Latina. R. G. Kent. 2 Vols.
Velleius Paterculus and Res Gestae Divi Augusti. F. W. Shipley.
Virgil. H. R. Fairclough. 2 Vols.
Vitruvius: De Architectura. F. Granger. 2 Vols.

3

Greek Authors

ACHILLES TATIUS. S. Gaselee.

AELIAN: ON THE NATURE OF ANIMALS. A. F. Scholfield. 3 Vols.

AENEAS TACTICUS. ASCLEPIODOTUS and ONASANDER. The Illinois Greek Club.

AESCHINES. C. D. Adams.

AESCHYLUS. H. Weir Smyth. 2 Vols.

ALCIPHRON, AELIAN, PHILOSTRATUS: LETTERS. A. R. Benner and F. H. Fobes.

ANDOCIDES, ANTIPHON. Cf. MINOR ATTIC ORATORS.

APOLLODORUS. Sir James G. Frazer. 2 Vols.

APOLLONIUS RHODIUS. R. C. Seaton.

THE APOSTOLIC FATHERS. Kirsopp Lake. 2 Vols.

APPIAN: ROMAN HISTORY. Horace White. 4 Vols.

ARATUS. Cf. CALLIMACHUS.

ARISTIDES: ORATIONS. C. A. Behr. Vol. I.

ARISTOPHANES. Benjamin Bickley Rogers. 3 Vols. Verse trans.

ARISTOTLE: ART OF RHETORIC. J. H. Freese.

ARISTOTLE: ATHENIAN CONSTITUTION, EUDEMIAN ETHICS, VICES AND VIRTUES. H. Rackham.

ARISTOTLE: GENERATION OF ANIMALS. A. L. Peck.

ARISTOTLE: HISTORIA ANIMALIUM. A. L. Peck. Vols. I.–II.

ARISTOTLE: METAPHYSICS. H. Tredennick. 2 Vols.

ARISTOTLE: METEOROLOGICA. H. D. P. Lee.

ARISTOTLE: MINOR WORKS. W. S. Hett. On Colours, On Things Heard, On Physiognomies, On Plants, On Marvellous Things Heard, Mechanical Problems, On Indivisible Lines, On Situations and Names of Winds, On Melissus, Xenophanes, and Gorgias.

ARISTOTLE: NICOMACHEAN ETHICS. H. Rackham.

ARISTOTLE: OECONOMICA and MAGNA MORALIA. G. C. Armstrong (with METAPHYSICS, Vol. II).

ARISTOTLE: ON THE HEAVENS. W. K. C. Guthrie.

ARISTOTLE: ON THE SOUL, PARVA NATURALIA, ON BREATH. W. S. Hett.

ARISTOTLE: CATEGORIES, ON INTERPRETATION, PRIOR ANALYTICS. H. P. Cooke and H. Tredennick.

ARISTOTLE: POSTERIOR ANALYTICS, TOPICS. H. Tredennick and E. S. Forster.

ARISTOTLE: ON SOPHISTICAL REFUTATIONS.
On Coming to be and Passing Away, On the Cosmos. E. S. Forster and D. J. Furley.

ARISTOTLE: PARTS OF ANIMALS. A. L. Peck; MOTION AND PROGRESSION OF ANIMALS. E. S. Forster.

ARISTOTLE: PHYSICS. Rev. P. Wicksteed and F. M. Cornford. 2 Vols.

ARISTOTLE: POETICS and LONGINUS. W. Hamilton Fyfe DEMETRIUS ON STYLE. W. Rhys Roberts.

ARISTOTLE: POLITICS. H. Rackham.

ARISTOTLE: PROBLEMS. W. S. Hett. 2 Vols.

ARISTOTLE: RHETORICA AD ALEXANDRUM (with PROBLEMS. Vol. II). H. Rackham.

ARRIAN: HISTORY OF ALEXANDER and INDICA. New Vol. I by P. A. Brunt. Vol. II by E. Iliffe Robson.

ATHENAEUS: DEIPNOSOPHISTAE. C. B. Gulick. 7 Vols.

BABRIUS and PHAEDRUS (Latin). B. E. Perry.

ST. BASIL: LETTERS. R. J. Deferrari. 4 Vols.

CALLIMACHUS: FRAGMENTS. C. A. Trypanis. MUSAEUS: HERO AND LEANDER. T. Gelzer and C. Whitman.

CALLIMACHUS: HYMNS and EPIGRAMS. LYCOPHRON. A. W. Mair. ARATUS. G. R. Mair.

CLEMENT OF ALEXANDRIA. Rev. G. W. Butterworth.

COLLUTHUS. Cf. OPPIAN.

DAPHNIS AND CHLOE. Thornley's Translation revised by J. M. Edmonds. PARTHENIUS. S. Gaselee.

DEMOSTHENES I: OLYNTHIACS, PHILIPPICS and MINOR ORATIONS I–XVII and XX. J. H. Vince.

DEMOSTHENES II: DE CORONA and DE FALSA LEGATIONE. C. A. Vince and J. H. Vince.

DEMOSTHENES III: MEIDIAS, ANDROTION, ARISTOCRATES, TIMOCRATES and ARISTOGEITON I and II. J. H. Vince.

DEMOSTHENES IV–VI: PRIVATE ORATIONS and IN NEAERAM. A. T. Murray.

DEMOSTHENES VII: FUNERAL SPEECH, EROTIC ESSAY, EXORDIA and LETTERS. N. W. and N. J. DeWitt.

DIO CASSIUS: ROMAN HISTORY. E. Cary. 9 Vols.

DIO CHRYSOSTOM. J. W. Cohoon and H. Lamar Crosby. 5 Vols.

DIODORUS SICULUS. 12 Vols. Vols. I–VI. C. H. Oldfather. Vol. VII. C. L. Sherman. Vol. VIII. C. B. Welles. Vols. IX and X. R. M. Geer. Vol. XI. F. Walton. Vol. XII. F. Walton. General Index. R. M. Geer.

DIOGENES LAERTIUS. R. D. Hicks. 2 Vols. New Introduction by H. S. Long.

DIONYSIUS OF HALICARNASSUS: ROMAN ANTIQUITIES. Spelman's translation revised by E. Cary. 7 Vols.

DIONYSIUS OF HALICARNASSUS: CRITICAL ESSAYS. S. Usher. 2 Vols.

EPICTETUS. W. A. Oldfather. 2 Vols.

EURIPIDES. A. S. Way. 4 Vols. Verse trans.

EUSEBIUS: ECCLESIASTICAL HISTORY. Kirsopp Lake and J. E. L. Oulton. 2 Vols.

GALEN: ON THE NATURAL FACULTIES. A. J. Brock.

THE GREEK ANTHOLOGY. W. R. Paton. 5 Vols.

GREEK ELEGY AND IAMBUS with the ANACREONTEA. J. M. Edmonds. 2 Vols.

THE GREEK BUCOLIC POETS (THEOCRITUS, BION, MOSCHUS). J. M. Edmonds.

GREEK MATHEMATICAL WORKS. Ivor Thomas. 2 Vols.

HERODES. Cf. THEOPHRASTUS: CHARACTERS.

HERODIAN. C. R. Whittaker. 2 Vols.

HERODOTUS. A. D. Godley. 4 Vols.

HESIOD and THE HOMERIC HYMNS. H. G. Evelyn White.

HIPPOCRATES and the FRAGMENTS OF HERACLEITUS. W. H. S. Jones and E. T. Withington. 4 Vols.

HOMER: ILIAD. A. T. Murray. 2 Vols.

HOMER: ODYSSEY. A. T. Murray. 2 Vols.

ISAEUS. E. W. Forster.

ISOCRATES. George Norlin and LaRue Van Hook. 3 Vols.

[ST. JOHN DAMASCENE]: BARLAAM AND IOASAPH. Rev. G. R. Woodward, Harold Mattingly and D. M. Lang.

JOSEPHUS. 9 Vols. Vols. I–IV. H. Thackeray. Vol. V. H. Thackeray and R. Marcus. Vols. VI–VII. R. Marcus. Vol. VIII. R. Marcus and Allen Wikgren. Vol. IX. L. H. Feldman.

JULIAN. Wilmer Cave Wright. 3 Vols.

LIBANIUS. A. F. Norman. Vol. I.

LUCIAN. 8 Vols. Vols. I–IV. A. M. Harmon. Vol. VI. K. Kilburn. Vols. VII–VIII. M. D. Macleod.

LYCOPHRON. Cf. CALLIMACHUS.

LYRA GRAECA. J. M. Edmonds. 3 Vols.

LYSIAS. W. R. M. Lamb.

MANETHO. W. G. Waddell. PTOLEMY: TETRABIBLOS. F. E. Robbins.

MARCUS AURELIUS. C. R. Haines.

MENANDER. F. G. Allison.

MINOR ATTIC ORATORS (ANTIPHON, ANDOCIDES, LYCURGUS, DEMADES, DINARCHUS, HYPERIDES). K. J. Maidment and J. O. Burtt. 2 Vols.

MUSAEUS: HERO AND LEANDER. Cf. CALLIMACHUS.

NONNOS: DIONYSIACA. W. H. D. Rouse. 3 Vols.

OPPIAN, COLLUTHUS, TRYPHIODORUS. A. W. Mair.

PAPYRI. NON-LITERARY SELECTIONS. A. S. Hunt and C. C. Edgar. 2 Vols. LITERARY SELECTIONS (Poetry). D. L. Page.

PARTHENIUS. Cf. DAPHNIS AND CHLOE.

PAUSANIAS: DESCRIPTION OF GREECE. W. H. S. Jones. 4 Vols. and Companion Vol. arranged by R. E. Wycherley.

PHILO. 10 Vols. Vols. I–V. F. H. Colson and Rev. G. H. Whitaker. Vols. VI–IX. F. H. Colson. Vol. X. F. H. Colson and the Rev. J. W. Earp.

PHILO: two supplementary Vols. (*Translation only.*) Ralph Marcus.

PHILOSTRATUS: THE LIFE OF APOLLONIUS OF TYANA. F. C. Conybeare. 2 Vols.

PHILOSTRATUS: IMAGINES. CALLISTRATUS: DESCRIPTIONS. A. Fairbanks.

PHILOSTRATUS and EUNAPIUS: LIVES OF THE SOPHISTS. Wilmer Cave Wright.

PINDAR. Sir J. E. Sandys.

PLATO: CHARMIDES, ALCIBIADES, HIPPARCHUS, THE LOVERS, THEAGES, MINOS and EPINOMIS. W. R. M. Lamb.

PLATO: CRATYLUS, PARMENIDES, GREATER HIPPIAS, LESSER HIPPIAS. H. N. Fowler.

PLATO: EUTHYPHRO, APOLOGY, CRITO, PHAEDO, PHAEDRUS. H. N. Fowler.

PLATO: LACHES, PROTAGORAS, MENO, EUTHYDEMUS. W. R. M. Lamb.

PLATO: LAWS. Rev. R. G. Bury. 2 Vols.

PLATO: LYSIS, SYMPOSIUM, GORGIAS. W. R. M. Lamb.

PLATO: REPUBLIC. Paul Shorey. 2 Vols.

PLATO: STATESMAN, PHILEBUS. H. N. Fowler. ION. W. R. M. Lamb.

PLATO: THEAETETUS and SOPHIST. H. N. Fowler.

PLATO: TIMAEUS, CRITIAS, CLITOPHO, MENEXENUS, EPISTULAE. Rev. R. G. Bury.

PLOTINUS. A. H. Armstrong. Vols. I–III.

PLUTARCH: MORALIA. 17 Vols. Vols I–V. F. C. Babbitt. Vol. VI. W. C. Helmbold. Vols. VII and XIV. P. H. De Lacy and B. Einarson. Vol. VIII. P. A. Clement and H. B. Hoffleit. Vol. IX. E. L. Minar, Jr., F. H. Sandbach, W. C. Helmbold. Vol. X. H. N. Fowler. Vol. XI. L. Pearson and F. H. Sandbach. Vol. XII. H. Cherniss and W. C. Helmbold. Vol. XV. F. H. Sandbach.

PLUTARCH: THE PARALLEL LIVES. B. Perrin. 11 Vols.

POLYBIUS. W. R. Paton. 6 Vols.

PROCOPIUS: HISTORY OF THE WARS. H. B. Dewing. 7 Vols.

PTOLEMY: TETRABIBLOS. Cf. MANETHO.

QUINTUS SMYRNAEUS. A. S. Way. Verse trans.

SEXTUS EMPIRICUS. Rev. R. G. Bury. 4 Vols.

SOPHOCLES. F. Storr. 2 Vols. Verse trans.

STRABO: GEOGRAPHY. Horace L. Jones. 8 Vols.

THEOPHRASTUS: CHARACTERS. J. M. Edmonds. HERODES, etc. A. D. Knox.

Theophrastus: De Causis Plantarum. B. Einarson and G. K. K. Link. Vol. I.

Theophrastus: Enquiry into Plants. Sir Arthur Hort, Bart. 2 Vols.

Thucydides. C. F. Smith. 4 Vols.

Tryphiodorus. Cf. Oppian.

Xenophon: Cyropaedia. Walter Miller. 2 Vols.

Xenophon: Hellenica. C. L. Brownson. 2 Vols.

Xenophon: Anabasis. C. L. Brownson.

Xenophon: Memorabilia and Oeconomicus. E. C. Marchant. Symposium and Apology. O. J. Todd.

Xenophon: Scripta Minora. E. C. Marchant and G. W. Bowersock.

IN PREPARATION

Latin Authors

Manilius. G. P. Goold.

Greek Authors

Plutarch: Moralia XIII 1–2. H. Cherniss.

DESCRIPTIVE PROSPECTUS ON APPLICATION

CAMBRIDGE, MASS.   HARVARD UNIVERSITY PRESS
LONDON   WILLIAM HEINEMANN LTD